2016

# Social Panorama
## of Latin America

UNITED NATIONS

ECLAC

**Alicia Bárcena**
Executive Secretary

**Antonio Prado**
Deputy Executive Secretary

**Laís Abramo**
Chief, Social Development Division

**Pascual Gerstenfeld**
Chief, Statistics Division

**Paulo Saad**
Chief, Latin American and Caribbean Demographic Centre (CELADE)-Population Division of ECLAC

**Nieves Rico**
Chief, Division for Gender Affairs

**Ricardo Pérez**
Chief, Publications and Web Services Division

This document is the 2016 edition of *Social Panorama of Latin America*, which is prepared each year by the Social Development Division and the Statistics Division of the Economic Commission for Latin America and the Caribbean (ECLAC), under the supervision of Laís Abramo and Pascual Gerstenfeld, respectively, and with participation by the Latin American and Caribbean Demographic Centre (CELADE)-Population Division of ECLAC, directed by Paulo Saad, and the ECLAC Division for Gender Affairs, directed by María Nieves Rico.

The 2016 edition was coordinated by Laís Abramo, who also worked on the preparation of the text together with Verónica Amarante, Ernesto Espíndola, Álvaro Fuentes, Carlos Maldonado, Xavier Mancero, Rodrigo Martínez, Vivian Milosavljevic, Fabiana del Popolo, Marta Rangel, Lucía Scuro, Varinia Tromben, Heidi Ullmann, Iliana Vaca Trigo, Alejandra Valdés and Pablo Yanes. Martín Abeles, John Anton, Agustín Arakaki, Miguel del Castillo Negrete, Andrés Espejo, Gabriel Kattan, Soledad Villafañe and Martina Yopo prepared substantive inputs; while Martín Brum, Ernesto Espíndola, Fabiola Fernández, Marco Galván, Laura García, Carlos Howes, Carlos Kroll, Vivian Milosavljevic, Rocío Miranda, Claudio Moris, Alynn Sánchez and Iliana Vaca Trigo worked on the statistical processing. Valuable contributions and comments relating to different sections of the document were received from Simone Cecchini, Antonio Prado, Guillermo Sunkel and Daniela Trucco.

Support was provided for the preparation of chapter II under the 2016-2018 cooperation programme between ECLAC, the Federal Ministry for Economic Cooperation and Development of Germany (BMZ) and the German Agency for International Cooperation (GIZ) "Support for the implementation of the 2030 Agenda for Sustainable Development in Latin America and the Caribbean", in the framework of the component "Institution-building for universal and sustainable social protection". Chapter V was prepared in the framework of the regional programme between ECLAC and the United Nations Population Fund (UNFPA) and the ECLAC-Ford Foundation project "Afrodescendent and indigenous peoples in Latin America: building knowledge and information for incidence on policies" (No. 0155-1388), with the support of the project "Promoting equality: strengthening the capacity of selected developing countries to design and implement equality-oriented public policies and programmes", financed by the ninth tranche of the United Nations Development Account.

United Nations publication

ISBN: 978-92-1-121963-0 (print)

ISBN: 978-92-1-058600-9 (pdf)

ISBN: 978-92-1-358066-0 (ePub)
Print ISSN: 1020-5160
Online ISSN: 1684-1425

Sales No.: E.17.II.G.6

Distr.: General

LC/PUB.2017/12-P

Explanatory notes:
-Three dots (...) indicate that data are not available or are not separately reported.
- A dash (-) indicates that the amount is nil or negligible.
- A full stop (.) is used to indicate decimals.
- The term "dollars" refers to United States dollars, unless otherwise specified.
- A slash (/) between years (e.g. 2013/2014) indicates a 12-month period falling between the two years.
- Figures and percentages in tables may not necessarily add up to the corresponding totals owing to rounding.

This publication should be cited as: Economic Commission for Latin America and the Caribbean (ECLAC), *Social Panorama of Latin America, 2016* (LC/PUB.2017/12-P), Santiago, 2017.

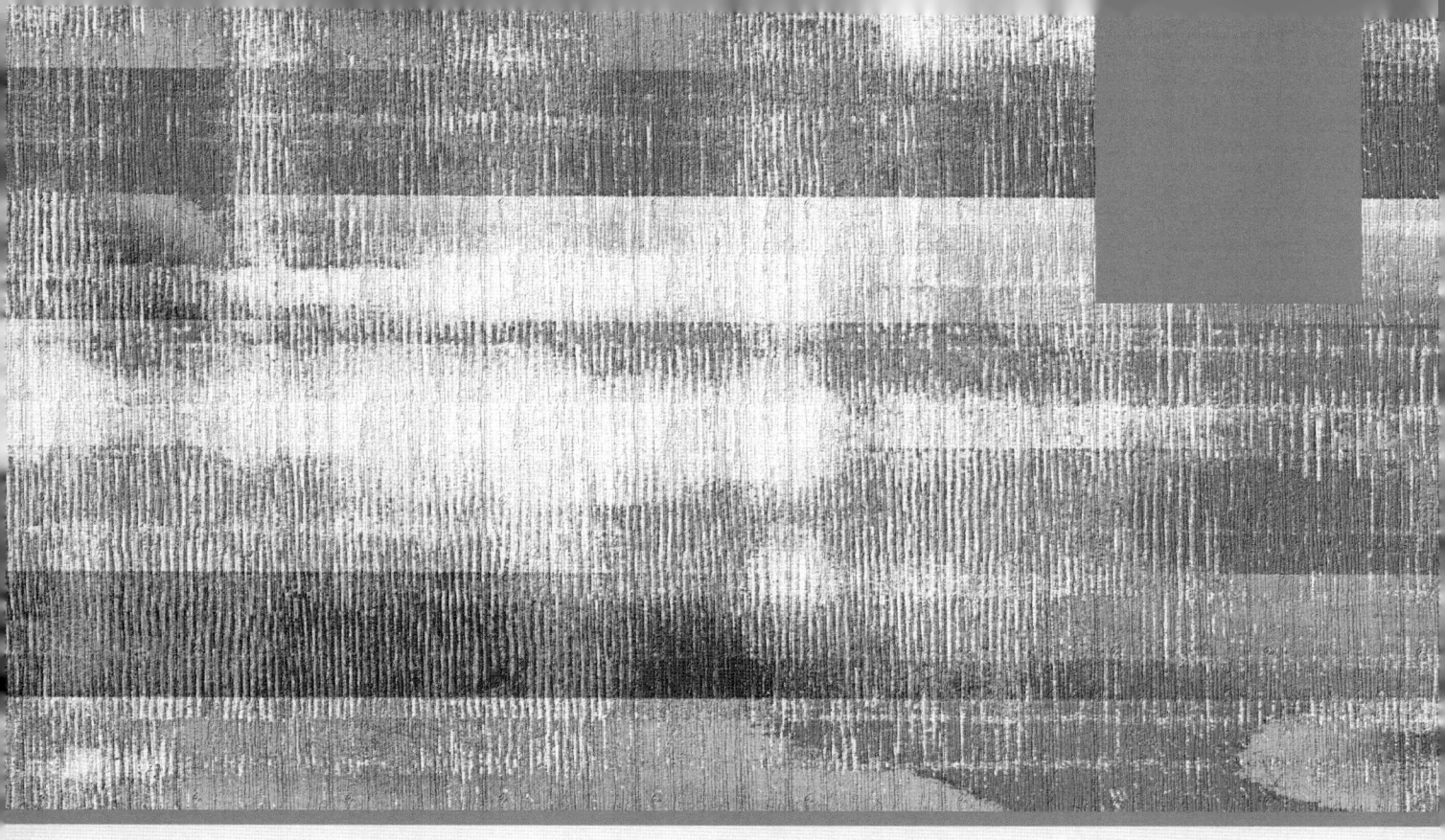

# Summary

# Introduction

While concerns about equality have been a historically constant element in the thinking of the Economic Commission for Latin America and the Caribbean (ECLAC), they have moved to the fore since 2010, as established and explained in the set of documents known as the equality trilogy (ECLAC, 2010, 2012 and 2014a), and in 2016 were expanded with the analysis of the main challenges that the region faces in accomplishing the Goals of the 2030 Agenda for Sustainable Development. Significantly reducing inequality is a commitment assumed by all the countries of the region (reflected in Sustainable Development Goal 10 of the 2030 Agenda, to "reduce inequality within and among countries"), and is clearly expressed in the commitment "to leave no one behind".

Economic and social development analysis conducted by ECLAC have determined that the Latin American and Caribbean economies have historically been defined by sharp structural heterogeneity, which is largely responsible for the high levels of social inequality found in the region's countries. Their scantly diversified and highly heterogeneous production structures, within which low-productivity sectors account for approximately 50% of all jobs, are a key determinant of social inequality. The labour market is the essential link between that production structure and high levels of income inequality between households, which are associated with a highly differentiated distribution of the fruits of productivity and with highly stratified access to good-quality employment and social protection (ECLAC, 2010, 2012, 2014a and 2016a).

There is growing recognition that inequality is a multidimensional phenomenon caused by many factors. The notion of equality used by ECLAC is not therefore constrained to economic or income equality alone. This is clearly a central dimension of equality, which refers both to the distribution of the monetary incomes people and their families have for ensuring their well-being and developing their capacities, and to the functional distribution of income between capital and labour and the distribution of ownership of financial and non-financial assets.

The ECLAC definition of equality also covers equality in the exercise of rights and the development of capacities (understood as the set of abilities, knowledge and skills that individuals acquire and that allow them to pursue life plans they deem valuable), the reciprocal recognition of actors and gender, ethnic and racial equality, among other fundamental aspects (Bárcena and Prado, 2016).

Equality of rights is, as ECLAC sees it, the basic axis of equality, covering the full realization of economic, social and cultural rights as the regulatory and practical horizon for all persons (without distinctions on the grounds of sex, race, ethnicity, age, religion, origin, socioeconomic situation or any other condition) and the inclusion of all citizens in the dynamics of development, which implies a genuine belonging to society and full exercise of citizenship. In contrast, inequality means that not all individuals can fully exercise their civil, political, economic, social and environmental rights and, consequently, that the principle of universality is violated.

Analysing social inequalities requires paying attention to how assets, means and opportunities, income and other outcomes, power and influence are distributed. Thus, inequality refers to asymmetries in the capacity to appropriate resources and productive assets (income, goods, services, etc.) that represent or create well-being among different social groups. It also refers to exclusion and to the unequal distribution of political and economic power, which empowers a reduced segment of society to take decisions that affect the majority and that enable or constrain the exercise of rights and the development of capacities of all. Inequality is, therefore, essentially relational in nature and, in addition, it is a phenomenon inherent to relations of power at the individual and collective levels. A multidimensional approach to inequality therefore implies analysing its economic, social, political and cultural aspects and taking into consideration the different structuring axes that shape social, political and economic relations in Latin American societies.

The central theme of this edition of *Social Panorama of Latin America* is social inequality, seen as a fundamental challenge and obstacle to sustainable development. Some of the axes and aspects of social inequality are addressed, drawing attention to how they intersect with and reinforce one another. The different chapters will examine inequalities in the distribution of income (personal and functional) and property; inequalities over the course of the life cycle; time-use inequalities between men and women; and the situation of Afrodescendent populations as an example of ethnic and racial inequalities. Recent trends in the amount of public resources available to finance social policies capable of tackling poverty and inequality and of promoting inclusive social development are also analysed.

# Chapter I
# Inequality in Latin America: a key challenge for sustainable development

This chapter analyses changes in certain aspects related to resource inequality and socioeconomic strata as the central axis of social inequality in Latin America. Analysis of income distribution among individuals and among households carried out in previous editions of *Social Panorama of Latin America* was expanded to include the functional distribution of income and recent developments in that regard. The chapter also covers the topic of concentration of ownership of financial and non-financial assets, based on a study of Mexico, which yields results that can be applied to other countries in the region.

## A. Inequality in income distribution[1]

In Latin America, the level of income distribution inequality in 2015 was similar to that seen in 2014. Nonetheless, taking into account the entire period since the global financial crisis, the income distribution gap narrowed between 2008 and 2015 in most of the region's countries. During this period, the income of the lowest income quintile increased more than that of the highest. This occurred generally across the various sources of household income, but mainly in labour income (both for wage jobs and self-employment), retirement and transfers.

## 1. Level of inequality and changes in the distribution of personal and household income

The Gini coefficient, which ranges from 0 (complete equality) to 1 (complete inequality), is 0.469 for Latin America, according to data available for 2015, practically unchanged from 2014, when the average stood at 0.473.[2] Most countries saw a decline in the Gini coefficient, mainly between 2008 and 2012, while variations were smaller between 2012 and 2015. In the regional average, the Gini coefficient fell only half as quickly between 2012 and 2015 (-0.6% per year), as it did between 2008 and 2012 (-1.2% per year) (see figure 1).

Income distribution can also be analysed on the basis of the ratio between the average per capita income of households in the highest income quintile (quintile V) and the lowest income quintile (quintile I). Between 2008 and 2015, the average ratio for 14 countries of the region fell 16.8%, from 14.7 to 12.2. Despite the decline, the differences remain very large; on average, in 2015, for every 100 monetary units received by each member of quintile I, each member of quintile V received 1,220 monetary units. This drop in the ratio in the 14 countries under review reflects an improvement in income distribution.

In 2015, for every 100 monetary units received by each member of quintile I, each member of quintile V received 1,220 monetary units.

---

[1]   The values of the inequality indicators presented in this edition of *Social Panorama of Latin America* correspond to an updated series and differ from those presented in previous editions of this publication. The process of updating the measurement included a conceptual and operational review of the different income items and the manner of imputing non-responses. It also meant putting aside the income adjustment process for the national accounts surveys.

[2]   Average for 15 countries, excluding Costa Rica, Guatemala and Nicaragua.

**Figure 1**

Latin America (17 countries): Gini coefficient, around 2008, 2012 and 2015[a][b]

## A. Around 2008 and 2012

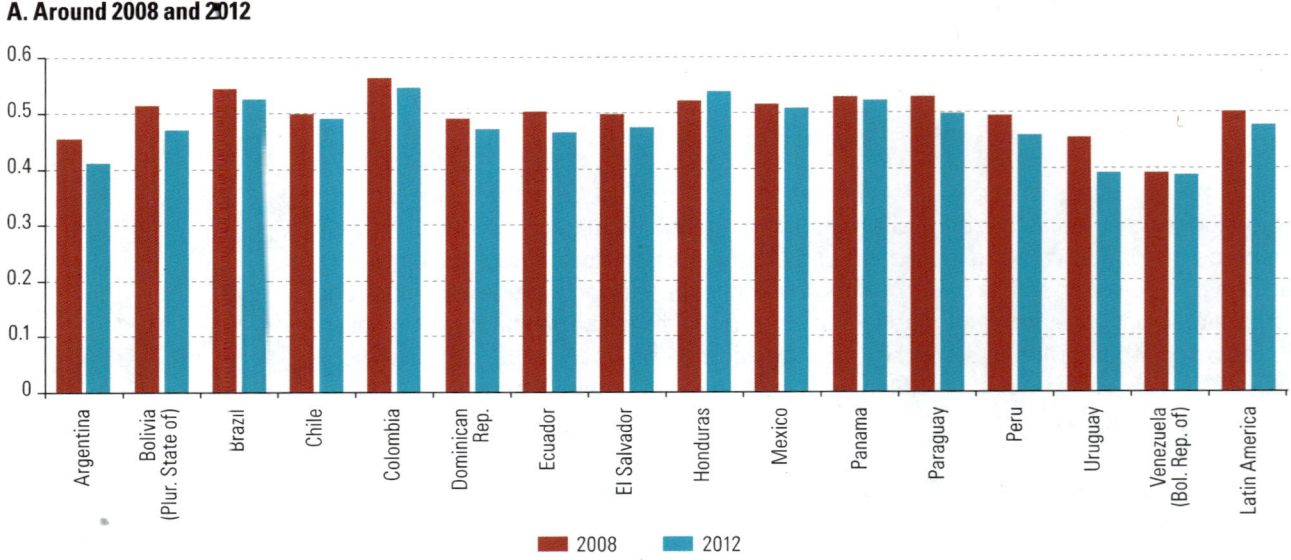

## B. Around 2012 and 2015

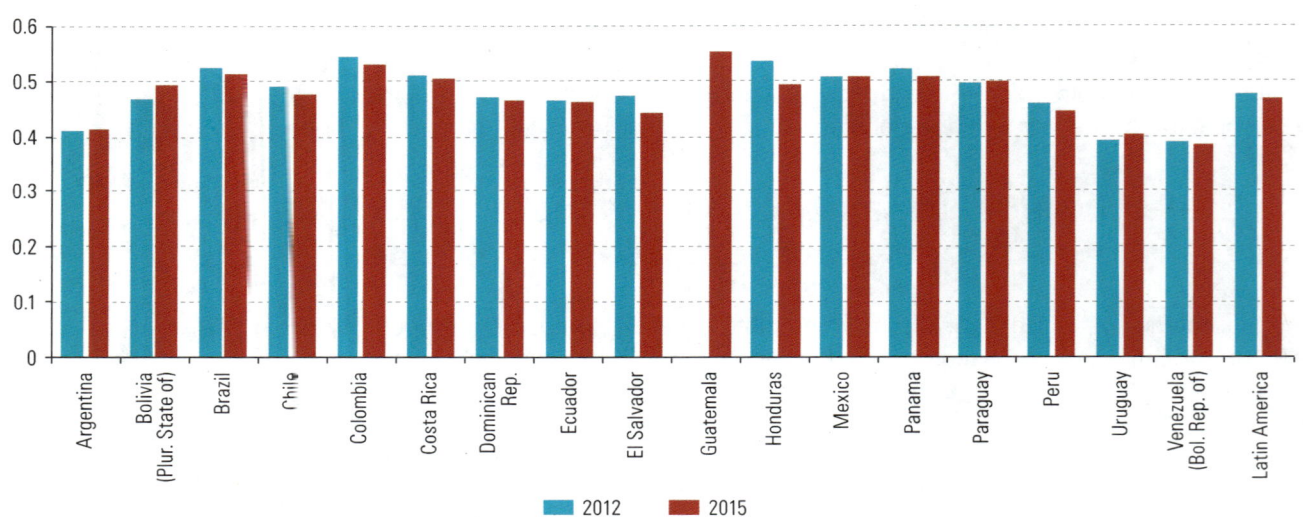

**Source**: Economic Commission for Latin America and the Caribbean (ECLAC), on the basis of Household Survey Data Bank (BADEHOG).
[a] Data refer to 2008, 2012 and 2015, except in the cases of Argentina (2009-2014), Bolivarian Republic of Venezuela (2008, 2012 and 2014), Chile (2009, 2011 and 2015), Colombia (2009, 2012 and 2015), Costa Rica (only 2012 and 2015), El Salvador (2009, 2013 and 2015), Guatemala (only 2014), Honduras (2009, 2013 and 2015), Mexico (2008, 2012 and 2014) and Plurinational State of Bolivia (2008, 2011 and 2014).
[b] The average for Latin America includes the 15 countries with information available for both subperiods. It does not include Costa Rica, Nicaragua or Guatemala.

The fall in inequality between 2008 and 2015 was linked, in general, to a higher relative increase in income for quintile I than for quintile V.[3] This occurred in the main sources of household income, that is, income from wage jobs and self-employment. In terms of the averages for a set of 14 countries, the real variation in per capita wage income in quintile I was 3% per year, compared to 2.3% per year in quintile V. There

---

3    An improvement in distribution does not automatically result in better well-being. In Honduras, for example, the improvement in income distribution between 2008 and 2015 came about within the framework of an overall decline in household income, which had a greater impact on quintile V households.

was a similar trend in income from self-employment, which grew at an annual rate of 2.8% (in real per capita terms) in quintile I, compared to an average variation of -0.3% in quintile V. Total retirement benefits and other transfers reflected the same pattern of differentiated increases benefitting quintile I households (up 6.4% per year, compared to 0.1% in quintile V). Transfers were very low in several countries in 2008, so although they posted strong growth over the period, their share of total per capita income of quintile I did not change significantly.

## 2. Income inequality from a gender perspective

Women's autonomy, in particular their economic autonomy, is a cornerstone of efforts to reduce inequality. There is ample empirical evidence that women's greater participation and labour income have a significant effect on reducing poverty and income inequality. In general, women have less access to production and financial resources, as well as to money, training and different technologies. Meanwhile, because they bear the brunt of unpaid domestic work, women have less time for their own use, which undermines their ability to train and maintain an unbroken presence in the labour market.

Low-income households contain a higher proportion of women of ages at which productive and reproductive demands are greatest. Without exception among the countries considered, women are overrepresented in the first two or three income quintiles. In particular, women aged between 20 and 59 are overrepresented in the poorest income quintile by up to 40% compared to men. This is because women tend to receive lower incomes, as a result of the difficulty of reconciling unpaid work in the home with labour market participation. Moreover, they generally work in typically low-wage occupations and are often overrepresented among the heads of single-parent households.

Meanwhile, the percentage of women who receive income from the labour market or in the form of pensions or other transfer is considerably lower than the percentage of men who do. An average figure for 15 countries shows that 44% of women in quintile I lack their own income, compared to just 23% of men.

With regard to the composition of personal income, transfers account for 16.8% of women's total income but less than 10% of men's income, whereas self-employment income accounts for 23.3% of women's total income compared to 33.7% of men's. The main source of income for both men and women is wages and salaries, accounting for 54% of all personal income. However, only one in two working-age women in the region are employed or seeking employment, and women's pay is still only 83.9% of men's.

In short, both the overrepresentation of women in the lower income quintiles and the higher proportion of women without their own income, especially in those quintiles, mean that a large group of women face deprivation and inequity. While progress has been made in recent years, the income gaps that women face, together with the differentiated composition of that income, remains a distinctive feature of inequality in all the countries of the region.

## B. Functional income distribution

The most commonly used approach to analysing income distribution in the region has been inequality between individuals or between households. The original concept of functional income inequality, which is reflected in aggregate indicators such as the wage share of gross domestic product (GDP), has received little attention at either the global or regional level. However, functional income distribution analysis provides very

> Functional income distribution analysis provides very valuable information for understanding the dynamics of labour income and capital yields and can be considered in conjunction with personal income inequality.

valuable information for understanding the dynamics of labour income and capital yields and can be considered in conjunction with personal income inequality.

A long-term series of the relationship between the wage bill and GDP in Latin America between 1950 and 2011, built by Alarco Tosoni (2014), shows that wage shares were highest in the late 1960s and early 1970s. They were also relatively high in the 1990s, albeit with lower values than the first cycle in the 1960s and 1970s. Smaller wage shares were identified during the 1980s and the first five years of the twenty-first century. In recent years, the wage share of GDP has risen in the regional aggregate, owing to an improvement in functional income distribution, chiefly in Argentina and Brazil.

It is useful to study changes in the wage share of GDP in conjunction with changes in personal income inequality, measured using the Gini coefficient. Personal income distribution inequality has decreased in the vast majority of Latin American countries since 2002, and the Gini coefficient declined between 2006 and 2014 in 13 of a total of 14 countries, with Costa Rica being the exception. Although wage share deterioration was widespread between 2002 and 2006, from 2006 onwards —alongside a decline in the Gini coefficient— this share improved, except in Guatemala, Mexico, Panama and the Plurinational State of Bolivia, where it continued to decrease (see figure 2). This indicates that the distributive improvements in the region since the middle of the previous decade may have been linked to a more equitable distribution of returns between labour and capital.[4]

**Figure 2**
Latin America (14 countries): wage share of GDP and Gini coefficient, 2002 and 2014
*(Percentages)*

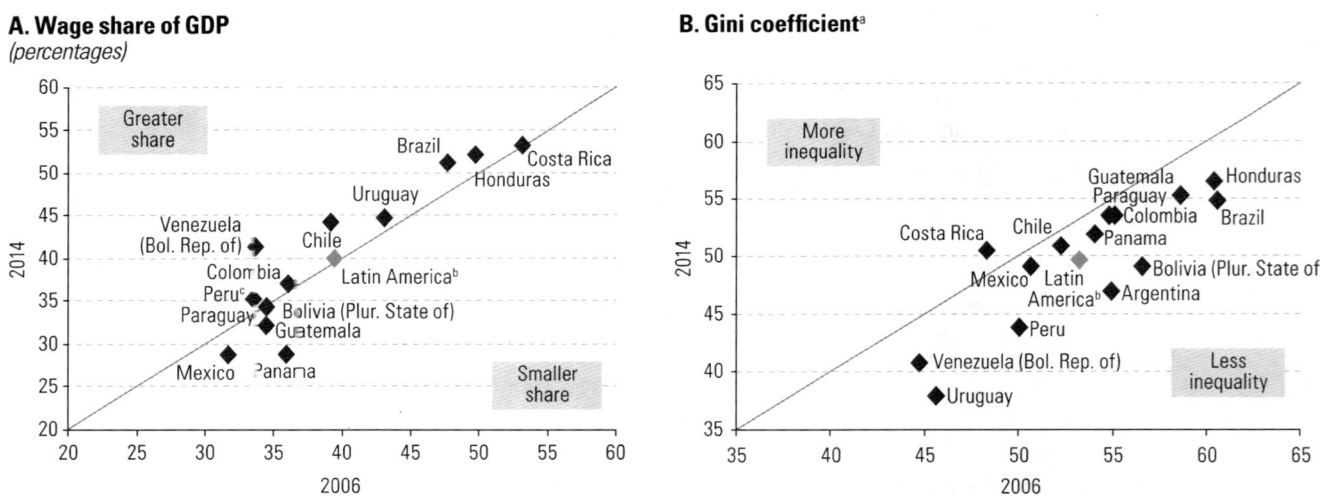

**Source:** Economic Commission for Latin America and the Caribbean (ECLAC), on the basis of information from CEPALSTAT, National Institute of Statistics and Censuses (INDEC) of Argentina, Central Bank of Costa Rica and Central Bank of Uruguay. .
[a] The Gini coefficients correspond to the previous series of inequality estimates produced by ECLAC, on the basis of an income aggregate that included the adjustment to national accounts.
[b] Simple average for the countries.
[c] Data correspond to 2007.

---

[4]   National accounts provide information on the wage bill (remuneration of wage workers), but do not usually cover mixed income. This refers to the remuneration of self-employed workers and implicitly contains an element of return on labour and an element of return on the capital involved in productive activities.

Sectoral-level analysis is also important for a better understanding of functional income inequality. The differences in the aggregate wage share of GDP between countries or variations in this ratio over time in a particular country may be due to changes in how value added is distributed between labour and capital in the different economic sectors, or to changes in the relative scale of value added among sectors. Analysis of the eight Latin American economies selected shows that the wage share of value added increased in four of them (Argentina, Brazil, Costa Rica and Honduras), decreased in three (Chile, Guatemala and Mexico) and stayed practically the same in one (Colombia). It also reveals shifts in the returns on labour and capital within sectors had stronger effects than changes in the relative size of the different sectors within in the economy. For example, more than 70% of the total change in the wage share of income was due to the intrasectoral effect (changes in the returns on labour and capital) in Argentina, Brazil, Colombia, Costa Rica and Guatemala, while the structural change effect (changes in the weight of different economic sectors) was greater in Chile, Costa Rica and Honduras.

# C. Inequality in the ownership of physical and financial assets

Putting efforts to combat inequality at the heart of government thinking will mean moving towards measurements that take into account the ownership structure of physical and financial assets. The document *The social inequality matrix in Latin America* (ECLAC, 2016c) states that one of the major structuring axes of inequality is social class, or socioeconomic stratum, which means that general wealth must be measured.

The ownership structure is one of the key variables involved in perpetuating —and even increasing— social inequality. For that reason, empirical studies that measure wealth or asset inequality tend to agree that this inequality is greater, more deeply rooted and more persistent than inequality measured solely on the basis of income.

According to the *Global Wealth Report 2016* by Credit Suisse, global wealth is very poorly distributed: 0.7% of adults (35 million people) hold almost half (45%) of the world's physical and financial assets; 9% of global wealth is concentrated in the hands of just 123,000 high net worth individuals (those who are worth more than US$ 30 million); and 1,722 people belong to the select group of billionaires.

The analysis below is based on a study of the situation in Mexico, but the finding may apply to other countries of the region. Between 2003 and 2014, the Mexican economy grew at an average annual rate of 2.6%. However, wealth grew at an average annual real rate of 7.9% over the same period. As a result, wealth in Mexico doubled between 2004 and 2014.

In addition, ownership of the physical assets held by production units listed in economic censuses is concentrated in very few hands, which demonstrates the high degree of structural heterogeneity in the Mexican economy: 10% of companies hold 93% of physical assets, while the remaining 90% have very few capital assets. As a result, the Gini coefficient of the distribution of physical assets is a record 0.93.

In 2015, the Government of Mexico managed 23% of assets, private companies 19%, autonomous public corporations 9% and financial institutions 5%, while 7% of financial assets were held by non-residents. Nevertheless, the largest share, 37% —equivalent to 280 billion Mexican pesos— is concentrated in the hands of families. Unfortunately, those 280 billion pesos are distributed very unequally.

Two thirds of these physical and financial assets are in the hands of the country's richest 10% of families and 1% of those families hold more than a third. By family, the Gini coefficient of total asset distribution (physical and financial) is 0.79. The distribution of financial assets is even more unequal: 80% is owned by the richest 10%.

## D. Challenges with regard to understanding inequality

The recent experience of the countries in their efforts to reduce and eliminate poverty indicates that achieving this goal will only be possible by combating and decreasing inequality in its various and interconnected manifestations.

ECLAC affirms the need for a new development style centred around equality and sustainability, and has reiterated the importance of reducing the high levels of inequality in the countries of Latin America and the Caribbean. The recent experience of the countries in their efforts to reduce and eliminate poverty indicates that achieving this goal will only be possible by combating and decreasing inequality in its various and interconnected manifestations.

The region has made significant progress in reducing inequality in personal income distribution since the start of the new millennium. A broader analysis indicates that this progress may derive from changes in labour relations. A functional approach to income distribution analysis in the region shows that in the past few years, the wage share of GDP grew in most countries, which suggests that the improvement in personal income distribution was linked to more equitable distribution of returns between capital and labour. Nonetheless, the partial analysis of inequality in wealth distribution among families indicates that it is higher than inequality measured solely on the basis of income and that the ownership structure of financial assets is even more concentrated, and this trend continues to deepen.

The study, analysis and measurement of wealth and of the ownership structure of physical and financial assets is a promising path to understanding the multidimensional nature of inequality and to achieving a more consistent analysis of the challenges to reducing it significantly in the region. Among the challenges of this research agenda is fine-tuning instruments and methodologies for measuring inequality. Improvements to household surveys to capture high incomes more accurately should be combined with analysis of other information sources, such as national accounts or personal tax records, to complement the findings of the surveys.

# Chapter II
# Social spending: trends and challenges in policy financing

One of the innovations of the 2030 Agenda for Sustainable Development is its focus on the means of implementation, with the explicit aim that this should be based on resources mobilized at the national and international levels. In this context, one of the most important tools for achieving the Sustainable Development Goals is social investment, which has been strongly associated with substantial progress in access to basic services such as sanitation, housing, education, health care and social protection systems, all areas in which the 2030 Agenda aims for guaranteed universal access. Social investment also includes spending on environmental protection and natural disaster prevention, essential for the progress towards environmental sustainability that is sought by the 2030 Agenda.

The chapter draws on the new ECLAC public social spending database and is divided into two sections. Section A uses the official data provided to ECLAC by the region's countries to describe recent trends in public social spending according to the functional classification, which considers the public resources allocated to policies associated with the following six functions: (i) environmental protection, (ii) housing and community amenities, (iii) health, (iv) recreation, culture and religion, (v) education, and (vi) social protection. Section B presents information on the social spending provided for in national budgets, describing the decisions that have been taken and the countries' plans for 2017.

## A. Public and social spending in 2000-2015

Central government and public sector social spending in the region's countries, calculated as a simple average, was worth 10.5% and 14.5% of GDP, respectively, in 2015 (see figure 3), the highest levels this century. For the first time, central government spending exceeded the level of disbursement in 2009 in response to the 2008 subprime crisis. Social spending in 2015 represented just over half of total public spending that year.

The countries spending most on social functions are Argentina, Brazil, Colombia and Costa Rica, at more than 20% of GDP, while the countries spending least are Guatemala and Haiti, at less than 8% of GDP. Taking the social functions separately, Argentina and Brazil spend most on social protection (over 13% of GDP in 2015), Costa Rica and the Plurinational State of Bolivia on education (over 7% of GDP in 2015) and Argentina and Costa Rica again on health care (over 6% of GDP in 2015).

When spending by social function at the public sector level is analysed, the official institutional coverage figures published by each country indicate that social protection, education and health are the top priorities in terms of resource allocation, at 5.0%, 4.6% and 3.4% of GDP, respectively, in 2015 (see figure 4).

Central government and public sector social spending in the region's countries, calculated as a simple average, was worth 10.5% and 14.5% of GDP, respectively, in 2015, the highest levels this century.

**Figure 3**

Latin America (19 countries): central government and public sector social spending, 2000-2015[a][b]
*(Percentages of GDP and of total public spending)*

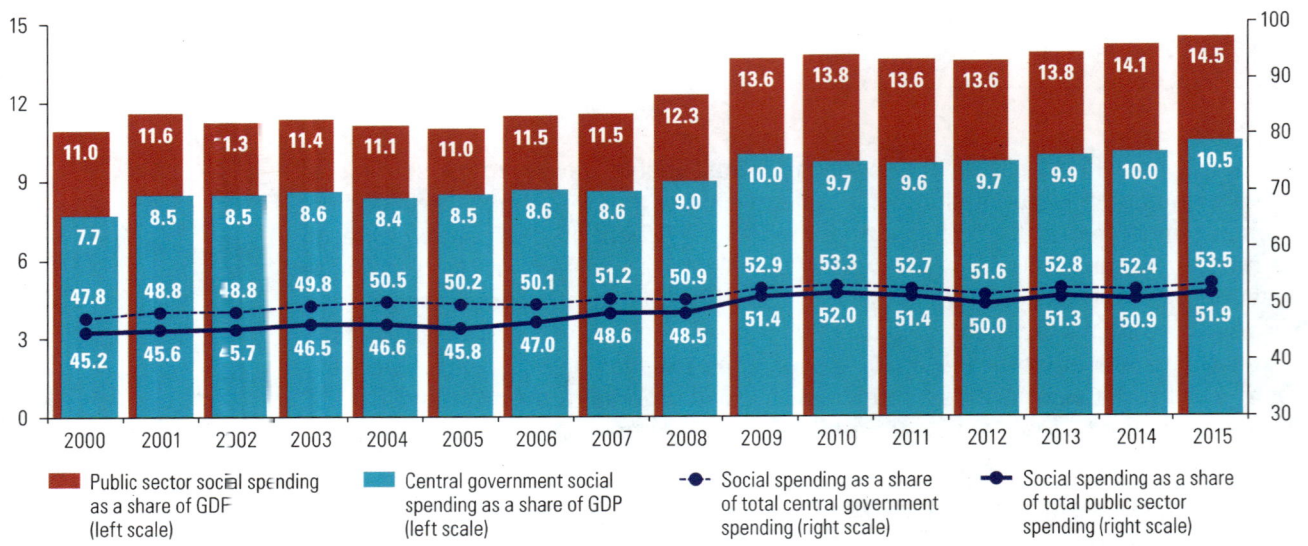

**Source:** Economic Commission for Latin America and the Caribbean (ECLAC), on the basis of official information from the respective countries.

[a] Simple average for 19 countries: Argentina, Bolivarian Republic of Venezuela, Brazil, Chile, Colombia, Costa Rica, Dominican Republic, Ecuador, El Salvador, Guatemala, Haiti, Honduras, Mexico, Nicaragua, Panama, Paraguay, Peru, Plurinational State of Bolivia and Uruguay. Information is available up to 2009 for the Bolivarian Republic of Venezuela and 2014 for Panama.

[b] The countries with coverage wider than central government are Argentina, Brazil, Colombia, Costa Rica, Ecuador, El Salvador, Mexico, Peru and the Plurinational State of Bolivia.

**Figure 4**

Latin America (19 countries): public sector social spending, by function, 2000-2015[a][b]
*(Percentages of GDP)*

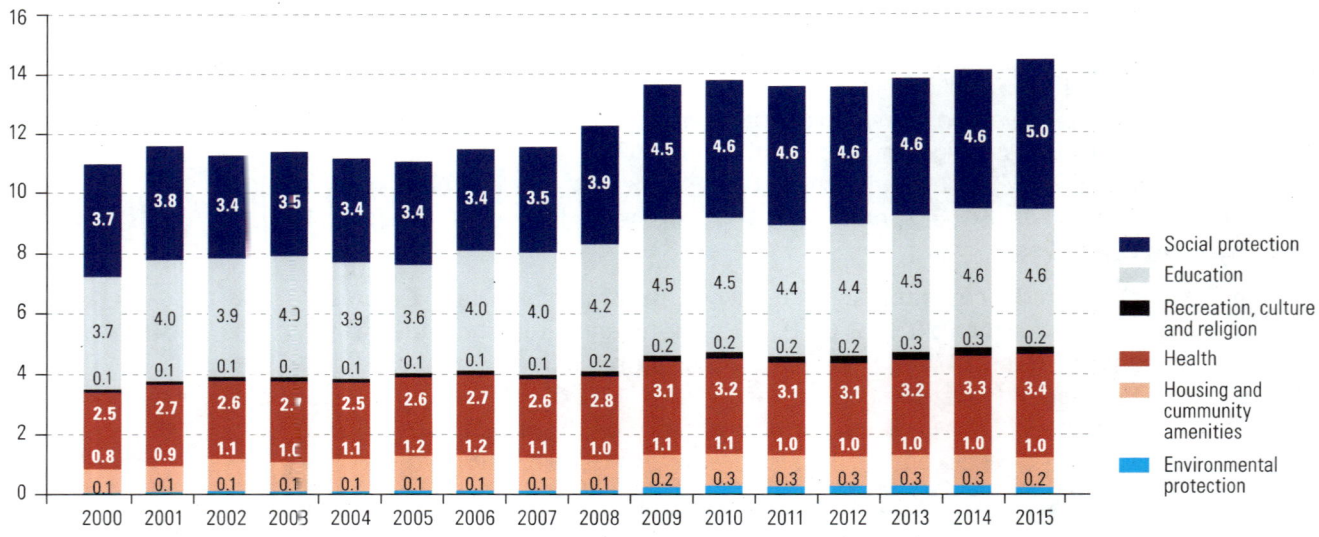

**Source:** Economic Commission for Latin America and the Caribbean (ECLAC), on the basis of official information from the respective countries.

[a] Simple average for 19 countries: Argentina, Bolivarian Republic of Venezuela, Brazil, Chile, Colombia, Costa Rica, Dominican Republic, Ecuador, El Salvador, Guatemala, Haiti, Honduras, Mexico, Nicaragua, Panama, Paraguay, Peru, Plurinational State of Bolivia and Uruguay. Information is available up to 2009 for the Bolivarian Republic of Venezuela and 2014 for Panama.

[b] The countries with coverage wider than central government are Argentina, Brazil, Colombia, Costa Rica, Ecuador, El Salvador, Mexico, Peru and the Plurinational State of Bolivia.

Comparing the 2014 social spending of the countries analysed in the region with that of the European Union countries and the United States reveals differences of 20 percentage points of GDP and almost 10 percentage points of GDP, respectively, in favour of the latter.

Central government per capita social spending averaged US$ 728 at 2010 prices in 2015, an increase of about 60% from 2000 and of over 20% in five years. Official information for the public sector as a whole yields an average of US$ 1,094 per capita for the region's countries, an increase of almost 50% from 2000 and almost 10% from 2010.

# B. Present and future social spending as budgeted in the 2015-2017 period

Analysis of social spending executed in the 2000-2015 period is supplemented by a review of the information in the budgets of the Latin American countries with a view to assessing governments' social policy priorities. This edition of the *Social Panorama of Latin America* analyses budgeted central government expenditure for fiscal years 2015, 2016 and 2017, and results are shown for 13 countries in the region.

Figure 5 shows that, on average, the region's countries have been cautious in preparing their 2016 and 2017 budgets, in that the total and social spending budgeted for is lower than in 2015. The chart also allows the spending implemented in 2015 to be compared to the amount budgeted for the year, and shows that actual total spending was 1 percentage point of GDP lower than planned (i.e. an average of 10% of the amount budgeted); furthermore, the shortfall was greatest for social functions.

**Figure 5**

Latin America (12 countries): executed and budgeted central government social spending, by function, 2015-2017[a]

*(Percentages of GDP)*

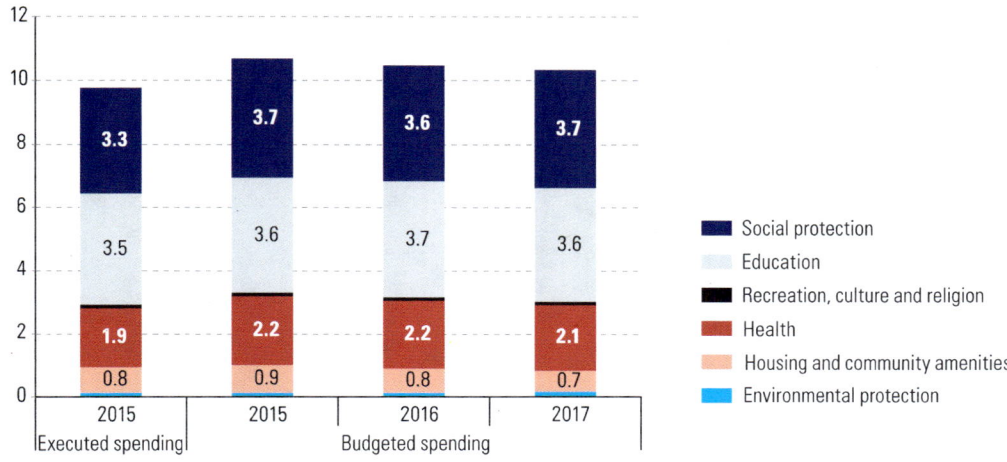

**Source**: Economic Commission for Latin America and the Caribbean (ECLAC).

[a] Simple average for 12 countries: Argentina, Brazil, Colombia, Costa Rica, Dominican Republic, El Salvador, Guatemala, Honduras, Mexico, Nicaragua, Panama and Peru.

The information in the countries' public budgets, and those of South America in particular, suggests budget cuts in social functions for 2017. This could have a direct impact on the population in a context of positive if low economic growth, compounding limitations in implementation, since budgets are not always executed as fully as they might be.

## C. Conclusions

ECLAC is calling once again for policy financing to be safeguarded and protected to ensure the sustainability of the progress made, deal with ongoing challenges and be able to advance towards the SDGs.

The 2030 Agenda for Sustainable Development represents an ambitious attempt by countries to establish a broad global consensus for simultaneous progress with the social, economic and environmental pillars of sustainable development. Any substantial advance will depend, among other implementation measures, on each country's ability to mobilize sufficient domestic resources not just for aspects linked directly to inclusion and social welfare, but for strengthened environmental protection and sustainability. In this context, ECLAC is calling once again for social policy financing to be safeguarded and protected to ensure the sustainability of the progress made, deal with ongoing challenges and be able to advance towards the Goals agreed on in the 2030 Agenda for Sustainable Development.

Because of this, measurement of the resources invested in social policies and analysis of their composition and evolution over time, and likewise of their redistributive effect and efficiency, must form part of the implementation process for the Sustainable Development Goals. The effort made in this chapter to expand and improve social spending information in collaboration with the region's countries is a major step in this direction. Better measurement is bound to mean better analysis and decision-making by the countries.

# Chapter III
# The social inequality matrix: age as an axis of social inequalities

Age is one of the axes of social inequality, an underlying determinant of the organization of social institutions such as the family and the structures that organize education and work. As such, it is also a determinant of the distribution of well-being, power and authority in the social structure and one of the foundations of social organization and its allocation of responsibilities and roles (ECLAC, 2016a).

The life cycle perspective is helpful for studying the progression of different stages that people pass through over the course of their lives, from birth to death, owing to the interaction of biological, relational and social factors (Carr, 2009). This perspective facilitates an analysis that not only incorporates age and its interaction with other axes of inequality but that can help identify the concatenation of inequalities at each stage of people's life histories and the critical junctures that contribute to the reproduction of social inequality at these different stages. Four basic stages in the life cycle have traditionally been distinguished: childhood and adolescence, youth, adulthood and old age (Cecchini and others, 2015), but there also are very important divisions within each of these.

Analysing the relationship between inequality and the life cycle requires drawing a distinction between stratifications over the life cycle, within each of its stages and between these different stages in different sociohistorical contexts. Stratification over the different stages of the life cycle has to do with the way institutions and systems that distribute resources, such as the State, market and family, generate processes of social differentiation between population groups by virtue of the stage of life they are in. Besides inequalities between people at different stages of the life cycle at any given time, there are also large gaps between people at the same stage, particularly in relation to socioeconomic status, gender, ethnic and racial origin and territory. An important part of this approach is that inequality is conceived as the outcome of processes that take place over time, being the cumulative result of decisions, needs, advantages, events and experiences interacting with institutional arrangements and the social and economic context (Gibbs and Eaton, 2014). Chapter III explores intra- and intergenerational inequalities at the different stages of the life cycle, seeking to emphasize the concatenation of inequality over these stages. It also emphasizes the inequalities experienced over the life cycle by indigenous people, a population segment historically discriminated against. Lastly, it provides an overview of institutions dedicated to specific population segments over the life cycle, highlighting the challenges of coordination for public policies.

Each stage of the life cycle presents specific opportunities, challenges and risks. Childhood, and early childhood in particular, is a stage of particular importance for human development: it is the period when the foundations for future cognitive, affective and social development are laid (ECLAC, 2016a). It is a stage at which risk factors converge in such sensitive areas for development as health and nutrition, early stimulation and education, and the opportunity to grow and develop in safe family and community settings. Infringements of rights at this stage can have deep and lasting effects.

In Latin America and the Caribbean, inequality is pervasive from the earliest stages of people's lives. Poverty in childhood is particularly critical because of children's greater dependence, lack of autonomy and vulnerability to the economic and social conditions of their environment and their families. Children are overrepresented in the lowest income quintiles and more likely to have multiple unmet needs than people at other stages of the life cycle. Furthermore, there are also large inequalities within the child population itself when other axes of social inequality such as socioeconomic status, gender, ethnic and racial origin and territory are considered, as illustrated in figure 6, which shows the gaps between the infant mortality rate of the indigenous population and that of the non-indigenous population.

The life cycle perspective facilitates an analysis that not only incorporates age and its interaction with other axes of inequality but that can help identify the concatenation of inequalities at each stage of people's life histories and the critical junctures that contribute to the reproduction of social inequality at these different stages.

**Figure 6**
Latin America (11 countries): infant mortality by ethnicity, around 2010
*(Per 1,000 live births)*

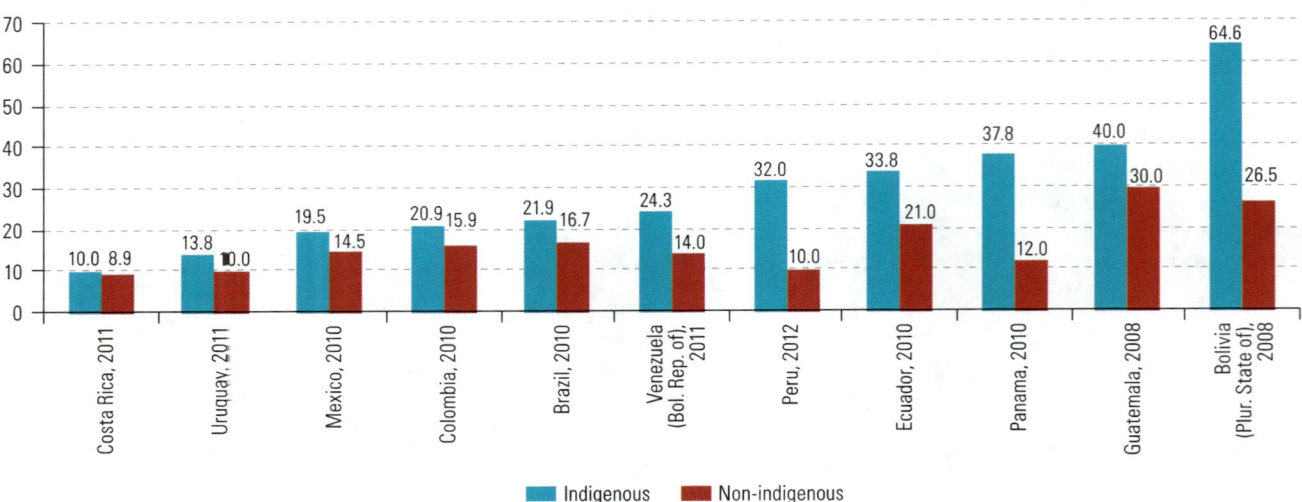

**Source**: Economic Commission for Latin America and the Caribbean (ECLAC), on the basis of Latin American and Caribbean Demographic Centre (CELADE)-Population Division of ECLAC.

Access to preschool education is another area that is critical to children's development. There is great heterogeneity here as well, with the gap between children in the different countries of the region being especially striking. Within each country, attendance at this level of schooling is usually higher in urban areas than in rural ones. Another major challenge is the quality of this level of education, on which its benefits largely depend. Consequently, as stated in target 4.2 of the Sustainable Development Goals and the Ibero-American commitment signed in 2010 in relation to the Educational Goals for 2021, there needs to be progress towards universalization of preschool education to mitigate inequalities in the accumulation of capabilities and skills, with all the repercussions these subsequently have for people's opportunities and well-being.

Youth is another critical stage during which social inequalities may be either widened or reduced. During this stage, issues that will mark adulthood are defined: young people are expected to complete their studies, acquire work skills, begin their working lives under suitable conditions and, in many cases, start or consolidate a family of their own. In Latin America, however, these phases and transitions often do not follow a linear sequence, and during them inequality is reproduced and magnified.

Individuals' level of education is one of the most important determinants of their opportunities in terms of employment, income, health, housing and other individual and social benefits over their lifetimes (Espínola and Claro, 2010). Completion of secondary school, in particular, not only affects later stages in adolescents' life cycle but also plays a fundamental role in interrupting the transmission of poverty and inequality to future generations. The percentage of young people aged 20 to 24 (both male and female) completing secondary education has risen across the region, and this growth has been particularly striking in rural areas, with rates rising from 18.7% to 38.4% for men and from 20.4% to 42.2% for women. At the same time, while the secondary school completion rate among young indigenous people has risen strongly (by about 50%, as compared to some 20% for non-indigenous young people), there are still very large ethnicity gaps in this indicator, and closing them will require specific public policy action.

Another major challenge for young Latin Americans, and an obstacle to their emancipation, is the transition from school to the labour market. A group of special concern are young people who are neither studying nor employed in the labour market. This situation is contributing to the reproduction of inequality down the generations and preventing the region from taking advantage of the window of opportunity represented by the demographic dividend. However, it is important to recognize and bring to light the great variety of situations within this group. It is a group composed mainly of women, as other studies have identified (ECLAC, 2016a; Trucco and Ullmann, 2015). Although the proportion of young people who were neither studying nor employed in the labour market dropped on average between 2002 and 2014 in the five countries of the region with information available on ethnicity (Brazil, Chile, Ecuador, Guatemala and the Plurinational State of Bolivia), the decline was not uniform across the different population groups, being much more modest for women than for men, while indigenous women made the least progress.

Access to income and well-being in adulthood depends even more on the ability to participate successfully in the job market, which derives in turn from the skills and capabilities people have acquired during earlier stages in life (Rossel and Filgueira, 2015, cited in ECLAC, 2016a). Furthermore, access to contributory social protection is heavily dependent on participation in the formal labour market. This is also the stage when the pressures of care are felt most keenly because of the presence of young dependants (children) and, in some cases, of older persons as well (parents or other family members). The combination of these demands —the need to generate adequate income and to reconcile labour market participation with care responsibilities— creates a particularly challenging situation for adult women. Lastly, the way individuals engage with the job market during adulthood, and in particular their access to social protection and security mechanisms, have implications for their well-being when they enter old age.

> Access to income and well-being in adulthood depends even more on the ability to participate successfully in the job market, which derives in turn from the skills and capabilities people have acquired during earlier stages in life.

The region is undergoing a period of profound demographic transformation, characterized by steady population ageing (ECLAC, 2016a). The most notable inequalities in old age are associated with alterations in family living arrangements, access to a stable pension and retirement income and changes in health and in physical and intellectual autonomy. At the same time, divides between older persons reflect the disadvantages (or advantages) they have accumulated over a lifetime.

For example, educational attainments during adolescence and youth substantially affect people's long-term position in the labour market, which in turn affects access to contributory pensions. Generally speaking, the proportion of both men and women aged 65 and over receiving a pension increased modestly in almost all the countries between 2002 and 2014. However, there are very large differences in contributory pension eligibility by education level: taking the simple average for the eight countries with information available, just 30% of men aged 65 and over with incomplete primary education had a pension in 2014, while 66% of those with secondary education or more did; the figures for women were 21% and 62%, respectively, which reveals a gender gap stemming from the weaker position of women in the labour market (see figure 7).

There is a high degree of inequality in people's prospects of having to live with some disability during the final stage of life, related in turn to other factors such as educational attainment and socioeconomic status. People who had secondary or tertiary education in their youth have a lower prevalence of disability than those with lesser educational attainments. As ECLAC (2016a) argues, those who go through the stages of life in a context of economic vulnerability and lesser access to social protection mechanisms are at high risk of any health problem becoming a disability because they cannot afford the health and support services and the assistance they need to mitigate the impact of limitations acquired with age, particularly considering that health and rehabilitation services are tending to rise in price over time and may be unaffordable.

**Figure 7**
Latin America (simple average for 8 countries): persons aged 65 and over receiving a pension, by sex and education level, 2002 and 2014
*(Percentages)*

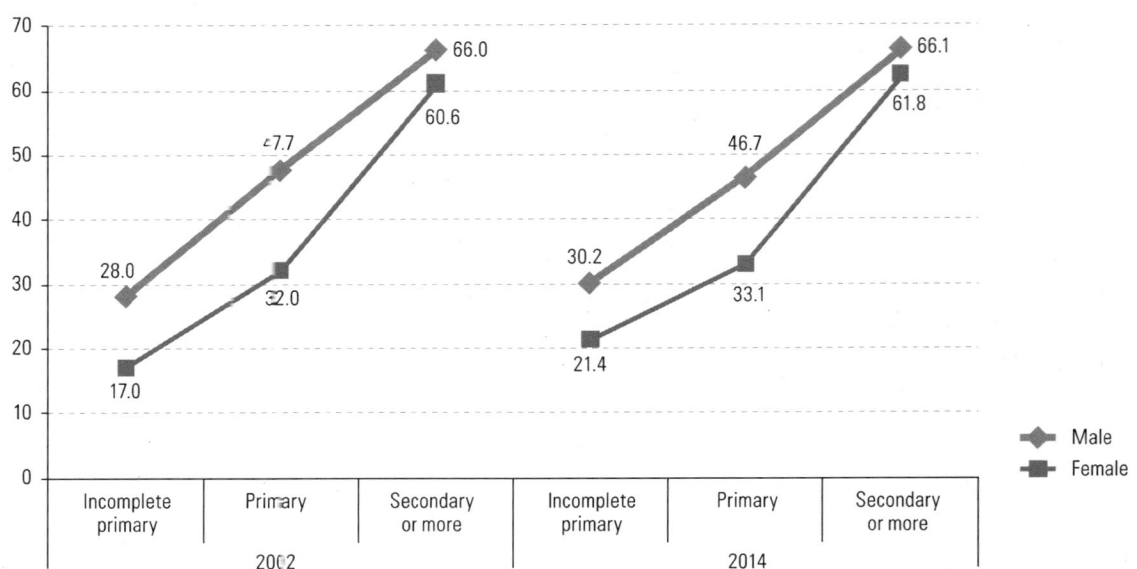

Source: Economic Commission for Latin America and the Caribbean (ECLAC), on the basis of special processing of census microdata using Retrieval of Data for Small Areas by Microcomputer (REDATAM) software.

As for indigenous people, their situation and the inequalities they experience over the life cycle are challenges for social inclusion in the region, despite the major progress made in recent decades. The inequality characterizing Latin America is manifested in the case of indigenous children and young adults by considerable disadvantages, particularly as regards health and education, two dimensions that are vital at this stage in the life cycle and that in turn have implications for later stages. Furthermore, this infringement of rights is compounded by interaction with other axes of social inequality (gender, socioeconomic, territorial and age inequalities), resulting in multiple forms of exclusion. These inequalities are manifested in spheres critical to the current and future development of indigenous children. In youth, indigenous people are affected by educational shortcomings and inequalities in health, including problems with mental health and substance abuse. In adulthood, indigenous women and men are faced with numerous difficulties, this being a stage in the life cycle when "productive" and "reproductive" decisions deriving from their social, cultural, environmental, territorial and spiritual environment have to be taken within a development paradigm characterized by a ransacking of natural, human and cultural resources that is categorically opposed to the indigenous concept of "living well". Lastly, old age truly begins for many indigenous people when they can no longer carry out tasks or activities for the maintenance of their families or the material reproduction of the community. A person's status and role in society may increase as they "age", as a high value is usually set on the collective wisdom and memory that have to be transmitted to young people to ensure the cultural reproduction of the group. The way the different axes of social inequality interact and reinforce each other in the situation of indigenous people can be seen at different stages in the life cycle. It is thus vital to design policies that genuinely reflect current international standards regarding the rights of indigenous peoples, conjoining individual and collective rights and incorporating gender, generational and territorial outlooks.

The corollary of an increased awareness of the need to adopt policy approaches that are sensitive to people's lifelong needs is the emergence of social institutions devoted to specific population segments such as children and adolescents, young adults and older people. These institutions have spread throughout Latin America and the Caribbean and are anchored in all cases both in international commitments and instruments and in national laws and specialized government agencies. Their organizational diversity notwithstanding, these agencies share a commitment to mainstreaming the specific needs and guaranteeing the rights of these population segments in all public action. To achieve this, the region's countries need to overcome the shared challenge of constantly increasing their capacity for intersectoral coordination.

The aims of the 2030 Agenda for Sustainable Development include not only ensuring that no one is left behind, but reaching the furthest behind first. To meet these aspirations, it is necessary to determine which population groups suffer most from marginalization, exclusion and infringements of their rights. These groups often experience a number of inequalities that overlap and compound each other, accumulating throughout their lives and across generations. Efforts to identify these groups are complicated by the statistical invisibility of certain populations and their needs and the limited potential to disaggregate information sources by multiple characteristics. Better information sources are urgently needed to look beyond national averages. In particular, longitudinal data, which are also lacking, are needed to better analyse trends and interrelationships in the different manifestations of social inequality over the whole of people's life cycles.

The life cycle approach places individuals at the centre of public action from birth to the end of life, recognizing that their needs change over a lifetime and that the individual is the starting and end point of social policy. From an institutional standpoint, this means recognizing and dealing with the specific needs and risks of each stage in the life cycle, while also coordinating policies focused on these different stages.

The life cycle approach places individuals at the centre of public action from birth to the end of life, recognizing that their needs change over a lifetime and that the individual is the starting and end point of social policy. From an institutional standpoint, this means recognizing and dealing with the specific needs and risks of each stage in the life cycle, while also coordinating policies focused on these different stages.

# Chapter IV
# Time distribution: a key element of the inequality analysis

Time is a finite resource that people use in different ways depending on a number of sociocultural factors that reflect social structure, power relationships and the prevailing gender order, among other things. The sexual division of labour in the region restricts some in using this time freely and autonomously, resulting in a lack of own time. As occurs with income, the lack of own time and of the ability to manage it freely is a significant contributor to inequality.

In Latin America and the Caribbean, the production structure, gender roles and family make-up have reinforced stark differences between men and women with respect to time distribution. This has led to inequalities in opportunities and outcomes for personal and professional development. In order to increase well-being and sustainable development, public policies must include time as a central element to guarantee better harmonization and balance between time spent on domestic, employment and personal activities. Just as the feminist movement's slogan "the personal is political" drew attention to domestic issues requiring public policies, advances in the region show that, now, time is political. It is essential to develop and implement public policies on the redistribution of time and work to foster gender equality and sustainable development (ECLAC, 2016b).

## A.   Time distribution and inequality

Ongoing discussions about the care economy and the sustainability of human life —from the perspective of feminist economics— clearly show that much of what is produced and what sustains people is neither considered nor accounted for in traditional economics (Carrasco and Tello, 2013). Social inequality in the region is strongly determined by the production matrix and ownership structure, as well as other structural determinants —like the prevailing gender system— which in turn intersects with factors such as life cycle stages, area of residence, ethnicity and race (ECLAC, 2016c).

According to ECLAC (2016b, 2016d), time use and the distribution of unpaid domestic work are a central element in the analysis of gender inequality. The achievement of women's autonomy depends heavily on the balanced distribution of unpaid domestic and care work between men and women, and between families, the market, the community and the State. For a complete and in-depth analysis of inequalities in Latin America and the Caribbean, more light must be shed on the distribution and use of time by men and women.

The Montevideo Strategy adopted by the governments of the region at the thirteenth Regional Conference on Women in Latin America and the Caribbean (2016) highlights time-use surveys as essential data-generating tools which provide input for the design of equality policies. These surveys are the ideal information source for the analysis of gender inequality; studies on the link between monetary poverty, income and time distribution and use; national, regional and international requirements for data on unpaid work and new labour statistics requirements. Nineteen countries in the region have already measured time use, mainly in the past 10 years. However, existing time-use surveys are not comparable owing to the different methodologies used in terms of the objectives, collection process, classification of activities, geographical scope and ability to disaggregate data. Nonetheless, it is hoped that the adoption of the Classification of

Time-Use Activities for Latin America and the Caribbean (CAUTAL) in 2015 will allow the region to move towards a common methodology that allows international comparability.

The analysis of the dimensions of inequality and how they interconnect is fundamental to the design of public policies that would allow society to achieve sustainable development and the Goals set forth in the 2030 Agenda for Sustainable Development (ECLAC, 2016e, 2016f). Sustainable Development Goal indicator 5.4.1 (Proportion of time spent on unpaid domestic and care work, by sex, age and location) was proposed at the global level to monitor the achievement of gender equality and the empowerment of women and girls. Although it is not one of the Sustainable Development Goal indicators that countries regularly produce (despite a clear concept and established methodology), the efforts of national statistical offices in Latin American to develop time-use measurement tools have made it is possible to calculate this indicator in 17 countries, as shown in figure 8. According to these data, women in the region spend between one fifth and one third of their time each day or each week on unpaid domestic and care work, while men spend about 10% of their time on this work. Although indicator 5.4.1 offers a perspective of the situation at the national level, efforts should be made to shed light on the inequalities affecting specific groups, which are concealed by average figures.

Figure 8
Latin America (17 countries): time spent on unpaid domestic and care work, by sex (Sustainable Development Goal indicator 5.4.1)
*(Percentages)*

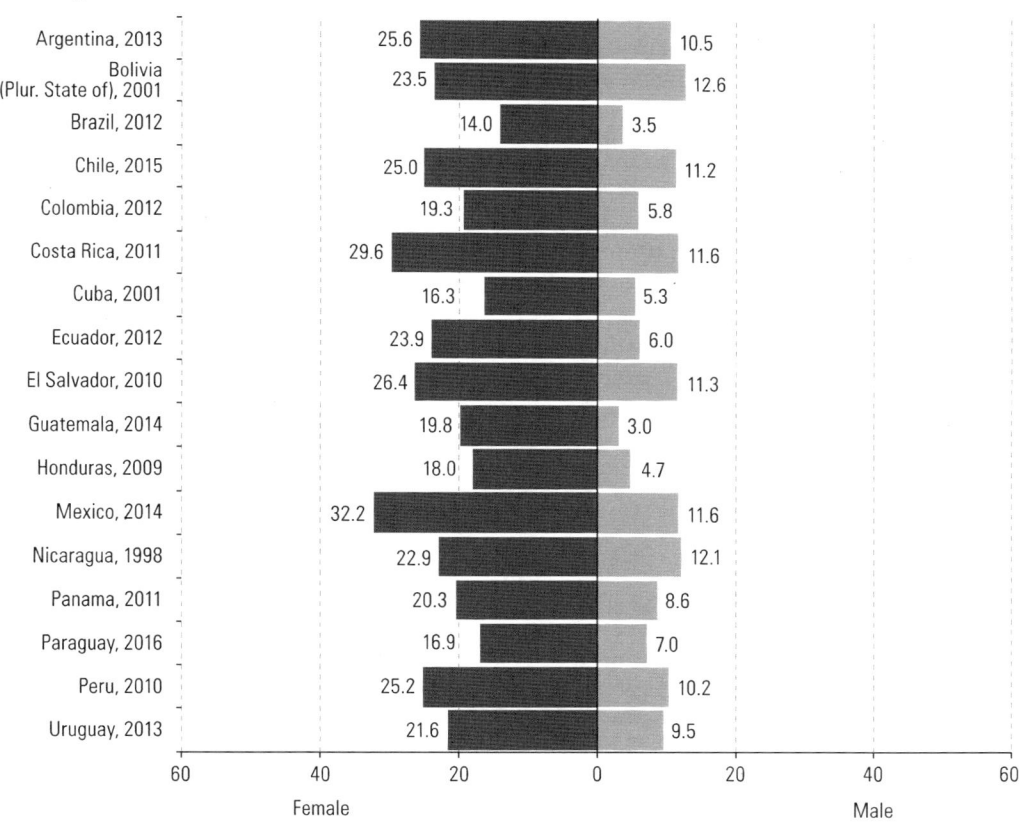

| Country | Female | Male |
|---|---|---|
| Argentina, 2013 | 25.6 | 10.5 |
| Bolivia (Plur. State of), 2001 | 23.5 | 12.6 |
| Brazil, 2012 | 14.0 | 3.5 |
| Chile, 2015 | 25.0 | 11.2 |
| Colombia, 2012 | 19.3 | 5.8 |
| Costa Rica, 2011 | 29.6 | 11.6 |
| Cuba, 2001 | 16.3 | 5.3 |
| Ecuador, 2012 | 23.9 | 6.0 |
| El Salvador, 2010 | 26.4 | 11.3 |
| Guatemala, 2014 | 19.8 | 3.0 |
| Honduras, 2009 | 18.0 | 4.7 |
| Mexico, 2014 | 32.2 | 11.6 |
| Nicaragua, 1998 | 22.9 | 12.1 |
| Panama, 2011 | 20.3 | 8.6 |
| Paraguay, 2016 | 16.9 | 7.0 |
| Peru, 2010 | 25.2 | 10.2 |
| Uruguay, 2013 | 21.6 | 9.5 |

**Source**: Economic Commission for Latin America and the Caribbean (ECLAC), on the basis of special tabulations from time-use surveys conducted in the respective countries.

**Note**: Figures take into account time spent on domestic and care work in one's own household, in other households, in the community and volunteer work, except in the case of Brazil, where the survey asks only one question relating to domestic work in one's own household, and of Honduras, which includes only information on care for members of one's own household. The data correspond to the national total except for Costa Rica (Greater Metropolitan Area) and Cuba (Old Havana). The population examined was 15 years and older, except in Argentina (18 years and older) and Nicaragua (6 years and older).

Time distribution varies during a person's life cycle. However, there is a common thread which is the greater burden of unpaid domestic and care work for women, in particular during their reproductive years.

Time distribution varies during a person's life cycle. However, there is a common thread which is the greater burden of unpaid domestic and care work for women, in particular during their reproductive years.

The division of public and private spaces for men and women occurs from a very early age. Although data from time-use surveys are not designed to measure child labour, they do shed light on the early construction of gender roles by showing that male children and adolescents spend more time on paid work than girl children and adolescents. They also show notable differences in the time spent on unpaid work, which ranges from 6.6 to 15.2 hours per week for male children and adolescents, compared with 13.6 to 23.3 hours per week for girl children and adolescents, depending on the country. Data on how boys, girls and adolescents spend their time also allows the measurement of their well-being. They indicate that boys aged 18 and under spend two to seven hours per week more than girls in the same age group on social activities, including leisure, sports and recreational activities with family and friends.

Data on time use by young people aged 15 to 29 who are not in education or employment helps break the stigma that they are inactive or unproductive members of society. On average, women who are not in education or employment spend at least 40 hours per week on unpaid domestic work, which means that they do work, but receive no compensation (ECLAC, 2016b).

Lastly, time-use data help to analyse the care that older persons provide and receive. Some surveys in the region (for example in Mexico and Uruguay) show the care provided to older persons at home and take account of activities such as assistance with personal hygiene, feeding or medical care, including transportation to health centres, and support in the use of information technology. In households where older persons are present, women spend 18 hours per week caring for them, compared with 15 hours for men.

The data indicate that women aged 65 and older spend between 9.8 and 32.5 hours per week caring for members of their own or other households, generally younger generations, so that other women (daughters, daughters-in-law, nieces, neighbours) can go to work. This is a clear example of the unequal distribution of time in old age. It also shows that the situation is worse for women who may not have been as active in the labour market during their adult lives and thus receive fewer social benefits relating to employment, which then results in greater difficulties for them to access care services. This is a perverse logic that deprives people of the very services that they provided to others throughout the course of their own lives (Gómez, 2008).

## B. The valuation of unpaid work and the System of National Accounts

Domestic and care work support societies and have a significant impact on countries' well-being and development potential. Nonetheless, the limited definition of the System of National Accounts (SNA) production boundary excludes the domestic and care services produced or consumed by members of a household from the central framework of macroeconomic analysis. This conceals the importance of these activities for the economy, and perpetuates economic and power relationships. Owing to the importance of national accounts in economic analysis, decision-making and policy formulation, the exclusion of these activities has repercussions for the distribution of resources and benefits stemming from that production. If this aspect of the economy is not recognized or its impact is not analysed, inequalities will persist or worsen.

The valuation of unpaid work in the framework of SNA provides a more precise measurement of what society produces (shedding light on a part of the economy that had remained hidden) and allows the contribution of this type of work to be incorporated into macroeconomic analysis and decision-making. Moreover, it aids the analysis of the interaction between the household and market economies. A revision of SNA carried out in 1993 introduced the possibility of adding satellite accounts to the central framework, in order to provide a comprehensive picture of a specific field of economic activity. This significantly expanded the analytical capacity of national accounting, without overburdening or disrupting the central system.

The countries that have determined the economic value of unpaid domestic work have shown that this type of work is equivalent to 15.2% to 24.2% of GDP and that there is a marked difference in the distribution of unpaid domestic responsibilities. In terms of the relative weight of men's and women's contributions to GDP, women contribute between 70% and 87%, depending on the country.

## C. The contribution of time-use data to equality policies

Today's apparently gender-neutral public policies disregard distribution of time as a fundamental resource for the social and economic well-being of people and society as a whole. The failure to recognize the contribution by both men and women to families' well-being and to sustainable development through unpaid work widens gaps and reproduces inequalities. States must address this problem through innovative public policies designed around time distribution and unpaid work and geared towards transforming the existing sexual division of labour.

This chapter describes a non-exhaustive research and recommendation agenda for public policies that highlights the potential utilization of time-use and distribution data for equality policies from a gender perspective. Although some sectoral applications are suggested, it is important to establish inter-institutional and intersectoral coordination and synergies, and there is an urgent need for comprehensive policies, especially on redistributive measures aimed at working in a cross-cutting manner towards equality between men and women and the recognition of women's contributions to countries' growth, well-being and development.

Time-use data gleaned from surveys, for instance, generate empirical data for policies to expand water networks, sanitation and drinking water distribution, which could improve gender equality by reducing the unpaid work done by women. In rural areas of Peru, data show that 57.3% of women spend time fetching water, and in Guatemala women spend six hours per week on this activity, which is almost two hours more than men.

Time distribution is closely linked to the organization of space in each territory; making activities compatible is linked to distances and means and conditions for covering them, particularly in cities (ECLAC, 2016e). Data on the time that men and women spend each week commuting between home and work in the capital cities of five Latin American countries (Colombia, Ecuador, Mexico, Peru and Uruguay) show that they spend one hour more than the national average on this activity, and that women spend less time than men commuting, owing to the nature of their participation in the labour market. With a view to building cities that provide a better quality of life for both men and women, helpful measures include planning spaces and defining time use for urban services (for example, timetables, waiting times, attention to and management

States must address this problem through innovative public policies designed around time distribution and unpaid work and geared towards transforming the existing sexual division of labour.

of procedures and distances) so that women and men can perform their daily tasks of caring for family members and paid work more easily and quickly (Segovia, 2016).

Time-use indicators establish a link between unpaid work (for households) and paid work (for the market) as the amount of time spent on the former limits the availability of time to perform the latter. Time use by the employed population shows that people have double working days (paid and unpaid) and that women have a heavier overall workload in all countries (on the whole, they work 6 to 21 hours more than men each week). Women's overrepresentation in unpaid work and underrepresentation in paid work show the link between unpaid work and women's lesser engagement in the labour market, as well as the fact that, compared with men, women tend to have more informal and precarious jobs. Hence, it is crucial to consider time distribution in the formulation of policies which, when combined with other sectoral policies, incentivize the redistribution of domestic work and promote labour practices that offer alternatives for the organization of time spent on market activities (Marco, 2012). Moreover, the balance between paid and unpaid work with shorter working days would allow men to participate more in domestic and care work and would increase women's employment and income-generation options (Batthyány, 2009).

Monetary poverty and lack of time sustain a vicious circle that is very difficult to break without policies focused on strengthening women's economic autonomy. An analysis of time-use data based on per capita income shows that women in the lowest-income households spend the most time on unpaid work. The differences are significant: women in quintile V households spend an average of 32 hours per week on unpaid work, compared with 46 hours per week for women in quintile I. For men, the difference between those in quintile V and quintile I households is generally not more than one hour per day. In order to eliminate poverty in all its forms, there is a need for public policies with a gender perspective that can eliminate the structural factors of the feminization of poverty in the lowest income households. In addition to monetary income redistribution policies, there is a need for policies targeting time redistribution, which is indispensable to eradicating poverty and achieving development.

Various studies on time use by beneficiaries of conditional transfer programmes (Gammage and Orozco, 2008; ECLAC, 2013 and 2016b) suggest that time spent on unpaid work and the workload itself increase for the women carrying out the activities required by these programmes. Time-use data should be taken into account to incorporate the gender perspective when designing poverty-eradication programmes or when evaluating the benefits of retaining conditionalities that represent an additional burden for those responsible for meeting them. They should also be used to encourage shared responsibility between men and women and between the State, the market and families (ECLAC, 2016b).

> Time-use data shed light on households' lack of autonomy to meet care needs and the debt the region owes to women who sustain the care economy.

That fact that the macroeconomic aggregates in the national accounts lack indicators on health services provided within the household limits the measurement of the economic value of health care to that provided in public and private institutions. This is prejudicial to health policies and to countries' economic and social growth (Ferrán, 2008). Hence, the information provided by time-use surveys is crucial to the monetary valuation of domestic health services. In Mexico, for example, the estimated monetary value of unpaid domestic health care is 167,536 million pesos, which is equivalent to roughly 1% of GDP, or 85.5% of the value added of hospital services; women contribute 72.2% of this monetary value (INEGI, 2014).

In order to support appropriate provision of care, public policies must recognize care work as an essential development activity that must be guaranteed by society (Gómez, 2008), as well as meet the challenge of providing the care required by dependent individuals and of protecting and promoting gender equality. Time-use data shed light on households' lack of autonomy to meet care needs and the debt the region owes to women who sustain the care economy. With respect to care for children under age 5, time-use surveys show that women in households with the means to send these children to day-care centres spend 3.2 to 7.6 fewer hours on care per week, compared with households that are unable to do so. In the case of men, there is no significant difference. The surveys that also provide information on the care of dependent persons with disabilities show that women are more involved in this activity and that they spend more time on average caring for this population segment (12 to 56 hours per week) than men. In households where a member has a disability of some sort, other members spend a significant amount of time meeting their care needs, given the demanding nature of the tasks required.

## D.  Conclusions

The region must take advantage of the progress made in the past few years in the production of statistics with a gender perspective. However, there is still much work to be done. On one hand, data collection instruments must be fine-tuned to provide information that can be disaggregated to reflect situations that affect men and women differently throughout their life cycles and in different socioeconomic situations and territories. Hence, planning by national statistical offices should include surveys such as those on time use, which must be adequately funded and conducted on a sufficiently regular basis. On the other hand, none of these advances in measurement will bring about real change unless the resulting data are used to guide the implementation of public policies for equality and unless they are supported by studies on the subjective well-being produced by the current time distribution. As well as stronger measurement tools, decision-makers need stronger analytical and statistical capacities to "transform data into information, information into knowledge and knowledge into political decisions", in line with the Montevideo Strategy.

## Chapter V
## Afrodescendent populations: guaranteeing rights through a broader approach to inequality

## A. Afrodescendent populations in Latin America and the framework for action

The existence of a large Afrodescendent population in Latin America and the Caribbean has a tragic and violent origin in the transatlantic trafficking of Africans carried out by the European conquerors for almost 400 years. It constituted the largest transoceanic deportation ever perpetrated. The economic interests of colonial metropolises gave rise to a growing demand for forced labour for a range of activities, with profound effects on the distribution of the Afrodescendent population that are felt even today in the countries of the region. Nonetheless, the magnitude of the Afrodescendent population in each country also reflects the relation between their demographic dynamics and political processes as, for example, when their numbers were decimated during the wars for the independence of the current Southern Cone countries.

Beyond the diversity of national and subregional situations and specifics, Afrodescendent people occupied a subordinate place in the hierarchical, class-based and racist structure of the colonial era and, together with indigenous peoples, suffered much greater poverty and social and political exclusion. The population descending from the African Diaspora remained in a disadvantageous position over the centuries, even after their release from slavery. This situation is perpetuated by the statistical invisibility and denial of the Afrodescendent presence in some of the region's countries, a process that was entrenched with the creation and consolidation of nation States that disregarded the Afrodescendent contribution to the social and cultural development of the Latin American nations.

In response, Afrodescendent communities have kept up a constant resistance and struggle, with collective action that has had impacts at different levels. A number of international steps and commitments have been made in this regard since the mid-twentieth century, especially under the auspices of the United Nations, most recently the proclamation of the International Decade for People of African Descent (2015-2024). This initiative marks out a path towards meeting the commitments and obligations incumbent on States for resolving the structural problems that perpetuate the exclusion and discrimination of Afrodescendent populations in Latin America. In the region, the Montevideo Consensus on Population and Development, adopted at the first meeting of the Regional Conference on Population and Development of Latin America and the Caribbean (Montevideo, 2013), contains a series of explicit priority measures for Afrodescendent populations. At the national level, the countries have undertaken constitutional reforms and applied policies and programmes in this regard. Nonetheless, although this progress is significant, large implementation gaps remain between these legal frameworks and the day-to-day life of Afrodescendent populations.

The inclusion of this chapter in the current edition of *Social Panorama* expresses the commitment of ECLAC to continue to support the region's countries in identifying actions to help progress towards equality in diversity, with a rights-based approach. Making the situation of Afrodescendent persons fully visible is necessary in order to achieve recognition, justice and development for these groups.

# B. Who are Afrodescendent people, what are their numbers and where are they?

Statistical visibility forms part of the Afrodescendent demand for recognition, on the basis that information is a fundamental tool for promoting their rights and for designing and monitoring policies and actions to tackle the various forms of inequality and discrimination they suffer. Accordingly, a necessary requirement for identifying the condition of Afrodescendancy is to include ethno-racial self-identification questions in all data sources, which thus far has not happened in most of the region's countries.

Greater progress has been made in the case of population and housing censuses, mainly during the current decade: by 2020, 17 of the 20 Latin American countries will have included a question offering Afrodescendent self-identification in questionnaires. Conversely, few countries include questions of this nature in household surveys and, with the exception of Brazil and Uruguay, these groups are still underrepresented in the samples. The lag is even greater in the case of continuous administrative records.

On the basis of census information, the region's Afrodescendent population was estimated at 111 million in 2010, or 21.1% of the total population. These figures are considered to be low, owing to the limitations that persist with regard to quantifying the Afrodescendent population. Nevertheless, on this basis, the 2015 Afrodescendent population is estimated at 130 million.

Brazil is the country with largest number of Afrodescendent inhabitants, in both absolute and relative terms, since they represent over half of the country's population. Cuba follows with Afrodescendants making up 35.5% of the population, or just over 4 million people. Colombia, Costa Rica, Ecuador and Panama have relatively smaller Afrodescendent populations of between 7% and 10%. Aside from relative sizes, in Colombia the Afrodescendent population is estimated at around 5 million, in Mexico about 1.5 million, in Ecuador and the Bolivarian Republic of Venezuela around 1 million and in Peru over half a million.

A characteristic feature of Afrodescendent populations is that they are eminently urban. The degree of urbanization of Afrodescendent people in the 12 countries with data available varies from 59.2% in Honduras to 96.6% in Uruguay; it exceeds 70% in all the countries except Honduras. Although censuses also show that the Afrodescendent population is distributed practically throughout national territory of each country, there are specificities in settlement areas related to the slave-period territories of arrival in the colonial era that persist to the present day. The figures also show that Afrodescendent populations are at an intermediate or advanced stage of the demographic transition, owing mainly to falling fertility rates, but also to reductions in mortality and longer lifespans. This information is essential for steering the design of public policies and the associated investment.

> On the basis of census information, the region's Afrodescendent population is estimated at 130 million in the 2015 figures.

# C. Intersecting inequalities: gaps in the exercise of economic and social rights

Ethno-racial and socioeconomic inequalities, together with those of gender, life cycle and territory, are axes of the social inequality matrix in Latin America. These inequalities are expressed in various spheres of social development, including socioeconomic status, health, education and employment, which are analysed in this chapter using a range of indicators.

In the four countries for which information is available, the Afrodescendent population is more heavily concentrated in quintile I than the non-Afrodescendent population (see figure 9).

**Figure 9**
Latin America (4 countries : distribution of the population by per capita household income (quintile), by ethno-racial status, 2014
*(Percentages)*

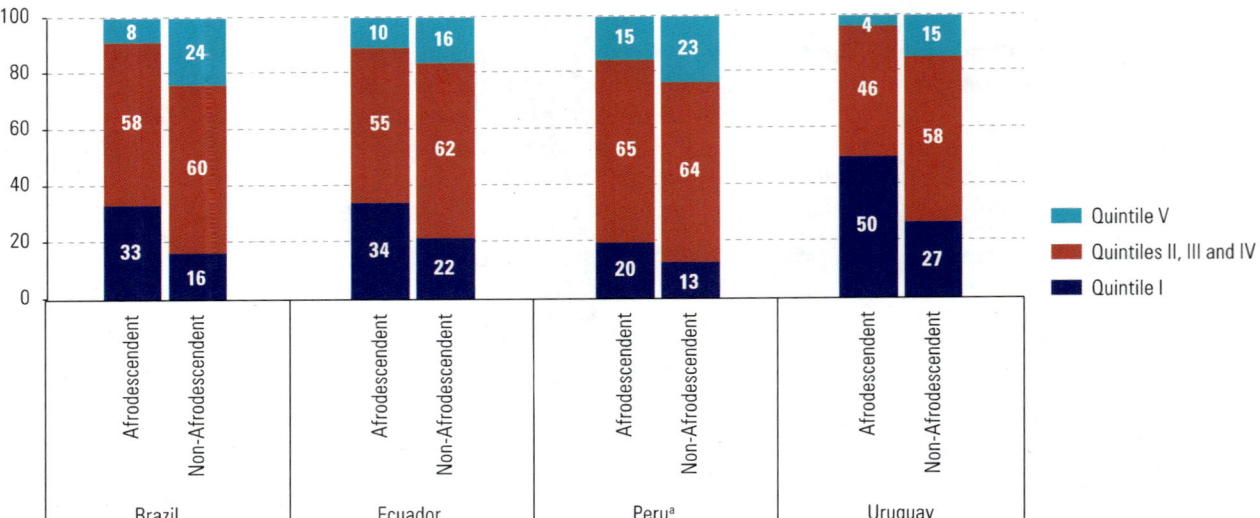

**Source**: Economic Commission for Latin America and the Caribbean (ECLAC), on the basis of data from the Household Survey Data Bank (BADEHOG).
**Note**:    The non-Afrodescendent population does not include those who self-identify as indigenous or cases where ethno-racial status is unknown.
[a] In Peru, the question on ethno-racial status is asked of persons aged 13 and older.

In the area of health, one of the most eloquent indicators is the inequality in child mortality rates between the Afrodescendent and non-Afrodescendent populations. In a group of eight countries for which this information is available, child mortality among the Afrodescendent population as estimated in 2010 varies from 10 per 1,000 live births in Costa Rica to 26 per 1,000 live births in Colombia. Irrespective of its magnitude, the chances that an Afrodescendent boy or girl will die before his or her first birthday are systematically higher than those of non-Afrodescendants, except in Argentina. The largest gaps occur in Colombia, Uruguay, Panama and Brazil, where the probability of an Afrodescendent child dying before his or her first birthday varies from 1.6 times to 1.3 times that of a non-Afrodescendent child. Moreover, these inequalities persist even after controlling by area of residence.

The conditions of poverty which Afrodescendent women endure in the region impair their health status, which is further compounded by limited access to and cultural accessibility of health services, including sexual and reproductive health. Pregnancy in adolescence is another manifestation of inequality to the disadvantage of Afrodescendent youth. Census figures show that the percentage of Afrodescendent mothers aged between 15 and 19 remains high and in 7 of 10 countries exceeds the figure for non-Afrodescendent adolescents. The largest disparities are seen in Brazil and Uruguay, showing that even countries that have implemented integrated and universal health services for youth care, including those aimed at reducing unwanted adolescent pregnancy, have not been able to eliminate the ethno-racial inequality.

Gaps are evident in the sphere of education, too, in most of the countries of the region. The proportion of young people aged 18-24 who are attending an educational establishment varies from 16.9% in Uruguay to 41.4% in Argentina and is lower than for non-Afrodescendent youth in most of the countries analysed. These gaps widen in tertiary education. In most of the countries, a larger proportion of Afrodescendent than non-Afrodescendent youth is neither in education nor employed in the labour market. Taking into account the intersection of gender and ethno-racial inequalities, it becomes evident that young Afrodescendent women are subjected to at least twice the exclusion that young non-Afrodescendent men are (see figure 10).

In most of the countries, a larger proportion of Afrodescendent than non-Afrodescendent youth is neither in education nor employed in the labour market.

**Figure 10**

Latin America (11 countries): proportion of Afrodescendent women and non-Afrodescendent men aged between 15 and 29 not in education or employed in the labour market
*(Percentages)*

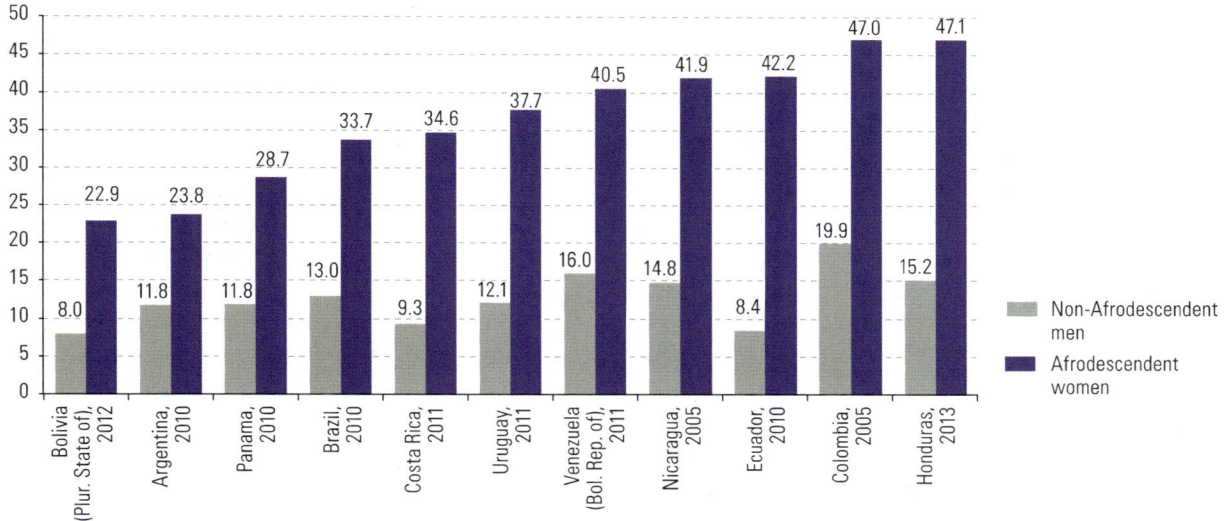

**Source**: Economic Commission for Latin America and the Caribbean (ECLAC), on the basis of special processing of census microdatabases using REDATAM.

Ethno-racial inequalities also arise in the labour market. Unemployment has been broadly documented to be one of the main indicators of labour market exclusion and affects women and youth disproportionately. Factoring in the ethno-racial dimension shows that Afrodescendants are worse affected by unemployment —again, women in youth in particular. Unemployment rates are higher among Afrodescendants than non-Afrodescendants in most of the countries analysed and, where the opposite is true, the gap in favour of Afrodescendants is smaller.

Work and education are essential for social inclusion and for reducing inequalities, but educational achievement does not translate automatically into successful labour market integration. Analysis of labour incomes, one of the most important indicators of employment quality, shows that shows that Afrodescendent women, whose levels of schooling are significantly higher than Afrodescendent men, are systematically lower on the salary scale, even after controlling for level of education and hours worked. The data show how ethno-racial and gender inequalities intersect in the labour market and that the higher the level of schooling, the larger the gaps. For example, among the employed with tertiary education, per hour worked, Afrodescendent women receive on average 58% of the income of a non-Afrodescendent man, Afrodescendent men, 73% and non-Afrodescendent women, 75%.

Lastly, one of the most telling pieces of evidence of the intertwining of socioeconomic, gender and ethno-racial inequalities is the situation of waged female domestic workers. Domestic service is one of the largest sources of employment for women in Latin America, and one of the least valued socially and economically, with a large deficit from the perspective of decent work. The percentage of waged female domestic workers runs from 3% (among non-Afrodescendent women Colombia) to 20% (Afrodescendent women in Brazil). In Brazil and Ecuador double the proportion of Afrodescendent women, in relation to non-Afrodescendent women, are employed as domestic workers.

# D. Institutional framework and policies for the Afrodescendent population

Since the turn of the century, and especially since the World Conference against Racism, Racial Discrimination, Xenophobia and Related Intolerance, held in Durban (South Africa) in 2001, government machineries devoted to the Afrodescendent population have risen steadily in number in Latin America and now exist in 14 countries. This progress is the outcome of lengthy work by Afrodescendent movements, other civil society organizations, governments and international agencies.

These machineries function within a legal framework based on institutional and regional human rights instruments and national legislation. Some countries have extensive legislation aimed at combating racism or directed towards Afrodescendants; others have less legislation of this sort and some none at all. More than a dozen countries have constitutional provisions prohibiting ethno-racial discrimination, while other constitutions refer to equality and non-discrimination in general or on other grounds. Ecuador's constitution devotes an entire chapter exclusively to "black or Afro-Ecuadorian peoples" and Brazil's defines racism as a crime punishable by jail, with no right to bail and no statute of limitations.

The region's racial equality machineries occupy different places in the State hierarchy, which in turn defines their area of influence. This is crucial, considering that they work on cross-cutting issues that need to be linked across different government departments and bodies, both sectorally and at the national, provincial and local levels, as well as coordinated with civil society. The fact that the situation of these machineries remains somewhat unstable in the Latin American countries not only jeopardizes the protection of Afrodescendent rights, but also influences the resources allocated to them, and thus their scope of action. Giving them more authority within the State apparatus could enhance their coordination function and help to make racial quality policies more effective.

Several Latin American countries have adopted policies to combat racism and promote racial equality over the past few years, in response to the Afrodescendent movement and in follow-up to the commitments they have undertaken at the international level.

In terms of preventing and tackling racism, most of the countries not only have constitutional provisions against ethno-racial discrimination, but several have also adopted legislation prohibiting racial discrimination and even classifying it as a crime punishable by imprisonment. Some countries have developed more comprehensive policies aimed at eliminating racial discrimination and have passed local laws.

A number of countries also have affirmative action policies, consisting chiefly of reserved places for Afrodescendent persons at university and in employment, and provide grants in private tertiary education institutions. Many have also adopted appreciation policies such as official days celebrating Afrodescendancy and the teaching of African history and culture in schools, and some have implemented policies that integrate ancestral views and practices into health care and have focused on diseases that particularly affect Afrodescendent persons, among other measures. There has also been notable recognition of distinguished Afrodescendent figures in national education and of Afrodescendent cultural practices as part of national heritage.

In relation to policy efforts to strengthen traditional Afrodescendent communities, Brazil and Ecuador stand out for having recognized collective ownership rights. Lastly, in some case action is under way, albeit incipient, to promote participation by Afrodescendent persons and organizations in decision-making by linking up government machineries and Afrodescendent social movements.

Several Latin American countries have adopted policies to combat racism and promote racial equality over the past few years, in response to the Afrodescendent movement and in follow-up to the commitments they have undertaken at the international level.

# E. Conclusions

In short, with the exception of only a few countries, such as Brazil, Colombia and Ecuador, Afrodescendants' disadvantages have been one of the least perceptible dimensions of social inequality in the region. Information is a key tool for ending that invisibility. Accordingly, national statistical systems need to be further developed to include self-identification of Afrodescendent persons and permit disaggregation of indicators.

While it is possible to identify, to a limited extent, systematic ethno-racial gaps that disadvantage Afrodescendent persons in different areas, including health, education and employment, in the few countries where the situation is the reverse, the advantage of the Afrodescendent population is very small. The intersection between ethno-racial and gender inequalities places Afrodescendent women at an even greater disadvantage.

The 2030 Agenda for Sustainable Development, with its commitment to "leave no one behind", the International Decade for People of African Descent and regional agreements, such as the Montevideo Consensus on Population and Development, make it all the more urgent to meet the challenge of ensuring the well-being of Afrodescendent persons and their full exercise of rights, by taking sustained action that is based on the recognition of equality in diversity.

# Bibliography

Alarco Tosoni, G. (2014), "Wage share and economic growth in Latin America, 1950-2011", *CEPAL Review*, No. 113 (LC/G.2614-P), Santiago, Economic Commission for Latin America and the Caribbean (ECLAC), August.

Batthyány, K. (2009), "Cuidado de personas dependientes y género", *Las bases invisibles del bienestar social. El trabajo no remunerado en Uruguay*, R. Aguirre (ed.), Montevideo, United Nations Development Fund for Women (UNIFEM).

Carr, D. (2009), "Life cycle", *Encyclopedia of the Life Course and Human Development*, vol. 3, D. Carr (ed.), Detroit, Gale Cengage Learning.

Cecchini, S. and others (2015), "Rights and the life cycle: reordering social protection tools", *Towards Universal Social Protection: Latin American pathways and policy tools*, S. Cechinni and others (eds.), ECLAC Books, No. 136 (LC/G. 2644-P), Santiago, Economic Commission for Latin America and the Caribbean (ECLAC).

ECLAC (Economic Commission for Latin America and the Caribbean) (2016a), *The social inequality matrix in Latin America* (LC/G.2690(MDS.1/2)), Santiago.

___(2016b), *Equality and women's autonomy in the sustainable development agenda* (LC/G.2686/Rev.1), Santiago.

___(2016c), *Inclusive social development: The next generation of policies for overcoming poverty and reducing inequality in Latin America and the Caribbean* (LC.L/4056/Rev.1), Santiago, January.

___(2016d), *Horizons 2030: equality at the centre of sustainable development* (LC/G.2660/Rev.1), Santiago, July.

___(2016e), "Territorio e igualdad: planificación del desarrollo con perspectiva de género", *Manuales de la CEPAL*, No. 4 (LC/L.4237), Santiago, October.

___(2016f), *40 years of the regional gender agenda* (LC/G.2682), Santiago.

___(2014), *Social Panorama of Latin America, 2014* (LC/G.2635-P), Santiago.

___(2013), *Gender Equality Observatory of Latin America and the Caribbean. Annual Report 2012: A look at grants, support and burden for women* (LC/G.2561/Rev.1), Santiago.

Espínola, V. and J. Claro (2010), "Estrategias de prevención de la deserción en la educación secundaria: perspectiva latinoamericana", *Revista de Educación*, special edition.

Ferrán, L. (2008), "Marco conceptual y lineamientos metodológicos de la cuenta satélite de los hogares para medir el trabajo no remunerado en salud", *La economía invisible y las desigualdades de género. La importancia de medir y valorar el trabajo no remunerado*, Washington, D.C., Pan American Health Organization (PAHO).

Gammage, S. and M. Orozco (2008), "El trabajo productivo no remunerado dentro del hogar: Guatemala y México", *Estudios y Perspectivas series-ECLAC subregional headquarters in Mexico*, No. 103 (LC/L.2983-P; LC/MEX/L.889), Mexico City, Economic Commission for Latin America and the Caribbean (ECLAC).

Gibbs, B. and T. Eaton (2014), "Drop out from primary to secondary school in Mexico: A life course perspective", *International Journal of Educational Development*, vol. 36, May.

Gómez, E. (2008), "La valoración del trabajo no remunerado: una estrategia clave para la política de igualdad de género", *La economía invisible y las desigualdades de género. La importancia de medir y valorar el trabajo no remunerado*, Washington, D.C., Pan American Health Organization (PAHO).

INEGI (National Institute of Statistics and Geography of Mexico) (2014), *Sistema de Cuentas Nacionales de México. Cuenta satélite del trabajo no remunerado de los hogares de México 2013. Preliminar. Año base 2008*, Mexico City.

Marco, F. (2016), "La nueva ola de reformas previsionales y la igualdad de género en América Latina", *Asuntos de Género series*, No. 139 (LC/L.4225), Santiago, Economic Commission for Latin America and the Caribbean (ECLAC) [online] http://www.cepal.org/es/publicaciones/40653-la-nueva-ola-reformas-previsionales-la-igualdad-genero-america-latina.

___(2012), "La utilización de las encuestas de uso del tiempo en las políticas públicas", *Mujer y Desarrollo series*, No. 119 (LC/L.3557), Santiago, Economic Commission for Latin America and the Caribbean (ECLAC), October.

Segovia, O. (2016), "¿Quién cuida en la ciudad? Oportunidades y propuestas en la comuna de Santiago (Chile)", *Asuntos de Género series*, No. 132 (LC/L.4127), Santiago, Economic Commission for Latin America and the Caribbean (ECLAC), January.

Trucco, D. and H. Ullmann (eds.) (2015), *Youth: realities and challenges for achieving development with equality*, ECLAC Books, No. 137 (LC/G.2647-P), Santiago, Economic Commission for Latin America and the Caribbean (ECLAC).

# Inequality in Latin America: a key challenge for sustainable development

# Introduction

Inequality is a historical and structural characteristic of Latin American and Caribbean societies that has been maintained and perpetuated even at times of growth and economic prosperity. In recent years, inequality in the distribution of income and in other areas has fallen (ECLAC, 2016a and 2016d) in a political context in which the region's governments have placed a high priority on social development goals and actively promoted redistributive and inclusive policies. In spite of that progress, high levels of inequality still exist, conspiring against development and posing a considerable barrier to the eradication of poverty, the expansion of citizenship, the exercise of rights and democratic governance. Significantly reducing inequality is a commitment set out in the 2030 Agenda for Sustainable Development, which has been assumed by all the countries of Latin America and the Caribbean, and is clearly expressed in the commitment "to leave no one behind".

The emphasis of the 2030 Agenda for Sustainable Development on the central challenge of reducing inequality both within and between countries represents the culmination of a global and regional process of analysis and reflection following on immediately from the partial progress made towards attaining the Millennium Development Goals. It reflects an international commitment of the greatest importance, one that is highly relevant for Latin America and the Caribbean, which, in spite of the progress made over the past decade, is still the world's most unequal region in terms of the distribution of income. This commitment is expressed in Sustainable Development Goal 10: "Reduce inequality within and among countries" (see box I.1 for more details).

While concerns about equality have been a historically constant element in the thinking of the Economic Commission for Latin America and the Caribbean (ECLAC), they have moved to the fore since 2010, as established and explained in the set of documents known as the equality trilogy (ECLAC, 2010, 2012a and 2014), and in 2016 were expanded with the analysis of the main challenges that the region faces in accomplishing the Goals of the 2030 Agenda for Sustainable Development (ECLAC, 2016b). Equality is seen as a guiding principle and strategic target for development (Bárcena and Prado, 2016, p. 54) and as a fundamental condition not only for overcoming poverty and ensuring the effective enjoyment of rights for the whole population, but also for advancing towards social, economic and environmentally sustainable development.

Economic and social development analysis conducted by ECLAC have determined that Latin American and Caribbean economies have historically been defined by sharp structural heterogeneity, which is largely responsible for the high levels of social inequality found in the region's countries. Their scantly diversified and highly heterogeneous production structures, within which low-productivity sectors account for approximately 50% of all jobs, are a key determinant of social inequality. The labour market is the essential link between that production structure and high levels of income inequality between households, which are associated with a highly differentiated distribution of the fruits of productivity and with highly stratified access to good-quality employment and social protection (ECLAC, 2010, 2012, 2014 and 2016c).

> Latin American and Caribbean economies have historically been defined by sharp structural heterogeneity, which is largely responsible for the high levels of social inequality found in the region's countries.

For decades, discussions and analysis of inequality in Latin America and the Caribbean have focused on income disparities among households and individuals. This is largely because income makes a direct contribution to the well-being of people and their families and therefore shapes both their opportunities and the future of their children, particularly in societies where market mechanisms for accessing goods and services predominate. ECLAC has made substantial contributions to this analysis by quantifying income inequality and studying its causes (ECLAC, 2014) and has also highlighted the structural nature and persistence of high levels of income concentration, which have remained in place even at times of economic prosperity and high rates of growth.[1]

ECLAC has also emphasized the importance of analysing functional income distribution as well as the concentration of assets (wealth) and not only that of income because, in spite of the dearth of information in that regard, there are several partial pieces of evidence that seem to indicate the existence of even deeper inequalities, in terms of ownership of both productive assets and of financial assets (Bárcena and Prado, 2016; ECLAC, 2016c).

There is growing recognition that inequality is a multidimensional phenomenon caused by many factors. Income inequality determined by participation in the labour market is compounded by other inequalities related to political, social and cultural phenomena and to mechanisms of discrimination that are reproduced in various socioeconomic environments in addition to the world of work, such as health, education, culture and political and citizen participation. Those inequalities are determining factors of poverty and pose major barriers to overcoming it (ECLAC, 2016a).

The notion of equality used by ECLAC is not therefore constrained to economic or income equality alone. This is clearly a central dimension of equality, which refers both to the distribution of the monetary incomes people and their families have for ensuring their well-being and developing their capacities, and to the functional distribution of income between capital and labour and the distribution of ownership of financial and non-financial assets.

The ECLAC definition of equality also covers equality in the exercise of rights and the development of capacities (understood as the set of abilities, knowledge and skills that individuals acquire and that allow them to pursue life plans they deem valuable), the reciprocal recognition of actors and gender, ethnic and racial equality, among other fundamental aspects (Bárcena and Prado, 2016).

Equality of rights is, as ECLAC sees it, the basic axis of equality, covering the full realization of economic, social and cultural rights as the regulatory and practical horizon for all persons (without distinctions on the grounds of sex, race, ethnicity, age, religion, origin, socioeconomic situation or any other condition) and the inclusion of all citizens in the dynamics of development, which implies a genuine belonging to society and full exercise of citizenship. In contrast, inequality means that not all individuals can fully exercise their civil, political, economic, social and environmental rights and, consequently, that the principle of universality is violated.

However, analysing social inequalities requires not only identifying those individuals whose access to that basic level of well-being has been infringed, but also paying attention to how assets, means and opportunities, income and other outcomes, power and influence are distributed. Thus, inequality refers to asymmetries in the capacity to appropriate resources and productive assets (income, goods, services, etc.) that represent or create well-being among different social groups. Ultimately, it underscores the concentration of a large proportion of wealth within a limited sector of the population. It also refers to exclusion and to the unequal distribution of political and economic power, which empowers a reduced segment of society to take decisions that affect the majority and that enable or constrain the exercise of rights and the development of capacities of all. Inequality is, therefore, essentially relational in nature and, in addition, it is a phenomenon inherent to relations of power at the individual and collective levels.

---

[1] There is a growing focus on measuring inequality, which has sparked a renewed academic and political interest in knowledge, analysis and quantification of the subject. Academics of different schools and with varied analytical approaches have highlighted the relevance of this issue and their data and conclusions are undeniably pertinent to the valuation of the current style of development and the consideration of adjustments and alternatives. The work of Wilkinson and Pickett (2009), Picketty (2014), Milanovic (2016), Atkinson (2015), Stiglitz (2012), Bourguignon (2015) and Deaton (2015), among others, has contributed significantly to calling attention to inequality as a fundamental problem of contemporary society.

To summarize, inequality is produced and reproduced in the production structure; it then moves from that field into employment and the social and cultural domains and intertwines with gender relations, ethnic and racial relations and relations over the entire life cycle and can even largely define patterns of territorial development (Bárcena and Prado, 2016). A multidimensional approach to inequality therefore implies analysing its economic, social, political and cultural aspects and taking into consideration the different structuring axes that shape social, political and economic relations in Latin American societies (ECLAC, 2016a and 2016c).

This chapter focuses on the analysis of some of the aspects relating to the inequality of resources and socioeconomic strata (and the heterogeneous nature of the productive system) as the structuring axis of social inequality. It is divided into three sections that address the following themes: (i) the distribution of income among people and households, (ii) functional income distribution and (iii) the distribution of financial and non-financial assets.

Box I.1
Sustainable Development Goal 10: reduce inequality within and among countries

Inequalities based on income, sex, age, disability, sexual orientation, race, class, ethnicity, religion and opportunity continue to persist across the world, within and among countries. Inequality threatens long-term social and economic development, harms poverty reduction and destroys people's sense of fulfilment and self-worth.

The 2030 Agenda for Sustainable Development expresses the international commitment to tackle this serious problem, as articulated in Sustainable Development Goal (SDG) 10, which proposes to "reduce inequality within and among countries". Its specific targets are as follows:

10.1    By 2030, progressively achieve and sustain income growth of the bottom 40 per cent of the population at a rate higher than the national average

10.2    By 2030, empower and promote the social, economic and political inclusion of all, irrespective of age, sex, disability, race, ethnicity, origin, religion or economic or other status

10.3    Ensure equal opportunity and reduce inequalities of outcome, including by eliminating discriminatory laws, policies and practices and promoting appropriate legislation, policies and action in this regard

10.4    Adopt policies, especially fiscal, wage and social protection policies, and progressively achieve greater equality

10.5    Improve the regulation and monitoring of global financial markets and institutions and strengthen the implementation of such regulations

10.6    Ensure enhanced representation and voice for developing countries in decision-making in global international economic and financial institutions in order to deliver more effective, credible, accountable and legitimate institutions

10.7    Facilitate orderly, safe, regular and responsible migration and mobility of people, including through the implementation of planned and well-managed migration policies

10.a    Implement the principle of special and differential treatment for developing countries, in particular least developed countries, in accordance with World Trade Organization agreements

10.b    Encourage official development assistance and financial flows, including foreign direct investment, to States where the need is greatest, in particular least developed countries, African countries, small island developing States and landlocked developing countries, in accordance with their national plans and programmes

10.c    By 2030, reduce to less than 3 per cent the transaction costs of migrant remittances and eliminate remittance corridors with costs higher than 5%

Because of its central role, the challenge to reduce inequality must be considered as a cross-cutting element of the 2030 Agenda for Sustainable Development and a necessary condition, in particular, for achieving the Goals and targets explicitly associated with its social pillar (Goals 1, 2, 3, 4, 5, 6, 8, 11 and 16).

**Source**: Economic Commission for Latin America and the Caribbean (ECLAC), on the basis of United Nations, "Transforming our world: the 2030 Agenda for Sustainable Development" (A/RES/70/1), New York, 2015.

# A. Inequality in income distribution

In Latin America, the level of income distribution inequality in 2015 was similar to that seen in 2014. Nonetheless, taking into account the entire period since the global financial crisis, the income distribution gap narrowed between 2008 and 2015 in most of the region's countries. During this period, the income of the lowest income quintile increased more than that of the highest. This occurred generally across the various sources of household income, but mainly in labour income (both for wage jobs and self-employment), retirement and transfers. With respect to gender inequality, recent figures confirm that women are overrepresented in lower-income households and that a large number of women still do not have their own income.

## 1.    Unequal distribution of personal and household income[2]

In existing economic structures, income —which is understood as the resources that a household obtains over a specific period— is the main means of accessing basic goods and services to ensure material well-being (see box I.2). Households require income to obtain food, shelter, clothing, transport, basic and recreational services, among other things, in order to meet the needs of their members. Hence, the analysis of disparities in income distribution is highly relevant to understanding inequalities in the region's countries.[3]

Box I.2
Measurement of income

The recommended concept of income to be used household surveys is that which was adopted at the seventeenth International Conference of Labour Statisticians and which appears in the Canberra Group Handbook on Household Income Statistics. In both cases, income is defined as all receipts, whether monetary or in kind, that are received by the household or by individual members of the household at annual or more frequent intervals, excluding windfall gains and other such irregular and typically one-time receipts. This definition is consistent with the System of National Accounts (SNA 2008), which defines disposable income as the "maximum amount that a household or other unit can afford to spend on consumption goods or services during the accounting period without having to finance its expenditures by reducing its cash, by disposing of other financial or non-financial assets or by increasing its liabilities" (United Nations, 2008, 8.25).

The income received by the household is the result of two processes: primary distribution between production factors and secondary distribution. Primary income refers to income from work and income from asset ownership, while secondary income corresponds to the transfers and subsidies that the household receives without providing anything to the donor in direct return. Overall household income, as routinely measured using household surveys in the region, includes the following components: income from employment (wages and salaries, and income from self-employment), income from asset ownership and transfers (retirement benefits, pensions and other transfers) and rent imputed for owner-occupied housing.

---

[2]    The values of the inequality indicators presented in this edition of *Social Panorama of Latin America* correspond to an updated series and differ from those presented in previous editions of this publication (see box I.2 for details). As outlined in *Social Panorama of Latin America, 2015*, there are limitations to determining income through household surveys that can lead to an underestimation of the level of concentration owing to the difficulties in determining high incomes, either because of underdeclaration by respondents or incomplete coverage of the wealthiest households (ECLAC, 2016d; Amarante and Jiménez, 2015).

[3]    In spite of this, it is important to remember that income is an incomplete indicator of the material well-being of individuals. Some of the population's needs are covered mainly by goods and services provided by the State, such as public goods, or by family members through unpaid domestic work; hence, income does not necessarily convey the access to these goods and services.

Box I.2 (concluded)

The imputation of non-response income also forms part of the income measurement procedure used by ECLAC. This situation occurs when, during the interview process, answers are provided for different sections of the questionnaire but no information is gathered on the respondent's income. On these occasions, the missing field is assigned a value, based on the information provided by other respondents with similar characteristics (provided that such a procedure is not already used by the country to produce its data).

In the 2016 edition of the *Social Panorama of Latin America*, ECLAC is initiating a new series of estimated household income, largely in line with the recommendations of International Labour Organization (ILO) and the Canberra Group. During the process, the definitions of income used for the different components of each survey were revised and reworded in accordance with the international recommendations. Furthermore, the adjustment of incomes to the national accounts, a procedure that involved individually modifying the different categories of income on the basis of the difference between the aggregated estimates of the surveys and the national accounts was abandoned. In the same way, as a consequence of methodological issues that made it hard to adequately estimate the rent imputed for owner-occupied housing, this type of income was excluded from the calculation of household income. Because of these changes, the household incomes corresponding to this new series are not comparable with those of the previous series.

**Source**: Economic Commission for Latin America and the Caribbean (ECLAC), on the basis of United Nations, *System of National Accounts 2008* [online] https://unstats.un.org/unsd/nationalaccount/docs/SNA2008.pdf, 2009.

A common method used to analyse income inequality is a synthetic index that describes the way income measured in household surveys is distributed. The Gini coefficient, which ranges from 0 (complete equality) to 1 (complete inequality), is 0.469 for Latin America, according to data available for 2015.[4] This indicator conveys a noticeable difference between countries: higher than 0.500 in Brazil, Colombia, Mexico and Panama, and around 0.400 in the Bolivarian Republic of Venezuela and Uruguay only, while the other countries fall somewhere in between.

The 2015 Gini coefficient was practically unchanged from that of 2014, when the average stood at 0.473. Nonetheless, this indicator fell 6.2% between 2008 (0.500) and 2015 (0.469), at a rate of -0.9% per year. Over the same period there were statistically significant declines in 12 of the countries under review, with the most notable seen in El Salvador (-2.0% per year), Argentina (-1.9%), Uruguay (-1.7%), Peru (-1.4%) and Ecuador (-1.2%) (see figure I.1).[5]

Over the course of 2008-2015, most countries saw a decline in the Gini coefficient, mainly between 2008 and 2012, while variations were smaller between 2012 and 2015 (see figure I.2).[6] Between 2008 and 2012 there were significant changes in this indicator in almost all the countries under review, notably in Uruguay (-3.7% per year), Argentina (-3.3%), the Plurinational State of Bolivia (-3.0%), Ecuador (-1.9%), Peru (-1.8%) and Paraguay (-1.5%). By contrast, between 2012 and 2015, there were significant declines only in Honduras (-4.2% per year), El Salvador (-3.5%), Colombia (-1.0%), Chile (-0.8%) and Brazil (-0.7%), and an increase of 0.9% in Uruguay. In the other countries, 2015 indicators remained at similar levels to those seen in 2012, as shown in figure I.2B.

---

[4]    Average for 15 countries, excluding Costa Rica, Guatemala and Nicaragua.

[5]    The statistical analysis was carried out by estimating variances through simulations, applying the bootstrapping method. The variations recorded between surveys in the same country were significant, at 95% in all countries except Mexico and the Plurinational State of Bolivia.

[6]    In 2008-2012, six of the recorded variations were not statistically significant (those corresponding to the Bolivarian Republic of Venezuela, Chile, the Dominican Republic, Honduras, Mexico and Panama). In 2012-2015, nine variations were not meaningful (for Bolivarian Republic of Venezuela, Costa Rica, Dominican Republic, Ecuador, Mexico, Panama, Paraguay, Peru and Plurinational State of Bolivia).

**Figure I.1**

Latin America (15 countries): Gini coefficient, around 2008 and 2015[a]

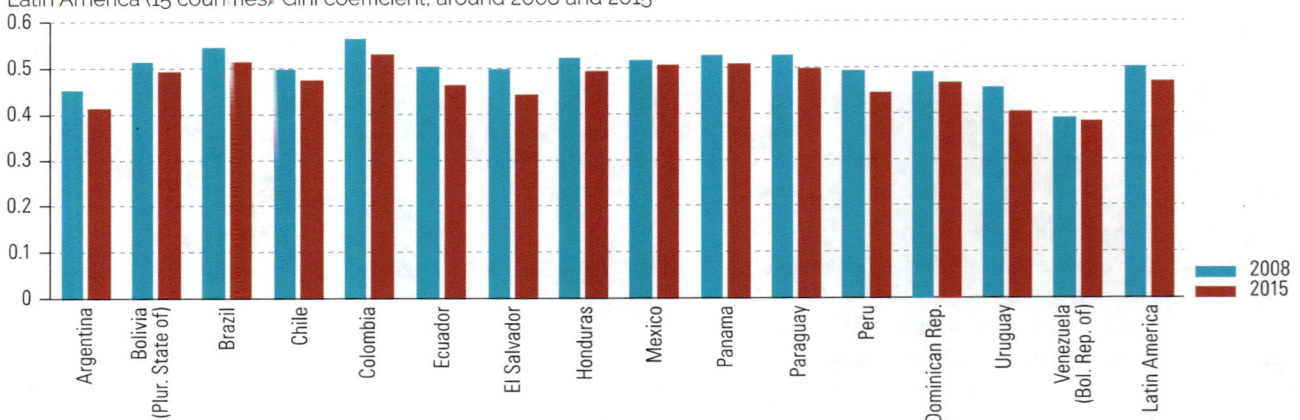

**Source**: Economic Commission for Latin America and the Caribbean (ECLAC), on the basis of Household Survey Data Bank (BADEHOG).
[a] Data refer to 2008 and 2015, except in the cases of Argentina (2009 and 2014), Bolivarian Republic of Venezuela (2008 and 2014), Chile (2009 and 2015), Colombia (2009 and 2015), El Salvador (2009 and 2015), Honduras (2009 and 2015), Mexico (2008 and 2014) and Plurinational State of Bolivia (2008 and 2014).

**Figure I.2**

Latin America (17 countries): Gini coefficient, around 2008, 2012 and 2015[a][b]

**A. Around 2008 and 2012**

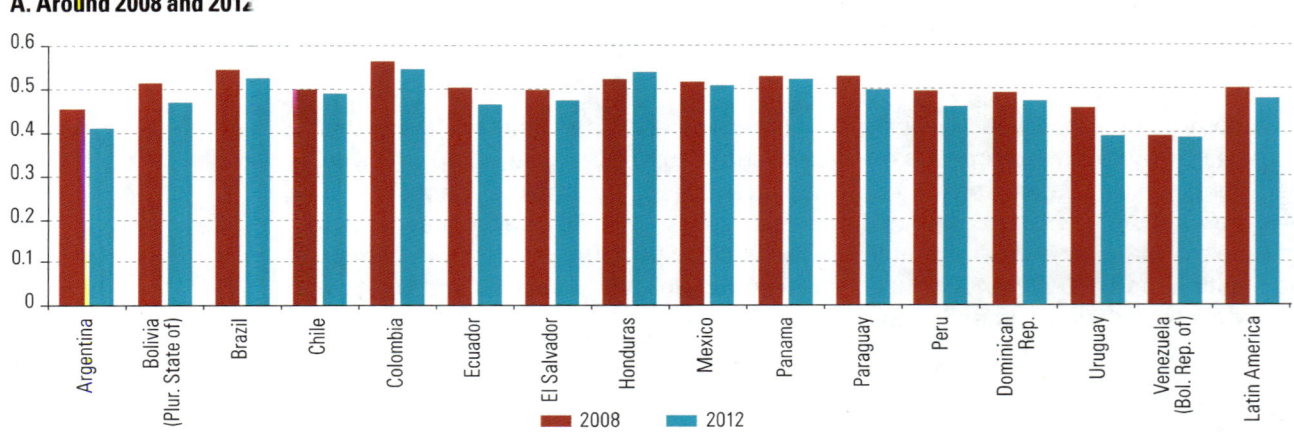

**B. Around 2012 and 2015**

**Source**: Economic Commission for Latin America and the Caribbean (ECLAC), on the basis of Household Survey Data Bank (BADEHOG).
[a] Data refer to 2008, 2012 and 2015, except in the cases of Argentina (2009-2014), Bolivarian Republic of Venezuela (2008, 2012 and 2014), Chile (2009, 2011 and 2015), Colombia (2009, 2012 and 2015), Costa Rica (only 2012 and 2015), El Salvador (2009, 2013 and 2015), Guatemala (only 2014), Honduras (2009, 2013 and 2015), Mexico (2008, 2012 and 2014) and Plurinational State of Bolivia (2008, 2011 and 2014).
[b] The average for Latin America includes the 15 countries with information available for both subperiods. It does not include Costa Rica, Nicaragua or Guatemala.

In the regional average, the Gini coefficient fell half as quickly between 2012 and 2015 (-0.6% per year) as it did between 2008 and 2012 (-1.2% per year).

Other inequality indicators confirm the downward trend in the Gini coefficient in 2008-2015. The Theil and Atkinson indices contain ideal features for measuring inequality that the Gini coefficient does not, which makes them relevant for use as complementary tools (see more details in box I.3). As seen in figure I.3, the annual variation in the Gini coefficient and Theil and Atkinson indices was negative in 15 of the countries under review, which shows an improvement in distribution. Furthermore, in most countries the declines in the Theil and Atkinson indices were larger than those in the Gini coefficient, which suggests that the improvement in inequality stemmed mainly from an increase in earnings for lower-income households.

Box I.3
Indicators for measuring
distribution inequality

A wide range of indicators can be used to measure the degree of concentration of a given income distribution. This chapter uses three of the best-known inequality indicators:

Gini coefficient:

$$G = \frac{1}{2n^2\,\mu} \sum_{i=1}^{n} \sum_{j=1}^{n} \left| y_i - y_j \right|$$

Theil index:

$$T = \frac{1}{n} \sum_{i=1}^{n} \frac{y_i}{\mu}\, \ln\left(\frac{y_i}{\mu}\right)$$

Atkinson index:

$$A_\varepsilon = 1 - \left[ \frac{1}{n} \sum_{i=1}^{n} \left(\frac{y_i}{\mu}\right)^{1-\varepsilon} \right]^{\frac{1}{1-\varepsilon}}$$

where $n$ = population size, $y_i$ = per capita income of the ith individual, $\mu$ = mean income, $\varepsilon$ is a parameter that represents "inequality aversion" (taking values ranging from 0 to infinity) and $ln$ = natural logarithm.

The Gini coefficient is the best-known of the indicators used to measure income distribution. Its formula is expressed graphically because it corresponds to the area between the Lorenz curve and the equidistribution line. The greater the income concentration, the larger the area and the higher the value of the indicator.

Despite its popularity, the Gini coefficient does not satisfy the transfer sensitivity axiom, which is a desirable property for inequality indicators. According to this principle, inequality should decrease more in response to a progressive transfer of income (that is, from a wealthier household to a poorer one) between poor individuals than when the transfer is between rich individuals. That is why the measure should be complemented with other indicators that meet this property, such as the Theil and Atkinson indices.

For all three indicators, the higher the value the greater the degree of inequality. Nevertheless, while the Gini coefficient and the Atkinson index take values in the range of zero to 1 (where zero is absolute equality and 1 is absolute inequality), the maximum Theil index value is the logarithm of population size, which exceeds the value 1. The Atkinson index formula uses an additional parameter, inequality aversion ($\varepsilon$). The greater the value used, the higher the weight given to observations in the lower part of the distribution.

All inequality indicators are ordinal, so their values cannot be compared. Because each of them measures partial aspects of inequality, they can generate different rankings for the same distribution. The ranking of a group of distributions can be considered definitive only if it does not vary between indices. It is therefore best to see inequality indices as complementary to each other and analyze the findings together.

**Source**: Economic Commission for Latin America and the Caribbean (ECLAC), on the basis of F. Cowell, "Measuring Inequality", *LSE Handbooks in Economics*, Prentice Hall, 1995.

**Figure I.3**
Latin America (15 countries): annual variation in inequality indexes (Gini coefficient and Theil and Atkinson indices),[a] 2008-2015[b]
*(Percentages)*

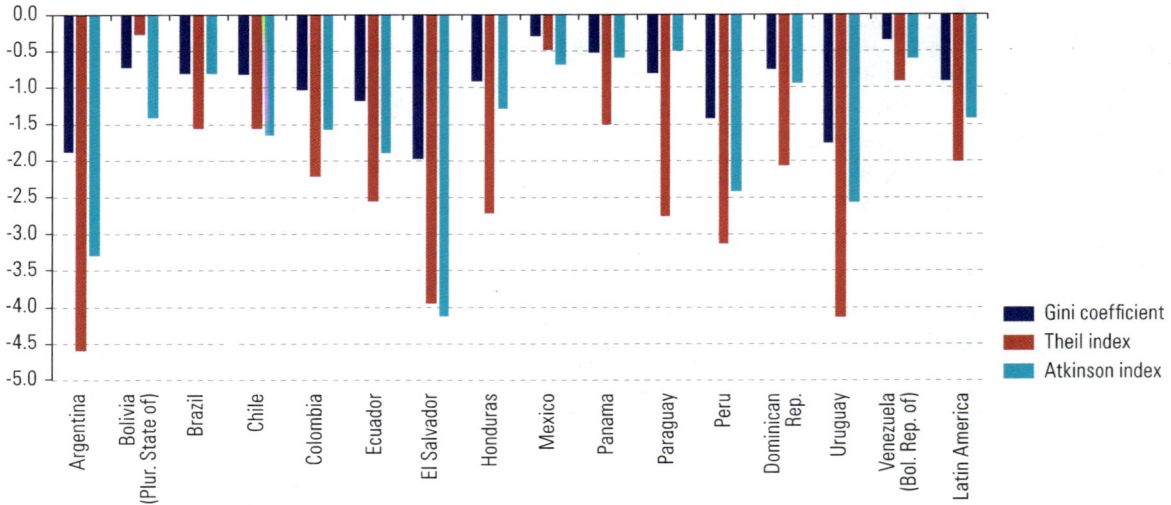

**Source:** Economic Commission for Latin America and the Caribbean (ECLAC), on the basis of Household Survey Data Bank (BADEHOG).
[a] Atkinson index with an inequality aversion coefficient equal to 1.5.
[b] Data refer to 2008 and 2015 except in the cases of Argentina (2009-2014), Bolivarian Republic of Venezuela (2008 and 2014), Chile (2009 and 2015), Colombia (2009 and 2015), El Salvador (2009 and 2015), Honduras (2009 and 2015), Mexico (2008 and 2014) and Plurinational State of Bolivia (2008 and 2014).

Income distribution can also be analysed on the basis of the share of the income of population grouped by its monetary resources. This analysis is discussed below, and uses as a basis for comparison quintiles for households according to per capita income.

For the countries under review, the lowest income quintile (quintile I) represented just 5.6% of total income in 2015 on average, compared with 46.2% for the highest income quintile (quintile V). The share of income for quintile I varied from one country to the next, with the lowest level seen in the Plurinational State of Bolivia (4.1%) and the highest in Uruguay (9.2%). Meanwhile, the share of income for quintile V recorded the lowest and highest levels in the Bolivian Republic of Venezuela (35.9%) and Guatemala (52.8%), respectively (see figure I.4).

**Figure I.4**
Latin America (16 countries): share of total income by income quintile, around 2015[a]
*(Percentages)*

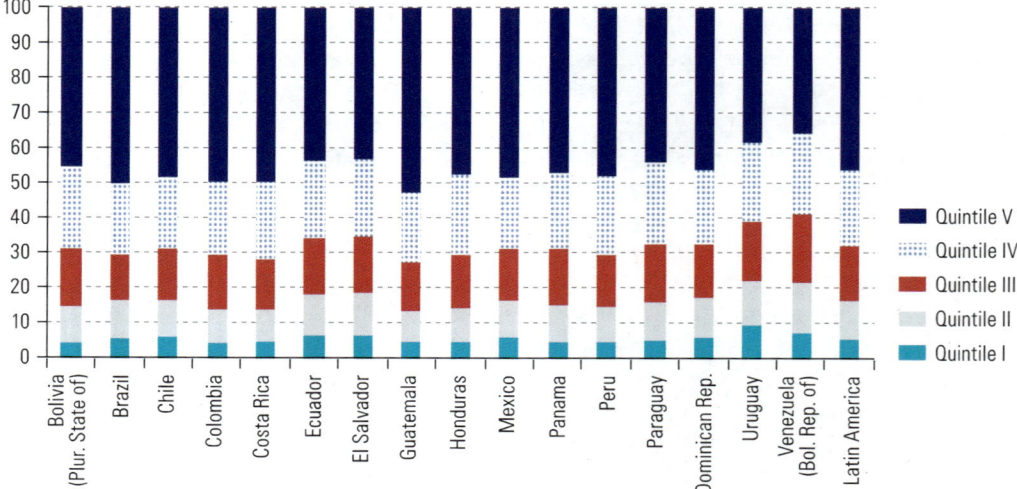

**Source:** Economic Commission for Latin America and the Caribbean (ECLAC), on the basis of Household Survey Data Bank (BADEHOG).
[a] Data refer to 2015, except in the cases of Plurinational State of Bolivia (2014), Guatemala (2014) and Bolivarian Republic of Venezuela (2014). The regional average is the arithmetic average of the percentage shares in the countries included.

Another relevant indicator is the gap between the average per capita income of households in quintiles V and I, which is shown in figure I.5. Between 2008 and 2015, the average ratio for 14 countries of the region fell 16.8%, from 14.7 to 12.2. Despite the decline, differences remain very large; on average, in 2015, for every 100 monetary units received by each member of quintile I, each member of quintile V received 1,220 units.

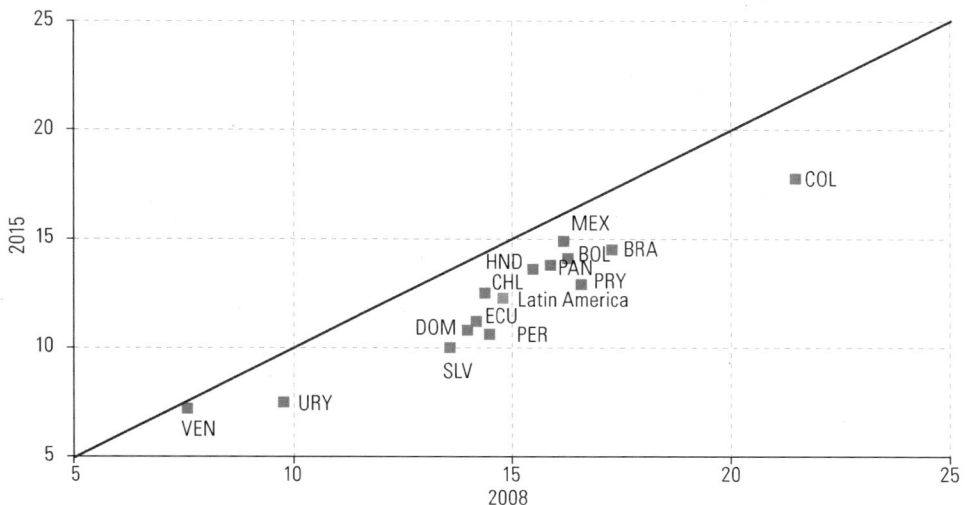

**Figure I.5**
Latin America (14 countries): ratio between the average income of income quintile V and income quintile I, around 2008 and 2015[a]

**Source**: Economic Commission for Latin America and the Caribbean (ECLAC), on the basis of Household Survey Data Bank (BADEHOG).
[a] Data refer to 2008 and 2015, except in the cases of Bolivarian Republic of Venezuela (2008 and 2014), Chile (2009 and 2015), Colombia (2009 and 2015), El Salvador (2009 and 2015), Honduras (2009 and 2015), Mexico (2008 and 2014) and Plurinational State of Bolivia (2008 and 2014).

In the 14 countries under review, this ratio narrowed in 2008-2015, reflecting an improvement in income distribution. Like the other indicators, trends varied considerably from one country to the next. In Colombia, for every 100 monetary units obtained on average by each household member of quintile I in 2015, the corresponding figure for quintile V was 1,780. This disparity in per capita income between the top and bottom quintiles was much smaller in the Bolivarian Republic of Venezuela and Uruguay, where for every 100 units received by members of quintile I, those in quintile V obtained 700.

As shown in box I.2, sources of household and individual income vary: employment (wage or independent), asset ownership, retirement and net transfers.

The portion of income from each of these sources varies according to per capita income. For the 17 countries under review, income from labour (wage and independent) represented, on average, 74% of per capita income for households in quintile I and 82% on average for those in quintile V. The main difference between these two quintiles was the share of income corresponding to wages, which represented 41% of total income in quintile I and 54% in quintile V. The situation is reversed with respect to income from independent employment, which is higher in quintile I (33% on average, compared with 28% for quintile V). Capital income represented 1% of the total in quintile I households versus 3% in quintile V homes (see figure I.6).[7]

---

[7] This type of income tends to be underestimated in household surveys. There are various alternatives to correct the estimates of size and the contribution to distributive inequality of capital income, even when they produce different results depending on the assumptions used.

**Figure I.6**

Latin America (17 countries): different sources' share of per capita income of income quintile I and income quintile V, around 2015[a][b]

**A. Income quintile I (lowest 20%)**

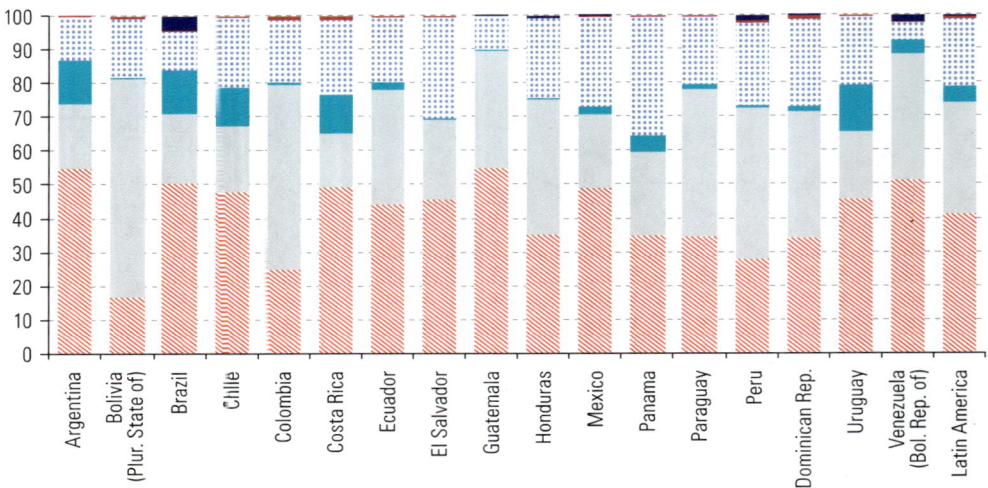

**B. Income quintile V (highest 20%)**

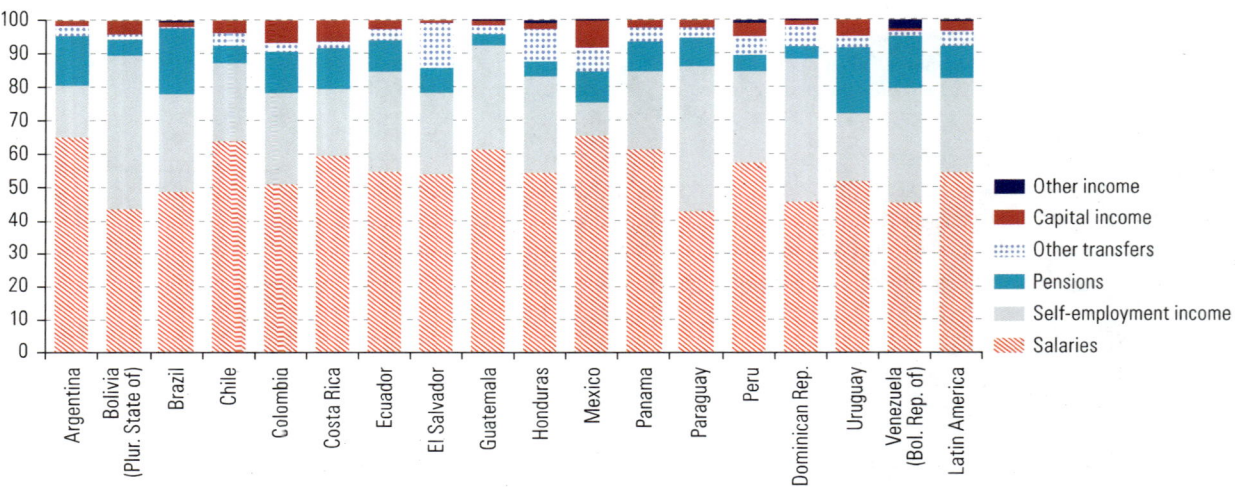

**Source**: Economic Commission for Latin America and the Caribbean (ECLAC), on the basis of Household Survey Data Bank (BADEHOG).

[a] Data refer to 2015, except in the cases of Argentina, the Bolivarian Republic of Venezuela, Guatemala, Mexico and the Plurinational State of Bolivia which refer to 2014.

[b] Other transfers are calculated as the net difference between transfers received and paid, insofar as the design of the survey allows it. Included, among other items, are remittances to other households, food costs and alimony payments and non-contributory transfers from the government and non-profit institutions, as well as direct tax payments and rebates.

With respect to the secondary distribution of income, there is a stark difference in the proportion of retirement benefits and pensions (which represent, on average, 10% of total income in quintile V and 5% in quintile I). On the contrary, other types of net transfers represent a larger share of income in quintile I households, amounting to 30% of total income on average, compared with 4% in quintile V.[8] In relative terms, quintile I households receive a larger portion of total income from both types of transfers (25%, on average, compared with 15% for quintile V households). Meanwhile, in absolute terms, quintile V households receive almost eight times the amount of per capita income from transfers received by quintile I households, on average.

---

[8] This item comprises mainly non-contributory transfers, maintenance payments and remittances received, free from payments for direct taxes and maintenance allowances, when these can be differentiated.

On the whole, there were no changes in the size of contributions from various sources to overall income in 2008-2015. On average, there was a slight decline in the share of income from independent employment in quintile I, along with an increase in weight of retirement benefits and other transfers. Meanwhile, in quintile V, there was a slight increase in the share of income from wage employment and retirement benefits, and declines of a similar magnitude in the share of income from independent employment and other transfers.

The fall in inequality between 2008 and 2015 meant, in general, a higher relative increase in income for quintile I than for quintile V.[9] This occurred in the main sources of household income, that is, income from wage jobs and self-employment. In terms of the averages for a set of 14 countries, the real variation in per capita wage income for quintile I was 3% per year, compared to 2.3% per year in quintile V. There was a similar trend in income from self-employment, which grew at an annual rate of 2.8% (in real per capita terms) in quintile I, compared to an average variation of -0.3% in quintile V. The changes over the period were not homogeneous across the countries, with sharp increases and decreases in income from one or both sources, albeit with a fairly steady trend of larger increases in quintile I households both from wage jobs and from self-employment (see figure I.7).

**A. Wage-employment income (wages and salaries)**

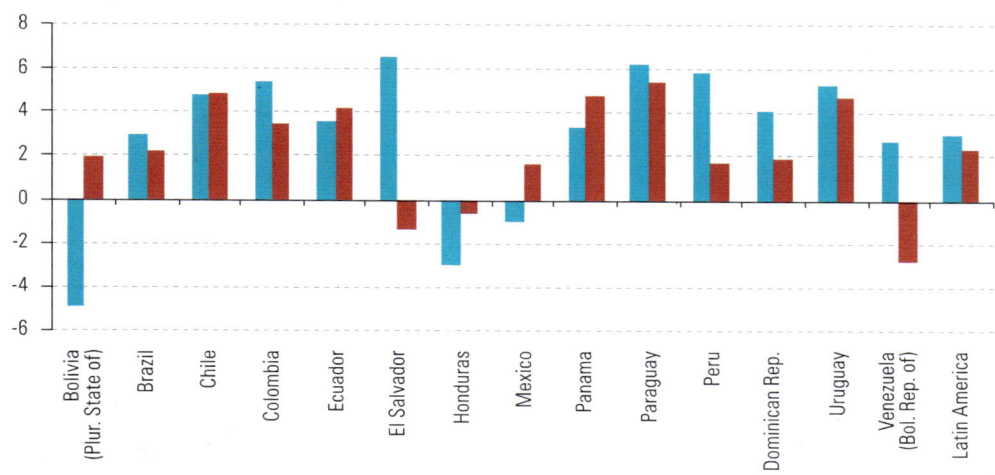

**Figure I.7**

Latin America (14 countries): annual growth per capita in wage income, income from self-employment and pensions and other transfers of income quintiles I and V, 2008-2015[a]
*(Percentages)*

**B. Income from self-employment**

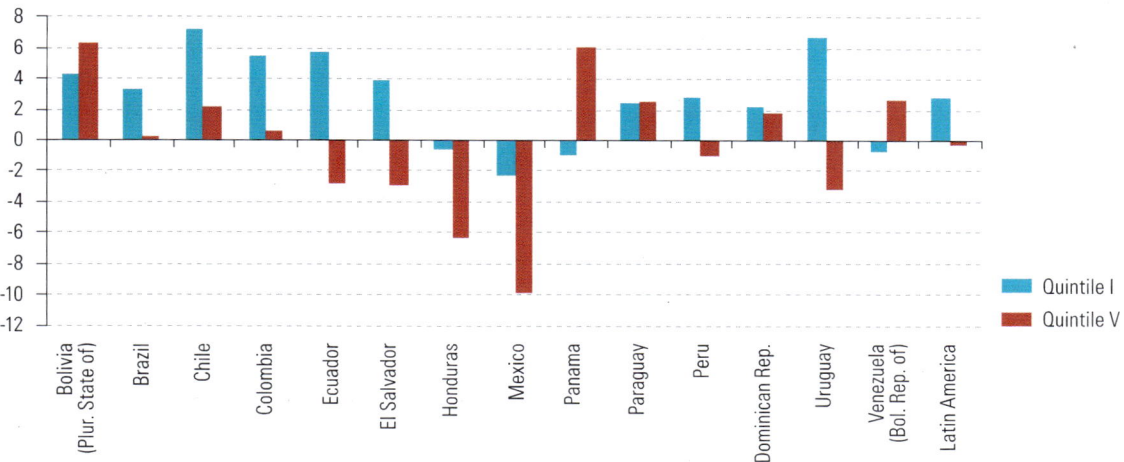

■ Quintile I
■ Quintile V

---

9　An improvement in distribution does not automatically result in better well-being. In Honduras, for example, the improvement in income distribution between 2008 and 2015 came about within the framework of an overall decline in household income, which had a greater impact on quintile V households.

Figure I.7 (concluded)

**C. Pensions and other transfers**

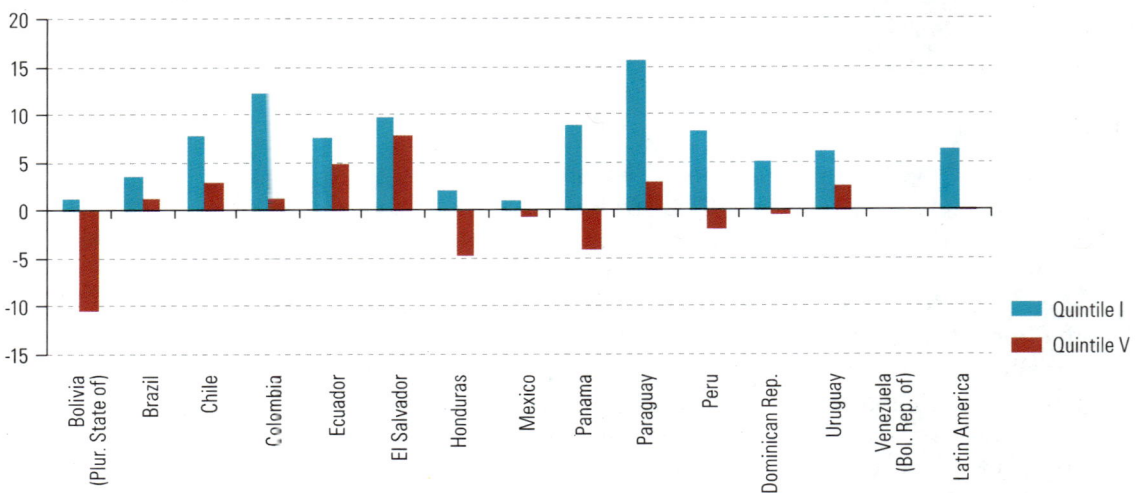

**Source**: Economic Commission for Latin America and the Caribbean (ECLAC), on the basis of Household Survey Data Bank (BADEHOG).
ª Data refer to 2008-2015, except in the cases of Chile (2009 and 2015), Colombia (2009 and 2015), El Salvador (2009 and 2015), Honduras (2009 and 2015), Mexico (2008 and 2014) and the Plurinational State of Bolivia (2008 and 2014).

Total retirement benefits and other transfers reflected the same pattern of differentiated increases benefitting quintile I households (up 6.4% per year, compared to 0.1% in quintile V). Transfers were very low in several countries in 2008, so although they posted strong growth over the period, their share of total per capita income of quintile I households did not change significantly (see figure I.7).

## 2. Income inequality from a gender perspective

Economic autonomy is a cornerstone of women's autonomy, which requires, among other things, that women receive enough income not only to overcome poverty, but also to have enough free time to realize their personal aspirations. Over the years, ample empirical evidence has been gathered to suggest that income is distributed unequally both in society and within households. In general, women have less access to production and financial resources, as well as to money, training and different technologies. Meanwhile, because they take care of their families, women have less time for their own use, which undermines their autonomy and their ability to train and maintain an unbroken presence in the labour market, which in turn undermines equality in households and in society as a whole (ECLAC, 2016e).

This section looks at aspects that illustrate the gender-based inequalities that affect individuals, based on four commonly used indicators: the number of women and men in low-income households; the percentage of women and men without their own income; the composition of women's incomes; and the wage gap between women and men who work 35 hours or more per week.

With regard to the first indicator, low-income households contain a higher proportion of women of ages at which productive and reproductive demands are greater than the population as a whole. Without exception, women are overrepresented in the first two or three income quintiles of the countries under consideration.

This can be seen in figure I.8, which shows the index constructed as the ratio between the proportion of women aged between 20 and 59 to men in the same age group and the total number of people in that age range in each income quintile. A value greater than 100 means that the ratio of women to men in a given quintile is greater than in the general population, while a value less than 100 indicates the opposite. According to the data, women are overrepresented in the poorest income quintile by up to 40%.

**Figure I.8**

Latin America (16 countries): ratio between the proportion of women to men in each income quintile and the proportion observed in the total population, persons aged between 20 and 59 years, 2015[a][b]

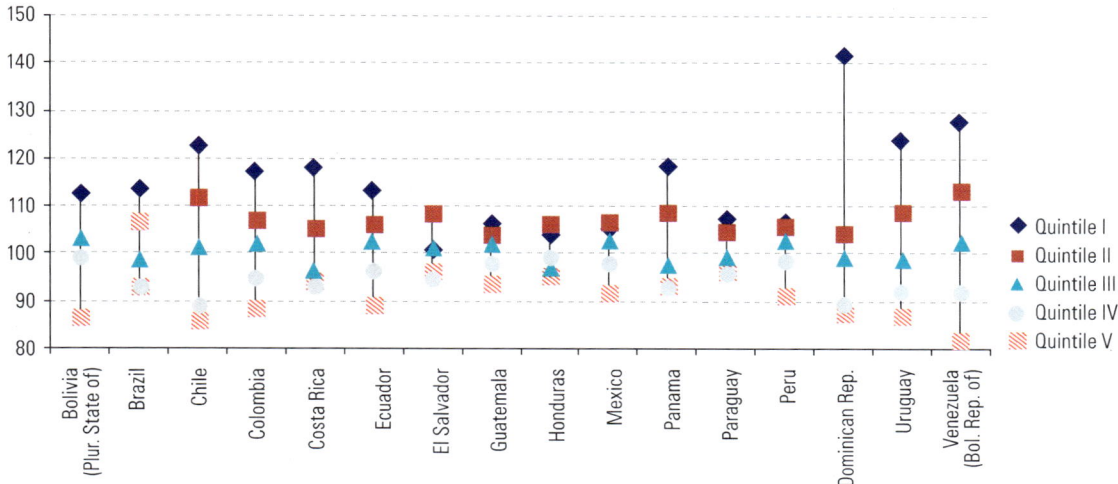

**Source**: Economic Commission for Latin America and the Caribbean (ECLAC), on the basis of Household Survey Data Bank (BADEHOG).
[a] Data refer to 2015, except in the cases of Argentina, the Bolivarian Republic of Venezuela, Guatemala, Mexico and the Plurinational State of Bolivia, which refer to 2014.
[b] A value greater than 100 indicates that the ratio of women to men in a given quintile is greater than in the general population, and a value less than 100 indicates the opposite.

The greater number of women in low-income groups is the result of various forms of discrimination. On the one hand, women tend to receive lower incomes, because of the difficulty of reconciling unpaid work in the home with labour market participation, and because they usually work in typically low-wage occupations.[10] Women also tend to be overrepresented among the heads of single-parent households, where low income and high dependency rates may not be mutually exclusive. On the other hand, the percentage of women who receive income from the labour market or in the form of pensions or other transfer is considerably lower than the percentage of men who do.[11] The high percentage of women without their own income or with insufficient income not only means that households have a one less source of income to meet their needs, it also undermines women's economic autonomy (ECLAC, 2016e).

The percentage of women without their own income is considerably higher than that of men without their own income. The simple average figure for the 15 countries studied, shows that 44% of women in quintile I lack their own income, compared to 23% of men. The highest percentages of women in quintile I without their own income are greater than 50% in Guatemala (69.6%), El Salvador (57.8%) and Costa Rica (53%), while, for men it is not higher than 30%. Brazil is an exception, as the percentage is similar for men and women in quintile I, around 41% (see figure I.9).

---

[10]  Chapter IV will examine how men and women use their time and its relationship with gender equality
[11]  One exception is the cash transfer programmes that seek to combat poverty, as in the vast majority of cases, women are the main beneficiaries of these programmes.

**Figure I.9**
Latin America (15 countries): people without their own income in income quintiles I and V, by sex, 2015[a]
*(Percentages)*

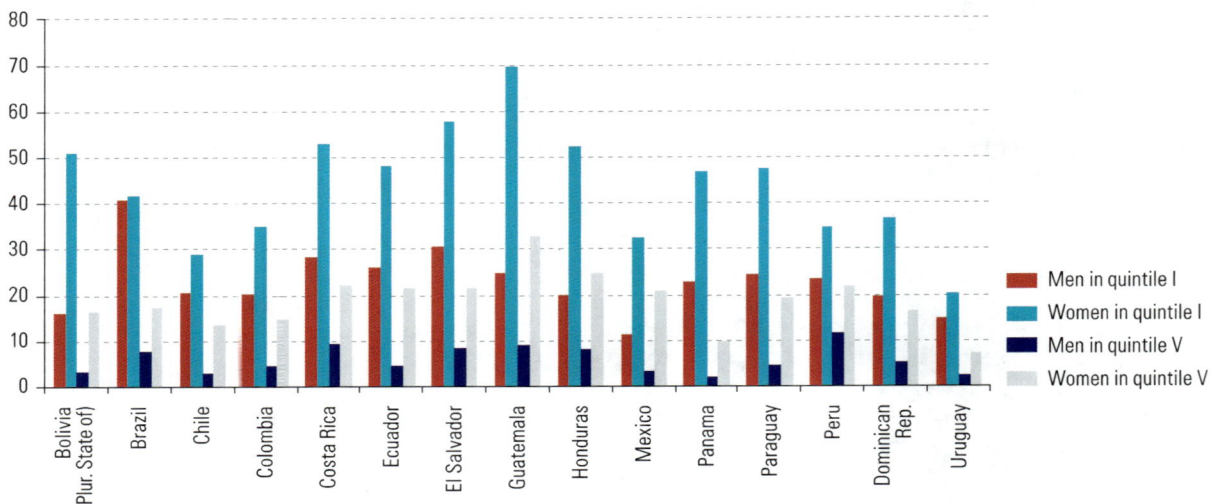

**Source**: Economic Commission for Latin America and the Caribbean (ECLAC), on the basis of Household Survey Data Bank (BADEHOG).
[a] Data refer to 2015, except in the cases of Guatemala, Mexico and Plurinational State of Bolivia, which refer to 2014.

As is to be expected, the percentage of people without their own income is considerably less among richer households. However, the gap between men and women remains or is even widening. On average, 19% of women in quintile V do not have their own income, while only 6% of men in this income group do not have their own income.

In 10 of the countries for which information is available, between 2008 and 2015, the percentage of women without their own income in quintile I declined, while it remained the same in two countries and in Chile and El Salvador it increased significantly (see figure I.10).

**Figure I.10**
Latin America (14 countries): women without their own income, income quintile I, 2008 and 2015[a]
*(Percentages)*

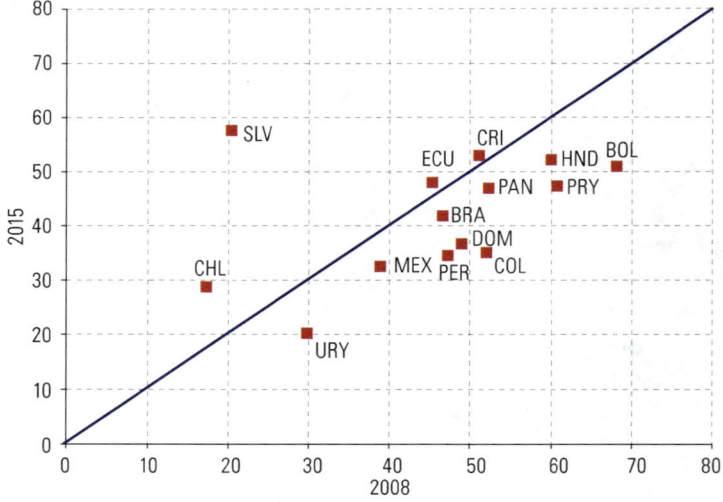

**Source**: Economic Commission for Latin America and the Caribbean (ECLAC), on the basis of the Household Survey Data Bank (BADEHOG).
[a] Data refer to 2008 and 2015, except in the cases of Chile (2009 and 2015), Colombia (2009 and 2015), El Salvador (2009 and 2015), Honduras (2009 and 2015), Mexico (2008 and 2014) and Plurinational State of Bolivia (2008 and 2014).

Meanwhile, a look at the composition of men's and women's personal income by source reveals that the biggest difference is in income from transfers (mainly from the government, but also from remittances and other households), which is particularly important because of its strong link with public policies. Transfers account for 16.8% of women's total income but less than 10% of men's income (see figure I.11).

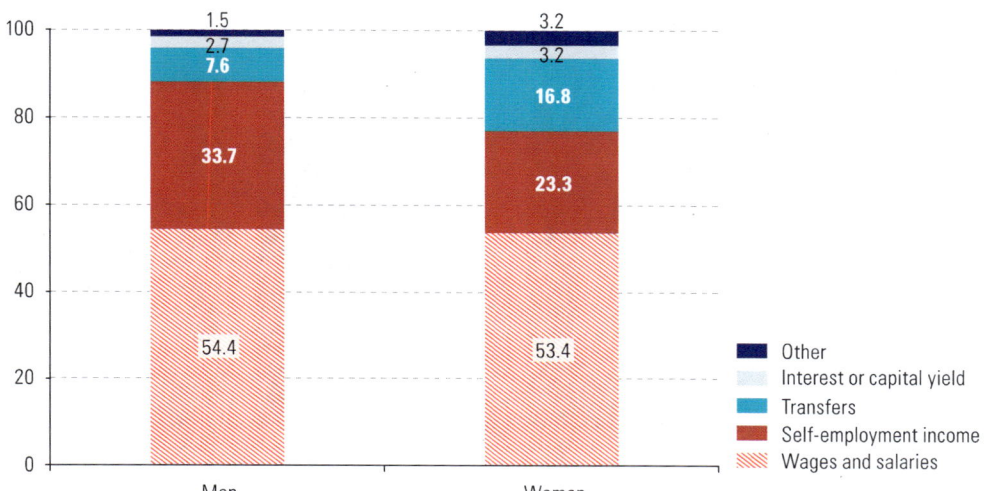

**Figure I.11**
Latin America (17 countries): composition of own income by source and sex, around 2014[a][b]
(Percentages)

**Source**: Economic Commission for Latin America and the Caribbean (ECLAC), *Equality and women's autonomy in the sustainable development agenda* (LC/G.2686/Rev.1), Santiago, 2016

[a] Personal income can come from a variety of sources: paid employment in the form of wages, salaries or self-employment income; income derived from ownership of physical or financial assets; or transfers related to a person's career or to circumstances for which they receive money personally. Transfers may come from the government or other agencies, in the form of contributory transfers (such as retirement benefits) or non-contributory transfers (such as disability pensions or special poverty alleviation programmes) or else they may derive from a tie with a family member or former family member in the form of remittances or obligations arising from dissolution of marriage.

[b] The countries included are: Argentina, the Bolivarian Republic of Venezuela, Brazil, Chile, Colombia, Costa Rica, Dominican Republic, Ecuador, El Salvador, Guatemala, Honduras, Mexico, Panama, Paraguay, Peru, the Plurinational State of Bolivia and Uruguay.

It is important to analyse the gender differences in independent income within the composition of personal income and how it relates to women's autonomy. Non-contributory government transfers whose receipt —as in the case of conditional cash transfers— is conditional upon performing a particular activity have been used in a number of Latin American countries as part of strategies to protect poor households with children by providing a cash income to women. There are diverse opinions today on whether such programmes have contributed to women's empowerment or, on the contrary, have reinforced traditional gender roles, increased the time women are forced to devote to unpaid domestic and care work and limited their participation in the labour market. It must also be considered that making autonomous income dependent on a conditional cash transfer from the State treats women as just another adjustment variable for the economic crises that the region's countries face on a cyclical basis. As many cases have confirmed, o+nce a crisis sets in and public spending is reduced to address it, cutbacks are very likely to be made in social programmes, where women are the main recipients. The result is income fragility with very little certainty of continuity.

Wide disparities exist between men and women in Latin America with regard to the weight of self-employment income in the composition of their income, with this source providing 33.7% of men's total income and 23.3% of women's.

The main source of income for both men and women is wages and salaries, accounting for 54% of all personal income. However, only one in two working-age women in the region are economically active, meaning they are employed or seeking employment. Another point of note is the discrimination and inequality currently faced by women in paid employment. Despite their skills and expertise, they continue to face obstacles in access to paid work and, when they succeed, they encounter a marked gender wage gap which, paradoxically, grows wider the more years of schooling they have, as is shown in figure I.12.

**Figure I.12**
Latin America (weighted average of 18 countries): average wage of urban female wage earners aged 20 to 49 years, working 35 hours or more per week, as a proportion of the average wages of men with the same characteristics, by years of schooling, 1990 and 2014[a]
*(Percentages)*

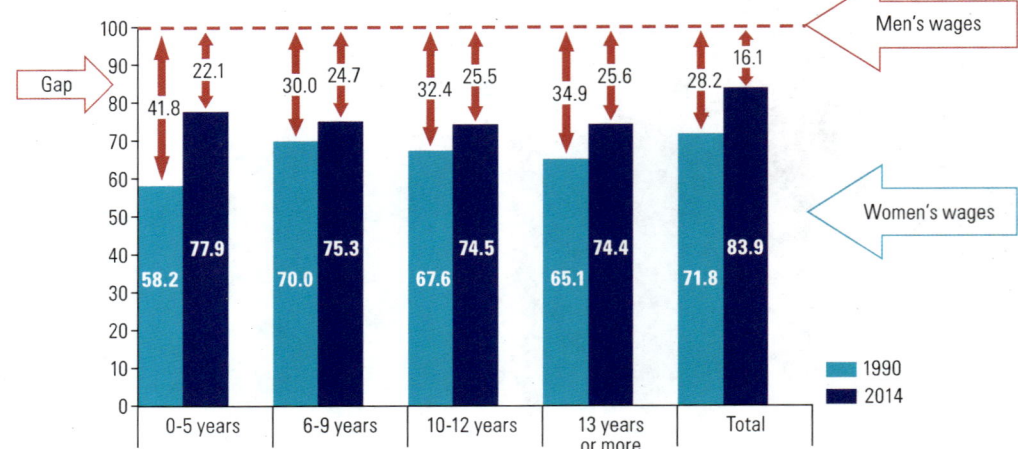

Source: Economic Commission for Latin America and the Caribbean (ECLAC), *Equality and women's autonomy in the sustainable development agenda* (LC/G.2686/Rev.1), Santiago, 2016.
[a] Argentina, Bolivarian Republic of Venezuela, Brazil, Chile, Colombia, Costa Rica, Dominican Republic, Ecuador, El Salvador, Guatemala, Honduras, Mexico, Nicaragua, Panama, Paraguay, Peru, Plurinational State of Bolivia and Uruguay.

Although the wage gap between women and men shrank by 12.1 percentage points between 1990 and 2014, women's pay is still only 83.9% of men's. The biggest decrease in the wage gap (19.7 percentage points) was observed in the group of women with the lowest educational level (those with 0-5 years of schooling). This is due to advances in legislation by countries in the region to regulate and formalize paid domestic work, and to an increase in the minimum wage.

For women with the highest educational level (13 years or more of education), the wage gap shrank by 9.3 percentage points. While the entry of women into such fields as science and technology, telecommunications and large enterprise may be helping to improve the situation, it has failed to create equality: the wage gap between women and men is still 25.6 percentage points, showing that investment in women's education and vocational training has not impacted their earnings in line with those of men with the same training.

In short, both the overrepresentation of women in the lower income quintiles and the higher proportion of women without their own income, especially in those quintiles, mean that a large group of women face deprivation and inequity. While progress has been made in recent years, the income gaps that women face, and the differentiated composition of that income, remains a distinctive feature of inequality in all the countries of the region.

Both the overrepresentation of women in the lower income quintiles and the higher proportion of women without their own income, especially in those quintiles, mean that a large group of women face deprivation and inequity.

# B. Functional inequality of income distribution in Latin America

The functional approach to income distribution analysis provides valuable information for understanding the dynamics of income from labour and capital, and can be considered in conjunction with personal income inequality. Comparing the wage share of GDP and the personal income inequality indicators of the region reveals that while the Gini coefficient fell in most of the countries between 2002 and 2014, the wage share of GDP increased in a small number of countries. This suggests that distributive gains in the region were not directly linked to a more equitable distribution between capital and labour. Lastly, sectoral-level analysis of the indicators in the selected countries shows that most of the changes are due to highly distributive factors and not to shifts in the composition of the production structure.

## 1. Functional analysis of income distribution

In recent years, there has been a renewed effort to tackle the problem of inequality. On the one hand, the imperative of equality has moved up the regional agenda of different stakeholders. On the other hand, several studies have attempted to understand the reasons for the fall in inequality in the 2000s, and why that downward trend recently stalled, as discussed in the first part of this chapter.

The most commonly used approach for analysing income distribution in the region has been inequality between individuals or between households. The original concept of functional income inequality, which is reflected in aggregate indicators such as the wage share of gross domestic product (GDP), has received little attention at either the global or regional level. However, functional income distribution analysis provides very valuable information for understanding the dynamics of labour income and capital yields and can be considered in conjunction with personal income inequality (see box I.4).

However, there are major data limitations in functional income distribution analysis. National accounts provide information on the wage bill (remuneration of wage workers) and, in the best case scenario, include the concept of mixed income, which reflects the remuneration of self-employed workers and implicitly contains an element of return on labour and an element of returns on the capital involved in the productive activities under consideration. Thus, in order to calculate the wag share of GDP correctly, the labour income received by self-employed workers must be estimated, as it is not included in the national accounts. An approximate figure can be arrived at by assuming that self-employed workers receive remuneration similar to the average salary (see, for example, Gollin, 2002) or, a more accurately, by estimating the wages that self-employed workers would receive on the basis of their individual skills and the economic sector they work in (instead of taking the average salary), as suggested by Young (1995). However, it is important to bear in mind that, more often than not, studies refer to the wage share and not total labour income, in other words, they concentrate on the wage workers' earnings as a share of GDP, based on the national accounts, which means that the labour share of GDP is seriously underestimated in developing countries where self-employment plays a substantial role in the economy (see Abeles and others, 2014).

Meanwhile, an essentially empirical approach has been taken to analysis of the link between personal and functional income distribution. In general, studies have shown that

National accounts provide information that implicitly contains an element of return on labour and an element of returns on the capital involved in the productive activities under consideration.

a greater labour income share of value added is associated with more egalitarian levels of personal income (Daudey and García-Peñalosa, 2007; García-Peñalosa and Orgiazzi, 2013, among others). It is therefore important to bear in mind the three reasons given by Atkinson (2009) for studying factor shares when examining income distribution: firstly, to make a link between incomes at the macroeconomic level (that is, from national accounts) and incomes at the level of the household; secondly, to help understand inequality in the personal distribution of income; and thirdly, to address the concern of social justice with the fairness of different sources of income, or in other words, the extent to which increased productivity is reflected in higher wages or earnings.

**Box I.4**
Functional and personal income distribution

Classical economists placed functional income distribution at the centre of economic debate, and its importance was later recognized by marginalist economists in the late-nineteenth century (such as William Jevons, Léon Walras and Carl Menger), although within a different conceptual and methodological framework whereby each factor of production (the social classes of the classical authors) represented a share of the product depending on its marginal contribution to the production process.

With the consolidation of neoclassical economics around the mid-1950s, and its emphasis on analysing the individual behaviour of economic agents, the focus of mainstream economists shifted from functional income distribution to personal income distribution (Goldfarb and Leonard, 2005). To start with, interest in examining personal income distribution was met with resistance from post-Keynesian and neo-Ricardian economists, who believed that distribution should be approached from a functional perspective, not only for analytical purposes but also with the stated aim of highlighting the central role played by the social conflict between capitalists and workers in the development of capitalist economies. From the 1960s, however, an unequivocal shift occurred towards personal income distribution and the functional approach found itself placed on the back burner (Atkinson, 2009).

While studies into personal income inequality often place emphasis on the characteristics of individuals and the behaviour of different income sources, thanks to the robust methodological tools that have been developed to this end, functional income distribution analysis draws links between distribution phenomena and other aspects including the relative prices of capital and work, market concentration, the global offshoring of production processes, the deregulation of labour markets, financialization and its deregulation, changes to institutions, and levels of unionization (Bentolila and Saint-Paul, 2003; Bernanke and Gürkaynak, 2002; Fichtenbaum, 2009; Gollin, 2002; Hogrefe and Kappler, 2013; IMF, 2007; Jayadev, 2007; Rodríguez and Ortega, 2006). Furthermore, following the contributions of authors from post-Keynesian or structuralist backgrounds, changes to functional income distribution have been linked to economic growth, with a distinction made between salary-based regimes and profit-based regimes (see Bhaduri and Marglin, 1990; Taylor, 1991).

To understand the headway made by the personal approach to distributional analysis, both historic and institutional factors must be considered, as well as other elements concerning the availability of data sources and the strengthening of statistical tools. As Atkinson (2009) points out, the complexity of modern production processes, as well as the significant heterogeneity within the social groups linked to the different production factors, mean that individuals and households receive income associated with more than one production factor (rather than exclusively from work or from capital). What's more, levels of inequality can be very high within one group (wage earners, for example). From an institutional perspective, the consolidation of welfare States brought with it the need to identify with more precision the most vulnerable social groups —the principal beneficiaries of public assistance— and to examine with greater rigour the distribution of income within the working class. The personal approach facilitates a more detailed analysis of the impact of the State's redistributive action, by using statistical information from household surveys to evaluate the effect that taxes and transfers have on income.

Box I.4 (concluded)

In recent years, there has been a new surge of interest in the functional approach, which has once more emerged as a topic of academic debate. This shift was at least partly caused by the declining labour share of income in the developed world since the 1980s, which has constituted a departure from the relative stability that had characterized this indicator since the end of the second world war. Different studies have attempted to identify the causes of this change in trend, highlighting the importance of globalization, financialization, capital-friendly technological changes and institutional modifications affecting the labour market (among others, Guscina, 2006; ILO, 2010 and 2012; OECD, 2012; Stockhammer, 2013; Berg, 2015; Autor and others, 2017).

**Source**: Economic Commission for Latin America and the Caribbean (ECLAC), on the basis of A. Atkinson, "Factor shares: the principal problem of political economy?" *Oxford Review of Economic Policy*, vol. 25, No. 1, Oxford University Press, 2009; D. Autor and others, "Concentrating on the fall of the labor share", *American Economic Review Papers and Proceedings*, 2017, forthcoming; R. Goldfarb and T. Leonard, "Inequality of what among whom?: Rival conceptions of distribution in the 20th century", *Research in the History of Economic Thought and Methodology*, vol. 23, part 1, 2005; S. Bentolila and G. Saint-Paul, "Explaining Movements in the Labor Share", *The B.E. Journal of Macroeconomics*, vol. 3, No. 1, 2003; J. Berg (ed), *Labour Markets, Institutions and Inequality: Building Just Societies in the 21st Century*, International Labour Organization, 2015; B. Bernanke and R. Gürkaynak, "Is growth exogenous? Taking Mankiw, Romer, and Weil seriously", *NBER Chapters*, National Bureau of Economic Research (NBER), 2002; A. Bhaduri and S. Marglin, "Unemployment and the real wage: the economic basis for contesting political ideologies", *Cambridge Journal of Economics*, No. 14, Academic Press Limited, 1990; R. Fichtenbaum, "The impact of unions on labor's share of income: a time-series analysis", *Review of Political Economy*, vol. 21, No. 4, 2009; International Monetary Fund (IMF), *Annual Report 2007: Making the Global Economy Work for All*, Washington, D.C., 2007; D. Gollin, "Getting income shares right", *Journal of Political Economy*, vol. 110, No. 2, 2002; A. Guscina, "Effects of globalization on labor's share in national income", *IMF Working Papers*, No. 294, International Monetary Fund, 2006; J. Hogrefe and M. Kappler, "The labour share of income: heterogeneous causes for parallel movements?", *The Journal of Economic Inequality*, vol. 11, No. 3, 2013; A. Jayadev, "Capital account openness and the labour share of income", *Cambridge Journal of Economics*, vol. 31, No. 3, 2007; Organization for Economic Cooperation and Development (OECD), *OECD Employment Outlook 2012*, Paris, 2012; International Labour Organization (ILO), *Global Wage Report 2010/11: Wage Policies in Times of Crisis*, Geneve, 2010; ILO, *Global Wage Report 2012/13: Wages and Equitable Growth*, Geneva, 2012; F. Rodríguez and D. Ortega, "Are capital shares higher in poor countries? Evidence from industrial surveys", *Wesleyan Economics Working Papers*, No. 2006-023, Wesleyan University, 2006; E Stockhammer, "Why have wage shares fallen? A panel analysis of the determinants of functional income distribution", *Conditions of Work and Employment Series*, No. 35, International Labour Organization, 2013; L. Taylor, *Income Distribution, Inflation, and Growth: Lectures on Structuralist Macroeconomic Theory*, London, MIT Press, 1991.

## 2. Functional income distribution in Latin America: a historical perspective

There are some regional, long-term studies that examine the wage share of GDP (Lindenboim, 2008; Frankema, 2009; Bértola and others, 2008). Among others, Alarco Tosoni (2014) focuses on 15 countries of the region between 1950 and 2011. The mean, the standard deviation, and the maximum and minimum values of the wage share are shown in table I.1. The highest averages for wage share are found in Panama, Costa Rica, Honduras, Brazil, Argentina, Uruguay and Chile; while Ecuador, El Salvador and Peru have the lowest. The Bolivarian Republic of Venezuela, Colombia, Mexico, Paraguay and the Plurinational State of Bolivia are in the middle. As Alarco Tosoni points out Panama, Ecuador, El Salvador, Peru, Uruguay, Argentina and the Bolivarian Republic of Venezuela show a higher standard deviation, i.e. greater volatility, than Costa Rica and Brazil, which have the lowest standard deviations. In general, the minimum wage share values tend to be seen after the debt crisis of the 1980s (except in Honduras and El Salvador). The wage share peaks at times of intensive import-substitution industrialization —Bolivarian Republic of Venezuela, 1960; Brazil, 1957; Peru, 1958; and Uruguay, 1963— and at certain sociopolitical junctures that were favourable to workers: Argentina, 1974; Chile, 1972; Colombia, 1993; Costa Rica, 1990; Ecuador, 2007; El Salvador, 1981; Honduras, 1986; Mexico, 1976; Panama, 1969; Paraguay, 2000; and the Plurinational State of Bolivia, 1984.

Table I.1
Latin America (15 countries): main characteristics of wage share in GDP, 1950-2011

| Country | Coverage | Number of observations | $\bar{x}$ (percentages) | $\bar{\sigma}$ | $\frac{\bar{\sigma}}{\bar{x}}$ | Maximum value (percentages) | Year of maximum value | Minimum value (percentages) | Year of minimum value |
|---|---|---|---|---|---|---|---|---|---|
| Argentina | 1950-2011 | 62 | 39.51 | 5.46 | 0.14 | 48.79 | 1974 | 28.06 | 1989 |
| Bolivia (Plurinational State of) | 1960-2011 | 52 | 33.98 | 3.88 | 0.11 | 43.12 | 1984 | 24.13 | 1986 |
| Brazil | 1950-2011 | 62 | 43.11 | 2.46 | 0.06 | 48.27 | 1957 | 39.31 | 2004 |
| Chile | 1950-2010 | 61 | 38.17 | 3.79 | 0.1 | 52.19 | 1972 | 30.88 | 1988 |
| Colombia | 1950-2010 | 61 | 36.82 | 3.35 | 0.09 | 44.07 | 1993 | 31.67 | 2008 |
| Costa Rica | 1953-2010 | 58 | 46.95 | 1.96 | 0.04 | 50.57 | 1990 | 39.10 | 1982 |
| Ecuador | 1953-2011 | 60 | 26.15 | 7.19 | 0.28 | 37.95 | 2007 | 11.51 | 1999 |
| El Salvador | 1960-2011 | 52 | 30.67 | 6.81 | 0.22 | 41.91 | 1981 | 15.80 | 1960 |
| Honduras | 1950-2011 | 62 | 43.31 | 3.52 | 0.08 | 50.36 | 1986 | 35.04 | 1953 |
| Mexico | 1950-2011 | 62 | 32.58 | 3.57 | 0.11 | 40.26 | 1976 | 26.84 | 1987 |
| Panama | 1950-2011 | 62 | 50.76 | 11.48 | 0.23 | 67.41 | 1969 | 30.15 | 2011 |
| Paraguay | 1962-2010 | 49 | 33.70 | 3.03 | 0.09 | 38.73 | 2000 | 24.34 | 1990 |
| Peru | 1950-2011 | 62 | 31.60 | 6.62 | 0.21 | 41.15 | 1958 | 20.91 | 2008 |
| Uruguay | 1955-2011 | 57 | 39.37 | 5.68 | 0.14 | 50.43 | 1963 | 27.75 | 1984 |
| Venezuela (Bolivarian Republic of) | 1957-2010 | 54 | 37.40 | 5.43 | 0.15 | 46.90 | 1960 | 25.52 | 1996 |
| Latin America[a] | 1950-2010 | 61 | 38.76 | 2.02 | 0.052 | 41.70 | 1967 | 33.69 | 2004 |

**Source**: G. Alarco Tosoni, "Wage share and economic growth in Latin America, 1950-2011", *CEPAL Review*, No. 113, August 2014.
[a] Average weighted by nominal GDP in current dollars.

The analysis performed by Alarco Tosoni (2014) reveals considerably different levels and fluctuations between countries, depending on the size of their economies. For example, in Argentina the cycles are more pronounced than in Brazil, while the pattern is less cyclical in Mexico. Among the medium-sized economies, the long-term downward trend from the 1970s peak in Peru, the cyclical pattern in Chile, and the cases of Colombia and Bolivarian Republic of Venezuela, with peaks in the 1990s and the 1960s, respectively, are all significant. Among the smaller Latin American economies, variability is remarkably low in the Plurinational State of Bolivia.

Alarco Tosoni also builds a series for Latin America as a whole, covering the period between 1950 and 2011, weighted by nominal GDP in current dollars (see figure I.13). The series shows that wage shares were highest in the late 1960s and early 1970s. They were also relatively high in the 1990s, albeit with lower values than the first cycle in the 1960s and 1970s. Smaller wage shares were identified during the 1980s and the first five years of the twenty-first century. In recent years, the wage share of GDP has risen in the regional aggregate, owing an improvement in functional income distribution, chiefly in Argentina and Brazil, although in the case of many countries the wage share is falling, which is analysed below.

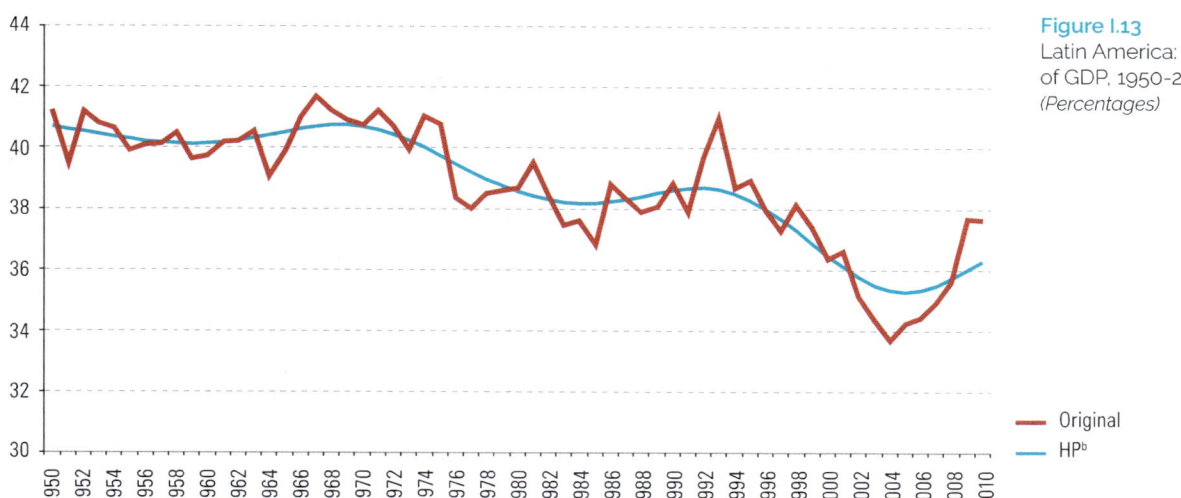

**Figure I.13**
Latin America: wage share
of GDP, 1950-2010[a]
*(Percentages)*

**Source**: G. Alarco Tosoni, "Wage share and economic growth in Latin America, 1950-2011", *CEPAL Review*, No. 113, August 2014.
[a] Average weighted by nominal GDP in current dollars.
[b] HP: series corrected using the Hodrick-Prescott filter. This filter is applied to time series to remove trend components and cyclical components.

It should be noted that Alarco Tosoni's study focuses on wage share and not on the ratio between total labour share of GDP. One of the distinguishing features of Latin American labour markets is the considerable weight of self-employment, which includes self-employed workers and employers, and accounts for a very large proportion of total employment in the region (almost 32%, with variations by country) (Abeles, Amarante and Vega, 2014). According to household survey data, income reported by self-employed workers represents a very substantial proportion of the per capita household income (about 31% in the region). As explained above, given the nature of the activities involved, some of this income is payment for labour and another part is capital yields. The fact that this income is not included in functional income distribution analysis is a major limitation that must be taken into account and an example of the basic statistical challenges that the region still faces.

## 3. Functional income distribution in Latin America: recent events

Before analysing the recent trend in wage share of GDP in Latin America, it is useful to compare figures for this indicator from countries of the region with that of other economies around the world, using information from the United Nations Statistics Division database, which calculates the indicator at market prices. There is wide variation between the countries analysed, ranging from 17% in Niger to 59% in Switzerland (see figure I.14). Of the 10 Latin American economies considered, seven are among the bottom third of countries, with wage shares below 40% of GDP: Uruguay, the Plurinational State of Bolivia, Colombia, the Bolivarian Republic of Venezuela, Guatemala, Mexico, and Panama. Two, Brazil and Chile, fall in the middle, between 40% and 45% of GDP, while only Costa Rica is in the upper third, with a wage share higher than 50% of GDP.

Despite the widespread fall in the wage share of GDP between 2002 and 2006, it began to rise again in most of the countries thereafter, alongside the fall in the Gini.

**Figure I.14**
Selected countries: wage share in GDP at market prices, around 2014

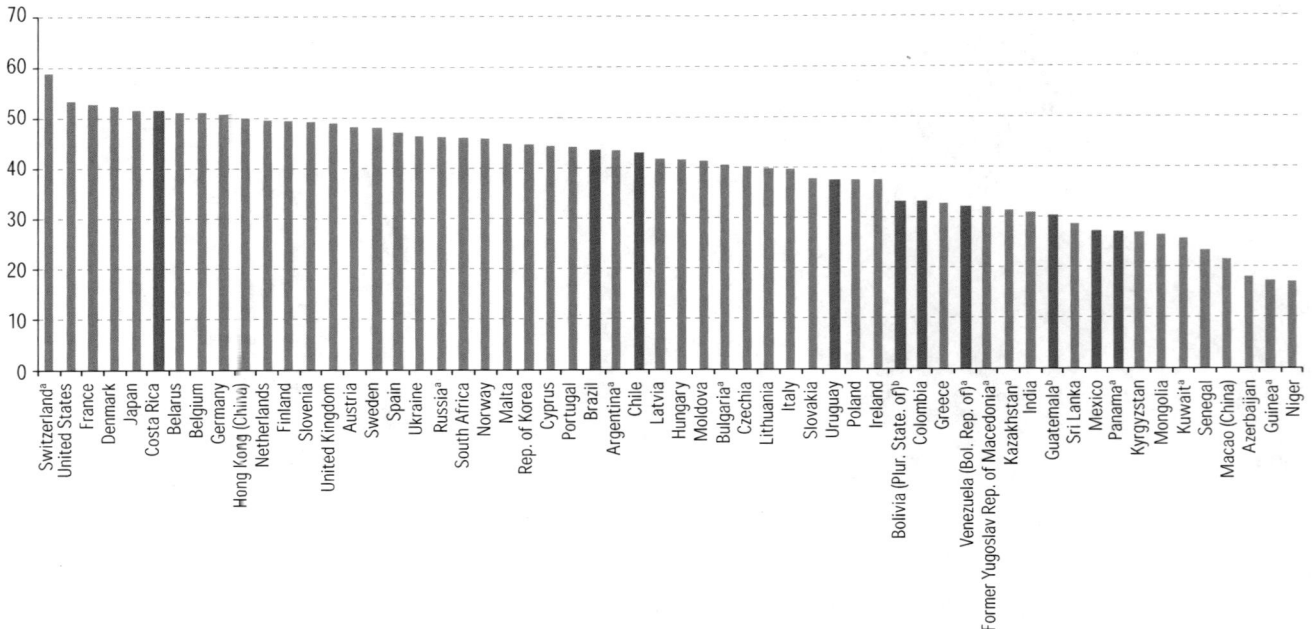

**Source**: Economic Commission for Latin America and the Caribbean (ECLAC), on the basis of United Nations, UNdata, [online database] http://data.un.org.
[a] Data from 2013.
[b] Data from 2012.

The national accounts information contained in CEPALSTAT, supplemented by the updated data obtained from the relevant official authorities for each country, allows for deeper analysis of the labour share of total income in each economy, at factor prices.[12] By 2014, wages as a share of income of Latin American countries was between 29% in Panama and 53% in Costa Rica (see table I.2). Since 2002, the share of income generated to pay workers' wages increased in only 4 of the 12 countries for which data are available for the whole period: the Bolivarian Republic of Venezuela, Brazil, Honduras and Uruguay. However, it should be noted that this masks two periods where the pattern was reversed. Between 2002 and 2006, the wage share fell in the vast majority of the countries studied (12 out of a total of 14), while between 2010 and 2014, the wage share of income increased in most countries. In particular, Chile, Colombia and Costa Rica saw recent increases in the wage bill that failed to offset the decrease prior to 2006.

Among the countries where wages accounted for the largest share of income, the most notable increases between 2002 and 2014 were in the Bolivarian Republic of Venezuela and Brazil (around 5 percentage points). In the Bolivarian Republic of Venezuela, the rise is simply a result of the most recent data, as the wage bill fell as a percentage of GDP both in the period 2002-2006 and in 2006-2010. Brazil is the only country in which the indicator rose in all the periods under consideration. Those increases have been relatively homogenous since 2002.

---

[12]   In the case of Uruguay, the wage ratio was updated in 2005 in line with the average nominal wage index, the employment rate and GDP at factor cost, as the Uruguayan system of national accounts does not contain up-to-date information on the wage bill.

Table I.2
Latin America (15 countries): wages as a share of GDP at factor prices, 2002-2014
(Percentages)

| | Wages as a share of GDP | | | | Change in the wage share of GDP (percentage points) | | | |
|---|---|---|---|---|---|---|---|---|
| | Around 2002 (a) | Around 2006 (b) | Around 2010 (c) | Around 2014 (d) | 2002-2006 (b)-(a) | 2006-2010 (c)-(b) | 2010-2014 (d)-(c) | 2002-2014 (d)-(a) |
| Argentina | 34.6 | 41.5 | ... | ... | 6.8 | ... | ... | ... |
| Bolivia (Plurinational State of) | 40.6 | 34.4 | 32.3 | 34.3 | -6.3 | -2.0 | 2.0 | -6.3 |
| Brazil | 46.2 | 47.6 | 49.6 | 51.2 | 1.5 | 2.0 | 1.5 | 5.0 |
| Chile | 46.7 | 39.1 | 40.2 | 44.1 | -7.6 | 1.1 | 3.9 | -2.6 |
| Colombia | 37.2 | 36.0 | 36.6 | 37.0 | -1.3 | 0.7 | 0.3 | -0.3 |
| Costa Rica | 54.3 | 53.1 | 56.9 | 53.3 | -1.2 | 3.8 | -3.6 | -1.1 |
| Guatemala | 35.5 | 34.4 | 32.9 | 32.2[a] | -1.1 | -1.5 | -0.6 | -3.3 |
| Honduras | 50.1 | 49.7 | 51.8 | 52.2 | -0.4 | 2.1 | 0.4 | 2.1 |
| Mexico | 35.6 | 31.6 | 31.3 | 28.9 | -4.0 | -0.3 | -2.4 | -6.7 |
| Nicaragua | 58.1 | 41.4 | 40.4 | ... | -16.6 | -1.1 | ... | ... |
| Panama | 38.6 | 35.9 | 31.0 | 28.8 | -2.6 | -4.9 | -2.2 | -9.8 |
| Paraguay | 36.1 | 34.4 | 32.7 | 34.5 | -1.7 | -1.7 | 1.8 | -1.6 |
| Peru | ... | 33.6[b] | 33.4 | 35.0 | ... | -0.2 | 1.6 | ... |
| Uruguay | 44.1 | 43.0 | 44.2 | 44.6 | -1.2 | 1.2 | 0.4 | 0.4 |
| Venezuela (Bolivarian Republic of) | 36.1 | 33.6 | 32.4 | 41.4 | -2.5 | -1.2 | 9.0 | 5.3 |
| Latin America[c] | 41.8 | 39.4 | 39.3 | 40.2 | -2.4 | -0.1 | 0.9 | -1.6 |

**Source**: Economic Commission for Latin America and the Caribbean (ECLAC), on the basis of information from CEPALSTAT, national statistical offices and central banks of the respective countries.
[a] Data refer to 2012.
[b] Data refer to 2007.
[c] Simple average. Does not include data for Argentina or Nicaragua.

By contrast, the sharpest falls were in Mexico, Panama and the Plurinational State of Bolivia. Mexico and Panama, as well as Guatemala, have seen sustained declines since 2002. It should also be noted that in those countries, the steepest declines occurred in the early years of the period under consideration. Moreover, in the Plurinational State of Bolivia, after falling between 2002 and 2010, the wage share has begun to show signs of recovery since 2011.

Lastly, it is useful to study changes in the wage share in conjunction with changes in personal income inequality. Personal income distribution inequality had decreased in the vast majority of Latin American countries since 2002. The Gini coefficient declined in 13 of a total of 14 countries between 2006 and 2014 (the exception was Costa Rica). Despite the widespread fall in the wage share of GDP between 2002 and 2006, it began to rise again in most of the countries thereafter, alongside the fall in the Gini (the exceptions were Guatemala, Mexico, Panama and the Plurinational State of Bolivia, where the wage share continued to fall) (see figure I.15). This suggests that the distributive improvements achieved in the region from 2005 onwards could have been partly associated with improvements the distribution of returns on labour versus capital which, in turn, may be linked to stronger job creation policies (especially those devised to tackle the effects of the 2008-2009 global financial crisis), labour formalization and labour inclusion, as well as rises in real minimum wages and, to a lesser extent, in average wages, among other factors.

Figure I.15
Latin America (14 countries): wage share of GDP and Gini coefficient, 2006 and 2014
*(Percentages)*

**A. Wage share of GDP**
*(percentages)*

**B. Gini coefficient**[a]

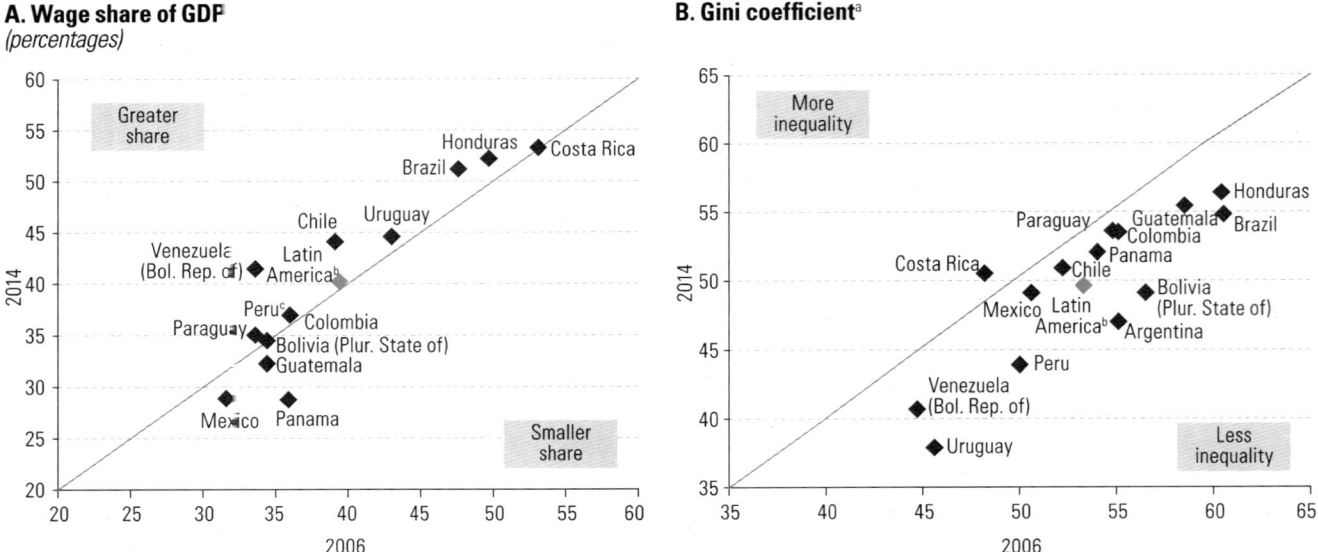

Source: Economic Commission for Latin America and the Caribbean (ECLAC), on the basis of information from CEPALSTAT, National Institute of Statistics and Censuses (INDEC) of Argentina, Central Bank of Costa Rica and Central Bank of Uruguay.
[a] The Gini coefficients correspond to the previous series of inequality estimates produced by ECLAC, based on an aggregate income that included the adjustment to the national accounts (see box I.2).
[b] Simple average for the countries.
[c] Refers to 2007.

As was already noted, the information presented above underestimates the true labour income share (labour share) of GDP, since it does not include the income of self-employed workers. The wage share adjustment put forward by Abeles, Amarante and Vega (2014) for the countries of the region, following the methodology developed by Young (1995), produces a much higher labour share of GDP. Using that methodology, the weight of labour income is 10 percentage points higher than if wages from the national accounts system alone are taken into account. After this adjustment, the labour share ranges from 31% of GDP in Peru to 65% of GDP in Costa Rica.[13] Changes in the wage bill after this adjustment are fairly similar across countries, albeit somewhat greater in countries where there is more self-employment (Colombia, for example).

In addition to the limitations arising from failing to include the income of self-employed workers, consideration of the wage share at the aggregate level hides the changes in the different components of national output. The magnitude of the wage share ratio depends on the composition of national output, and changes in that ratio may be due to shifts in the composition of GDP or in sectoral rates. That is why sectoral-level analysis is extremely useful, as it allows functional income inequality to be linked to productive economic activity. These aspects are addressed in the next section.

## 4.    Factor analysis by branches of activity

The differences in the aggregate wage share of GDP between countries or variations in this ratio over time in a particular country may be due to changes in how value added is distributed between labour and capital in the different economic sectors, or to changes

---

[13]   It should be noted that the values are lower than those arrived at by imputing the average wage, an adjustment also calculated in Abeles, Amarante and Vega (2014).

in the relative scale of value added among sectors. Therefore, sectoral-level analysis is important for a better understanding of functional income inequality. A recent study by Abeles, Arakaki and Villafañe (2017), the main results of which are summarized below, analyses the wage share of value added in eight countries of the region (Argentina, Brazil, Chile, Colombia, Costa Rica, Guatemala, Honduras y Mexico), based on nine major divisions of economic activity.[14]

The most striking finding is that the share of value added used to pay workers varies considerably from one sector to another (see figure I.16), ranging from 77.8% in the division that includes public administration, education, health and other social services to 19.5% in mining.[15]

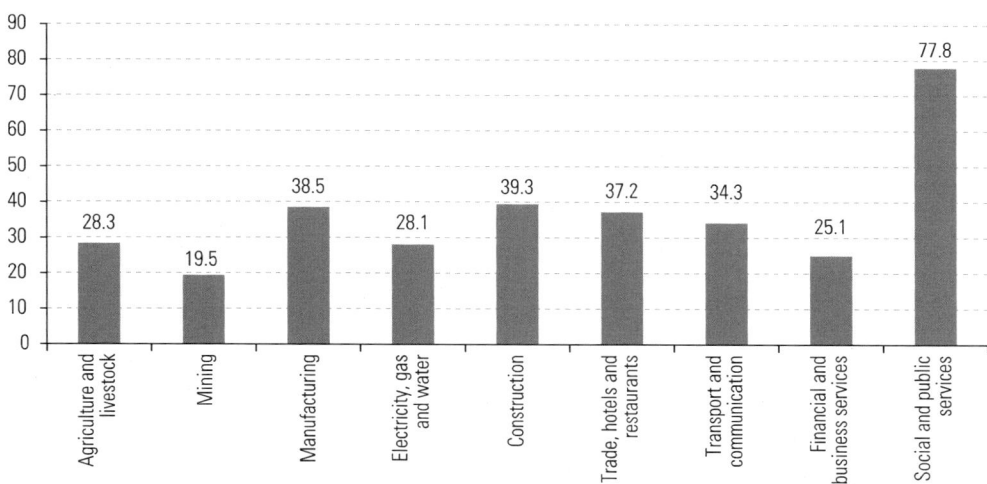

Figure I.16
Latin America (average of 8 countries): wage share of value added, by major division of economic activity, 2010[a]
(Percentages)

**Source**: M. Abeles, A. Arakaki and S. Villafañe, "Distribución funcional del ingreso en América Latina desde una perspectiva sectorial", *serie Estudios y Perspectivas-Oficina de la CEPAL en Buenos Aires*, No. 52, 2017, forthcoming.
[a] Includes Argentina, Brazil, Chile, Colombia, Costa Rica, Guatemala, Honduras and Mexico.

Figure I.17A shows the average wage share of value added for each major division of economic activity for eight countries, as well as the overall maximum and minimum values for each sector from among that group of countries. The differences among countries at the sectoral level are generally greater than aggregate differences at the national level, which suggests that the behaviour of a particular sector may vary from country to country. This may be due to the volumes of capital and the technology involved, or to aspects such as the organization of work and labour market institutions. The aggregate wage share depends not only on its level in each major division, but also on the weight that each division has in the total value added. Figure I.17B sets out the average share of each sector in the added value for eight countries and the overall maximum and minimum values from among that group of countries. While the differences are smaller than in figure I.17A, as expected, the weight of some branches in value added differs from country to country. This is the case, for example, for the value added share of the major division of public and social services, which ranges from 13.4% (Mexico) to 32.0% (Brazil).

---

[14]  These are taken from revision 2 of the International Standard Industrial Classification of All Economic Activities (ISIC, Rev. 2) and comprise the following sectors: (i) agriculture, livestock, forestry and fishing; (ii) mining and quarrying; (iii) manufacturing; (iv) electricity, gas and water; (v) construction; (vi) trade and repairs, hotels and restaurants; (vii) transport, storage and communication; (viii) financial intermediation, real estate, business and rental activities; and (ix) public administration and defence, compulsory social security plans, education, social and health services, other community, social and personal services, and private households with domestic service.

[15]  Even when public administration is excluded, there are almost 20 percentage points between the highest (39.3% in construction) and the lowest values.

**Figure I.17**
Latin America (8 countries): labour share of value added by sector and each sector's share of total value added, 2010[a]
*(Percentages)*

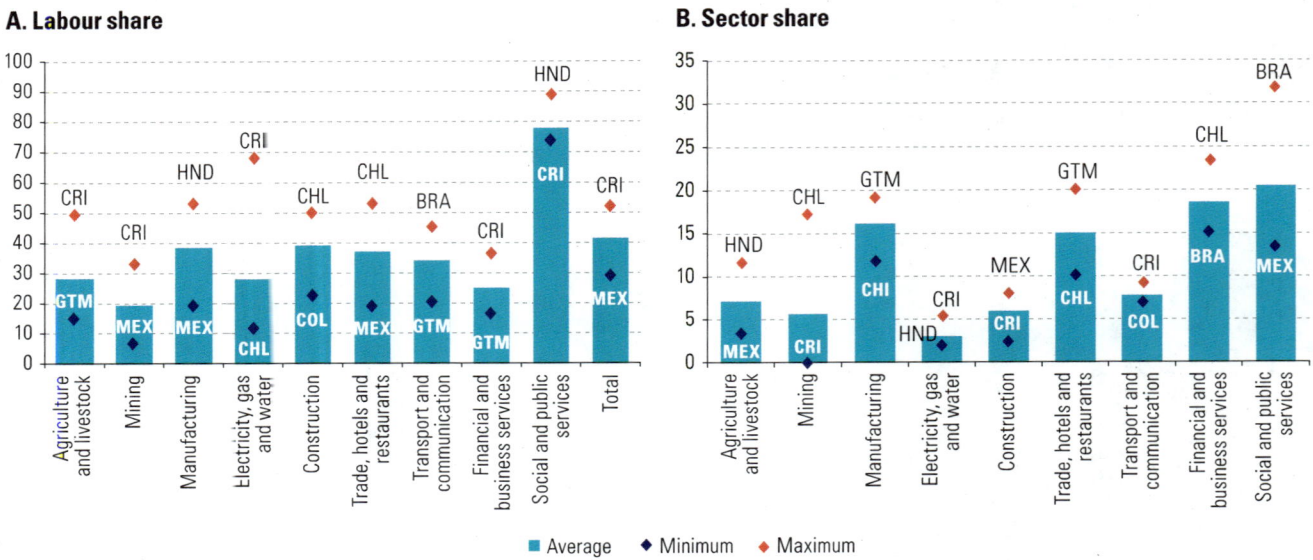

**Source**: M. Abeles, A. Arakak and S. Villafañe, "Distribución funcional del ingreso en América Latina desde una perspectiva sectorial", *serie Estudios y Perspectivas-Oficina de la CEPAL en Buenos Aires*, No. 52, 2017, forthcoming.
[a] Includes Argentina, Brazil, Chile, Colombia, Costa Rica, Guatemala, Honduras and México.

To determine the importance of each of these two factors (the differences in the wage share of the value added of different sectors, as shown in figure I.17A, and the differences in the share of each sector in the total value added, as shown in figure I.17B), a shift-share analysis is used. This methodology reveals to what extent the differences in the wage share in income (between countries or in the same country at two different points in time) are the result of strictly distributive effects or of structural changes in industry composition.[16] These differences can be disaggregated by two main components: by a strictly intra-sectoral distributive effect, quantifying the difference that would be observed at the aggregate level if different sectors share of total value added remained constant and only the distribution between capital and labour changed within each sector, and by a structural change effect, which indicates the difference that would be observed at the aggregate level as a result of changes in sectors' weight in GPD (in which the remuneration for wage work is higher or lower), if the wage share of value added of each industry remained constant. A residual effect is also defined, the so-called "interaction effect", which refers to the difference observed at the aggregate level when different sectors' share of total value added and their wage share of value added vary.

Comparing countries through a shift-share decomposition of data from 2010, taking as a reference the average of the eight countries considered, reveals that, in five of the eight countries (Colombia, Costa Rica, Guatemala, Honduras and Mexico), the difference between the wage share of income and the regional average is largely due to distributive or intra-sectoral effects (see figure I.18). This means that even if their GDP structure was similar to that of the hypothetical example (the regional average calculated using data from eight countries), Costa Rica and Honduras would have a higher-than-average wage share, while Colombia, Guatemala and Mexico would have a lower wage share. The aggregate value of the countries analysed is the result of a higher wage share in the vast majority of sectors in the first two countries, and a lower wage share in the last three countries. Meanwhile,

---

16    Similar studies of the United States have been carried out by Young (2010) and by Elsby, Hobijn and Sahin (2013); of the countries of the Organization for Economic Cooperation and Development (OECD) by ILO (2010) and OECD (2012); and of Latin America by Quaresma de Araujo (2013).

the structural change effect is greater in Brazil (improving its relative position) and Chile (making it worse). In particular, the effect has been most pronounced in the major division that includes public and social services in the broadest sense, as 8.9 percentage points of Brazilian GDP and -3.2 percentage points of Chilean GDP are attributed to the effect in that sector. It should be noted that the results are similar when this sector is excluded from the calculation, even though the impact of the structural change effect is lower in all the countries. In short, in the most of the countries analysed, the differences in the wage share apppear to be due to eminently distributive (or intra-sectoral) effects.

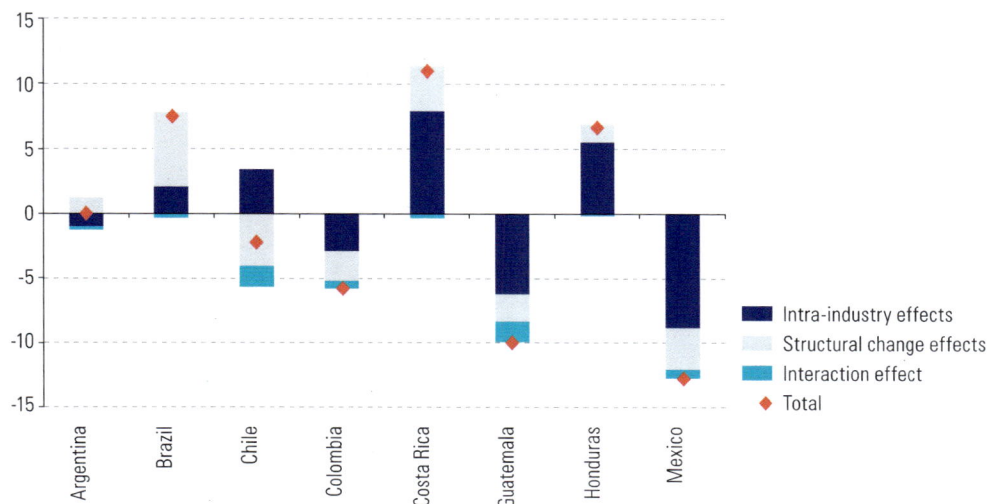

**Figure I.18**
Latin America (selected countries): cross-cutting shift-share decomposition of the difference between the wage share of value added in each country and the regional average, 2010[a]
*(Percentage points)*

**Source**: M. Abeles, A. Arakaki and S. Villafañe, "Distribución funcional del ingreso en América Latina desde una perspectiva sectorial", *serie Estudios y Perspectivas-Oficina de la CEPAL en Buenos Aires*, No. 52, 2017, forthcoming.

[a] The bars show the difference, in percentage points, between the wage share of value added in the country and a regional reference figure for that share, calculated from the average of eight countries. The segments in each bar indicate how much of that difference is attributable to inter-industry effects, structural change effects and interaction effects.

The same decomposition approach can be used to analyse aggregate changes in the wage share in each country between 2000 and 2010 (see figure I.19). This share increased in four countries (Argentina, Brazil, Costa Rica and Honduras), decreased in three (Chile, Guatemala and Mexico) and stayed practically the same in one (Colombia).

The decomposition shows the predominance of distributive (intra-sectoral) effects over structural change effects. For example, more than 70% of the total change in the wage share of imcome was due to shifts in the intra-sectoral effect in Argentina (5.4 percentage points), Brazil (3.2 percentage points), Colombia (2.0 percentage points), Costa Rica (3.6 percentage points) and Guatemala (3.0 percentage points). In contrast, the structural change effect had, on the whole, less of an impact, except in Chile, Costa Rica and Honduras.

It should be noted that what happens at the sectoral level is in turn a consequence of the market structure and the characteristics of the companies in that sector. A recent study by Autor and others (2017) of the United States argues that the decline in the labour income share of GDP between 1982 and 2012 is due to greater industry concentration, as a result of the emergence of large corporations. The higher the level of concentration in a small number of firms within each sector, the sharper the fall in the wage share, as labour earnings account for a relatively small part of the wage share compared with high profits. With regard to the research agenda, the link between market structures and the wage share of GDP should also be an area of regional interest.

**Figure I.19**
Latin America (selected countries): longitudinal shift-share decomposition of the difference between the wage share of value added in each country in 2000 and in 2010[a]
*(Percentage points)*

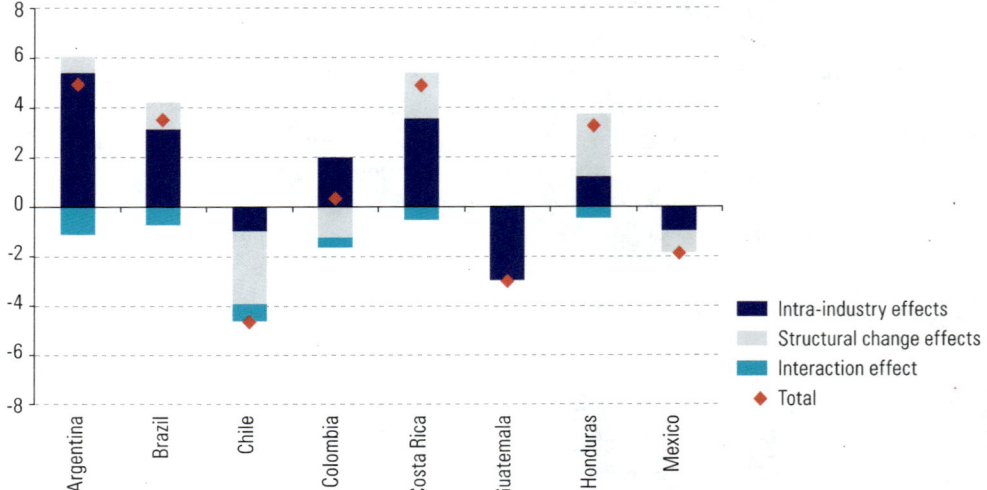

**Source**: M. Abeles, A. Arakaki and S. Villafañe, "Distribución funcional del ingreso en América Latina desde una perspectiva sectorial", *serie Estudios y Perspectivas-Oficina de la CEPAL en Buenos Aires*, No. 52, 2017, forthcoming.

[a] The bars show the difference, in percentage points, between the wage share of value added of the country in 2000 and 2010. The segments in each bar indicate how much of that difference is attributable to inter-industry effects, structural change effects and interaction effects. Due to the limits imposed by the information available, this period is not fully covered in every case. The exceptions are Chile and Mexico, whose data start in 2003, and Guatemala, whose series starts in 2001.

# C. Distribution of physical and financial assets

The ownership of physical and financial assets is a key variable to consider in the effort to increase the public's focus on inequality. ECLAC emphasizes the importance of social class or socioeconomic stratum as one of the axes structuring inequality (ECLAC, 2016c), which makes the measurement of overall wealth indispensable. A study of the situation in Mexico has produced results that could be extrapolated to other countries or to the region: a comparison of families based on wealth and on income shows a higher level of inequality with respect to the former, while a similar comparison can be drawn in terms of financial asset ownership versus physical asset ownership.

## 1. Measuring wealth: relevance and difficulties

In *The social inequality matrix in Latin America* (ECLAC, 2016c), the Commission emphasized the importance of an inequality analysis that takes into account the complexity and multidimensional nature of this issue, as well as the significance of social class, or socioeconomic stratum, as one of its structuring axes. It is becoming increasingly evident that measuring income is not sufficient, and that there should be a focus on overall wealth, ownership, or if preferred, financial and non-financial assets.

Income is highly sensitive to the economic cycle, particularly the characteristics of the labour market and its changes, and the country's employment structure. Wealth however, is a collection of assets (stock) that are less sensitive to these changes, more permanent and not dependent on the labour market structure alone, but also on the general social structure, meaning that they are often inherited and, starting from a certain threshold, tend to be preserved, reproduced and accumulated independently of the employment activity of their owners.

According to Del Castillo Negrete Rovira (2012), income increases wealth, but when countries, families and individuals face situations in which the sum of their income is not enough to meet their needs, they either sell their assets or take on debt, which creates greater economic inequality.

Hence, it is no coincidence that ownership structure is a key variable involved in perpetuating —and even increasing— social inequality. For that reason, empirical studies that measure wealth or asset inequality tend to show that this inequality is greater, more deeply rooted and more persistent than inequality measured solely on the basis of income.

This is relevant because the inequality trends in a society cannot be determined by examining just one dimension, income, without considering another central factor, ownership, and the resulting asset inequality.

The use of various income inequality indicators (see the first section of this chapter) is valuable but not enough to explain the extent and causes of inequality, owing to the lack of analysis of the accumulated wealth.

Nonetheless, the methodological challenges of measuring wealth are complex (Del Castillo Negrete Rovira, 2017). The first challenge is establishing a precise definition of wealth. Kuznets (1938) defined national wealth as the stock of economic goods that allows individuals to access services which they are willing to pay for because they are of some use.

According to the same author, the first step in measuring wealth is to identify these goods. Some are material and can be divided into two categories: durable and non-durable. Others are immaterial, for example patents, business monopolies or the skills of a population. They may be reproducible, such as goods created through a productive process, or not (non-renewable), for example land, minerals and oil. Most of these goods are transferable, while others are not, such as an individual's intellectual capital (Kuznets, 1938).

Davies (2008) uses a simpler definition as a starting point. He defines wealth as the value of physical and financial assets minus debt. However, he does recognize a certain level of complexity in measuring wealth. The problems stem mainly from assets, and to a lesser extent, debt. For example, pension plans may be considered as deferred compensation for labour.[17] Meanwhile, it is not clear whether certain assets belong to the State or to families, for example, a dwelling classified as a national monument that belongs to a family which is still living there.

Moreover, asset valuation is difficult. So far there have been two approaches: one based on the income generated by assets (going concerns) and the other on their realizable (sale) value.[18] The second approach is normally applied in income and spending surveys. The unit of analysis varies: sometimes the wealth of households is examined, while that of individuals or adults is the focus in other cases. One relevant question is whether the money invested in countries, tax havens or foreign investment (in physical or financial assets) should be attributed to the host nation or the asset holder's country of citizenship. If the latter were to be taken into account, the value of assets present in the country would exceed the country's actual wealth (Davies, 2008).[19] Further questions could be raised, such as: Who do government assets belong to? Is it feasible to distribute assets among citizens? Who owns the assets of a cooperative? Should the debt of each country be distributed to each citizen and subtracted from their assets?

Income is highly sensitive to the economic cycle, particularly the characteristics of the labour market and its changes and the country's employment structure. Wealth however, is a collection of assets (stock) that are less sensitive to these changes and more permanent.

---

[17]   When they are considered on an individual basis. Otherwise, calculation becomes more complicated.
[18]   See Atkinson and Harrison (1978).
[19]   As in the case of Mexico for example, which will be discussed later on.

With a view to simplifying this analysis without ignoring all the conceptual and methodological challenges, national wealth includes only transferable goods, either material or immaterial, reproducible or non-renewable; in other words, all real estate, automobiles, household goods and other items owned by individuals and companies (physical assets), plus bank deposits and financial investments (financial assets), minus debt relating both to mortgages and durable goods (vehicles) and to consumer spending (credit cards).

## 2.    Sources of the studies on inequality in asset ownership[20]

Measuring inequality in asset ownership not only poses major methodological and conceptual challenges but also involves limits in the availability of suitable and sufficient data.

Data on the distribution of wealth among families in a country comes from at least five types of sources: (i) the balance sheets of the System of National Accounts, specifically capital and financial accounts, which are part of the accumulation account; (ii) economic censuses, for production units; (iii) administrative records, for example, on payment of taxes on assets and inheritances, for families, in countries where these apply; (iv) household surveys to measure income and spending as well as those specifically designed to determine households' assets (which are rare); and (iv) other sources, such as global rich lists prepared by editorial groups such as Forbes and wealth studies by asset managers (for example Credit Suisse and Knight Frank).

National accounts data can be used to determine the wealth of each institutional sector: businesses, financial services companies, governments, households, and organizations serving households. Unfortunately, there is no way of determining distribution within each sector, except through economic censuses for the years they focus on and only for industry, trade and agriculture activities.

The limitation of data on the payment of taxes on assets and inheritances is that they do not apply in all countries and the information is not publicly available in some where they do. Moreover, they refer to individuals who are obligated to pay taxes and not to families, and exclude assets that are not subject to tax. Surveys on households' assets are carried out in very few countries and those on income and spending, which are more common, only reveal family-owned assets indirectly. Lastly, the lists published by some magazines are limited to a small number of billionaires and provide approximate figures of the wealth of these individuals and their families. Hence, estimating a country's wealth is a major challenge (see box I.4).

Box I.5
The challenge
of improving data sources
to measure wealth

Although the working group comprising the European Commission, the International Monetary Fund (IMF), the Organization for Economic Cooperation and Development (OECD), the World Bank and the United Nations suggested the creation of a balance sheet for the System of National Accounts as early as 1968, in 2000 only 22 countries had balance sheet data (with complete financial and non-financial information) and 15 had only financial account data (Davies and others, 2009, p. 36).

The OECD published data corresponding to 2012 on household wealth using the national account balance sheets of 21 of its 34 member countries.

The administrative records used most frequently by researchers are those pertaining to inheritance and wealth taxes. However, few countries levy an inheritance tax and furthermore make these data public. Data on wealth obtained from inheritance tax records also pose their share of problems.

---

[20]    Sections 2 and 3 are based on the study carried out by Del Castillo Negrete Rovira (2017).

Box I.5 (concluded)

Only a small number of countries levy a wealth tax and in most cases data disaggregated by source are not available to the public.[a] Moreover, this source of information also poses problems. The definition of the source varies from one country to the next, as well as the assets that are subject to this tax, and tax evasion may skew results (Slemrod and Yitzhaki, 2002).

There are other administrative records which are not used frequently by wealth researchers but which provide very useful information; for example, in Mexico: information on the contracts of financial services companies (investment companies and brokerage firms), as well as statistics on bank deposits and investments.

The census and statistical offices of 14 countries, as well as the European Community (through the European Central Bank) carry out surveys on household assets. Although these surveys provide very useful information on wealth distribution, they face the problem of underreporting, stemming from the fact that wealthy families or individuals tend to declare less than what they really own (mainly with respect to financial assets). Moreover, the definition of wealth used varies. For example, some countries only collect information on financial assets. Similarly, the questions included in surveys on households' personal property may vary.

Global billionaire lists are a source used by some researchers and non-governmental organizations focused on wealth (for example Oxfam), newspapers and magazines. The most popular is the Forbes list, which has been published since 1987.[b] Other companies also prepare similar lists, including: Bloomberg Billionaires,[c] Sunday Times Rich List for the United Kingdom[d] and Business Review Weekly Rich List for Australia.[e] Although these lists are impressive, which explains why they are used by the press, the information they contain does not always allow for a serious analysis of global wealth.

Asset managers also prepare studies on multimillionaires to determine the size of their market. The best known report is Crédit Suisse's *Global Wealth Report*. Similar reports are also published by Capgemini (*World Wealth Report*), Citi Private Bank and Knight Frank (*The Wealth Report*).

The methodology of these reports is more solid, which allows a better analysis of countries' wealth. Crédit Suisse's report is based on the work of Anthony Shorrocks and James Davies (Crédit Suisse Research Institute, 2010, p. 3; Davies, 2008). Instead of presenting a list of the wealthiest people, including names and surnames, they provide statistical tables with the number of adults (individuals aged 20 and over) who fit the criteria, in two categories: high net worth individuals (HNWI) whose wealth ranges from US$ 1 to US$ 50 million, and ultra high net worth individuals (UHNWI) whose wealth exceeds US$ 50 million (Del Castillo Negrete Rovira, 2017).[f]

**Source**: Economic Commission for Latin America and the Caribbean (ECLAC), on the basis of J. B. Davies and others, "The Level and Distribution of Global Household Wealth", *NBER Working Paper Series*, N° 15508 [online] http://www.nber.org/papers/w15508.pdf, 2009; Slemrod, J. and S. Yitzhaki, "Tax avoidance, evasion and administration", *Handbook of Public Economics*, vol. 3, A. Auerbach y M. Feldstein (eds.), Elsevier, 2002; Credit Suisse Research Institute, *Global Wealth Report* [online] https://publications.credit-suisse.com/tasks/render/file/index.cfm?fileid=88DC32A4-83E8-EB92-9D57B0F66437AC99, 2010; J. B. Davies, *Personal Wealth from a Global Perspective*, Oxford, Oxford University Press, 2008; and M. Del Castillo Negrete Rovira, "La distribución y la desigualdad en los activos financieros y no financieros en México", unpublished, 2017.

[a] Disaggregated data is available on Denmark, France, Norway and Switzerland (Ohlsson, Roine and Waldenström, cited in Davies, 2008).

[b] See "The World's Billionaires" [online] www.forbes.com/billionaires/list/.

[c] See [online] www.bloomberg.com/billionaires.

[d] See [online] thesundaytimes.co.uk.

[e] See [online] http://www.afr.com.

f According to the ranges used by Crédit Suisse. Capgemini and Knight Frank define very rich individuals as adults who are worth more than US$ 30 million.

### 3.    Measuring inequality in the ownership of financial and non-financial assets in Mexico[21]

The data analysed below are for Mexico only, but they still provide insight into the situation in Latin America as a whole, since it is the second largest economy in the region, has one of the highest levels of product diversification, industrialization and openness to international trade and investment, and its primary sector is relatively smaller in terms of export volume. These results are consistent, but to obtain them a set of information sources had to be used, in order to overcome the difficulties and limitations with regard to both the content of and access to sources for measuring wealth and estimating inequality in the ownership of physical and financial assets.

According to the *Global Wealth Report 2016* by Credit Suisse, global wealth is very poorly distributed: 0.7% of adults (35 million people) hold almost half (45%) of the world's physical and financial assets; 9% of global wealth is concentrated in the hands of just 123,000 high net worth individuals; and 1,722 people belong to the select group of billionaires. Mexico is no exception to this trend.

In 2015, Mexico was twentieth in the Credit Suisse's list of countries with the highest number of high net worth individuals (wealth holdings above US$ 1 million). The United States, Japan, France, the United Kingdom and Germany topped the list. Mexico has more wealthy people than Denmark, Hong Kong (Special Administrative Region of China), Singapore, Israel, New Zealand, the United Arab Emirates, Finland and Saudi Arabia. Mexico was fourteenth on the Forbes 2016 billionaires list, with 14 billionaires worth US$ 100 billion (1.5% of global wealth). In the 16 years between 1996 and 2012, their wealth increased sevenfold, from US$ 1.7 billion to US$ 11.8 billion, indicating an average annual growth rate of 12.8%, five times greater than the rate of growth of the economy.

According to the closing balance (net value) of the national accounts, in 2014 Mexico had wealth, both physical and financial assets, in the amount of 76.6 billion Mexican pesos. This is a large amount for a developing country, for example, it was equivalent to 60% of France's wealth in purchasing power parity (PPP).[22] This level of wealth is linked, in large part, to the size and magnitude of the country's population. If this wealth were evenly distributed among the inhabitants of Mexico, the per capita amount, according to 2014 data, would be 640,000 pesos per year (US$ 80,842, expressed in purchasing power parity), just over a third (34%) of the average wealth of a citizen of France.

In Mexico, total wealth (all physical and financial assets) was 4.6 times national income in 2014; a ratio that has worsened as in 2003 it was 2.6 times greater.

It is positive for Mexico that its physical and financial assets grew, in the light of the country's continuing needs. However, failure to distribute assets, particularly financial assets, properly, as is the case in Mexico, gives rise to what Piketty describes as the "fundamental force for divergence" of inequality (Piketty, 2014): the rate of return on capital is higher than the rate of growth of wages.

In Mexico, in nominal terms, the average rate of return on capital has fluctuated over the last 11 years (2003-2014) by around 15% per year (ranging from 12% to 22%), while the minimum wage and average salary of workers in the manufacturing sector

Global wealth is very poorly distributed: 0.7% of adults (35 million people) hold almost half (45%) of the world's physical and financial assets; 9% of global wealth is concentrated in the hands of just 123,000 high net worth individuals.

---

[21]    There are other relatively recent studies on the concentration of wealth in Chile and Uruguay, albeit with goals and methodologies that are not necessarily comparable. See López, Figueroa and Gutiérrez (2013) and De Rosa (2016).

[22]    To compare countries' wealth, conversion factors are used to convert local currencies into US dollars at the World Bank's 2011 purchasing power parity. The figures for France are taken from the OECD.Stat database [online] http://stats.oecd.org/.

has not increased by more than 5% per year in the same period. This is one of the sources of growing inequality in income distribution (Del Castillo Negrete Rovira, 2015).

In developed countries, capital accounts for 30% of national income on average and wealth is up to six times greater than income, indicating a 5% annual rate of return, a situation that even those countries find worrying. In Mexico, capital accounted for 54% of national income in 2014, according to conservative estimates,[23] with wealth close to 4.6 times greater than income, which translates into a much higher average rate of return on capital (12%) for that year.

Between 2003 and 2014, the Mexican economy grew at an average annual rate of 2.6%, which is a cause for concern. However, the average real rate of growth of wealth has been much higher —7.9% per year over the same period (and 10.1% per year between 2003 and 2009, before the effects of the international financial crisis were felt). When an amount grows at an average annual rate of 7%, it doubles every 10 years. As a result, wealth in Mexico doubled between 2004 and 2014.

Most of the country's wealth is made up of non-financial produced assets (75.9%), that is mainly machinery, industrial facilities, business property, livestock, houses and automobiles. They are followed by non-financial non-produced assets, agricultural land, woods and urban plots, among others (24.7%). While financial assets account for a much smaller share (0.4%), it must be understood that, in this case, they cover both assets and liabilities (debt).

It is important to note that the average wealth of financial companies is considerable —75 billion pesos per institution, according to data from 2014— compared with the situation of just over 4 million industrial firms, which hold 19% of national wealth, but have an average of 3.6 million pesos worth of assets each. The high average wealth of financial companies comes from the fact that they hold public resources (liabilities) and they invest by providing loans (assets), as part of their financial brokerage services.

Although there is consensus over the low economic growth warning for Mexico, the growth figures are averages that mask the differences among the various economic players. Analysis of how physical and financial assets are distributed among institutional sectors clarifies the situation. By 2014, 37% of wealth was owned by 31 million households, which had assets worth an average of 900,000 pesos.

The largest increases in total wealth (physical and financial assets) between 2003 and 2014, in real terms, occurred in the following subsectors: (i) investment funds and the money market (33% annually and 24% annually, respectively); (ii) federal and municipal governments (26% annually); and (iii) institutions serving households and parastatal companies (23% annual average).

Of the total activities surveyed in 2014, manufacturing held 26% of physical assets, the majority of which are machinery and equipment (68%). Next was electricity generation, transmission and distribution and the mains supply of water and gas, activities that hold 23% of total physical assets. These industries' main assets are buildings and fixed installations (55%). In third place was mining, which holds 14% of physical assets, consisting primarily of buildings and facilities (71%), as is the case in the previous sector. Transport, storage and postal services have a smaller share (9% of physical assets), as does trade (7% held by retail trade and 3% by wholesale trade), mass media information services (4%) and hotels (3%). The other sectors together hold 11% of physical assets (see figure I.20).

In Mexico, in nominal terms, the average rate of return on capital has fluctuated over the last 11 years (2003-2014) by around 15% per year, while the minimum wage and average salary of workers in the manufacturing sector has not increased by more than 5% per year in the same period.

---

[23]   Not including the share of capital in mixed income.

Figure I.20
Mexico: distribution of
physical assets of production
units, by sector, 2013
(Percentages)

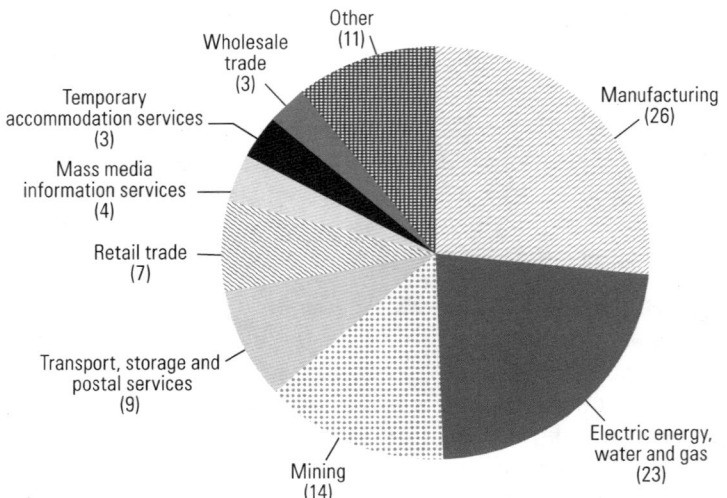

**Source**: Economic Commission for Latin America and the Caribbean (ECLAC), on the basis of National Institute of Statistics and Geography (INEGI) of Mexico, "Censos Económicos 2014" [online] http://www.beta.inegi.org.mx/proyectos/ce/2014/.

This distribution is due, to a certain extent, to the number of establishments that operate in each branch of activity. If the average assets per production unit are calculated based on 2013 data, the energy, water and gas sector tops the list, with physical assets valued at 675 million pesos per company, followed by mining, with assets worth 371 million pesos per firm. These activities require large amounts of capital. In many countries they are therefore the preserve of the State, as was the case in Mexico for many years and remains true for certain activities. Governments generally have to borrow from international financial institutions to finance them.

Ownership of the physical assets held by production units listed in economic censuses is concentrated in very few hands; 10% of companies hold 93% of physical assets, while the remaining 90% have very few capital assets. As a result, the Gini coefficient of the distribution of physical assets is a record 0.93. This inequality is very high, regardless of the specific characteristics of each branch of activity and their needs for investment in physical assets.

The activities that have, on average, greater inequality in terms of physical asset distribution (with a Gini coefficient higher than 0.90) are electricity, water and gas, financial and insurance services, mass media information services, mining and manufacturing. The distribution of physical assets (a Gini coefficient lower than 0.60) is better in real estate and rental services, corporate services and wholesale trade (see figure I.21).

Mexico is a country with great natural wealth; it has minerals and oil, an extensive coastline, water resources, forests and enough agricultural land to feed its inhabitants, and a complex relationship with its neighbour the United States, which is still the world's largest producer. Mexico's natural wealth has increased as a result of physical asset production and higher financial assets. However, not all wealth belongs to families. In 2015, the Government of Mexico managed 23% of assets, private companies 19%, public corporations 9% and financial institutions 5%, while 7% of financial assets were held by non-residents. Nevertheless, a larger share, 37% —equivalent to 280 billion Mexican pesos— is concentrated in the hands of families.

Unfortunately, those 280 billion pesos are distributed very unequally. Two thirds of total wealth is in the hands of the country's richest 10% of families and 1% of those families hold more than a third. By family, the Gini coefficient of total asset distribution (physical and financial) is 0.79. The distribution of financial assets is even more unequal: 80% is owned by the richest 10%. Because very few people are able to invest in an investment fund or the market, the dramatic increase in financial assets has resulted in a heavy concentration of wealth.

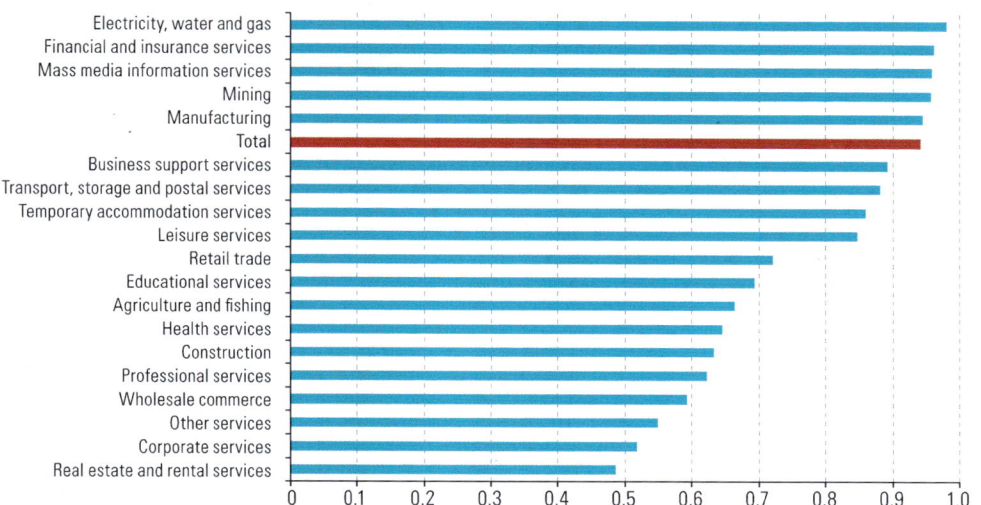

**Figure I.21**
Mexico: Gini coefficient of
the distribution of physical
assets by sector, 2013

**Source**: Economic Commission for Latin America and the Caribbean (ECLAC), on the basis of National Institute of Statistics and Geography (INEGI) of Mexico, "Censos Económicos 2014" [online] http://www.beta.inegi.org.mx/proyectos/ce/2014/.

Financial assets held by foreigners have increased in recent years, reaching US$ 687.5 billion (PPP) in 2014, more than double the amount in 2003. The amount of resources transferred abroad every year also increased (the difference between GDP and national income); it has more than tripled, up from US$ 20 billion (PPP) at the beginning of the century to more than US$ 60 billion (PPP) in recent years (see figure I.22).

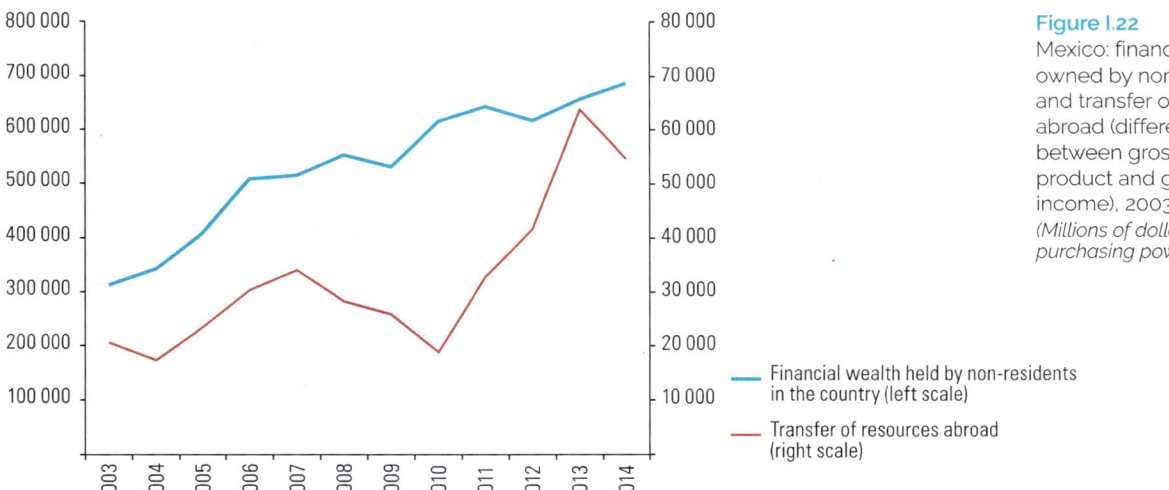

**Figure I.22**
Mexico: financial wealth
owned by non-residents
and transfer of resources
abroad (differences
between gross domestic
product and gross national
income), 2003-2014
*(Millions of dollars in
purchasing power parities)*

**Source**: Economic Commission for Latin America and the Caribbean (ECLAC), on the basis of National Institute of Statistics and Geography (INEGI) of Mexico, "Censos Económicos 2014" [online] http://www.beta.inegi.org.mx/proyectos/ce/2014/ and World Bank, "World Bank Open Data" [online] http://data.worldbank.org/.

According to figures from the National Banking and Securities Commission (CNBV), 221,816 brokerage contracts were concluded in Mexico in 2015 to invest in shares for a total amount of 17.5 trillion pesos. Of those contracts, 78% (174,531 contracts) were signed by natural persons.

Although the average amount per contract was 79 million pesos in 2015, 11% of the contracts were for an investment exceeding 500 million pesos and accounted for 79.5% of total investment. That means that 23,000 people (if each contract is linked to one person) account for 80% of investment in the Mexican stock exchange. A conservative estimate, assuming that just one contract corresponds to each person, is that in Mexico for every 1,000 adults (aged 18 or over) only 2.2 invest in the stock exchange. However, this figure should be added to the number of clients of investment companies managed by banks.

In 2015, banks had 374,690 clients who had investments with investment companies or in the capital market or private bank deposits (CNBV, 2016). If they are added to the number of brokerage firms' contracts, assuming that they are not the same people, in all Mexico there would be only 549,221 people with equity investments, a very small figure for a country of 80.8 million adults: only 7 out of every 1,000 adults would have invested in shares or investment funds.

The high degree of asset concentration tends to borne out by analysis of other sources such as Mexico's National Survey of Household Living Standards (ENNVIH).[24] According to the survey, the percentage of total assets held by the richest 10% increased to 69% and the Gini coefficient of asset distribution rose to 0.79. This level of inequality would be equivalent to that of a society in which 80% of families (eight out of ten) do not have any type of asset and all the wealth is distributed among the remaining 20%.

In order to analyse the segment of the wealthiest individuals, two procedures have been carried out. The first calculates the centiles (i.e. divides the population into 100 groups), from the lowest to the highest value of the assets they own, based on data from the ENNVIH. The second applies the Pareto formula,[25] based on the income ratio of the last two deciles.[26] According to these calculations, 58% of the wealth is concentrated in the hands of the wealthiest 5% of families, who have an average of 5 million pesos in physical and financial assets. At the top end of the scale, about 240,000 families (the richest 1%) hold almost 40% of the total and are worth, on average, 14 million pesos (see figure I.23).

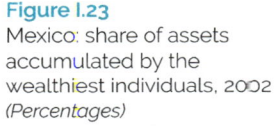

**Figure I.23**
Mexico: share of assets accumulated by the wealthiest individuals, 2002 *(Percentages)*

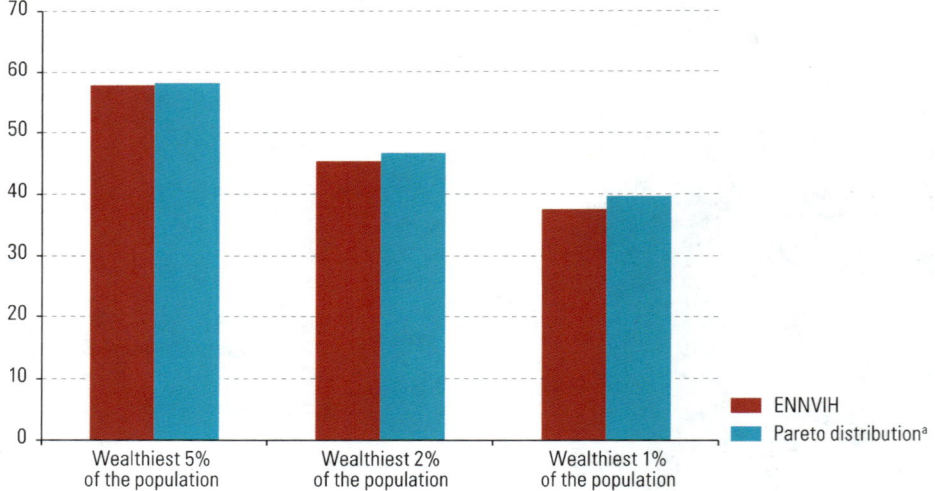

**Source**: Economic Commission for Latin America and the Caribbean (ECLAC), on the basis of information from National Survey of Household Living Standards (ENNVIH) 2002.
[a] Continuous probability distribution put forward by the sociologist, Vilfredo Pareto, that allows the wealth of the richest end of the distribution to be estimated.

---

[24]  While this survey is not exempt from issues of underreporting due to inaccurate declarations of assets, mainly financial, it is possible to make an adjustment for the first round of the 2002 survey using data from the system of national accounts, specifically the household sector balance sheet. The adjustment consists of distributing the difference between the amount of financial assets identified by the survey and the figures from the balance sheet at the beginning of 2003 among those households that declared having money or investments in the financial system. Each household is assigned a share of the difference in proportion to the size of its financial assets.

[25]  The Pareto distribution is a continuous probability distribution put forward by the sociologist, Vilfredo Pareto, that allows the wealth of the richest end of the distribution (known as the "upper tail") to be estimated.

[26]  The Pareto distribution is often used to estimate the wealthiest end of the distribution, although it is important to confirm whether the mathematical procedure generates good approximations of the figures. In this case, it has been observed that, for wealth data, the Pareto distribution yields a reasonable estimate, since the percentages of income held by the wealthiest 5%, 2% and 1% of households are practically the same as those obtained using the other procedure.

This suggests that the distribution of total assets in Mexico is deeply inequitable, which affects income distribution. More wealth means more income and vice versa, especially among those who receive income from renting out property, since it is very difficult to join the richest 1% in large part or just on the basis of saving employment income.

If financial institutions' sources are used, the very high concentration and inequality in the ownership of assets is confirmed. According to studies by Capgemini, Knight Frank and Credit Suisse, the number of wealthy people in Mexico, who are worth US$ 1 million or more, was between 125,000 and 202,000 in 2014. Credit Suisse estimates that there were 804 very wealthy adults, who have US$ 50 million or more. Meanwhile, individuals worth US$ 100 million or more totalled approximately 300 and there are between 12 and 19 billionaires. Knight Frank estimates that by 2025 there will be 441 people worth US$ 100 million or more and 28 billionaires. However, the vast majority of Mexicans, according to Credit Suisse, have very few assets: 57% have less than US$ 10,000 and 40% between US$ 10,000 and US$ 100,000. According to the bank, the Gini coefficient of asset distribution rose in 2015 to 0.79.

Credit Suisse estimates that the average wealth per adult in Mexico is US$ 25,000, 72% held in physical assets and 28% in financial assets. As a result of the global financial crisis that began in 2008, the value of assets plummeted. The value of financial assets fell by 24% and that of physical assets by 18%. However, the value of financial assets recovered quickly, growing by 32% the following year.

The Swiss financial institution also provides decile-level data for 2014 and 2015. The wealthiest 1% of adults (754,000 people) held more than a third of national wealth (36% of the total) in 2015. In contrast, the poorest 50% (37.7 million adults) have only 5.7% of physical and financial assets. The Gini coefficient of total asset distribution is 0.79, equivalent to that of a society in which four-fifths of the population have no wealth and all assets are distributed among the remaining 20%.

## D. Closing considerations

ECLAC affirms the need for a new development style that places equality and sustainability at the centre of policies, and has reiterated the importance of reducing the high levels of inequality in Latin American and Caribbean countries. The various dimensions and expressions of inequality not only result in significant dissatisfaction and disaffection with democracies, but also represent obstacles to a sustained and sustainable development process that looks after the planet as well as its inhabitants. The importance of this theme for ECLAC is reflected in the publication of a collection of position papers known as the equality trilogy at three successive sessions of the Commission (2010, 2012 and 2014).

Inequality has become a key focus in discussions about global development, as is reflected in the fact that this issue is now at the centre of the 2030 Agenda for Sustainable Development, whose aims include ending poverty in all its forms everywhere. The recent experience of Latin American and Caribbean countries in their efforts to reduce and eliminate poverty indicates that achieving this goal will only be possible by combating and decreasing inequality in its various and interconnected manifestations (ECLAC, 2016a and 2016c).

Early in the new millennium, the region made progress in reducing inequality in personal income distribution (monthly income measured through countries' household surveys). Recent evidence confirms the trend: income inequality decreased in most countries between 2008 and 2015. In particular, there was a larger relative increase in the income of

In Mexico in 2015 there were only 549,221 people with equity investments, a very small figure for a country of 80.8 million adults: only 7 out of every 1,000 adults would have invested in shares or investment funds.

the lowest income quintile than that of the highest. This increase was reflected generally in the various sources of household income, mainly earnings (wages and salaries and income from independent work), and also in retirement benefits and transfers.

A broader analysis indicates that this progress may be linked to certain changes in labour relations. A functional approach to income distribution shows that the wage share of GDP, which had been deteriorating since the 1970s, trending upwards in most of the countries over the past few years, which suggests that the improvement in personal income distribution was partly associated with a more equitable distribution of returns between capital and labour. Nevertheless, personal income equality remains very sharp and the wage share of GDP is low compared to other world regions. Moreover, the partial analysis of inequality in wealth distribution among families indicates that this is higher than inequality measured solely on the basis of current income and that the ownership structure of financial assets is even more concentrated and becoming more so.

Wealth and extreme wealth are central themes of development and public policy. Hence, the deepest understanding possible of the characteristics, magnitude and dynamics of flows and of assets, and of the correlation between them, is essential. The ownership structure of physical and financial assets and the way they are distributed between the State, families and companies, is one of the most significant indicators of the level of polarization, concentration or equality of the social structure, which is one of the key components of the socioeconomic inequality matrix in the region.

The study, analysis and measurement of wealth and of the ownership structure of physical and financial assets is a promising path to understanding the multidimensional nature of inequality and to achieving a more consistent analysis of the challenges to reducing it significantly in the region.

Among the challenges of the research agenda is fine-tuning instruments and methodologies for measuring inequality. Improvements to household surveys to capture high incomes more accurately should be combined with analysis of other information sources, such as personal tax records, to complement the findings of the surveys. Lastly, it is important to revive the classical analyses of the functional distribution of income and their contributions, including the link between market structures and wage share of GDP.

This process, replete with conceptual and methodological challenges, calls for robust and creative solutions in the coming years, and the commitment of all the region's countries to achieving the Sustainable Development Goals.

# Bibliography

Abeles, M., V. Amarante and D. Vega (2014), "The earnings share of total income in Latin America, 1990-2010", *CEPAL Review*, No. 114 (LC/G.2629-P), Santiago, Economic Commission for Latin America and the Caribbean (ECLAC), December.

Abeles, M., A. Arakaki and S. Villafañe (2017), "Distribución funcional del ingreso en América Latina desde una perspectiva sectorial", *Estudios y Perspectivas series-ECLAC Office in Buenos Aires*, No. 52, forthcoming.

Alarco Tosoni, G. (2014), "Wage share and economic growth in Latin America, 1950-2011", *CEPAL Review*, No. 113 (LC/G.2614-P), Santiago, Economic Commission for Latin America and the Caribbean (ECLAC), August.

Alvaredo, F., A. B. Atkinson and S. Morelli (2016), "The challenge of measuring UK wealth inequality in the 2000s", *Fiscal Studies*, vol. 37, No. 1.

Amarante, V. and J. P. Jiménez (2015), "Desigualdad, concentración y rentas altas en América Latina", *Desigualdad, concentración del ingreso y tributación sobre las altas rentas en América Latina*, J. P. Jiménez (ed.), Libros de la CEPAL, No. 134 (LC/G.2638-P), Santiago, Economic Commission for Latin America and the Caribbean (ECLAC).

Atkinson, A. B. (2015), *Inequality: What Can Be Done?*, Harvard University Press.

____(2009), "Factor shares: the principal problem of political economy?", *Oxford Review of Economic Policy*, vol. 25, No. 1, Oxford University Press.

Atkinson, A. B. and A. Harrison (1978), *Distribution of Personal Wealth in Britain*, Cambridge, Cambridge University Press.

Autor, D. and others (2017), "Concentrating on the fall of the labor share", *American Economic Review Papers and Proceedings*, forthcoming.

Bárcena, A. and A. Prado (2016), *El imperativo de la igualdad: por un desarrollo sostenible en América Latina y el Caribe*, Buenos Aires, Siglo XXI.

Bentolila, S. and G. Saint-Paul (2003), "Explaining Movements in the Labor Share", *The B.E. Journal of Macroeconomics*, vol. 3, No. 1.

Berg, J. (ed) (2015), *Labour Markets, Institutions and Inequality: Building Just Societies in the 21st Century*, International Labour Organization (ILO).

Bernanke, B. S. and R. S. Gürkaynak, (2002), "Is growth exogenous? Taking Mankiw, Romer, and Weil seriously", *NBER Chapters*, National Bureau of Economic Research (NBER).

Bértola, L. and others (2008), "Income distribution in the Latin American Southern Cone during the first globalization boom, ca: 1870-1920", *Working Papers in Economic History*, No. 08-05, Madrid, Universidad Carlos III, April.

Bhaduri, A. and S. Marglin (1990), "Unemployment and the real wage: the economic basis for contesting political ideologies", *Cambridge Journal of Economics*, No. 14, Academic Press Limited.

Bourguignon, F. (2015), *The Globalization of Inequality*, Princeton University Press.

CNBV (National Banking and Securities Commission) (2016), "Portafolio de información: banca múltiple" [online] http://portafolioinfo.cnbv.gob.mx/BM/Paginas/default.aspx.

Cole, A. (2015), "Estate and inheritance taxes around the world", *Fiscal Fact*, No. 458, Washington, D.C., Tax Fundation,

Daudey, E. and C. García-Peñalosa (2007), "The personal and the factor distributions of income in a cross-section of countries", *The Journal of Development Studies*, vol. 43, No. 5, Taylor & Francis.

Davies, J.B. (ed.) (2008), *Personal Wealth from a Global Perspective*, Oxford, Oxford University Press.

Davies, J.B. y otros (2009), "The level and distribution of global household wealth", *NBER Working Paper Series*, No. 15508 [online] http://www.nber.org/papers/w15508.pdf.

Deaton, A. (2015), *El gran escape: salud, riqueza y los orígenes de la desigualdad*, Fondo de Cultura Económica.

Del Castillo Negrete Rovira, M. (2012), "La distribución del ingreso en México", *Este País* [online] http://archivo.estepais.com/site/2012/la-distribucion-del-ingreso-en-mexico/.

____(2015), "La magnitud de la desigualdad en el ingreso y la riqueza en México: una propuesta de cálculo", *Estudios y Perspectivas series-ECLAC Subregional Headquarters in Mexico*, No. 167 (LC/L.4108; LC/MEX/L.1199), Mexico City, Economic Commission for Latin America and the Caribbean (ECLAC).

____(2017), "La distribución y la desigualdad en los activos financieros y no financieros en México", unpublished.

De Rosa, M. (2016), "Distribución de la riqueza en Uruguay: una aproximación por el método de capitalización", paper presented at "VIII Jornadas de la Red sobre Desigualdad y Pobreza de América Latina y el Caribe", Montevideo, 5-6 October.

ECLAC (Economic Commission for Latin America and the Caribbean) (2016a), *Inclusive Social Development: The next generation of policies for overcoming poverty and reducing inequality in Latin America and the Caribbean* (LC.L/4056/Rev.1), Santiago.

____(2016b), *Horizons 2030: Equality at the Centre of Sustainable Development* (LC/G.2660/Rev.1), Santiago.

____(2016c), *The social inequality matrix in Latin America* (LC/G.2690(MDS.1/2)), Santiago.

____(2016d), *Social Panorama of Latin America, 2015* (LC/G.2691-P), Santiago.

____(2016e), *Equality and Women's Autonomy in the Sustainable Development Agenda* (LC/G.2686/Rev.1), Santiago.

____(2014), *Compacts for Equality: Towards a Sustainable Future* (LC/G.2586(SES.35/3)), Santiago.

____(2012a), *Structural Change for Equality: An Integrated Approach to Development* (LC/G.2524(SES.34/3)), Santiago.

____(2012b), *Eslabones de la desigualdad: heterogeneidad estructural, empleo y protección social* (LC/G.2539), Santiago.

____(2010), *Time for Equality: Closing Gaps, Opening Trails* (LC/G.2432(SES.33/3)), Santiago.

Elsby, M., B. Hobijn and A. Sahin (2013), "The decline of the U.S. labor share", *Brookings Papers on Economic Activity, No. 2*.

Fichtenbaum, R. (2009), "The impact of unions on labor's share of income: a time-series analysis", *Review of Political Economy,* vol. 21, No. 4.

Frankema, E. (2009), *Reconstructing Labour Income Shares in Argentina, Brazil and Mexico, 1870-2000*, Utrecht, Utrecht University.

García-Peñalosa, C. and E. Orgiazzi (2013), "Factor components of inequality: a cross-country study", *The Review of Income and Wealth,* vol. 59, No. 4.

Goldfarb, R. S. and T.C. Leonard (2005), "Inequality of what among whom?: Rival conceptions of distribution in the 20th century", *Research in the History of Economic Thought and Methodology,* vol. 23, part I.

Gollin, D. (2002), "Getting income shares right", *Journal of Political Economy,* vol. 110, No. 2.

Guscina, A. (2006), "Effects of globalization on labor's share in national income", *IMF Working Papers,* No. 294, International Monetary Fund (IMF).

Hogrefe, J. and M. Kappler (2013), "The labour share of income: heterogeneous causes for parallel movements?", *The Journal of Economic Inequality,* vol. 11, No. 3.

ILO (International Labour Organization) (2012), *Global Wage Report 2012/13: Wages and Equitable Growth*, Geneva.

____(2010), *Global Wage Report 2010/11: Wage Policies in Times of Crisis,* Geneva.

IMF (International Monetary Fund) (2007), *Annual Report 2007: Making the Global Economy Work for All,* Washington, D.C.

Jayadev, A. (2007), "Capital account openness and the labour share of income", *Cambridge Journal of Economics*, vol. 31, No. 3.

Kuznets, S. (1938), "On the measurement of national wealth", *Studies in Income and Wealth,* vol. 2, New York, National Bureau of Economic Research (NBER) [online] www.nber.org/chapters/c10561.

Lindenboim, J. (2008), "Distribución funcional del ingreso, un tema olvidado que reclama atención", *Problemas del Desarrollo. Revista Latinoamericana de Economía*, vol. 39, No. 153, Mexico City, National Autonomous University of Mexico (UNAM).

López, R., E. Figueroa and P. Gutiérrez (2013), "La 'parte del león': nuevas estimaciones de la participación de los súper ricos en el ingreso de Chile", *serie de Documentos de Trabajo*, No. 379, Santiago, Department of Economics, University of Chile.

Milanovic, B. (2016), *Global Inequality: A New Approach for the Age of Globalization*, Cambridge, Harvard University Press.

OECD (Organization for Economic Cooperation and Development) (2012), *OECD Employment Outlook 2012*, Paris.

Piketty, T. (2014), *Capital in Twenty-First Century*, Cambridge, Harvard University Press.

Piketty, T. and G. Zucman (2015), "Wealth and Inheritance in the Long Run", *Handbook of Income Distribution*, A. B. Atkinson and F. Bourguignon (eds.), Oxford, North Holland.

Quaresma de Araujo, P. (2013), "Productive structure and the functional distribution of income: an application of the input-output model", *CEPAL Review*, No. 109 (LC/G.2556-P), Santiago, Economic Commission for Latin America and the Caribbean (ECLAC).

Rodríguez, F. and D. Ortega (2006), "Are capital shares higher in poor countries? Evidence from industrial surveys", *Wesleyan Economics Working Papers*, No. 2006-023, Wesleyan University.

Rubalcava, L. and G. Teruel (2013), "Encuesta Nacional sobre Niveles de Vida de los Hogares" [online] http://www.ennvih-mxfls.org.

___(2006), "Encuesta Nacional sobre Niveles de Vida de los Hogares" [online] http://www.ennvih-mxfls.org.

___(2002), "Encuesta Nacional sobre Niveles de Vida de los Hogares" [online] http://www.ennvih-mxfls.org.

Slemrod, J. and S. Yitzhaki (2002), "Tax avoidance, evasion and administration", *Handbook of Public Economics*, vol. 3, A. Auerbach and M. Feldstein (eds.), Elsevier.

Stiglitz, J. E. (2012), *The Price of Inequality: How Today's Divided Society Endangers Our Future*, Nueva York, W. W. Norton & Company.

Stockhammer, E. (2013), "Why have wage shares fallen? A panel analysis of the determinants of functional income distribution", *Conditions of Work and Employment Series*, No. 35, International Labour Organization (ILO).

Taylor, L. (1991), *Income Distribution, Inflation, and Growth: Lectures on Structuralist Macroeconomic Theory*, London, MIT Press.

Wilkinson, R. and K. Pickett (2009), *The Spirit Level: Why More Equal Societies Almost Always Do Better*, London, Allen Lane.

Young, A. (2010), "One of the things we know that ain't so: is the US labor's share relatively stable?", *Journal of Macroeconomics*, vol. 32, No.1.

___(1995), "The tyranny of numbers: confronting the statistical realities of the East Asian growth experience", *The Quarterly Journal of Economics*, vol. 110, No. 3.

# Annex I.A1

Table I.A1.1

Latin America (17 countries): household income distribution, 2008-2015[a]
(Percentages)

| Country | Year | Share in total income (percentages) | | | | | Ratio of average per capita household income (times)[b] | |
|---|---|---|---|---|---|---|---|---|
| | | Quintile I (poorest 20%) | Quintile II | Quintile III | Quintile IV | Quintile V (richest 20%) | $D^{10}/D^{(1\ to\ 4)}$ | $Q^5/Q^1$ |
| Argentina | 2009 | 7.4 | 14.6 | 18.0 | 22.8 | 37.2 | 10.2 | 5.0 |
| | 2012 | 8.7 | 15.3 | 17.3 | 23.9 | 34.8 | 7.8 | 4.0 |
| | 2014 | 8.9 | 15.2 | 17.4 | 23.0 | 35.5 | 7.8 | 4.0 |
| Bolivia (Plurinational State of) | 2008 | 4.1 | 9.8 | 15.4 | 23.1 | 47.6 | 16.2 | 11.6 |
| | 2011 | 4.6 | 11.3 | 17.0 | 24.4 | 42.7 | 12.2 | 9.3 |
| | 2013 | 3.2 | 10.1 | 16.7 | 24.5 | 45.5 | 14.9 | 14.2 |
| | 2014 | 4.1 | 10.6 | 16.6 | 23.4 | 45.3 | 14.1 | 11.0 |
| Brazil | 2008 | 4.9 | 9.7 | 12.6 | 19.7 | 53.1 | 17.2 | 10.8 |
| | 2012 | 5.2 | 10.5 | 12.9 | 20.0 | 51.4 | 15.6 | 9.9 |
| | 2014 | 5.5 | 11.0 | 12.8 | 19.8 | 50.9 | 14.4 | 9.3 |
| | 2015 | 5.6 | 10.9 | 13.0 | 20.3 | 50.2 | 14.5 | 9.0 |
| Chile | 2009 | 5.5 | 9.9 | 13.6 | 19.9 | 51.1 | 14.3 | 9.3 |
| | 2011 | 5.8 | 10.0 | 14.1 | 19.9 | 50.2 | 13.4 | 8.7 |
| | 2013 | 5.9 | 10.2 | 14.2 | 19.8 | 49.9 | 13.5 | 8.5 |
| | 2015 | 6.0 | 10.5 | 14.5 | 20.6 | 48.4 | 12.5 | 8.1 |
| Colombia | 2009 | 3.6 | 8.9 | 13.6 | 21.3 | 52.6 | 21.4 | 14.6 |
| | 2012 | 3.9 | 9.3 | 14.3 | 21.5 | 51.0 | 19.1 | 13.1 |
| | 2014 | 4.0 | 9.4 | 14.6 | 21.0 | 51.0 | 19.6 | 12.8 |
| | 2015 | 4.3 | 9.6 | 15.3 | 21.2 | 49.6 | 17.8 | 11.5 |
| Costa Rica | 2010 | 4.8 | 9.0 | 14.1 | 22.6 | 49.5 | 15.7 | 10.3 |
| | 2012 | 4.7 | 9.0 | 14.3 | 21.8 | 50.2 | 15.2 | 10.7 |
| | 2014 | 4.5 | 9.0 | 14.3 | 22.6 | 49.6 | 14.6 | 11.0 |
| | 2015 | 4.5 | 9.4 | 14.3 | 22.3 | 49.5 | 14.9 | 11.0 |
| Dominican Republic | 2003 | 5.8 | 10.7 | 15.1 | 21.8 | 46.6 | 13.9 | 8.0 |
| | 2012 | 6.2 | 10.8 | 14.9 | 22.1 | 46.0 | 12.1 | 7.4 |
| | 2014 | 6.3 | 11.4 | 15.7 | 21.8 | 44.8 | 10.2 | 7.1 |
| | 2015 | 6.1 | 11.0 | 15.2 | 21.3 | 46.4 | 10.8 | 7.6 |
| Ecuador | 2008 | 5.1 | 10.1 | 14.9 | 21.6 | 48.3 | 14.1 | 9.5 |
| | 2012 | 5.2 | 10.9 | 16.3 | 22.9 | 44.7 | 11.5 | 8.6 |
| | 2014 | 6.8 | 11.8 | 15.9 | 22.3 | 43.2 | 10.4 | 6.4 |
| | 2015 | 6.3 | 11.8 | 16.1 | 22.0 | 43.8 | 11.2 | 7.0 |
| El Salvador | 2009 | 4.6 | 10.5 | 15.8 | 21.8 | 47.3 | 13.5 | 10.3 |
| | 2011 | 5.3 | 11.4 | 15.9 | 21.9 | 45.5 | 11.7 | 8.6 |
| | 2013 | 5.7 | 11.7 | 16.4 | 22.5 | 43.7 | 10.6 | 7.7 |
| | 2015 | 6.3 | 12.2 | 16.1 | 22.3 | 43.1 | 10.0 | 6.8 |

Table I.A1.1 (concluded)

| Country | Year | Share in total income (percentages) | | | | | Ratio of average per capita household income (times)[b] | |
|---|---|---|---|---|---|---|---|---|
| | | Quintile I (poorest 20%) | Quintile II | Quintile III | Quintile IV | Quintile V (richest 20%) | $D^{10}/D^{(1\ to\ 4)}$ | $Q^5/Q^1$ |
| Guatemala | 2014 | 4.4 | 8.8 | 13.9 | 20.1 | 52.8 | 19.4 | 12.0 |
| Honduras | 2009 | 4.4 | 9.3 | 14.2 | 22.3 | 49.8 | 15.8 | 11.3 |
| | 2013 | 4.0 | 8.8 | 13.9 | 21.9 | 51.4 | 17.7 | 12.8 |
| | 2014 | 4.5 | 9.7 | 14.8 | 22.3 | 48.7 | 14.7 | 10.8 |
| Mexico | 2008 | 5.3 | 9.9 | 14.7 | 21.0 | 49.1 | 16.1 | 9.3 |
| | 2012 | 5.4 | 10.4 | 15.1 | 21.2 | 47.9 | 15.6 | 8.9 |
| | 2014 | 5.9 | 10.5 | 14.8 | 20.6 | 48.2 | 14.9 | 8.2 |
| Panama | 2008 | 4.8 | 9.7 | 15.3 | 21.5 | 48.7 | 15.4 | 10.1 |
| | 2012 | 4.5 | 10.0 | 15.7 | 22.3 | 47.5 | 14.8 | 10.6 |
| | 2014 | 4.9 | 10.4 | 16.3 | 23.1 | 45.3 | 13.8 | 9.2 |
| | 2015 | 4.7 | 10.3 | 16.1 | 22.0 | 46.9 | 13.6 | 10.0 |
| Paraguay | 2008 | 4.9 | 9.8 | 14.9 | 21.3 | 49.1 | 16.5 | 10.0 |
| | 2012 | 4.3 | 10.0 | 15.9 | 22.6 | 47.2 | 14.8 | 11.0 |
| | 2014 | 4.4 | 9.2 | 14.3 | 20.4 | 51.7 | 16.2 | 11.7 |
| | 2015 | 4.6 | 9.9 | 14.9 | 22.5 | 48.1 | 12.9 | 10.5 |
| Peru | 2008 | 4.1 | 9.7 | 15.6 | 23.4 | 47.2 | 14.4 | 11.5 |
| | 2012 | 4.6 | 10.4 | 16.1 | 23.6 | 45.3 | 11.6 | 9.8 |
| | 2014 | 5.1 | 10.5 | 16.6 | 23.6 | 44.2 | 10.7 | 8.7 |
| | 2015 | 5.2 | 10.8 | 16.6 | 23.2 | 44.2 | 10.6 | 8.5 |
| Uruguay | 2008 | 8.1 | 11.7 | 15.1 | 21.2 | 43.9 | 9.7 | 5.4 |
| | 2012 | 9.5 | 13.4 | 17.3 | 23.1 | 36.7 | 7.1 | 3.9 |
| | 2014 | 9.2 | 13.0 | 16.9 | 22.4 | 38.5 | 7.4 | 4.2 |
| | 2015 | 9.2 | 12.9 | 17.0 | 22.3 | 38.6 | 7.5 | 4.2 |
| Venezuela ((Bolivarian Republic of) | 2008 | 7.3 | 13.2 | 18.3 | 24.5 | 36.7 | 7.5 | 5.0 |
| | 2012 | 7.3 | 13.8 | 19.4 | 23.9 | 35.6 | 7.4 | 4.9 |
| | 2013 | 7.0 | 13.9 | 19.4 | 23.7 | 36.0 | 7.6 | 5.1 |
| | 2014 | 7.4 | 14.0 | 19.7 | 23.0 | 35.9 | 7.2 | 4.9 |

**Source**: Economic Commission for Latin America and the Caribbean (ECLAC), on the basis of tabulations from Household Survey Data Bank (BADEHOG).

[a] Households in the country as a whole, in order of per capita income.

[b] D(1 to 4) refers to the 40% lowest-income households, while D10 refers to the 10% highest-income households. The same notation is used for quintiles (Q), which refer to 20% segments of all households.

Table I.A1.2
Latin America (17 countries): household income distribution,Gini coefficient and Theil and Atkinson indexes, 2008-2015[a]
(Percentages)

| Country | Year | Concentration indices | | | | |
|---|---|---|---|---|---|---|
| | | Gini[b] | Theil | Atkinson | | |
| | | | | ($\varepsilon$=0.5) | ($\varepsilon$=1.0) | ($\varepsilon$=1.5) |
| Argentina | 2009 | 0.455 | 0.373 | 0.168 | 0.310 | 0.435 |
| | 2012 | 0.411 | 0.287 | 0.135 | 0.257 | 0.371 |
| | 2014 | 0.414 | 0.295 | 0.138 | 0.259 | 0.368 |
| Bolivia (Plurinational State of) | 2008 | 0.515 | 0.513 | 0.225 | 0.413 | 0.587 |
| | 2011 | 0.470 | 0.399 | 0.186 | 0.354 | 0.517 |
| | 2013 | 0.495 | 0.470 | 0.210 | 0.398 | 0.589 |
| | 2014 | 0.493 | 0.505 | 0.211 | 0.380 | 0.539 |
| Brazil | 2008 | 0.545 | 0.588 | 0.243 | 0.415 | 0.547 |
| | 2012 | 0.526 | 0.570 | 0.229 | 0.391 | 0.519 |
| | 2014 | 0.516 | 0.529 | 0.220 | 0.380 | 0.508 |
| | 2015 | 0.515 | 0.527 | 0.221 | 0.384 | 0.517 |
| Chile | 2009 | 0.500 | 0.500 | 0.207 | 0.353 | 0.475 |
| | 2011 | 0.491 | 0.475 | 0.199 | 0.342 | 0.460 |
| | 2013 | 0.488 | 0.482 | 0.198 | 0.337 | 0.449 |
| | 2015 | 0.476 | 0.455 | 0.188 | 0.322 | 0.430 |
| Colombia | 2009 | 0.564 | 0.638 | 0.264 | 0.451 | 0.599 |
| | 2012 | 0.546 | 0.590 | 0.247 | 0.428 | 0.574 |
| | 2014 | 0.546 | 0.599 | 0.248 | 0.426 | 0.568 |
| | 2015 | 0.530 | 0.558 | 0.233 | 0.405 | 0.545 |
| Costa Rica | 2010 | 0.510 | 0.497 | 0.213 | 0.375 | 0.509 |
| | 2012 | 0.512 | 0.496 | 0.215 | 0.380 | 0.518 |
| | 2014 | 0.510 | 0.468 | 0.209 | 0.375 | 0.512 |
| | 2015 | 0.506 | 0.462 | 0.207 | 0.372 | 0.516 |
| Dominican Republic | 2008 | 0.491 | 0.480 | 0.201 | 0.345 | 0.457 |
| | 2012 | 0.472 | 0.418 | 0.182 | 0.321 | 0.434 |
| | 2014 | 0.451 | 0.361 | 0.164 | 0.298 | 0.410 |
| | 2015 | 0.466 | 0.415 | 0.179 | 0.316 | 0.428 |
| Ecuador | 2008 | 0.503 | 0.503 | 0.209 | 0.363 | 0.489 |
| | 2012 | 0.465 | 0.419 | 0.179 | 0.320 | 0.444 |
| | 2014 | 0.452 | 0.403 | 0.170 | 0.298 | 0.404 |
| | 2015 | 0.463 | 0.420 | 0.177 | 0.312 | 0.428 |
| El Salvador | 2009 | 0.498 | 0.471 | 0.208 | 0.386 | 0.560 |
| | 2013 | 0.475 | 0.475 | 0.195 | 0.354 | 0.516 |
| | 2014 | 0.455 | 0.384 | 0.173 | 0.326 | 0.483 |
| | 2015 | 0.442 | 0.370 | 0.164 | 0.301 | 0.435 |
| Guatemala | 2014 | 0.554 | 0.722 | 0.267 | 0.438 | 0.576 |
| Honduras | 2009 | 0.522 | 0.526 | 0.226 | 0.398 | 0.534 |
| | 2013 | 0.538 | 0.599 | 0.244 | 0.418 | 0.554 |
| | 2014 | 0.505 | 0.480 | 0.209 | 0.372 | 0.503 |
| | 2015 | 0.494 | 0.446 | 0.199 | 0.360 | 0.494 |

Table I.A1.2 (concluded)

| Country | Year | Gini[b] | Theil | Atkinson ($\varepsilon$=0.5) | Atkinson ($\varepsilon$=1.0) | Atkinson ($\varepsilon$=1.5) |
|---------|------|---------|-------|-------------------------------|-------------------------------|-------------------------------|
| Mexico | 2008 | 0.516 | 0.566 | 0.225 | 0.381 | 0.502 |
| | 2012 | 0.508 | 0.518 | 0.215 | 0.370 | 0.490 |
| | 2014 | 0.507 | 0.550 | 0.218 | 0.366 | 0.482 |
| Panama | 2008 | 0.528 | 0.547 | 0.232 | 0.410 | 0.552 |
| | 2012 | 0.522 | 0.514 | 0.228 | 0.416 | 0.576 |
| | 2014 | 0.505 | 0.470 | 0.212 | 0.390 | 0.543 |
| | 2015 | 0.509 | 0.492 | 0.215 | 0.387 | 0.530 |
| Paraguay | 2008 | 0.528 | 0.592 | 0.235 | 0.399 | 0.529 |
| | 2012 | 0.498 | 0.511 | 0.212 | 0.375 | 0.517 |
| | 2014 | 0.532 | 0.660 | 0.247 | 0.407 | 0.538 |
| | 2015 | 0.499 | 0.487 | 0.208 | 0.369 | 0.511 |
| Peru | 2008 | 0.494 | 0.467 | 0.204 | 0.369 | 0.509 |
| | 2012 | 0.459 | 0.392 | 0.176 | 0.323 | 0.454 |
| | 2014 | 0.445 | 0.369 | 0.165 | 0.304 | 0.428 |
| | 2015 | 0.447 | 0.374 | 0.167 | 0.305 | 0.429 |
| Uruguay | 2008 | 0.456 | 0.395 | 0.171 | 0.301 | 0.404 |
| | 2012 | 0.392 | 0.263 | 0.123 | 0.229 | 0.322 |
| | 2014 | 0.401 | 0.285 | 0.130 | 0.239 | 0.333 |
| | 2015 | 0.403 | 0.294 | 0.132 | 0.242 | 0.337 |
| Venezuela (Bolivarian Republic of) | 2008 | 0.391 | 0.263 | 0.123 | 0.233 | 0.336 |
| | 2012 | 0.388 | 0.264 | 0.122 | 0.231 | 0.335 |
| | 2013 | 0.390 | 0.260 | 0.121 | 0.229 | 0.332 |
| | 2014 | 0.383 | 0.249 | 0.117 | 0.223 | 0.324 |

**Source**: Economic Commission for Latin America and the Caribbean (ECLAC), on the basis of tabulations from Household Survey Data Bank (BADEHOG).
[a] Calculated on the basis of the distribution of per capita income for individuals in the country as a whole.
[b] Includes people with income equal to zero.

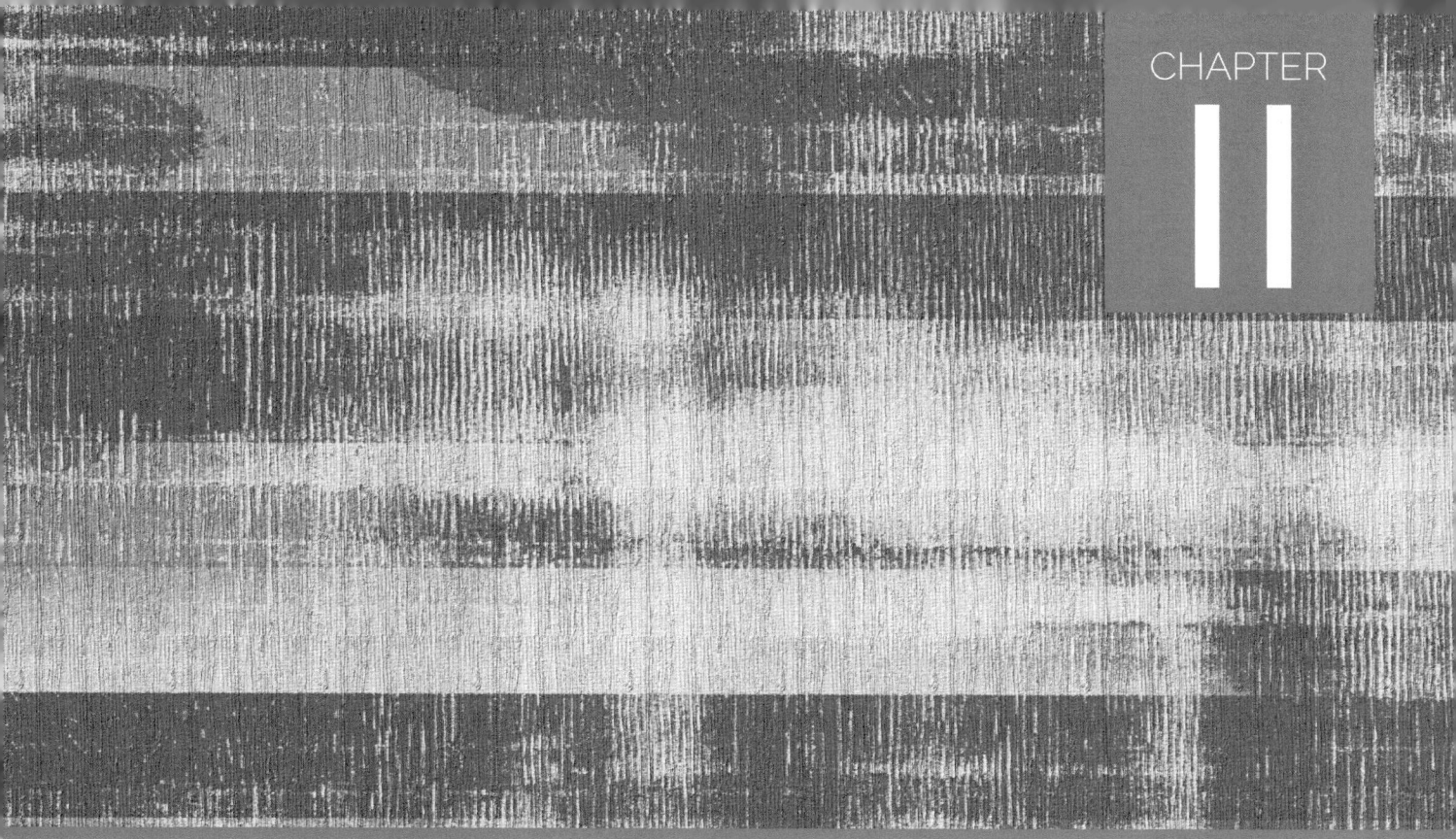

# Social spending: trends and challenges in policy financing

# Introduction

In 2016, low growth in the global economy (2.2%) for the eighth year in a row, global trade volume growth that was even lower and a moderate decline in commodity prices formed the backdrop to economic and social policymaking in the region's countries. The region's economies face major headwinds in these circumstances, as the Economic Commission for Latin America and the Caribbean (ECLAC) argued in its recent *Preliminary Overview of the Economies of Latin America and the Caribbean*, and after recording negative growth in the aggregate in 2016 (estimated at -1.1%), they are expected to recover only modestly (1.1%) in 2017 (ECLAC, 2016b).[1] The impact of this performance on the labour market has included a deterioration in the quality and quantity of jobs (urban unemployment in 2016 is estimated at 9%), especially in the South American countries. As analysed in other chapters of this edition of the *Social Panorama of Latin America,* high levels of inequality persist in the region.

One of the innovations of the 2030 Agenda for Sustainable Development is its focus on the means of implementing the various Sustainable Development Goals. In particular, it explicitly sets out to mobilize resources at the national and international levels so that countries have adequate and predictable funding for policy implementation. Social investment could be said to be becoming one of the most important implementation tools for achieving the Goals, as it is strongly associated with substantial advances in access to basic services such as sanitation, housing, education, health care and social protection systems, all areas in which the 2030 Agenda aims for guaranteed universal access. Social investment also includes spending on environmental protection and on the prevention of natural disasters, areas in which the 2030 Agenda also calls for greater resources and efforts to be invested in pursuit of environmental sustainability.

For progress to be made towards the Goals overall at a time of lower economic growth, "countries must have more resources for social investment, ensure that the tax burden is more progressive, enhance the countercyclical bias of fiscal policy and protect the financing of the core social policies (in particular poverty eradication, a basic social protection floor to guarantee rights, and access to high-quality health and education services, decent housing and decent work)" (ECLAC, 2016c).

This chapter is divided into two sections. Section A describes recent trends in public social spending according to the functional classification, drawing on the official data provided to ECLAC by the region's countries.[2] This type of spending is defined as the public resources allocated to policies relating to the following six functions: (i) environmental protection, (ii) housing and community amenities, (iii) health, (iv) recreation, culture and religion, (v) education and (vi) social protection. The technical work carried out with the countries on this theme has been stepped up in the past two years within the framework of the agreements adopted at the Regional Conference on Social Development in Latin America and the Caribbean, held in Lima in November 2015, with the aim of making more information available on public social spending as categorized by the functional classification (see box II.1).

Section B presents information on the social spending provided for in national budgets, describing the decisions that have been taken and the countries' plans for 2017.

---

[1] See "Economic activity in Latin America and the Caribbean will expand 1.1% in 2017" [online] http://www.cepal.org/en/pressreleases/economic-activity-latin-america-and-caribbean-will-expand-11-2017.

[2] There are many types of budget classification (economic, functional, administrative, by currency, by programme, etc.). The functional classification indicates the function or purpose of government spending, regardless of which government agency implements the programme.

Box II.1
Updating public social
spending information

Information on social spending has been updated in this edition of the *Social Panorama of Latin America*, with a new series for the years from 2000 to 2015. This draws on a new database developed following the guidelines agreed with the countries that participated in the workshop seminars on the measurement of social spending held by the Social Development Division of ECLAC in 2015 and 2016. According to these guidelines: (i) the countries and ECLAC will work with the Classification of the Functions of Government (COFOG), which is the international standard (United Nations, 2001; IMF, 2001 and 2014); (ii) the countries agree to report all spending (functions 701 to 710) and not just spending on social functions; (iii) the following functions are considered "social": environmental protection (705), housing and community amenities (706), health (707), recreation, culture and religion (708), education (709) and social protection (710). "Non-social" functions are: general public services (701), defence (702), public order and safety (703) and economic affairs (704), including labour affairs. This classification provides information about the overall functions of government and does not necessarily coincide with the information from satellite accounts for specific functions.

With respect to institutional coverage, ECLAC argues that the best way of capturing governments' whole social spending effort is for them to report public spending in accordance with the functional classification, using the fuller coverage of the public sector. In other words, the aim should be to report on the entire non-financial public sector (which incorporates the consolidated spending of the central government, subnational governments and non-financial public corporations). However, many of the region's countries only report central government public spending, which is the most limited public sector coverage. Countries therefore face a difficult choice between reporting the widest coverage and reporting internationally comparable data. A major effort has been made in this edition of the *Social Panorama of Latin America* to provide data that are comparable between countries by presenting an institutional coverage common to all, which is that of central government. The following table lists the availability of data on public spending for each country and year, by type of institutional coverage.

Latin America and the Caribbean (22 countries): availability of public spending data based on the functional classification, by institutional coverage and year

| Country | Central administration | Central government | General government | Non-financial public sector | Public sector |
|---|---|---|---|---|---|
| Argentina | | 1980-2015 | | 1980-2015 | |
| Bolivia (Plurinational State of) | 1990-2015 | | 1996-2014 | | |
| Brazil | | 2001-2015 | 2000-2015 | | |
| Chile | | 1990-2015 | | | |
| Colombia | 2000-2015 | | 2009-2015 | | |
| Costa Rica | | 1994-2015 | | | 1987-2015 |
| Cuba | | 2002-2015 | 1996-2015 | | |
| Dominican Republic | | 1990-2015 | | | |
| Ecuador | 1990-2008 | 2009-2015 | | | |
| El Salvador | | 2002-2015 | | 2002-2015 | |
| Guatemala | 1995-2015 | | | | |
| Haiti | | 2012-2015 | | | |
| Honduras | | 1990-2015 | | | |
| Jamaica | | 1992-2014 | | | |
| Mexico | | 1998-2015 | | 1990-2015 | |
| Nicaragua | | 1998-2015 | | | |
| Panama | | 2000-2014 | | | |
| Perú | | 2005-2015 | 1999-2015 | | 1999-2015 |
| Paraguay | 2007-2015 | | | | |
| Trinidad and Tobago | | 2008-2015 | | | |
| Uruguay | | 2011-2015 | | | |
| Venezuela (Bolivarian Republic of) | | 1999-2009 | | | |

**Source**: Economic Commission for Latin America and the Caribbean (ECLAC).

Box II.1 (concluded)

## Averages for Latin America

The decision was taken to use simple arithmetic means for 19 countries of the region in the tables, figures and text of this edition of the *Social Panorama of Latin America*. This change from previous editions of the *Social Panorama*, which presented arithmetic means weighted by the countries' GDP and public spending, was made for two main reasons: first, because economic and social policy decisions are taken at the country level and the use of GDP-weighted means would not give a picture of what is happening across the region; and second, in the interests of consistency with the other ECLAC flagship publications, particularly the *Preliminary Overview of the Economies of Latin America and the Caribbean* and the *Economic Survey of Latin America and the Caribbean*. These publications also work with government finance statistics, and it is likewise considered important for them to be able to present an indicator of State size measured by the level of public spending (on the economic classification) that is similar to the amount of public spending (on the functional classification). The number of countries covered by the average was matched to the 19 included in those publications for the same reason.

## Indicators

The following indicators are calculated:

- public spending according to the functional classification as a percentage of GDP (both series, spending and GDP, are measured in local currency and current prices for each year and each country).

- public spending according to the functional classification in constant 2010 dollars per capita. This indicator is produced in two stages. In the first, the local-currency series at current prices is deflated using the national accounts expenditure deflator at constant 2010 prices estimated by the ECLAC Statistics Division (except in the case of Jamaica, where this deflator is not available, so the GDP deflator is used instead). In the second stage, it is divided by the 2010 exchange rate and by population. The source of the 2010 exchange rate data is the International Monetary Fund (IMF), while the population data are projections by the Latin American and Caribbean Demographic Centre (CELADE)-Population Division of ECLAC.

## The online database

The data used in this edition of the *Social Panorama of Latin America* are available from the CEPALSTAT database (see [online] http://estadisticas.cepal.org/cepalstat/WEB_CEPALSTAT/Portada.asp?idioma=i) and from the database portal of the Social Development Division of ECLAC (see [online] http://observatoriosocial.cepal.org /inversion/en).

Lastly, there is the work done by ECLAC with the 18 countries which validated, corrected and completed the public social spending questionnaire between November and December 2016 in a process of dialogue and constructive collaboration. The development of social spending measurement tools has not ended with this edition of the *Social Panorama*. In 2017, ECLAC will continue working to expand the available data in an effort to include more information from Caribbean countries and to increase institutional coverage and supplementary data sources (National Accounts and administrative records) so as to be able to produce estimates for social spending in the private sector. These developments are a precondition for eventually producing more specific analyses, for example of public spending targeted at particular population segments (differentiated by sex, age group or racial or ethnic origin).

**Source**: Economic Commission for Latin America and the Caribbean (ECLAC), on the basis of data from International Monetary Fund (IMF), *Government Finance Statistics Manual 2001* [online] https://www.imf.org/external/pubs/ft/gfs/manual/pdf/all.pdf and *Government Finance Statistics Manual 2014* [online] https://www.imf.org/external/Pubs/FT/GFS/Manual/2014/gfsfinal.pdf; United Nations, *System of National Accounts 2008*, 2009 [online] https://unstats.un.org/unsd/nationalaccount/docs/SNA2008.pdf; M.P Collinao and others, "Estimación de las erogaciones sociales a partir del sistema de cuentas nacionales: una propuesta para las funciones de educación, salud y protección social", *Manuales de la CEPAL*, No. 5 (LC/L.4273), Santiago, ECLAC, 2016; United Nations, "Classifications of expenditure according to purpose", *Statistical Papers Series M*, No. 84 (ST/ESA/STAT/SER.M/84), New York, 2001.

Information on social spending has been updated in this edition of the *Social Panorama of Latin America*, with a new series for the years from 2000 to 2015.

# A. Public and social spending in 2000-2015

In response to the adverse economic climate, the countries of the region chose to increase the funding they allocated to social policies in 2015. As a result, average public social spending rose to a record high of 10.5% of GDP for central government and 14.5% of GDP for the public sector that year.

Taking all the Latin American countries together, the weighted average share of regional GDP allocated to public social policies rose from 15.4% in 2000 to 20.7% in 2015. Collating these figures with regional population sizes shows that per capita spending in this area rose from US$ 1,397 to US$ 2,031 (in constant 2010 dollars) over the same period.

This information gives a general idea of resources relative to population, but is not enough for an in-depth analysis of the priority given to social policies when funds are being distributed and spent within each country, or for a comparative analysis between the region's countries. For this reason, data on social spending will be given from now on in the form of simple regional averages for two different types of institutional coverage, central government and the public sector.

Central government coverage is vast and complex. As indicated in the International Monetary Fund (IMF) *Government Finance Statistics Manual 2001* and *Government Finance Statistics Manual 2004* (IMF, 2001 and 2014), it comprises a core group of ministries and secretariats along with administrative units that act under the authority of the central government, even though they may have their own autonomous legal authority. To make the figures comparable, this section presents central government social spending, figures for which are available from all the region's countries. Total public sector coverage[3] is even more complex, as it involves a combination of different types of institutional coverage, and figures for the various countries are not comparable: some only have data on the functional classification for central government (10 countries) and others for general government (3 countries), the non-financial public sector (4 countries) or the public sector (1 country). This point is particularly important in the case of federal countries, where subnational governments are responsible for much social spending. Notwithstanding these comparability issues, the figures are presented here to give an idea of countries' efforts with respect to social spending.

## 1. Social spending in the region

Central government social spending in the region's countries, calculated as a simple average, was worth 10.5% of GDP in 2015 (see figure II.1). This was the highest level this century,[4] exceeding for the first time the 10.0% of GDP spent in 2009 in response to the 2008 subprime crisis. Social spending in 2015 represented 53% of total central government spending that year, again taking a simple average of 19 countries. This figure was also a small increase on the previous year and matched other peaks in the fiscal priority given to social policies since 2000.

Central government social spending in the region's countries, calculated as a simple average, was worth 10.5% of GDP in 2015.

---

[3]   A country's public sector is analysed by subsector or type of institutional coverage: (i) central government, which comprises the ministries, secretariats and public institutions exercising authority over the entire territory of the country; (ii) general government, which includes central government and subnational governments (first territorial subdivision and local governments); (iii) the non-financial public sector, which consists of general government and non-financial public corporations; and (iv) the public sector, which comprises the non-financial public sector plus financial public corporations.

[4]   As indicated in box II.1, the Latin American averages presented in this chapter are arithmetic means for 19 countries.

Figure II.1
Latin America (19 countries): central government social spending, 2000-2015[a]
*(Percentages of GDP and of total central government spending)*

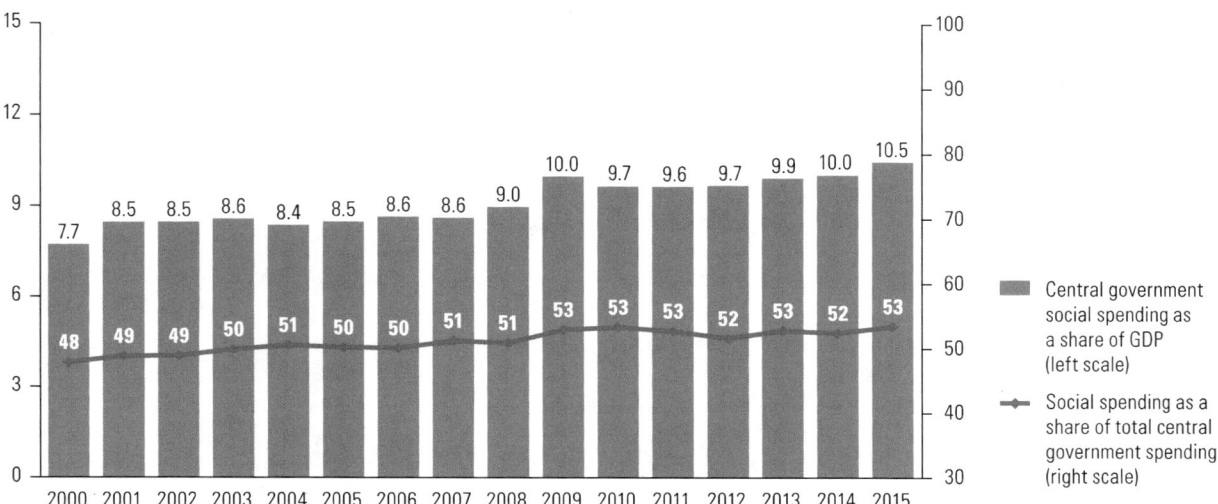

**Source**: Economic Commission for Latin America and the Caribbean (ECLAC), on the basis of official information from the respective countries.
[a] The averages are arithmetic means of the values for 19 countries: Argentina, Bolivarian Republic of Venezuela, Brazil, Chile, Colombia, Costa Rica, the Dominican Republic, Ecuador, El Salvador, Guatemala, Haiti, Honduras, Mexico, Nicaragua, Panama, Paraguay, Peru, the Plurinational State of Bolivia and Uruguay. The most recent data are from 2009 for the Bolivarian Republic of Venezuela and from 2014 for Panama.

The same trend can be seen in an analysis of broader institutional coverage, namely that of the public sector (see figure II.2): taking a simple average of the same 19 Latin American countries, social spending was higher than ever before in 2015, at 14.5% of GDP. This came after five years of sluggish growth in social spending as a share of GDP.

Figure II.2
Latin America (19 countries): public sector social spending, 2000-2015[a]
*(Percentages of GDP and of total public spending)*

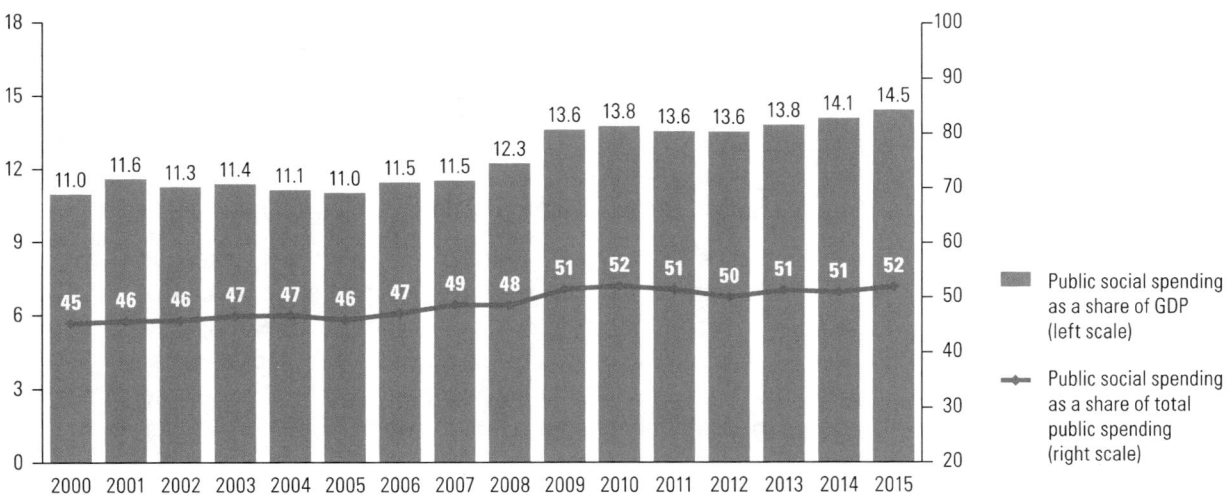

**Source**: Economic Commission for Latin America and the Caribbean (ECLAC), on the basis of official information from the respective countries.
[a] The averages are arithmetic means of the values for 19 countries. The countries for which coverage is broader than central government are Argentina, Brazil, Colombia, Costa Rica, Ecuador, El Salvador, Mexico, Peru and the Plurinational State of Bolivia, while coverage is central government only for the Bolivarian Republic of Venezuela, Chile, the Dominican Republic, Guatemala, Haiti, Honduras, Nicaragua, Panama, Paraguay and Uruguay. The most recent data are from 2009 for the Bolivarian Republic of Venezuela and from 2014 for Panama and the Plurinational State of Bolivia.

## 2. Social spending by function

When public social spending is analysed by social function, it transpires that education, social protection and health are still the most important functions at the central government level in the region, with averages of 3.9%, 3.7% and 2.0% of GDP, respectively, in 2015 (see figure II.3). These same functions posted the strongest increases between 2000 and 2015, with the spending shares of education and health rising by 0.7 percentage points of GDP and that of social protection by 1.1 percentage points of GDP.

**Figure II.3**
Latin America (19 countries): central government social spending, by function, 2000-2015[a]
*(Percentages of GDP)*

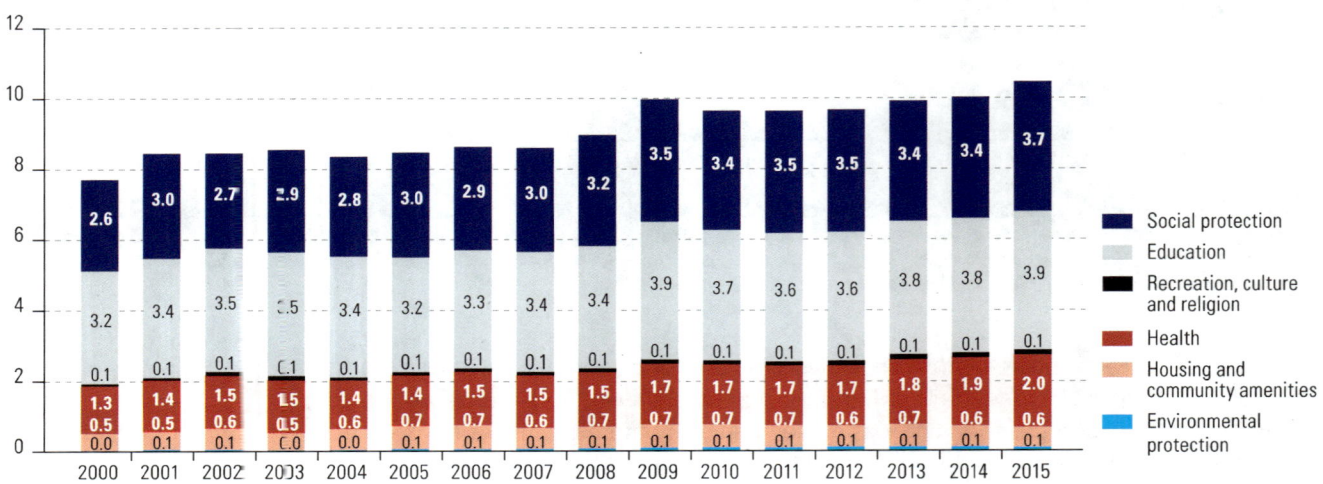

**Source**: Economic Commission for Latin America and the Caribbean (ECLAC), on the basis of official information from the respective countries.
[a] The averages are arithmetic means of the values for 19 countries: Argentina, the Bolivarian Republic of Venezuela, Brazil, Chile, Colombia, Costa Rica, Dominican Republic, Ecuador, El Salvador, Guatemala, Haiti, Honduras, Mexico, Nicaragua, Panama, Paraguay, Peru, the Plurinational State of Bolivia and Uruguay. Information is available up to 2009 for the Bolivarian Republic of Venezuela and 2014 for Panama.

When developments over the past five years are analysed, it is striking that whereas education spending held fairly steady at around 3.7% of GDP, the trend has been somewhat different for social protection spending, since although it did not change much between 2010 and 2014, it rose by 0.3 percentage points of GDP between 2014 and 2015. Spending on health also edged up towards the end of the period, rising by 0.1 percentage points of GDP per year from 2012.

If the fullest institutional coverage reported by the countries is taken (see figure II.4), social protection, education and health are once again found to be the top priorities in terms of resource allocation, at 5.0%, 4.6% and 3.4% of GDP, respectively, in 2015, with an increase of at least 0.9 percentage points of GDP in each of these areas since 2000. Whereas education is the best-funded function in central government coverage, social protection is in this fuller coverage, the reason being that a number of countries have public sector social protection bodies that are not part of central government. Trends in public sector social spending by function will now be described and analysed in order of importance.

**Figure II.4**
Latin America (19 countries): public sector social spending, by function, 2000-2015[a]
*(Percentages of GDP)*

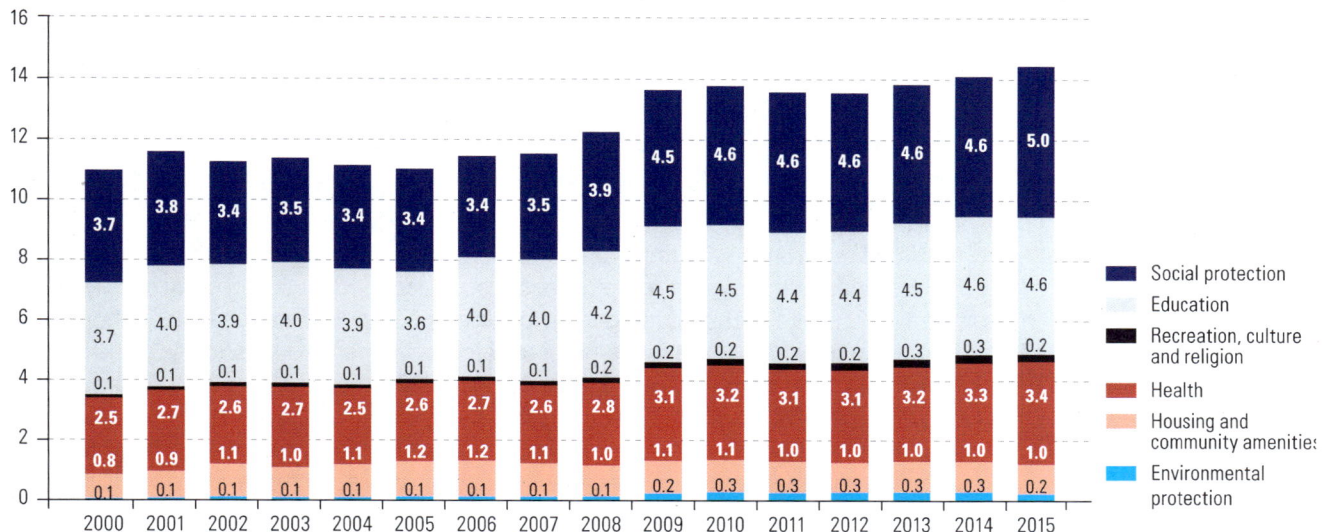

**Source**: Economic Commission for Latin America and the Caribbean (ECLAC), on the basis of official information from the respective countries.
[a] The averages are arithmetic means of the values for 19 countries. The countries for which coverage is broader than central government are Argentina, Brazil, Colombia, Costa Rica, Ecuador, El Salvador, Mexico, Peru and the Plurinational State of Bolivia, while coverage is central government only for the Bolivarian Republic of Venezuela, Chile, the Dominican Republic, Guatemala, Haiti, Honduras, Nicaragua, Panama, Paraguay and Uruguay. The most recent data are from 2009 for the Bolivarian Republic of Venezuela and 2014 for Panama and the Plurinational State of Bolivia.

## (a) Social protection

Social protection spending goes on services and transfers to individuals and families that cover the following subfunctions of social protection: illness and disability, old age, survivors,[5] families and children, unemployment, housing and social exclusion. This function covers risks that may be faced by the population as a whole (for example illness, old age and unemployment) but also risks associated with structural problems such as poverty and inequality (the social exclusion subfunction, which involves conditional transfer programmes, for instance). The region's social protection spending averaged 5% of GDP in 2015. At the country level, Argentina and Brazil allocated proportionally the largest amounts to this function, spending 14.1% and 13.2% of GDP, respectively, in 2015.

Although the subcategories of social protection spending are not shown, spending on policies for the elderly represents more than half the total in countries for which this information is available.

Meanwhile, spending relating to social exclusion represents 25% of the total for this function. Conditional transfer programmes are one component. As indicated by Cecchini and Atuesta (2017), both the population coverage and spending of these programmes have increased considerably over the past 20 years, and in 2015 they reached a fifth of the region's population (132 million people and 30 million households) for an outlay of 0.27% of regional GDP, or US$ 114 per capita (at constant 2010 prices).

Further disaggregation of the data associated with this function is essential for a thorough analysis, given that it includes both contributory social protection programmes (for old age and unemployment) and non-contributory programmes (for social exclusion and for families and children).

---

[5]  Spending on survivors includes benefits in cash or in kind for the family members of deceased persons, such as the spouse, former spouse, children, grandchildren, parents and others.

## (b) Education

Education spending is the funding that goes to the different levels of the education system, from preschool to tertiary, including education-related support services and research and development. This function ranks second for spending at the public sector level, with a regional average of 4.6% of GDP, according to 2015 data, as compared with 3.7% in 2000. The Plurinational State of Bolivia invests the most in education in the region, spending 8.2% of GDP in 2014, followed by Costa Rica with 7.5% of GDP (see annex and figure II.8). Article 78 of Costa Rica's constitution establishes a floor for education financing.[6]

This upward trend in spending on education policies stems from legal changes made by the countries of the region (more years of compulsory education in most of them[7]) and from improvements in the coverage and quality of compulsory education. Although the net primary school enrolment rate[8] remained almost unchanged at 92.3%, the secondary education enrolment rate increased from 60.8% in 2000 to 75.7% in 2013. The quality of education has also improved: the Third Regional Comparative and Explanatory Study (TERCE) showed average regional scores for learning attainment improving across all the grades and areas evaluated (see Cetrángolo and Curcio, 2017). Even so, a major effort is still needed to increase secondary education coverage and reach the most excluded sections of the population, and to improve quality at all levels, it being in this that the region really lags.

## (c) Health

Health spending goes on services for individuals and groups. This is one of the three most important social functions, representing an average of 3.4% of GDP in the region according to 2015 data, and has been on a rising trend as mentioned earlier (the share in 2000 was 2.5% of GDP). This is partly explained by two things: (i) the increase in non-communicable and chronic diseases resulting from population ageing and the epidemiological transition,[9] and (ii) the expansion of health coverage.[10] Health is undoubtedly one of the functions that will see a continued increase in spending in the coming years.

Of the countries included in the analysis, Argentina and Costa Rica recorded the highest levels of health spending in 2015, at 7.1% and 6.6% of GDP, respectively, followed by Brazil (5.1%), Colombia (4.9%) and Chile (4.4%).

## (d) Environmental protection

Environmental protection spending includes outlays on waste and sewage treatment, pollution control, biodiversity and landscape protection, and research for environmental protection purposes. It is important to analyse this function at the public sector level, i.e. including subnational governments (which are generally responsible for waste management) and public sector sewage treatment companies, owing to the manner in which policies are managed and funded.

---

[6]    According to the text as amended in 2011, "public spending on State education, including higher education, will be no less than eight per cent (8%) of gross domestic product each year".

[7]    Of the 19 countries of the region included in this analysis, only five (Colombia, Costa Rica, Cuba, the Dominican Republic and Panama) have left the number of years' compulsory education unaltered since 2000 (see Cetrángolo and Curcio, 2017).

[8]    The net primary school enrolment rate shows the extent to which children of an age at which primary school attendance is compulsory are actually enrolled. It is calculated by dividing the number of children enrolled in primary school who are of the appropriate age for the level by the total population in this age group and multiplying the result by 100.

[9]    According to Gottret and Schieber (2006), health needs are changing in all the world's countries, regardless of their level of economic development, in response to lower fertility rates, longer life expectancies and the shift in the burden of illness toward chronic diseases. These demographic and epidemiological transitions pose challenges for public health systems and the funding they receive.

[10]   Dmytraczenko and Almeida (2015) emphasize that the Latin American countries have made considerable progress towards universal health care by extending population coverage and access to health services and increasing public spending on health.

Although average spending on this function is relatively low in the region as a share of GDP (0.2% in 2015), it is on a rising trend, having been just 0.1% of GDP in 2000. Of all the countries analysed (see annex II.A1 and the ECLAC social investment database), Peru allocates the most, with public sector spending of 1.4% of GDP, followed by the Plurinational State of Bolivia with 1.1% of GDP and Colombia with 0.6% of GDP, both at the general government level.[11]

It is not only to meet their sustainable development commitments that the countries must continue to increase public spending on environmental protection;[12] access to sanitation is also fundamental because it prevents gastrointestinal diseases that can cause death, particularly among children, and reduce years of healthy life. There is still a long way to go and much work to be done to ensure that households have this basic service and to ease the enormous territorial inequalities that still exist in this area (see ECLAC, 2016c, particularly chapter IV).

### (e) Housing and community amenities

Spending on housing and community amenities encompasses outlays on urbanization (including the administration of urbanization issues, slum clearance for residential development, construction and remodelling of homes for the public in general or for persons with special needs, and acquisition of land for housebuilding), community development, water supply and street lighting. The countries of the region invested an average of 1.0% of GDP in this function in 2015. Argentina invests the most, with 2.7% of GDP in 2015, followed by Costa Rica and Nicaragua with 2.3% of GDP each.

Access to drinking water, like sanitation, is essential. Although very considerable progress has been made in the Latin American countries, there are still profound territorial inequalities in this area as well.

Health spending, representing an average of 3.4% of GDP, has been on a rising trend for two reason: the increase in non-communicable and chronic diseases and the expansion of health coverage.

### (f) Recreation, culture and religion

Spending on recreation, culture and religion encompasses leisure pastimes (sporting and cultural activities, radio and television) and religious services. This function accounted for 0.2% of GDP region-wide in 2015. The countries investing most in this area as a share of GDP were the Plurinational State of Bolivia at 1.1% and Colombia at 0.9%. The Ibero-American Cultural Charter adopted in 2006 by the sixteenth Ibero-American Summit of Heads of State and Government affirms the fundamental character of cultural rights and recognizes that the traditional cultures of the indigenous, Afrodescendent and migrant populations are an important part of culture and an essential heritage of humanity. The culture ministers and high-level officials who attended the tenth Ibero-American Conference on Culture, held in Valparaiso (Chile) in July 2007, agreed that "each State should progressively allocate at least 1% of its general budget to the promotion of culture" (ECLAC/OEI, 2014), a commitment that calls for additional efforts in the region.

---

[11]  These values are not equivalent to those arising from ECLAC estimates performed on the basis of satellite accounts on environmental protection, which are available for some Latin American countries.

[12]  In the 2030 Agenda for Sustainable Development, the following Sustainable Development Goals relating to the environmental sustainability of development and environmental protection should be noted: Goal 6, "ensure availability and sustainable management of water and sanitation for all"; Goal 7, "ensure access to affordable, reliable, sustainable and modern energy for all"; Goal 12, "ensure sustainable consumption and production patterns"; Goal 13, "take urgent action to combat climate change and its impacts"; Goal 14, "conserve and sustainably use the oceans, seas and marine resources for sustainable development"; and Goal 15, "protect, restore and promote sustainable use of terrestrial ecosystems, sustainably manage forests, combat desertification, halt and reverse land degradation, and halt biodiversity loss".

# 3. Public funding for social policies in the region

Analysing social spending in absolute terms can create a picture that complements the overview based on GDP shares that has already been provided. Central government social spending as a simple average for 19 countries in the region came out at US$ 728 per capita in 2015. As shown in figure II.5, this average represents an increase of roughly 60% from 2000 and more than 20% over five years.

**Figure II.5**

Latin America (19 countries): central government social spending per capita, by function, 2000-2015[a]

*(2010 dollars)*

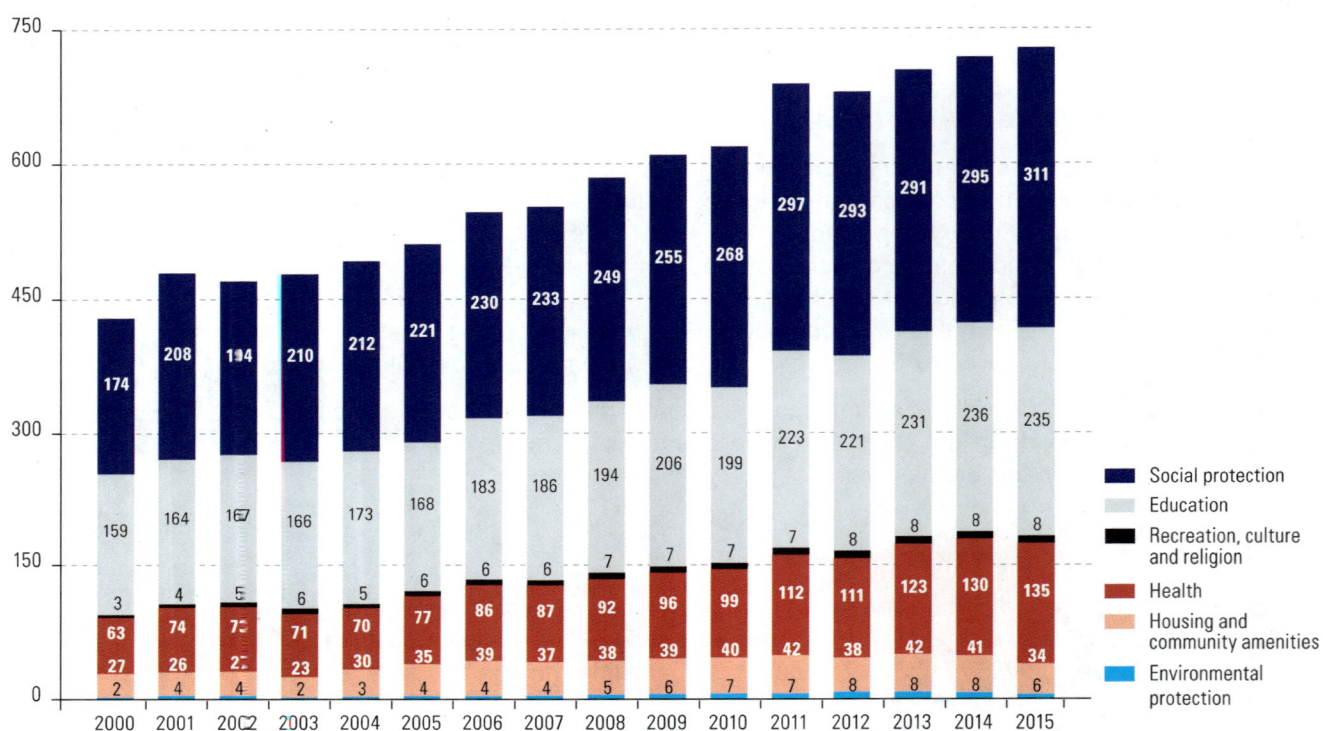

**Source**: Economic Commission for Latin America and the Caribbean (ECLAC), on the basis of official information from the respective countries.

[a] The averages are arithmetic means of the values for the 19 countries: Argentina, Bolivarian Republic of Venezuela, Brazil, Chile, Colombia, Costa Rica, Dominican Republic, Ecuador, El Salvador, Guatemala, Haiti, Honduras, Mexico, Nicaragua, Panama, Paraguay, Peru, the Plurinational State of Bolivia and Uruguay. Information is available up to 2009 for the Bolivarian Republic of Venezuela and 2014 for Panama.

When official information for the whole public sector is taken, average social spending by the region's countries comes out at US$ 1,094 per capita in 2015 (see figure II.6), an increase of almost 50% from 2000 and almost 10% from 2010.

**Figure II.6**

Latin America (19 countries): public sector social spending per capita, by function, 2000-2015[a]
*(2010 dollars)*

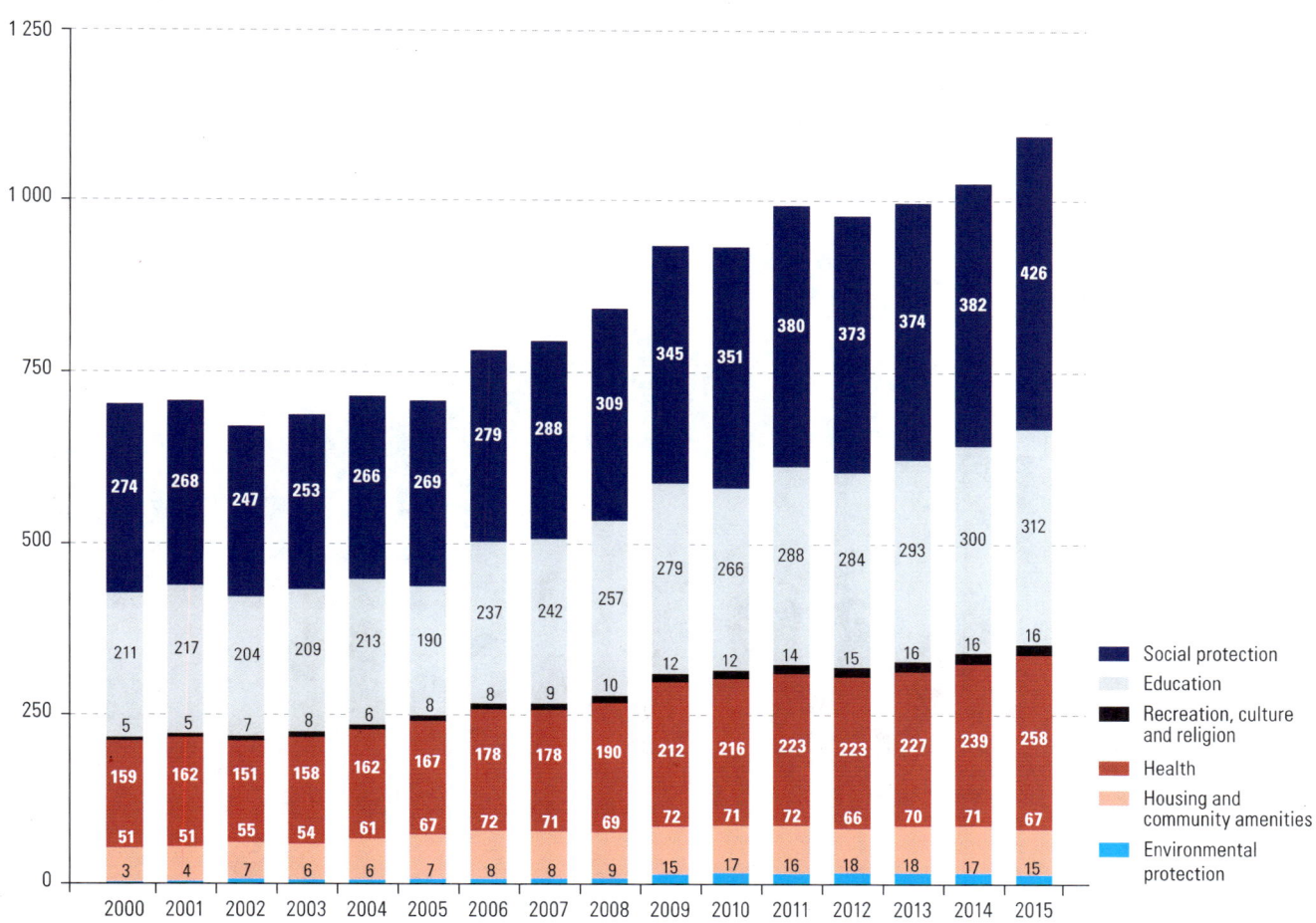

**Source**: Economic Commission for Latin America and the Caribbean (ECLAC), on the basis of official information from the respective countries.
[a] The averages are arithmetic means of the values for 19 countries. The countries for which coverage is broader than central government are Argentina, Brazil, Colombia, Costa Rica, Ecuador, El Salvador, Mexico, Peru and the Plurinational State of Bolivia, while coverage is central government only for the Bolivarian Republic of Venezuela, Chile, the Dominican Republic, Guatemala, Haiti, Honduras, Nicaragua, Panama, Paraguay and Uruguay. The most recent data are from 2009 for the Bolivarian Republic of Venezuela and 2014 for Panama and the Plurinational State of Bolivia.

## 4.    A comparative analysis of the region's countries

At the central government level, Chile and Trinidad and Tobago invest the most in social functions in the region, at more than 16% of GDP, followed by Uruguay with 14.9% of GDP (see figure II.7). Meanwhile, Central American countries (with the exception of Costa Rica) generally appear to have the lowest levels of total public spending and social spending relative to GDP.

**Figure II.7**

Latin America and the Caribbean (21 countries): central government social spending, by function, 2015[a]
*(Percentages of GDP)*

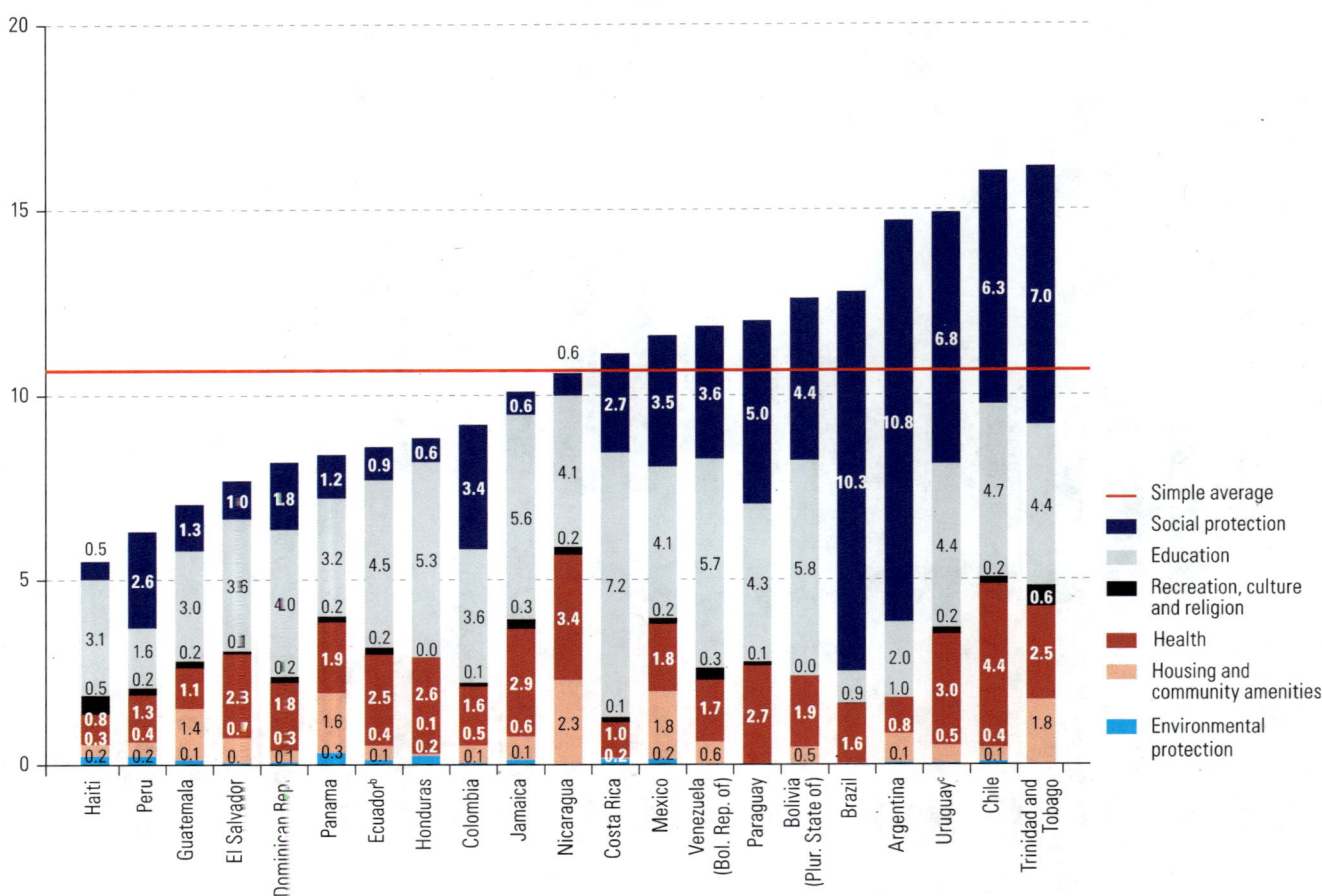

**Source**: Economic Commission for Latin America and the Caribbean (ECLAC), on the basis of official information from the respective countries.

[a] The data on the Bolivarian Republic of Venezuela are from 2009 and those on Panama from 2014. Three countries' fiscal years do not match the calendar year: that of Haiti and Trinidad and Tobago runs from 1 October to 30 September, and Jamaica's from 1 April to 31 March. The Plurinational State of Bolivia only reports on central administration coverage for social functions.

[b] The data refer to the institutional coverage of the general State budget, which includes the central administration and decentralized and autonomous entities. It does not include information from the Ecuadorian Social Security Institute (IESS).

[c] The information comes from the Office of the Accountant-General and includes only institutional coverage of the central government. It does not include information from quasi-public pension funds, the social protection agency or the State-owned water utilities company, Obras Sanitarias del Estado (OSE). This information does not coincide with the historical series prepared jointly by the Ministry of Social Development and the Ministry of Economic Affairs and Finance.

When official information on the coverage of the whole public sector is considered, Argentina, Brazil, Costa Rica, Colombia and the Plurinational State of Bolivia emerge as the region's largest investors in social functions, spending over 20% of GDP in each case (see figure II.8).

**Figure II.8**

Latin America and the Caribbean (21 countries): public sector social spending, by function, 2015[a]
*(Percentages of GDP)*

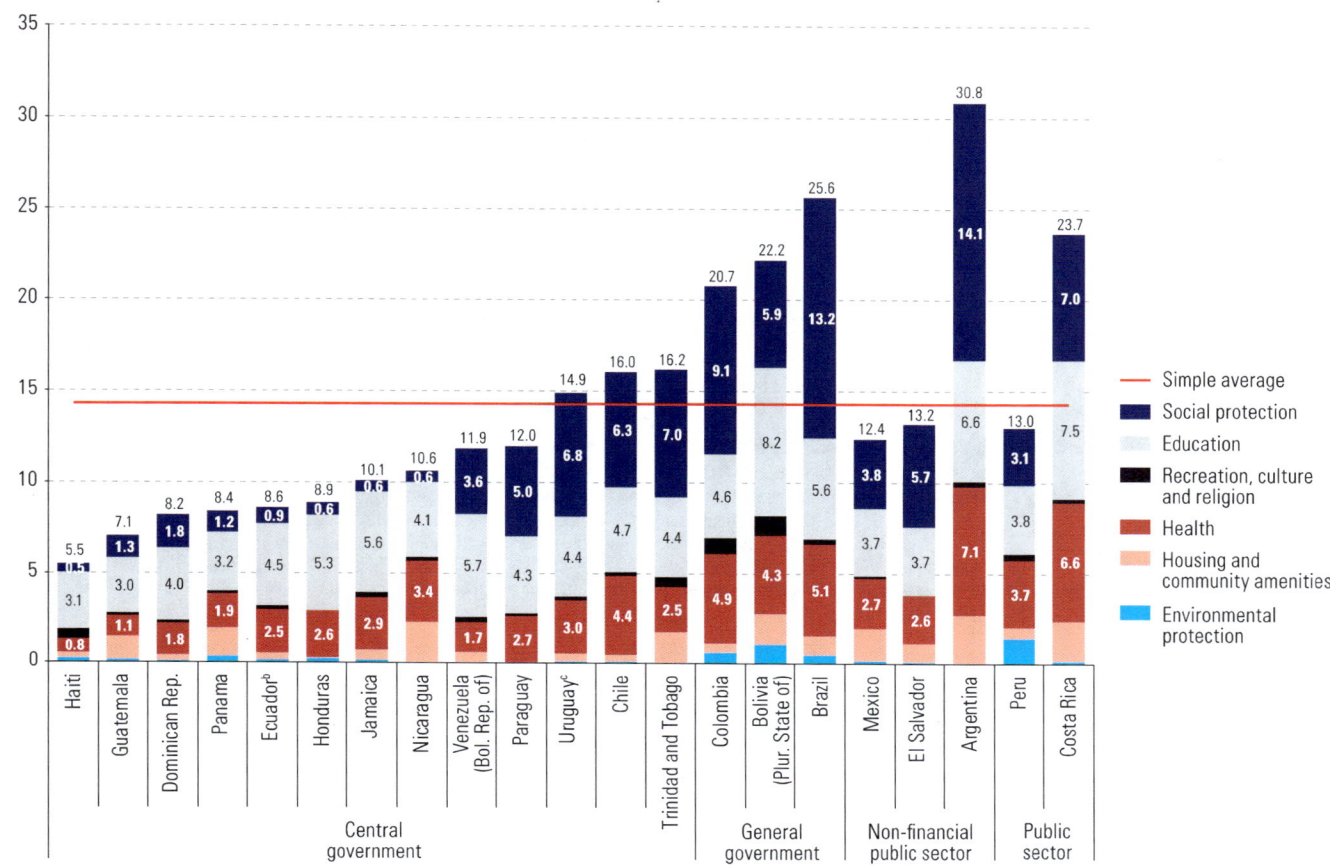

**Source**: Economic Commission for Latin America and the Caribbean (ECLAC), on the basis of official information from the respective countries.
[a] The data on the Bolivarian Republic of Venezuela are from 2009 and those on Panama from 2014. Three countries' fiscal years do not match the calendar year: that of Haiti and Trinidad and Tobago runs from 1 October to 30 September, and Jamaica's from 1 April to 31 March. Coverage is central government for the following countries: Bolivarian Republic of Venezuela, Chile, Dominican Republic, Ecuador, Guatemala, Haiti, Honduras, Jamaica, Nicaragua, Panama, Paraguay, Trinidad and Tobago and Uruguay.
[b] The data refer to the institutional coverage of the general State budget, which includes the central administration and decentralized and autonomous entities. It does not include information from the Ecuadorian Social Security Institute (IESS).
[c] The information comes from the Office of the Accountant-General and includes only institutional coverage of the central government. It does not include information from quasi-public pension funds, the social protection agency or the State-owned water utilities company, Obras Sanitarias del Estado (OSE). This information does not coincide with the historical series prepared jointly by the Ministry of Social Development and the Ministry of Economic Affairs and Finance.

# 5.　International comparisons

How does Latin America compare with other regions of the world, groupings or countries outside the region for public social spending? Unsurprisingly, it spends much less than the European Union or the United States: in 2014, average social spending in Latin America was 20 percentage points of GDP below the European Union's and almost 10 percentage points below that of the United States, but very similar to the average for six selected Asian countries for which comparable information is available on social spending by functional classification (Japan, Malaysia, the Philippines, the Republic of Korea, Singapore and Thailand) (see figure II.9). Where the composition of social spending is concerned, Latin America is very similar to the Asian countries but different from the European Union and the United States. For example, the health function attracts the most spending in the United States, at 8.8% of GDP, while the largest function in the European Union is social protection, at 19.4% of GDP.

**Figure II.9**
European Union
(28 countries), United States,
Latin America (19 countries)
and Asia (6 countries): public
social spending, 2014[a]
*(Percentages of GDP)*

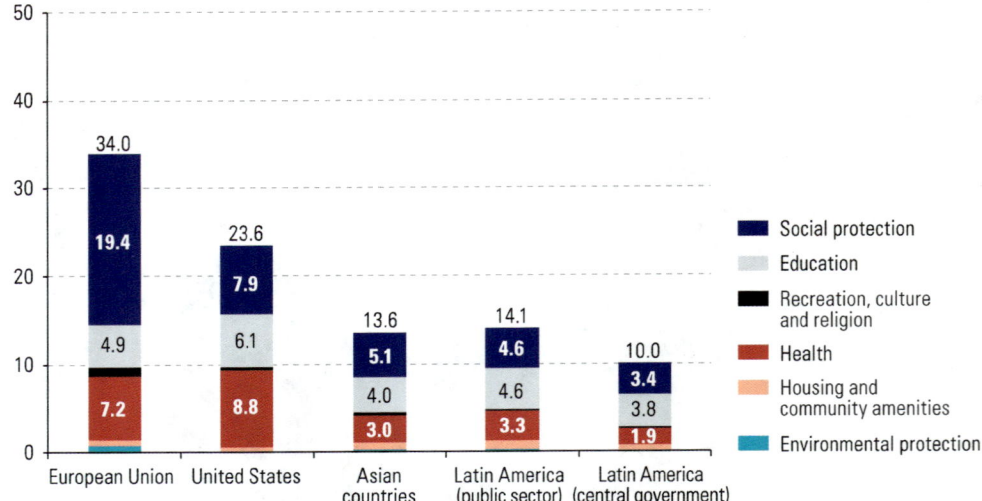

Source: Economic Commission for Latin America and the Caribbean (ECLAC), on the basis of official information from the respective countries, the Organization for Economic Cooperation and Development (OECD) and the International Monetary Fund (IMF).
[a] Coverage is general government for the European Union and the United States. The selected countries of Asia are Japan (general government), Malaysia (central administration), the Philippines (central administration), the Republic of Korea (general government), Singapore (central government) and Thailand (central government). The Latin American countries with coverage broader than central government in the public sector column are Argentina, Brazil, Colombia, Costa Rica, Ecuador, El Salvador, Mexico, Peru and the Plurinational State of Bolivia, while coverage is central government in both columns for the Bolivarian Republic of Venezuela (where the data are from 2009), Chile, the Dominican Republic, Guatemala, Haiti, Honduras, Nicaragua, Panama, Paraguay and Uruguay.

Wagner's law is one of the oldest theories concerning growth of the State relative to a country's economy (Wagner, 1893). According to this "law of expanding State activity", if an economy grows, so will the public sector, for three reasons: (i) the State's administrative and protective functions will grow owing to the substitution of public activities for private ones; (ii) there will be a greater need for social and cultural goods and services and an increase in public redistributive and educational functions (these being superior goods whose consumption rises by more than income); and (iii) more State intervention will be needed to regulate markets (given that technological changes and the larger amounts of capital needed to carry out certain activities create private sector monopolies) (Bird, 1971). Hence, according to Wagner, growth in public spending can be seen as the result of economic growth, in contrast to the Keynesian theory that economic growth is driven by public spending. As discussed by Rodríguez, Venegas and Lima (2013), there has been a great deal of theoretical and empirical research into the relationship between public spending and economic growth in a large number of both developed and developing countries because of its major implications for economic policy, although the findings have been mixed and contradictory.

It is therefore interesting to examine the long-term trend in social spending and GDP per capita in different regions. To this end, a series running from 1990 to 2015 was analysed for Latin America and one running from 1990 to 2012 for the countries of the Organization for Economic Cooperation and Development (OECD). The series are comparable because they include the same six social functions as are considered by ECLAC. They also reveal the tax burden needed for the sustainable funding of public expenditure. As previously mentioned, the gap separating Latin America from the European Union and United States is wide: GDP per capita and the tax burden were already higher in the OECD countries by 1965 than they were in the Latin American countries in 2014 (see figure II.10 and Arenas de Mesa, 2016).

As their per capita GDP rises, it may be said that the countries of the region could also increase their social spending and their capacity to fund public policy. The need for higher spending looks even clearer in the light of the commitments made within the framework of the Sustainable Development Goals.

**Figure II.10**
Latin America and countries of the Organization for Economic Cooperation and Development (OECD): public social spending, tax burdens and GDP per capita,[a] 1990-2015
*(Percentages of GDP and 2010 dollars at purchasing power parity)*

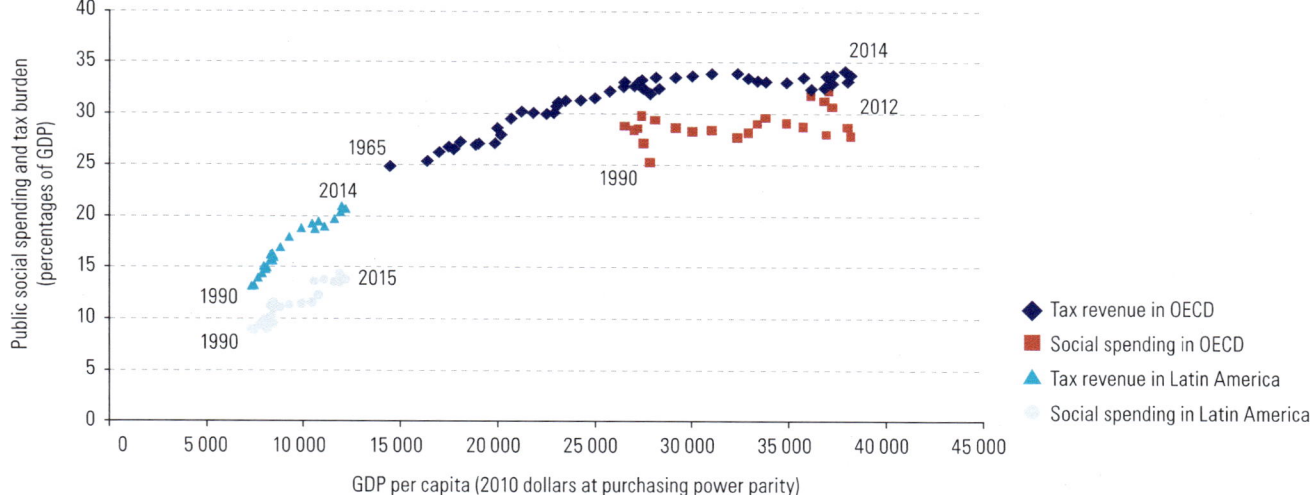

**Source:** Economic Commission for Latin America and the Caribbean (ECLAC), on the basis of official information from the respective countries, the Organization for Economic Cooperation and Development (OECD) and the International Monetary Fund (IMF).

[a] The following are deemed to be social functions in both the Latin American and OECD series: (i) environmental protection, (ii) housing and community amenities, (iii) health, (iv) recreation, culture and religion, (v) education and (vi) social protection.

# B. Present and future social spending as budgeted in the 2015-2017 period

Information in the budgets of the Latin American countries for 2016 and 2017 indicates that the South American countries are reducing their public social spending whereas those of Central America are increasing it.

This section presents the information contained in the budgets of the Latin American countries from a functional perspective, in order to assess governments' prioritization of the various social policies for the current year, analyse them in the light of the present phase in the economic cycle and be able to contrast planned and actual spending.

A country's public budget is its most important fiscal policy instrument. It summarizes the availability of resources for each government sector, unit and programme, and is governed by an established legal framework (Marcel, Guzmán and Sanginés, 2014). The budget cycle comprises five successive stages: (i) planning, which focuses on identifying the main priorities; (ii) formulation, leading to the government's executive branch submitting the budget proposal to the legislative branch for discussion; (iii) approval of the proposed budget by the legislature so that it becomes law;[13] (iv) execution of the budget act; (v) oversight and assessment (see table II.1 for a description of each stage). A budget incorporates decision-making and negotiation processes that involve the executive and legislative branches in their entirety as well as different stakeholders in civil society.

---

[13]    The legislature may reject the budget proposal put forward by the executive branch. Depending on the country, this situation has three possible outcomes: (i) the government suspends its functions until the legislature approves the budget (this option does not exist in any Latin American country), (ii) the previous year's budget is adopted, or (iii) the budget proposed by the president's office is enacted.

Table II.1
The budget cycle

| Stage | Timetable[a] | Objective | Inputs | Outputs | Actors |
|---|---|---|---|---|---|
| Planning | Year 1: April-May | Identification of resource allocation priorities | Government programme, development plan, sectoral proposals | Programmatic structure of the budget, priority sectors | Ministries of finance and planning, president's office |
| Formulation | Year 1: June-August | Effective allocation of resources within the macroeconomic context | Programmatic priorities, previous financial year's performance, legal commitments, sectoral proposals and expected outcome | Budget proposal | Line ministries, public entities, ministry of finance, president's office |
| Approval | Year 1: September-December | Legal authorization of access to public funds | Proposals by the executive, reports from external agencies, opinions of parliamentarians | Budget act | Legislature, pundits, civil society, ministry of finance |
| Execution | Year 2: January-December | Use of public resources | Approved budget, rules on financial management, changes in conditions, contingencies | Executed budget | Line ministries, public entities |
| Oversight and assessment | Year 3: January-March | Verification that legal obligations and management commitments have been met | Budget execution, management indicators, impact assessments, audits | Reports, accountability, impact assessment | Internal and external oversight bodies, assessment and planning bodies |

**Source**: Economic Commission for Latin America and the Caribbean (ECLAC), on the basis of M. Marcel, M. Guzmán and M. Sanginés, *Presupuestos para el desarrollo en América Latina*, Washington, D.C., Inter-American Development Bank (IDB), 2014.
[a] This is a generic timetable for countries whose budget cycles coincide with the calendar year (1 January to 31 December).

> The region's governments have been cautious in their 2016 and 2017 budgets, in that the total and social spending budgeted for is lower than in 2015.

With a view to developing the functional analysis of social spending further and ascertaining the outlook for the countries' future policy decision-making, it is necessary to determine whether budgets present information based on the functional classification, indicating what the money is to be spent on regardless of the government entity doing the spending.

ECLAC did not previously seek to determine whether countries reported budgeted spending by purpose, i.e. whether spending figures at the formulation and approval stages of the budget cycle were disaggregated by function. Nor did it compile this information, but only had estimates of actual expenditure, like those presented in section A of this chapter. As shown in annex II.A1, 15 of the region's countries do compile these data. It is worth noting that in many cases they use a classification of their own (not the internationally recommended one), or an institutional/administrative classification. Only five countries (Colombia, Costa Rica, Dominican Republic, Guatemala and Trinidad and Tobago) apply the internationally used Classification of the Functions of Government (COFOG).

This analysis covers budgeted spending for the 2016 and 2017 fiscal years and shows results for 12 of the 15 countries under review. Data are not included for Paraguay because it presents its budget act in functional terms for the public sector including financial corporations, and this is not comparable with actual spending, whose institutional coverage is narrower (central administration). Data are likewise not included for Trinidad and Tobago owing to a lack of official information on macroeconomic assumptions for 2017. In the case of Uruguay, data are not included because of lack of information needed to process it.

Figure II.11 shows data on total and social spending for the 12 countries, obtained from their budgets. The region's governments have been cautious in their 2016 and 2017 budgets on average, in that the total and social spending budgeted for is lower than in 2015. The chart also allows the spending implemented in 2015 to be compared to the amount budgeted for the year, and shows that actual total spending was 1 percentage point of GDP lower than planned. Strikingly, the whole shortfall was accounted for by the social functions.

**A. Total and social spending**

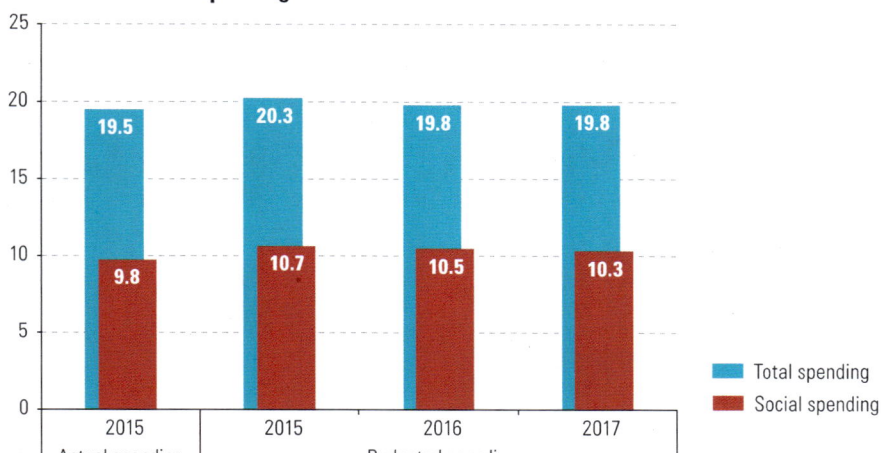

**B. Social spending by function**

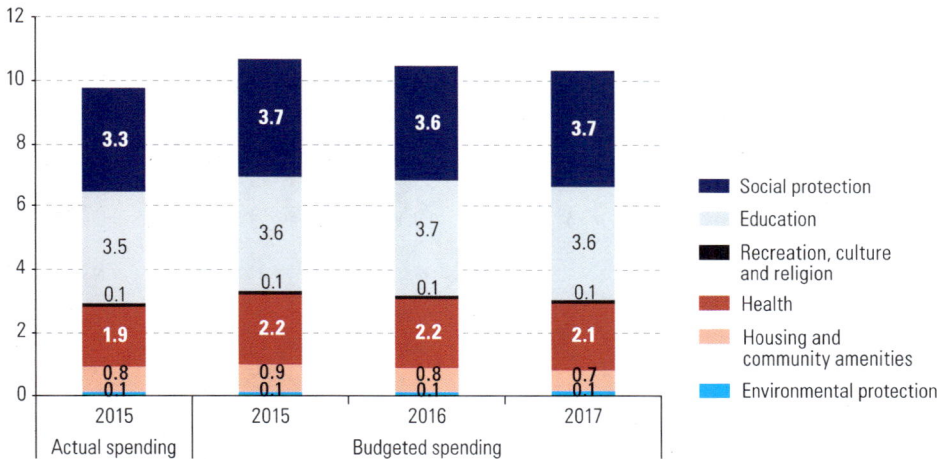

Figure II.11
Latin America (12 countries): executed and budgeted spending, by function, 2015-2017[a]
*(Percentages of GDP)*

**Source**: Economic Commission for Latin America and the Caribbean (ECLAC).
[a] Simple average of 12 countries: Argentina, Brazil, Colombia, Costa Rica, Dominican Republic, El Salvador, Guatemala, Honduras, Mexico, Nicaragua, Panama and Peru.

According to ECLAC figures, the GDP of Latin America and the Caribbean dipped by 1.1% in 2016 and will rise by 1.1% in 2017. The region has been caught in a process of economic slowdown and contraction since 2011. Its negative performance in 2016 was essentially due to weaker growth in most South American economies and contractions in some, such as Argentina, the Bolivarian Republic of Venezuela, Brazil and Ecuador, amid economic uncertainty. Meanwhile, Central American countries (Costa Rica, Cuba, the Dominican Republic, El Salvador, Guatemala, Haiti, Honduras, Nicaragua and Panama) maintained a substantial pace of growth in 2016 (3.6%), albeit weaker than in 2015 (4.7%). They are expected to post growth of 3.6% once again in 2017. The situation is very different in South America, where GDP growth stood at -2.4% in 2016 and is expected to be just 0.6% in 2017.

The social spending budgeted by each country for 2016 and 2017 against this economic backdrop is shown by function in table II.2, which also includes budgeted and actual spending for 2015. Three countries are planning to increase social spending in 2017 (Argentina, the Dominican Republic and Guatemala), six to reduce it (Brazil, Colombia, El Salvador, Mexico, Nicaragua and Peru), and three to keep it unchanged (Costa Rica, Honduras and Panama).

Table II.2
Latin America (12 countries: executed and budgeted central government social spending, by function, 2015-2017[a]
(Percentages of GDP)

| Country | Function | Executed spending | Executed spending | | |
|---|---|---|---|---|---|
| | | 2015 | 2015 | 2016 | 2017 |
| Argentina | Social spending | 14.7 | 14.0 | 13.7 | 15.5 |
| | Environmental protection | 0.1 | 0.1 | 0.1 | 0.1 |
| | Housing and community amenities | 0.8 | 0.8 | 0.7 | 0.5 |
| | Health | 1.0 | 0.9 | 0.9 | 0.9 |
| | Recreation, culture and religion | 0.0 | 0.0 | 0.0 | 0.0 |
| | Education | 2.0 | 2.1 | 2.0 | 2.0 |
| | Social protection | 10.8 | 10.2 | 10.1 | 12.1 |
| | GDP growth rate | | 2.5 | -2.0 | 2.0 |
| Brazil | Social spending | 12.8 | 13.8 | 13.5 | 12.2 |
| | Environmental protection | 0.0 | 0.2 | 0.0 | 0.0 |
| | Housing and community amenities | 0.0 | 0.1 | 0.1 | 0.1 |
| | Health | 1.6 | 1.9 | 1.8 | 1.6 |
| | Recreation, culture and religion | 0.0 | 0.1 | 0.0 | 0.0 |
| | Education | 0.9 | 1.2 | 0.9 | 0.9 |
| | Social protection | 10.3 | 10.4 | 10.6 | 9.6 |
| | GDP growth rate | | -3.9 | -3.6 | 0.4 |
| Colombia | Social spending | 9.2 | 14.7 | 13.4 | 13.1 |
| | Environmental protection | 0.1 | 0.2 | 0.1 | 0.1 |
| | Housing and community amenities | 0.5 | 0.3 | 0.3 | 0.3 |
| | Health | 1.6 | 2.8 | 2.9 | 2.8 |
| | Recreation, culture and religion | 0.1 | 0.2 | 0.2 | 0.2 |
| | Education | 3.6 | 3.2 | 3.1 | 3.1 |
| | Social protection | 3.4 | 8.0 | 6.9 | 6.7 |
| | GDP growth rate | | 3.1 | 2.0 | 2.4 |
| Costa Rica | Social spending | 11.1 | 13.0 | 12.9 | 12.8 |
| | Environmental protection | 0.2 | 0.1 | 0.1 | 0.1 |
| | Housing and community amenities | 0.0 | 0.1 | 0.1 | 0.1 |
| | Health | 1.0 | 0.9 | 0.9 | 0.9 |
| | Recreation, culture and religion | 0.1 | 0.2 | 0.2 | 0.2 |
| | Education | 7.2 | 7.6 | 7.6 | 7.6 |
| | Social protection | 2.7 | 4.2 | 4.1 | 4.0 |
| | GDP growth rate | | 3.7 | 4.1 | 4.1 |
| Dominican Republic | Social spending | 8.2 | 8.3 | 8.2 | 8.4 |
| | Environmental protection | 0.1 | 0.1 | 0.1 | 0.1 |
| | Housing and community amenities | 0.3 | 0.3 | 0.3 | 0.3 |
| | Health | 1.8 | 1.9 | 1.8 | 2.0 |
| | Recreation, culture and religion | 0.2 | 0.2 | 0.2 | 0.1 |
| | Education | 4.0 | 4.1 | 4.1 | 4.2 |
| | Social protection | 1.8 | 1.8 | 1.8 | 1.7 |
| | GDP growth rate | | 7.0 | 6.4 | 5.3 |
| El Salvador | Social spending | 7.7 | 7.2 | 6.9 | 6.2 |
| | Environmental protection | 0.1 | 0.1 | 0.1 | 0.1 |
| | Housing and community amenities | 0.7 | 0.5 | 0.1 | 0.1 |
| | Health | 2.3 | 2.4 | 2.4 | 2.2 |
| | Recreation, culture and religion | 0.1 | 0.0 | 0.0 | 0.0 |
| | Education | 3.6 | 3.6 | 3.5 | 3.4 |
| | Social protection | 1.0 | 0.7 | 0.9 | 0.4 |
| | GDP growth rate | | 2.5 | 2.2 | 2.5 |
| Guatemala | Social spending | 7.1 | 8.0 | 7.2 | 7.6 |
| | Environmental protection | 0.1 | 0.2 | 0.2 | 0.2 |
| | Housing and community amenities | 1.4 | 1.8 | 1.4 | 1.4 |
| | Health | 1.1 | 1.1 | 1.0 | 1.2 |
| | Recreation, culture and religion | 0.2 | 0.2 | 0.2 | 0.2 |
| | Education | 3.0 | 3.1 | 3.1 | 3.1 |
| | Social protection | 1.3 | 1.6 | 1.3 | 1.4 |
| | GDP growth rate | | 4.1 | 3.3 | 3.4 |

Table II.2 (concluded)

| Country | Function | Executed spending | Year Executed spending | | |
|---|---|---|---|---|---|
| | | 2015 | 2015 | 2016 | 2017 |
| Honduras | Social spending | 8.9 | 8.9 | 9.5 | 9.6 |
| | Environmental protection | 0.2 | 0.2 | 0.2 | 0.1 |
| | Housing and community amenities | 0.1 | 0.1 | 0.3 | 0.1 |
| | Health | 2.6 | 2.8 | 3.1 | 2.7 |
| | Recreation, culture and religion | 0.0 | 0.0 | 0.0 | 0.0 |
| | Education | 5.3 | 5.0 | 5.2 | 5.1 |
| | Social protection | 0.6 | 0.8 | 0.8 | 1.6 |
| | GDP growth rate | | 3.6 | 3.5 | 3.7 |
| Mexico | Social spending | 12.4 | 12.2 | 12.1 | 11.3 |
| | Environmental protection | 0.2 | 0.2 | 0.1 | 0.1 |
| | Housing and community amenities | 1.8 | 1.4 | 1.4 | 1.0 |
| | Health | 2.7 | 2.8 | 2.8 | 2.6 |
| | Recreation, culture and religion | 0.2 | 0.2 | 0.1 | 0.1 |
| | Education | 3.7 | 3.9 | 3.8 | 3.5 |
| | Social protection | 3.8 | 3.7 | 3.9 | 4.0 |
| | GDP growth rate | | 2.5 | 2.0 | 1.9 |
| Nicaragua | Social spending | 10.6 | 10.8 | 10.9 | 10.6 |
| | Environmental protection | 0.0 | 0.0 | 0.0 | 0.0 |
| | Housing and community amenities | 2.3 | 2.3 | 2.2 | 2.2 |
| | Health | 3.4 | 3.4 | 3.5 | 3.3 |
| | Recreation, culture and religion | 0.2 | 0.2 | 0.2 | 0.3 |
| | Education | 4.1 | 4.2 | 4.6 | 4.4 |
| | Social protection | 0.6 | 0.6 | 0.6 | 0.5 |
| | GDP growth rate | | 4.9 | 4.8 | 4.6 |
| Panama | Social spending | 8.4 | 10.3 | 10.1 | 10.0 |
| | Environmental protection | 0.3 | 0.0 | 0.1 | 0.1 |
| | Housing and community amenities | 1.6 | 2.3 | 2.0 | 2.1 |
| | Health | 1.9 | 3.8 | 3.7 | 3.6 |
| | Recreation, culture and religion | 0.2 | 0.0 | 0.0 | 0.0 |
| | Education | 3.2 | 3.6 | 3.8 | 3.7 |
| | Social protection | 1.2 | 0.5 | 0.5 | 0.5 |
| | GDP growth rate | | 5.8 | 5.2 | 5.2 |
| Peru | Social spending | 6.3 | 7.1 | 7.0 | 6.5 |
| | Environmental protection | 0.2 | 0.4 | 0.5 | 0.8 |
| | Housing and community amenities | 0.4 | 0.5 | 0.4 | 0.2 |
| | Health | 1.3 | 1.4 | 1.3 | 1.2 |
| | Recreation, culture and religion | 0.2 | 0.1 | 0.1 | 0.2 |
| | Education | 1.6 | 2.2 | 2.4 | 2.1 |
| | Social protection | 2.6 | 2.5 | 2.3 | 2.1 |
| | GDP growth rate | | 3.3 | 3.9 | 3.5 |

**Source**: Economic Commission for Latin America and the Caribbean (ECLAC), on the basis of official information.

[a] The information on GDP growth rates was provided by ECLAC. The countries reporting central government budget information are Argentina (national administration), Brazil (federal government), Colombia (general national budget), Costa Rica, Dominican Republic, El Salvador, Mexico (federal expenditure budget), Nicaragua, Panama and Peru (national government), while Guatemala and Honduras report central administration budget information.

The data show that Argentina and Brazil were the two South American countries where GDP contracted in 2016. Difficult economic conditions there have affected social spending, as shown in table II.2. In Argentina, the devaluation of the peso in December 2015 (by roughly 40% in one day) heavily affected wages, pensions and social protection system transfers, which are estimated to have shrunk by 3.3% in real terms between 2015 and 2016 (ECLAC, 2016b). Argentina has budgeted for an increase in the social protection function in 2017 to take it up to 12.07% of GDP, with plans to maintain and expand various cash transfer programmes (such as the universal child allowance and family allowances) and to create a programme of historical redress for retirees and pensioners (Ministry of Treasury and Public Finances, 2017). Meanwhile, Brazil has presented an austerity budget and negotiated a constitutional amendment bill (known as PEC 95, 2016)[14] whose purpose is to establish a 20-year cap on public spending growth in order to rein in the increase of the public debt. It is interesting to note that Argentina and Brazil, both in recession, have taken opposite approaches to social spending for 2017, with Brazil's stance being clearly procyclical and Argentina's countercyclical. The other two South American countries, Colombia and Peru, have also presented austerity budgets for 2017, with both total and adjusted social spending lower than in their 2016 budgets as percentages of GDP.

For 2017, Mexico has presented a spending budget that aims at fiscal consolidation for the second year in a row, with lower discretionary spending than the previous year. Nonetheless, the cuts are in line with the budgetary considerations submitted by the National Council for the Evaluation of Social Development Policy (CONEVAL), which identifies priority budget programmes for reducing need in each dimension of the official poverty measurement in Mexico, as well as programmes to fulfil each of the social rights established in the Social Development Act. Even so, the budget cuts funding for all functions except social protection.

The Central American countries budgeting for higher total spending in 2017 than in 2016 are Costa Rica, the Dominican Republic, Guatemala, Honduras and Panama. These countries are maintaining or slightly increasing their social spending as a percentage of GDP in 2017, which means a rise in funding for social policies. Particularly strong growth in education spending is planned for 2016 and 2017 in the Dominican Republic, in line with the National Education Reform Pact (2014-2030), and in particular its article 8.1 on minimum funding for pre-university education, set at 4% of GDP. Meanwhile, the 2017 budgets for El Salvador and Nicaragua show decreases in total and social spending.

---

[14]    See the text of the amendment at [online] https://www.planalto.gov.br/ccivil_03/constituicao/Emendas/Emc/emc95.htm.

# C.  Conclusions

The 2030 Agenda for Sustainable Development represents an ambitious attempt by countries to establish a broad global consensus for simultaneous progress with the social, economic and environmental pillars of sustainable development. Any substantial advance will depend, alongside any other implementation resources mobilized, on each country's ability to raise sufficient funding not just for aspects linked directly to inclusion and social welfare, but for strengthened environmental protection and sustainability. Hence, implementation of the Sustainable Development Goals needs to be supported by efforts to measure social investment and analyse its composition and development over time, as well as the redistributive biases and efficiency characterizing it. The effort made in this chapter to expand and improve social spending information in collaboration with the region's countries is a major step in this direction. Better measurement can mean better analysis and decision-making by the countries.

Implementation of the SDGs needs to be supported by efforts to measure social investment and analyse its composition and development over time, as well as the redistributive biases and efficiency characterizing it.

Section A of this chapter showed that in 2015 the countries of the region allocated an average of 10.5% of GDP to funding for public social policies at the central government level and 14.5% at the public sector level, these being in both cases the highest levels of social spending in the region since the change in 2009 in response to the subprime mortgage crisis of 2008. The countries spending most on social functions were Argentina, Brazil, Colombia and Costa Rica, at more than 20% of GDP. Guatemala and Haiti spent the least, at less than 8% of GDP. Taking the social functions separately, Argentina and Brazil spent most on social protection in 2015 (over 13% of GDP), Costa Rica and the Plurinational State of Bolivia on education (over 7% of GDP) and Argentina and Costa Rica again on health care (over 6% of GDP).

Section B closely examined the information in the countries' public budgets from a functional perspective, with the indications being that spending on social functions will be lower in 2017, especially in South American countries, something that could have a direct impact on the population in the event of an economic slowdown.

Against this backdrop, ECLAC is calling once again for social policy financing to be safeguarded and protected with a view to ensuring the sustainability of the progress made, dealing with ongoing challenges and advancing towards the Goals agreed in the 2030 Agenda for Sustainable Development.

# Bibliography

Arenas de Mesa, A. (2016), *Sostenibilidad fiscal y reformas tributarias en América Latina* (LC/G.2688-P), Santiago, Economic Commission for Latin America and the Caribbean (ECLAC).

Bird, R. M. (1971), "Wagner's Law of Expanding State Activity", *Public Finance*, vol. 26, No. 1.

Bry, G. and C. Boschan (1971), *Cyclical Analysis of Time Series: Selected Procedures and Computer Programmes*, New York, National Bureau of Economic Research (NBER).

Carvallo, P., E. Perez and D.Titelman (2013), "Weak expansions. A distinctive feature of the business cycle in Latin America and the Caribbean", *Financiamiento para el Desarrollo series*, No. 243 (LC/L.3656), Santiago, Economic Commission for Latin America and the Caribbean (ECLAC).

Cecchini, S. and B. Atuesta (2017), "Programas de transferencias condicionadas en América Latina y el Caribe: tendencias de cobertura e inversión", unpublished.

Cetrángolo, O. and J. Curcio (2017), "Financiamiento y gasto educativo en América Latina y el Caribe con especial referencia a su impacto sobre la equidad", unpublished.

Collinao, M.P. and others (2016), "Estimación de las erogaciones sociales a partir del sistema de cuentas nacionales: una propuesta para las funciones de educación, salud y protección social", *Manuales de la CEPAL*, No. 5 (LC/L.4273), Santiago, Economic Commission for Latin America and the Caribbean (ECLAC).

Daude, Ch., A. Melguizo and A. Neut (2011), "Fiscal policy in Latin America: countercyclical and sustainable?", *Economics: The Open Access, Open-Assessment E-Journal*, vol. 5.

Dmytraczenko, T. and G. Almeida (2015), *Towards Universal Health Coverage and Equity in Latin America and the Caribbean: Evidence from Selected Countries. Directions in Development-Human Development*, Washington, D.C., World Bank.

Dubois, É. and E. Michaux (2016), "Grocer: an econometric toolbox for Scilab" [online] http://dubois.ensae.net/grocer.html.

ECLAC (Economic Commission for Latin America and the Caribbean) (2016a), *Social Panorama of Latin America, 2015* (LC/G.2691-P), Santiago.

____(2016b), *Preliminary Overview of the Economies of Latin America and the Caribbean* (LC/G.2698-P), Santiago.

____(2016c), *The social inequality matrix in Latin America* (LC/G.2690(MDS.1/2), Santiago.

ECLAC/OEI (Economic Commission for Latin America and the Caribbean/Organization of Ibero-American States for Education, Science and Culture) (2014), *Cultura y desarrollo económico en Iberoamérica*, Madrid.

Gavin, M. and R. Perotti (1997), "Fiscal policy in Latin America", *NBER Macroeconomics Annual*, vol. 12.

Girouard, N. and C. André (2005), "Measuring cyclically adjusted budget balances for OECD countries", *OECD Economics Department Working Papers*, No. 434.

Gottret, P. and G. Schieber (2006), *Health Financing Revisited: a Practitioner's Guide*, World Bank.

IMF (International Monetary Fund) (2014), *Government Finance Statistics Manual 2014* [online] https://www.imf.org/external/Pubs/FT/GFS/Manual/2014/gfsfinal.pdf.

____(2001), *Government Finance Statistics Manual 2001* [online] https://www.imf.org/external/pubs/ft/gfs/manual/pdf/all.pdf.

Klemm, A. (2014), "Fiscal policy in Latin America over the cycle", *Working Paper*, No. 14/59, Washington, D.C., International Monetary Fund (IMF).

Marcel, M., M. Guzmán and M. Sanginés (2014), *Presupuestos para el desarrollo en América Latina*, Washington, D.C., Inter-American Development Bank (IDB).

Martner, R. (2007), "La política fiscal en tiempos de bonanza", *Gestión Pública series*, No. 66, (LC/L.2736-P), Santiago, Economic Commission for Latin America and the Caribbean (ECLAC).

___(2000), "Automatic fiscal stabilizers", *CEPAL Review*, No. 70 (LC/G.2095-P), Santiago, Economic Commission for Latin America and the Caribbean (ECLAC).

Martner, R., A. Podestá and I. González (2014), "Políticas fiscales para el crecimiento y la igualdad", *Inestabilidad y desigualdad: la vulnerabilidad del crecimiento en América Latina*, J.A. Fuentes, Santiago, Economic Commission for Latin America and the Caribbean (ECLAC).

Ministry of Treasury and Public Finances (2017), "Mensaje presidencial del Proyecto de Presupuesto 2017 de la República Argentina", Buenos Aires [online] http://www.mecon.gov.ar/onp/html/presutexto/proy2017/mensaje/mensaje2017.pdf.

Musgrave, R. (1959), *The Theory of Public Finance*, New York, McGraw Hill.

Price, R., T. Dang and J. Botev (2015), "Adjusting fiscal balances for the business cycle: New tax and expenditure elasticity estimates for OECD countries", *OECD Economics Department Working Papers*, No. 1275, Paris, OECD Publishing.

Rodríguez, D., F. Venegas and V. Lima (2013), "La ley de Wagner versus la hipótesis keynesiana: el caso de México, 1950-2009", *Investigación Económica*, vol. LXXII, No. 283, January-March.

Tromben, V. (2016), "Gasto social y ciclo económico en América Latina y el Caribe", *Políticas Sociales series*, No. 219 (LC/L.4245), Santiago, Economic Commission for Latin America and the Caribbean (ECLAC).

United Nations (2001), "Classifications of expenditure according to purpose", *Statistical Papers Series M*, No. 84 (ST/ESA/STAT/SER.M/84), New York.

Wagner, A. (1893), *Grundlegung der politischen Ökonomie*, Leipzig.

# Annex II.A1

Table II.A.1
Latin America (15 countries : budget classification (draft budget approval phase) for analysing spending by function

| Country | Classification | Document | Source (government body) |
|---|---|---|---|
| Argentina | Purpose-function | Budget Act | Ministry of Treasury and Public Finances, National Budget Office |
| Brazil | Functional | Act | Federal Senate, Federal Public Budget |
| Colombia | Functional (Classification of the Functions of Government (COFOG)) | Act | Ministry of Finance, annex to President's message on the Budget Bill |
| Costa Rica | Functional (Classification of the Functions of Government (COFOG)) | Approved budget | Ministry of Finance, 2017 Budget Act |
| Dominican Republic | Functional (Classification of the Functions of Government (COFOG)) | Approved budget | Budget Department of the Ministry of Finance, Budget Act |
| El Salvador | Area-institution | Voted | Ministry of Finance, Budget Bill message |
| Guatemala | Purpose (Classification of the Functions of Government (COFOG)) | Approved | Ministry of Public Finances, budget |
| Honduras | Purpose-function | Approved by Congress | Finance Secretariat, Budget Department |
| Mexico | Functions | Expenditure budget | Secretariat of Finance and Public Credit, federal expenditure budget |
| Nicaragua | Functional | Updated budget | Ministry of Finance and Public Credit, report on the execution of the general budget |
| Panama | Institutional | Budget | Ministry of Economy and Finance, online official gazette 2015-2016 |
| Paraguay | Functional | Budget Act | Ministry of Finance, Budget Department |
| Peru | Functional | Budgetary approval | Ministry of Economy and Finance, public sector budget |
| Trinidad and Tobago | Functional (Classification of the Functions of Government (COFOG)) | Reviewed | Ministry of Finance, *Draft Estimates of Expenditure for the Financial Year 2017* |
| Uruguay | Programme area | Budget allocation | National Accounting Office, accountability report and budget execution report |

**Source**: Economic Commission for Latin America and the Caribbean (ECLAC), on the basis of official information from the respective countries.

Table II.A.2

Latin America and the Caribbean (22 countries): social public spending as a proportion of GDP in local currency at current prices, 2000-2015
*(Percentages of GDP)*

| Country | Coverage | Period | | | | | | | | | | | | | | | |
|---|---|---|---|---|---|---|---|---|---|---|---|---|---|---|---|---|---|
| | | 2000 | 2001 | 2002 | 2003 | 2004 | 2005 | 2006 | 2007 | 2008 | 2009 | 2010 | 2011 | 2012 | 2013 | 2014 | 2015 |
| Argentina | CG | 9.5 | 9.4 | 8.1 | 7.8 | 7.9 | 8.2 | 8.6 | 9.3 | 9.4 | 11.6 | 11.4 | 11.6 | 12.5 | 13.4 | 13.4 | 14.7 |
| | NFPS | 20.1 | 20.7 | 18.3 | 17.9 | 17.7 | 14.3 | 19.2 | 20.9 | 21.8 | 26.0 | 24.8 | 25.6 | 27.1 | 28.3 | 28.1 | 30.8 |
| Bolivia (Plurinational State of) | CG | 11.5 | 12.4 | 13.3 | 13.3 | 12.9 | 12.4 | 11.8 | 11.7 | 11.5 | 13.0 | 12.3 | 11.2 | 11.0 | 10.9 | 11.6 | 12.6 |
| | GG | 15.7 | 17.1 | 17.1 | 17.5 | 16.9 | 17.5 | 16.5 | 17.1 | 18.0 | | 18.1 | 17.5 | 18.3 | 20.1 | 22.2 | |
| Brazil | CG | | 11.3 | 11.2 | 11.5 | 8.8 | 11.5 | 11.8 | 11.8 | 11.4 | 12.5 | 12.0 | 12.0 | 11.7 | 11.9 | 12.2 | 12.8 |
| | GG | 20.0 | 20.3 | 20.1 | 21.3 | 21.2 | 21.2 | 22.2 | 22.7 | 23.0 | 24.5 | 23.7 | 23.2 | 23.6 | 21.6 | 24.2 | 25.6 |
| Chile | CG | 14.2 | 14.4 | 14.4 | 13.7 | 12.8 | 12.3 | 11.5 | 11.8 | 13.6 | 15.7 | 14.9 | 14.3 | 14.7 | 14.7 | 15.1 | 16.0 |
| Colombia | CG | 4.6 | 6.0 | 6.4 | 6.5 | 7.0 | 7.6 | 7.6 | 7.7 | 8.0 | 8.7 | 8.6 | 8.2 | 8.7 | 8.8 | 9.6 | 9.2 |
| | GG | | | | | | | | | | 18.6 | 19.0 | 18.8 | 19.3 | 19.7 | 20.1 | 20.7 |
| Costa Rica | CG | 6.0 | 6.0 | 8.2 | 8.4 | 8.1 | 7.8 | 7.6 | 7.5 | 8.2 | 9.7 | 10.4 | 10.0 | 10.6 | 10.8 | 10.8 | 11.1 |
| | PS | 16.9 | 18.2 | 18.3 | 18.1 | 17.4 | 16.8 | 16.5 | 17.0 | 18.8 | 21.8 | 22.0 | 21.9 | 22.4 | 23.1 | 23.0 | 23.7 |
| Cuba | CG | | | | | | 16.1 | 12.0 | 17.4 | 20.9 | 20.7 | 18.4 | 19.5 | | | | |
| | GG | 23.1 | 24.3 | 25.9 | 27.2 | 27.6 | 34.3 | 32.0 | 36.9 | 40.7 | 40.7 | 38.2 | 35.8 | | | | |
| Dominican Republic | CG | 5.3 | 6.3 | 6.1 | 5.5 | 5.4 | 5.8 | 6.4 | 6.6 | 7.3 | 6.7 | 6.3 | 6.2 | 7.3 | 8.2 | 7.8 | 8.2 |
| Ecuador[a] | CG | 2.5 | 3.9 | 3.8 | 3.6 | 3.8 | 4.2 | 4.2 | 5.3 | 6.6 | 8.1 | 8.2 | 8.2 | 8.3 | 8.5 | 8.8 | 8.6 |
| El Salvador | CG | | | 6.6 | 7.3 | 7.3 | 7.8 | 7.6 | 5.5 | 5.9 | 8.0 | 6.9 | 7.0 | 7.3 | 7.9 | 7.5 | 7.7 |
| | NFPS | | | 8.9 | 8.2 | 7.5 | 8.0 | 7.5 | 7.6 | 11.2 | 12.7 | 12.5 | 12.7 | 13.1 | 13.6 | 12.8 | 13.2 |
| Guatemala | CG | 6.5 | 7.1 | 7.0 | 7.6 | 7.0 | 7.6 | 7.8 | 7.2 | 7.0 | 8.1 | 8.0 | 7.5 | 7.6 | 7.6 | 7.5 | 7.1 |
| Haiti | CG | | | | | | | | | | | | | 4.6 | 5.1 | 5.4 | 5.5 |
| Honduras | CG | 7.8 | 8.9 | 8.8 | 10.3 | 10.0 | 9.8 | 9.7 | 10.4 | 10.7 | 11.2 | 11.6 | 10.7 | 10.8 | 10.9 | 9.7 | 8.9 |
| Jamaica | CG | 7.0 | 8.1 | 9.4 | 8.9 | 8.8 | 8.7 | 9.6 | 10.5 | 11.0 | 11.3 | 10.8 | 10.8 | 10.7 | 10.5 | 10.1 | |
| Mexico | CG | 7.0 | 7.4 | 7.7 | 7.4 | 8.1 | 8.2 | 8.5 | 9.4 | 12.0 | 10.0 | 10.4 | 10.3 | 10.0 | 10.7 | 10.8 | 11.6 |
| | NFPS | 8.6 | 9.1 | 9.3 | 9.1 | 9.0 | 9.3 | 9.5 | 10.0 | 10.9 | 11.2 | 11.2 | 11.4 | 11.4 | 11.8 | 11.9 | 12.4 |
| Nicaragua | CG | 6.6 | 5.9 | 6.6 | 7.8 | 8.0 | 8.6 | 8.7 | 8.9 | 9.2 | 9.6 | 9.3 | 9.1 | 9.6 | 9.8 | 10.3 | 10.6 |
| Panama | CG | 8.5 | 9.3 | 8.6 | 7.4 | 7.5 | 7.2 | 8.6 | 8.7 | 8.8 | 9.7 | 10.2 | 9.3 | 9.0 | 8.7 | 8.4 | |
| Paraguay | CG | | | | | | | | 8.1 | 7.7 | 9.9 | 8.7 | 9.8 | 11.7 | 11.2 | 11.2 | 12.0 |
| Peru | CG | | | | | | 6.0 | 5.5 | 5.4 | 5.0 | 5.4 | 5.1 | 4.9 | 4.8 | 5.4 | 6.0 | 6.3 |
| | GG | 8.2 | 9.0 | 9.3 | 10.3 | 9.2 | 9.1 | 8.3 | 9.1 | 9.4 | 10.2 | 9.6 | 9.2 | 9.5 | 10.4 | 11.2 | 11.1 |
| | PS | 10.7 | 10.9 | 11.6 | 12.3 | 12.1 | 12.2 | 11.3 | 11.2 | 11.2 | 12.7 | 11.7 | 11.0 | 11.2 | 11.9 | 13.2 | 13.0 |
| Trinidad and Tobago | CG | | | | | | | | | 9.5 | 14.3 | 12.9 | 13.1 | 13.0 | 15.7 | 16.7 | 16.2 |
| Uruguay[b] | CG | | | | | | | | | | | | 13.5 | 13.9 | 14.2 | 14.3 | 14.9 |
| Venezuela (Bolivarian Republic of) | CG | 10.1 | 10.2 | 10.1 | 10.6 | 10.9 | 10.7 | 12.3 | 10.9 | 10.5 | 11.9 | | | | | | |
| Latin America and the Caribbean (weighted average) | CG | 7.9 | 9.7 | 9.7 | 9.6 | 8.6 | 9.9 | 10.1 | 10.4 | 10.9 | 11.5 | 11.2 | 11.1 | 11.0 | 11.3 | 11.6 | 12.1 |
| Latin America and the Caribbean (simple average) | CG | 7.7 | 8.4 | 8.5 | 8.6 | 8.4 | 8.9 | 8.9 | 9.2 | 9.7 | 10.8 | 10.3 | 10.4 | 9.9 | 10.2 | 10.4 | 10.8 |
| Latin America and the Caribbean (weighted average) | PS | 15.4 | 15.8 | 15.5 | 16.1 | 15.9 | 16.2 | 16.7 | 17.2 | 17.9 | 19.3 | 19.3 | 18.9 | 19.0 | 18.4 | 19.6 | 20.7 |
| Latin America and the Caribbean (simple average) | PS | 11.5 | 12.2 | 12.0 | 12.2 | 12.0 | 12.5 | 12.6 | 12.9 | 13.5 | 15.0 | 14.9 | 14.5 | 13.4 | 13.8 | 14.0 | 14.6 |

**Source:** Economic Commission for Latin America and the Caribbean (ECLAC), on the basis of official information from the countries. For further information see Database on Social Investment in Latin America and the Caribbean [online] http://observatoriosocial.cepal.org/inversion/en.

**Note:** Coverage corresponds to: CG: central government; GG: general government; NFPS: non-financial public sector; PS: public sector.

[a] The data refer to the institutional coverage of the general State budget, which includes the central administration and decentralized and autonomous entities. It does not include information from the Ecuadorian Social Security Institute (IESS).

[b] The information comes from the Office of the Accountant-General and includes only institutional coverage of the central government. It does not include information from quasi-public pension funds, the social protection agency or the State-owned water utilities company, Obras Sanitarias del Estado (OSE). This information does not coincide with the historical series prepared jointly by the Ministry of Social Development and the Ministry of Economic Affairs and Finance.

Table II.A.3
Latin America and the Caribbean (22 countries): social public spending per capita in dollars at constant prices, 2000-2015
*(Dollars per capita)*

| Country | Coverage | Period | | | | | | | | | | | | | | | |
|---|---|---|---|---|---|---|---|---|---|---|---|---|---|---|---|---|---|
| | | 2000 | 2001 | 2002 | 2003 | 2004 | 2005 | 2006 | 2007 | 2008 | 2009 | 2010 | 2011 | 2012 | 2013 | 2014 | 2015 |
| Argentina | CG | 864 | 806 | 756 | 780 | 831 | 852 | 901 | 988 | 992 | 1 095 | 1 179 | 1 203 | 1 242 | 1 375 | 1 390 | 1 392 |
| | NFPS | 1 831 | 1 779 | 1 713 | 1 795 | 1 854 | 1 488 | 2 011 | 2 234 | 2 299 | 2 465 | 2 575 | 2 659 | 2 702 | 2 907 | 2 924 | 2 921 |
| Bolivia (Plurinational State of) | CG | 185 | 186 | 200 | 196 | 195 | 195 | 210 | 215 | 230 | 238 | 245 | 235 | 245 | 252 | 265 | 261 |
| | GG | 253 | 257 | 257 | 259 | 256 | 274 | 293 | 316 | 359 | | 359 | 367 | 408 | 466 | 510 | |
| Brazil | CG | | 1 052 | 1 045 | 1 113 | 900 | 1 162 | 1 211 | 1 253 | 1 223 | 1 312 | 1 342 | 1 373 | 1 371 | 1 368 | 1 374 | 1 361 |
| | GG | 1 896 | 1 892 | 1 867 | 2 065 | 2 171 | 2 144 | 2 274 | 2 404 | 2 476 | 2 571 | 2 642 | 2 659 | 2 760 | 2 494 | 2 718 | 2 728 |
| Chile | CG | 1 359 | 1 385 | 1 383 | 1 382 | 1 428 | 1 475 | 1 528 | 1 608 | 1 683 | 1 876 | 1 895 | 1 878 | 1 974 | 1 959 | 2 021 | 2 180 |
| Colombia | CG | 222 | 288 | 312 | 325 | 365 | 411 | 439 | 466 | 497 | 525 | 537 | 555 | 596 | 615 | 685 | 660 |
| | GG | | | | | | | | | | 1 130 | 1 189 | 1 270 | 1 323 | 1 373 | 1 431 | 1 486 |
| Costa Rica | CG | 577 | 542 | 716 | 738 | 728 | 710 | 714 | 729 | 754 | 805 | 848 | 811 | 868 | 871 | 889 | 923 |
| | PS | 1 615 | 1 642 | 1 604 | 1 598 | 1 571 | 1 535 | 1 556 | 1 641 | 1 736 | 1 812 | 1 801 | 1 767 | 1 829 | 1 867 | 1 895 | 1 963 |
| Cuba | CG | | | | | | 744 | 627 | 912 | 995 | 1 028 | 1 046 | 1 074 | | | | |
| | GG | 890 | 926 | 926 | 1 051 | 1 100 | 1 590 | 1 669 | 1 932 | 1 937 | 2 017 | 2 165 | 1 968 | | | | |
| Dominican Republic | CG | 201 | 234 | 235 | 223 | 257 | 280 | 315 | 341 | 355 | 318 | 343 | 371 | 416 | 493 | 448 | 450 |
| Ecuador[a] | CG | 128 | 185 | 177 | 149 | 163 | 185 | 192 | 242 | 302 | 355 | 383 | 426 | 450 | 472 | 504 | 480 |
| El Salvador | CG | | | 216 | 245 | 254 | 279 | 270 | 207 | 224 | 276 | 239 | 243 | 256 | 278 | 262 | 271 |
| | NFPS | | | 291 | 276 | 263 | 284 | 265 | 287 | 422 | 436 | 434 | 441 | 457 | 478 | 445 | 466 |
| Guatemala | CG | 174 | 180 | 181 | 188 | 174 | 193 | 207 | 197 | 199 | 227 | 232 | 226 | 233 | 237 | 237 | 228 |
| Haiti | CG | | | | | | | | | | | | | 32 | 37 | 40 | 43 |
| Honduras | CG | 149 | 161 | 156 | 186 | 185 | 189 | 197 | 211 | 214 | 216 | 228 | 227 | 229 | 227 | 209 | 204 |
| Jamaica | CG | 293 | 338 | 395 | 384 | 385 | 383 | 432 | 548 | 571 | 553 | 520 | 529 | 516 | 510 | 491 | |
| Mexico | CG | 708 | 683 | 686 | 636 | 749 | 771 | 825 | 916 | 1 150 | 877 | 936 | 945 | 918 | 951 | 966 | 1 026 |
| | NFPS | 870 | 843 | 828 | 786 | 836 | 872 | 922 | 979 | 1 048 | 977 | 1 015 | 1 045 | 1 040 | 1 045 | 1 064 | 1 097 |
| Nicaragua | CG | 86 | 71 | 76 | 90 | 94 | 104 | 104 | 120 | 137 | 143 | 142 | 148 | 159 | 166 | 185 | 203 |
| Panama | CG | 446 | 492 | 457 | 411 | 432 | 435 | 564 | 639 | 692 | 775 | 816 | 829 | 865 | 865 | 879 | |
| Paraguay | CG | | | | | | | | 235 | 235 | 275 | 281 | 325 | 386 | 389 | 400 | 422 |
| Peru | CG | | | | | | 215 | 221 | 232 | 225 | 242 | 255 | 264 | 264 | 299 | 323 | 339 |
| | GG | 266 | 282 | 301 | 332 | 311 | 327 | 331 | 389 | 421 | 460 | 484 | 495 | 522 | 574 | 601 | 599 |
| | PS | 348 | 342 | 375 | 394 | 408 | 438 | 453 | 481 | 502 | 569 | 589 | 595 | 618 | 660 | 704 | 699 |
| Trinidad and Tobago | CG | | | | | | | | | 1 623 | 2 319 | 2 157 | 2 175 | 2 163 | 2 667 | 2 786 | 2 567 |
| Uruguay[b] | CG | | | | | | | | | | | | 1 648 | 1 724 | 1 812 | 1 842 | 1 933 |
| Venezuela (Bolivarian Republic of) | CG | 478 | 444 | 457 | 508 | 628 | 726 | 850 | 795 | 826 | 809 | | | | | | |
| Latin America and the Caribbean (weighted average) | CG | 666 | 833 | 830 | 854 | 798 | 913 | 958 | 1 008 | 1 060 | 1 063 | 1 116 | 1 139 | 1 142 | 1 165 | 1 177 | 1 189 |
| Latin America and the Caribbean (simple average) | CG | 419 | 470 | 466 | 472 | 486 | 517 | 545 | 571 | 656 | 713 | 717 | 774 | 745 | 792 | 810 | 830 |
| Latin America and the Caribbean (weighted average) | PS | 1 388 | 1 374 | 1 352 | 1 448 | 1 524 | 1 537 | 1 624 | 1 723 | 1 791 | 1 820 | 1 937 | 1 956 | 2 003 | 1 908 | 2 012 | 2 034 |
| Latin America and the Caribbean (simple average) | PS | 689 | 698 | 669 | 691 | 718 | 767 | 814 | 845 | 927 | 1 044 | 1 040 | 1 078 | 1 014 | 1 056 | 1 087 | 1 181 |

**Source**: Economic Commission for Latin America and the Caribbean (ECLAC), on the basis of official information from the countries. For further information see Database on Social Investment in Latin America and the Caribbean [online] http://observatoriosocial.cepal.org/inversion/en.

**Note**: Coverage corresponds to: CG: central government; GG: general government; NFPS: non-financial public sector; PS: public sector.

[a] The data refer to the institutional coverage of the general State budget, which includes the central administration and decentralized and autonomous entities. It does not include information from the Ecuadorian Social Security Institute (IESS).

[b] The information comes from the Office of the Accountant-General and includes only institutional coverage of the central government. It does not include information from quasi-public pension funds, the social protection agency or the State-owned water utilities company, Obras Sanitarias del Estado (OSE). This information does not coincide with the historical series prepared jointly by the Ministry of Social Development and the Ministry of Economic Affairs and Finance.

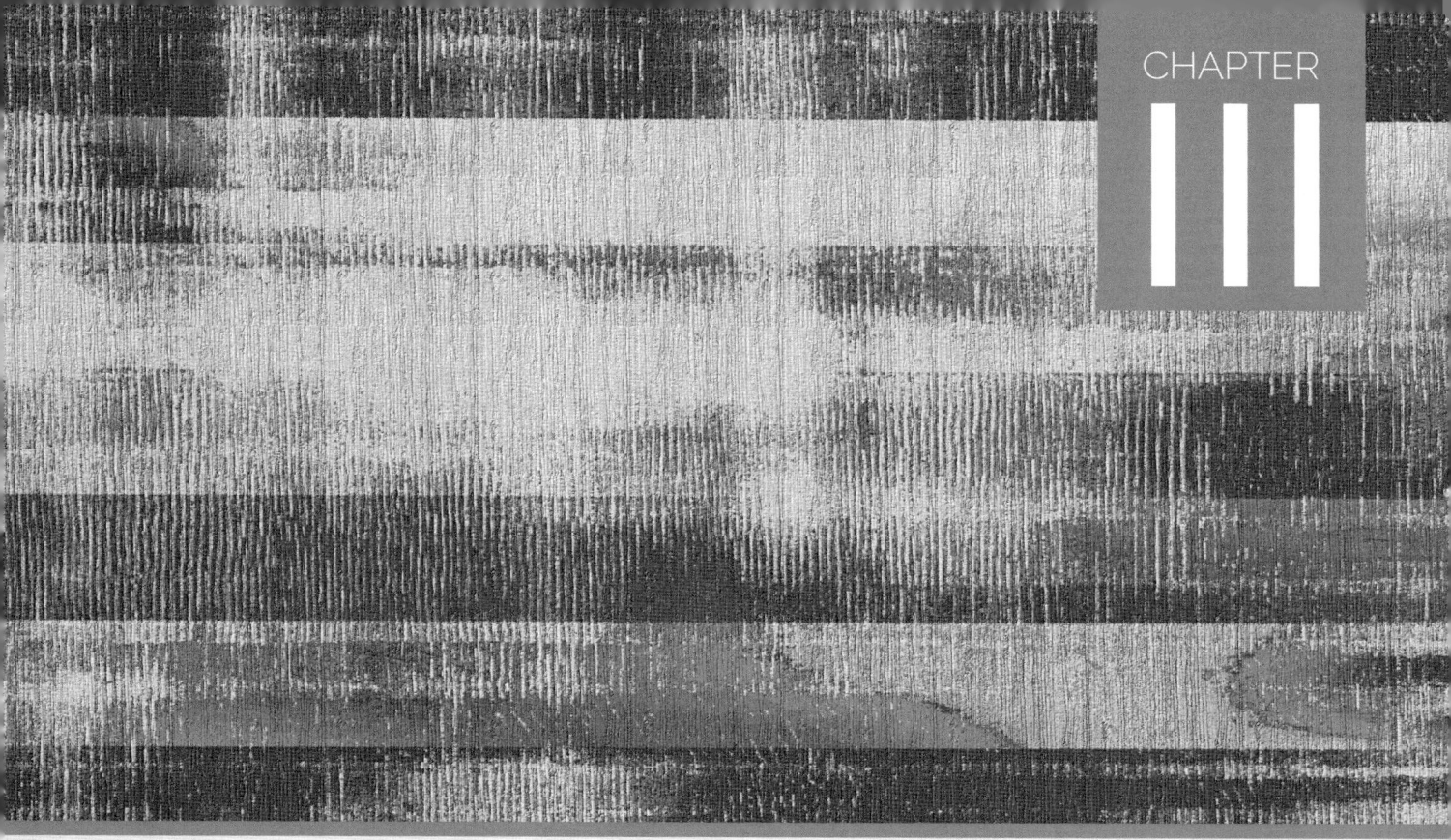

# The social inequality matrix: age as an axis of social inequalities

# Introduction

Social inequality is a phenomenon with multiple causes and an array of manifestations that go well beyond the matter of income and its distribution. ECLAC has recently stressed the importance of identifying and analysing the axes of social inequality that are present in areas of great importance for economic and social inclusion relating to the enjoyment of economic, social and cultural rights, such as access to education, health services, sanitation, housing, care, income, opportunities for decent work, social protection and political participation, and that translate into major disparities in well-being and agency in people's lives (ECLAC, 2016a). Bringing these inequalities to light makes it easier to identify the specific ways in which public policies can be used to overcome poverty reproduction mechanisms and bring equality closer.

In Latin America, socioeconomic status, gender, racial or ethnic origin, territory and age are mutually reinforcing axes of social inequality. Each has particular historical roots and manifests itself in different ways and through different mechanisms. The accumulation and interaction of inequalities associated with each of these axes create a complex structure of social relations in which numerous forms of discrimination manifest themselves as inequalities in autonomy, well-being and empowerment and as disparities in treatment and stark differences in the exercise of rights, the acquisition of capacities and the enjoyment of opportunities (ECLAC, 2016a). These mechanisms of discrimination are also embedded in the stereotypes that exist in different spheres of society and indeed permeate institutions, which reproduce them.

The purpose of this chapter is to revisit the concept of the social inequality matrix as presented in *The social inequality matrix in Latin America* (ECLAC, 2016a) and to carry forward the analysis of age as one of its structuring axes. It will examine inter- and intragenerational inequalities at each stage (childhood and adolescence, youth, adulthood and old age) in dimensions related to education, work and social protection, three areas that are critical to inclusion in both its aspects, social and economic. The chapter is structured into four sections. Section A offers a conceptual reflection on the topic. Section B presents examples of gaps in key development indicators at each stage of the life cycle and identifies links which are critical from the point of view of intragenerational gaps and in which the stage in the life cycle interacts with other axes of inequality, as well as intergenerational gaps. Section C analyses the specific situation of indigenous peoples over the life cycle, and section D provides an overview of the social institutions devoted to particular population segments at the main stages of the life cycle.

# A.  Age as a structuring axis of the social inequality matrix

Age is an axis that determines the distribution of well-being and power within the social structure and one of the foundations of social organization and its allocation of responsibilities and roles. The life cycle perspective is a theoretical approach for studying the different stages people progressively pass through over the course of their lives owing to the interaction of biological, relational and social factors (Carr, 2009). This perspective facilitates an analysis that not only incorporates age and its interaction with other axes of inequality but that can help identify the concatenation of inequalities at each stage of people's life histories and the critical circumstances that contribute to the reproduction of social inequality at these different stages.

Age is an underlying determinant of the social organization of institutions such as the family and the structures of education and work. It is an axis that determines the distribution of well-being and power within the social structure and one of the foundations of social organization and its allocation of responsibilities and roles (ECLAC, 2016a). Many laws and policies define rights on the basis of age, both explicitly through structured rules and via implicit judgments about the nature of different periods of life. Similarly, social institutions like school play an important role in structuring time, the sequence of events and the transitions individuals experience over the course of their lives. Individually, people organize their lives and expectations into age-determined times or phases. Thus, age moulds the interactions of daily life through the expectations of the individuals involved (Settersten Jr., 2003). In our society, the normative understanding of age can operate as a major criterion of discrimination, since there are stereotypes and prejudices based on age that manifest themselves in spheres such as health and work. Age tends to be one of the determinants for full enjoyment of civil and political rights, an example being the requirement for voters and candidates for office to have reached a given age to participate in elections. In addition to taking age as an explanatory variable for inequality, the life cycle perspective identifies particular stages characterized by specific opportunities, challenges and risks.

The life cycle perspective is a theoretical approach for studying the different stages people progressively pass through over the course of their lives, from birth to death, owing to the interaction of biological, relational and social factors (Carr, 2009). This perspective facilitates an analysis that not only incorporates age and its interaction with other axes of inequality but that can help identify the concatenation of inequalities at each stage of people's life histories and the critical circumstances that contribute to the reproduction of social inequality at these different stages. Four basic stages in the life cycle have traditionally been distinguished: childhood and adolescence, youth, adulthood and old age (Cecchini and others, 2015).[1] Lastly, it needs to be emphasized that there are very important internal divisions within these stages that differ greatly from one another: early childhood, puberty, adolescence and young adulthood are distinct phases at the earlier stages, just as there are large differences within the older adult population. The complexity of designing policies from a life cycle perspective means that all these considerations have to be taken seriously.

---

[1]    There are no standardized age definitions for these categories, and they sometimes overlap. For example, although the Convention on the Rights of the Child (United Nations, 1989) defines childhood as lasting until the age of 17 inclusive, youth is often defined as starting at 15. Besides the difficulty of delimiting age bands conceptually, their meaning, being a social construct, varies by context. In recent times there has also been a tendency towards postponement or extension of the stages, youth for example, beyond the age ranges traditionally considered specific to them.

The relationship between inequality and the life cycle requires three different types of stratification to be distinguished: (i) between the different stages of the life cycle, (ii) within the stages of the life cycle and (iii) at the different stages of the life cycle in different socio-historical contexts. Stratification between the different stages of the life cycle has to do with the way institutions and systems that distribute resources such as the State, market and family generate processes of social differentiation between population groups by virtue of the stage of life they are in. This age stratification principle is a major underpinning of social differentiation and inequality, since political and economic institutions may allocate resources asymmetrically to the different age groups in society. In turn, the different age groups also differ in their weight and bargaining power in society, so that decisions about policy and resource allocation priorities may be said to be taken in a complex age-based political economy. The advantages or disadvantages associated with phases in the life cycle are manifested in inequality divides between age groups, termed "intergenerational divides" in this chapter.[2]

Besides inequalities between people at different stages of the life cycle at any given time, there are also large gaps between people in the same stage of the life cycle, particularly in relation to the axes already identified (socioeconomic status, gender, ethnic and racial origin and territory). These intragenerational disparities have consequences subsequently. The notion of stratification within the different stages of the life cycle relates to the longitudinal dimension of inequality and to the process of differentiation or heterogeneity that unfolds during an individual's life cycle as a result of socially structured pathways of inequality (O'Rand, 1995). An important part of this approach is the way inequality is conceived of as the outcome of processes that take place over time, being the cumulative result of decisions, needs, advantages, events and experiences interacting with institutional arrangements and the social and economic context (Gibbs and Eaton, 2014).

The focus on the accumulation of advantages and disadvantages over the life cycle entails a perspective according to which inequalities at the outset tend to be amplified over time because of the early structure of opportunities and the individual behaviour determined by this structure of opportunities (Dewilde, 2003; O'Rand, 1996). This implies that initial inequalities, combined with unequal structures of opportunity and the historical and social background, affect the potential for people to acquire capabilities and accumulate resources over the life cycle. Another implication is that social differentiation is an increasing function of age, since this reflects the cumulative experience of a cohort's members over time, structuring different life paths (O'Rand, 1995). Thus, a number of empirical studies have shown that income inequalities (Deaton and Paxson, 1998) and health inequalities (Halliday, 2009; Jones, Mitchel and Goza, 2014) increase with age, and that inequalities in income and wealth largely stem from differences in starting conditions, and not just from crises experienced over the life cycle (Huggett, Yaron and Ventura, 2011).[3]

The relationship between inequality and the life cycle requires three different types of stratification to be distinguished: (i) between the different stages of the life cycle, (ii) within the stages of the life cycle and (iii) at the different stages of the life cycle in different socio-historical contexts. Stratification between the different stages of the life cycle has to do with the way institutions and systems that distribute resources such as the State, market and family generate processes of social differentiation between population groups by virtue of the stage of life they are in.

---

[2]  The intergenerational dimension of inequality may be synchronic or diachronic. Synchronicity refers to disparities between people at different stages of the life cycle at a single point in time (an example might be current levels of unemployment among young people and adults). Diachronic intergenerational inequality, meanwhile, means disparities between people at different stages of the life cycle (for example, differing levels of unemployment among young people and adults) at two different points in time. This chapter focuses especially on synchronic intergenerational divides.

[3]  Although the latter aspects (inter- and intragenerational inequalities) are stressed in what follows, the life cycle perspective also exposes inequalities between stages of the life cycle in different socio-historical contexts, e.g., between the experience of being an adolescent now and five decades ago. This approach stresses the different levels of well-being and development opportunities available to people in different socio-historical contexts and periods (Erikson and Goldberg, 2002; OECD, 2010)".

# B.   Inter- and intragenerational divides

Each stage of the life cycle presents specific opportunities, challenges and risks. This section will reflect on these different stages and look more closely at the multiple axes of social inequality, emphasizing the interaction between age, gender, territory and ethnic and racial origin, which are particularly important in three key dimensions of economic and social inclusion: education, paid work and social protection.

## 1.   Childhood and adolescence: setting out from dissimilar conditions

All children are born with the same inalienable rights, enshrined in the Convention on the Rights of the Child and other international, regional and national human rights instruments. Nonetheless, not all children are able to exercise these rights, since their enjoyment in practice is heavily dependent on their place of birth, the socioeconomic situation of their families, their sex, their ethnic and racial background and their disability status, among other factors. Consequently, childhood, and early childhood in particular, is a stage of particular importance for human development: it is the period when the foundations for future cognitive, affective and social development are laid (ECLAC, 2016a). First, this stage involves dimensions of risk in such sensitive areas for development as health and nutrition, early stimulation and education, and the opportunity to grow and develop in safe and supportive family and community settings. By the same token, infringements of rights at this stage can have deep and lasting effects on a person's well-being and future development possibilities. The particular vulnerability of children and adolescents is due to a number of factors, including their high levels of dependence on others (their families in particular) for their well-being and adequate physical, intellectual and emotional development. That vulnerability is also related to their invisibility as rights-holders and political actors.

In the region, the chances of surviving the first years of life and enjoying well-being, rights and an appropriate environment are not the same for a boy as for a girl; nor are they the same for a girl born in the Andean highlands as for one born on the coast, or for an indigenous or Afrodescendent girl as for a "white" one. Attached to each of these differentiations are a number of scenarios of possible discrimination and multidimensional exclusion that mark children's experiences, life paths and development opportunities.

The region has made substantial progress with respect to the welfare of its child population in the last few decades, improving key indicators such as child mortality and chronic malnutrition rates, particularly among the poor (UNICEF, 2016). Nonetheless, there are still large inequalities in dimensions that are crucial to early childhood development, marked in turn by the axes of inequality referred to earlier, as will now be seen.

### (a) Poverty in childhood and throughout the life cycle

Poverty in childhood is particularly critical because of children's greater level of dependence, lack of autonomy and vulnerability to the economic and social conditions of their environment and their families. Childhood poverty is expressed in deprivations in the material conditions and basic services children need for all-round development, in exclusion from the full exercise of rights, in the denial of dignity and in vulnerability to change and to economic crises (Saunders and others, 2015).

Children are overrepresented in the first income quintiles, in other words, in households with the lowest incomes, and are thus exposed to more deficiencies of various kinds, which can generate severe and lasting harm to their development, with consequences throughout the life cycle (see figure III.1). This age imbalance, which places children at a clear disadvantage, is due to a number of factors, including a stratified decline in fertility and changes in family structures, particularly an increase in single-parent households that are often supported financially by just one adult, making it more difficult to both generate income and provide care, i.e., to reconcile paid work and unpaid domestic work.

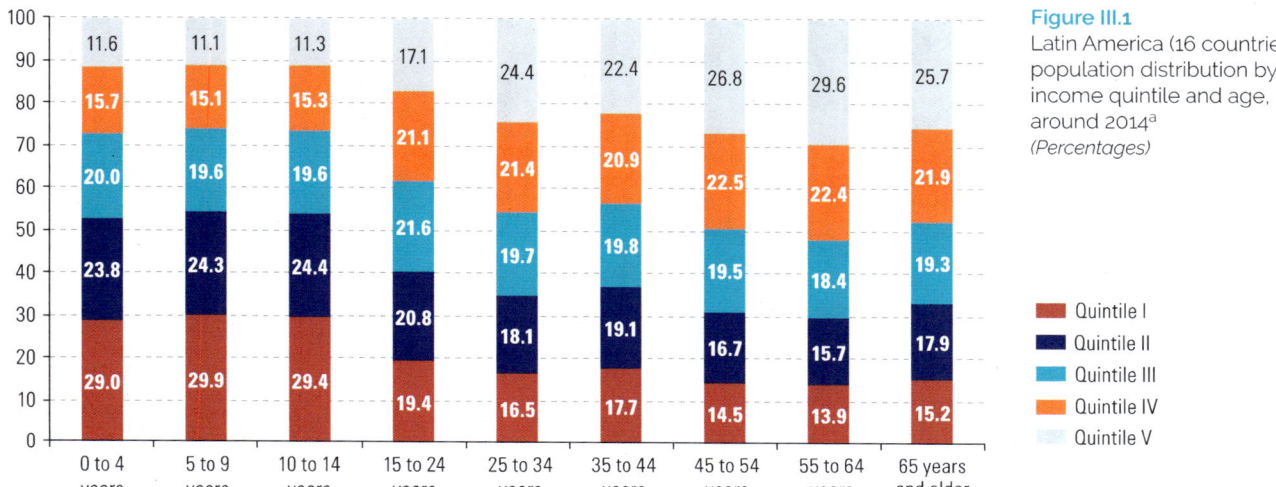

**Figure III.1**
Latin America (16 countries): population distribution by income quintile and age, around 2014[a]
*(Percentages)*

**Source:** Economic Commission for Latin America and the Caribbean (ECLAC), on the basis of special tabulations of household surveys conducted in the respective countries.
[a] Simple average of the countries.

Besides gaps in well-being between childhood and other stages of the life cycle, there are also large inequalities within the child population itself when other axes of social inequality such as gender, ethnic and racial origin and territory are considered.[4]

As for population distribution by income quintile and ethnicity, two region-wide trends stand out, despite the diversity of national situations (see figure III.2). First, if intragenerational disparities (within the child population) are considered, a significantly higher percentage of indigenous children live in quintile I households compared with non-indigenous children: roughly 50% of indigenous children aged 0 to 4 and 5 to 9 live in quintile I households, compared with less than one third of their non-indigenous peers. As regards intergenerational divides (between the child population and those at other stages of the life cycle), a gap of 10 percentage points or more is found between indigenous children in the lowest income quintile and indigenous youths and adults (those aged between 15 and 54) in the same quintile. Nonetheless, the ethnicity gap in income quintile I is also distinctive in youths and adults. For example, the percentage of indigenous people in quintile I is almost double that of non-indigenous people in the same quintile in the oldest age groups (45 to 54, 55 to 64 and 65 and older).

---

4       In this chapter, territory as an axis of social inequality is analysed by distinguishing between residence in rural areas and urban areas. Although the manifestation of social inequalities at the territorial level is much more complex, in light of limited data, the analysis is restricted to this aspect.

**Figure III.2**
Latin America (7 countries): income quintile I population, by age group and ethnicity, around 2014[a][b]
*(Percentages)*

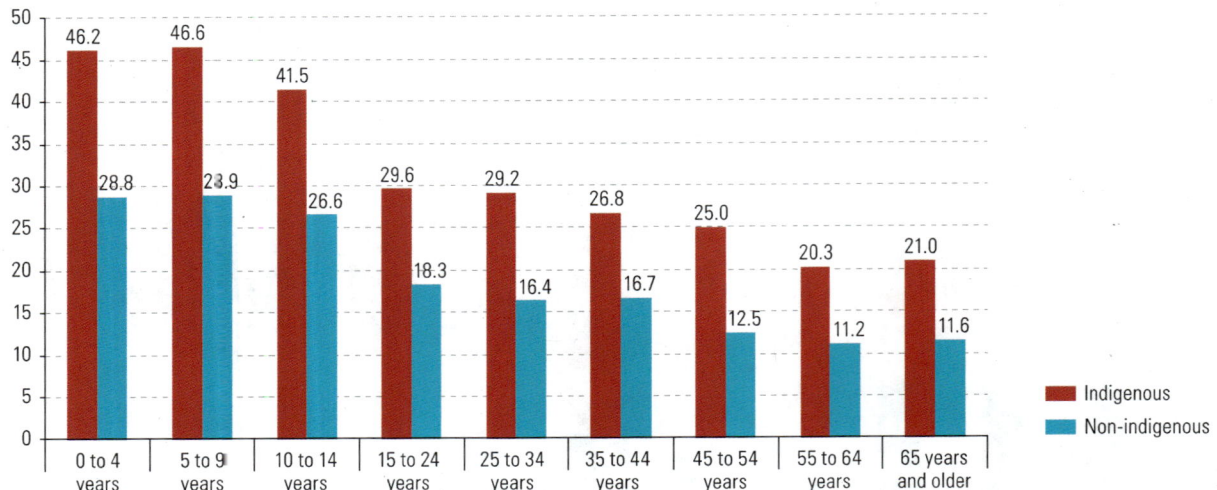

Source: Economic Commission for Latin America and the Caribbean (ECLAC), on the basis of special tabulations of household surveys conducted in the respective countries.
[a] Simple average based on information from Brazil (2014), Chile (2013), Ecuador (2014), Guatemala (2014), Mexico (2014), the Plurinational State of Bolivia (2013) and Uruguay (2014).
[b] The "non-indigenous" category does not include Afrodescendants.

## (b) Access to preschool education

As part of the 2030 Agenda for Sustainable Development, agreed on by the international community in 2015, target 4.2 states that all girls and boys should have access to quality early childhood development, care and pre-primary education so that they are ready for primary education. This aspiration is also expressed in the Educational Goals for 2021 adopted by the Ibero-American countries (SITEAL, 2009). From an intergenerational perspective, investing in capacity-building in the early years is vital to reducing inequalities over the life cycle.[5] Accordingly, expanding the coverage of high-quality preschool education should be a priority on the regional policy agenda for achieving greater equality. Preschool education consists of offerings at the initial stage of organized education designed to prepare children aged 3 and up for the school environment and to help them make the transition from home to school. This provision is of the greatest importance because it fulfils functions in children's education and rearing that may incorporate elements of care, security, health and nutrition, besides helping women cope with the burden of domestic and care work so that they may participate in the labour market (UNICEF, 2001). A comprehensive approach to needs at this stage makes it possible to combine and coordinate simultaneous actions in the areas of health, education, nutrition and decent treatment, with large positive effects in later phases, both individually and collectively.

There are social inequalities that develop at the beginning of life and cannot always be reversed later, the development of cognitive and non-cognitive skills being an example (Alarcón and others, 2015). In fact, the evidence shows large gaps in children's cognitive development at early ages by the socioeconomic level of their households. For example, a number of studies have revealed disparities in language skills as early as the age of 3 and shown that children living in poor households know fewer words

From an intergenerational perspective, investing in capacity-building in the early years is vital to reducing inequalities over the life cycle. Accordingly, expanding the coverage of high-quality preschool education should be a priority on the regional policy agenda for achieving greater equality.

---

[5]    It is worth emphasizing the importance of the first 1,000 days of life, the critical time between birth and the start of preschool education. Inequalities arise not just in access to preschool education, but earlier. Access to services and the enjoyment of rights in the first two or three years of life are critical.

than children from higher-income households, which places them at a disadvantage when they start school (Paxson and Schady, 2007; Schady, 2011). This tenuous start can adversely affect the educational paths of the poorest children and cause them to lose motivation, fall behind, repeat years and perhaps even drop out. Conversely, attendance at a preschool educational institution has been associated with a better subsequent school performance, irrespective of pupils' socioeconomic status (UNESCO, 2015; Bos, Ganimian and Vegas, 2014). Early intervention in terms of coverage and quality, which starts with preschool education, is vital to ensure that these gaps are not perpetuated and widened and that all children start their school trajectories on a sound footing and in less unequal conditions.

Notwithstanding, there is great heterogeneity in access to preschool education, with the differences in attendance between the various countries of the region being especially striking (see table III.1).[6] The attendance rate at this level of schooling for children aged 3 to 5 ranges from a low of 38% in Honduras to a high of 86% in Uruguay.[7] The rate is usually higher in urban areas than rural ones in each country, but the difference does not tend to be very large, a finding that is consistent with earlier analyses (Bos, Ganimian and Vegas, 2014). Table III.1 also illustrates the significant increase in preschool attendance when only the year prior to the start of primary school is considered (age 5 in most cases) and the positive effect on attendance at these ages when this is compulsory.

Table III.1
Latin America (8 countries): preschool education attendance among children aged 3 to 5 by place of residence, around 2014
(Percentages)

| Country | Children aged 3 to 5 | | | Total for year prior to start of primary cycle[a] |
|---|---|---|---|---|
| | National total | Urban areas | Rural areas | National total |
| Brazil | 79.1 | 81.0 | 69.2 | 90.2 |
| Chile | 76.6 | 78.3 | 64.3 | 95.8 |
| Colombia | 60.8 | 67.5 | 43.3 | 88.7 |
| Costa Rica | 42.6 | 46.6 | 34.6 | 81.7 |
| Honduras | 37.6 | 40.7 | 35.2 | 81.9 |
| Mexico | 71.8 | 72.0 | 71.5 | 96.1 |
| Peru | 64.2 | 66.3 | 58.3 | 79.4 |
| Uruguay | 86.0 | 86.6 | 72.7 | 98.8 |
| Latin America[b] | 64.8 | 67.4 | 56.1 | 89.1 |

**Source**: Economic Commission for Latin America and the Caribbean (ECLAC), on the basis of special tabulations of household surveys conducted in the respective countries.
[a] The age preceding the start of the primary cycle is 5 in all the countries considered.
[b] Simple average of the countries.

Access to preschool education still presents large shortfalls in the region, and progress needs to be made towards universalization of this educational level, as stated in target 4.2 of the Sustainable Development Goals. To achieve this and the Educational Goals for 2021, attendance will have to be expanded among the youngest children, who have the lowest levels of attendance and the largest gaps by area of residence (see figure III.3). Among three-year-olds, for example, the preschool attendance rate is below 25% in rural areas and 40% in urban areas. For five-year-olds, preschool attendance rates by area of residence converge at high levels.

---

[6]  Attendance at a preschool educational institution is compulsory in almost all the region's countries. The age at which compulsion begins varies from country to country, but is usually 5 (SITEAL, 2009).
[7]  Attendance is a proxy for preschool education coverage.

**Figure III.3**
Latin America (8 countries):
preschool education
attendance, by age ar d area
of residence, around 2014[a]
*(Percentages)*

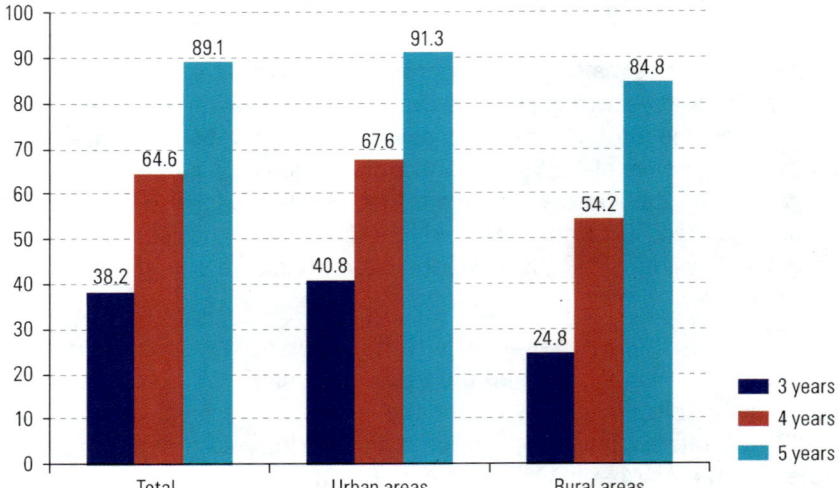

**Source**: Economic Commission for Latin America and the Caribbean (ECLAC), on the basis of special tabulations of household surveys conducted in the respective countries.

[a] Simple averages based on information from Brazil (2014), Chile (2013), Colombia (2014), Costa Rica (2014), Honduras (2013), Mexico (2014), Peru (2014) and Uruguay (2014).

Another major challenge concerns the quality of preschool education, on which its potential benefits largely depend. The entrenchment of social inequalities from early ages in Latin America is due not only to the inadequate (and often unaffordable) supply of preschool education, but also to large differences in the quality of the teaching available to different socioeconomic groups in the population. Preschool education access and quality are issues of equality for children in the present, and a failure to ensure them undermines equality in future between people from different strata and territories (Marco, 2014). This is vital for fulfilling Sustainable Development Goal 4 of ensuring inclusive, equitable and quality education for all and promoting lifelong learning, pursuant to the principle that no one should be left behind.[8]

Lastly, child labour is another factor for inequality in early life, being detrimental to well-being and rights (see box III.1).

In summary, the inequalities that manifest in early life need not condemn children to a lifetime of exclusion. They are avoidable if governments commit themselves to measures aimed at improving opportunities for all children, especially the most disadvantaged (UNICEF, 2016). For that, child well-being policies need to act on intertwined inequalities at this stage in the life cycle and comprehensive approaches need to be adopted that help limit the concatenation of deprivations at early ages. Early childhood development programmes are the foundation for successful social investments over the lifetime of an individual, especially for those experiencing poverty, discrimination and exclusion. Investing more in this area is one of the most effective ways of improving social mobility and reducing social inequalities (IDB, 2015).

---

[8]   Another challenge is cultural resistance to the institutionalization of care in early childhood, to the detriment of the traditional roles of women in this respect.

Box III.1
Child labour: a serious violation of children's and adolescents' rights

Child labour, which still persists in the region, not only prevents children from enjoying other rights (such as the rights to education and leisure) but is itself a serious violation of their rights (Ullmann and Milosavljevic, 2016). Recognizing the profound negative consequences of child labour, 27 countries in the region, alongside union and employers' organizations, have been conducting the Latin America and the Caribbean Free of Child Labour Regional Initiative, whose aim is to speed the pace of eradication of this serious problem in order to meet target 8.7 of the Sustainable Development Goals, the ending of child labour in all its forms.

The countries of Latin America and the Caribbean have been striving to eliminate child labour for over 20 years. Their efforts have included the ratification of international instruments (in particular the International Labour Organization (ILO) Minimum Age Convention, 1973 (No. 138) and Worst Forms of Child Labour Convention, 1999 (No. 182)), considerable national legislative progress, the development of a knowledge base on the subject and the pursuit of prevention and eradication policies and programmes. All this has led to a substantial reduction in child labour, leaving Latin America and the Caribbean well placed to become the first developing region free of child labour (ILO, 2016c). According to estimates by ILO (2013), the number of children and adolescents aged between 5 and 17 in the labour market dropped from 14.1 million in 2008 to 12.5 million in 2012, a reduction of 1.6 million people. This is still an alarming figure, though, and the rate of decline tailed off in the period, while there was a worrying increase in dangerous child working —a warning to the countries to redouble their eradication efforts (ILO, 2013).

As can be seen in the following table, Brazil, Mexico, Peru and Colombia are the countries with the largest numbers of children working in absolute terms. In relative terms, the countries with the greatest prevalence of child labour are Haiti (34%), the Plurinational State of Bolivia (26%), Paraguay (22%) and Peru (19%). The inequalities manifested in patterns of child labour include disparities by gender, racial and ethnic origin and place of residence.

Latin America and the Caribbean (18 countries): children and adolescents in work, latest year available
*(Numbers and percentages)*

| Country | Age range considered | Approximate population | Percentage | Year |
|---|---|---|---|---|
| Argentina (urban area) | 5 to 17 | 456 207 | 10.6 | 2004 |
| Belize | 5 to 17 | 3 528 | 3.2 | 2013 |
| Bolivia (Plurinational State of) | 5 to 17 | 800 000 | 26.4 | 2008 |
| Brazil | 5 to 17 | 2 827 959 | 6.7 | 2014 |
| Chile | 5 to 17 | 229 510 | 6.9 | 2013 |
| Colombia | 5 to 17 | 1 019 000 | 9.1 | 2015 |
| Costa Rica | 5 to 17 | 20 896 | 2.1 | 2016 |
| Dominican Republic | 5 to 17 | 338 000 | 14.0 | 2014 |
| Ecuador | 5 to 17 | 360 000 | 8.6 | 2012 |
| El Salvador | 5 to 17 | 144 168 | 8.5 | 2013 |
| Guatemala | 7 to 14 | 732 430 | 16.9 | 2014 |
| Haiti | 5 to 14 | 815 993 | 34.4 | 2012 |
| Honduras | 5 to 17 | 328 000 | 12.3 | 2013 |
| Mexico | 5 to 17 | 2 217 648 | 7.5 | 2015 |
| Panama | 5 to 17 | 23 855 | 2.5 | 2016 |
| Paraguay | 5 to 17 | 416 425 | 22.4 | 2011 |
| Peru | 5 to 17 | 1 672 900 | 19.0 | 2015 |
| Uruguay | 5 to 17 | 68 500 | 9.9 | 2010 |

**Source**: A. Espejo, "Propuesta de implementación de modelos predictores del trabajo infantil para la orientación de acciones de políticas preventivas a nivel subnacional", *Documento de Trabajo*, Santiago, Economic Commission for Latin America and the Caribbean (ECLAC), 2017, unpublished.

Child labour is sharply divided by sex: boys and male adolescents have higher rates than girls, and most of their work is done in production activities outside the home, especially agriculture. In El Salvador, for example, 76% of child labour is carried out by boys and male adolescents, particularly in agriculture, stockbreeding and forestry (ILO, 2013). Conversely,

Box III.1 (concluded)

girls are largely employed as paid domestic workers. In Brazil, for example, some 214,000 children and adolescents are engaged in domestic work, and 94.2% of these are female, a proportion that also holds among adults, marking a stark gender divide in this occupation.

Another salient feature of child labour in the region is its geographic variability and its concentration in rural areas, since many children are employed in agricultural activities. In Ecuador, for example, the findings of the 2013 Child Labour Survey show that 71% of children who work do so on the land, while 21% are employed in the service sector and 8% in industry.

The reports reviewed similarly reveal that a high percentage of child employment is informal, being concentrated particularly in unpaid family work. In Guatemala, for example, over half of all working children are in the informal sector and more than 95% are employed as unpaid family workers, according to the 2016 National Employment and Income Survey (ENEI). In many countries, furthermore, working children are completely unpaid, and those that do receive some wage earn far less than their country's legal minimum.

National reports also point out that child labour disproportionately affects indigenous and Afrodescendent populations. In the Plurinational State of Bolivia, almost half of all boys who work are indigenous and many of them carry out dangerous activities. Similarly in Brazil, roughly 60% of child labourers between the ages of 5 and 13 are Afrodescendants.

In sum, the pace of progress and indicators achieved thus far raise concerns about the ability to honour national and international commitments, particularly the 2030 Agenda for Sustainable Development. In order to meet the ambitious target of eliminating all forms of child labour by 2025, action is required on various fronts, including poverty reduction, improvement in education access, relevance and quality, creation of decent work opportunities for adult family members (men, women and young people of working age), promotion of gender and ethno-racial equality and strengthening of social protection policies, paying special attention to the populations that are most vulnerable to child labour, and taking territorial, gender and ethno-racial dimensions into consideration.

**Source:** A. Espejo, "Propuesta de implementación de modelos predictores del trabajo infantil para la orientación de acciones de políticas preventivas a nivel subnacional", *Documento de Trabajo*, Santiago, Economic Commission for Latin America and the Caribbean (ECLAC), 2017, unpublished; H. Ullmann and V. Milosavljevic, "Time use in adolescence", *Challenges*, No. 19, Santiago, Economic Commission for Latin America and the Caribbean (ECLAC)/United Nations Children's Fund (UNICEF), August 2016; International Labour Organization (ILO), *Cinco claves para acelerar la reducción del trabajo infantil en América Latina y el Caribe*, Lima, 2016, and *World Report on Child Labour: Economic vulnerability, social protection and the fight against child labour*, Geneva, 2013.

## 2. Youth: a crossroads at which exclusion pathways can be solidified or reversed

Youth is another critical stage during which social inequalities may either widen or reduce, particularly when it comes to ensuring a proper transition to working life so that a pathway towards greater well-being and lesser inequality is created from the outset (ECLAC, 2016a). During this stage, issues that will mark adulthood are defined: young people are expected to complete their studies, acquire working skills, start their working lives and, in many cases, start or consolidate a family of their own. In Latin America, these phases and transitions often do not follow a linear sequence, and during them inequality is reproduced and magnified.

### (a) The evolution of disparities in completion of secondary education by ethnicity and area of residence

Education is a social right and is vital to build skills and capabilities for the world of paid work and life in general. Thus, it acts as a lever for social and economic inclusion and for citizenship and participation in society.

Individuals' level of education is one of the most important determinants of their opportunities in terms of employment, income, health, housing and other individual and social benefits over their lifetimes (Espínola and Claro, 2010). Although almost all 11-year-olds are studying, high drop-out rates in secondary education are an ongoing challenge in Latin

America (Rico and Trucco, 2014). This indicates that prevailing conditions in the region still induce young people of both sexes to leave school before completing secondary education, something that is crucial to their prospects of a better position in the labour market later.[9]

As Rico and Trucco (2014) point out, the capabilities required for social inclusion in a complex globalized society like today's are greater than before and are associated not only with opportunities for integrating into the labour force but also with important development factors such as social mobility, poverty reduction, the construction of citizenship and social identity and the strengthening of social cohesion and integration. This is why secondary education is now vital for people's future.

In addition, completion of secondary education not only affects later stages in adolescents' life cycle but also plays a fundamental role as regards the transmission of poverty and inequality to future generations. The mother's education level, in particular, has been consistently associated with numerous child well-being outcomes and indicators, such as children's attendance at preschool educational institutions, the presence of malnutrition and levels of child mortality, among other health outcomes (IDB, 2015), as well as the incidence of poverty (ECLAC/UNICEF, 2010 and 2012). Consequently, helping young people to complete their secondary studies is a strategy for reversing the inequalities that build up over the life cycle and preventing their transmission to the new generations.

The percentage of young people (both male and female) completing secondary education has risen in most of the region's countries (see figure III.4). This growth has been particularly striking in percentage terms in rural areas of certain countries. In rural parts of the Plurinational State of Bolivia, for example, the percentage of men aged between 20 and 24 who had completed secondary education rose from 16.9% in 2002 to 58.1% in 2014, while the proportion of women was up from 9.8% to 45.5%. In Brazil, increases for young people in rural areas were also remarkable, with the rate rising from 9.6% to 35.8% for men and from 13.3% to 44.5% for women. Despite the scale of this progress in secondary education completion in rural areas, there are still large disparities, and rural adolescents are worst placed in most of the countries.

Completion of secondary education is socially segmented to a high degree. Those who fail to complete this crucial stage of education tend to experience multiple forms of exclusion. Thus, the percentages not completing secondary school are highest among young people of both sexes belonging to the lowest-income households (ECLAC, 2016b) and those living in rural areas, together with indigenous people and Afrodescendants. As figure III.5 shows, in five countries of the region (Brazil, Chile, Ecuador, Guatemala and the Plurinational State of Bolivia) there was a large increase in secondary school completion between 2002 and 2014 in all the groups considered. The changes have been greatest for young indigenous people (around 64%, as compared to 29% for non-indigenous people), the very group that had the lowest coverage at the start of the period. Ethnic divides are still very large, however, and targeted action will be required to close them.

Secondary education can be a catalyst for reducing social inequalities. Because of large differences in the quality and efficiency of the education available to young people, however, there are great disparities in learning. As a result, social inequalities may actually widen during secondary education, even with a relatively high level of access. This requires determined action on two fronts. First, coverage needs to be expanded, with particular attention paid to the most excluded groups. Second, it is imperative to improve education quality and relevance, thereby narrowing gaps.

Individuals' level of education is one of the most important determinants of their opportunities in terms of employment, income, health, housing and other individual and social benefits over their lifetimes (Espinola and Claro, 2010). Although almost all 11-year-olds are studying, high drop-out rates in secondary education are an ongoing challenge in Latin America (Rico and Trucco, 2014). This indicates that prevailing conditions in the region still induce young people of both sexes to leave school before completing secondary education, something that is crucial to their prospects of a better position in the labour market later.

---

[9]   It is important to stress that one of the conditions that may induce young people to leave the school system at the secondary level is the segmentation of education quality at earlier stages of education, particularly primary school.

Figure III.4
Latin America (14 countries): people aged 20 to 24 who completed secondary education,
by sex and area of residence, around 2002 and 2014[a]
*(Percentages)*

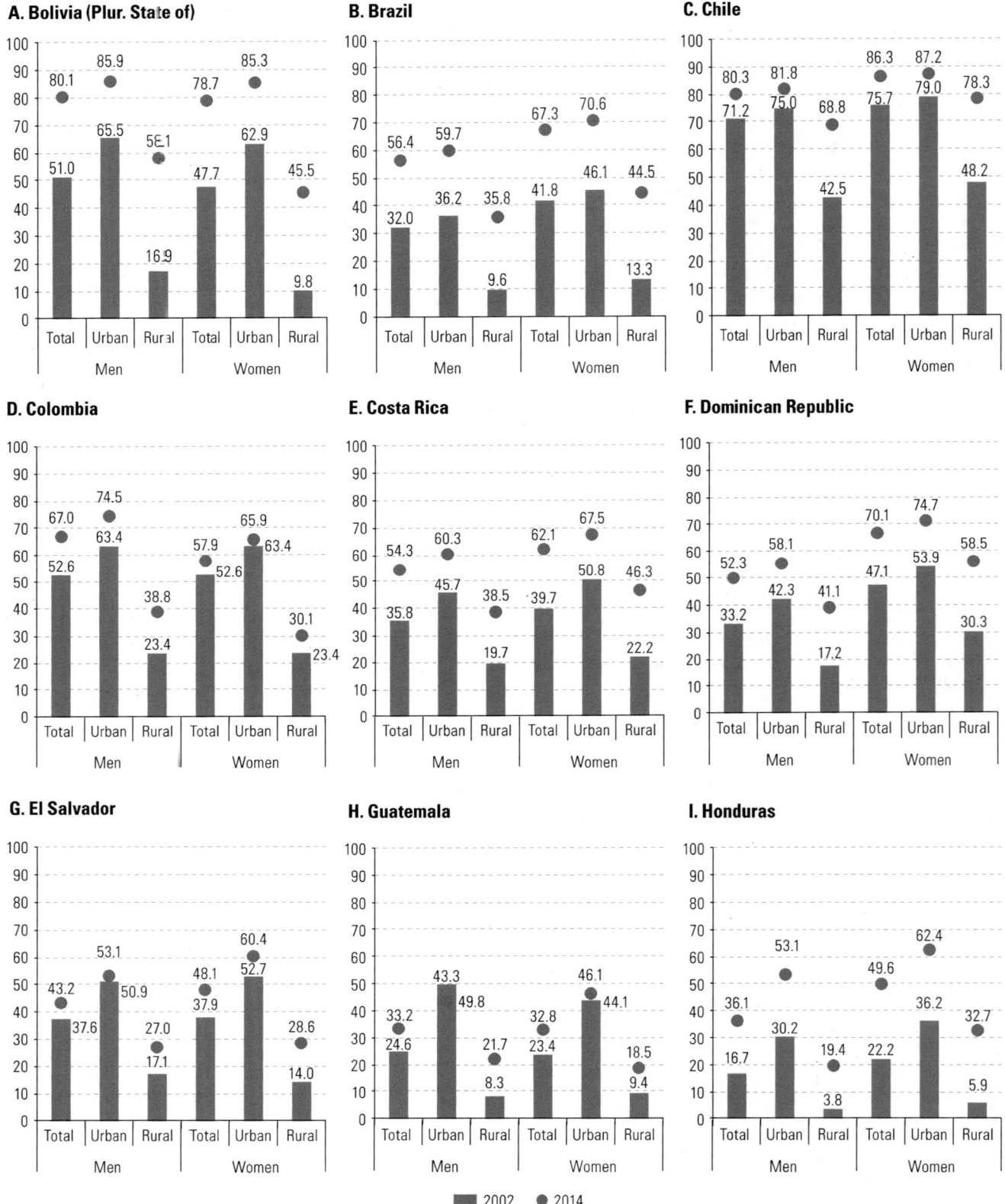

Figure III.4 (concluded)

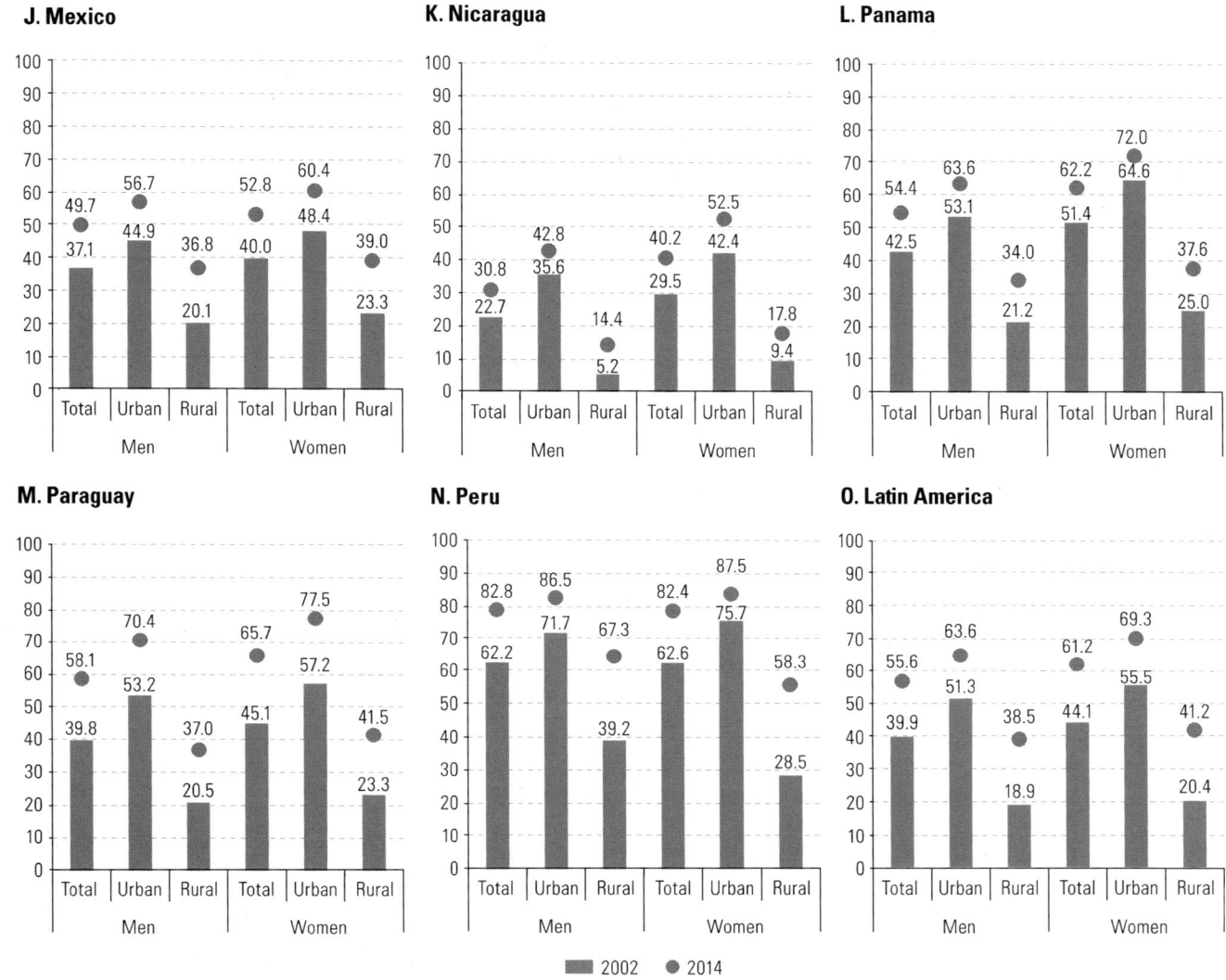

**J. Mexico**

**K. Nicaragua**

**L. Panama**

**M. Paraguay**

**N. Peru**

**O. Latin America**

■ 2002    ● 2014

**Source:** Economic Commission for Latin America and the Caribbean (ECLAC), on the basis of special tabulations of household surveys conducted in the respective countries.
[a] The Latin America figures are simple averages of the country figures.

**Figure III.5**
Latin America (5 countries): people aged 20 to 24 who completed secondary education, by sex and ethnicity, around 2002 and 2014[a] [b]
*(Percentages)*

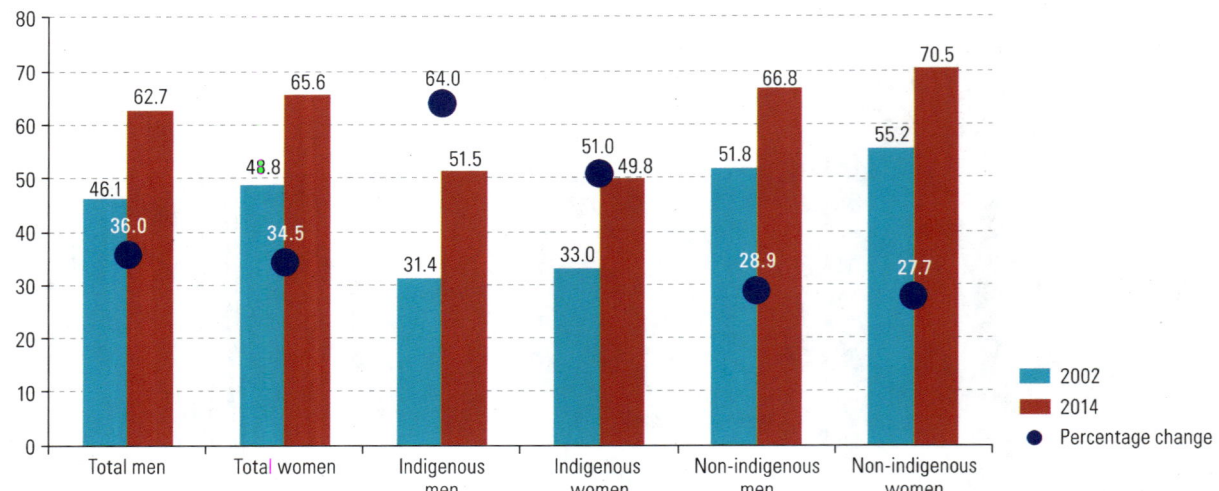

**Source**: Economic Commission for Latin America and the Caribbean (ECLAC), on the basis of special tabulations of household surveys conducted in the respective countries.
[a] Simple average based on information from Brazil (2001, 2014), Chile (2003, 2013), Ecuador (2002, 2014), Guatemala (2002, 2014) and the Plurinational State of Bolivia (2002, 2013).
[b] The "non-indigenous" category does not include Afrodescendants.

## (b) Young people who neither study nor work in the labour market: a multidimensional problem

A major challenge for young people in the region, and an obstacle to their emancipation, is the transition from school to the labour market. This passage from education to work is obstructed both by the difficulties young people face in completing their education and acquiring the skills needed in the labour market and by the barriers that prevent them from entering the labour market on the right terms. A group of special concern, not just in Latin America and the Caribbean but worldwide, are young people who are neither studying nor employed in the labour market. In recognition of the risk of long-term occupational and social exclusion that this entails, and the consequences that may ensue for society at large, target 8.6 of Goal 8 of the Sustainable Development Goals calls upon countries to reduce the percentage of young people in this situation considerably by 2030.

It is a situation that is contributing to the reproduction of inequality across generations and preventing the region from taking advantage of the window of opportunity represented by the demographic dividend. However, it is important to recognize and demonstrate that this phenomenon presents great variations, being more structural in some cases and more temporary in others, and to avoid stigmatizing these young people. With this more nuanced approach, different policy paths can be found for integrating them into society on better terms. As figure III.6 shows, it is a group composed mainly of women, with very substantial differences in some countries, something that earlier studies have identified (ECLAC, 2016a; Trucco and Ullmann, 2016).

## Figure III.6
Latin America (14 countries): young people aged 15 to 29 who are neither studying nor employed in the labour market, by sex and area of residence, around 2002 and 2014[a]
*(Percentages)*

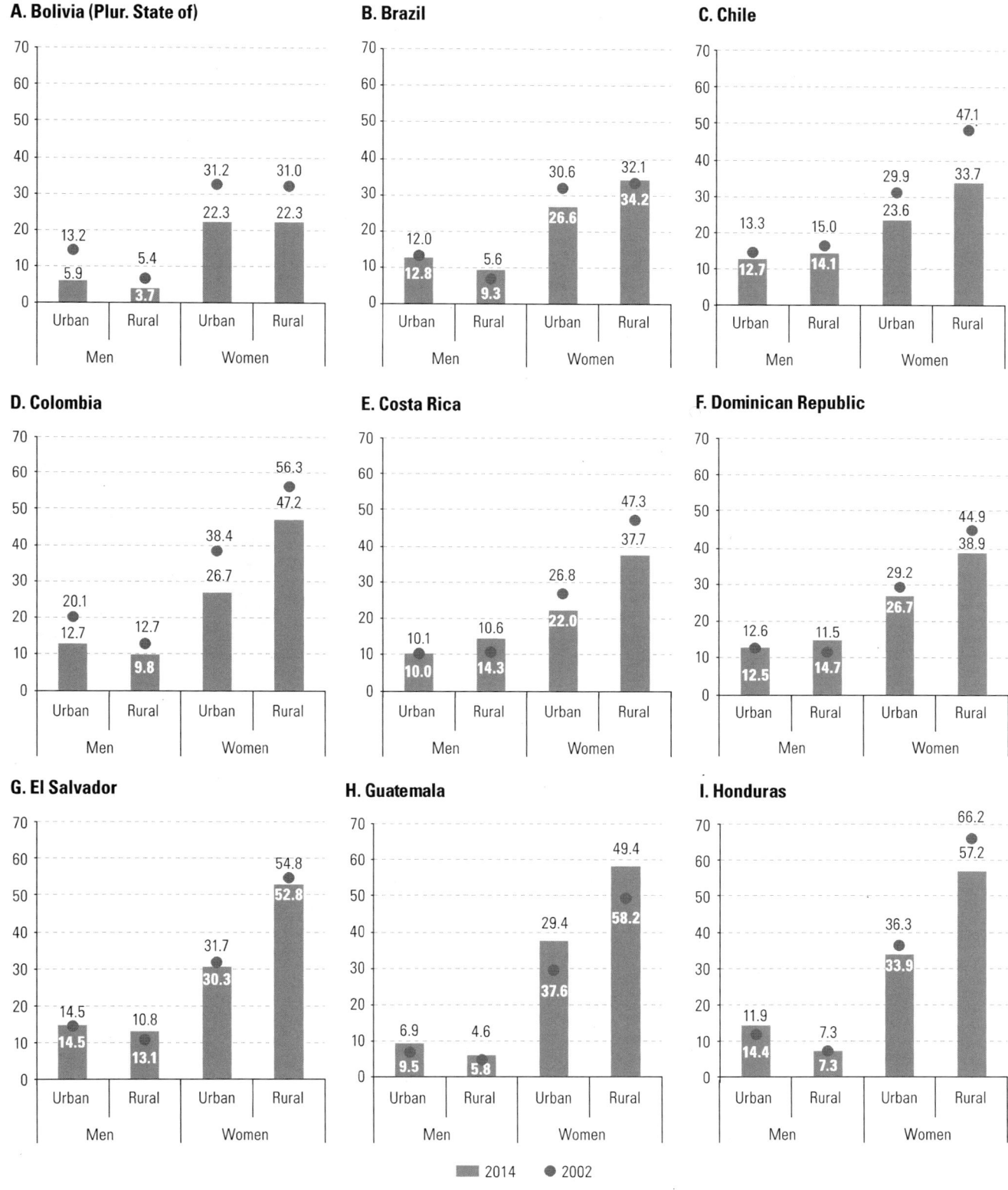

Figure III.6 (concluded)

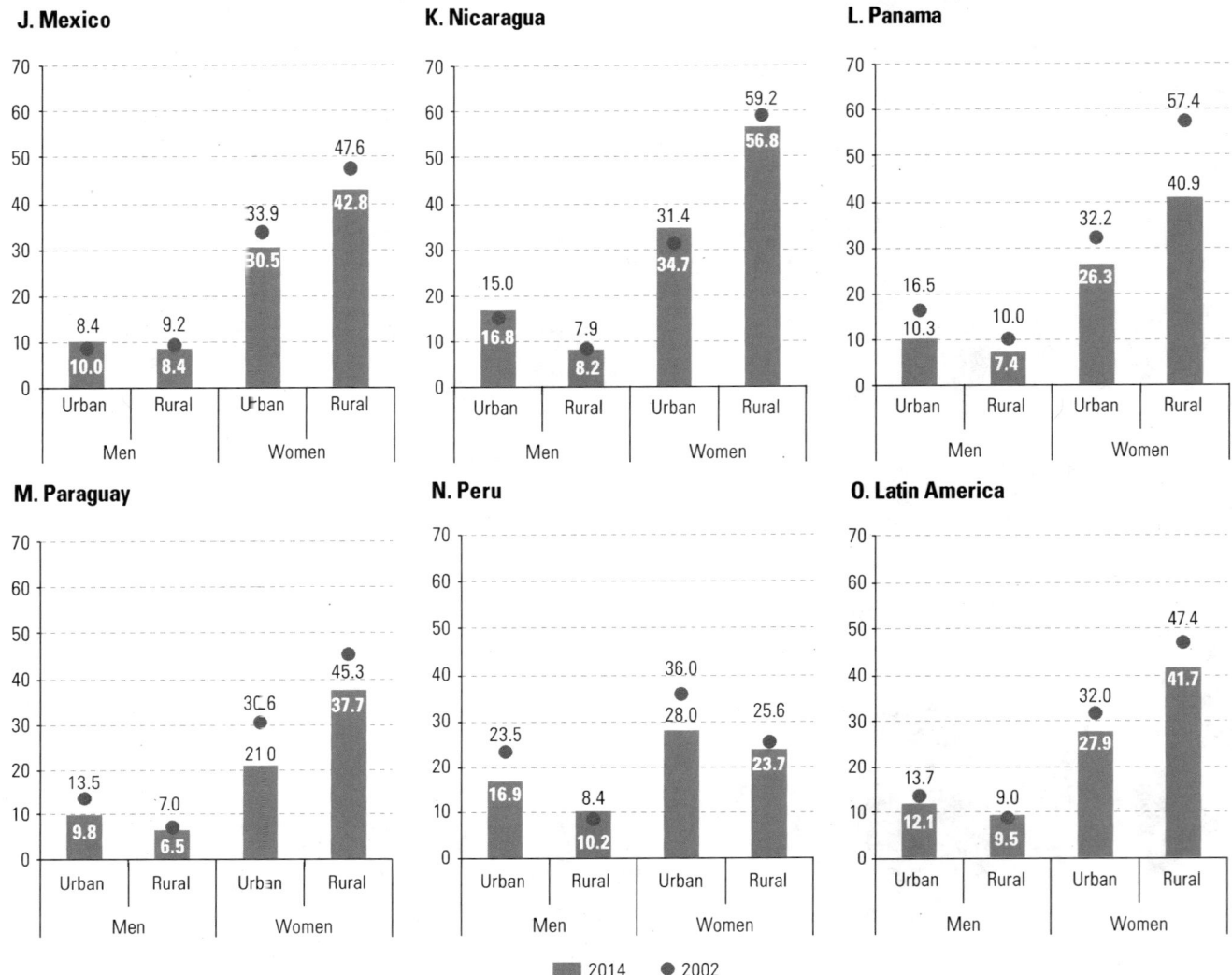

**Source:** Economic Commission for Latin America and the Caribbean (ECLAC), on the basis of special tabulations of household surveys conducted in the respective countries.
a The Latin America figures are simple averages of the country figures.

Educational opportunities, the characteristics of the local labour market, patterns of fertility and other cultural features of rural areas relative to urban ones increase the risk of young people being in a situation where they are neither studying nor employed in the labour market (see figure III.6). Three trends can be observed here. First, irrespective of the area of residence or year, a significantly higher proportion of women than of men are neither studying nor employed in the labour market in all the countries. In rural areas of El Salvador, for example, about 53% of young women were in this situation in 2014, as compared to 13% of young men. Second, there is a clear gradient for women depending on the area of residence: the percentage of those who are not in school or in employment is much higher in rural areas than in urban areas. The gap between women by area of residence is very large in some countries. In Colombia, for example, 47% of young women in rural areas are in this position, compared with 26% in urban areas. A possible explanation is that this is partly because young women in urban areas have lower fertility rates and greater expectations of completing education or entering the labour market than those in rural areas. Conversely, the patterns for young men display the opposite trend: in most of the countries, they are least likely to fall into this category in the countryside, and gaps between young men by area of residence are smaller, which may be due to early entry into the labour market. A third element is that this is an indicator that changed very little between 2002 and 2014, particularly where young men are concerned, with the figures for these actually rising in many cases over the most recent period. In 2014, on average, the percentage of young men not in school or in employment stood at 12.1% in urban areas and 9.5% in rural areas, while the corresponding figures for young women were 27.9% and 41.7%, respectively.

When the ethnic dimension is brought into the analysis, it can be seen that in the five countries of the region with information available (Brazil, Chile, Ecuador, Guatemala and the Plurinational State of Bolivia), although the proportion of young people who were neither studying nor employed in the labour market dropped on average between 2002 and 2014, the decline was not uniform across the different population groups, but was much more modest for women than for men, while indigenous women made the least progress (see figure III.7). By and large, these gaps derive from the greater obstacles women face in trying to do unpaid domestic and care work while simultaneously studying and participating in paid employment and, in the case of indigenous women, also from cultural factors and differentiated fertility patterns.

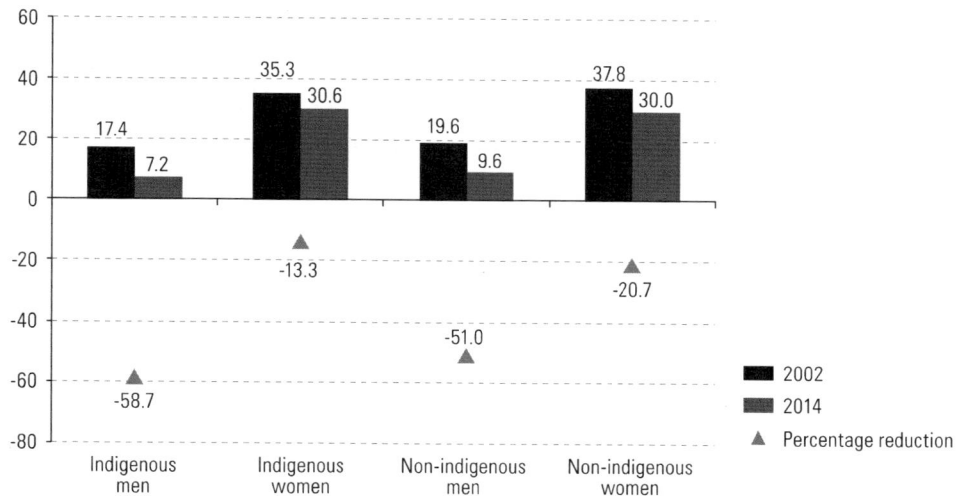

**Figure III.7**
Latin America (5 countries): young people aged 15 to 29 who are neither studying nor employed in the labour market, by sex and ethnicity, around 2002 and 2014[a][b]
*(Percentages)*

**Source**: Economic Commission for Latin America and the Caribbean (ECLAC), on the basis of special tabulations of household surveys conducted in the respective countries.
[a] Simple average based on information from Brazil (2001, 2014), Chile (2003, 2013), Ecuador (2002, 2014), Guatemala (2002, 2014) and the Plurinational State of Bolivia (2002, 2013).
[b] The "non-indigenous" category does not include Afrodescendants.

Despite its importance, the youth stage of life is largely invisible in public policy, and when references are made to young people, they are presented as the object of policies and not as rights-holders or agents of development and productive change (ECLAC, 2016a). Given the demographic weight the young still have in the vast majority of the region's countries and the demographic dividend these could be benefiting from, now is a particularly propitious time to invest in this stage of the life cycle and ensure young people are fully included, in order to construct fairer and more egalitarian societies. This is also vital because of the important role the new generations will play in bringing about the structural and productive change that the new sustainable development model requires in the region.

Despite its importance, the youth stage of life is largely invisible in public policy, and when references are made to young people, they are presented as the object of policies and not as rights-holders or agents of development and productive change (ECLAC, 2016a). Given the demographic weight the young still have in the vast majority of the region's countries and the demographic dividend these could be benefiting from, now is a particularly propitious time to invest in this stage of the life cycle and ensure young people are fully included, in order to construct fairer and more egalitarian societies.

## 3.    Adulthood: entrenched inequalities in the labour market

Access to income and well-being in adulthood depends even more on the ability to participate in the job market (Rossel and Filgueira, 2015, cited in ECLAC, 2016a), which derives in turn from the skills and capabilities people acquired during earlier stages in life. Furthermore, access to contributory social protection is heavily dependent on participation in the formal labour market. This is also the stage when the pressures of care are felt most keenly, because of the presence of young dependants (children) and, in some cases, of older ones (parents or other family members). The combination of these demands —the need to generate adequate income and reconcile labour market participation, personal projects and care responsibilities— creates a particularly challenging situation for adult women. Lastly, the way individuals engage with the job market during adulthood has consequences for their well-being in the immediate future as they enter old age: if they work informally, they will not be entitled to a contributory pension or, in many cases, to health services. For these reasons, the main challenges during this stage concern labour market participation and job quality, in terms of income and other working conditions and of access to employment rights (such as maternity, paternity and sick leave and paid holidays) and to social protection mechanisms, including care services (ECLAC, 2016a).

### (a) The evolution of unemployment among men and women, young people and adults, by area of residence

The effects of the economic slowdown and contraction in the region since 2015 are already visible in Latin American labour markets, reverting some of the positive trends seen in the past decade. On average, unemployment rates are rising, while job quality is deteriorating and wage growth and formality are stagnating (OECD/ECLAC/CAF, 2016). As highlighted by ECLAC (2016a), the decline in unemployment contributed to lower poverty and inequality levels between 2002 and 2014. Hence, in the current complex economic environment, measures must be put in place to create and protect jobs and to improve job quality, as well as to expand access to unemployment insurance and other social protection mechanisms.

The unemployment rate is one of the key indicators of labour market exclusion and it reflects the intertwining of the pillars of social inequality in the region. Although there has been substantial progress towards greater gender equality across the region over recent decades in areas such as physical autonomy and participation in decision-making (ECLAC, 2016c), there are still large disparities between men and women for example in the labour market, including gaps in participation and higher rates of unemployment, informality and wage discrimination experienced by women.

These inequalities have a great impact on women's financial autonomy and on their own and their children's well-being. It also has major consequences for the future financial security of women and their families, since disadvantages in the labour market have a cumulative effect on their careers, opportunities to generate resources and ability to save over a lifetime, ultimately translating into large pension shortfalls (Marco, 2016; ECLAC, 2014a). Lower earnings, combined with working careers that are usually more discontinuous and prone to informality and insecurity, mean lesser coverage in employment-related contributory regimes, which tends to reproduce gender equalities in the sphere of social protection (ILO, 2016a). This means not only that fewer women receive pensions, but any pensions they do receive are of a lower amount, which relates to the higher incidence of poverty among women in old age (ECLAC, 2016c).

The intergenerational gap between young people and adults is also clear in labour market indicators. Despite the fact that young people in Latin America currently have a higher level of education and socioeconomic status than in the past decade, they continue to experience higher unemployment levels than adults (OECD/ECLAC/CAF, 2016). This contradiction is especially evident among young women who, in spite of greater academic achievements than their male counterparts (as shown previously in this chapter), are unable to translate this into success in the labour market. Figure III.8 shows trends in unemployment by sex, age group and area of residence, between 2002 and 2014. Gender and age gaps exist regardless of area of residence, as young women who live in both urban and rural areas experience the highest unemployment levels.

Figure III.8

Latin America (17 countries): unemployment by sex, age group and area of residence, around 2002 and 2014[a]

(Percentages)

**A. National total**

**Men**

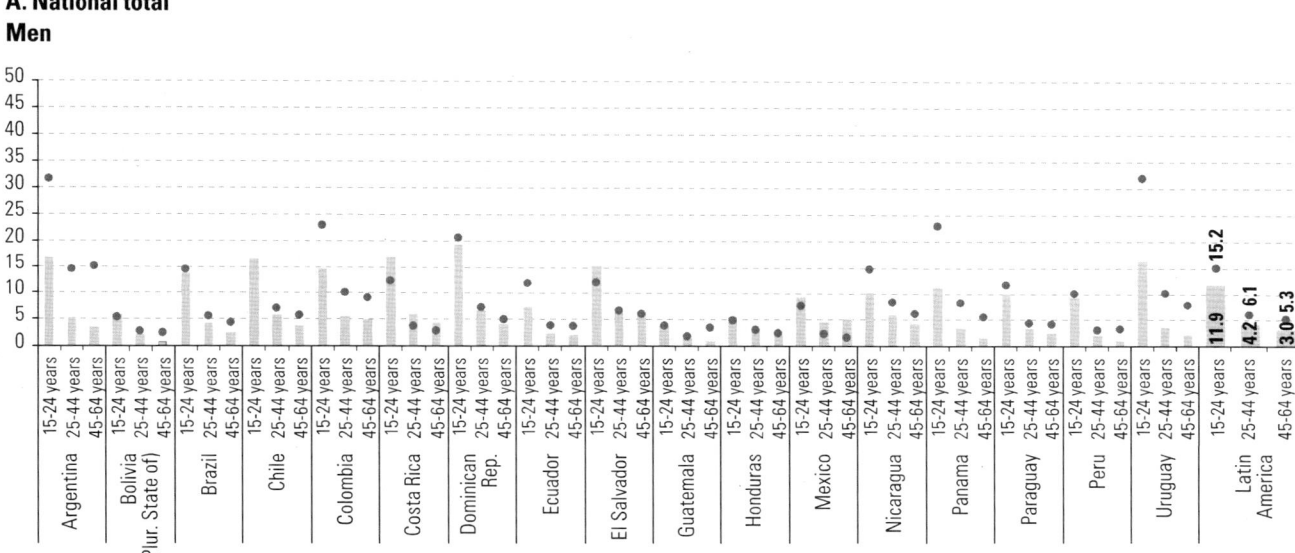

**Women**

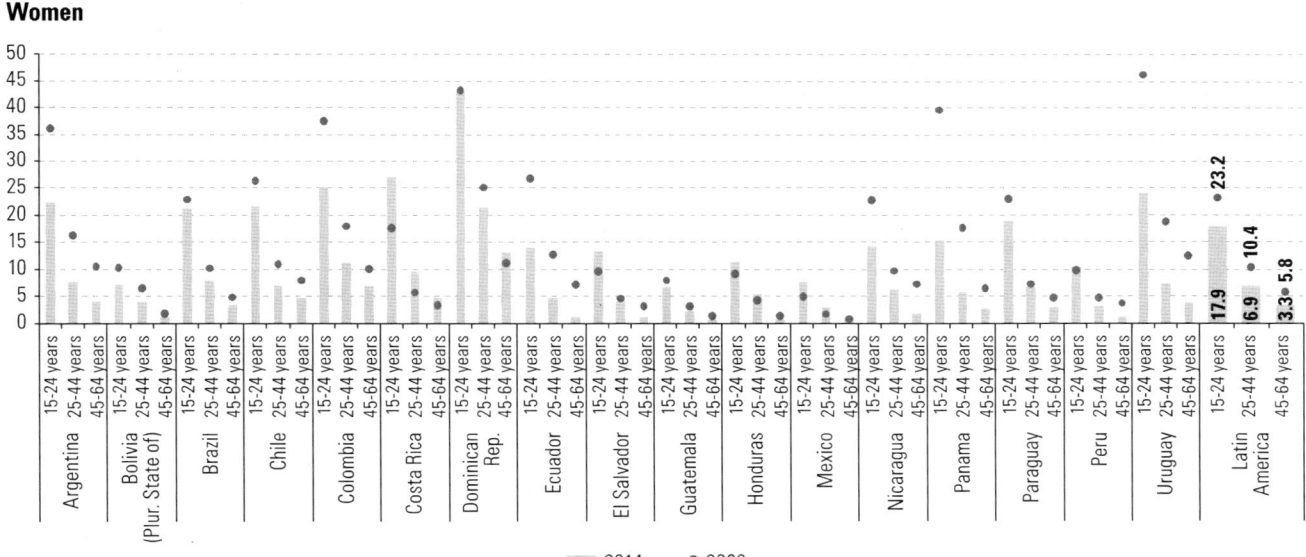

2014          2002

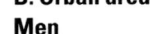

Figure III.8 (continued)

## B. Urban areas
### Men

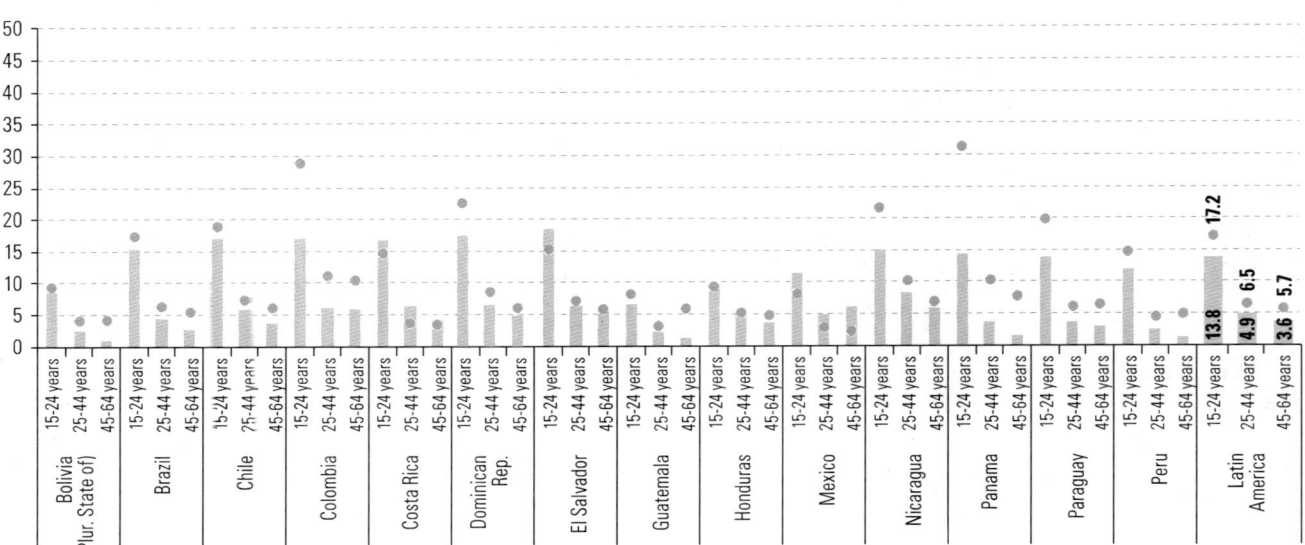

### Women

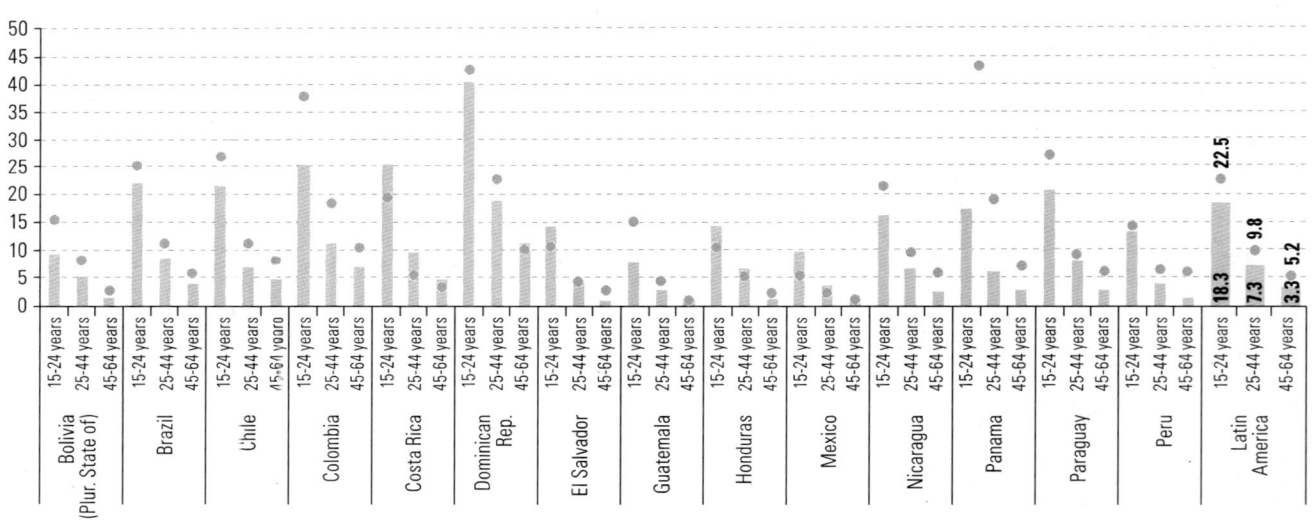

2014    ● 2002

Figure III.8 (concluded)

## C. Rural areas
### Men

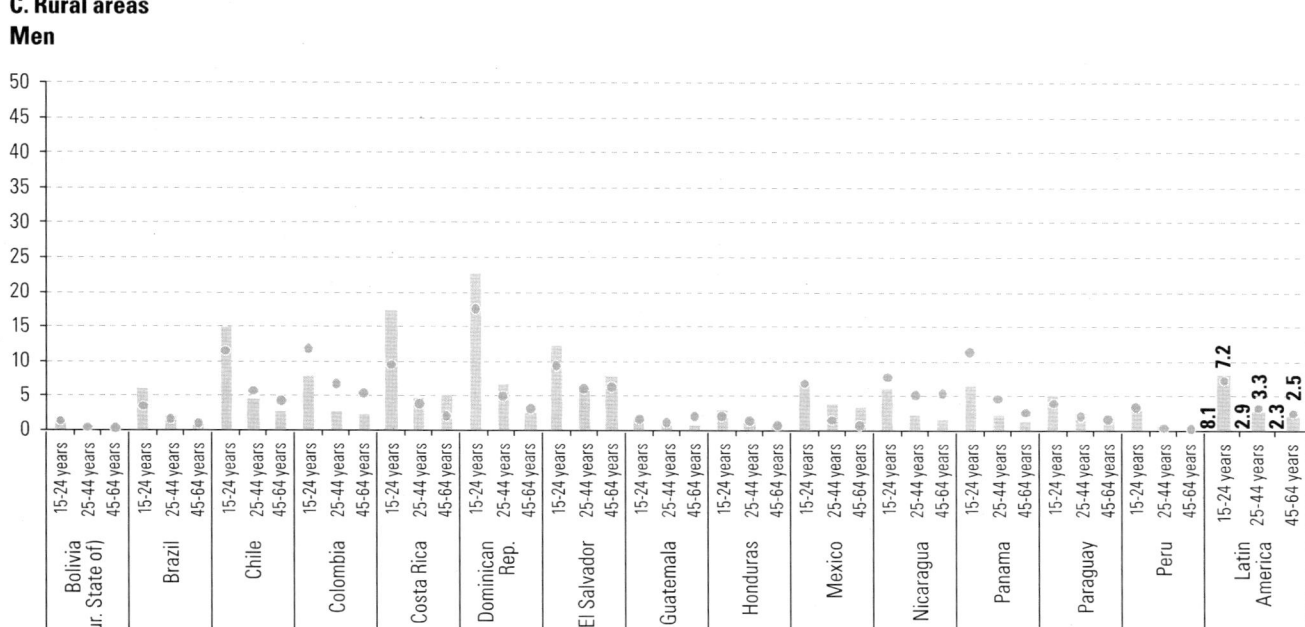

### Women

2014　　2002

Source: Economic Commission for Latin America and the Caribbean (ECLAC), on the basis of special tabulations of household surveys conducted in the respective countries.
a Simple averages of the countries.

The unemployment trend between 2002 and 2014 in 14 of the region's countries shows that it remained lower in rural areas than in urban areas, a finding which is consistent with previous studies (ECLAC/ILO, 2016). According to ECLAC and ILO, this trend stems from a surplus of rural labour supply that results in migratory flows to the cities and in a higher incidence of low-paid jobs with less social protection coverage, rather than showing through as open unemployment. Moreover, the chance of obtaining a paid job varies according to the agricultural cycle, which means greater labour inactivity in periods when labour demand is weak (ILO, 2014, as cited in ECLAC/ILO, 2016). Nonetheless, the figure also shows how this indicator has stalled in rural areas, unlike in urban areas.

Figure III.8 also shows the inequalities between women and men in the labour market, regardless of age or area of residence. In rural areas, the high rates of unemployment among women in comparison with men stem from the greater difficulties women face in finding employment, the invisibility of rural women workers (given that in many cases unpaid female family workers are not recognized as employed in surveys), and the traditional assignment of gender roles, according to which men have the main responsibility for production, while women are confined to the domain of reproduction and related tasks (ECLAC/ILO, 2016).

Lastly, figure III.8 shows significant differences in unemployment by age group, which was not unexpected, but nonetheless striking. Unemployment rates are highest among young people in all the region's countries. On the basis of regional averages, in 2014, 12% of young men and 18% of young women were unemployed, compared with 3% of adults, men and women, aged 45 to 64. However, some countries have made progress in this area. Colombia and Panama, for example, managed to reduce youth unemployment significantly between 2002 and 2014. In Colombia, considering the national total, unemployment fell from 23% in 2002 to 14% in 2014 among young men, and from 37% to 25% among young women in the same period. From a life-cycle perspective, youth unemployment is especially worrying as it can affect future career paths. Prolonged unemployment at this age can also lead to inactivity, with serious effects on young people, their families, and the region's societies.

### (b) Working people with labour income lower than the national minimum wage, by sex and area of residence

Decent, high-quality work is essential for individuals and their families to earn what they need to maintain an adequate living standard and to have access to social protection systems. Accordingly, decent work is vital to reduce poverty and inequality and promote well-being and social inclusion (ILO, 2016b). However, precisely because the production structure is heterogeneous, with high levels of unstable and informal employment, a substantial proportion of the working population in Latin America does not earn enough to achieve an adequate living standard.

Figure III.9 shows three general trends. First, in all the region's countries, among men and women, the percentage of workers in rural areas whose income is below the minimum wage is higher than that of workers in urban areas in the same situation (see box III.2), except in the case of men aged 25 to 44 and 45 to 64 in Uruguay. These data, along with the information in figure III.8, show that among workers in rural areas, unemployment rates are lower, but job quality is poor. The disadvantages faced by women and young people are also clear. The percentage of women with income below the minimum wage is higher than that of men in the same situation in both urban and rural areas and of all ages, although the difference between men and women is particularly striking in the 25 to 45 age group, in which 30% of men and 40% of women are in this situation. With respect to age, there is a U-shaped relationship in which the percentages of workers with income below the minimum wage are higher among young men and women, decline significantly in the 25 to 45 age group and later increase slightly in the 45 to 64 age group.

Figure III.9
Latin America (16 countries): workers with income lower than the national minimum wage,
by sex, age group and area of residence, around 2014[a]
*(Percentages)*

**A. Men**

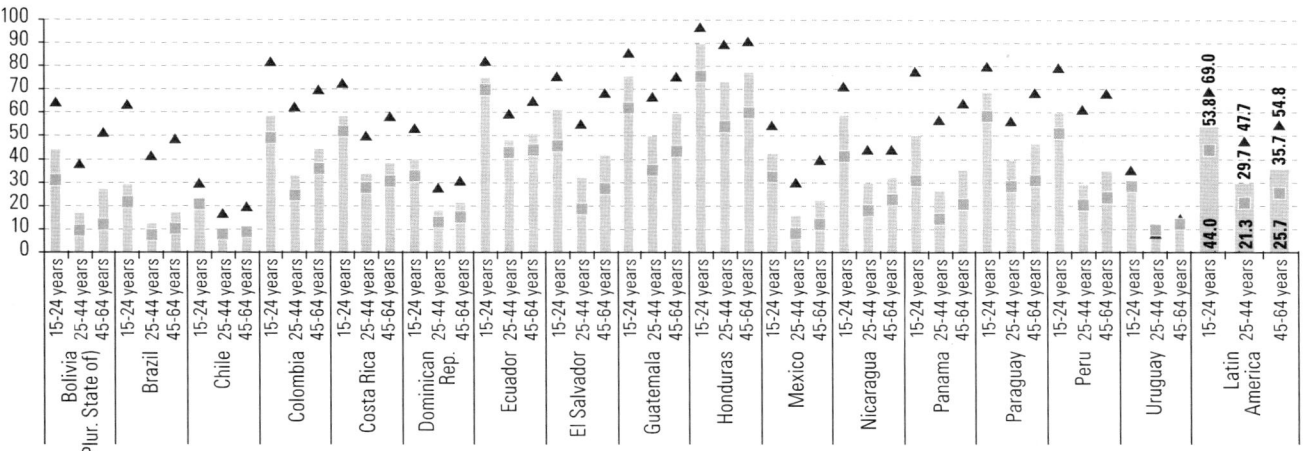

**B. Women**

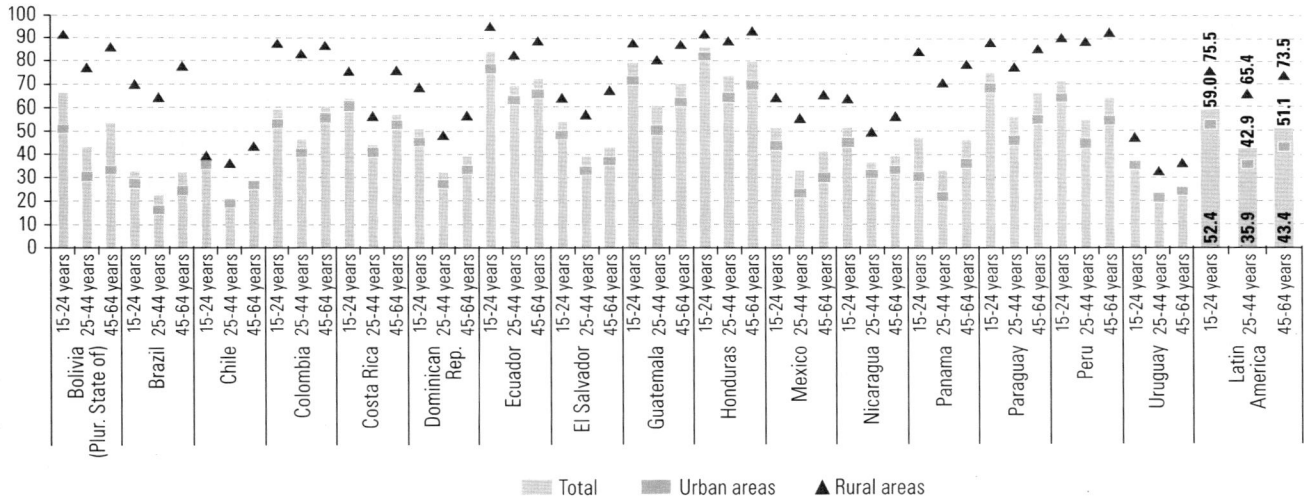

Total　　Urban areas　　▲ Rural areas

**Source**: Economic Commission for Latin America and the Caribbean (ECLAC), on the basis of special tabulations of household surveys conducted in the respective countries.
**Note**:　Information for the main city and other urban areas was available for Argentina, Ecuador and Uruguay, while for the Dominican Republic data for the main city and
rural areas were used.
[a] The Latin America figures are simple averages of the country figures.

Box III.2
Comparison of labour income with minimum wage in the region

The minimum wage is an important labour market institution that aims to reduce the incidence of low wages in order to protect the purchasing power of the most vulnerable workers (Maurizio, 2014). The vast majority of countries have ratified the ILO Minimum Wage Fixing Convention, 1970 (No. 131) and there are mechanisms to put one in place even in countries that have not. Practically all the region's countries have some form of minimum wage, although there is significant variation with respect to how these wages are set and how coverage is determined, the interaction with collective bargaining, periodicity of adjustments and level of implementation (Marinakis, 2014; Maurizio, 2014). The weakness of collective bargaining in some countries has contributed to the minimum wage playing a key role in wage determination (Marinakis, 2008), particularly in its use as a benchmark for wages that are established as multiples of that rate. In some countries, the minimum wage has nationwide coverage, while others establish a level for professional categories. There are also other criteria for fixing the minimum wage, such as differentiation on the basis of the level of development of regions within the country.

In order for the minimum wage to achieve its objectives, its value must guarantee a decent income for workers, as it is "the minimum sum payable to a worker for work performed or services rendered, within a given period, whether calculated on the basis of time or output, which may not be reduced either by individual or collective agreement, which is guaranteed by law and which may be fixed in such a way as to cover the minimum needs of the worker and his or her family, in the light of national economic and social conditions" (ILO, 1992), "so that it can be used to secure adequate food, decent housing, education, clothing, health care, transport and recreation, vacation and insurance against unforeseen events" (Maurizio, 2014). The minimum wage is a threshold which can be used to compare labour income (wages or income from independent work) to assess job quality in the region.

In this chapter, the figures used for comparison correspond to the annual average of the official monthly minimum wage of each country, in local currency, corresponding to the year of the survey of households studied, as shown in the following table.

Latin America (16 countries): monthly minimum wage, annual average, 2009-2014[a]
(Local currencies)

| Country | Year | Amount | Currency | In PPP dollars at 2010 prices[b] |
|---|---|---|---|---|
| Bolivia (Plurinational State of) | 2013 | 1 200 | Bolivianos (Bs) | 362 |
| Brazil | 2014 | 724 | Reais (R$) | 355 |
| Chile | 2013 | 200 083 | Pesos (Ch$) | 497 |
| Colombia | 2014 | 616 000 | Pesos (Col$) | 461 |
| Costa Rica[c] | 2014 | 272 575,18 | Colones (¢) | 669 |
| Dominican Republic[d] | 2014 | 6 880 | Pesos (RD$) | 287 |
| Ecuador[e] | 2014 | 396,51 | Dollars (US$) | 628 |
| El Salvador[f] | 2014 | 198 975 | Dollars (US$) | 351 |
| Guatemala[g] | 2014 | 2 096,01 | Quetzales (Q) | 468 |
| Honduras[h] | 2013 | 6 819,04 | Lempiras (L) | 593 |
| Mexico[i][j] | 2014 | 1 738 | Pesos (Mex$) | 169 |
| Nicaragua[k] | 2009 | 2 075,43 | Córdobas (C$) | 251 |
| Panama[l] | 2014 | 390,08 | Balboas (B) | 606 |
| Paraguay | 2014 | 1 796 418 | Guaraníes (G) | 674 |
| Peru | 2014 | 750 | Soles (S/.) | 421 |
| Uruguay | 2014 | 8 960 | Pesos (Ur$) | 414 |

[a] In cases where not otherwise specified, countries have a single minimum wage.
[b] Conversion to purchasing power parity (PPP) dollars at 2010 prices, for private sector consumption (for example, households' final consumption).
[c] Minimum wage for unskilled workers.
[d] Corresponds to non-agricultural small businesses in the private sector. There is a different (daily) minimum wage for agricultural workers.
[e] The monthly minimum wage corresponds to US$ 340. Workers receive bonuses in August and December.
[f] Simple average of the monthly minimum wage in four large sectors: trade and services, industry, maquila textile production and agriculture.
[g] Minimum wage for specific companies or geographical areas (maquila).
[h] Average monthly minimum wage for 10 areas of activity, for four business sizes, and the regionalized minimum wage (in effect for Choluteca, Valle, El Paraíso, Santa Bárbara and Olancho).
[i] Daily minimum wage multiplied by 26.5 days.
[j] Average minimum wage in three geographical areas, in force in 2014, weighted by the number of employees (official data).
[k] Corresponds to the manufacturing industry.
[l] Corresponds to small manufacturing businesses (45 hour work week), average of the two regions into which the country's districts are divided, for this purpose. The minimum wage in small agricultural businesses is 292.56.

**Source:** A. Marinakis, *Evolución de los salarios en América Latina, 1995-2006*, Santiago, International Labour Organization (ILO), 2008; A. Marinakis, (ed.), *Incumplimiento con el salario mínimo en América Latina. El peso de los factores económicos e institucionales*, Santiago, ILO, 2014; R. Maurizio, "El impacto distributivo del salario mínimo en la Argentina, el Brasil, Chile y el Uruguay", *Políticas Sociales* series, No. 194 (LC/L.3825), Santiago, Economic Commission for Latin America and the Caribbean (ECLAC), 2014; ILO, "Minimum wages: Wage-fixing machinery, application and supervision", *Report III (Part 4 B)*, International Labour Conference, 79th Session, Geneva, 1992 [online] http://www.ilo.org/public/libdoc/ilo/P/09661/09661%281992-79-4B%29.pdf and official information from the countries.

Adulthood is when investments made during the earlier stages of life by society as a whole, whether individually or through public policies, should bear fruit and enhance people's productive capacity for their present and future benefit, for future generations and for society at large, with a view to attaining long-run sustainability. When these investments have not been made and labour market constraints remain, many people reach adulthood under conditions of inequality. Meanwhile, structural gaps in labour markets and large differences between different population groups in access to opportunities, rights and benefits perpetuate deeply entrenched social inequalities in the adult population.

## 4.  Old age: promoting the well-being and autonomy of older people

We live in a period of profound demographic transformation, characterized by steady population ageing that has resulted from sharp declines in fertility and increases in life expectancy. From a life cycle perspective, this is manifested in an old age that is longer and more complex.[10] This demographic milestone, which is the result of improvements in nutrition, health and sanitation, technological changes and other factors, means that the number of people aged 60 years and over will increase steadily over the coming decades. The number of older persons is expected to grow faster in Latin America and the Caribbean than anywhere else in the world, with a projected 71% increase over the next 15 years (United Nations, 2015, cited in ECLAC, 2016a). As ECLAC points out, these new configurations will create new social, economic, political and cultural needs and aspirations among different age groups, and those must be addressed and resolved through public policies that guarantee everyone social inclusion and the full enjoyment of rights (ECLAC, 2016a).It is also important to note that as life expectancy increases, including healthy life expectancy, the elderly population becomes more heterogeneous, encompassing people of different ages with different capacities and needs.

The most notable inequalities at this stage in the life cycle are associated with alterations in family living arrangements, access to stable pension income and changes in health and in physical and intellectual autonomy. At the same time, divides between older persons reflect the disadvantages (or advantages) they have built up over a lifetime.

For example, educational attainments during adolescence and youth substantially affect the likelihood of receiving a pension during this last stage of the life cycle (see figure III.10).[11]

Generally speaking, the proportion of men and women aged 65 and over in receipt of a pension increased in almost all the countries between 2002 and 2014. The average proportion of adults aged 65 and over in receipt of a pension rose from 38.2% to 42.3% for men and from 25.1% to 30.8% for women in the period. One of the largest rises was for women in Costa Rica (up from 28% to 61%). As can be seen, however, there is still a large gender divide. Furthermore, educational gradients in pensions affect both men and women in all the countries. In some countries, there are very striking differences between people with very low levels of education (incomplete primary) and those with complete secondary education or above. For example, just 15% of uneducated women in Panama receive pensions, as against 82% of those with complete secondary education or better; the equivalent figures for men are 31% and 90%. Well-documented gender inequalities also persist, even when women and men with the same level of education are considered. Thus, 63% of women with a secondary education or better receive a

The number of older persons is expected to grow faster in Latin America and the Caribbean than anywhere else in the world, with a projected 71% increase over the next 15 years (United Nations, 2015, cited in ECLAC, 2016a). As ECLAC points out, these new configurations will create new social, economic, political and cultural needs and aspirations among different age groups, and those must be addressed and resolved through public policies that guarantee everyone social inclusion and the full enjoyment of rights.

---

[10]  This development tends to present a gender bias in the region's societies, as women have a higher life expectancy.
[11]  The discussion refers to contributory pensions, including survivors' pensions.

pension in Chile, while 74% of men with this level of education do. This suggests that differences by sex in access to pensions are the result of gender inequalities in the labour market and factors associated with the design of contributory pension systems (Marco, 2016).[12] Lastly, it is interesting to note that the impact of educational divides on the likelihood of receiving a pension was greater for women than for men at the end of the period considered (around 2014). In other words, the difference between uneducated people and those with secondary education or more in the likelihood of receiving a pension was greater for women than for men.

Figure III.10
Latin America (8 countries): adults aged 65 and over in receipt of a pension, by sex and education level attained, 2002 and 2014[a]
(Percentages)

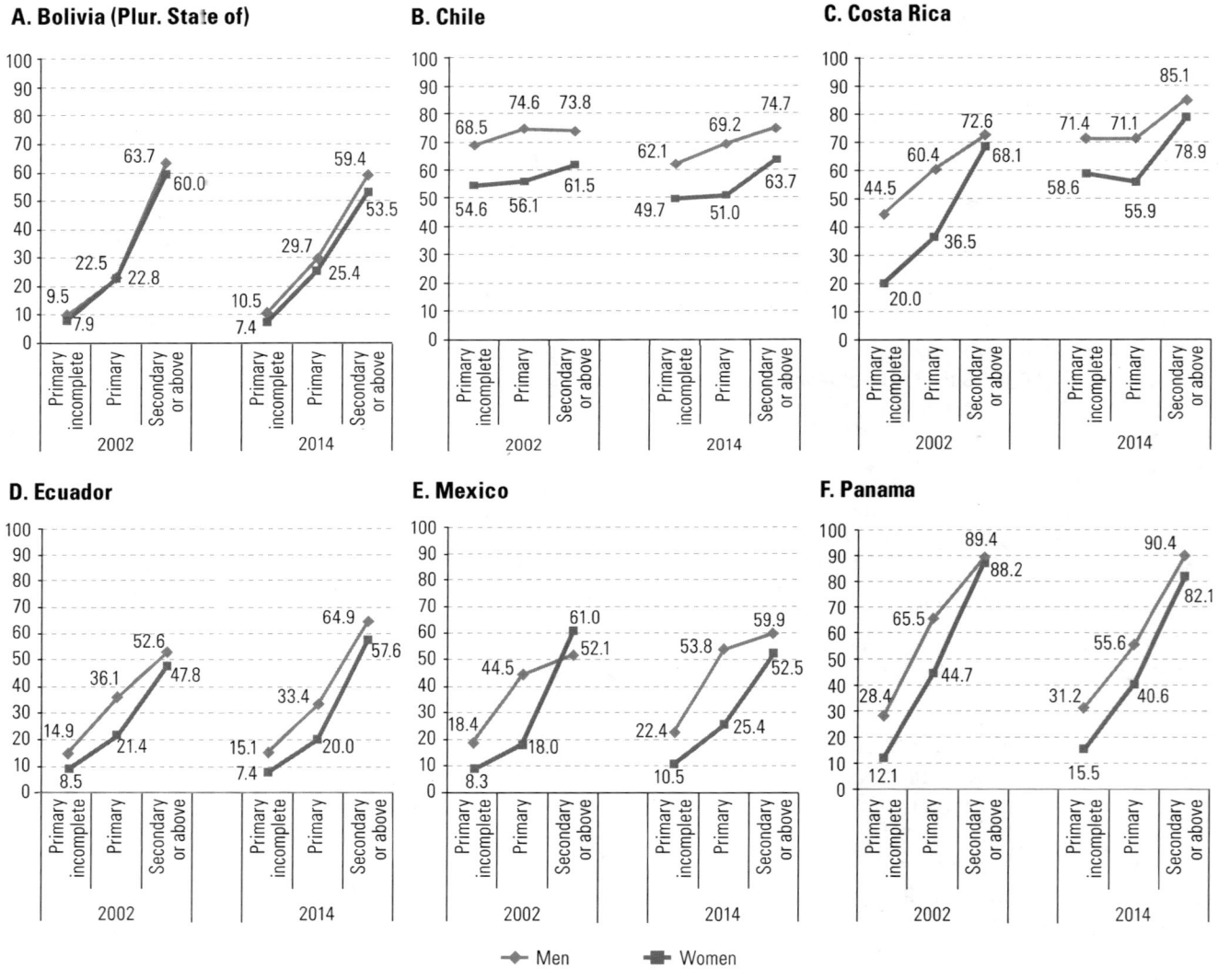

---

[12]    This analysis focuses on coverage, but there is also evidence of divides between men and women in the size of pensions, although these have been narrowing (Amarante, Colacce and Manzi, 2016).

Figure III.10 (concluded)

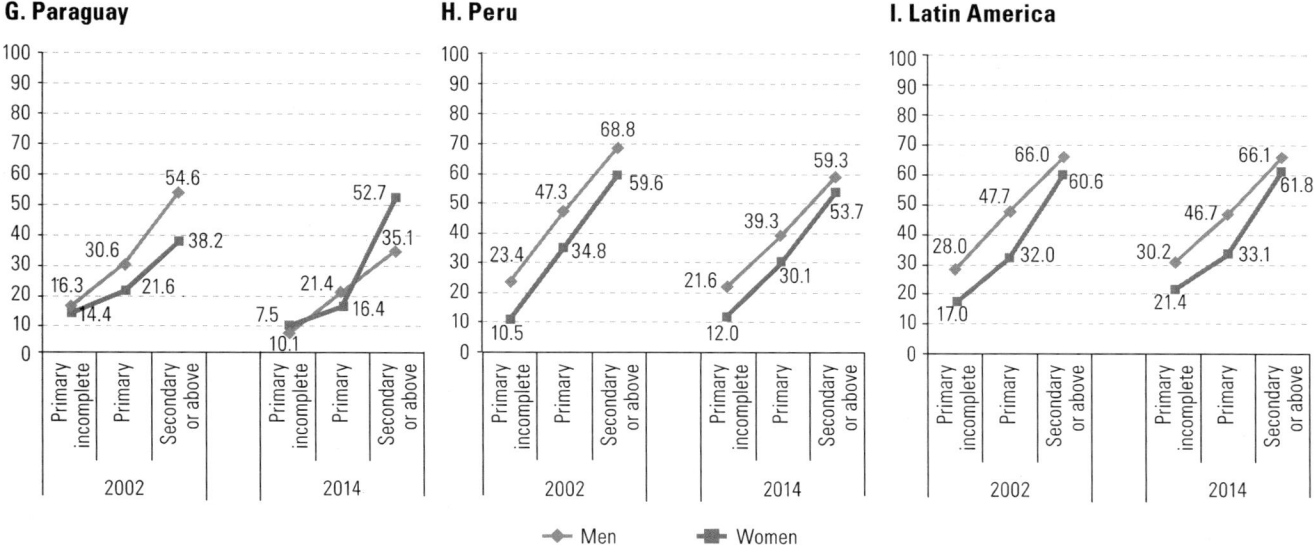

**G. Paraguay**　　**H. Peru**　　**I. Latin America**

◆ Men　　■ Women

**Source**: Economic Commission for Latin America and the Caribbean (ECLAC), on the basis of special tabulations of household surveys conducted in the respective countries.
[a] Simple average of the countries.

As this chapter has shown, social disparities over the life cycle are intensified by interaction with other axes of inequality such as sex and ethnic or racial origin. When the situations of indigenous and non-indigenous men and women with the same levels of education are compared in four countries (Chile, Mexico, Peru and the Plurinational State of Bolivia), the percentage of indigenous women receiving pensions is found to be systematically lower than the percentages receiving them in all the other groups considered (indigenous men and non-indigenous men and women), rising with years of education. Bearing out the findings of ECLAC (2015b and 2016a), the gap between indigenous women and non-indigenous men in the upper education band (secondary and over) ranges from some 11 percentage points in Mexico and Peru to over 20 percentage points in the Plurinational State of Bolivia (see figure III.11).

Figure III.11
Latin America (4 countries): adults aged 65 and over in receipt of a pension, by sex, ethnicity and education level attained, 2014[a]
*(Percentages)*

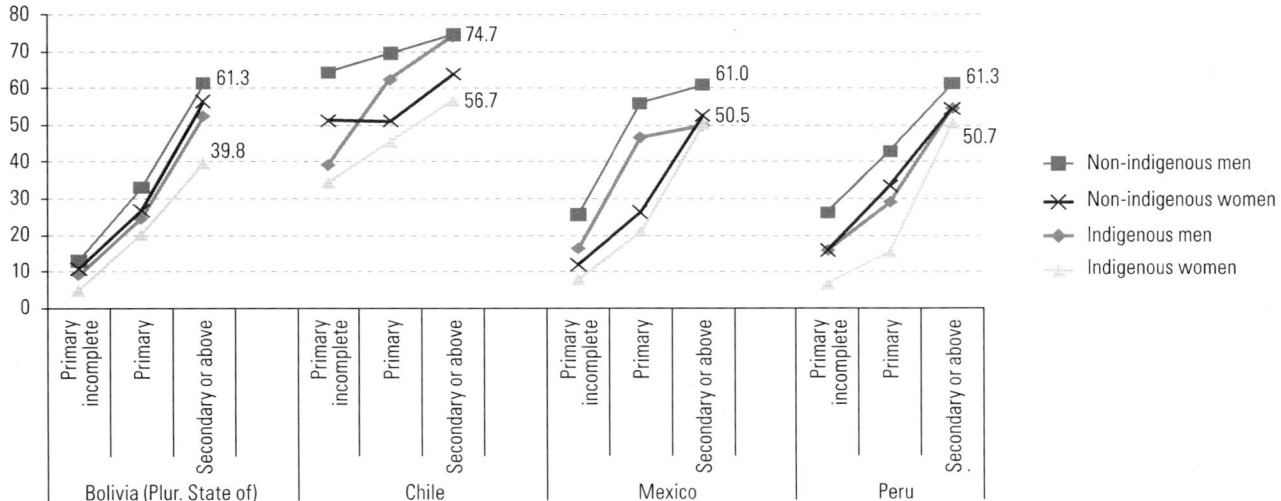

■ Non-indigenous men
✕ Non-indigenous women
◆ Indigenous men
▲ Indigenous women

**Source**: Economic Commission for Latin America and the Caribbean (ECLAC), on the basis of special tabulations of household surveys conducted in the respective countries.
[a] The "non-indigenous" category does not include Afrodescendants.

Educational attainment, along with other factors associated with socioeconomic status, also strongly influences the likelihood of having some disability in the final stage of life (see figure III.12). People who had secondary or tertiary education in their youth have a lower prevalence of disability later on in life than those with lesser educational attainments. If we treat the level of education attained as indicative of a person's socioeconomic level, their prior participation in the labour market and their access to the social protection system, it is reasonable to think that the career paths of people with no education or only primary education left them more vulnerable to disability in old age.[13] As ECLAC (2016a) argues, those who go through these stages of life in a context of economic vulnerability and reduced access to social protection mechanisms (potentially associated with low educational attainments at earlier stages of the life cycle) are at a greater risk of any health problem becoming a disability because they lack the resources to pay for the support services and technical assistance they need to mitigate the impact of limitations acquired with age, particularly in view of the rising cost of health and rehabilitation services, which may be unaffordable for some older people.

**Figure III.12**
Latin America (7 countries): people aged 60 and over with disabilities, by education level attained, sex, area of residence and ethnicity or race, around 2010
*(Percentages)*

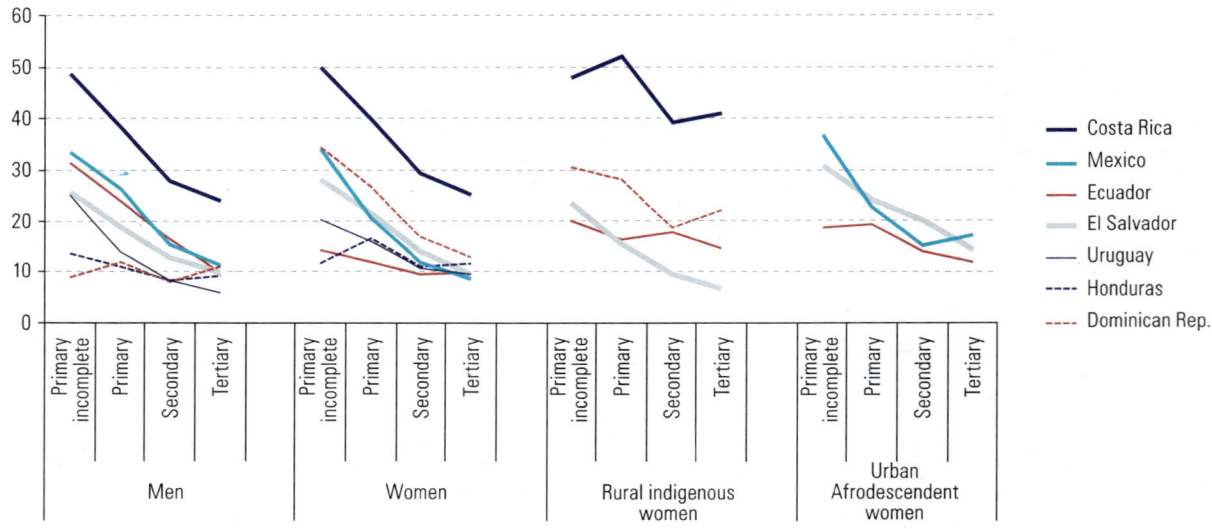

**Source**: Economic Commission for Latin America and the Caribbean (ECLAC), on the basis of special tabulations of censuses from the 2010 round conducted in the respective countries.

States should act to level out and correct the inequalities that accumulate over people's lifetimes by applying social policies designed to limit the reproduction and growth of these disparities. However, given the large inequalities in levels of education attained during adolescence or youth and two indicators critical for well-being in old age, namely access to income and physical autonomy, the region's countries clearly need to exert themselves to deal with disparities in education access and quality.

---

[13] An alternative explanation for this trend is that children with disabilities are much less likely to go to school. That was particularly true six decades ago, when this group of older people would have started education. In one way or another, this reflects the accumulation of inequalities over a lifetime.

# C. The experience of indigenous peoples over the life cycle: differentiated approaches to the pursuit of equality

The accumulation of disadvantages over the life cycle in the case of indigenous people illustrates the longitudinal dimension of inequality in the region. Despite major advances driven by policies and programmes designed to put into practice a rights-based approach grounded in current standards, there are still great challenges when it comes to the inclusion of indigenous persons over the whole life cycle. A priority, then, is to persevere with the development of ethnically relevant policies, starting with the systematic identification of indigenous peoples in all data sources.

This section will deal with the challenges and inequalities facing indigenous people over the life cycle with a view to underscoring the specificity of this population and illustrating the longitudinal dimension of the inequality that develops over an individual's life cycle.

There are over 800 indigenous peoples in Latin America, and while they show enormous territorial, demographic and sociocultural diversity, they also have a common denominator: the exclusion and material poverty that affects them more than the rest of the population.[14] The disadvantages indigenous peoples experience derive from long historical processes that began with the arrival of the European conquerors and were entrenched during the colonial period and the founding of nation-States.

Indigenous peoples have certain demographic and sociocultural peculiarities of relevance to the analysis of the life cycle. One characteristic of indigenous populations that undoubtedly influences and is expressed in different stages of the life cycle is that they are still younger than non-indigenous populations. As table III.2 shows, the proportion of children aged 15 and under is systematically higher among the indigenous population than among the non-indigenous population in all countries with available data, except Uruguay. At the same time, the share of older people is smaller in indigenous populations than in the rest of the population in the great majority of the countries. The "youngest" indigenous populations are in Colombia, Honduras and Panama. The contrasts are particularly striking in Panama, as it is a country whose non-indigenous population presents a high level of ageing, while about half the indigenous population (some 45%) is under the age of 15. Ethnic differences in age composition are also marked in the Bolivarian Republic of Venezuela and Brazil.

Notwithstanding, indigenous populations have also entered upon the so-called "demographic transition", and the population share of the new generations is now declining as indigenous fertility rates descend (ECLAC, 2014b).[15] This indicates a shift in reproductive patterns, at least as regards the average number of children indigenous women are now having.

---

[14]  As of 2015, the indigenous population in Latin America was estimated at no less than 48 million people distributed in 17 of the region's 20 countries. This is a lower bound estimate, as quantifying the indigenous population through censuses still presents problems of underestimation in some countries.

[15]  A detailed analysis of age structures using population pyramids derived from the 2010 census round shows that Ecuador, Mexico, Nicaragua and Peru have begun to go through the demographic transition. Lower fertility in these countries is reflected in a narrowing of the base of the pyramid as the share of children in indigenous populations declines. This development is more evident in Argentina, Costa Rica and Uruguay, in the last of which the indigenous population clearly has an aged structure (ECLAC, 2014).

Table III.2
Latin America (12 countries): population distribution by age group and by ethnicity, around 2010
(Percentages)

| Country and census date | Ethnicity | Age group | | | | Total | Absolute total |
|---|---|---|---|---|---|---|---|
| | | 0 to 14 | 15 to 29 | 30 to 59 | 60 and over | | |
| Argentina, 2010 | Indigenous | 28.4 | 26.4 | 36.2 | 9.0 | 100.0 | 955 032 |
| | Non-indigenous | 25.4 | 24.8 | 35.4 | 14.4 | 100.0 | 39 162 064 |
| Brazil, 2010 | Indigenous | 36.1 | 26.6 | 29.0 | 8.3 | 100.0 | 821 501 |
| | Non-indigenous | 24.0 | 26.9 | 38.3 | 10.8 | 100.0 | 189 898 247 |
| Colombia, 2005 | Indigenous | 39.5 | 26.2 | 26.8 | 7.4 | 100.0 | 1 392 623 |
| | Non-indigenous | 30.4 | 26.3 | 34.4 | 9.0 | 100.0 | 39 214 785 |
| Costa Rica, 2011 | Indigenous | 26.1 | 25.0 | 36.3 | 12.6 | 100.0 | 104 143 |
| | Non-indigenous | 24.6 | 27.9 | 37.1 | 10.4 | 100.0 | 4 102 429 |
| Ecuador, 2010 | Indigenous | 37.3 | 27.7 | 26.5 | 8.6 | 100.0 | 1 018 176 |
| | Non-indigenous | 30.8 | 27.0 | 32.9 | 9.3 | 100.0 | 13 465 323 |
| Honduras, 2013 | Indigenous | 40.0 | 29.2 | 24.4 | 6.4 | 100.0 | 601 815 |
| | Non-indigenous | 35.2 | 29.9 | 27.6 | 7.3 | 100.0 | 7 701 956 |
| Mexico, 2010 | Indigenous | 31.5 | 25.7 | 32.6 | 10.1 | 100.0 | 16 927 762 |
| | Non-indigenous | 28.6 | 26.7 | 35.4 | 9.3 | 100.0 | 94 041 188 |
| Nicaragua, 2005 | Indigenous | 40.9 | 28.8 | 24.4 | 6.0 | 100.0 | 311 704 |
| | Non-indigenous | 37.2 | 30.2 | 26.5 | 6.1 | 100.0 | 4 668 146 |
| Panama, 2010 | Indigenous | 45.1 | 26.1 | 23.4 | 5.4 | 100.0 | 417 547 |
| | Non-indigenous | 27.0 | 24.7 | 37.0 | 11.3 | 100.0 | 2 987 714 |
| Peru, 2007 | Indigenous | 33.6 | 26.4 | 30.1 | 10.0 | 100.0 | 6 489 109 |
| | Non-indigenous | 29.9 | 27.7 | 33.5 | 8.9 | 100.0 | 20 564 285 |
| Uruguay, 2011 | Indigenous | 16.9 | 21.2 | 44.8 | 17.1 | 100.0 | 76 452 |
| | Non-indigenous | 21.9 | 22.2 | 37.3 | 18.6 | 100.0 | 3 066 193 |
| Venezuela (Bolivarian Republic of), 2011 | Indigenous | 36.8 | 29.0 | 28.3 | 5.9 | 100.0 | 724 592 |
| | Non-indigenous | 26.8 | 27.6 | 36.4 | 9.2 | 100.0 | 26 325 411 |

**Source**: Economic Commission for Latin America and the Caribbean (ECLAC), on the basis of Latin American and Caribbean Demographic Centre (CELADE)-Population Division of ECLAC, special processing of available census microdata using Retrieval of Data for Small Areas by Microcomputer (REDATAM) software.

A study conducted by the Latin American and Caribbean Demographic Centre (CELADE)-Population Division of ECLAC (ECLAC, 2014b) shows age discontinuities in some countries' population pyramids, suggesting that the extent to which people declare an indigenous identity differs by sex and age. The behaviours observed thus seem to be influenced both by structural elements of the demographic dynamic and by identity factors that ought to be investigated in greater depth. It should also be remembered that age composition differs from one indigenous people to another, since demographic dynamics, and the behaviour of fertility in particular, are closely linked to the cultural and social organization of each indigenous people in its particular territorial context (ECLAC, 2007 and 2014b).

# 1.　The build-up of inequalities and disadvantages over the life cycle

## (a) Childhood

Indigenous children join adult activities as much as they can from an early age, learning the different manifestations of their identity. Broadly speaking, the primary socialization process is combined with incorporation into the family and community production system (Del Popolo, López and Acuña, 2009). As a traditional socialization mechanism, young people of both sexes work from a very early age, helping their parents with household tasks, crops, animal husbandry, fishing and other activities that support the family. Another manifestation of this form of socialization is marriage, whereby they acquire the responsibilities that forming a family entails. The transition from one stage of the life cycle to the next is clearly marked in many indigenous peoples, being often delimited by rites of passage or initiation. Notwithstanding, indigenous peoples are also experiencing sociocultural changes, and in general it can be seen that young people are at the centre of a number of tensions as a result: even as they are expected to bear responsibility for the biological and cultural continuity of the indigenous way of life, they are demanding greater inclusion and opportunities to access some degree of economic and social development and greater scope for participation (Del Popolo, López and Acuña, 2009; ECLAC, 2014b).

The inequality characterizing the region is manifested in the case of indigenous children and young adults by considerable disadvantages, particularly as regards health and education, two dimensions that are vital at this stage in the life cycle and that in turn have implications for later stages. Furthermore, as has been argued over the course of the chapter, this infringement of rights is compounded by interaction with other axes of the inequality matrix, resulting in exclusion based on multiple aspects: ethnicity (because they are indigenous), class (because they are poor), age (because they are young), gender (when they are female) and geography (because they live mainly in rural or marginal periurban localities). These inequalities are manifested in spheres critical to the current and future development of indigenous children.

The right to life is unquestionably a fundamental right, without which no other right can be enjoyed. Infant mortality (within the first year of life) and child mortality (before the age of 5) are very direct manifestations of the inequities affecting indigenous children from the start of life. The region has made progress, with infant and child mortality being reduced substantially in the last 10 years. Where childhood mortality is concerned, for example, the Bolivarian Republic of Venezuela and Mexico achieved a reduction of about 64% between 2000 and 2010, while in the same period Brazil, Costa Rica, Ecuador and Peru reduced the indicator by over half (ECLAC, 2014b). Even so, there are still deep divides affecting indigenous children. As figure III.13 shows, indigenous infant mortality is still systematically higher than non-indigenous infant mortality and far from reaching parity (Costa Rica is the only exception). The greatest inequalities are in Panama and Peru, where indigenous infant mortality is three times as high as non-indigenous infant mortality, and in the Plurinational State of Bolivia, where it is over twice as high. These inequalities are found in both urban and rural areas, being generally higher in the countryside, irrespective of the mortality level; child mortality behaves similarly (ECLAC, 2014b). Inequalities in infant and child mortality reflect the structural inequities suffered by indigenous peoples in the region, and thus will not be eliminated unless the issue of indigenous children's health (and health in general) is addressed synergistically with all other sectoral policies, without neglecting the collective dimension represented by the special sociocultural characteristics of indigenous peoples.

> The inequality characterizing the region is manifested in the case of indigenous children and young adults by considerable disadvantages, particularly as regards health and education, two dimensions that are vital at this stage in the life cycle and that in turn have implications for later stages.

**Figure III.13**
Latin America (11 countries): infant mortality by ethnicity, around 2010
*(Per 1,000 live births)*

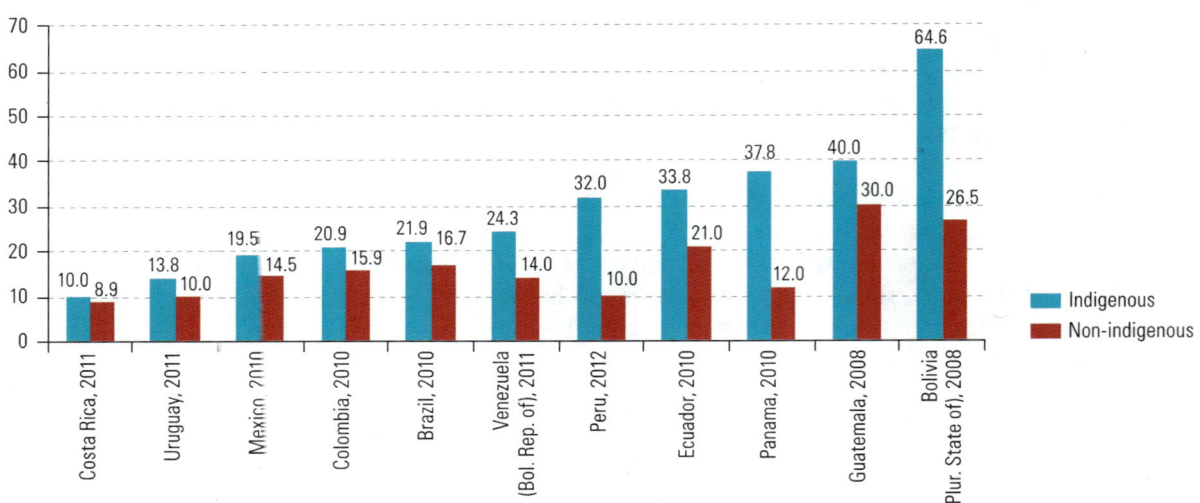

**Source**: Economic Commission for Latin America and the Caribbean (ECLAC), on the basis of Latin American and Caribbean Demographic Centre (CELADE)-Population Division of ECLAC.

Another key indicator of a deficit in childhood well-being that affects future development potential is malnutrition. Food insecurity is clearly greater in the indigenous population than in the non-indigenous population. This is a paradox, because it is the indigenous territories that are home to the greatest genetic diversity and wealth. In addition to explaining how the original communities survived, these resources have been the basis of food systems for modern societies throughout the world. Indigenous children are the worst affected, and the figures are telling. According to information from seven countries in the region from around 2010, the rate of chronic malnutrition is over twice as high for indigenous children under five as for the non-indigenous child population, ranging from 22.3% in Colombia to 58% in Guatemala. Ethnic disparities are even wider in the case of severe chronic malnutrition, while overall malnutrition behaves similarly (ECLAC, 2014b). Chronic malnutrition is recognized as having an adverse effect on children's cognitive development, affecting their future educational attainment (see, for example, Adair and others, 2013), something that in turn can limit their potential for social and economic inclusion at subsequent stages of the life cycle.

## (b) Youth

There are at least 10 million indigenous adolescents and youths aged between 10 and 24 in Latin America, most of them living in rural areas (ECLAC/PAHO, 2011).[16] Besides the educational gaps that they face, as detailed in section B of this chapter, young indigenous people in the region face inequalities in health, including mental health and substance abuse.

Problems such as alcoholism, drug abuse, depression and suicide among young indigenous people are a great source of concern. The United Nations Permanent Forum on Indigenous Issues has repeatedly drawn attention to the high rates of mental illness and suicide in indigenous communities, particularly among adolescents and young

---

[16]    This is the sum total of the figures available from censuses in the 2000 round for 14 countries of the region: Argentina, the Bolivarian Republic of Venezuela, Brazil, Chile, Costa Rica, Ecuador, Guatemala, Honduras, Mexico, Nicaragua, Panama, Paraguay, Peru and the Plurinational State of Bolivia. The actual number of indigenous young people undoubtedly exceeds this, as those in Colombia, the Dominican Republic and El Salvador were excluded for lack of data.

people. Alarming numbers of suicides among indigenous children, adolescents and young adults in Argentina, the Bolivarian Republic of Venezuela, Brazil, Chile, Colombia, Nicaragua and Paraguay have been noted for years now (ECLAC, 2014b).

Sexual and reproductive health divides between indigenous and non-indigenous young people are also marked. Indicators such as age of sexual initiation, institutional delivery, maternal mortality and knowledge about the transmission of HIV and other sexually transmitted diseases show differentiated patterns depending on ethnicity (ECLAC/PAHO, 2011; Pasqualini and Llorens, 2010). Rates of adolescent motherhood still differ strikingly between the indigenous and non-indigenous populations, undermining the development potential and rights of indigenous young women and their children (see figure III.14). Notwithstanding, these differences need to be understood in each socio-territorial context, since they involve both factors of structural inequality and others of a cultural nature that need to be understood for effective policies to be designed.

**Figure III.14**
Latin America (6 countries): young women aged 15 to 19 who are mothers, by area of residence and ethnicity, around 2010
*(Percentages)*

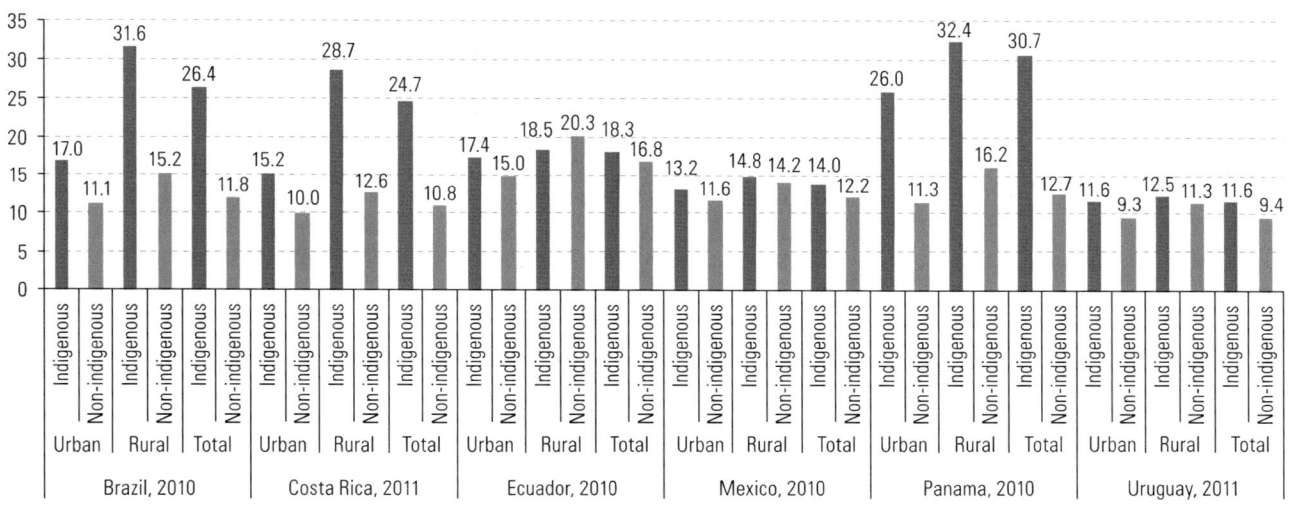

**Source**: Economic Commission for Latin America and the Caribbean (ECLAC), on the basis of *Mujeres indígenas en América Latina: dinámicas demográficas y sociales en el marco de los derechos humanos* (LC/W.558), Santiago, 2013, table 11, p. 69.

## (c) Adulthood: interlinked inequalities and cultural diversity

Both indigenous women and indigenous men experience numerous difficulties in adulthood, a stage in the life cycle when "productive" and "reproductive" decisions deriving from their social, cultural, environmental, territorial, spiritual and cosmic environment have to be taken within a development paradigm that has been challenged for its ransacking of natural, human and cultural resources, categorically opposed as this is to the indigenous concept of "living well". Accordingly, the premise of ECLAC is to consider the contribution indigenous peoples can make to the construction of a new development paradigm based on a structural shift towards equality and sustainability and including the ancestral knowledge, innovations and traditional practices of these peoples in the conservation and sustainable use of biological diversity, as well as the development of the different collective modalities of indigenous economies.

In the area of employment, although the information provided by censuses and surveys on economic participation and employment characteristics provides an important frame of reference, it also presents limitations in that the subsistence activities that predominate in the working world of many indigenous peoples are not included. Less recognized still is the work of indigenous women, especially in rural areas, where they are employed in occupations that are not treated as such in the context of the market economy. With this proviso, the figures on indigenous women's economic participation yielded by censuses are well below men's and even, in most cases, non-indigenous women's (ECLAC, 2013).

These factors also influence where and how indigenous men and women participate in the world of work. The censuses of this decade show that employed indigenous men work most of all in the primary sector, unlike their non-indigenous peers, who are more likely to be in the tertiary sector. Indigenous women, meanwhile, are mainly employed in the tertiary sector of the economy, including commerce and service activities in particular, while they also have a lesser but still important role in the primary sector (ECLAC, 2013). Most of these women are wage earners, and while this is usually viewed as positive from the perspective of social protection, the price that is paid is that traditional indigenous activities are relinquished in favour of other sectors of the economy in which, furthermore, they have greater comparative disadvantages. Thus, in urban areas, indigenous women are systematically more likely than non-indigenous ones to be in domestic service. The earnings of indigenous women also reflect the disparities that exist in the world of work, where they earn less than other population groups even when they have the same levels of education (ECLAC, 2016b). Lastly, indigenous women are at a disadvantage with respect to access to social protection mechanisms: just 28% of indigenous women aged 15 and over and in work were covered by a pension plan in 2013 or thereabouts, as compared to 44% of non-indigenous, non-Afrodescendent women (ECLAC, 2016b). This can leave indigenous women unprotected and vulnerable in the final stage of the life cycle.

### (d) Indigenous older persons

For many indigenous people, old age truly begins when they can no longer carry out tasks or activities for the maintenance of their families or the material reproduction of the community. A person's status and role in society may increase as they age, since older people accumulate the wisdom and collective memory that has to be transmitted to young people to ensure the cultural reproduction of the group or people. Consequently, old age is not seen as something negative but as part of the continuity of the culture. Furthermore, many of these people provide the link between local authorities and the community. In addition, the migration of young people and adults means that older people are the ones who are left in the countryside employing economic strategies to sustain families' life plans.

Conceptions of old age in the indigenous world may differ in relation to men and women, with older women having a subordinate role. Older indigenous people may actually be more vulnerable in cities because of the force of modernity, which erodes their social status and respect and results in a loss of traditional roles and the value set on them, all this being compounded by the poverty and marginalization experienced by indigenous people throughout their lives.

Discussion of gender inequalities in old age usually sets out from the fact that women have had to cope with unequal access to opportunities throughout their lives, with a negative cumulative effect on their social, financial and psychological well-being. Unfortunately, few studies have investigated how far these conceptions are equally valid for indigenous men and women and to what degree the factors protecting traditional indigenous cultures have been maintained, something that would require examination of the territorial, cultural and demographic situation of each people.

Although the information provided by censuses and surveys on economic participation and employment characteristics provides an important frame of reference, it also presents limitations in that the subsistence activities that predominate in the working world of many indigenous peoples are not included. Less recognized still is the work of indigenous women, especially in rural areas, where they are employed in occupations that are not treated as such in the context of the market economy.

Although the data sources available are clearly able to provide some evidence of the social inequality matrix through consideration of life cycles, little use has been made of them, particularly population and housing censuses, to analyse the situation of indigenous older persons. For example, considering that the structural factors of material poverty and exclusion affecting indigenous peoples tend to increase cumulative health risks or harm, and that this is compounded by disproportionate exposure to environmental degradation and the impact of major development projects, it is reasonable to think that elderly indigenous persons may be more disadvantaged in terms of their well-being.

The census-derived figures in table III.3 on the prevalence of disability offer some evidence. Although the prevalence of disability increases substantially with age irrespective of ethnicity, it is striking that generational increases are larger among indigenous peoples than among non-indigenous individuals. Furthermore, virtually no ethnic inequalities are observed in the early stages of the life cycle, but these are clearly present in adulthood and old age to the detriment of indigenous persons.

| Country and census year | Age groups and ethnicity | | | | | |
|---|---|---|---|---|---|---|
| | 0 to 18 | | 19 to 59 | | 60 and over | |
| | Indigenous | Non-indigenous | Indigenous | Non-indigenous | Indigenous | Non-indigenous |
| Brazil, 2010 | 5.9 | 8.5 | 25.3 | 24.9 | 66.0 | 63.4 |
| Colombia, 2005 | 2.9 | 3.2 | 6.8 | 5.9 | 25.8 | 23.9 |
| Costa Rica, 2011 | 3.7 | 3.7 | 13.7 | 9.6 | 45.4 | 36.4 |
| Ecuador, 2010 | 3.2 | 3.0 | 6.0 | 5.5 | 24.2 | 22.4 |
| Mexico, 2010 | 1.8 | 1.8 | 4.7 | 3.7 | 30.3 | 25.7 |
| Panama, 2010 | 2.2 | 2.1 | 7.6 | 6.8 | 32.7 | 32.0 |
| Uruguay, 2011 | 8.3 | 5.6 | 18.3 | 12.1 | 52.8 | 44.2 |

Table III.3
Latin America (7 countries): persons with disabilities, by ethnicity and by age group, around 2010
(Percentages)

**Source**: Economic Commission for Latin America and the Caribbean (ECLAC), on the basis of Latin American and Caribbean Demographic Centre (CELADE)-Population Division of ECLAC, special processing of census microdata using Retrieval of Data for Small Areas by Microcomputer (REDATAM) software.

As with the disability-related education gaps presented in section B of this chapter, the high prevalence of disability among indigenous older persons relative to non-indigenous older persons points to contextual factors having an increasingly pronounced effect (ECLAC, 2016a). It is clear that financial and social resources heavily influence prospects of enjoying a relatively autonomous old age.

## 2.    Closing reflections

Although the region has made great progress, there are still major challenges to the inclusion of indigenous persons throughout the life cycle. The progress has been due to the intensification in the past decade of a number of policies and programmes that, to differing degrees, have sought to include a rights approach based on current standards. Notwithstanding, the availability of timely, high-quality information disaggregated for indigenous peoples is an urgent need that the region must address if it is to continue making progress in this area and succeed in implementing ethnically relevant policies. For this, it is important to ensure that the identification of indigenous peoples is increasingly included in all data sources. Apart from indigenous (self-)identification, essential variables that need to be present in all the information sources of national statistical systems are indigenous individuals' age, sex and geographic location and the indigenous people they belong to. Another challenge is to generate complementary statistical tools for monitoring the requirements of indigenous peoples and their collective rights.

# D. The life cycle as reflected in the social institutions of Latin America

Most of the countries have adopted institutional frameworks centred on the needs of population segments over the life cycle, and this is reflected in laws and government bodies explicitly focused on childhood, youth and older adulthood, and in the adoption of policies and programmes oriented specifically towards these groups. The main obstacles and challenges for these institutions are very similar and can be summed up as the difficulty of effectively mainstreaming the needs of these population segments across public policy as a whole and using the latter to respond to them comprehensively.

In recent decades, most of the region's countries have adopted institutional frameworks emphasizing the needs of specific population segments over the life cycle. This is reflected in laws and government bodies explicitly focused on childhood, youth and old age. At the same time, the incorporation of the life cycle approach has been manifested in the adoption of policies and programmes in different areas. The difficulties and challenges of this institutional structure, in turn, reflect the difficulties of mainstreaming the needs of these segments in public policy as a whole.

An overview of the institutions dealing with these population segments will now be presented, after which some of the policy challenges involved in coordinating and incorporating the life cycle approach will be examined. As ECLAC (2016b) notes, two analytical dimensions (the legal and regulatory dimension and the organizational dimension) provide a way to characterize social institutions.[17] One of the challenges for the latter in the region is to be able to take comprehensive action via interinstitutional and intersectoral coordination of the different government actors participating in social policy implementation (Repetto, Cunill Grau and Bronzo, 2015).

## 1. Laws and authorities focused on children and adolescents

Most of the 33 countries in the region that adopted the 1990 Convention on the Rights of the Child have progressively introduced specific legislation and set up specialized agencies to safeguard the rights of the child and adolescent population under its auspices (see table III.4). This instrument installed a new approach, individualizing children as subjects of rights and generating new mechanisms that have renewed agencies whose main policy focus was originally on the traditional family.

There is great heterogeneity in the region when it comes to the institutions coordinating children's and adolescents' affairs, as they include ministries (Trinidad and Tobago), deputy ministers' offices (Plurinational State of Bolivia) and secretariats attached to ministries (Argentina, Guatemala, Panama and Paraguay), institutes (Uruguay), departments (Cuba and Honduras) and inter-agency councils (Brazil, Chile, Colombia, Costa Rica, the Dominican Republic, El Salvador and Nicaragua), among others.

---

[17] The information in this section is updated to February 2017.

Table III.4
Latin America and the Caribbean (23 countries): institutions leading the protection of children's and adolescents' rights

| Country | Legislation or children's code | Main agency responsible for protecting children's and adolescents' rights | Lead or coordinating authority |
|---|---|---|---|
| Argentina | Law No. 26061 on the Comprehensive Protection of the Rights of Children and Adolescents and Decree 415/2006 | National Secretariat for Childhood, Adolescence and the Family (SENNAF) | Ministry of Social Development |
| Bahamas | Early Childhood Care Act (2004) | Early Childhood Development Center-Ministry of Social Services and Community Development | Social development or inclusion ministry |
| Belize | n.a. | Early Childhood and Education Unit | Ministry of Education, Youth, Sports and Culture |
| Bolivia (Plurinational State of) | Code on Children and Adolescents Law No. 2026 (October 1999) | Office of the Deputy Minister for Equal Opportunities (Department of Children, Youth and Older Adults) | Ministry of Justice |
| Brazil | Statute on Children and Adolescents Law No. 8069 (1990) Law No. 8242 (1991) | National Council for Children's and Adolescents' Rights (CONANDA) | Ministry of Human Rights |
| Chile | Law No. 20032 establishing a system of provision for children and adolescents | National Children's Council | Social development or inclusion ministry |
| Colombia | Law No. 1804 establishing a State policy for all-round development in early childhood "from zero to forever" (2016) Law No. 1098 - Code on Children and Adolescents (2006), corrected by Decrees 4840 of 2007, 4652 of 2006, 578 of 2007 and 4011 of 2006 | Inter-Agency Commission for Comprehensive Early Childhood Care | Office of the president or vice-president or presidential appointee |
| Costa Rica | Law No. 7739 - Code on Children and Adolescents (1998) | National Council on Children and Adolescents | Office of the president or vice-president or presidential appointee |
| Cuba | Family Code (1975) Code on Children and the Young (1978) | Department of Minors of the Ministry of the Interior | Ministry of the Interior |
| Dominican Republic | Law No. 136-03 - Code for the System of Children's and Adolescents' Protection and Fundamental Rights | National Council on Children and Adolescents (CONANI) | Office of the president or vice-president or presidential appointee |
| Ecuador | Law No. 100 - Code on Children and Adolescents (2003) | Ministry of Economic and Social Inclusion (MIES) - Child and Family Service (INFA) National Council on Children and Adolescents (CNNA) | Social development or inclusion ministry |
| El Salvador | Law on Comprehensive Protection of Children and Adolescents (March 2009) | National Council on Children and Adolescents (CONNA) | Office of the president or vice-president or presidential appointee |
| Guatemala | Decree No. 27-2003 - Law on Comprehensive Protection of Children and Adolescents (2003) | Social Welfare Secretariat | Office of the president or vice-president or presidential appointee |
| Honduras | Code on Children and Adolescents (1996) | Department for Children, Adolescents and the Family (DINAF) | Social development or inclusion ministry |
| Jamaica | Child Care and Protection Act (2005) | Early Childhood Commission | Ministry of Education |
| Mexico | Law for the Protection of Children's and Adolescents' Rights (2014) | National System for Comprehensive Protection of Children and Adolescents | Office of the president or vice-president or presidential appointee |
| Nicaragua | Law No. 287 - Code on Children and Adolescents (1998) (CONAPINA) | Council for the Comprehensive Care and Protection of Children and Adolescents - Ministry of the Family | Social development or inclusion ministry |
| Panama | Family Code | National Secretariat for Children, Young Persons and the Family | Social development or inclusion ministry |
| Paraguay | Law No. 1680/01 - Code on Children and Adolescents (2001) | National Secretariat for Children and Adolescents (SNNA) | Office of the president or vice-president or presidential appointee |
| Peru | Code on Children and Adolescents (2000) | Department of Children and Adolescents | Ministry of Women and Vulnerable Populations |
| Trinidad and Tobago | Children Act (2012) | Ministry of Gender, Youth and Child Development | Ministry of Gender, Youth and Child Development |
| Uruguay | Law No. 17823 - Code on Children and Adolescents (2004) Regulatory Decree 475/2006 | Uruguayan Institute for Children and Adolescents (INAU) | Office of the president or vice-president or presidential appointee |
| Venezuela (Bolivarian Republic of) | Organic Law for the Protection of Children and Adolescents (LOPNA) (2000) | Ministry of People's Power of the Office of the President through the Autonomous Institute of the National Council for Children's and Adolescents' Rights | Office of the president or vice-president or presidential appointee |

**Source**: Economic Commission for Latin America and the Caribbean (ECLAC), on the basis of official information from the countries.
**Note**: n.a.: No official information available.

With a view to inter-agency coordination, the highest authority in a number of countries are children's councils formed of different social ministries, sometimes with the participation of private sector and civil society bodies as well. This method is followed in seven countries, with coordination being carried out in the great majority by the office of the president or vice-president or some presidential appointee. A great challenge in these cases is to achieve the leadership needed to coordinate the wide array of organizations represented on these councils, particularly with a view to implementing comprehensive systems for the protection of children's rights as suggested by international guidelines, one example being the National System for Comprehensive Protection of Children and Adolescents adopted by Mexico in 2014 (see box III.3).

Box III.3
Desirable aspects of institutions dealing with children and adolescents

According to the recommendations of the United Nations Children's Fund (UNICEF), the construction of a comprehensive system of protection for children's and adolescents' rights involves a set of necessary laws, policies and services in all social areas, but especially social welfare, education, health and justice, to support the prevention of protection-related risks and the response in this area (Morlachetti, 2013, p. 11). It should include the following in particular:

- A legal framework compatible with the principles and provisions of the Convention on the Rights of the Child, which requires an exhaustive review of domestic legislation.

- Institutions involving the different levels of government (central, provincial and local) and all three branches of the State, in dialogue with civil society and with a view to the multidimensional character of children's issues.

- A management model for public policies on children and adolescents that serves to coordinate institutions, preferably a systemic management model rather than one centred on a single coordinating or lead agency.

- A national action strategy for children and adolescents that reflects the provisions of the Convention in practice.

- Adequate, timely and equitable budgetary resourcing of policies and programmes designed to benefit children and adolescents.

- A children's rights information and knowledge base with up-to-date, disaggregated high-quality data to provide solid evidence for policy and programme design.

- An institutional children's rights-focused capacity-building strategy so that children and adolescents are properly served.

**Source**: Economic Commission for Latin America and the Caribbean (ECLAC), on the basis of A. Morlachetti, "Comprehensive national child protection systems: legal basis and current practice in Latin America and the Caribbean", *Project Documents* (LC/W.515), Santiago, ECLAC/United Nations Children's Fund (UNICEF), 2013; and UNICEF, "Infancia y leyes" [online] https://www.unicef.org/mexico/spanish/17042.html.

Of a total of 23 countries, the main agency responsible for children and adolescents comes under the social development or inclusion ministry in 7, the office of the president or vice-president or a presidential appointee in 9, and some other portfolio in another 7 (such as the justice, education or interior ministry).[18] Departments or national institutes are what predominate in these cases. Meeting the challenge of coordination depends

---

[18]    There has been a degree of institutional volatility in some cases, with changes in the institutional reporting lines and functions of the bodies responsible. In Brazil between 2003 and 2015, for example, there was a Secretariat for Children and Adolescents forming part of the National Secretariat of Human Rights, coming directly under the office of the President. In 2015 this body became a National Secretariat of the Ministry for Women, Racial Equality and Human Rights. This ministry ceased to exist during a political crisis in May 2016, and the Secretariat was placed under the Ministry of Justice and Citizenship. Finally, in February 2017, Provisional Measure 768/17 created the Ministry of Human Rights, which incorporates responsibilities relating to children and adolescents and policies for women's rights, racial equality, people with disabilities and older persons, among other functions (for further information, see [online] http://www2.camara.leg.br/camaranoticias/noticias/522670.html).

on the ability of these institutes or secretariats for children (and the ministry to which they are attached) to coordinate and mobilize the resources and programmes of other departments that, sectorally speaking, are not under their jurisdiction.

In all cases, the challenge is to coordinate sectoral policies, in both social and other areas, to meet the needs and safeguard the rights of children, as well as adopting models that make provision for processes associated with people's needs during the different phases of childhood and the transition from childhood and adolescence to adult life. Given some of the critical situations associated with the reproduction of inequality in this phase of the life cycle and the longitudinal linkages that arise subsequently, institutions are clearly called upon to promote greater coordination and awareness of issues such as protection and good treatment within the family and less uneven access to care, preschool education, health and nutrition services.

## 2.    Laws and agencies for youth

Although there is no international instrument that entails the adoption of a comprehensive system for protecting the rights of youth in particular, the Global Forum on Youth Policies, held in Baku in 2014, agreed on basic guidelines for such policies, such as that they should be rights-based, inclusive, comprehensive, participatory, gender-responsive, knowledge-based and evidence-informed, accountable and fully resourced (ECLAC, 2015b). Many countries in the region have developed strategies in which the youth perspective is taken as a type of citizenship, and young people as strategic development actors, and which incorporate some elements of the Baku Commitment.

Latin America has two regional instruments of relevance to youth. One is the 2007 Ibero-American Convention on the Rights of Youth, which enshrines the rights of youth on issues ranging from health and sexuality to work, taking in education and culture, among other things. Each of the signatory States committed itself to progressively incorporating concrete decisions and measures in which young people would be treated as crucial actors in the countries' development in the context of current challenges.[19] More recently, the Ibero-American Youth Covenant was agreed upon during the twenty-fifth Ibero-American Summit of Heads of State and Government, held in Cartagena de Indias (Colombia) in October 2016. The Covenant is meant to promote initiatives in the areas of education, employment, innovation and the culture of peace, among other areas of importance for the well-being of youth in Ibero-America.[20] In the Caribbean, the Caribbean Community (CARICOM) also has a youth development agenda.[21]

Most of these initiatives to institutionalize actions aimed at youth have been established since the 2000s. The different countries in the region have strongly committed themselves to pursuing youth development and protection, mainly by encouraging young people to participate in social, economic and political development. Nonetheless, there are still large gaps in implementation. A key tension is the inability of increasingly highly educated youth populations to participate successfully in the labour market, finding decent jobs commensurate with their level of schooling.

In all cases, the challenge is to coordinate sectoral policies, in both social and other areas, to meet the needs and safeguard the rights of children, as well as adopting models that make provision for processes associated with people's needs during the different phases of childhood and the transition from childhood and adolescence to adult life.

---

[19]    See International Youth Organization for Ibero-America [online] http://www.oij.org/es_ES/noticia/convencion-iberoamericana-de-derechos-de-los-jovenes.

[20]    See [online] http://segib.org/documento/pacto-iberoamericano-de-juventud/.

[21]    See [online] http://cms2.caricom.org/documents/13930-cydap_2012-2017_rev.pdf.

The existence of a body of law in a country reflects a social consensus about the need to deal with an issue and the best way to do so. Sixteen countries in the region have general legislation dealing with youth, and this is important because a legal framework contributes to stability, permanent standards, institutional continuity and the resourcing of public policies for youth.

As ECLAC (2014a) notes, setting aside differences in the types of agencies and the work they do to promote the development of the youth population in their respective countries, institutions tend to be weak, certainly by comparison with the solidity of related sectoral ministries such as those for education, labour and health. In this situation, the key functions that should be performed by governmental youth institutions essentially involve playing a coordinating role and mainstreaming and joining up initiatives to dynamize processes and thereby bring about improvements in youth policies within each sector, maintaining a comprehensive view of the needs of this population in its respective contexts and at the different levels of government. Building themselves up into genuine governing or standard-setting authorities in this area is probably the greatest challenge they face.

All this suggests that governments are increasingly aware of the importance of having the right legislation and policies in place to meet the needs, aspirations and demands of youth.

In this context, and given how intractable some features of the reproduction of social inequality during youth can be, the core missions for the institutions responsible for this population should include providing adequate resources for the implementation of specific policies or programmes to ensure the conditions are in place for young people of both sexes to mobilize their capabilities so that they can autonomously achieve their life plans, and working to give greater prominence and coherence to their particular needs, particularly issues relating to the completion of schooling, the transition from school to work, training for work, support for and access to sexual and reproductive health and care services, protection from and prevention of violence, and access to culture. In other words, youth policies should meet needs, ensure real access to rights and be organized around the idea of emancipation for youth. These are issues whose level of priority will differ from one situation to another, but which it is up to institutions to bring to light and deal with in a coordinated fashion.

In most of the countries, the social institutions devoted to this group include specific laws and specialized agencies tasked with safeguarding the rights of youth (see table III.5).

The core missions for the institutions responsible for this population should include providing adequate resources for the implementation of specific policies or programmes to ensure the conditions are in place for young people of both sexes to mobilize their capabilities so that they can autonomously achieve their life plans, and working to give greater prominence and coherence to their particular needs.

Table III.5
Latin America and the Caribbean (24 countries): institutional position and governance of agencies responsible for young people

| Country | Youth legislation or code | Main agency tasked with protecting youth | Coordinating or governing authority |
|---|---|---|---|
| Argentina | Law creating the National Youth Department, S-1434 (2003) | National Youth Department | Ministry of Social Development |
| Bahamas | n.a. | Ministry of Youth, Culture and Sports | Ministry of Youth, Culture and Sports |
| Belize | n.a. | Ministry of Education, Youth, Sports and Culture | Ministry of Education, Youth, Sports and Culture |
| Bolivia (Plurinational State of) | Supreme Decree 2114 - Youth Act (2014) | Plurinational Youth Council | Ministry of Justice |
| Brazil | Law No. 12852 on the Youth Statute (2013) Law No. 11129 creating the National Youth Secretariat (2005) | National Youth Secretariat | Office of the president or vice-president or presidential appointee |
| Chile | Law No. 19042 creating the National Institute for Youth (1991) | National Institute for Youth | Social development or inclusion ministry |
| Colombia | Statutory Law No. 1622 adopting the Youth Citizenship Statute (2013) | Directorate of the "Young Colombia" National Youth System | Office of the president or vice-president or presidential appointee |
| Costa Rica | Law No. 8261 - Young Persons Act (2002) | Office of the Deputy Minister for Youth | Ministry of Culture and Youth |
| Dominica | n.a. | Ministry of Youth, Sports, Culture and Constituency Empowerment | Ministry of Youth, Sports, Culture and Constituency Empowerment |
| Dominican Republic | Law No. 49-2000 - General Youth Act (2000) | Ministry of Youth | Ministry of Youth |
| Ecuador | Youth Act (2001) | National Department for Youth and Adolescence | Social development or inclusion ministry |
| El Salvador | General Youth Act (2012) | National Institute for Youth | Office of the president or vice-president or presidential appointee |
| Guatemala | Government Order 405-96 Decree 114-97 (1997) | National Youth Council | Office of the president or vice-president or presidential appointee |
| Guyana | n.a. | Ministry of Education-Department of Culture, Youth and Sport | Other ministry |
| Honduras | Decree No. 260-2005 - Framework Act for the Comprehensive Development of Young People (2006) | National Youth Council | Office of the president or vice-president or presidential appointee |
| Jamaica | n.a. | Ministry of Culture, Gender, Entertainment and Sport | Ministry of Culture, Gender, Entertainment and Sport |
| Mexico | Mexican Youth Institute Act (1999) | Mexican Youth Institute | Office of the president or vice-president or presidential appointee |
| Nicaragua | Law No. 392 promoting the Comprehensive Development of Youth and its Regulations (2002) | Ministry of Youth | Other ministry |
| Panama | Law No. 42 creating the Ministry of Youth, Children, Women and the Family (1997) | Ministry of Social Development | Social development or inclusion ministry |
| Paraguay | National Law on Youth and Public Agencies for Youth (2005) | National Youth Secretariat | Office of the president or vice-president or presidential appointee |
| Peru | Law No. 27802 - National Youth Council Act (2002) | National Youth Secretariat | Ministry of Education |
| Trinidad and Tobago | n.a. | Ministry of Gender, Youth and Child Development | Ministry of Gender, Youth and Child Development |
| Uruguay | Law No. 17866 Creation of the Ministry of Social Development (2005) | National Institute for Youth | Social development or inclusion ministry |
| Venezuela (Bolivarian Republic of) | Law No. 37404 - National Youth Act (2002) | National Institute of People's Power for Youth | Ministry of People's Power for Youth and Sport |

**Source**: Economic Commission for Latin America and the Caribbean (ECLAC), on the basis of official information from the countries.
**Note**:    n.a.: No official information available.

The ambition of interinstitutional coordination implied by the inter-agency council format is less in evidence here than in the case of institutions dealing with the child population. Instead, ministries specializing in youth feature prominently: of the 24 countries for which information is available, 8 have an institution of this type. This may be deceptive, however, since in many cases they encompass a number of areas (such as sport and culture) or priority groups (women and children) and do not have great technical or financial resources.

Of a total of 24 countries, the main youth agency is attached to the ministry responsible for social development in just 5 cases, while in 12 it reports to a different portfolio: a ministry devoted exclusively to youth (the Dominican Republic and Nicaragua), the education ministry (Guyana and Peru), the justice ministry (Plurinational State of Bolivia) or, as in the cases already mentioned, ministries dealing with multiple social or other areas (Bahamas, Belize, the Bolivarian Republic of Venezuela, Costa Rica, Dominica, Jamaica and Trinidad and Tobago). What predominate in these cases are directorates or national institutes of youth, and they are faced with the difficulty of coordinating effectively with other ministerial bodies. Lastly, in 7 of the 24 countries, the governing authority is the office of the national president or vice-president.

Thus, there is also heterogeneity in the region as regards the institutions for youth affairs. According to ECLAC (2009), the objectives of these bodies include at least four key tasks: systematic appreciation of the situation of youth, professionalization of technical personnel, innovation in programme design and implementation and development of communication skills to build consensus among leaders and public opinion.

Lastly, the role of a national youth policy or plan is also critical, as it provides the vision for all a country's youth-related programmes and activities (see table A.1 of the annex) and helps to clarify the tasks involved in coordinating different government bodies.

## 3.    Laws and agencies for older persons

International statutes designed to guarantee the rights of older adults include a number of legal instruments of global and regional scope. Among the former, particular mention may be made of the United Nations Principles for Older Persons (1991), the Proclamation on Ageing (1992) and the Madrid Political Declaration and International Plan of Action on Ageing (2002). The latter include the Regional Strategy for the Implementation in Latin America and the Caribbean of the Madrid International Plan of Action on Ageing (2003), the Brasilia Declaration (2007), the Pan-American Health Organization (PAHO) Plan of Action on the Health of Older Persons, including Active and Healthy Aging (2009), the Declaration of Commitment of Port of Spain (2009) and the San José Charter on the Rights of Older Persons in Latin America and the Caribbean (2012). This last instrument was a major step towards the emergence of national commitments, with guarantees for the social and political rights of older persons. A legally binding instrument finalized recently is the Inter-American Convention on Protecting the Human Rights of Older Persons (2015), currently being signed and ratified by the countries (see box III.4).

International progress in this area has been matched at the national level. Currently, 19 of the 23 countries for which information is available have specific legislation and specialized agencies for the protection of older persons (see table III.6). In federal countries, there is also important legislation at the subnational level.

Box III.4
The Inter-American
Convention on Protecting
the Human Rights
of Older Persons

The Convention is a regional legal instrument designed to promote, protect and ensure the recognition and the full enjoyment and exercise, on an equal basis, of all human rights and fundamental freedoms of older persons, in order to contribute to their full inclusion, integration, and participation in society.

As a binding regional agreement, the Convention commits the American States that have signed it to adopt and generate any changes needed in their constitutions to adapt to the provisions of the Convention and so ensure that the legislative measures required to promote and uphold the rights and freedoms of older persons are taken. One of the general principles that the Convention seeks to uphold is recognition for older persons, with particular emphasis on their role in society and their valuable contributions to countries' development. Protection for the dignity, independence and autonomy of older persons is meant to create an atmosphere of equality and non-discrimination, bringing about a favourable situation for this group and ensuring their physical, economic and social well-being.

The States undertake to safeguard the human rights and fundamental freedoms of older persons, and to that end will adopt measures to prevent, punish, and eradicate practices that contravene the Convention, such as isolation, abandonment, prolonged physical restraint, overcrowding, expulsion from the community, deprivation of food, infantilization, medical treatments that are, inter alia, inadequate or disproportional or that constitute mistreatment or cruel, inhuman, or degrading treatment or punishment that jeopardizes the safety and integrity of older persons.

The Convention also provides that States should strengthen such legislative, administrative, judicial, budgetary and any other measures, including adequate access to justice, as may be necessary to ensure differentiated and preferential treatment for older persons in all areas. Other duties include the creation of public institutions specializing in the protection and promotion of the rights of older persons and their all-round development and transparent measures to promote the gathering of appropriate information, including statistical and research data, for designing and applying policies.

**Source**: Inter-American Convention on Protecting the Human Rights of Older Persons.

Table III.6
Latin America and the Caribbean (23 countries): lead institutions coordinating protection for the rights of older persons

| Country | Legislation or code regarding older persons | Main agency tasked with protecting older persons | Coordinating or governing authority |
| --- | --- | --- | --- |
| Argentina | Old Age Protection Act – S3844/12 (2012) | National Directorate of Policies for Older Adults | Social development or inclusion ministry |
| Bahamas | n.a. | Department of Social Services - Senior Citizens Division | Social development or inclusion ministry |
| Belize | n.a. | Ministry of Human Development, Social Transformation and Poverty Alleviation - Family Support Services Division | Social development or inclusion ministry |
| Bolivia (Plurinational State of) | Older Adults Act Law No. 369 (2013) | Directorate-General for Children and Older Adults | Ministry of Justice |
| Brazil | Law No. 10741 (2003) | National Council for the Rights of the Elderly (CNDI) | Ministry of Human Rights |
| Chile | Law No. 19828 creating the National Service for Older Adults (2002) | National Service for Older Adults (SENAMA) | Social development or inclusion ministry |
| Colombia | Law No. 1251 (2008) | National Council for Older Adults | Ministry of Health and Social Protection |
| Costa Rica | Law No. 7935 - Comprehensive Older Adults Act (1999) | National Council for Older Adults | Office of the president or vice-president or presidential appointee |
| Cuba | Law No. 41 - Public Health Act (1983) | National Directorate for Older Adult Services | Ministry of Public Health |
| Dominican Republic | Law No. 352-98 - Elderly Protection Act (1998) | National Council for the Elderly (CONAPE) | Ministry of Public Health |
| Ecuador | Elderly Act (2006) | National Council for Intergenerational Equality (CNII) | Office of the president or vice-president or presidential appointee |
| El Salvador | Older Adults Comprehensive Services Act (2002) | National Council for Comprehensive Care for Programmes for Older Persons (CONAIPAM) | Social development or inclusion ministry |

Table III.6 (concluded)

| Country | Legislation or code regarding older persons | Main agency tasked with protecting older persons | Coordinating or governing authority |
|---|---|---|---|
| Guatemala | Decree No. 80-96 - Third Age Protection Act (1996) | Social Welfare Secretariat of the Office of the First Lady (SOSEP) - National Committee for Protection of the Elderly (CONAPROV) | First family |
| Guyana | n.a | National Commission for the Elderly | Ministry of Labour, Human Services and Social Security |
| Honduras | Older Adult and Pensioner Protection Act (2006) | Older Adults Department | Social development or inclusion ministry |
| Jamaica | n.a. | National Council for Senior Citizens | Ministry of Labour and Social Security |
| Mexico | Rights of Older Adults Act (2002) | National Institute of Older Persons | Social development or inclusion ministry |
| Nicaragua | Law No. 720 - Older Adults Act (2010) | National Council for Older Adults | Social development or inclusion ministry |
| Panama | Law No. 15 (1992) | National Council for Older Adults | Social development or inclusion ministry |
| Paraguay | Law No. 1885 - Adult Persons Act (2002) | Council for Older Adults | Ministry of Public Health and Social Welfare |
| Peru | Law No. 28803 - Older Adults Act (2006) | Older Adults Department (DIPAM) | Ministry of Women and Social Development (MIMDES) |
| Uruguay | Law No. 17796 - Comprehensive Support for Older Adults Act (2004) | National Institute for Older Persons | Social development or inclusion ministry |
| Venezuela (Bolivarian Republic of) | Social Services for Older Adults Act (2005) | Presidential Council for Older Adults | Office of the president or vice-president or presidential appointee |

**Source**: Economic Commission for Latin America and the Caribbean (ECLAC), on the basis of official information from the countries.
**Note**:    n.a.: No official information available.

The institutions devoted to older persons are very diverse and include services (Chile), subsecretariats or institutes (Mexico and Uruguay), departments (Argentina, Cuba, Honduras, Peru and Plurinational State of Bolivia), national councils (Bolivarian Republic of Venezuela, Brazil, Colombia, Costa Rica, Dominican Republic, Ecuador, El Salvador, Jamaica, Nicaragua, Panama and Paraguay) and others.

In contrast to agencies dealing with the child and adolescent population, which usually come under the authority of the national president's or vice-president's office, the most common situation (10 of the 23 countries observed) is for institutions dealing with older persons to come under the social development or inclusion ministry. The responsible authorities are other ministries in 9 cases (health or justice ministries or social security institutions of various kinds), while in only 3 instances are these agencies governed from the office of the president or vice-president or the first family.

These institutions are mostly recent, however. Only a few countries (those of the Caribbean plus Argentina, Costa Rica, Cuba and Mexico) have older institutions, usually associated with health or interior ministries or social security institutes. As noted by Huenchuan (2013 and 2016), the relative frequency with which agencies dealing with older persons are attached to social development ministries bespeaks a transformation characterized by the abandonment of an initial biomedical approach in favour of a broader spectrum of actions guided by the aim of mainstreaming issues associated with ageing and enforcement of older people's rights in all public-sector activities. In particular, when dealing with some of the social inequality dimensions analysed, the institutions responsible for this population should work for greater coordination and visibility, particularly as regards access to special health and care services and to contributory and non-contributory pensions.

In contrast to agencies dealing with the child and adolescent population, which usually come under the authority of the national president's or vice-president's office, the most common situation (10 of the 23 countries observed) is for institutions dealing with older persons to come under the social development or inclusion ministry.

# E.    Final comments

The aims of the 2030 Agenda for Sustainable Development include not only ensuring that no one is left behind, but reaching the furthest behind first. To meet these aspirations, it is necessary to determine which population groups experience most marginalization, exclusion and infringements of their rights. These populations often experience a number of inequalities that overlap and compound each other, accumulating throughout their lives and across generations. Efforts to identify these groups are complicated by the statistical invisibility of certain populations and their needs and the limited potential to disaggregate information sources by multiple characteristics. Better information sources are urgently needed to make it possible to look beyond national averages and to obtain longitudinal data, which are also in short supply, in order to study trends over the whole of people's life cycles.

The proposed social inequality matrix is intended to shed light on the combinations of axes that entrench inequality and to strengthen actions at those intersections which are visible but have not seen improvements over time. Possible combinations include, in particular: (i) intersections that have not yet been given enough consideration but are of great importance because they affect people's well-being and (ii) intersections that are of great importance and highly visible (perhaps because they have been the subject of public policies), but that persist with no reduction in the gaps observed.

This chapter has analysed the life cycle as one of the axes of social inequalities, examining inter- and intragenerational divides at each stage (childhood and adolescence, youth, adulthood and old age) in dimensions related to poverty, education, work and social protection, all key areas in social and economic inclusion and the exercise of rights. It has sought to illustrate how gender, racial, ethnic and geographical disparities interact and intensify the inequalities observed at the different stages of the life cycle.[22] It has also examined the links between inequalities experienced at the different stages, considering the importance of the paths people follow throughout the life cycle and the manner in which an array of social disadvantages accumulate and consolidate over time.

Just as the axes structuring inequality intersect and reinforce one another, it is likewise necessary to analyse the connections between the rights that are infringed. Lack of education, poor health, unemployment and a lack of decent working opportunities, social vulnerability, housing deprivations, poverty and political invisibility also intersect and reinforce one another.

The situation of indigenous people is of particular interest when it comes to illustrating these relationships. On the whole, the indigenous population still has higher fertility, implying greater potential growth. Policy and programme design should take account of these distinctive demographic profiles, in which there is a substantial presence of children, adolescents and youth, as this is essential for adequate resources to be allocated, mainly to address challenges associated with health and education, responding to both individual and collective rights. The greatest progress on policies and programmes with an intercultural perspective in the region has been in the areas of health and education, centring precisely on indigenous women and children.

---

[22]    The particular case of Afrodescendants and race as a structuring factor in inequality is explored in chapter V.

Indigenous persons are faced with greater disadvantages at different stages of the life cycle, and these intersect with gender and territory, sometimes building up over a lifetime and deepening ethnic divides. It is thus vital to design policies that genuinely reflect current international standards regarding the rights of indigenous peoples, conjoining individual and collective rights and incorporating gender, generational and territorial outlooks. This is why it is so important for States to renew and strengthen their commitment to applying the United Nations Declaration on the Rights of Indigenous Peoples, among other current international and regional agreements, as a way of starting to break up the social inequality matrix.

The life cycle approach places individuals at the centre of public action from birth to the end of life, recognizing that their needs change over a lifetime and that the individual is the starting and end point of social policy. From an institutional standpoint, this means recognizing and dealing with the specific needs and risks of each stage in the cycle, but also the transitions between the different stages.

The corollary of an increased awareness of the need to adopt policy approaches that are sensitive to people's lifelong needs and to mainstream the gender perspective is the emergence of social institutions devoted to specific population segments (especially children and adolescents, youth and older people). These institutions have spread throughout Latin America and the Caribbean and are anchored both in international commitments and instruments and in specialized national laws and agencies. Their organizational diversity notwithstanding, these agencies share a commitment to mainstreaming the specific needs and guaranteeing the rights of these segments in all public-sector activities, showing where there are gaps and exclusions. Consequently, they also share the challenge of fomenting greater all-round (inter-agency) coordination between different government actors as a way of ensuring that the approaches adopted are sensitive to people's rights and stage in the life cycle. Nonetheless, these are incipient institutions for which social authority and coordination models are still being developed. It must be recognized that consistency in promoting the rights of all population groups from an intergenerational and life cycle perspective needs to be developed with an emphasis on the specific risks and vulnerabilities of each stage.

The life cycle approach places individuals at the centre of public action from birth to the end of life, recognizing that their needs change over a lifetime and that the individual is the starting and end point of social policy. From an institutional standpoint, this means recognizing and dealing with the specific needs and risks of each stage in the cycle, but also the transitions between the different stages.

# Bibliography

Adair, L. S. and others (2013), "Associations of linear growth and relative weight gain during early life with adult health and human capital in countries of low and middle income: findings from five birth cohort studies", *The Lancet*, vol. 382, No. 9891.

Alarcón, J. and others (2015), "Desafíos de la educación preescolar en Chile: ampliar cobertura, mejorar la calidad y evitar el acoplamiento", *Estudios Pedagógicos*, vol. XLI, No. 2.

Amarante, V., M. Colacce and P. Manzi (2016), "La brecha de género en jubilaciones y pensiones: los casos de Argentina, Brasil, Chile y Uruguay", *Asuntos de Género series*, No. 138 (LC/L.4223), Santiago, Economic Commission for Latin America and the Caribbean (ECLAC).

Bos, M.S., A. J. Ganimian and E. Vegas (2014), "América Latina en PISA 2012: ¿cómo se desempeñan los estudiantes que asistieron a pre-escolar?", Inter-American Development Bank (IDB) [online] https://publications.iadb.org/handle/11319/6467.

Carr, D. (2009), "Life cycle", *Encyclopedia of the Life cycle and Human Development*, vol. 3, D. Carr (ed.), Detroit, Gale Cengage Learning.

Cecchini, S. and others (2015), "Rights and the life cycle: reordering social protection tools," *Towards Universal Social Protection: Latin American pathways and policy tools*, S. Cecchini and others (eds.), ECLAC Books, N° 136 (LC/G. 2644-P), Santiago, Economic Commission for Latin America and the Caribbean (ECLAC).

Deaton, A. and C. Paxson (1998), "Health, income and inequality over the life cycle", *The Economics of Ageing*, D. A. Wise (ed.), Chicago, University of Chicago Press.

Del Popolo, F., M. López and M. Acuña (2009), *Juventud indígena y afrodescendiente en América Latina: inequidades sociodemográficas y desafíos de políticas*, Madrid, Ibero-American Youth Organization (OIJ) [online] http://www.oij.org/file_upload/publicationsItems/document/EJ1264093002.pdf.

Dewilde, C. (2003), "A life-course perspective on social exclusion and poverty", *British Journal of Sociology*, vol. 54, No. 1, March.

ECLAC (Economic Commission for Latin America and the Caribbean) (2016a), *The social inequality matrix in Latin America* (LC/G.2690(MDS.1/2)), Santiago.

___(2016b), *Social Panorama of Latin America, 2015* (LC/G.2691-P), Santiago.

___(2016c), *Equality and women's autonomy in the sustainable development agenda* (LC/G.2686/Rev.1), Santiago.

___(2015), *Inclusive social development: The next generation of policies for overcoming poverty and reducing inequality in Latin America and the Caribbean* (LC.L/4056(CDS.1/3)), Santiago.

___(2014a), *Social Panorama of Latin America, 2014* (LC/G.2635-P), Santiago.

___(2014b), *Los pueblos indígenas en América Latina: avances en el último decenio y retos pendientes para la garantía de sus derechos* (LC/L.3902), Santiago.

___(2013), *Mujeres indígenas en América Latina: dinámicas demográficas y sociales en el marco de los derechos humanos* (LC/W.558), Santiago [online] http://repositorio.cepal.org/bitstream/handle/11362/4100/1/S2013792_es.pdf.

___(2009), *Social Panorama of Latin America, 2008* (LC/G.2402-P), Santiago.

___(2007), *Social Panorama of Latin America, 2006* (LC/G.2326-P), Santiago.

ECLAC/ILO (Economic Commission for Latin America and the Caribbean/International Labour Organization) (2016a), "Recent improvements and persistent gaps in rural employment", *Employment Situation in Latin America and the Caribbean*, No. 14 (LC/L.4141), Santiago, May.

ECLAC/PAHO (Economic Commission for Latin America and the Caribbean/Pan American Health Organization) (2011), "Salud de la población joven indígena en América Latina: un panorama general" (LC/R.2171), Santiago.

ECLAC/UNICEF (Economic Commission for Latin America and the Caribbean/United Nations Children's Fund) (2012), "Pobreza infantil en pueblos indígenas y afrodescendientes de América Latina", *Project Documents* (LC/W.477), Santiago.

___(2010), "Pobreza infantil en América Latina y el Caribe" (LC/R.2168), Santiago.

Erikson, R. and J. H. Goldberg (2002), "Intergenerational inequality: A sociological perspective", *Journal of Economic Perspectives*, vol. 16, No. 3.

Espejo, A. (2017), "Propuesta de implementación de modelos predictores del trabajo infantil para la orientación de acciones de políticas preventivas a nivel subnacional", *Documento de Trabajo*, Santiago, Economic Commission for Latin America and the Caribbean (ECLAC), unpublished.

Espínola, V. and J. Claro (2010), "Estrategias de prevención de la deserción en la educación secundaria: perspectiva latinoamericana", *Revista de Educación*, special issue.

Gibbs, B. and T. Eaton (2014), "Drop out from primary to secondary school in Mexico: A life cycle perspective", *International Journal of Educational Development*, vol. 36, May.

Halliday, T. (2009), "Health inequality over the life-cycle", *IZA Discussion Paper*, No. 4369.

Huenchuan, S. (ed.) (2016), *Envejecimiento e institucionalidad pública en América Latina y el Caribe: conceptos, metodologías y casos prácticos* (LC/L.4175), Santiago, Economic Commission for Latin America and the Caribbean (ECLAC), June.

____(2013), *Ageing, Solidarity and Social Protection in Latin America and the Caribbean: time for progress towards equality*, ECLAC Books, No. 117 (LC/G.2553-P), Santiago, Economic Commission for Latin America and the Caribbean (ECLAC).

Huggett, M., A. Yaron and G. Ventura (2011), "Sources of lifetime inequality", *American Economic Review*, vol. 101, December.

IDB (Inter-American Development Bank) (2015), *Los primeros años: el bienestar infantil y el papel de las políticas públicas*, S. Berlinski and N. Schady (eds.), Washington, D.C.

ILO (International Labour Organization) (2016a), *Women at Work. Trends 2016. Executive summary*, Geneva [online] http://www.ilo.org/wcmsp5/groups/public/---dgreports/---dcomm/---publ/documents/publication/wcms_457317.pdf.

(2016b), *World Employment and Social Outlook 2016. Transforming jobs to end poverty*, Geneva.

(2016c), *Cinco claves para acelerar la reducción del trabajo infantil en América Latina y el Caribe*, Lima, International Programme on the Elimination of Child Labour.

____(2013), *World Report on Child Labour: Economic vulnerability, social protection and the fight against child labour*, Geneva.

Irwin, L.G. and others (2007), *Desarrollo de la primera infancia. Un potente ecualizador. Informe final para la Comisión sobre los determinantes sociales de la salud de la Organización Mundial de la Salud* [online] http://www.who.int/social_determinants/publications/early_child_dev_ecdkn_es.pdf?ua=1.

Jones, A., D. Mitchel and F. Goza (2014), "Lifecourse socioeconomic status and cardiovascular illness in Latin America", *Current Sociology*, vol. 62, No. 7.

Marco, F. (2016), "La nueva ola de reformas previsionales y la igualdad de género en América Latina", *Asuntos de Género series*, No. 139 (LC/L.4225), Santiago, Economic Commission for Latin America and the Caribbean (ECLAC) [online] http://www.cepal.org/es/publicaciones/40653-la-nueva-ola-reformas-previsionales-la-igualdad-genero-america-latina.

____(2014), "Calidad del cuidado y la educación para la primera infancia en América Latina: igualdad para hoy y mañana", *Políticas Sociales series*, No. 204 (LC/L.3859), Santiago, Economic Commission for Latin America and the Caribbean (ECLAC) [online] http://repositorio.cepal.org/bitstream/handle/11362/36822/1/S1420230_es.pdf.

Marinakis, A. (ed.) (2014), Incumplimiento con el salario mínimo en América Latina. El peso de los factores económicos e institucionales, Santiago, International Labour Organization (ILO).

Maurizio, R. (2014), "El impacto distributivo del salario mínimo en la Argentina, el Brasil, Chile y el Uruguay", *Políticas Sociales series*, No. 194 (LC/L.3825), Santiago, Economic Commission for Latin America and the Caribbean (ECLAC).

Morlachetti, A. (2013), "Comprehensive national child protection systems: legal basis and current practice in Latin America and the Caribbean", *Project Documents* (LC/W.515), Santiago, Economic Commission for Latin America and the Caribbean (ECLAC)/United Nations Children's Fund (UNICEF).

OECD (Organization for Economic Cooperation and Development) (2016), "Gender pay gaps for full-time workers and earnings differentials by educational attainment", Social Policy Division [online] https://www.OCDE.org/els/family/LMF_1_5_Gender_pay_gaps_for_full_time_workers.pdf.

____(2013), *Iniciativa para una vida mejor. México* [online] http://www.oecd.org/centrodemexico/Working%20draft%20Mexico%20Report_FINAL.pdf.

____(2010), "A family affair: intergenerational social mobility across OECD countries", *Economic Policy Reforms: Going for Growth 2010*, Paris, OECD Publishing.

OCDE/CEPAL/CAF (Organization for Economic Cooperation and Development/Economic Commission for Latin America and the Caribbean/Development Bank of Latin America) (2014), *Latin American Economic Outlook 2017: Youth, Skills and Entrepreneurship* (LC/G.2689), Santiago.

O'Rand, A. M. (1996), "The precious and the precocious: understanding cumulative disadvantage and cumulative advantage over the life cycle", *The Gerontologist*, vol. 36, No. 2.

____(1995), "The cumulative stratification of the life cycle", *Handbook of Aging and the Social Sciences*, R.H Binstock and L. K. George (eds.), San Diego, Academia Press.

Pasqualini, D. and A. Llorens (2010), *Salud y bienestar de los adolescentes y jóvenes: una mirada integral,* Buenos Aires, Pan American Health Organization (PAHO)/Universidad de Buenos Aires.

Paxson, C. and N. Schady (2007), "Cognitive development among young children in Ecuador: the roles of wealth, health, and parenting", *Journal of Human Resources*, vol. 42, No. 1.

Repetto, F., N. Cunill Grau and C. Bronzo (2015), "Coordinating sectors and institutions for building comprehensive social protection", *Towards Universal Social Protection: Latin American pathways and policy tools*, S. Cecchini and others (eds.), ECLAC Books, No. 136 (LC/G.2644-P), Santiago, Economic Commission for Latin America and the Caribbean (ECLAC).

Rico, M.N. and D. Trucco (2014), "Adolescentes. Derecho a la educación y bienestar futuro", *Políticas Sociales series*, No. 190 (LC/L.3791), Santiago, Economic Commission for Latin America and the Caribbean (ECLAC)/United Nations Children's Fund (UNICEF).

Saunders, F. and others (2015), "Pobreza infantil en Honduras: análisis de progresividad y redistribución de las transferencias dirigidas a la niñez", *Revista Economía y Administración,* No. 5.

Schady, N. (2011), "Parental education, vocabulary, and cognitive development in early childhood: longitudinal evidence from Ecuador", *American Journal of Public Health*, vol. 101, No. 12.

Sen, A. (1997), *On Economic Inequality. Enlarged edition with a substantial annex by James E. Foster and Amartya Sen*, Oxford, Clarendon Press.

Settersten Jr., R.A. (2003), "Age structuring and the rhythm of the life cycle", *Handbook of the Life cycle*, J.T. Mortimer and M.J. Shanahan (eds.), New York, Kluwer Academic Publishers.

SITEAL (Information System on Educational Trends in Latin America) (2009), *Primera infancia en América Latina: la situación actual y las respuestas del Estado* [online] http://www.siteal. iipe-oei.org/informe/228/informe-2009.

Tomaselli, A. (2017), "Caracterización de la participación laboral en Chile. Análisis para el fortalecimiento de los programas de capacitación y empleo", unpublished.

Trucco, D. and H. Ullmann (eds.) (2016), *Youth: realities and challenges for achieving development with equality*, ECLAC books, No. 137 (LC/G.2647-P), Santiago, Economic Commission for Latin America and the Caribbean (ECLAC).

Ullmann, H. and V. Milosavljevic (2016), "Time use in adolescence", *Challenges*, No. 19, Santiago, Economic Commission for Latin America and the Caribbean (ECLAC)/United Nations Children's Fund (UNICEF).

UNESCO (United Nations Educational, Scientific and Cultural Organization) (2015), *Informe de resultados TERCE. Factores asociados: laboratorio latinoamericano de evaluación de la calidad de la educación*, Santiago, Regional Office for Education in Latin America and the Caribbean [online] http://unesdoc.unesco.org/images/0024/002435/243533s.pdf.

UNICEF (United Nations Children's Fund) (2016), *The State of the World's Children 2016: A fair chance for every child* [online] https://www.unicef.org/publications/index_91711.html.

____(2001), *Impacto educativo de la enseñanza preescolar: resultados, causas y desafíos,* Desafíos de la Política Educacional, No. 7, Santiago [online] http://www.unicef.cl/web/wp-content/ uploads/doc_wp/impacto_educativo.pdf.

United Nations (1989), Convention on the Rights of the Child [online] http://www.ohchr.org/EN/ ProfessionalInterest/Pages/CRC.aspx.

# Annex III.A1

Table III.A1.1
Latin America and the Caribbean (19 countries): main national strategy for protecting the rights of the young

| Country | Name of the national youth plan or policy | Institution coordinating the national youth plan or policy |
|---|---|---|
| Argentina | National Youth Plan (2016) | Ministry of Social Development, through the National Youth Department |
| Bolivia (Plurinational State of) | Plurinational Youth Plan 2008-2012 | Ministry of Justice, through the Office of the Deputy Minister for Equal Opportunities and the Plurinational Youth Department |
| Brazil | National Youth Policy: guidelines and outlook 2006 | National Youth Secretariat |
| Chile | Chile commits to the young: Youth Action Plan 2004-2006 | National Institute for Youth |
| Colombia | National Youth Policy: bases for the 10-year youth plan 2005-2015 | Directorate of the "Young Colombia" National Youth System |
| Costa Rica | Public Youth Policy and Action Plan 2014-2019 | Office of the Deputy Minister for Youth, Ministry of Culture and Youth |
| Cuba | n.a. | Union of Young Communists |
| Dominican Republic | Strategic Plan of the Ministry of Youth 2015-2019 | Ministry of Youth |
| Ecuador | National Youth Plan 2004-2008 | National Directorate for Youth and Adolescence |
| El Salvador | National Youth Policy 2011-2024 and Action Plan 2011-2014 | National Institute for Youth |
| Guatemala | Youth Policy 2012-2020: building a plurinational, inclusive and equitable nation | National Youth Council |
| Honduras | National Youth Policy 2007-2021: towards full citizenship | National Institute for Youth |
| Mexico | National Youth Programme 2014-2018 | Mexican Youth Institute |
| Nicaragua | National Comprehensive Youth Development Policy and Action Plan 2005-2015 | Ministry of Youth |
| Panama | Inter-Agency Strategic Youth Plan 2015-2019 | Ministry of Social Development |
| Paraguay | National Youth Plan "Don Félix de Guarania" 2011-2013: towards the new generation of leaders | National Youth Secretariat, created in 2013 and reporting to the Office of the President |
| Peru | National Strategic Youth Plan 2015-2021: towards the bicentenary | National Youth Secretariat |
| Uruguay | Youth Action Plan 2015-2025 | National Institute for Youth |
| Venezuela (Bolivarian Republic of) | Youth of the Nation Mission 2013-2014 (programme) | National Institute of People's Power for Youth |

**Source**: Economic Commission for Latin America and the Caribbean (ECLAC), on the basis of official information from the countries.

# Time distribution: a key element of the inequality analysis

# Introduction

Humankind has always reflected on and attempted to measure time, which is generally defined as the duration of things that are subject to change, through various and very distinct disciplines such as physics, history, psychology, theology and literature. From the era of the ancient Greeks until now, philosophical notions of time have revolved mainly around two ideas: (i) physical time, as a natural and absolute element, and (ii) relative social time, as a subjective interpretation of human existence and the occurrence of various events. The first is a variable that represents an objective, observable, continuous, homogenous, measurable and independent exteriority, while the second is a social, subjective, heterogeneous construction that can occur simultaneously or discontinuously.

For many years, economic and social research focused on the analysis of income as one of the main sources of a person's well-being. However, since the last third of the twentieth century, the study of time use has become crucial to understanding the key components of societies' social and economic structures. The analysis of time use and distribution has developed along three main lines of research: sociopolitical, aiming for social change; humanistic, focused on the philosophical and anthropological understanding of temporality; and empirical, targeting, in particular, the measurement of time distribution in households and by people on a daily basis (Durán, 2012a).

Time consists of a series of events and personal or social experiences organized into sequences that shape a person's identity and integration into a particular society. Time is also a finite resource and, as such, its use for certain activities inevitably means less is set aside for others. Moreover, people use their time in different ways, depending on a number of sociocultural factors that adapt to the context they live in and the roles they play. Hence the distribution of time includes a voluntary component and another imposed by culture, the dominant gender order, social structure and power relationships. Free and autonomous time use and management are restricted in some cases, where time distribution —which is considerably influenced by the current sexual division of labour— is a barrier to well-being or the exercise of certain rights. As occurs with income, the lack of own time and of the ability to manage it freely creates social inequality.

In Latin America and the Caribbean, the production structure, gender roles and family make-up have reinforced stark differences between men and women with respect to time distribution. This has led to inequalities in opportunities and outcomes for personal and professional development. Research on time use, and particularly the analysis of time-use survey data, has revealed patterns of inequality in time distribution and allowed the quantification of time allocated to daily activities. It has also identified the conditions that affect time distribution and allocation for specific tasks according to the rules of the patriarchal system within families and the dominant gender system in the public arena, providing statistics to reflect unpaid domestic and care work and their effects on the lives of women and on gender relationships. Time can be converted into goods and services of monetary value that contribute to society's well-being through work. Hence, time-use surveys provide important valuation inputs. This analysis is reinforced by the gender perspective, through which the sexual division of labour is identified as a key factor in understanding people's behaviour, needs and contributions to development.

The new social and economic realities represent multiple challenges for the improvement of opportunities available to the population and for the reduction of inequality. In order to increase well-being and sustainable development, public policies must include time as a central element to guarantee better harmonization and balance between time spent on domestic, professional and personal activities. Just as the feminist movement's slogan "the personal is political" drew attention to the fact that domestic issues require public policies, advances in the region show that, now, time is political as well. It is essential to develop and implement public policies on the redistribution of time and work to foster gender equality and sustainable development (ECLAC, 2016a).

Under article 206 of the Beijing Declaration and Platform for Action adopted in 1995, United Nations Member States agreed to develop a more comprehensive awareness of all forms of work and public policies on equality by improving data compilation and developing new measurement tools in different areas. These include: (i) other types of non-market production activities; (ii) the quantitative assessment of the value of unpaid work that is not included in national accounts, for example, caring for dependent family members, so that it may be included in special, satellite or other official accounts with a view to recognizing the economic contribution of women; (iii) an international classification of activities for time-use statistics which reveals the differences between men and women in terms of paid and unpaid work; (iv) periodic time-use studies to quantitatively measure unpaid work, especially the activities carried out simultaneously with paid work or other unpaid activities (United Nations, 1995).

The Commission on the Measurement of Economic Performance and Social Progress reiterated these recommendations in its 2009 report, emphasizing the need to pay more attention to the distribution of resources, incorporate time-use and satisfaction indicators into analyses of inequality and well-being, and establish household satellite accounts (Stiglitz, Sen and Fitoussi, 2008).

> In order to increase well-being and sustainable development, public policies must include time as a central element to guarantee better harmonization and balance between time spent on domestic, professional and personal activities.

As will be discussed later in this chapter, Latin America and the Caribbean's movement in this direction in the past two decades has been decisive (albeit heterogeneous from one country to the next) in overcoming (not without difficulty) institutional inertia and the limits of statistical instruments. Significant measures have been taken to address each of these commitments, especially over the past 10 years: developing time-use measurement tools, quantifying unpaid domestic work and unpaid care work, and promoting satellite accounts that allow the value of this type of work to be included in national accounts. Time-use data analyses have been very useful in the development of public policies targeting the recognition and redistribution of unpaid work, which represent one of the main determining factors of inequality between men and women in the region, even more so when other determinants of time distribution are taken into account, such as a person's place of residence, ethnicity, race and age, from an intersectional perspective. Time-use data also provides input for the design and evaluation of policies for the labour market, social security, poverty alleviation, health, education, transport and other areas, as analysed in the last section of this chapter.

# A.  Time distribution and inequality

The excessive burden of unpaid work is a significant barrier to women's economic autonomy as it complicates their entry into the labour market and development in other areas of their personal and social lives. This phenomenon has the greatest impact on women in the lowest-income households, which fuels a vicious circle of monetary poverty and lack of own time. The time-use surveys carried out in the region have played a key role in shedding light on this problem.

Ongoing discussions about the care economy and the sustainability of human life —from the perspective of feminist economics—, and on the basis of a heterodox view, clearly show that much of what is produced and what sustains people's lives is neither considered nor accounted for in traditional economics (Carrasco and Tello, 2013). For a complete and in-depth analysis of inequalities in Latin America and the Caribbean, more light must be shed on the distribution and use of time by men and women.

According to ECLAC, inequality is a historical and structural feature of the region, which has been maintained and reproduced even in times of growth and economic prosperity. Social inequality in the region is strongly determined by the production matrix and ownership structure, as well as other structural determinants like the dominant gender system, which in turn intersects with factors such as life cycle stages, area of residence, ethnicity and race (ECLAC, 2016f). The analysis of inequality, its dimensions and how they interconnect is fundamental to the design of public policies that would allow society to achieve sustainable development and the Goals set forth in the 2030 Agenda for Sustainable Development (ECLAC, 2016c, 2016d).

The gender perspective must be incorporated into the analysis of inequality in the region in order to ensure that the issue is understood and to take steps to transform the unequal power relationships between men and women, tackling structural barriers that hamper women's exercise of their rights and autonomy in the public and private spheres. A transformative approach that incorporates the entire development agenda is needed to make real progress towards reducing inequality. This implies taking a number of steps that, in addition to eliminating discrimination and violence, increase the number of women with sufficient income of their own, shatter the glass ceiling, increase women's access to the labour market, make personal and work life compatible for men and women, and ensure that domestic care work is shared fairly, among other measures. Gender equality is integral to sustainable development; without gender equality it is neither development nor sustainable.

The regional gender agenda[1] recognizes that achieving gender equality means overcoming structural challenges, which include: (i) socioeconomic inequality and the persistence of poverty; (ii) discriminatory, violent and patriarchal cultural patterns and the predominance of a culture of privilege; (iii) the sexual division of labour and the unfair social organization of care; and (iv) the concentration of power and hierarchical relations in the public sphere (ECLAC, 2017). Hence, relevant and timely information that helps to identify these challenges and guides policy is fundamental. According to the *Montevideo Strategy for Implementation of the Regional Gender Agenda within the Sustainable Development Framework by 2030*, which was adopted by the governments of the region at the thirteenth Regional Conference on Women in Latin America and the Caribbean (held in October 2016), one of the pillars for implementing the regional gender agenda is the development and strengthening of information

---

[1]  The regional gender agenda refers to the commitments made by Latin American and Caribbean governments to the rights and autonomy of women and gender equality adopted at the meetings of the Regional Conference for Women in Latin America and the Caribbean, from the first conference in Havana in 1977 until the present day (ECLAC, 2016d).

systems that highlight and quantify gender inequalities and contribute to the design of policies to overcome the existing sexual division of labour, as well as other factors that perpetuate inequality (ECLAC, 2017). In particular, time-use surveys are essential tools for generating data which, analysed from a gender perspective, provide input for the design of equality policies.

## 1.    Time-use surveys: the considerable potential of a statistical instrument

According to the Classification of Time-Use Activities for Latin America and the Caribbean (CAUTAL) (ECLAC/INEGI/INMUJERES/UN-Women, 2016), time-use surveys provide information on the various activities carried out by persons over a specified period and on how they distribute the time spent on them. These surveys are highly relevant owing to the broad analytical capacity they provide for various areas of research, including analysis of gender issues; studies on the link between monetary poverty, income and time distribution and use; national, regional and international requirements for data on unpaid work and new labour statistics requirements.

Time-use surveys are an ideal information source for the comprehensive analysis of all types of work, as they measure the amount of time —in hours per day or per week— that people spend on activities relating to unpaid domestic and care work, paid work, community work and volunteer work. Nonetheless, there are other sources, such as surveys on employment, living conditions, origin and destination, health, child labour, prevalence and characteristics of disability, and multi-purpose surveys, which provide information on time-use relating to specific population groups or activities.

The adoption of CAUTAL was a big step towards the harmonization of time-use statistics and comparability between countries thanks to homogenous criteria, and paved the way for a common methodology at the regional level (ECLAC, 2015b). Although a number of countries now implement time-use surveys, these are still not incorporated systematically into official statistics, which complicates the construction of time series. With a view to fine-tuning data collection tools that can shed light on situations that affect men and women differently, this type of survey should be included in statistical offices' planning, carried out on a regular basis and receive funding.

Various methods have been used to collect data from respondents in the region. For example, seven countries used surveys that employed the diary method (Argentina, Bolivarian Republic of Venezuela, Brazil, Chile, Cuba, Mexico and Plurinational State of Bolivia), but these early experiments were discontinued. Some results were discouraging owing to high non-response rates and costs, and in some instances, to the lack of adaptation to the country's cultural characteristics, which are especially evident in the functioning of households. Meanwhile, 15 countries used a list of activities in the form of questions or modules attached to existing household and multipurpose surveys, which are based on specific methodologies and which generally address themes of employment or living conditions. There are some advantages to including modules or questions on time use in household surveys, such as lower implementation costs, as the methodology and sample design are part of a regular survey, which also ensures periodicity and comparability with other indicators in the national statistical system (Milosavljevic and Tacla, 2007). This methodology also allows cross-referencing with other survey modules.

Box IV.1
Time-use surveys in Latin America

There is a wealth of information and experience in time-use measurement in Latin America. The Regional Gender Agenda has driven the gradual development of time-use measurement since the 1980s. In addition to the consensus reached by governments at the Regional Conferences for Women in Latin America and the Caribbean, the Working Group on Gender Statistics of the Statistical Conference of the Americas (SCA)[a] has played a notable role in conceptual and methodological development, and in the production and dissemination of analytical documents relating to time use.

To date, 19 countries in the region have already carried out at least one time-use measurement, mainly in the past 10 years. Cuba pioneered the field with its national time-use surveys in 1985 and 1988 (Aguirre and Ferrari, 2014). The methodologies used were heterogeneous in terms of the objectives, legal fundamentals, collection process, classification of activities, geographic scope and calculated and disseminated indicators.

Latin America and the Caribbean: surveys, modules or questions on time use and unpaid work, 1985-2016

| Country | Year | Type of survey |
|---|---|---|
| Argentina | 2013 | Module in the Annual Survey of Urban Households (EAHU) |
| | 2010-2011 (Rosario) | Survey on time use and volunteer work |
| | 2005 (Buenos Aires) | Independent survey |
| Bolivia (Plurinational State of) | 2011, 2010 | Survey of time use in Households |
| | 2001 | Module in the Continuous Survey of Households |
| Brazil | 2009-2010 | Pilot survey in five States |
| | Desde 1992 | Questions in the National Survey of Households (PNAD) |
| Chile | 2015 | National Time-use Survey |
| | 2008-2009 | Experimental survey of time use in Greater Santiago |
| Colombia | 2012 | National time-use survey |
| | 2010, 2009, 2008, 2007 | Questions in the Comprehensive Survey of Households |
| Costa Rica | 2011 | Survey of time use in the Greater Metropolitan Region |
| | 2004 | Module in the Multipurpose Household Survey (EHPM) |
| Cuba | 2001 | Survey administered in five provinces |
| | 1997, 1988, 1985 | National time-use survey |
| Dominican Republic | 2016 | Module on time use in the National Multipurpose Household Survey |
| | 2006-2007 | Question in the Demographic and Health Survey |
| Ecuador | 2012 | Time-use survey (EUT) |
| | 2012, 2010, 2007, 2005 | Module in the National Survey of Employment, Unemployment and Underemployment (ENEMDU) |
| El Salvador | 2010-2011 | Module in the Multipurpose Household Survey |
| | 2005 | Short list of questions in the Multipurpose Household Survey (EHPM) |
| Guatemala | 2014 | Module in the National Survey of Employment and Income |
| | 2014, 2011, 2006, 2000 | Module in the National Survey of Living Conditions (ENCOVI) |
| Honduras | 2011, 2009 | Module in the Permanent Survey of Households |
| Mexico | 2014, 2009, 2002, 1998 | National time-use survey (ENUT) |
| | 2010 | Module in the National Survey of Household Income and Expenditure |
| | 1996 | Module in the National Survey of Work, Contributions and Time Use (ENTAUT) |
| Nicaragua | 1998 | Module in the National Household Survey of Living Standards (ENHMNV) |
| Panama | 2011 | National time-use survey |
| | 2006 | Module in the Multipurpose Survey |
| Paraguay | 2016 | Time-use survey (EUT) |
| Peru | 2010 | National time-use survey |
| | 2006 | Questions included in the Continuous Household Survey |
| Uruguay | 2013, 2007 | Module in the Continuous Household Survey |
| | 2003 | Survey in the Metropolitan Region (Universidad de la República) |
| Venezuela (Bolivarian Republic of) | 2011, 2008 | Time-use survey |

**Source**: Economic Commission for Latin America and the Caribbean (ECLAC), Gender Equality Observatory for Latin America and the Caribbean, on the basis of information from the time-use surveys conducted in the respective countries; R. Aguirre and F. Ferrari, "Las encuestas sobre uso del tiempo y trabajo no remunerado en América Latina y el Caribe: caminos recorridos y desafíos hacia el futuro", *Asuntos de Género series*, No. 122 (LC/L.3678/Rev.1), Santiago, ECLAC, February 2014.

[a] The member countries of the Working Group on Gender Statistics of the Statistical Conference of the Americas are: Argentina, Bahamas, Bolivarian Republic of Venezuela, Brazil, Chile, Colombia, Costa Rica, Cuba, Dominican Republic, Ecuador, El Salvador, Guatemala, Guyana, Haiti, Honduras, Jamaica, Mexico, Panama, Peru and Plurinational State of Bolivia. Mexico is the group coordinator, through the National Institute of Statistics and Geography of Mexico (INEGI) and the ECLAC Gender Affairs Division acts as the secretariat. The National Women's Institute of Mexico (INMUJERES) and the United Nations Entity for Gender Equality and the Empowerment of Women (UN Women) act as advisory agencies of the working group.

The most recent experiences have produced information through independent surveys that provide wider thematic coverage of all aspects and activities relating to time use and distribution. The countries that carried them out are Chile, Colombia, Costa Rica, Ecuador, Mexico, Panama, Paraguay and Peru. These surveys cost more than questions or modules but are much more exhaustive with respect to the inclusion of details about activities and subcomponents of each type of unpaid work (care, domestic and voluntary), as well as personal activities.

Aside from the use of different activity classification systems, the disaggregation of activities and the representativeness of specific population groups may limit comparability between countries. Sometimes, despite the fact that surveys include questions that are relevant to the analysis, the resulting indicators are not truly representative of respondents owing to sample design limitations, as occurs in some countries with Afrodescendent populations. This problem also arises with territorial disaggregation to distinguish the urban situation from the rural, or conditions in cities of different sizes.

Box IV.2
Time-use classification for Latin America and the Caribbean (CAUTAL)

At the eighth meeting of the Statistical Conference of the Americas of the Economic Commission for Latin America and the Caribbean, held in 2015, member States adopted CAUTAL to classify time-use activities with a focus on gender and suitable for the regional context, which is a milestone in the harmonization and standardization of time-use surveys and the production of statistics regarding this theme.

This classification is a crucial tool for optimizing time-use surveys in the region, which are highly relevant as they provide information on the differences between time use by men and women, as well as empirical data and input for the design of public policies that promote and broaden women's economic autonomy. Moreover, standardized classification surveys incorporate the new labour statistics requirements stemming from the resolution on Statistics of Work, Employment and Labour Underutilization adopted at the nineteenth International Conference of Labour Statisticians of the International Labour Organization, held in 2013, and improve the measurement of unpaid work, as well as produce indicators to follow up the Sustainable Development Goals.

CAUTAL, which was initially launched in 2010, was developed by María Eugenia Gómez Luna of the National Institute of Statistics and Geography of Mexico, with the participation of ECLAC, the National Women's Institute of Mexico and the United Nations Entity for Gender Equality and the Empowerment of Women (UN Women), and received feedback from member countries of the Working Group on Gender Statistics of the Statistical Conference of the Americas (Gómez Luna, 2010). It is a dynamic and flexible instrument that can be adapted to the social and economic characteristics of each country, and presents a comprehensive blueprint of all the activities carried out within a reference period through a conceptual framework incorporating economic criteria based on the System of National Accounts (SNA). Human activities are organized into two categories: activities within the SNA general production boundary (relating to the production of goods and services) and those outside it (personal activities).

Until now, this classification has been used by several countries in the region: Chile, Colombia, Costa Rica, Ecuador, El Salvador, Guatemala, Paraguay and the Plurinational State of Bolivia. It is hoped that once it is adopted more countries will use this tool, which will strengthen international comparability through the harmonized dissemination of time-use statistics and indicators and the creation of satellite accounts for unpaid work in households.

Box IV.2 (concluded)

Diagram 1
Conceptual framework of the Classification of Time-use Activities for Latin America and the Caribbean (CAUTAL):
sections and main divisions

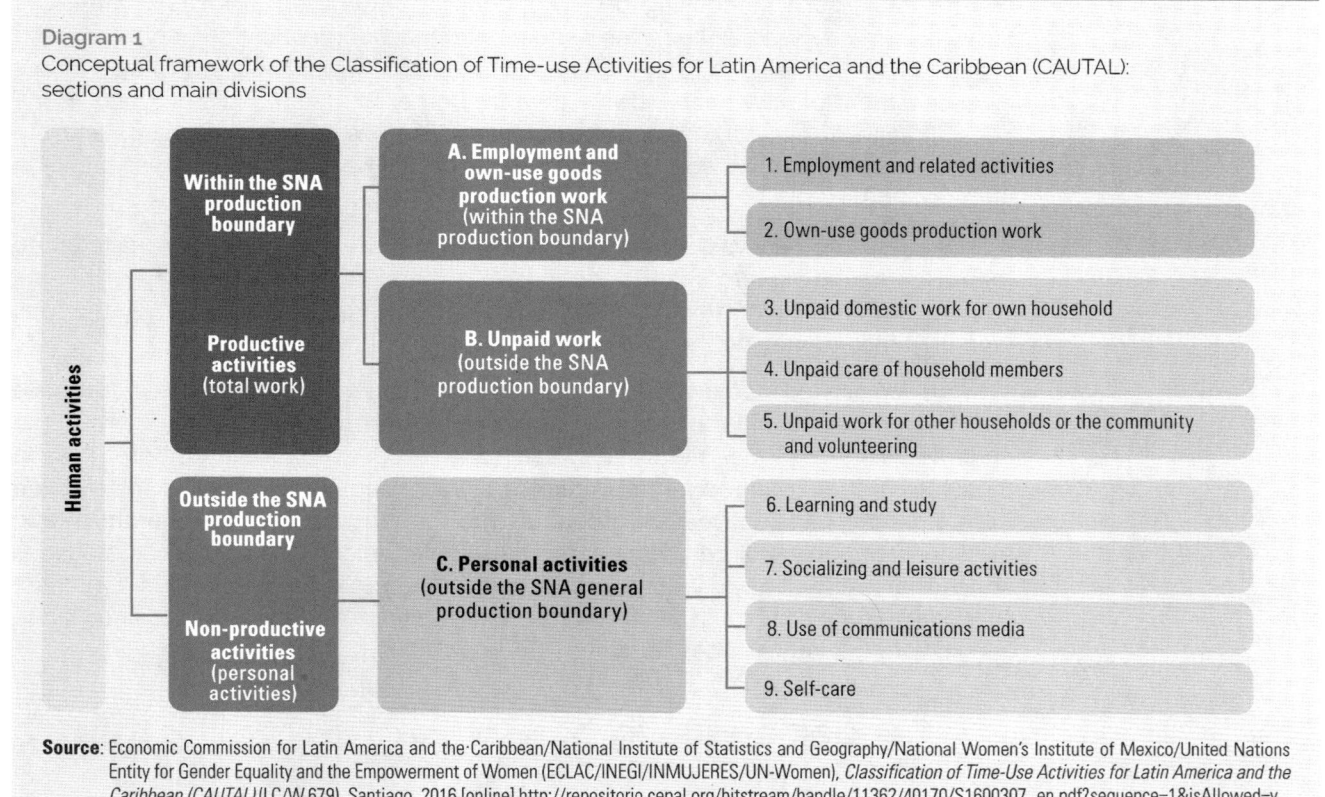

**Source:** Economic Commission for Latin America and the·Caribbean/National Institute of Statistics and Geography/National Women's Institute of Mexico/United Nations Entity for Gender Equality and the Empowerment of Women (ECLAC/INEGI/INMUJERES/UN-Women), *Classification of Time-Use Activities for Latin America and the Caribbean (CAUTAL)* (LC/W.679), Santiago, 2016 [online] http://repositorio.cepal.org/bitstream/handle/11362/40170/S1600307_en.pdf?sequence=1&isAllowed=y.

With respect to the classification of activities, eight countries in the region have used CAUTAL or a national adaption of this system until now (Chile, Colombia, Costa Rica, Ecuador, El Salvador, Guatemala, Paraguay and Plurinational State of Bolivia). In addition to CAUTAL, there is also the International Classification of Activities for Time-Use Statistics (ICATUS), which was presented for the first time in 1997 and adopted by United Nations Member States 20 years later, in March 2017, at the forty-eighth session of the United Nations Statistical Commission (United Nations, 2017a, 2017b). This classification covers a wide range of activities, and the early versions were adopted to measure time use in some of the region's countries, such as the Bolivian Republic of Venezuela, Brazil, Cuba, Peru and Uruguay. Although there were considerable differences between the two types of classification initially, especially in terms of structure and the conceptual framework of paid and unpaid work, they are now more coherent, owing to the active participation of the region's countries in the various versions of ICATUS.

Time-use surveys in the region generally cover the national territory and are representative at the urban level, and in some cases also at the rural level. Other differences stem from the minimum age of the population under review. In most surveys, questions target the activities of all members of a household from ages 10, 12 or 15 and older. However, the minimum age falls outside this range in two countries: Argentina (18 years) and Guatemala (6 years).

The major difference between countries is the level of detail of the activities. In Brazil for example, only one question is asked about the total amount of time spent on domestic work in one's own household, while independent time-use surveys contain a more detailed breakdown and sometimes even include questions on simultaneous

Thanks to Latin
American countries'
efforts to develop
time-use measurement
tools, it is possible to
calculate indicator 5.4.1
in a large number of
countries in the region,
as shown in figure V.1.

activities (for example, minding a dependent household member while carrying out another task, such as cooking or doing laundry). Although the focus of time-use surveys in the region has been the analysis of unpaid domestic work, some surveys include questions relating to the time spent on personal activities, which also allows an assessment of how people divide their free time. This represents progress in the consideration of non-commercial activity in the analysis of living standards and the establishment of comparisons of these standards in time and space (Stiglitz, Sen and Fitoussi, 2008).

Results have been presented in several ways. While most countries have opted for publishing data in terms of hours per week, others present the hours spent on one working day and one non-working day. Published indicators normally convey the total working time, identifying the paid work time and unpaid work time.

The region's academic sector and civil society have produced studies that have enriched the discussion about time-use analysis and its potential to improve the understanding of gender inequalities (Batthyány, 2009, 2015). All the progress made thus far will not change women's current situation unless the use of information from a gender perspective is incorporated into the formulation, implementation and evaluation of public policies. Hence, the dissemination and use of existing statistics and indicators must be broadened, reflection on the potential uses of this data must continue, and capacity must be strengthened to "transform information into knowledge and knowledge into political decisions" (ECLAC, 2017).

## 2.    Gender inequality

According to ECLAC (2016a, 2016e), time use and the distribution of unpaid domestic work in households, a concrete form of the sexual division of labour, is a central element in the analysis of gender inequality. The achievement of women's autonomy depends heavily on the balanced distribution of unpaid domestic and care work between men and women, and between families, the market, the community and the State. This balance in turn depends on the agreement between members of a household to share roles and responsibilities, the availability of and access to public services to care for dependent family members, the ability to pay for private services, the flexibility and benefits provided by paid work, labour policies that allow the harmonization of roles of women and men with respect to work in the public and private spheres, and lastly, the absence of coercion, intimidation and violence against women stemming from the dominant gender order.

### (a) Sustainable Development Goals and time use

The 2030 Agenda for Sustainable Development represents a significant step towards gender equality and empowerment for all women and girls, mainstreamed in the entire agenda and particularly highlighted in Goal 5, which is crucial to sustainable development (United Nations, 2015). Of particular note are the targets focused on eliminating all forms of gender discrimination and on promoting the recognition and valuation of unpaid care work, which would empower women in the public and private spheres. Indicator 5.4.1 (Proportion of time spent on unpaid domestic and care work, by sex, age and location)[2] has been proposed to monitor this Goal at the global level (United Nations, 2017c). It is currently one of the global indicators being used to follow

---

[2]    The amount of time spent on unpaid domestic and care work is calculated by dividing the average amount of time spent per day or per week on domestic and care work by 24 hours or 168 hours (one week), according to the survey's reference period. The average time, following the criterion used in the ECLAC Gender Equality Observatory for Latin America and the Caribbean, is calculated on the basis of the entire population aged 15 years and older.

up the Sustainable Development Goals. Despite a clear concept and an established methodology, these indicators are not regularly produced by countries. That said, and thanks to Latin American countries' efforts to develop time-use measurement tools, it is possible to calculate indicator 5.4.1 in a large number of countries in the region, as shown in figure IV.1.

As shown in figure IV.1, women in the region spend much more time per day and per week than men on unpaid work. Although time-use surveys are still not comparable owing to methodological differences, even the lowest percentage of time that women spend on unpaid work (14% in Brazil) is still higher than the highest percentage of time that men spend on this activity (12.6% in the Plurinational State of Bolivia). Women dedicate between one fifth and one third of their time each day or each week on unpaid domestic and care work, compared with about 10% for men.

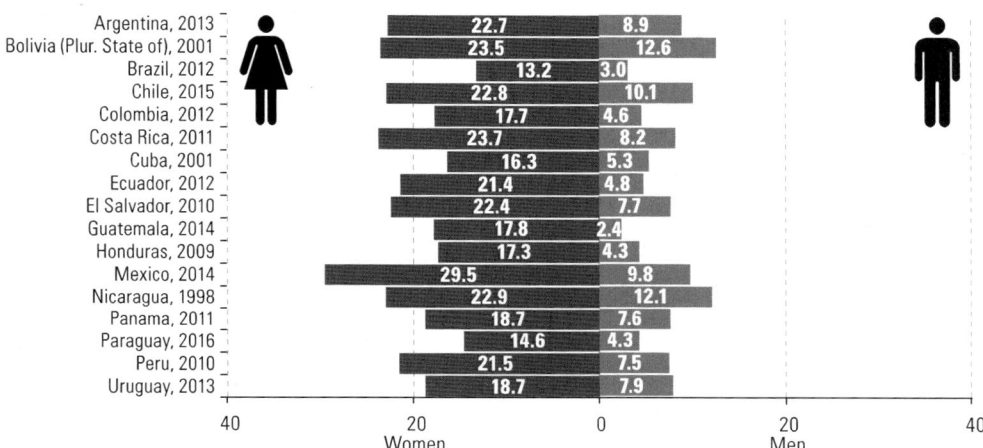

Figure IV.1
Latin America
(17 countries): time spent
on unpaid domestic
and care work, by sex
(Sustainable Development
Goal indicator 5.4.1)
(Percentages)

**Source**: Economic Commission for Latin America and the Caribbean (ECLAC), on the basis of special tabulations from time-use surveys conducted in the respective countries.
**Note**:    Figures take into account time spent on domestic and care work in one's own household, in other households, in the community and volunteer work, except in the case of Brazil, where the survey only asks one question relating to domestic work in one's own household, and of Honduras, which only includes information on care of members of one's own household. The data correspond to the national total except for Costa Rica (Greater Metropolitan Area) and Cuba (Old Havana). The population examined was 15 years and older, except in Argentina (18 years and older) and Nicaragua (6 years and older).

Although Sustainable Development Goal indicator 5.4.1 offers a perspective of the global situation, the average figures hide many specific situations. As is evident throughout this chapter, and as highlighted by the 2030 Agenda, the universal focus should be accompanied by a perspective that sheds light on the inequalities affecting specific groups, which are concealed by average figures. An important discussion relating to the Sustainable Development Goals is the disaggregation of data. With a view to ensuring that "no one is left behind" the most vulnerable population groups and those affected by various factors of inequality should be identified. With respect to the region, it is crucial to compile and analyse data that consider the specific characteristics of the entire population.

In Latin America, the notions of race and ethnicity serve as a conceptual platform for mobilizing the political identity processes of Afrodescendants and indigenous people, and have made it possible to create the basis for these populations to self-identify in censuses and surveys, and thus overcome the statistical invisibility that is another form of discrimination (ECLAC, 2016b). Hence, it is not only important to include questions on identity but also to ensure that the relevant populations are well represented. For example, the time-use survey carried out in Mexico in 2014 included an additional

2,000 households in areas where 90% or more of the indigenous-language-speaking population lived, to ensure the representation of ethnic groups.

Figure IV.2 shows data on four countries in the region (Colombia, Ecuador, Mexico and Peru). In this case, the selection of time-use survey respondents allows the disaggregation of data according to ethnicity, which should produce more accurate estimates. The gender gap is wider within indigenous populations in all countries with respect to the amount of time spent on unpaid work. Indigenous women may spend up to eight hours more per week on unpaid work than non-Indigenous women, as is the case in Mexico. This underscores the importance of considering the strict sexual division of labour in indigenous households, the need for care policies and basic infrastructure to support indigenous families, particularly those living in rural areas, and the barriers to women's economic autonomy.

**Figure IV.2**
Latin America (4 countries) time spent on unpaid work[a] by people aged 15 and older, by gender and ethnicity[b]
*(Hours per week)*

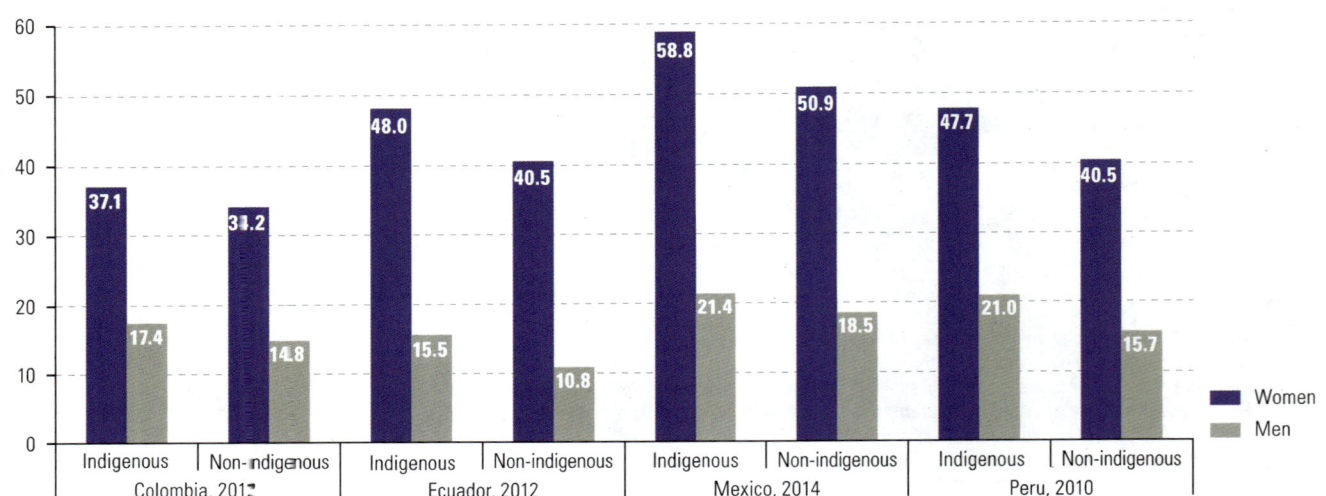

Source: Economic Commission for Latin America and the Caribbean (ECLAC), on the basis of special tabulations from time-use surveys conducted in the respective countries.
Note:    In light of the heterogeneous nature of data sources, comparisons between countries are still not possible; hence, the aim of this figure is to show the trends within each country.
[a] Unpaid work refers to work done without payment and is measured by quantifying the time a person spends on own-use goods production work, unpaid domestic work, unpaid care of household members, and unpaid work for other households or for the community and volunteering.
[b] In Colombia, the population was selected according to the cultures, towns or physical features recognized as indigenous. In Ecuador, the population that self-identified as indigenous according to their culture and customs was selected. In Mexico, indigenous people identified themselves in the survey, in accordance with their culture. The indigenous population in Peru identified themselves based on the question about their first spoken language (Quechua, Aymara, Asháninka and other native languages).

Time-use studies relating to Afrodescendent populations in Brazil (IPEA, 2011) and Colombia (Ayala Hernández and Cardona Arango, 2015; Huertas and Mola, 2015) do not provide conclusive evidence of the impact of unpaid work on time use in this group compared with the non-Afrodescendent population. In Brazil, there is practically no difference between the White and Afrodescendent populations in this respect. The study in Colombia, however, shows that indigenous and Afrodescendent peoples in areas affected by violence spend more time on personal activities, while for the population older than 50, being an Afrodescendant increases the probability of spending less time on personal activities. Although four time-use surveys in the region (in Brazil, Colombia, Ecuador and Uruguay) include questions that allow the self-identification of Afrodescendants, each one poses difficulties for analysis for various reasons, including sample size (Uruguay), the lack of cultural relevance of the questions and activities included in the questionnaires (Colombia and Ecuador), and the failure to specify care as a component of unpaid domestic work (Brazil). With a view to ensuring that the information obtained describes time use in Afrodescendent populations, race should be a focus of analysis from the design stage of measurement tools and methodologies.

## (b) Broadening the concept of work and time use

In the regional gender agenda, governments and women's movements in the region have deepened the global perception of the importance of measuring unpaid work to shed light on gender inequalities. Since 2008 and with the creation of the Gender Equality Observatory for Latin America and the Caribbean, ECLAC has systematically updated a total work time indicator, which comprises the amount of time spent on paid work and on unpaid work,[3] to show the amount and distribution of work done outside and inside the home, and women's daily contribution to countries' growth, economy and well-being. This effort was consolidated thanks to the global discussion about the measurement of labour statistics in line with the message underscored by the feminist economy for decades. The definition of "work" was broadened in the resolution of the nineteenth International Conference of Labour Statisticians in 2013: "work comprises any activity performed by persons of any sex and age to produce goods or to provide services for use by others or for own use" (ILO, 2013).

Figure IV.3 shows gender inequality in the distribution of time between paid work on the labour market and unpaid work for the household. A look beyond the averages shows the reality of the employed population with a double working shift consisting of two types of work: paid and unpaid. In all countries, women have a heavier total workload and while they are overrepresented in the unpaid work category, they are underrepresented in the paid work category. María Ángeles Durán calls this the never-ending working day, which corresponds to two socioeconomic behavioural models based on traditional gender roles: one in which men represent low production of domestic services, medium-high consumption of these services and a high economic contribution to the family as the only (or at least the main) source of household income; and the other, in which women, in extreme cases, spend all their time on unpaid work, and represent very high production of services for the entire family and low consumption of these services (as they consume much less than they produce) (Durán, 1986).

In addition to the information provided by time-use measurements, household surveys in the region show that on average,[4] 43.4% of women between the ages of 20 and 59 cite family (care for children, dependent persons, domestic work or prohibition by members of the household) as the main reason for not carrying out paid work or actively seeking employment (ECLAC, 2016a). The overburden of unpaid work lessens women's participation in decision-making and progress in their professional careers and employment opportunities, which in turn reduces their income and prospects for access to social security which is still directly linked to formal wage employment.

---

[3]  Paid work refers to work done for the production of goods and services for the market and unpaid work refers to work done without payment and develops mainly in the private sphere.

[4]  Weighted average of the 10 countries for which data are available: Bolivarian Republic of Venezuela, Chile, Costa Rica, Dominican Republic, Ecuador, El Salvador, Honduras, Panama, Plurinational State of Bolivia and Uruguay.

**Figure IV.3**
Latin America (14 countries): total paid[a] and unpaid[b] work of the employed population aged 15 and older[c], by gender
(Hours per week)

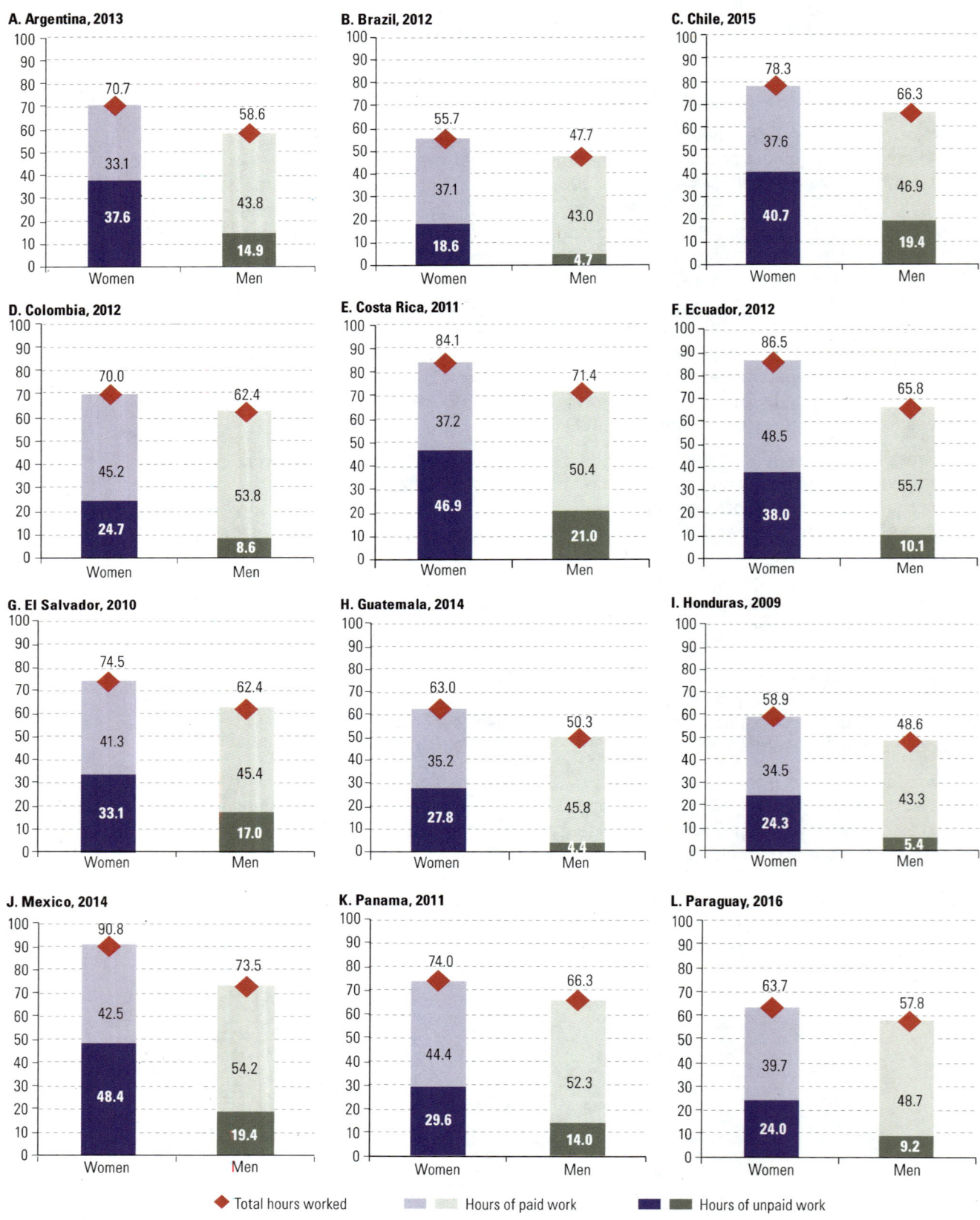

Legend: ◆ Total hours worked    Hours of paid work    Hours of unpaid work

**Figure IV.3 (concluded)**

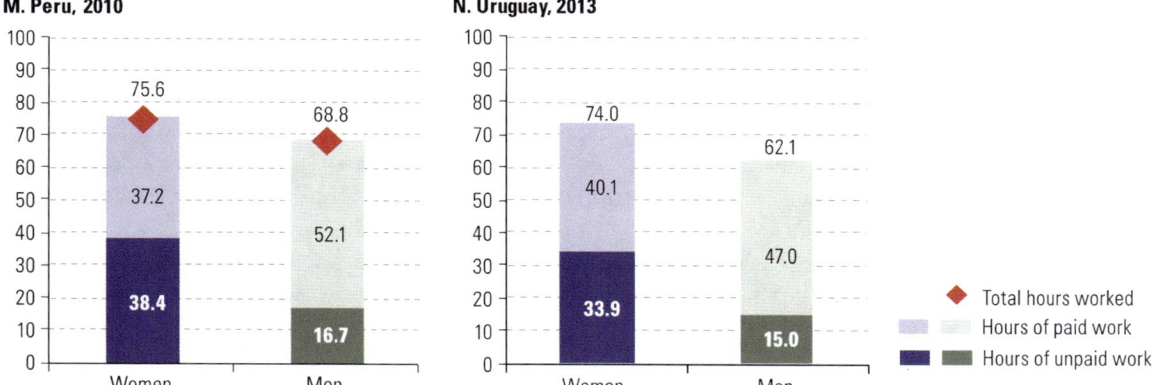

**Source**: Economic Commission for Latin America and the Caribbean (ECLAC), on the basis of special tabulations from time-use surveys conducted in the respective countries.
**Note**:    In light of the heterogeneous nature of data sources, comparisons between countries are still not possible; hence, the aim of this figure is to show the trends within each country. Data correspond to the national total except in the case of Costa Rica (Greater Metropolitan Area).
[a] Paid work refers to work done for the production of goods or services for the market and is calculated as the total amount of time devoted to employment, job-hunting and commuting. Argentina, Guatemala and Honduras do not ask about the time spent commuting to and from work; Argentina, Brazil, El Salvador, Guatemala and Uruguay do not ask about the time spent on employment seeking or setting up a business.
[b] Unpaid work refers to work done without payment developed mainly in the private sphere; it is measured by quantifying the time a person spends on own-use goods production work, unpaid domestic work, unpaid care of household members, unpaid work for other households or for the community and volunteering. The survey in Argentina does not include any questions relating to own-use goods production work; in Brazil only one question about domestic work is included and Honduras does not include any questions about own-use goods production work or activities for other households, the community or volunteer work.
[c] Surveys target the population aged 15 and older, except in Argentina (18 years and older).

Time-use surveys consider the household as an economic production and distribution unit, and the analysis of this unit helps establish a link between labour market adjustments and the sexual division of labour within households. The surveys also help to redefine the conflict between capital and work, which goes beyond tensions between only capital and wage employment, and instead encompasses both types of labour, paid and unpaid (Marco and Rico, 2013). Hence, these surveys not only help determine the distribution of time and provide an understanding of work in all of its complexity and scope; they are also an instrument that can be used to develop positions and proposals to improve the functioning of the labour market and growth within the framework of a heterodox economy.

## 3.    Time distribution in the reproduction of poverty and inequality

Poverty is more than an insufficient level of income or consumption. It is a multidimensional phenomenon stemming from a social and economic process —with political and cultural components— in which people and households lack access to essential assets and opportunities owing to various causes and circumstances, both individual and collective (ECLAC, 2004). One of the dimensions of poverty is time, a finite resource, and its unbalanced use for various activities.

The Beijing Declaration and Platform for Action (11995) already pointed out that women "contribute to the economy and to combating poverty through both remunerated and unremunerated work at home, in the community and in the workplace" (United Nations, 1995, paragraph 49). It also identified households as areas of inequality: "While poverty affects households as a whole, because of the gender division of labour and responsibilities for household welfare, women bear a disproportionate burden, attempting to manage household consumption and production under conditions of increasing scarcity" (United Nations, 1995, paragraph 50). This idea contradicts the many social policies that consider households as benchmarks for homogeneity and harmony.

An analysis of time-use data on the basis of households' income per capita as a stratification variable shows that women in the lowest-income households spend more time on unpaid work. This is partly related to the size and dependency ratio of these households, which tend to have specific family structures (Espejo, Filgueira and Rico, 2010). The differences are significant considering that while in households in quintile I women spend an average of 46 hours per week on unpaid work, those in quintile V spend almost 32 hours. Meanwhile, the differences in the amount of time spent on unpaid work between men in quintile I and V households are not significant; they are generally less than one hour per day. This shows that men's contribution to domestic and care work is generally independent of socioeconomic stratum, and that the gender gap is even wider and more unjust in the lowest-income households.

Monetary poverty and lack of time sustain a vicious circle that is very difficult to break without policies focused on strengthening women's economic autonomy. The burden of unpaid work which is culturally assigned to women hinders their access to the labour market and generation of their own income, and is worse in households with children under the age of five. The households in the lowest-income deciles have the highest number of dependents, who require a greater amount of time for care, and have the greatest need of income (ECLAC, 2016a). Moreover, women in poor households are unable to acquire goods and services on the market that could save them time on domestic and care work. There is also a lack of good-quality public services providing care for children, older persons, persons with disabilities and chronic illnesses, which is clearly a regressive situation that is set to worsen owing to the ongoing demographic changes in the region. The strong link between time and income means that the lack of time worsens or reproduces poverty, so the time-use analysis is fundamental for more comprehensive and multidimensional management of this phenomenon (Marco, 2012).

The 2030 Agenda for Sustainable Development aims to eliminate poverty everywhere and in all its forms, but this goal cannot be achieved if there are no public policies with a gender perspective that eradicate the structural factors of the feminization of poverty in the lowest-income households. In addition to monetary income redistribution policies, there is a need for policies on the redistribution of time as an indispensable resource to eliminate poverty and ensure development. Hence, in order to overcome gender inequality in the distribution of workloads, there is a need for policies focused on making family responsibilities compatible with generating income and on achieving a cultural transformation that prompts greater participation of men in domestic and care work. These policies should stimulate the sharing of responsibility between men and women within households and between families, society and the State.

Time-use data allows the evaluation of public policies from an innovative perspective, as will be discussed later on. Thus, it is important for this information to be used to monitor public policies and programmes to eradicate poverty and ensure that these neither reinforce current gender roles nor further intensify women's workload. During the programme design process, this data helps to establish criteria that can be used to redefine the sexual division of labour and responsibilities within the household, and that can support the autonomy and economic rights of women through care services and job creation.

## Figure IV.4

Latin America (7 countries): unpaid work[a] by population aged 15 and older[b], by sex and household income quintile
*(Hours per week)*

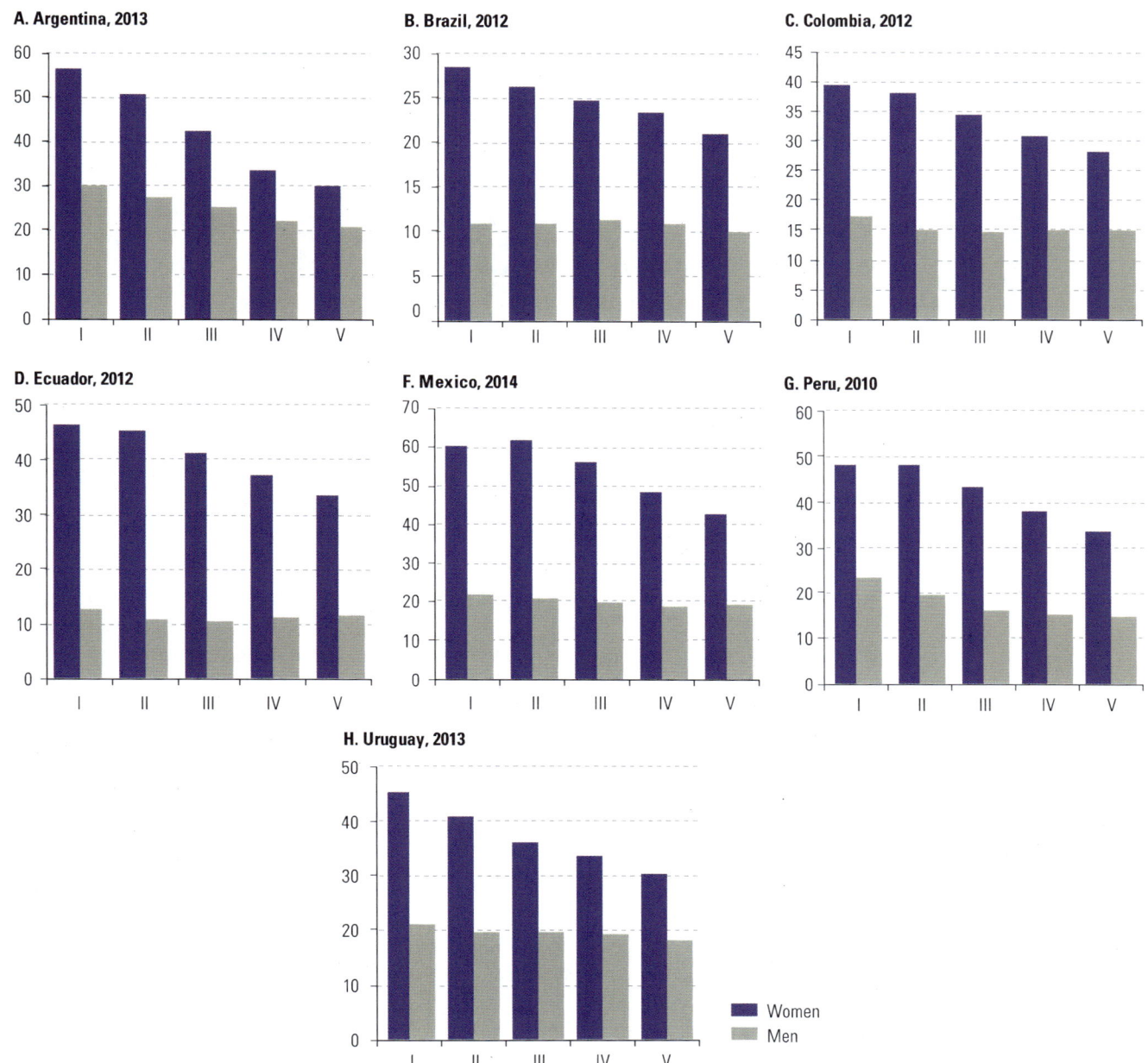

**A. Argentina, 2013**

**B. Brazil, 2012**

**C. Colombia, 2012**

**D. Ecuador, 2012**

**F. Mexico, 2014**

**G. Peru, 2010**

**H. Uruguay, 2013**

■ Women
■ Men

**Source**: Economic Commission for Latin America and the Caribbean (ECLAC), on the basis of special tabulations from time-use surveys conducted in the respective countries.

**Note**:    In light of the heterogeneous nature of data sources, comparisons between countries are still not possible; hence, the aim of this figure is to show the trends within each country.

[a] Unpaid work is measured by quantifying the time a person spends on own-use goods production work, unpaid domestic work, unpaid care of household members, unpaid work for other households or for the community and volunteering. The survey in Argentina does not include any questions relating to own-use goods production work; in Brazil only one question about domestic work is included.

[b] Surveys target the population aged 15 and older, except in Argentina (18 years and older).

# 4. Time at different stages of the life cycle: worsening inequalities

Time distribution varies during a person's life cycle. However, there is a common thread which is the heavier burden of unpaid domestic and care work on women, particularly during their reproductive age. Time-use analysis helps to identify gender inequalities at specific stages of the life cycle, such as childhood, adolescence and old age, and thus helps to provide crucial information for the formulation of public policies for equality.

## (a) Time for childhood and adolescence

Traditional gender roles are expressed from a young age and have an impact on the time available to boys and girls for their childhood development and well-being.

Article 31 of the Convention on the Rights of the Child recognizes children's right to "to rest and leisure, to engage in play and recreational activities appropriate to the age of the child and to participate freely in cultural life and the arts" (United Nations, 1989). Traditional gender roles are expressed from a young age and have an impact on the time available to boys and girls for their childhood development and well-being (Rico, 2013). Although it is not possible to make strict comparisons between countries as both the level of detail of the questions and the age ranges used in time-use surveys vary, there are some noticeable patterns in time use among girls, boys and adolescents that indicate limits to the exercise of women's rights.

Figure IV.5 shows that there are no significant gaps between men and women in terms of the amount of time spent on studying and learning. Nonetheless, when considering the amount of time spent on work, paid or unpaid, the difference between genders is clear. In all countries, the average time spent by boys and adolescent boys on paid work exceeds that of girls and adolescent girls. Meanwhile, the most notable difference is in the time spent on unpaid work, which is 6.6 to 15.2 hours per week for boys and adolescent boys compared with 13.6 to 23.3 hours per week for girls and adolescent girls. Although the time-use surveys are not designed to measure child labour, they do provide empirical data on the early construction of gender roles and on the dynamic of socialization according to which existing social norms and gender awareness —including their stereotypes on the division of labour— determine that from an early age, women carry out most of the reproductive work.

The data on time use among boys, girls and adolescents also allows the measurement of their well-being. The time spent on activities unrelated to formal academic, employment and domestic obligations facilitates the development of different physical, intellectual, social and creative skills (Ullmann and Milosavljevic, 2016). The data indicate that males younger than 18 spend two to seven hours per week more than females in the same age range on socializing activities, including recreational and sports activities and sharing recreational spaces with family and friends. The division of public and private spaces for men and women occurs from a very early age. Although very subtle, there are gender differences in the use of the media, which from the perspective of skill requirements in the information and knowledge society, are crucial to academic success and labour market integration for these generations. Time-use indicators can provide timely information to follow up on policies for expanding access to the Internet and other appropriate platforms during this stage of the life cycle.

## Figure IV.5

Latin America (6 countries): time spent by population aged 18 or younger[a] on paid[b] and unpaid[c] work and personal activities, by gender
*(Hours per week)*

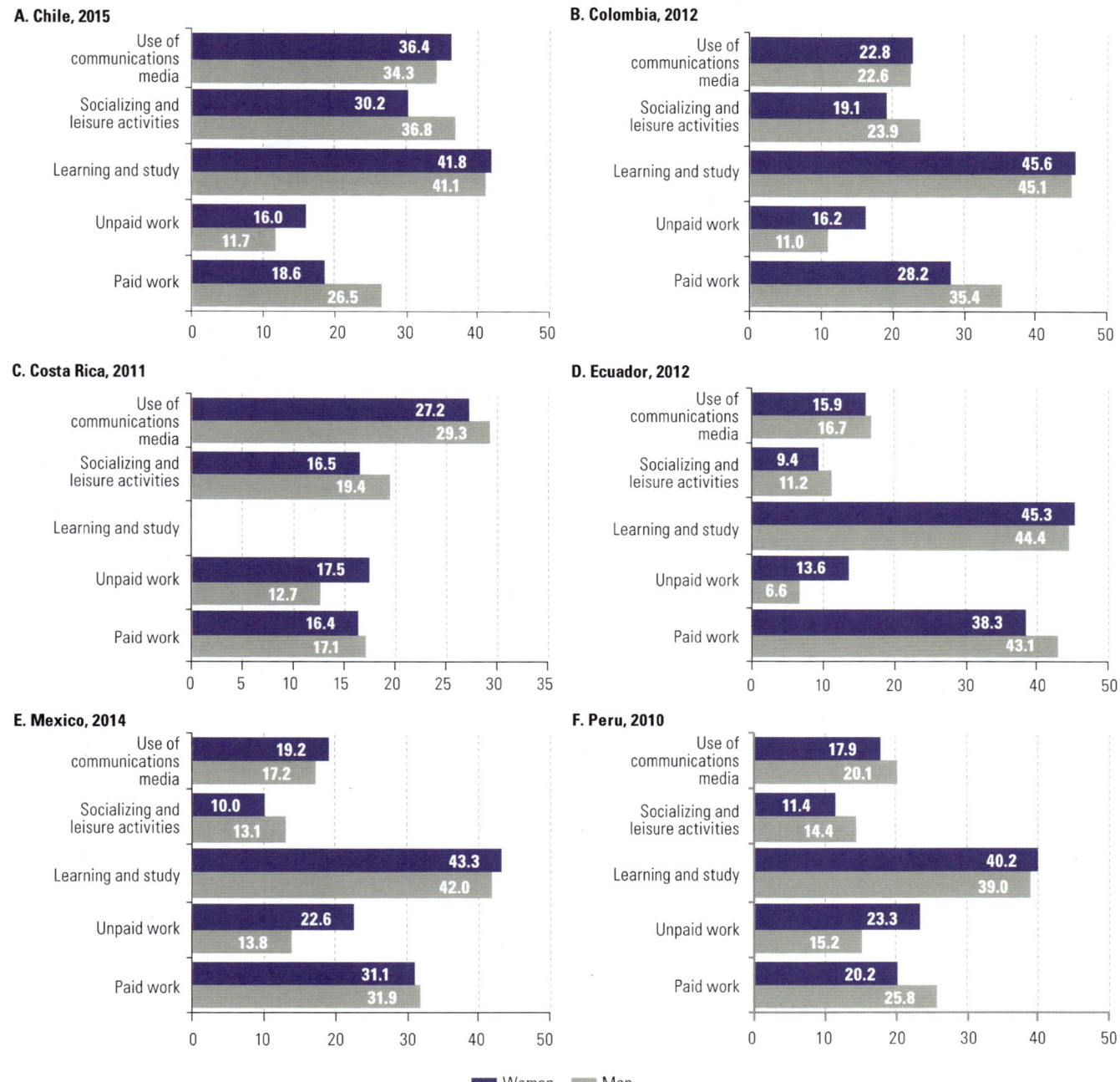

**Source:** Economic Commission for Latin America and the Caribbean (ECLAC), on the basis of special tabulations from time-use surveys conducted in the respective countries.
**Note:**   In light of the heterogeneous nature of data sources, comparisons between countries are still not possible; hence, the aim of this figure is to show the trends within each country. Data correspond to the national total except in the case of Costa Rica (Greater Metropolitan Area).
[a] The minimum age limit is 12 years in all countries except Colombia (10 years).
[b] Paid work refers to work done for the production of goods or services for the market and is calculated as the total amount of time devoted to employment, employment-seeking and commuting.
[c] Unpaid work refers to work done without payment and is measured by quantifying the time a person spends on own-use goods production work, unpaid domestic work, unpaid care of household members, unpaid work for other households or for the community and volunteering.

## (b) Time use among young people

Youth and the beginning of adulthood are a crucial period for eliminating gender inequalities. Nonetheless, as discussed in chapter III of this edition of *Social Panorama of Latin America*, the countries of Latin America and the Caribbean have not yet succeeded in ensuring that young women and men have the same rights and opportunities in training and labour market integration.

It is estimated that 22% of young people in the region between the ages of 15 and 29 do not benefit from the main pillars of social inclusion —the education system and labour market— and 73.5% of this group are women (ECLAC, 2016a). One of the targets of Goal 8 of the 2030 Agenda for Sustainable Development is the reduction in the number of young people in this situation, which means there is a need for information that explains the barriers to their integration into the labour market and the education system.

More than half (55%) of young people who are not in school or in employment spend their time on unpaid care and domestic work (Trucco and Ullman, 2015). The time-use data for this age group show that, on average, women who are out of school and the labour market spend at least 40 hours per week on unpaid domestic work, which confirms that they are not in school and not being paid for their work (ECLAC, 2016a). For example, in Costa Rica and Mexico, young people spend more than 70 hours per week on domestic and care work (see figure IV.6). This use of time for household work limits their possibilities for development in educational activities, opportunities for generating income and participation in public life and decision-making. They also miss out on building skills that would allow them to find good-quality jobs, which makes them more vulnerable to poverty and keeps them out of reach of the main social protection mechanisms.

**Figure IV.6**
Latin America (9 countries): unpaid work[a] by population aged 15 to 29 by activity and gender
*(Hours per week)*

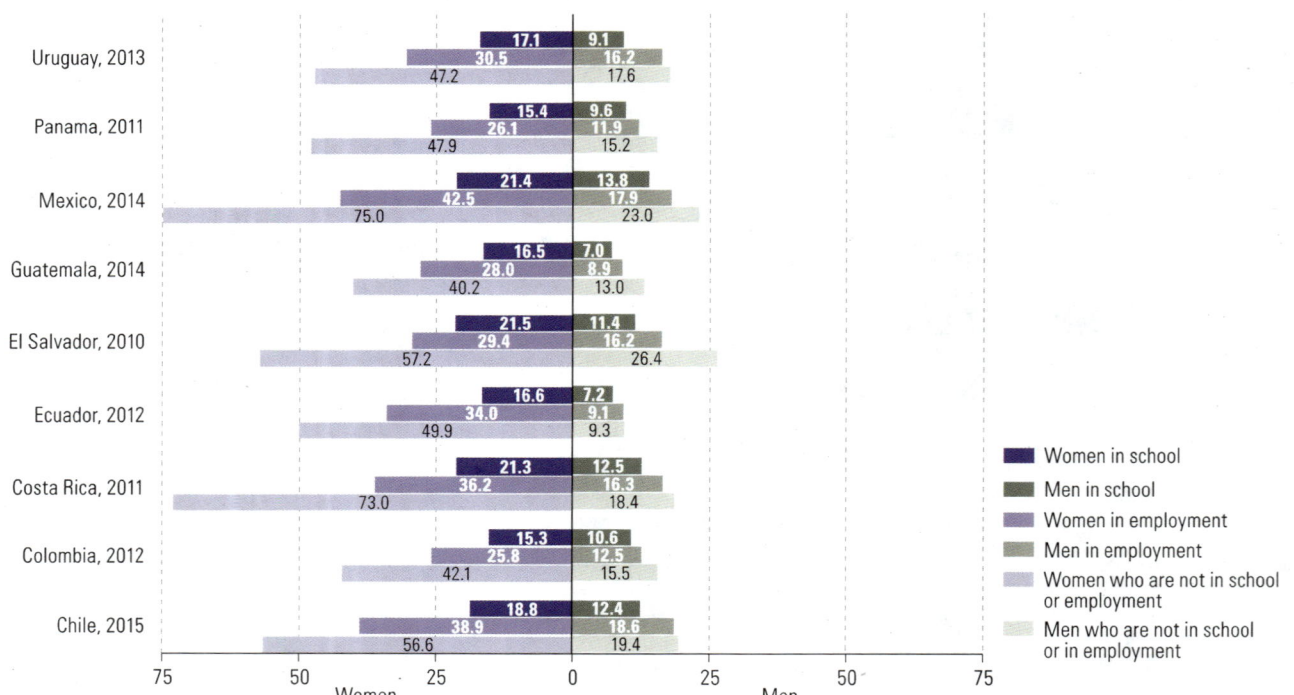

**Source**: Economic Commission for Latin America and the Caribbean (ECLAC), on the basis of special tabulations from time-use surveys conducted in the respective countries.
**Note**:    In light of the heterogeneous nature of data sources, comparisons between countries are still not possible; hence, the aim of this figure is to show the trends within each country. Data correspond to the national total except in the case of Costa Rica (Greater Metropolitan Area).
[a] Unpaid work refers to work done without payment and is measured by quantifying the time a person spends on own-use goods production work, unpaid domestic work, unpaid care of household members, unpaid work for other households or for the community and volunteering.

Time-use data on for this population segment contradicts the perception that young people are inactive or unproductive members of society, as they spend a significant amount of time providing services that are indispensable to the well-being of their households and the economy of their countries, but receive no payment and do not benefit from any form of social coverage. This information is relevant to policies on the social and economic inclusion of young people with a gender perspective that allows women in this age group to take advantage of academic and professional opportunities without being restricted by the demands of unpaid domestic and care work. In this context, it is also important to address the care responsibilities assigned to young mothers which significantly reduce the amount of time they are able to spend on other activities, which reproduces poverty.

Given the dynamic and flexible nature of the link between the different stages of the life cycle, the analysis of the situation among Latin American adolescents is a prelude to that among young men and women. Less than two thirds of adolescents between the ages of 15 and 17 are occupied only with school. Most of them work, and are either paid (mainly the men) or unpaid (primarily the women), showing a trend of early and unequal sexual division of labour (Rico and Trucco, 2014). According to the information garnered from time-use surveys, like the situation among older persons, adolescent girls spend more hours per week on work overall (paid and unpaid) than adolescent boys, which also reflects the limited time available for leisure and recreational activities, sports and community participation (Céspedes and Robles, 2016).

## (c) Old age: providing and receiving care

Demographic changes have had a significant impact on care supply and demand. As highlighted in *Social Panorama of Latin America 2015* (ECLAC, 2016g), accelerated population ageing will become the most relevant demographic trend in the region; the number of dependent older persons is expected to increase more than the number of people who can provide the care they potentially need. Given the lack of a culture of shared care responsibilities and of suitable public policies with a gender perspective, these changes in demand for care exacerbate the family responsibilities taken on by women (Rossel, 2016).

Several studies have been carried out in the region on the impact of demographic changes and the increase in demand for care (ECLAC, 2007; Calderón, 2013; Rossel, 2016). Time-use data is key in this analysis, considering that it helps identify people who require care and the services being provided at present. Mostly importantly, it helps determine the social organization of care and estimate the impact of future demographic changes on existing supply conditions.

Some time-use surveys in Latin America shed light on the care that older persons receive at home. The modalities with respect to the type of activities surveyed and the persons receiving care vary considerably from one country to the next. In Uruguay for example, data is collected on care provided to dependent persons aged 65 or older and questions focus on care for adults who require assistance with personal hygiene, feeding or medical care, including transportation to health centres. The national time-use survey in Mexico collects information on the time spent caring for persons aged 60 or older, including support in the use of information technology, transportation and accompaniment, even when the older person is not dependent or does not have a disability. In households where persons in this age range are present, women spend 18 hours per week on average caring for them, compared with 15 hours spent by men. The relevant module of the survey in Guatemala examines the total amount of time spent caring for persons aged 60 or over, but does not provide details on specific activities. In the same country, women spend 15 hours per week caring for older persons while men spend 13 hours per week.

The analysis of time-use surveys reveals a model of care provision by families that is maintained thanks to the unpaid work of women and which is not sustainable in the light of the new demographic challenges facing the region. Although demographic trends are a macrosocial phenomenon with a specific process, the region's countries can prepare for new care needs through comprehensive policies relating to health and equality, and to reduce vulnerabilities in old age, for example in the retirement and pension systems. These policies should consider gender equality as a core element to avoid the current overburden on women, who act as primary care providers.

Older persons require not only policies associated with care, but new social policy proposals that guarantee active ageing.[5] Time-use data based on life cycle stage also show that the division of tasks within the household changes little even after retirement. Figure IV.7 shows that despite the narrowing of the gender gap in participation as people grow older, the differences between men and women with respect to the time spent on unpaid work persist, including after retirement.

Unlike wage employment, reproductive work includes personal and emotional elements and lasts throughout a person's lifetime. While the career of employees (mainly men) is perceived as a long-term, individual, ascendant project that culminates in retirement, for women, the trajectory of unpaid domestic and care work represents a collective project that includes their families and does not end until old age or their death (Durán, 1986). Older men, who are accustomed to participating in public spaces, seek new models that allow them to transition from their activities on the labour market to recreation and participation in the public sphere (Durán, 2008a). It is more difficult for women to detach themselves from the obligations of domestic and care work (as shown in figure IV.7), which limits their participation in public spaces and activities that would allow them to build social ties and continue to develop their personal interests. It is important to use time-use data relating to older persons to adapt available programmes to the differentiated needs of men and women and thus guarantee their continued mental, physical, social and emotional growth. It is essential to include activities that allow them to adapt to this stage of their lives through the acquisition of new knowledge on health and capacities that help them to maintain a sense of identity, control and purpose that allows them to build social relationships (WHO, 2015).

The time-use analysis also provides information on older women as providers as well as receivers of care. Figure IV.8 shows that in all countries for which data is available on persons aged 65 or older, women provide most of the unpaid care for either members of their own household or of other households.

One of the phenomena resulting from longer life expectancy is different generations living under the same roof at the same time, which, along with greater participation of women in the labour market, has led to families adopting different arrangements for the care needed in the home. One of these arrangements is grandmothers or older women caring for younger generations so that other women (daughters, daughters-in-law, nieces or neighbours) are able to join the labour market. Although this care work is often considered voluntary, it reflects society's expectations of how older women should spend their time and perception of these women as ideal carers, as they have experience in this area. This is a clear example of the exacerbation of inequalities with respect to time distribution among older women. It also shows that the situation is worse for women who may not have been as active in the labour market during their adult lives and thus receive fewer social benefits relating to employment, which then results in greater difficulties for them to access care services. This is a perverse logic that deprives people of services that they provided to others throughout the course of their own lives (Gómez, 2008).

---

[5]　The World Health Organization defines active ageing as "the process of optimizing opportunities for health, participation and security to enhance quality of life as people age" (WHO, 2015).

**Figure IV.7**

Latin America (8 countries): time spent on unpaid work[a] and participation rate among retirees, by gender
*(Hours per week and percentages)*

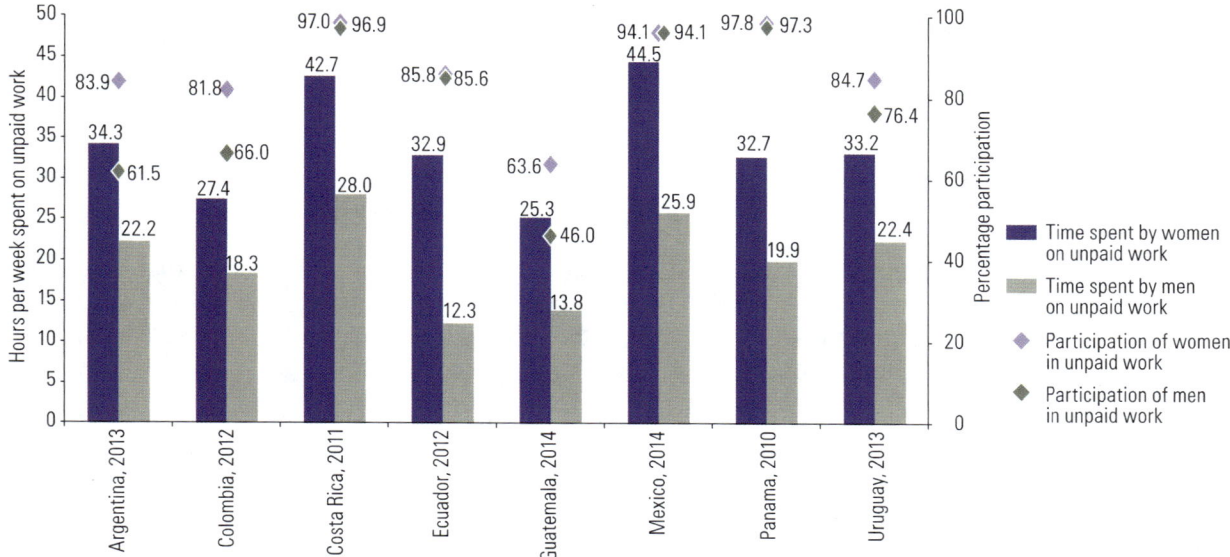

**Source**: Economic Commission for Latin America and the Caribbean (ECLAC), on the basis of special tabulations from time-use surveys conducted in the respective countries.

**Note**:   In light of the heterogeneous nature of data sources, comparisons between countries are still not possible; hence, the aim of this figure is to show the trends within each country. Data correspond to the national total except in the case of Costa Rica (Greater Metropolitan Area).

[a] Unpaid work refers to work done without payment and is measured by quantifying the time a person spends on own-use goods production work, unpaid domestic work, unpaid care of household members, unpaid work for other households or for the community and volunteering. The survey in Argentina does not include questions about own-use goods production work. Participation in unpaid work is calculated as the percentage of people who declared at least one activity in this category out of the total retiree population of each gender.

**Figure IV.8**

Latin America (6 countries): care provided[a] by persons aged 65 or older to members of their own or other households, by gender
*(Hours per week and percentages)*

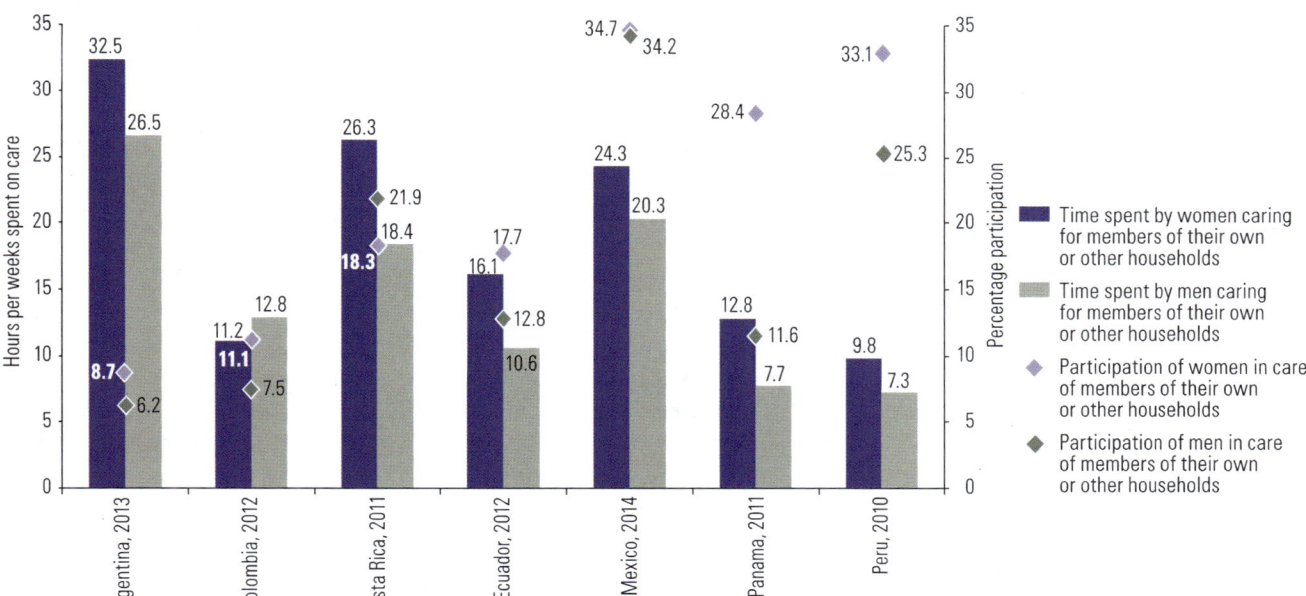

**Source**: Economic Commission for Latin America and the Caribbean (ECLAC), on the basis of special tabulations from time-use surveys conducted in the respective countries.

**Note**:   In light of the heterogeneous nature of data sources, comparisons between countries are still not possible; hence, the aim of this figure is to show the trends within each country. Data correspond to the national total except in the case of Costa Rica (Greater Metropolitan Area).

[a] Care refers to all activities relating to support for members of one's own household or other households classified within major division 4 and group 512 of the CAUTAL. Participation in care is calculated as the percentage of people who declared at least one activity relating to care for members of one's own household or other households out of the total population aged 65 and older of each gender.

# B. The valuation of unpaid work and the System of National Accounts (SNA)

The economic value determined by applying market prices to the goods and services produced in households through unpaid work represents, on average, between one fifth and one quarter of the total gross domestic product of countries that make this calculation by taking into account the contribution made to national economies, particularly by women, through their time and work.

Ensuring women's economic autonomy calls for a restructuring of the existing distribution of work through new policies that favour equality. This means recognizing and determining the value of the contribution made by men and women to the country's overall output through unpaid household work.

Domestic and care work support societies and have a significant impact on countries' well-being and development potential. Nonetheless, the limited definition of the System of National Accounts (SNA) production boundary excludes the domestic and care services produced or consumed by members of a household from the central framework of macroeconomic analysis. This conceals the importance of these activities for the economy, and perpetuates economic and power relationships. Owing to the importance of national accounts in economic analysis, decision-making and policy formulation, the exclusion of these activities has repercussions for the distribution of resources and benefits stemming from that production. If this aspect of the economy is not recognized or its impact is not analysed, inequalities will persist or worsen. Hence, the invisibility of women's contribution to the economy and to development becomes a disadvantage with respect to access to economic resources and protection, and impedes gender equality (Gómez, 2008).

The valuation of unpaid work in the framework of SNA provides a more precise measurement of what society produces (shedding light on a part of the economy that had remained hidden) and allows the contribution of this type of work to be incorporated into macroeconomic analysis and decision-making. Moreover, it aids the analysis of the interaction between the household and market economies.

A revision of SNA carried out in 1993 introduced the possibility of adding satellite accounts to the central framework, in order to provide a comprehensive picture of a specific field of economic activity. This significantly expanded the analytical capacity of national accounting, without overburdening or disrupting the central system. These satellite accounts allow the use of complementary elements or alternative concepts to highlight and provide more detailed descriptions of aspects concealed or not highly visible within the central framework. The steps required to include unpaid work in the SNA are: (i) quantifying unpaid work, (ii) valuing unpaid work and (iii) constructing a satellite account for unpaid household work (ECLAC, 2016a). Time-use surveys provide the information needed to quantify unpaid work. Countries have used several methodologies to value this type of work, as shown in table IV.1.

Table IV.1

Latin America (8 countries): economic value of unpaid household work

| Country | Year | Wages used for the economic valuation unpaid domestic household work | Contribution of unpaid work as a percentage of GDP (percentages) | | |
|---------|------|------|------|------|------|
| | | | Total | Women | Men |
| Colombia | 2012 | Replacement cost. specialist wage obtained from the Comprehensive Survey of Households | 20.4 | 16.3 | 4.1 |
| Costa Rica[a][b] | 2011 | Replacement cost. hybrid wage obtained from the national household survey | 15.7 | 11.5 | 4.3 |
| Ecuador | 2012 | Replacement cost. hybrid wage obtained from supply and use tables of the Central Bank of Ecuador | 15.2 | 11.8 | 3.4 |
| El Salvador | 2010 | Replacement cost. hybrid wage obtained from the Multipurpose Household Survey | 18.3 | 14.5 | 3.9 |
| Guatemala | 2014 | Replacement cost. general wage obtained from the National Survey of Employment and Income | 18.8 | 16.3 | 2.5 |
| Mexico | 2014 | Replacement cost. hybrid wage obtained from the average compensation by economic activity of the System of National Accounts of Mexico | 24.2 | 18.0 | 6.2 |
| Peru | 2010 | Replacement cost. hybrid wage obtained from supply and use tables and the equivalent employment matrix | 20.4 | 14.1 | 6.3 |
| Uruguay[a] | 2013 | Replacement cost. hybrid wage obtained from the Continuous Household Survey | 22.9 | 16.3 | 6.6 |

**Source**: Economic Commission for Latin America and the Caribbean (ECLAC), on the basis of the valuation of unpaid work in each country; National Statistics and Censuses Institute of Ecuador (INEC), "Cuentas satélite de trabajo no remunerado de los hogares 2011-2013, Ecuador", 2014 [online] http://www.ecuadorencifras.gob.ec/cuenta-satelite-de-trabajo-no-remunerado/; Mexican National Institute of Statistics and Geography (INEGI), "Trabajo no remunerado de los hogares", Mexico City [online] http://www.inegi.org.mx/est/contenidos/proyectos/cn/tnrh/default.aspx; National Institute of Statistics and Informatics of Peru (INEI), *Cuenta satélite del trabajo doméstico no remunerado*, Lima, Minister for Women's Affairs and Vulnerable Populations (MIMP)/United Nations Population Fund (UNFPA)/United Nations Entity for Gender Equality and the Empowerment of Women (UN-Women), 2016 [online] https://www.inei.gob.pe/media/MenuRecursivo/publicaciones_digitales/Est/Lib1358/libro.pdf; Salvadoran Institute for the Advancement of Women/Department of Statistics and Censuses/Central Reserve Bank of El Salvador (ISDEMU/DIGESTYC/BCR), "Principales resultados del ejercicio de valorización del trabajo no remunerado de los hogares", paper presented at the Seminar "Reconocimiento y Provisión de Cuidados: Desafíos para una Política Integrada en El Salvador", San Salvador, 2016; I. Sandoval and L. Gónzalez, "Estimación del valor económico del trabajo no remunerado en Costa Rica. Resultados e ilustración metodológica", *Estudios Demográficos y Urbanos*, vol. 30, No. 3, Colegio de México, September-December 2015 [online] http://www.scielo.org.mx/scielo.php?script=sci_arttext&pid=S0186-72102015000300691&lng=es&nrm=iso&tlng=es.

[a] The country's governing body for national accounts did not contribute to this calculation.
[b] Greater Metropolitan Area.

In order for the measurements to serve as policy inputs and lead to more equal distribution of unpaid work between men and women, they must be included in official statistics and developed using an interdisciplinary, interinstitutional and periodic approach. The countries of the region that have developed economic valuation exercises for unpaid domestic work and incorporated them into satellite accounts have built valuable partnerships between statistical offices and central banks in their capacity as data producers, and mechanisms for the advancement of women, as principal users of the information. Using an interinstitutional approach, they have evaluated how to make calculations, what information sources to use and how to disseminate data. The process has been difficult at times considering that it requires a common language to eliminate institutional mistrust, strengthen the capacity of the institutions involved and enable both to take ownership of the process and the results that will be disseminated and used.

Mexico was the first country in the region to build a satellite account for unpaid household work to show the economic contribution of households to the well-being of individuals and of the economy. The economic value of unpaid domestic work in Mexico in 2014 stood at 24.2% of GDP, which was higher than the individual contribution of any other economic activity in the country.

With a view to complementing the information contained in the central framework of national accounts, Colombia, Ecuador, Guatemala and Peru have also developed satellite accounts that quantify the economic contribution of unpaid activities in households providing domestic services and care to members of one's own household, other households or the community. El Salvador is now creating a satellite account for unpaid household work, while Costa Rica and Uruguay have made significant progress in studying methodologies and exercises for the valuation of unpaid work using the data collected from their respective time-use surveys.

The political will of decision-makers, efforts of civil society and legal framework play a crucial role in strengthening the production and use of data (Marco, 2012). For example, Law 1.413 (2010) in Colombia regulates the inclusion of the care economy in the System of National Accounts with the aim of measuring women's contribution to the country's economic and social development. Under this law, the National Administrative Department of Statistics (DANE) is responsible for conducting the national time-use survey and calculating a satellite account for the care economy. Articles 325 and 333 of the 2008 Constitution of Ecuador include in the definition of the economic system: unpaid subsistence or care work in the household, family labour and independent work. The adoption of Law No. 29.700 in Peru was crucial to the first official calculation in 2016 of the economic value of unpaid household work in the country and to ensuring that this measurement would be included in Peru's official statistics.

Table IV.1 shows that the economic value of unpaid household work ranges from 15.2% to 24.2% of GDP in the region.

The results obtained by the countries show a clear gap in the distribution of unpaid care and domestic work inside households. Considering the relative weight of the contribution of men and women to GDP, women's contribution represents between 70% (Peru) and 87% (Guatemala). This shows the significant contribution of women to countries' economies and the well-being of their populations. By carrying out unpaid work, women provide services that would otherwise have to be supplied by other household members and/or guaranteed by the State.

It is crucial for countries to continue pushing for the development of the necessary statistics for an economic analysis with a gender perspective. The statistical challenge is better harmonization of data that allows comparability over time and between countries. Hence, it makes sense to highlight the knowledge accumulated in the region on the measurement of unpaid work and the adoption of the CAUTAL as a tool to harmonize time-use statistics. As established in the System of National Accounts 2008: "When a number of countries develop similar satellites, exchanging experience can lead to beneficial refinements and the establishment of international guidelines in a particular topic and ultimately the possibility of changes in the central system itself" (United Nations, 2009).

Building a satellite account for unpaid care and domestic work is not an end in itself, but provides a better understanding of the economic dynamics within and among households, and between households and the rest of the economy, which is crucial for incorporating the care economy perspective into the analysis of the entire economic system. The information gleaned from this type of account supports the design of policies that favour more equitable distribution of work between men and women, fair access to income and other social protection benefits for women, and the allocation of resources and establishment of public policy priorities.

# C. The contribution of time-use data to equality policies

Designing public policies for equality that are timely and gender-balanced continues to present a challenge for Latin America and the Caribbean. In order to achieve equality, the matrix of social and economic policies must include development policies with transformative objectives relating to women's economic autonomy and that offer quality services, in the framework of the design of policies for the care of dependent persons.

States must address this problem through innovative public policies designed around time distribution and unpaid work and geared towards transforming the existing sexual division of labour.

Today's apparently gender-neutral public policies disregard distribution of time as a fundamental resource for the social and economic well-being of people and society as a whole. As shown in this chapter, there are inequalities in time use and the contribution of unpaid work to families' well-being and sustainability in the context of a broad and unorthodox economy (ECLAC, 2016a). The failure to recognize this contribution widens gaps and reproduces inequalities. States must address this problem through innovative public policies designed around time distribution and unpaid work and geared towards transforming the existing sexual division of labour. Time-use surveys, the valuation of unpaid work and satellite accounts represent key inputs for the formulation, follow-up and evaluation of these policies.

In the effort to coordinate activities in the public and private sphere, policies should not reinforce current gender roles and stereotypes, and should be based on a redistributive equation in which the responsibilities and benefits associated with unpaid work are shared equally between men and women, with the community and the State also sharing responsibility for the well-being of all members of society.

A study of time-use surveys in South Africa, Asia and Latin America highlights the difficult process of creating the right political conditions to carry out these surveys and their impact —which has been limited until now— on the development and evaluation of public policies (Esquivel and others, 2008). According to Budlender (2008) the results of the time-use survey in South Africa were barely incorporated into the formulation of public policies as their revelations were not surprising to decision-makers, such as the time spent by women and children collecting water and fuel for their homes, which was not regarded as a public concern requiring a response from the State.[6] This experience shows there is much work needed to ensure that the gender perspective is incorporated into the public agenda, and that even in the light of sufficient empirical evidence, the time spent on unpaid work and care is not recognized as a public problem that should be resolved (Marco and Rico, 2013). Time-use surveys are still not sufficiently factored into the adoption of decisions, allocation of resources and determination of priorities, but they are a valuable tool for a wide range of public policies that can achieve equality and sustainable development.

Although time-use data for the region has focused mainly on the recognition and distribution of unpaid work, this information can also be used in different areas considering that time is an indispensable resource for carrying out all human activities. Time is a finite economic and social resource and provides evidence on how society and people work, as well as the microphysics of power (Foucault, 1993) that regulates relationships within households. Generally speaking, all social policies focusing on families and households would benefit from an analysis of the use and allocation of time by their members.

---

[6]    In any case the results were incorporated into the Child Labour Programme of Action.

What follows is the description of a non-exhaustive research and recommendation agenda for public policies that highlights the potential utilization of time-use and distribution data for economic and social equality policies from a gender perspective. Although some sectoral applications are suggested, it is important to establish interinstitutional and intersectoral coordination and synergies, and there is an urgent need for comprehensive policies, especially on redistributive measures aimed at working in a cross-cutting manner towards equality between men and women and the recognition of women's contributions to countries' growth, well-being and development.

First, and considering the topology of time, attention is paid to policies relating to economic conditions and the production structure of the region's countries, such as rural development and natural resources, urban development and transport, and employment. Second, there is an analysis of the potential use of information for social policies such as health and eradicating poverty. Lastly, attention is paid to care policies, with a focus on those targeting persons with disabilities and young children, which include innovative features and to some extent attempt to transform economic conditions and have an impact on women's autonomy, as well as address social aspects linked to the initial stages of socialization of boy and girls, the development of capacities and skills in early childhood and better social inclusion.

## 1. Policies for natural resources and rural development

The sexual division of labour and dominant cultural patterns contribute to environmental problems and the consequences of climate change. Rural, indigenous and campesino women are guardians of biodiversity but, under conditions of significant fragility and exploitation, they have less access to and control over land and production resources, and they shoulder the main responsibility for providing food for their families, collecting water and firewood, and tending vegetable plots and animals. Their responsibilities and disempowerment thus worsen their vulnerability and prevent them from developing adaptation and response capacities (ECLAC, 2017).

Households without drinking water face additional costs with respect to finances, time, health and opportunities. The lack of access to better drinking water sources results in health problems, including gastrointestinal disorders that remain a major cause of death and healthy life years lost in the region. It also affects school attendance and academic performance and means a greater burden of unpaid work, which reduces the time available for paid work. Despite the progress that several countries have made in improving access to drinking water, there are significant differences by territory and income quintile in access to piped water and sanitation (ECLAC, 2016b).

Access to better drinking water sources is key to reducing the burden of unpaid work, as it would decrease the time spent collecting water, a task often carried out by women and girls (see figure IV.9). For example, in rural areas of Peru, 57.3% of women are responsible for fetching water, while in Guatemala, women spend six hours per week on this activity, one hour more than men. Hence, policies that extend water networks, sanitation and drinking water distribution could have a much larger than expected impact on gender equality and, in particular, reduce women's workload.

Meanwhile, the lack of access to modern energy sources means that many households, mainly those with the lowest incomes and in rural areas, continue to use solid fuels which generate high levels of atmospheric pollution, which in turn causes illness and death owing to respiratory problems. The use of wood as fuel represents a significant opportunity cost, especially for women who are responsible for collecting it, in terms of the time they could spend on other activities, such as paid work, and the effects that could result from handling the heavy weights involved. Time-use surveys have incorporated questions that help to determine the rate of participation and time spent by the population on this type of activity. Activities linked to collecting wood are included in the surveys for Colombia, Costa Rica, Ecuador, Guatemala, Mexico, Panama, Paraguay and Peru.

The analysis of gender relations within the framework of dominant production, consumption and energy-use patterns is crucial to promoting actions that would mitigate the effects of climate change and reduce greenhouse gas emissions. Time-use data sheds light on women's contribution to mitigation as producers, workers and consumers, and allows authorities to choose measures that contribute to sustainable development and women's economic autonomy (ECLAC, 2017).

**Figure IV.9**
Latin America (4 countries): time spent collecting water and participation rate of population aged 15 and older, by gender
*(Hours per week and percentages)*

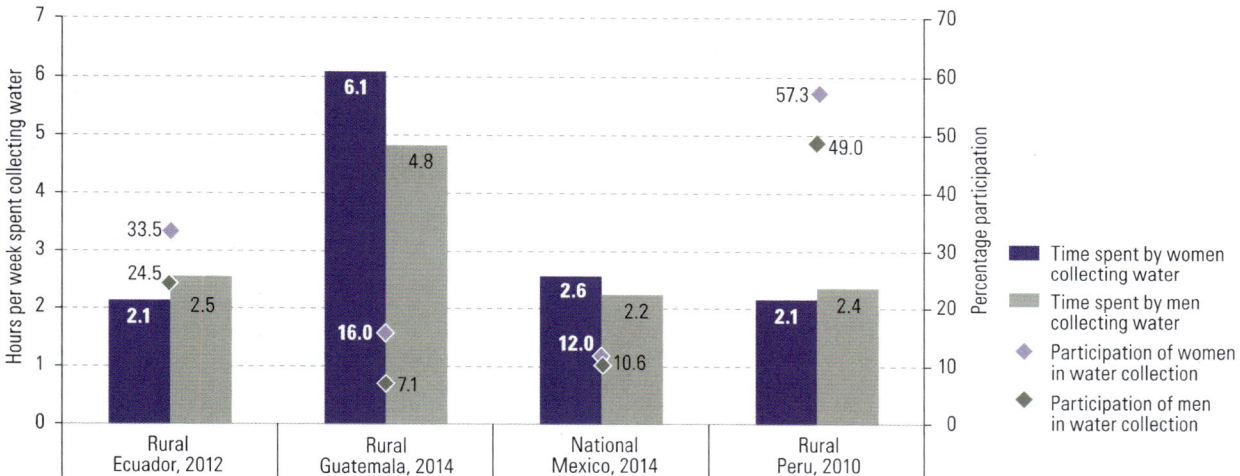

**Source**: Economic Commission for Latin America and the Caribbean (ECLAC), on the basis of special tabulations from time-use surveys conducted in the respective countries.
**Note**:    In light of the heterogeneous nature of data sources, comparisons between countries are still not possible; hence, the aim of this figure is to show the trends within each country. Participation in collecting water is calculated as the percentage of people who have stated that they carry out this activity out of the total population aged 15 and older of each gender. Data correspond to the information on water collection in rural areas, except in Mexico, where they correspond to the country as a whole.

In a regional context where gender inequality worsens food insecurity, malnutrition and poverty, rural development strategies do not always benefit women (with respect to income, land ownership and water rights, for example) and, on the contrary, exacerbate existing inequalities (ECLAC, 2016c). It is important to implement rural development measures with a gender perspective that take into account women's diverse needs and that, with a view to achieving equality, consider the data on time distribution and allocation in addition to identifying changes in the sector, technology modernization and necessary sociocultural transformations. The gender strategy for the Plan on Food Security, Nutrition and Eradication of Hunger of the Community of Latin American and Caribbean States —the FNS-CELAC plan[7]— is an example of this type of regional initiative (FAO, 2016). With a view to achieving greater equality and inclusive development, it is crucial to reduce the concentration of basic deficiencies and lack of public services in the most disadvantaged subnational territories given that these deficits, among other things, take up a disproportionate amount of women's time, forcing them to work to offset the loss (ECLAC, 2016b).

[7]    One of the strategic measures of the FNS-CELAC plan is to establish synergies with the Montevideo Strategy adopted at the thirteenth Regional Conference on Women in Latin America and the Caribbean, and strengthen intersectoral work to guarantee the rights and economic, physical and decision-making autonomy needed to ensure women's development, and the relationships between these types of autonomy. For this reason, emphasis is placed on the importance of time-use data in this plan.

## 2. Policies for urban development and transport

The *New Urban Agenda*, which was adopted by United Nations Member States at the third United Nations Conference on Housing and Sustainable Urban Development (Habitat III) held from 17 to 20 October 2016 in Quito, aims to build cities and human settlements where people can enjoy the same rights and opportunities (United Nations, 2017d). To that end, commitments were focused on changing the urban paradigm to achieve social inclusion, poverty eradication, sustainable and inclusive urban prosperity, opportunities for all and resilient and sustainable urban development from an environmental perspective. With equality as the ultimate goal, sustainable territorial development should be approached from a gender perspective that ensures that women's needs are met, so that existing gaps are closed.

Time distribution is closely linked to the organization of space in each territory; making activities compatible is linked to distances and means and conditions for covering them, particularly in cities (ECLAC, 2016c). There should be a focus on trends in cities to understand inequality and overcome it: as a result of the urbanization process, more than 80% of the regional population is concentrated in urban areas (ECLAC, 2016b). The common problems of Latin America cities are congestion, socio-spatial segregation, the lack of basic services, scarcity of adequate housing and deteriorating infrastructure. These problems must be addressed by proper planning of cities and their public and private services, taking into account how people use their time so that these cities can continue to prosper and grow, and to make better use of resources and reduce pollution, poverty and inequality, and socioterritorial division.

Time-use surveys are designed to provide information that helps to establish or adapt urban services suited to the population's needs, particularly those relating to transport and zoning of public community services. Sample designs should help to make inferences about geographical areas of interest, which could require financial resources for data production by municipalities, provinces or States. Nonetheless, once the necessary resources are available to prepare national surveys, the cost of expanding the samples to guarantee representativeness is usually not high.

The structure of urban spaces and policies, programmes and projects that shape cities affect the private and public lives of inhabitants in different ways. The availability and quality of transport, condition of public spaces, and safety while moving around and accessing urban services and the workplace or school are crucial factors in the lives of women and therefore affect their chances of increasing their autonomy comprehensively (Segovia, 2016).

Time-use data has been utilised to a large extent to identify transport needs and the factors that determine how they are decided. There are also studies on gender inequality in access to transport (United Nations, 2005). Hence, there is a dynamic approach to time use linked to the spatial dimension, to the degree that it takes into account the schedules and time necessary to carry out certain activities or access and effectively use public services, spaces for recreation and participation, educational institutions and places where paid work is carried out. This is reinforced when, as policies are being designed, attention is paid to inequalities in access and effective use that affect households and persons (particularly poor women) whose social and geographical positions seriously compromise their ability to manage time as an asset to take full advantage of opportunities and resources and to achieve autonomy and well-being (Rossel and Hernández, 2013).

Figure IV.10 shows the amount of time men and women spend per week commuting to and from work in the capital cities of five Latin American countries.[8] Although this time is classified in CAUTAL under paid work, it is generally not paid or considered part of the working day, although in some countries it is protected by health care coverage. As seen in the figure, commuting time in capital cities amounts to at least one hour more per week than the national average, and owing to the nature of women's participation in the labour market, the participation of women in the activity commuting to and from work is less than that of men. Women spend more time than men accessing health services or care and academic institutions, and are the main users of public transport (Figueroa and Waintrub, 2015; Hernández, 2012; Díaz and Jiménez, 2002).

**Figure IV.10**

Latin America (5 countries): time invested in commuting to and from work and participation of population aged 15 and older, by gender
*(Hours per week and percentages)*

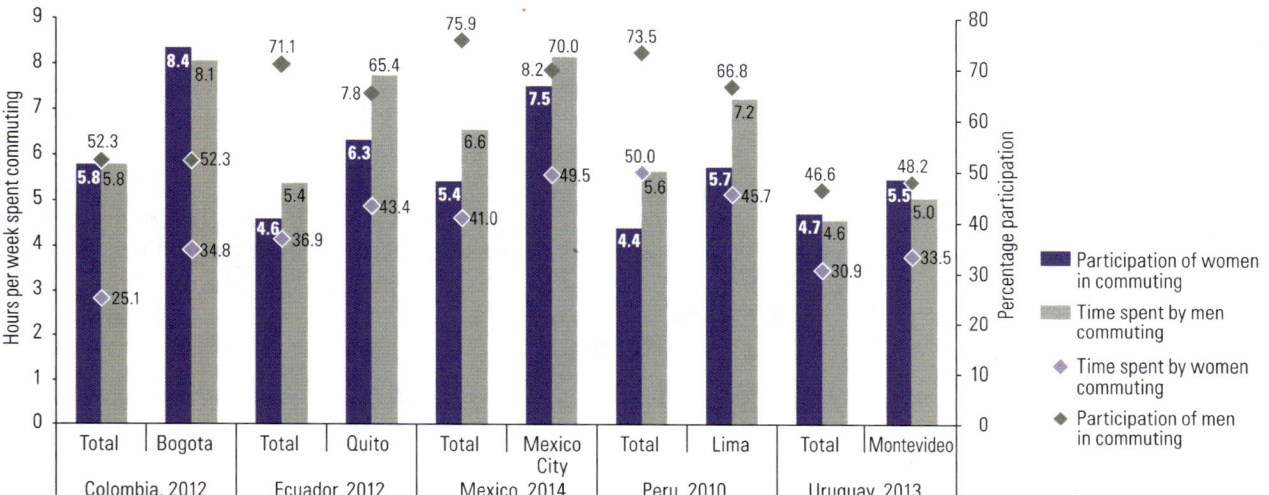

**Source**: Economic Commission for Latin America and the Caribbean (ECLAC), on the basis of special tabulations from time-use surveys conducted in the respective countries.
**Note**:    In light of the heterogeneous nature of data sources, comparisons between countries are still not possible; hence, the aim of this figure is to show the trends within each country. Participation in commuting to and from work is calculated as the percentage of people who said that they had participated in this activity out of the total population aged 15 and older, by gender.

With a view to building cities that provide a better quality of life for both men and women, helpful measures include planning spaces and defining time use for urban services (for example, timetables, waiting times, attention to and management of procedures and distances) so that women and men can perform their daily tasks of caring for family members and paid work more easily and quickly (Segovia, 2016). Moreover, data on time-use and transport contribute to the progressive structural change focused on the environmental big push with policies that favour the building of smart cities and good-quality, greener and more inclusive transport systems (ECLAC, 2016e).

Gender inequalities in time use affect women's participation in local development initiatives. The sexual division of labour affects women's level of involvement in matters of public interest aimed at improving living conditions for families and the community: they are often limited to participating in basic community improvement tasks and they occupy few positions of power in the political sphere (ECLAC, 2016c). Time-use studies help identify inequalities and propose innovative and transformative policies to eliminate them.

---

8    The aim of this section is to show the potential of time-use surveys for urban mobility policies. In addition to the selected countries, Brazil, Chile, Costa Rica, El Salvador, Guatemala, Panama and Paraguay also included questions on time spent commuting.

## 3.    Policies for the labour market

As previously mentioned, the way time is distributed currently limits women's access to social, political and community life. Time-use indicators establish a link between unpaid and paid work, as the amount of time spent on the former limits the availability of time to perform the latter. These data reveal the relationship between unpaid work and women's lesser engagement in the labour market and their tendency to have more informal and precarious jobs. Hence, it is crucial to consider time distribution in the formulation of policies which, when combined with other sectoral policies, incentivize the redistribution of domestic and care work and promote labour practices that offer alternatives for the organization of time spent on market activities (Marco, 2012). Moreover, the analysis of time spent on care helps to evaluate the importance of reinforcing maternity and paternity leave and the relevance of implementing leave for the care of older persons and household members with some form of disability or chronic illness.

According to feminist economics, work is not limited to demand on the market, but extends to production within households. Hence market and household needs should be met by everyone, with no advantages for some at the expense of others. With a view to avoiding the strengthening of gender roles, public policies must consider households' demand for goods and services for their own consumption and for collective well-being, as well as the fact that this demand is met by the unpaid work of women. This implies establishing a balanced relationship between the paid and unpaid work of men and women and promoting shared responsibility of care, both in the private sphere and in working relationships, as well as in the provision of goods and services by the market and the State (ECLAC, 2016; ECLAC, 2017).

A large percentage of employed women find themselves under pressure: on one hand, they put in long hours working and commuting and on the other hand, they face constant demands to care for family members. As a result of men's limited participation, insufficient public supply and segmented private supply of care, some women involuntarily decide to reduce their time at work (which affects their income), spend a part of their wages on care services, abandon the labour market, avoid the role of caregiver, or turn to other women in family and social networks to provide care, while others, anticipating these tensions, delay having children or reduce the number of children they have. Although the length of the working day has always been a central theme of the labour market, consideration of the double working day is more recent. In Latin America, the Hours of Work (Industry) Convention (ILO, 1919) had a significant impact on the adoption of labour laws; nonetheless, working days —paid and unpaid— are still very long, particularly for women (as shown in figure IV.3).

The organization of time is crucial to families' well-being. As outlined in the document *Equality and women's autonomy in the sustainable development agenda*, shorter working days would have a number of positive effects on the redistribution of time and work within households (ECLAC, 2016a). Balancing paid and unpaid work with shorter working days would allow men to participate more in domestic and care work and increase women's options for employment and income generation (Batthyány, 2009).

Time-use data helps to identify demand for domestic and care work in households as a result of demographic and epidemiological changes. This knowledge should guide policies and regulations relating to employment in domestic services, one of the main sectors providing paid employment to women in the region, and to employment in public and private service sectors that currently address only a small percentage of the total demand for care in the society. With a view to overcoming inequalities and ensuring decent, protected and inclusive work, there is a need for comprehensive and coordinated policies on shared responsibility and employment (ILO/UNDP 2009; Cecchini and Rico, 2015).

> Time-use data helps to identify demand for domestic and care work in households as a result of demographic and epidemiological changes.

The conditions in which paid work is carried out and the quality of jobs have direct impacts on the right to social security. Moreover, the overburden of unpaid work on women affects their economic autonomy by limiting their participation in the labour market. This reduces their ability to generate their own income and restricts their access to social security, which is strongly linked to formal employment in the region.

On one hand, a large percentage of women spend their lives outside the labour market or only participate in this market on an irregular or informal basis in order to meet the demand for care in their households (Marco, 2016). This limits their access to social protection, which they may only receive thanks to their relationship with an employed spouse (Gómez, 2008) or through non-contributory transfers. As shown previously, time-use data sheds light on women's economic contribution to countries through unpaid work. These data should allow people who carry out only unpaid work to receive social security benefits —an outstanding debt to women in the region— through programmes that aim for universal social protection and which are not necessarily linked to labour market participation (ECLAC, 2016a).

On the other hand, unpaid work by women is a central element of care as well as a type of social protection subsidy.[9] During this period of weakening economies, it makes sense to recall previous crises and structural adjustments, during which public services deteriorated and the impact of social spending cuts was absorbed by women through the unpaid provision of care, mainly with respect to health (Gómez, 2008). Hence, in order to avoid setbacks in existing policies and programmes and to continue advancing towards comprehensive care systems, the economic invisibility of unpaid domestic and care work in households must not become a factor of social exclusion.

Unpaid work is not only a barrier to women's economic autonomy during their reproductive age, but also until old age. Studies have been carried out in the region that show deficiencies in pension and retirement benefit coverage that have a larger impact on women, who receive roughly 20% less than men, on average (Marco, 2016; CEPAL, 2016a).

## 4.    Policies for overcoming poverty

Time-use data allows a comprehensive and multidimensional approach to poverty-alleviation policies. In recent years, time has become the subject of study as a measure of well-being: the problem of poverty has been analysed from various unconventional perspectives and a vicious circle involving poverty and time spent on unpaid work has been revealed (Vaca-Trigo, 2015; CEPAL, 2016a). Hence, in order to achieve sustainable development, it is important to consider this dimension when designing public policies.

Time-use surveys in Ecuador and Mexico include questions relating to time spent obtaining social programme benefits, which helps to determine whether these procedures, which are generally carried out by women, have a negative impact on recipients' burden of unpaid work.

Mothers in situations of poverty or extreme poverty in Latin America are the effective recipients of conditional transfer programmes. Although such programmes have given these women access to monetary income and other benefits (Cecchini and Madariaga, 2011), they have not managed to challenge the sexual division of labour and the role of women who are mothers as caregivers (ECLAC, 2013). A 2013 ECLAC

---

[9]    Owing to limited good-quality public services and a segmented private market, women are tasked with providing domestic care work to households, for which they are not paid. As a result, welfare systems in many Latin American and Caribbean countries are supported by the unpaid work of women, who subsidize the cost of care and hence part of the social protection required by the population. In the Brasilia Consensus, the region's governments agreed that unpaid domestic work was a burden that fell disproportionately on women and, in practice, constituted an invisible subsidy to the economic system (ECLAC, 2010).

study of time-use data for Ecuador and Mexico showed differences between women in poverty who received conditional transfers and those who did not. As shown in figure IV.11, poor women receiving transfers in both countries spend more hours per week on unpaid domestic and care work.

**Figure IV.11**
Ecuador and Mexico: average working time of women in poverty, based on conditional transfers received, 2010
*(Hours per week)*

Source: Economic Commission for Latin America and the Caribbean (ECLAC), *Gender Equality Observatory of Latin America and the Caribbean, Annual Report 2012. A look at grants support and burden for women* (LC/G.2561/Rev.1), Santiago, 2013.

A quasi-experimental evaluation of time-use surveys revealed that Colombia's Families in Action programme decreased the time spent by boys in paid work and increased their leisure time, but reduced the leisure time of girls and increased the time they spent on domestic work (Canavire-Bacarreza and Ospina, 2015, cited in ECLAC, 2016a). With respect to the programme's impact on adults, the time spent by men on paid work increased at the expense of domestic work, and the time spent by women on domestic and care work increased at the expense of leisure time. The unequal distribution of productive and reproductive work creates further inequality in the use of free time. According to María Ángeles Durán (2005), "women usually continue to be the main persons responsible for unpaid domestic and care work even when they find paid employment", which implies that some of the tasks that are not carried out during the week or are not done well as women are doing paid work occupy the time that should theoretically be spent resting. A study of Mexico's Oportunidades programme (now called Prospera), based on the results of the 2002 national time-use survey, calculated that households spent 18 hours and 24 minutes per year on average carrying out activities relating to health and nutrition, and an estimated 92% of this time was spent by women (Gammage and Orozco, 2008). Moreover, through a quasi-experimental analysis of this Mexican programme, there was an increase in domestic and care work by women owing to children's decreased participation in these activities (Espejo, 2013, cited in ECLAC, 2016a).

These studies suggest that the time spent on unpaid domestic and care work increases for women who must carry out activities required by conditional transfer programmes. Time-use data should be taken into account to incorporate the gender perspective when designing poverty-eradication programmes, or when evaluating the benefits of such conditions, and to promote shared responsibility between men and women and between the State, the market and families (ECLAC, 2016a), and when coordinating these programmes with others and strengthening health and education policies so that they reach the poorest sectors and are not supported by conditional transfer programmes and the unpaid work of women.

# 5.    Policies for health

In the region, it is often up to family members to complement or assume responsibility for health care for other members, either by buying medication, paying for private services, caring directly for the ill, or other means. The reasons vary, and include the cost and organization of health services, which complicate access to medical care, especially for people in the lowest-income households (Ferrán, 2008).

People's physical and mental well-being depend on a number of conditions (Gómez, 2008). In order to produce estimates of the activities that directly affect the health of household members, time-use surveys must distinguish between care activities relating specifically to health care and other activities. Figure IV.12 shows data for five Latin American countries where surveys clearly identify this type of work.[10] The analysis reveals clear gender gaps in household members' participation in health care: women's declared participation is three to nine percentage points higher than that of men. If this heavy burden is maintained over time, it can influence the physical and mental health of the caregiver, who will then also need care. No single overall trend can be identified in the time spent on care in the countries under review. In Colombia and Uruguay, men who provide health care spend more hours per week than women on this activity, while in Ecuador, Mexico and Peru, women spend more time on this type of care, which involves administering medication, providing therapy or rehabilitation, accompanying sick persons to health service facilities and providing special care to persons with disabilities and chronic illnesses.

The data provided by time-use surveys contributes to the building of indicators of supply and demand for unpaid health care work in households and should be considered by those responsible for formulating this type of policy. This will help to put an end to the perception that women who spend their time caring for family members with health problems are inactive and to grant them social security benefits that they currently do not receive. Nonetheless, estimating the time spent on unpaid health care relating to uncommon illnesses is a challenge that generally cannot be addressed through time-use surveys, as samples do not capture this type of information. Therefore, detailed studies are needed to complement more general information with a specific focus on care, by type of illness, and to distinguish between the time invested in prevention from time spent on care relating to an illness (Durán, 2008b).

Health care is one of the most complex unpaid activities in households and commands some of the highest prices on the market. Good health policies are hard to formulate if the distribution of the workload relating to this type of care is not known. Moreover, the absence of domestic health service indicators in the macroeconomic totals of national accounts limits the consideration of this service's economic value to public and private health care, with negative repercussions for health policies and for countries' economic and social growth (Ferrán, 2008). Hence, the information provided by time-use surveys is crucial to the monetary valuation of domestic health services. In Mexico, for example, the estimated monetary value of unpaid domestic health care is 167,536 million pesos, which is equivalent to roughly 1% of GDP, twice the total budget of conditional monetary transfer programmes, or 85.5% of the value added of hospital services. Women contribute 72.2% of this monetary value (INEGI, 2014).

---

[10]    In Colombia, the survey identifies activities such as administering medication; providing therapy, rehabilitation or treatments; accompanying ill persons to medical and dental appointments, emergency services or therapy sessions; and providing other types of health care for household members who are not permanently dependent. In Ecuador, surveys include special therapies or exercises for children in the household; transporting and accompanying persons to receive medical or hospital care (including alternative therapies) and preparing remedies and providing special care for household members with disabilities. In Mexico, the activities identified are: special therapy or assistance with exercises for children in the household; transportation of a household member to receive health care, and special care for household members with disabilities or chronic or temporary illness. In Peru, therapy for children is considered, as well as care for household members with any type of symptom, ailment or illness, including transport to health centres, and care for household members with physical and mental difficulties, chronic illnesses, or who are older persons and totally dependent. In Uruguay, activities such as providing therapy, feeding, accompanying and transporting household members to health centres and providing special care for persons with disabilities are incorporated.

**Figure IV.12**
Latin America (5 countries): time spent providing health care to family members and participation rate of population aged 15 and older, by gender
*(Hours per week and percentages)*

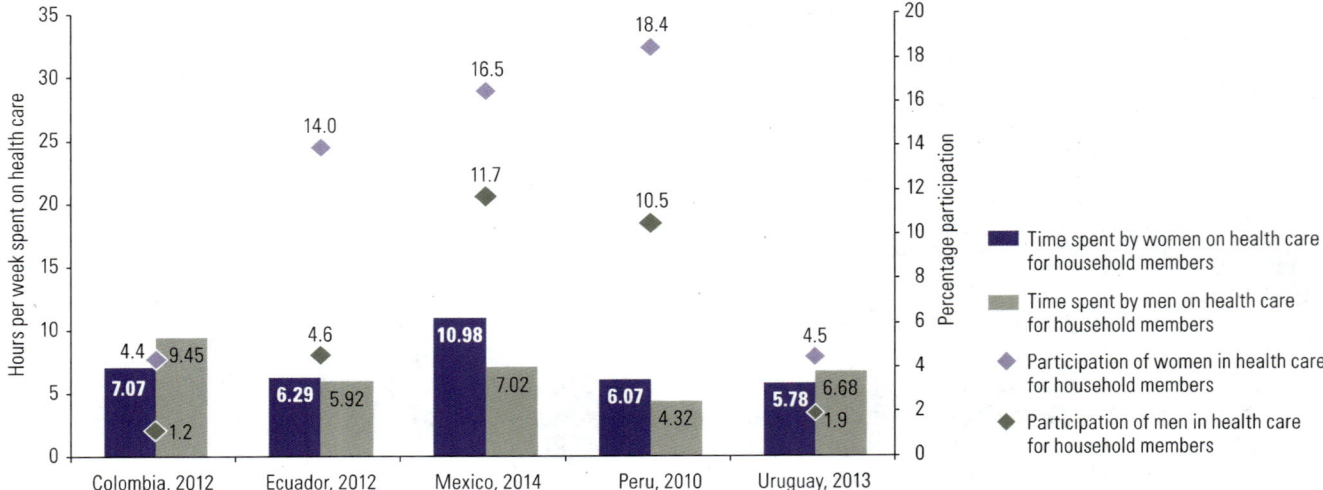

**Source**: Economic Commission for Latin America and the Caribbean (ECLAC), on the basis of special tabulations from time-use surveys conducted in the respective countries.
**Note**:    In light of the heterogeneous nature of data sources, comparisons between countries are still not possible; hence, the aim of this figure is to show the trends within each country. Participation in health care is calculated as the percentage of people who said that they had participated in this activity out of the total population aged 15 and older, by gender.

# 6.    Policies for care

According to ECLAC, care is understood as the activity of caring for others in the household throughout the life cycle, which requires an enormous amount of time and energy. It consists of indirect care —production of goods and services— but also direct personal care. Whether for reasons of age (either end of the life cycle) or health, a disability or emotional and affective needs, all individuals require care, including people who are healthy (ECLAC, 2015a).

The public policies that facilitate the appropriate provision of care should recognize care work as an essential development activity that must be guaranteed by society (Gómez, 2008), as well as meet the challenge of providing the care required by dependent individuals and of protecting and promoting gender equality. Efforts must be made to redistribute care responsibilities and benefits to transform the current model, which is sustained by women's unpaid work. These efforts should shed light on the contribution of domestic care, particularly by women, to the economy, and the effects of this workload on their autonomy.

Time-use data shed light on households' lack of autonomy to meet care needs and the debt the region owes to women who sustain the care economy. There is a need for specific studies on the quality of domestic care provided and on families' support structures.

According to the CAUTAL and recommendations by academics and experts in gender studies and work, it is important to create indicators that specify the separation of hours dedicated to domestic activities on one hand and the time spent on care on the other, in order to ensure that public policies are more effective. Figure IV.13 shows that women spend more hours per week on unpaid work than men, while men spend more time on activities relating to care work than on tasks relating to domestic work, which are more routine and less recognized.

**Figure IV.13**
Latin America (8 countries): time spent on unpaid domestic[a] and care[b] work by population aged 15 and older[c] in households where care is required, by gender
*(Hours per week)*

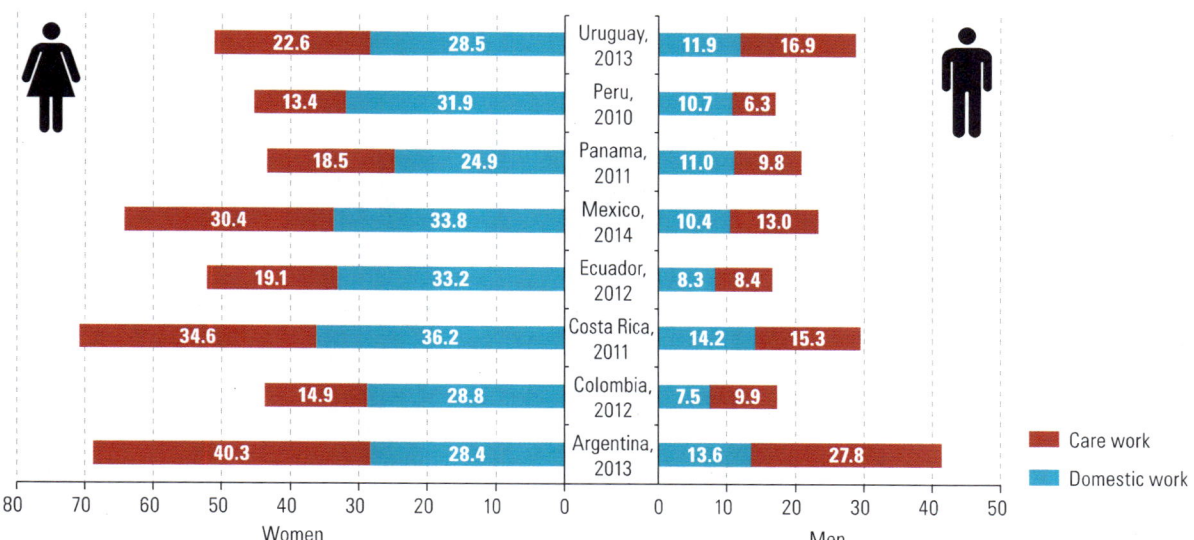

**Source**: Economic Commission for Latin America and the Caribbean (ECLAC), on the basis of special tabulations from time-use surveys conducted in the respective countries.
**Note**:   In light of the heterogeneous nature of data sources, comparisons between countries are still not possible; hence, the aim of this figure is to show the trends within each country. Data correspond to national totals, except in the case of Costa Rica (Greater Metropolitan Area). Only households that declare participation in some time of care activity are taken into consideration.
[a] Domestic work refers to the activities relating to the production of goods and services for household consumption classified within major division 3 of the CAUTAL.
[b] Care refers to all activities that directly support household members classified within major division 4 of the CAUTAL.
[c] Data correspond to the population aged 15 and older, except in Argentina (18 years and older).

Public policies must promote the sharing of responsibilities between men and women, more flexible working hours in paid jobs (for better coordination of responsibilities and benefits associated with paid and unpaid work) and better quality public services that would lighten households' workloads. The redistribution of unpaid work is one of the pillars for achieving gender equality in Latin America and the Caribbean by 2030 (Bidegain Ponte, 2017).

## (a) Care for young children

The provision of care for young children in Latin America continues to pose major challenges. The ability to place young children in day care depends in large part on households' purchasing power or on programmes catering for poor or vulnerable households or women. In many cases, these services are not regulated or under strict State supervision, which means that the conditions and quality of care in the different centres are mixed. Some time-use surveys in the region identify the time spent on this type of care and compare attendance at day-care centres. As shown in figure IV.14, women in households where children are in day care spend less time on care than women in households where children are not. There is no significant difference when comparing men in the two groups, as the activities that fathers carry out with their children (playing, going for walks, transporting them from place to place) are not affected by the hours that children spend at home. Women, however, are responsible for compulsory activities that need to be carried out on a daily basis and at set times (feeding, cleaning, health care) (Batthyány, 2009).

**Figure IV.14**
Mexico and Uruguay: time spent on care and participation rate, by gender and presence of children in the household
*(Hours per week and percentages)*

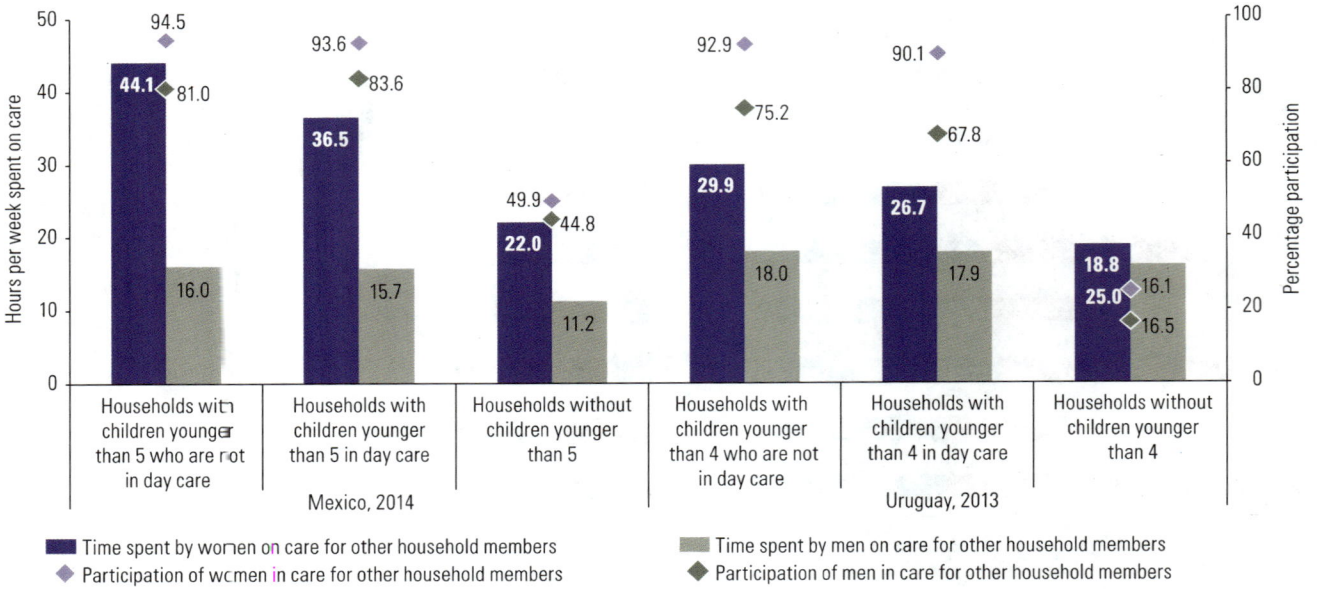

**Source**: Economic Commission for Latin America and the Caribbean (ECLAC), on the basis of special tabulations from time-use surveys conducted in the respective countries.
**Note**:   In light of the heterogeneous nature of data sources, comparisons between countries are still not possible; hence, the aim of this figure is to show the trends within each country. Participation in care is calculated as the percentage of people who said that they participated in these activities out of the total population aged 15 and older, by gender.

The time-use survey in Uruguay shows that most children younger than four in day care are supervised five days a week for four hours per day on average. Although this provides them with the right amount of stimulation, the number of hours is not convenient for mothers working outside the home, who have to make additional child care arrangements. The information on the time that the adults of a household spend on care is a crucial input for the design of educational strategies that would avoid placing a burden on women.

## (b) Care for persons with disabilities

The ageing population and the subsequent increase in the prevalence of chronic degenerative and debilitating diseases lead to greater demand for care. Although the region has made progress in legislation relating to health-care access for persons with disabilities (ECLAC, 2016g), national statistical systems still do not reflect the pervasiveness of these illnesses. Despite the notable progress in including disabilities in measurement tools in order to understand the potential demand for care, determining the supply of specialized care continues to pose a challenge, especially the care provided by households which is not included in statistical records. There are other factors that complicate measurement, such as the fact that the care available is not only dependent on demographic factors, but includes political and social components that affect the division of responsibilities in the household (Durán, 2008b).

Figure IV.15 shows that despite the different methodologies used by countries, it is clear that care provided by women for dependent persons with disabilities and the average time they spend caring for this population segment exceed that of men in all countries which identify this type of activity. In households with disabled persons, other members spend a significant amount of time meeting their care needs, which are demanding.

**Figure IV.15**
Latin America (5 countries): time spent on care of dependent household members or those with disabilities or chronic illnesses and participation rate of population aged 15 and older, by gender
*(Hours per week and percentages)*

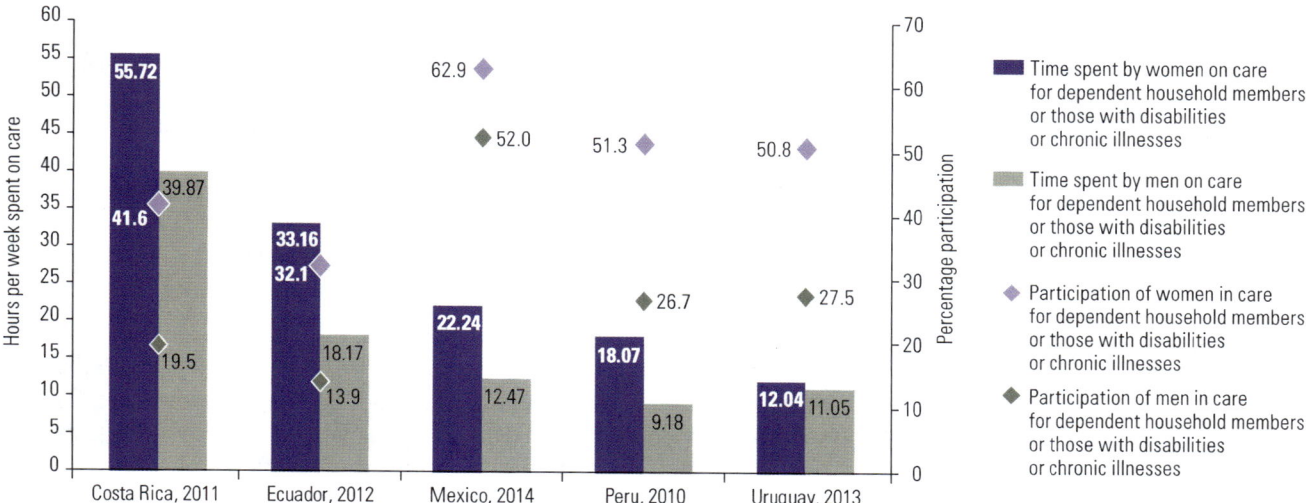

**Source**: Economic Commission for Latin America and the Caribbean (ECLAC), on the basis of special tabulations from time-use surveys conducted in the respective countries.
**Note**:    In light of the heterogeneous nature of data sources, comparisons between countries are still not possible; hence, the aim of this figure is to show the trends within each country. Participation in care for dependent household members or those with disabilities is calculated as the percentage of people who said that they had participated in these activities out of the total population aged 15 and older, by gender.

The time-use survey in Ecuador examines the reasons for which persons with disabilities fail to benefit from the care programmes catering to them. The most common causes are the lack of economic resources to cover the associated costs and the lack of awareness that they exist. The survey also identifies people who receive Joaquín Gallegos Lara grants to care for household members with disabilities: 84% of recipients are women. In addition to revealing the gender gap in the provision of care, the survey shows that women who receive these grants end up spending 66.7 hours per week on average caring for dependent family members with disabilities, compared with 30.5 hours per week on average for those who do not receive them. Time-use data should be taken into consideration in the design and implementation of public policies that favour the integration of dependent persons, and that also help to correct the gender-related injustices in the provision of care by combining economic transfers and good-quality social services (Marco, 2012).

# D. Conclusions

With a view to guaranteeing sustainable development in Latin America and the Caribbean, it is necessary to consolidate inclusive, solidarity-based and fair societies (ECLAC, 2016a). As outlined by ECLAC, the current development model has become unsustainable and progressive structural change is needed that would allow to transform a culture of privilege into a culture of equality, not just in terms of distribution and opportunities, but also from the point of view of rights, capacities and means (ECLAC, 2016e). In order to achieve this goal, the State must play a more active and decisive role in universalist policies. There is a crucial need for statistical instruments that can identify the critical areas for consideration in the implementation of transformative public policies and that can account for progress and setbacks in the implementation of policies based on empirical data, to help the region's States to play a central role in progressive structural change (Bárcena, 2017).

The Regional Gender Agenda recognizes that overcoming the sexual division of labour is one of the four fundamental pillars of achieving gender equality and moving towards development patterns based on human rights, women's autonomy and sustainability (ECLAC, 2017). As seen throughout this chapter, the assignment of roles based on unequal power relationships and the unfair social organization of care have strong implications for gender inequality between men and women, between women of different socioeconomic groups and between territories (Bidegain Ponte, 2017).

The Montevideo Strategy adopted by the region's governments at the thirteenth Regional Conference on Women in Latin America and the Caribbean held in Montevideo in October 2016 highlights that information systems are needed to achieve sustainable development, and establishes a series of measures focused on producing statistics and indicators with a gender perspective. In particular, it underscores time-use surveys as a key instrument for generating data that would serve as inputs for public policies aiming to significantly improve the measures adopted to guarantee women's right and autonomy (ECLAC, 2017).

Time-use data in the region has allowed a comprehensive and systematic approach to the multiple dimensions of inequality, providing empirical data on the unequal distribution of paid and unpaid work (Aguirre and Ferrari, 2014). These data also serve as inputs to calculate the economic value of unpaid work and show that through domestic and care work, women finance and sustain national economies and often subsidize limited social policies in this area (Bidegain Ponte, 2017).

The region must take advantage of the progress made in the past few years in the production of statistics with a gender perspective. However, there is still much work to be done. On one hand, data-collection instruments must be fine-tuned to provide information that can be disaggregated to reflect situations that affect men and women differently throughout their life cycles and in different socioeconomic situations and territories. Hence, surveys such as those focusing on time use should be included in national statistical offices' planning, with the appropriate periodicity and funding.

On the other hand, all of these advances in measurement will not bring about real change if data is not used to guide the implementation of public policies for equality and if they are not accompanied by studies on subjective well-being associated with the current distribution of time. In addition to strengthening measurement tools, there is a need for reinforced analytical and statistical capacity among decision-makers to "transform data into information, information into knowledge and knowledge into political decisions", in line with the Montevideo Strategy (ECLAC, 2017).

# Bibliography

Aguirre, R. and F. Ferrari (2014), "Las encuestas sobre uso del tiempo y trabajo no remunerado en América Latina y el Caribe: caminos recorridos y desafíos hacia el futuro", *Asuntos de Género series*, No. 122 (LC/L.3678/Rev.1), Santiago, Economic Commission for Latin America and the Caribbean (ECLAC), February.

Ayala Hernández, J. M. and D. Cardona Arango (2015), "Uso del tiempo libre de la población mayor de 50 años en la socialización", *Investigas. Siete estudios realizados a partir de la Encuesta Nacional de Uso del Tiempo, Colombia, 2012-2013*, National Administrative Department of Statistics (DANE).

Bárcena, A. (2017), "Intervención de Alicia Bárcena, Secretaria Ejecutiva de la CEPAL en la inauguración del XVI Comité Ejecutivo de la Conferencia Estadística de las Américas" [online] http://www.cepal.org/es/discursos/inauguracion-xvi-comite-ejecutivo-la-conferencia-estadistica-americas.

Batthyány, K. (ed.) (2015), *Los tiempos del bienestar social. Género, trabajo no remunerado y cuidados en Uruguay*, Montevideo, National Women's Institute (INMUJERES)/Ministry of Social Development (MIDES)/Universidad de la República del Uruguay/United Nations Population Fund (UNFPA)/United Nations Entity for Gender Equality and the Empowerment of Women (UN-Women)/Economic Commission for Latin America and the Caribbean (ECLAC), June.

___(2009), "Cuidado de personas dependientes y género", *Las bases invisibles del bienestar social. El trabajo no remunerado en Uruguay*, R. Aguirre (ed.), Montevideo, United Nations Development Fund for Women (UNIFEM).

Bidegain Ponte, N. (2017), "La Agenda 2030 y la Agenda Regional de Género. Sinergias para la igualdad en América Latina y el Caribe", *Asuntos de Género series*, No. 143 (LC/TS.2017/7), Santiago, Economic Commission for Latin America and the Caribbean (ECLAC), March.

Budlender, D. (2008), "Time-use in South Africa", Explorations: Time-use surveys in the South, V. Esquivel and others, *Feminist Economics*, vol. 14, No. 3, July.

Calderón, C. (coord.) (2013), "Redistributing care: the policy challenge", *Cuadernos de la CEPAL*, No. 101 (LC/G.2568-P), Santiago, Economic Commission for Latin America and the Caribbean (ECLAC), September.

Canavire-Bacarreza, G. and M. Ospina (2015), "Intrahousehold time allocation: An impact evaluation of conditional cash transfer programs", *Documentos de Trabajo, Economía y Finanzas*, No. 15-17, Bogota, Centre for Economic and Financial Research, Universidad EAFIT.

Carrasco, C. and E. Tello (2013), "Apuntes para una vida sostenible", *Tejiendo alianzas para una vida sostenible. Consumo crítico, feminismo y soberanía alimentaria*, X. Montagut, C. Murias and L. Vega (coords.), Barcelona, Xarxa de Consum Solidari/Marcha Mundial de las Mujeres [online] http://www.xarxaconsum.net/mm/file/LIBROS/Tejiendo_alianzas_para_una_vida_sostenible.pdf.

Cecchini, S. and A. Madariaga (2011), *Conditional cash transfer programmes: the recent experience in Latin America and the Caribbean*, Cuadernos de la CEPAL, No. 95 (LC/G.2497-P), Santiago, Economic Commission for Latin America and the Caribbean (ECLAC).

Cecchini, S. and M.N. Rico (2015), "The rights-based approach in social protection", *Towards universal social protection: Latin American pathways and policy tools*, ECLAC Books (LC/G.2644-P), S. Cecchini and others (eds.), Santiago, Economic Commission for Latin America and the Caribbean (ECLAC).

Céspedes, C. and C. Robles (2016), "Niñas y adolescentes en América Latina y el Caribe: deudas de igualdad", *Asuntos de Género series*, No. 133 (LC/L.4173), Santiago, Economic Commission for Latin America and the Caribbean (ECLAC), June.

Díaz, M. Á. and F. J. Jiménez (2002), "Transportes y movilidad: ¿necesidades diferenciales según género?", paper presented at Second International Seminar on Gender and Urban Development: Infrastructure for daily living, Madrid, 27-28 May.

Durán, M. (2012a), "La investigación sobre el uso del tiempo", paper presented at Tenth International Meeting of Experts on Time Use and Unpaid Work, entitled: "Public policies, time use and the care economy: the importance of national statistics" , Mexico City, 11-12 October.

___(2012b), *El trabajo no remunerado en la economía global*, Bilbao, Fundación BBVA.

___(2008a), *La ciudad compartida. Conocimiento, afecto y uso*, Santiago, Ediciones SUR.

____(2008b), "Integración del trabajo no remunerado en el análisis de los sectores de salud y bienestar social", *La economía invisible y las desigualdades de género. La importancia de medir y valorar el trabajo no remunerado*, Washington, D.C., Pan American Health Organization (PAHO).

____(2005), "Mujeres y hombres en el siglo XXI", *Cuenta y razón*, vol. 138.

____(1986), *La jornada interminable*, Barcelona, Icaria Editorial.

ECLAC (Economic Commission for Latin America and the Caribbean) (2017), *Montevideo Strategy for Implementation of the Regional Gender Agenda within the Sustainable Development Framework by 2030* (LC/CRM.13/5), Santiago, Mach.

____(2016a), *Equality and women's autonomy in the sustainable development agenda* (LC/G.2686/Rev.1), Santiago, December.

____(2016b), *The social inequality matrix in Latin America* (LC/G.2690(MDS.1/2)), Santiago, October.

____(2016c), "Territorio e igualdad: planificación del desarrollo con perspectiva de género", *Manuales de la CEPAL*, No. 4 (LC/L.4237), Santiago, October.

____(2016d), *40 years of the regional gender agenda* (LC/G.2682), Santiago.

____(2016e), *Horizons 2030: Equality at the Centre of Sustainable Development* (LC/G.2660/Rev.1), Santiago, July.

____(2016f), *Inclusive Social Development: The next generation of policies for overcoming poverty and reducing inequality in Latin America and the Caribbean* (LC.L/4056/Rev.1), Santiago, January.

____(2016g), *Social Panorama of Latin America, 2015* (LC/G.2691-P), Santiago.

____(2015a), *Regional review and appraisal of implementation of the Beijing Declaration and Platform for Action and the outcome of the twenty-third special session of the General Assembly (2000) in Latin American and Caribbean countries* (LC/L.3951), Santiago.

____(2015b), "Resolution 9(VIII)", eighth meeting of the Statistical Conference of the Americas of the Economic Commission for Latin America and the Caribbean, Quito, 17-19 November.

____(2013), *Gender Equality Observatory of Latin America and the Caribbean. Annual Report 2012: A look at grants, support and burden for women* (LC/G.2561/Rev.1), Santiago.

____(2010), "Brasilia Consensus", *Report of the eleventh session of the Regional Conference on Women in Latin America and the Caribbean* (LC/L.3309), Santiago.

____(2007), *Women's contribution to equality in Latin America and the Caribbean* (LC/L.2738(CRM.10/3)), Santiago.

____(2004), *Social Panorama of Latin America, 2004* (LC/G.2259-P), Santiago.

ECLAC/INEGI/INMUJERES/UN-Women (Economic Commission for Latin America and the Caribbean/ National Institute of Statistics and Geography/National Women's Institute of Mexico/United Nations Entity for Gender Equality and the Empowerment of Women) (2016), *Classification of Time-Use Activities for Latin America and the Caribbean (CAUTAL)* (LC/W.679), Santiago [online] http://repositorio.cepal.org/bitstream/handle/11362/40170/S1600307_en.pdf?sequence=1&isAllowed=y.

Espejo, A. (2013), "The impact of conditional cash transfer programs on the time allocation of beneficiaries: The case of "Oportunidades" program in Mexico", master's thesis in social policies and development, London School of Economics

Espejo, A., F. Filgueira and M.N. Rico (2010), "Familias latinoamericanas: organización del trabajo no remunerado y de cuidado", *Project Documents* (LC/W.354), Santiago, Economic Commission for Latin America and the Caribbean (ECLAC).

Esquivel, V. and others (2008), "Explorations: time-use surveys in the south", *Feminist Economics*, vol. 14, No. 3.

FAO (Food and Agriculture Organization of the United Nations) (2016), *Gender Strategy for the FNS-CELAC PLAN*, Santiago, Regional Office for Latin America and the Caribbean.

Ferrán, L. (2008), "Marco conceptual y lineamientos metodológicos de la cuenta satélite de los hogares para medir el trabajo no remunerado en salud", *La economía invisible y las desigualdades de género. La importancia de medir y valorar el trabajo no remunerado*, Washington, D.C., Pan American Health Organization (PAHO).

Figueroa, C. and N. Waintrub (2015), "Movilidad femenina en Santiago de Chile: reproducción de inequidades en la metrópolis, el barrio y el espacio público", *Urbe. Revista Brasileira Gestão Urbana*, vol. 7, No. 1

Foucault, M. (1993), *Microfísica del poder*, Madrid, Ediciones de la Piqueta.

Gammage, S. and M. Orozco (2008), "El trabajo productivo no remunerado dentro del hogar: Guatemala y México", *Estudios y Perspectivas series-ECLAC Subregional Headquarters in Mexico*, No. 103 (LC/L.2983-P; LC/MEX/L.889), Mexico City, Economic Commission for Latin America and the Caribbean (ECLAC).

Gómez, E. (2008), "La valoración del trabajo no remunerado: una estrategia clave para la política de igualdad de género", *La economía invisible y las desigualdades de género. La importancia de medir y valorar el trabajo no remunerado*, Washington, D.C., Pan American Health Organization (PAHO).

Gómez Luna, M. E. (2010), *Directrices y referentes conceptuales para armonizar las encuestas sobre uso del tiempo en América Latina y el Caribe. Documento para discusión*, Mexico City, National Institute of Statistics and Geography of Mexico (INEGI).

Hernández, D. (2012), *Políticas de tiempo, movilidad y transporte público: rasgos básicos, equidad social y de género*, United Nations Development Programme (PNUD)/Municipality of Montevideo/Territorial policies division of the Office of Planning and the Budget, noviembre.

Huertas, N. and J. Mola (2015), "Estudio del uso del tiempo en las poblaciones vulnerables como elemento para la inclusión social", *Investigas. Siete estudios realizados a partir de la Encuesta Nacional de Uso del Tiempo, Colombia, 2012-2013*, National Administrative Department of Statistics (DANE).

ILO (International Labour Organization) (2013), "Resolution concerning statistics of work, employment and labour underutilization", nineteenth International Conference of Labour Statisticians (ICLS), Geneva, October [online] http://www.ilo.org/wcmsp5/groups/public/---dgreports/---stat/documents/normativeinstrument/wcms_230304.pdf.

____(1919), "Hours of Work (Industry) Convention (No. 1), 1919", Washington, D.C., November [online] http://www.ilo.org/dyn/normlex/en/f?p=NORMLEXPUB:12100:0::NO::P12100_ILO_CODE:C001.

ILO/UNDP (International Labour Organization/United Nations Development Programme) (2009), *Work and Family: Towards new forms of reconciliation with social co-responsibility*, Santiago.

INEC (National Statistics and Census Institute of Ecuador) (2014), "Cuentas satélite de trabajo no remunerado de los hogares 2011-2013, Ecuador" [online] http://www.ecuadorencifras.gob.ec/cuenta-satelite-de-trabajo-no-remunerado/.

INEGI (National Institute of Statistics and Geography of Mexico) (2014), *Sistema de Cuentas Nacionales de México. Cuenta satélite del trabajo no remunerado de los hogares de México 2013. Preliminar. Año base 2008*, Mexico City.

____(2016), "Trabajo no remunerado de los hogares", Mexico City [online] http://www.inegi.org.mx/est/contenidos/proyectos/cn/tnrh/default.aspx.

INEI (National Institute of Statistics and Informatics of Peru) (2016), *Cuenta satélite del trabajo doméstico no remunerado*, Lima, Ministry for Women's Affairs and Vulnerable Populations of Peru (MIMP)/United Nations Population Fund (UNFPA)/United Nations Entity for Gender Equality and the Empowerment of Women (UN-Women) [online] https://www.inei.gob.pe/media/MenuRecursivo/publicaciones_digitales/Est/Lib1358/libro.pdf.

IPEA (Institute of Applied Economic Research) (2011), *Retrato das desigualdades de gênero e raça*, Brasilia [online] http://www.ipea.gov.br/retrato/pdf/revista.pdf.

ISDEMU/DIGESTYC/BCR (Salvadoran Institute for the Development of Women/Department of Statistics and Censuses/Central Reserve Bank of El Salvador) (2016), "Principales resultados del ejercicio de valorización del trabajo noremunerado de los hogares", paper presented at the Seminar "Reconocimiento y provisión de cuidados: desafíos para una política integrada en El Salvador", San Salvador.

Marco, F. (2016), "La nueva ola de reformas previsionales y la igualdad de género en América Latina", *Asuntos de Género series*, No. 139 (LC/L.4225), Santiago, Economic Commission for Latin America and the Caribbean (ECLAC).

____(2012), "La utilización de las encuestas de uso del tiempo en las políticas públicas", *Mujer y Desarrollo series*, No. 119 (LC/L.3557), Santiago, Economic Commission for Latin America and the Caribbean (ECLAC), October.

Marco, F. and M.N. Rico (2013), "Cuidado y políticas públicas: debates y estado de situación a nivel regional", *Las fronteras del cuidado. Agenda, derechos e infraestructura*, L. Pautassi and C. Zibecchi (coords.), Buenos Aires, Editorial Biblios.

Milosavljevic, V. and O. Tacla (2007), "Incorporando un módulo de uso del tiempo a las encuestas de hogares: restricciones y potencialidades", *Mujer y Desarrollo series*, No. 83 (LC/L.2709-P), Santiago, Economic Commission for Latin America and the Caribbean (ECLAC).

Rico, M. N. (2013), "Derechos de la infancia. Enfoque, indicadores y perspectivas", *Seminario Internacional: Indicadores de Derechos Económicos, Sociales y Culturales (DESC); y seguimiento de las políticas sociales para la superación de la pobreza y el logro de la igualdad*, Santiago, National Human Rights Institute.

Rico, M. N. and D. Trucco (2014), "Adolescentes. Derecho a la educación y al bienestar futuro", *Políticas Sociales series*, No. 190 (LC/L.3791), Santiago, Economic Commission for Latin America and the Caribbean (ECLAC).

Rossel, C. (2016), "Desafíos demográficos para la organización social del cuidado y las políticas públicas", *Asuntos de Género series*, No. 135 (LC/L.4186), Santiago, Economic Commission for Latin America and the Caribbean (ECLAC).

Rossel, C. and D. Hernández (2013), "Cuidado infantil, tiempo y espacio: el transporte y la frontera del acceso", *Las fronteras del cuidado. Agenda, derechos e infraestructura*, L. Pautassi and C. Zibecchi (coords.), Buenos Aires, Editorial Biblos.

Sandoval Carvajal, I. and L. M. González Vega (2015), "Estimación del valor económico del trabajo no remunerado en Costa Rica. Resultados e ilustración metodológica", *Estudios demográficos y urbanos*, vol. 30, No. 3.

Segovia, O. (2016), "¿Quién cuida en la ciudad? Oportunidades y propuestas en la comuna de Santiago (Chile)", *Asuntos de Género series*, No. 132 (LC/L.4127), Santiago, Economic Commission for Latin America and the Caribbean (ECLAC), January.

Stiglitz, J., A. Sen and J. Fitoussi (2009), "Report by the Commission on the Measurement of Economic Performance and Social Progress" [online] http://library.bsl.org.au/jspui/bitstream/1/1267/1/Measurement_of_economic_performance_and_social_progress.pdf.

Trucco, D. and H. Ullmann (eds.) (2015), *Youth: realities and challenges for achieving development with equality*, ECLAC Books, No. 137 (LC/G.2647-P), Santiago, Economic Commission for Latin America and the Caribbean (ECLAC).

Ullmann, H. and V. Milosavljevic (2016), "The right to free time in childhood and adolescence", *Challenges*, No. 19, Santiago, Economic Commission for Latin America and the Caribbean (ECLAC)/(United Nations Children's Fund (UNICEF), August.

United Nations (2017a), "International Classification of Activities for Time Use Statistics 2016 (ICATUS 2016). Prepared by the Secretariat (13 February 2017)" [online] https://unstats.un.org/unsd/statcom/48th-session/documents/BG-3h-ICATUS-2016-13-February-2017-E.pdf.

____(2017b), "Statistical Commission. Report on the forty-eighth session (7-10 March 2017)", *Official Records 2017, Supplement*, No. 4 (E/2017/24-E/CN.3/2017/35), New York.

____(2017c), "Report of the Inter-agency and Expert Group on Sustainable Development Goal Indicators" (E/CN.3/2017/2), New York.

____(2017d), "New Urban Agenda" (A/RES/71/256), New York, December.

____(2015), "Transforming our world: the 2030 Agenda for Sustainable Development" (A/RES/70/1), New York, October.

____(2009), *System of National Accounts, 2008* [online] https://unstats.un.org/unsd/nationalaccount/docs/SNA2008.pdf.

____(2006), *Guide to Producing Statistics on Time Use: Measuring Paid and Unpaid Work* (ST/ESA/STAT/SER.F/93), New York.

____(1995), "Beijing Declaration and Platform for Action", Fourth World Conference on Women [online] [online] http://www.unwomen.org/~/media/headquarters/attachments/sections/csw/pfa_e_final_web.pdf.

____(1989), Convention on the Rights of the Child [online] http://www.ohchr.org/Documents/ProfessionalInterest/crc.pdf.

Vaca-Trigo, I. (2015), "Pobreza y tiempo destinado al trabajo no remunerado: un círculo vicioso", paper presented at sixteenth International Meeting on Gender Statistics: statistical challenges for implementing the sustainable development agenda, Aguascalientes, México, 9-11 September.

WHO (World Health Organization) (2015), World Report on Ageing and Health, Geneva.

# Peoples of African descent: broadening the scope of inequality to make progress in guaranteeing their rights

## A.  Afrodescendent populations in Latin America and the framework for action

The existence of a large Afrodescendent population in the region has its origins in the slave trade that was plied across the Atlantic for nearly 400 years. In Latin American countries, persons of African descent remain disadvantaged by structural inequality and multiple forms of discrimination, a phenomenon that began in the colonial period and became entrenched during the creation of the nation States. Their resistance and struggle have made people of African descent political and social activists, as they strive to position their historical demands on international, regional and national agendas. One expression of this is the establishment by the United Nations of the International Decade for People of African Descent, spanning 2015-2024, with its three pillars of recognition, justice and development.

The existence of a large Afrodescendent population in Latin America and the Caribbean has an undeniably tragic and violent origin. Although slavery has been present in all eras of human history, the transatlantic trafficking of Africans carried out by the European conquerors is unparalleled, and is distinguished by its scale and eminently racial nature (UNESCO, 2010). An estimated 12.5 million people were enslaved and trafficked from Africa to America between 1500 and 1867; with almost half of this traffic occurring in the eighteenth century, representing the largest transoceanic deportation enterprise in history (UNESCO, 2010).

During the period of conquest and then in the colonial era, the economic interests of the colonial metropolises led to a growing demand for forced labour, for a variety of activities, such as the extraction of natural resources, crop and livestock farming, manual labour and handicraft and domestic work. Initially, the slaves were indigenous populations, but the European invasion rapidly changed the originating peoples and their culture. The most exposed indigenous population groups, such as those living on the coasts, suffered more devastating changes than living in more remote areas (such as Amazonia). The conjunction of wars and diseases imported from the "old continent" caused a demographic collapse, with the result that the "supply" of slave labour started to dwindle.

The geographical destinations of the deportations from Africa to America were often associated with the economic dynamic: the greater the degree of capitalistic accumulation, the greater were the needs for forced labour. This had a profound effect on the distribution of the Afrodescendent population, which persists until today in the region's countries. Nonetheless, the size of the Afrodescendent population in each country also reflects the relation between the political processes and demographic dynamics of these groups. For example, during the wars of independence of today's Southern Cone countries, the enslaved Africans were offered the chance to join the struggle in exchange for their freedom; but very few manage to survive, because they were placed in the front lines of the battles. There were also large-scale internal and intraregional displacements of Afrodescendent population groups throughout the slavery process, related to their struggles, survival and resistance (UNESCO, 2010; UNDP, 2010). As a result, mortality and birth rates, together with the impact of territorial mobility, gradually moulded the current population map of African descent in Latin America and the Caribbean.

Beyond the diversity of national and subregional situations and specifics, the hierarchical, class-based and racist structure of the colonial era meant that Afrodescendants occupied a subordinate place on that map, displaying, together with the indigenous peoples, higher levels of material poverty and social and political exclusion. In the region, the population descending from the African Diaspora remained in a disadvantageous position over the centuries, even after their liberation from slavery. Thus, poverty, destitution, disease, access barriers to education, lack of social security, lack of opportunities for decent work and exclusion from political decision-making combined to form the pillars of structural racism. This panorama is aggravated by the invisibility and denial of the Afrodescendent presence in some of the region's countries, especially since the creation of nation States, which also disregards the contribution made by these groups to the social and cultural development of the Latin American nations.

As a result of these circumstances, the Afrodescendent population has had to overcome structural problems that restrict its citizenship status and the exercise of its civil, political, economic, social and cultural rights. In response, Afrodescendent civil society has deployed mobilization strategies in the public domain, articulating political demands vis-à-vis the States and human rights institutions, and gaining a position on national, regional and international agendas. In the international arena, the most significant developments include the International Convention on the Elimination of All Forms of Racial Discrimination, adopted by the United Nations General Assembly in resolution 2106 (XX) of 21 December 1965, which entered into force on 4 January 1969. This Convention is particularly important, because it is based on the belief "that any doctrine of superiority based on racial differentiation is scientifically false, morally condemnable, socially unjust and dangerous and that there is no justification for racial discrimination, in theory or in practice, anywhere." The Convention also, for the first time, articulates the need for affirmative action, by stating that "Special measures taken for the sole purpose of securing adequate advancement of certain racial or ethnic groups or individuals requiring such protection as may be necessary in order to ensure such groups or individuals equal enjoyment or exercise of human rights and fundamental freedoms shall not be deemed racial discrimination, provided, however, that such measures do not, as a consequence, lead to the maintenance of separate rights for different racial groups and that they shall not be continued after the objectives for which they were taken have been achieved" (article 1.4).

Subsequently, important resolutions were adopted in the United Nations system in relation to the three decades of struggle against racism and racial discrimination, which began in 1973, 1983 and 1993, respectively, as well as two World Conferences to Combat Racism and Racial Discrimination, and the World Conference against Racism, Racial Discrimination and Xenophobia, and Related Forms of Intolerance convened in 1997 and held in 2001 in Durban (South Africa). One of the key outcomes of the latter was the Durban Declaration and Programme of Action, which provides a framework for the design and implementation of policies aimed at historical reparation in the development and well-being of Afrodescendent people. Although most of the international instruments agree on the need to expand the scope of recognition of the various forms of racism and discrimination, it was not until the Durban Conference that specific victims were recognized, along with the causes and consequences of racism. In fact, the Durban Conference made a historical reading of racism, stressing slavery and colonialism as causes of the current status of Afrodescendent men and women (Antón and others, 2009).

The Durban Conference ratified earlier thinking more precisely, asserting the need to recognize Afrodescendent peoples' rights to culture and their own identity; to participate freely and in equal conditions in political, social, economic and cultural life; to development in the context of their own aspirations and customs; to keep, maintain and foster their own forms of organization, their mode of life, culture, traditions and religious expressions;

to maintain and use their own languages; to the protection of their traditional knowledge and their cultural and artistic heritage; to the use, enjoyment and conservation of the natural renewable resources of their habitat and to active participation in the design, implementation and development of educational systems and programmes, including those of a specific and characteristic nature; and where applicable to their ancestrally inhabited land (Durban Declaration, paragraph 34). At the same time, the Durban Programme of Action urges States to adopt positive measures to enable Afrodescendent people to participate in all political, economic, social and cultural spheres of society and in the advancement and economic development of their countries.

More recently, the United Nations declared 2011 the International Year for People of African Descent, and then decreed the period 2015-2024 the International Decade for People of African Descent. This initiative, which continues the processes outlined above, marks out a path for States and civil society to fulfil their commitments and obligations in resolving the structural problems that persist the world over, including in Latin America, and perpetuate exclusion and discrimination against Afrodescendent populations. The proposal of an International Decade is a moral, ethical and political imperative to meet the demands that have been made of the international community since the 1970s. The justification of the Decade lies in the situation being endured by Afrodescendent people in the countries that have still not resolved problems of inequality, exclusion and discrimination against them.

The objectives of the International Decade for People of African Descent focus on recognition, justice and development, and usher in a new stage of crucial historical and political importance in the struggles against slavery, inequality, colonization and racism that have long mobilized Afrodescendent people throughout the world. Accordingly, they pose major challenges to recognize and resolve the problems inherent to the matrix of social inequality in the region, of which one of the structural pillars is the ethno-racial issue, as discussed by the countries at the Regional Conference on Social Development in Latin America and the Caribbean (ECLAC, 2015 and 2016b).

In the regional domain, the periodic reviews of progress made on the different international agreements signed by States in the 1990s gradually included the situation of Afrodescendent people, in particular in reference to the Fourth World Conference on Women (Beijing, 1995) and the International Conference on Population and Development (Cairo, 1994). The corollary of this process was the Montevideo Consensus on Population and Development, the outcome of the first session of the Regional Conference on Population and Development of Latin America and the Caribbean, held in Montevideo in 2013. This consensus included a specific chapter on Afrodescendent populations, which establishes seven priority measures in addition to considering this issue throughout the document (ECLAC, 2013).[1] Accordingly, the Montevideo Consensus is a complementary instrument that will strengthen implementation of the Programme of Activities of the International Decade for People of African Descent and the 2030 Agenda for Sustainable Development. Although the 2030 Agenda does not explicitly mention the Afrodescendent population, its premise of "no one left behind" implies consideration and inclusion of the most disadvantaged and vulnerable population groups. Thus, the attainment of the Sustainable Development Goals for all, without ethnic or racial distinction, forms part of the principles of the 2030 Agenda and is made explicit in Sustainable Development Goal target 10.2 : "by 2030 empower and promote the social, economic and political inclusion of all irrespective of age, sex, disability, race, ethnicity, origin, religion or economic or other

> The objectives of the International Decade for People of African Descent focus on recognition, justice and development, and usher in a new stage of crucial historical and political importance in the struggles against slavery, inequality, colonization and racism that have long mobilized Afrodescendent people throughout the world.

---

[1]   The first priority measure in the chapter on Afrodescendants states "Respect and implement the provisions of the Durban Declaration and Programme of Action adopted at the World Conference against Racism, Racial Discrimination, Xenophobia and Related Intolerance, by adapting the legal frameworks and formulating the policies necessary for their implementation, with the full participation of Afrodescendent persons." (Priority measure 92 of the Montevideo Consensus on Population and Development).

status"; and in target 17.18: "by 2020, enhance capacity building support to developing countries, including for least developed countries (LDCs) and small island developing states (SIDS), to increase significantly the availability of high-quality, timely and reliable data disaggregated by income, gender, age, race, ethnicity, migratory status, disability, geographic location and other characteristics relevant in national contexts".

In addition, Afrodescendent women have been considered in the construction of the Regional Gender Agenda of Governments and women's organisations, heavily influenced by Afrodescendent women's organisations, particularly since 2000 (see box V.1).

**Box V.1**
Afrodescendent women and the concept of intersectionality in the Regional Gender Agenda

In its 40 years of existence, the Regional Conference on Women of Latin America and the Caribbean have contributed to the formation of the Regional Gender Agenda (ECLAC, 2016h), which identify 36 agreements that reflect the concern of Governments and civil society on the situation of inequality in which Afrodescendent women live. In addition, the Agenda includes the inter-sectionality of the racial, ethnic and gender conditions, which has generated a body of agreements and recommendations for generating public policies.

The agreements entered into by the Governments at the sessions of the Regional Conference (particularly those held in Lima in 2000; Mexico City in 2004; Quito in 2007; Brasilia in 2010; Santo Domingo in 2013 and Montevideo in 2016) entail commitments to develop active policies in relation to the labour market and productive employment, the reduction of unemployment, women's access to positions of power, promoting and ensuring the mainstreaming of gender, race and ethnicity in all policies, particularly in economic and cultural policies; adopting preventive, punitive measures of protection and care that helped to eradicate all forms of violence against women in public and private spheres, and to implement affirmative-action policies paying special attention to Afrodescendent women.

The concern felt by social movements as to the need to effectively address the diversity that exists within the heterogeneous group of "women" gained ground in the institutional framework, leading to the explicit adoption of the inter-sectionality concept at the twelfth session of the Regional Conference on Women of Latin America and the Caribbean, held in Santo Domingo in 2013. That consensus formally asserts that full guarantee of women's human rights is based on recognizing the cultural diversity of the countries and posing challenges to address the inequalities that Afrodescendent women endure (ECLAC, 2013b).

The Regional Gender Agenda, along with the global agenda on this subject, supports an inter-sectional view of the different categories, positions or situations (identity, social, age-group, racial, economic, among others), which represents the diversity of women in the countries' female population and reflects the interaction and overlapping of different pillars of discrimination, which aggravate their subordination. This vision opens the debate with Ministers for Women's Affairs and other authorities in this area on the complexity of the effects, as noted by Brah (2012), of the intersection of the different pillars of economic, political, cultural and subjective difference that are part and parcel of Afrodescendent women's experience in the different contexts in which they live.

Discussing gender and autonomy gaps among women in one of the most unequal regions of the world (Bárcena and Byanyima, 2016) requires an approach that considers the intersections that exist between the social class and ethnic-racial condition, to enable a more precise diagnostic study of reality and propose effective measures aimed at equality.

**Source:** Economic Commission for Latin America and the Caribbean (ECLAC), *40 Years of the Regional Gender Agenda* (LC/G.2682), Santiago, 2016; A. Bárcena and W. Byanyima, "Latin America is the world's most unequal region. Here's how to fix it", Santiago, ECLAC, 2016 [online] http://www.cepal.org/en/articles/2016-latin-america-worlds-most-unequal-region-heres-how-fix-it [online], http://www.cepal.org/es/articulos/2016-america-latina-caribe-es-la-region-mas-desigual-mundo-como-solucionarlo; Brah, Avtar (2012), "Pensando en y a través de la interseccionalidad", in: La interseccionalidad en debate, Martha Zapata Galindo; Sabina García Peter; Jennifer Chan de Avila (orgs.), Berlin, Lateinamerika-Institut der Freien Universität Berlin, 2013.

In national domains, the constitutional reforms implemented by the region's countries in the 1990s recognized the multicultural nature of nations and, in some cases, they defined plurinationality, as in Ecuador or in the Plurinational State of Bolivia. In addition, Brazil's 1988 Constitution defined racism as a crime for which there is no possibility of bail or statute of limitations. This launched a period of promulgation of laws and decrees, creation of institutions responsible for matters pertaining to the Afrodescendent population, and establishment of policies and programmes on this subject, which represents a major step forward.

Those achievements are largely the outcome of the collective action of Afrodescendent groups and movements, which from within their national domains have gradually forged important regional alliances. For example, in 1977, the first Congress of Black Culture in the Americas was held in Cali (Colombia), attended by over 200 delegates from Africa and America. The experience was repeated in Panama in 1980 and in São Paulo (Brazil) in 1982. These meetings consolidated the experience of Afrodescendent continental articulation in the region, which was strengthened in the 1990s with the commemoration of the 500th anniversary of the arrival of the European conquistadors in America, which formed a general communication framework for several subregional networks of Afrodescendent organizations (Antón, 2011). In 1992, the First Meeting of Afro-Latin American and Afro-Caribbean Women was held in the Dominican Republic, resulting in the creation of the Network of Afro-Latin American, Afro-Caribbean and Diaspora Women, which has played a fundamental role in constructing the regional agenda on this subject, particularly in the context of the Regional Conference on Women in Latin America and the Caribbean and the Regional Conference on Population and Development in Latin America and the Caribbean. In 1994, the First Continental Seminar on Racism and Xenophobia, held in Montevideo, led to the creation of the Continental Network of Afro-American Organizations. Then, throughout the 1990s and early in the 2000 decade, various continental networks of Afrodescendent organizations were set up, responding to various ecclesiastical, cultural and academic interests.

Early in the twenty-first century, three continental networks played a fundamental role in consolidating a regional Afrodescendent social movement: the Strategic Latin American and Caribbean Afrodescendent Alliance (previously known as the Continental Network of Afro-American Organizations); the Afro-América XXI Network, coordinated from the United States, and the Global Afro-Latin and Caribbean Initiative (GALCI) (Anton, 2011). In 2003, a process of political coordination of Afrodescendent parliamentary representatives in the region began, resulting in the formation of the Network of Afrodescendent Parliamentarians of the Americas and the Caribbean, which has held five regional meetings thus far.

The joint action of Afrodescendent organizations in the region helped to consolidate a transnational agenda, in which the strategic pillar is combating racism, with actions targeted on social inclusion, reducing poverty and guaranteeing human rights by advocating for policies on racial and cultural equality and demanding participation both in political spaces for citizen participation and in public development agendas. Thus, the first World Summit of Afrodescendants was held as part of the International Year for People of African Descent (18-21 August 2011 in La Ceiba, Honduras), along with the Forum of Afro-Descendants in Our America: Fourth International Forum of Afro-Descendants and Revolutionary Transformations in America and the Caribbean (19 and 22 June 2011). These events represent a milestone in the recent history of Afrodescendent mobilization, reaffirming the commitment of the social movement to continue promoting local, national and international actions that bring about substantial improvements for Afrodescendent population groups.

Nonetheless, those advances have been insufficient to overcome the historical and structural gaps in fulfilment of the rights of Afrodescendent individuals and communities, as will be shown in later sections of this chapter. Hence the persistent and urgent need to redouble efforts in line with international standards and existing commitments.

Within this framework, one of the worrying aspects in terms of effectively guaranteeing the rights of Afrodescendants and thus enabling them to exercise full citizenship, is that, even now, too little is known about their sociodemographic and socioeconomic status in the region, owing, firstly, to a lack of regular and reliable statistics on those population groups in most countries. Statistical invisibility is another manifestation of the denial and lack of recognition of these population groups. There are large gaps in the information that is crucial for promoting the human rights, well-being and social development of Afrodescendent people; and a shortage of information to serve as an input in the design, monitoring and evaluation of public policies, and for the exercise of oversight by Afrodescendent organizations on government actions that affect their populations. Hence, the disaggregation of data by ethno-racial status forms part of the 2030 Agenda for Sustainable Development (through the aforementioned target 17.18), and is emphatically established in the Montevideo Consensus on Population and Development, where, as priority measure 98, the countries of the region agreed to "Generate knowledge and reliable and timely information with a gender perspective and disaggregated by sex, age and socioeconomic status, among other variables, on Afro-descendent populations through participatory processes, paying attention to the international requirements and recommendations relating to the issue".

Since the beginning of this century, the Economic Commission for Latin America and the Caribbean (ECLAC) has systematically carried out a series of activities to produce information and knowledge about indigenous and Afrodescendent peoples, including technical assistance for the countries of the region in these matters. The inclusion of this chapter in the current edition of *Social Panorama of Latin America* expresses the commitment of ECLAC to continue working in this area and help the region's countries design actions to move towards equality in diversity, centred on a rights approach. Making the situation of Afrodescendent persons in the region visible is the first step towards achieving their recognition, justice and historical reparation.

## B. Who are Afrodescendent people, what are their numbers and where are they?

In order to guarantee the rights of people of African descent and to fulfil the relevant international and regional commitments, it is necessary to break the statistical silence. To do this, the starting point is to include ethno-racial self-identification in all data sources. While the countries of the region have made progress in this regard, challenges in coverage and quality of information persist. Nevertheless, it is estimated that there were at least 130 million Afrodescendants in Latin America in 2015, representing 21% of the population. They are present in all countries, albeit with varying population sizes —in both absolute and relative terms— residing mainly in urban areas.

Raising the statistical profile of Afrodescendent populations in Latin America forms part of these groups' demands for recognition, on the basis that information is a fundamental tool for promoting their rights and for designing and monitoring policies and actions to close gaps in their implementation. Calls for greater information have become louder precisely since the World Conference against Racism, Racial Discrimination, Xenophobia and Related Intolerance, whose outcome, the Durban Programme of Action, expressly urged the region's countries to redouble efforts to obtain official data on Afrodescendent people, for the purpose of evaluating and formulating policies targeting them.

For that reason, the need to include and raise the profile of Afrodescendent populations in statistical systems is a recurrent topic in the periodic reviews of the various international and regional conferences and in the reports of human rights committees. It is also a regular feature in technical meetings relating to strengthening data sources, particularly population and housing censuses, at the national, regional and international levels. More recently, this subject has been reiterated and emphasized in the Montevideo Consensus on Population and Development, particularly in the aforementioned priority measure 98.

The concept of Afrodescendent, which refers to populations that are descended from the African Diaspora around the world, was coined in 2000 during the preparatory process of the World Conference against Racism, Racial Discrimination, Xenophobia and Related Intolerance held in Durban, an event for which Afrodescendent organizations mobilized vigorously. In Latin America and the Caribbean, this concept has acquired a specific connotation, because it refers to the different "Black" or Afro-American" cultures formed by the descendants of Africans who survived slave trafficking across the Atlantic between the sixteenth and nineteenth centuries. Nonetheless, at the present time, owing to migratory phenomena that generate very high rates of mobility worldwide, the concept of Afrodescendent has expanded to encompass new African populations that are not necessarily the descendants of victims of slavery. This process is fuelling important debates in the region, which have their impact on the operational definitions of statistical instruments.

Based on the above, one of the challenges facing the region over the last few years has been to translate this concept into a set of variables and categories that enable the statistical instruments to distinguish between Afrodescendants and non-Afrodescendants. The issue is made even more complex if one considers that the concepts of ethnicity or race (the latter claimed by Afrodescendent scholars and movements as a social category)[2] are not fixed notions; but their interpretation goes beyond a technical and methodological issue applicable to censuses and other data sources. In fact, these are concepts linked to the process of identity construction and politicization in the different countries, and the construction of repertoires of action among the Afrodescendent movements (Antón, 2007).

Population and housing censuses and household surveys show that, in the case of Afrodescendent people, priority has been given to the racial perspective through self-perceived phenotype categories. Nonetheless, this approach is changing in some of the region's countries, reflecting the fact that some racial groups adopt an ethnic identity and claim it collectively.[3] Moreover, in several cases, they claim ancestral lands associated with their places of arrival during the slave trafficking period,[4] which makes it possible to infer at least four dimensions of Afrodescendancy: (i) identity recognition; (ii) common origin, which refers to descendancy from common ancestors; (iii) territoriality; and (iv) the linguistic-cultural dimension (ECLAC, 2009). Although it is desirable to have indicators for each of these dimensions, an international consensus has been reached over the years that the self-identification criterion, associated with the dimension of identity recognition, has preeminence over other criteria, since it is consistent with a rights approach (ECLAC, 2009; Del Popolo and Schkolnik, 2011).

The concept of Afrodescendent, which refers to populations that are descended from the African Diaspora around the world, was coined in 2000 during the preparatory process of the World Conference against Racism, Racial Discrimination, Xenophobia and Related Intolerance held in Durban, an event for which Afrodescendent organizations mobilized vigorously.

---

[2]   See the discussion on this in ECLAC (2016b).

[3]   See, for example, the cases of Colombia, Ecuador, Honduras and Nicaragua discussed in Mosquera and others (2002 Hooker (2012), and Agudelo (2012).

[4]   Ibid 1.

A requirement for identifying the status of Afrodescendancy is to include ethno-racial self-identification questions in all data sources, which thus far has not happened in most of the region's countries.

Accordingly, a requirement for identifying the status of Afrodescendancy is to include ethno-racial self-identification questions in all data sources, which thus far has not happened in most of the region's countries.[5] Although greater progress has been made in the case of population and housing censuses, until the 1980s, only Brazil and Cuba had that type of question; Colombia joined in the censuses of the 1990s, and another five countries were added in the 2000 decade. Nonetheless, the greatest quantum leap has occurred in this decade, in which a total of 17 countries have or will have included questions on Afrodescendent self-identification.[6] Conversely, few countries include questions of this nature in household surveys, as discussed in ECLAC (2016b),[7] and, with the exception of Brazil, shortcomings persist in terms of the representativeness of the samples for these groups, particularly when it comes to breaking the information down by gender, age group or territorial location. In the case of continuous administrative records, the lag is even greater: only Brazil has systematic information, particularly on health and education, although Colombia and Ecuador have also made some progress and significant achievements in these areas.

Given the foregoing, this chapter uses population and housing censuses as its main source of quantitative information, while also tapping the potential of household surveys wherever possible. Although in countries with information available the criterion adopted has been self-identification, semantic problems persist in relation to the formulation of the questions and the categories considered (Del Popolo and Schkolnik, 2013). The terms used refer to different dimensions of the definition of ethnic group (for example, asking whether the person "descends from" or considers himself/herself"); or else they imply different degrees of rigour in terms of a commitment of subjective belonging (for example, when one alludes to "people" or "culture"). A third element concerns the different local meanings of the categories used and their social and territorial variations (in some countries, use of the term "black" generally has a stigmatizing intention among the "white" population, whereas among some Afrodescendent groups, it acquires a social-claim connotation. Ultimately, the conceptual and methodological decisions adopted by each country, which make up the classification system used, have a direct impact on the quantification and sociodemographic characteristics of Afrodescendent persons, and in the comparisons that can be made between countries.[8]

---

[5]   Progress made on the inclusion of Afrodescendent self-identification in the censuses is accompanied by the sociopolitical processes through which these population groups have acquired greater protagonism and recognition. Thus, statistical institutes have shown greater openness to such inclusion, with support from academia and international organizations; but, fundamentally, it has been the Afrodescendent organizations that have exerted pressure and insisted on being made statistically visible. ECLAC has been systematically supporting these processes since the start of the century.

[6]   Of the 12 Latin American countries that have conducted censuses in the 2010 decade, 11 included questions on Afrodescendent self-identification: Argentina, the Bolivarian Republic of Venezuela, Brazil, Costa Rica, Cuba, Ecuador, Honduras, Panama, Paraguay, the Plurinational State of Bolivia and Uruguay; Paraguay's census results are not yet available. Although Colombia, El Salvador, Guatemala and Nicaragua have not yet held censuses in this decade, they intend to include Afrodescendent self-identification, along with Peru, which will do so for the first time in a population census. Mexico included questions on this in the 2015 inter-census survey. Accordingly, in the region, Afrodescendent inclusion remains a challenge in the censuses of Chile, Dominican Republic and Haiti.

[7]   The countries that incorporated Afrodescendent self-identification in 2014 are Brazil, Ecuador, Peru and Uruguay. The Plurinational State of Bolivia included the alternative reply "Afro-Bolivian" in 2013, in the question relating to ethnic self-identification; but the number of people who self-identified with that category was very small, so it was impossible to work with the information. Colombia in 2014 included the question "according to your culture, people or physical features ... are you, or do you self-identify as ..." in the large-scale integrated household survey, but the data in question were not available when this document was being prepared.

[8]   In addition, there are methodological and operational problems that can affect the estimations, such as lack of training of the interviewers on this topic, communication difficulty in multilingual areas, the lack of participation by Afrodescendent people in the census processes (ECLAC, 2009). In addition, self-identification is influenced by the countries' sociopolitical context; simplifying matters, in an environment of structural discrimination, Afrodescendent persons may not declare themselves as such, particularly in the urban environment and large cities; in contexts of ethnic revitalization, on the other hand, persons who do not belong to a specific ethno-racial group may self affiliate to it by affinity, or through access to specific policies, among other reasons, although the latter situation seems to be less common than the former (ECLAC, 2009).

Even with the shortcomings in the available data, the population census remains the best source for quantifying and characterizing these groups from a Latin American perspective and for highlighting the equity gaps that still persist in the region. Ascertaining the numbers of Afrodescendent people in Latin America remains one of the most basic and urgent challenges: obtaining an accurate figure is hindered by problems of ethno-racial identification in the data sources, which range from a failure to include relevant questions to the quality of the data collected. For that reason, the information shown in table V.1 is considered a minimum estimate, according to which the Afrodescendent population of the region amounted to 111 million in 2010, representing 21.1% of the total population. On the basis of the figures shown in table V.1, the Afrodescendent population is forecast at 130 million by 2015.

> The Afrodescendent population is forecast at 130 million by 2015.

Table V.1

Latin America (16 countries): Afrodescendent population according to the latest census and estimates as of 2010
(Number of people)

| Country | Total population | Total Afrodescendent population | Afrodescendent percentage |
|---|---|---|---|
| **Results by census year** | | | |
| Argentina, 2010 | 40 117 096 | 149 570 | 0.4 |
| Bolivia (Plurinational State of), 2012 | 10 059 856 | 23 330 | 0.2 |
| Brazil, 2010 | 190 755 799 | 97 171 614 | 50.9 |
| Costa Rica, 2011 | 4 301 712 | 334 437 | 7.8 |
| Cuba, 2012 | 11 167 325 | 4 006 926 | 35.9 |
| Ecuador, 2010 | 14 483 499 | 1 041 559 | 7.2 |
| Honduras, 2013 | 8 303 772 | 115 802 | 1.4 |
| Mexico, 2010[a] | 112 336 538 | 1 348 038 | 1.2 |
| Panama, 2010 | 3 405 813 | 300 551 | 8.8 |
| Uruguay, 2011[b] | 3 251 654 | 149 689 | 4.6 |
| Venezuela (Bolivarian Republic of), 2011 | 27 227 930 | 936 770 | 3.4 |
| **Estimates as of 2010[c]** | | | |
| Colombia | 46 448 000 | 4 877 040 | 10.5 |
| El Salvador | 6 218 000 | 8 083 | 0.1 |
| Guatemala[d] | 14 334 000 | 5 734 | 0.04 |
| Nicaragua | 5 813 000 | 29 065 | 0.5 |
| Peru | 29 272 000 | 585 440 | 2.0 |
| **Total** | **527 495 994** | **111 083 648** | **21.1** |

**Source**: Economic Commission for Latin America and the Caribbean (ECLAC), on the basis of special tabulations of population censuses; Cuba: National Office of Statistics and Information (ONEI), *El color de la piel según el Censo de Población y Viviendas 2012*, Havana; Mexico: "Encuesta Intercensal 2015" [online] http://www.beta.inegi.org.mx/proyectos/enchogares/especiales/intercensal/.

[a] To maintain a degree of comparability through time, the percentage Afrodescendent population reported by the 2015 inter-census survey was used, and the total was estimated by applying this percentage to the 2010 census population.

[b] The question on recognition of ascendance with multiple response categories produces a total Afrodescendent population of 255,074, representing 7.8% of the national population. The figure shown in the table refers to people who responded that there main ascendance is "Afro or black".

[c] These countries have not yet held the censuses of the 2010 decade. Accordingly, the Afrodescendent population percentages obtained from the last available census were used, except in the case of Peru where the percentage was obtained from the National Household Survey-Living Conditions and Poverty 2012. These percentages were applied to the total population estimated in 2010, based on population estimates prepared by the Latin American and Caribbean Demography Centre (CELADE), Population Division of ECLAC (ECLAC 2013c). The census dates are: Colombia, 2005; El Salvador, 2007; Guatemala, 2002; and Nicaragua, 2005.

[d] In the case of the Afrodescendent peoples, the figures only represent the Garifuna population, the only group descending from the African Diaspora that was identified in the 2002 census.

Brazil is the country with the largest number of Afrodescendent residents, both in absolute and in relative terms, since they represent over half the country's inhabitants. Cuba follows with Afrodescendants making up 36% of the population, with just over 4 million people; while Colombia, Costa Rica, Ecuador and Panama have relatively smaller Afrodescendent populations of between 7% and 10%. Apart from relative sizes, in Colombia the Afrodescendent population is estimated at around 5 million people, while in the Bolivarian Republic of Venezuela, Ecuador and Mexico, there are about 1 million, and in Peru over half a million.[9]

A feature of Afrodescendent populations is that they are eminently urban; in fact the proportion of these groups living in cities is higher than that of the non-Afrodescendent population in over half the countries (see figure V.1). The degree of urbanization of Afrodescendent people in the 12 countries with data available varies between 59.2% in Honduras and 96.6% in Uruguay; apart from Honduras, all exceed 70%.

**Figure V.1**
Latin America (12 countries): degree of urbanization of the Afrodescendent and non-Afrodescendent populations
*(Percentages)*

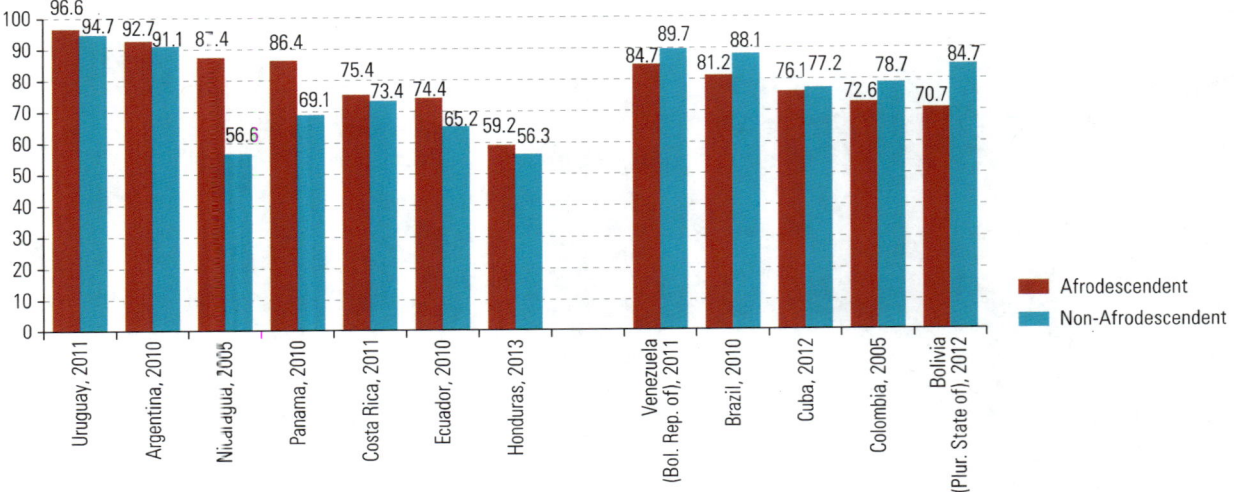

Source: Economic Commission for Latin America and the Caribbean (ECLAC), on the basis of special tabulations of population censuses and Cuba: National Office of Statistics and Information (ONEI), special tabulations of Population and Housing Census, 2012.
Note:    The non-Afrodescendent population does not include the indigenous population or cases of unknown ethno-racial status.

The censuses also show that the Afrodescendent population is distributed practically throughout the national territory of each country. Nonetheless, an analysis of distributions by major administrative divisions reveals significant differences vis-à-vis the rest of the population. In general, three Afrodescendent population settlement poles can be identified: settlement areas related to the slave-period territories of arrival in the colonial era; areas associated with international migration from neighbouring countries (for example, in Central America the migration of Afro-Caribbean people in the late nineteenth and early twentieth centuries); and other settlement areas that reflect a territorial redistribution resulting from internal migratory processes, generally towards the main cities of each country or metropolis. Some of these situations are described in box V.2. Moreover, at smaller territorial scales it is possible to identify areas

---

[9]    The figures on the Afrodescendent population remain controversial, for the reasons mentioned herein. To illustrate, in the case of Peru, Valdivia (2013) estimates an Afrodescendent population of 669,143 in 2006, on the basis of the National Continuous Survey. In the case of Colombia, Urrea-Giraldo (2006) estimates an Afrodescendent population of almost 8 million in 2001, representing 18.6% of the total population, on the basis of household surveys.

of Afrodescendent concentration, which, in the past, provided a safe haven for slaves who obtained their freedom by fleeing to remote areas. These settlements, known as *palenques* or *quilombos*, were areas of political and cultural resistance by the so-called "negros cimarrones", a name used since the sixteenth century to refer to slaves who took refuge in these areas and fought against the slavery regime.

Box V.2
Territorial distribution of the Afrodescendent population: slavery's footprints

The following examples briefly illustrate how the distribution of the Afrodescendent population across the administrative areas of each country reflects the historical settlement patterns of these groups. This does not mean, however, that they have been immune from spatial redistribution processes that are similar to those affecting the population at large. The censuses of this decade show that in Brazil the states that account for just over half the Afrodescendent population are São Paulo, home to 15% of the country's total Afrodescendants, followed by Bahia (11%), Minas Gerais (11%), Rio de Janeiro (8.5%) and Pará (6%). This pattern differs from that of the non-Afrodescendent population, for which the main states of concentration are São Paulo (29%), Minas Gerais (9.7%), Rio Grande do Sul (9.6%), Rio de Janeiro (8.3%) and Paraná (8%).

The Brazilian economy was developed and sustained with slave labour throughout the colonial and imperial periods, in a wide variety of economic activities —mainly in sugar and coffee plantations and gold mines, but also in domestic service. The main centre from which the Portuguese distributed slaves to the interior of Brazil was Salvador, the capital of the state of Bahia, where 76.5% of the population claimed to be Afrodescendent in the 2010 census. Another of the main slave disembarkation ports was Río de Janeiro. Large contingents of African slaves were also taken to Minas Gerais in the eighteenth century to work in gold mines and in the mining of precious stones. Although the transportation of African slaves to Amazonia was on a smaller scale, the first slaves arrived in the state of Pará with the English in the seventeenth century; and the process intensified under the Portuguese in the second half of the eighteenth century, partly because the Catholic Church opposed the enslavement of indigenous populations. In this state, 77% of the population self-identified as Afrodescendent in the 2010 census.[a]

According to the 2010 census, in Panama, 61.3% of the Afrodescendent population is settled in Panama province; the second largest provincial concentration being Colón, with 23%, followed by Bocas del Toro, which holds 4% of the country's total Afrodescendent people. In contrast, the main provincial concentrations of non-Afrodescendent and non-indigenous populations are Panamá (54%), Chiriquí (14%) and Coclé (8%). African slaves arrived in Panama from the outset of the colonial period, with the city of Portobelo, in Colón, serving as one of the main arrival and distribution ports. From there slaves were transported overland to Panama City, where some of them remained; while others were sold on and embarked again for cities in South America, mainly on the Pacific coast. These African slaves sustained the construction of Panama City, pearl fishing, mining and quarrying and domestic service, among other activities. A second "generation" of Afrodescendants arrived from the mid-nineteenth to the early twentieth century, from Trinidad, Jamaica, Barbados, Grenada, Saint Vincent and Saint Kitts, to build the railway and the Panama Canal. This group settled mainly in the provinces of Colón, Panamá and Darién. In addition, with the expansion of banana growing and the installation of a United States multinational enterprise in Bocas del Toro in the late nineteenth century, a large Afro-Antillean contingent arrived in that province.

**Source**: Economic Commission for Latin America and the Caribbean (ECLAC), on the basis of R. Castro, "La negritud en Salvador de Bahía, una ciudad africana fuera de África", *África América Latina, Cuadernos 21*, 1996; United Nations Development Programme (UNDP), *Derechos de la población Afrodescendiente de América Latina: desafíos para su implementación*, Panamá, 2010 and United Nations Educational, Scientific and Cultural Organization (UNESCO) (2010), "Slave Routes: A Global Visión. Documentary", 2010 [excerpt online] http://www.unesco.org/new/es/social-and-human-sciences/themes/slave-route/right-box/related-information/slave-routes-a-global-vision/.

[a] In Brazil, self-identification of Afrodescendants in censuses and household surveys is done through two of the five skin colour categories established in those instruments: "black" (*preto* or *negro*) and "brown" (*pardo* or mixed race). The combination of those two categories comprises the "black" or Afrodescendent category.

In terms of demographic profiles, which are fundamental in guiding the design of public policies and the associated investment, the census figures show that Afrodescendent populations are in the middle or at an advanced stage of the demographic transition, owing mainly to declining fertility rates, but to also reductions in mortality and longer lifespans. This is reflected in the sex and age structures of those population groups, which is summarized in table V.2 —based on major age groups. This information can be interpreted in at least two ways, depending on whether the comparison is based on the situation of Afrodescendent populations across countries or on ethno-racial differences within them.

Table V.2
Latin America (13 countries): distribution of the Afrodescendent and non-Afrodescendent populations by major age groups, around 2010
(Percentages)

| Country and census year | Ethno-racial status | Major age groups | | | Total |
|---|---|---|---|---|---|
| | | 0-14 years | 5-59 years | 60 years and over | |
| Countries in which the Afrodescendent population has relatively more children and fewer older adults than the non-Afrodescendent population | | | | | |
| Brazil, 2010 | Afrodescendent | 25.6 | 65.4 | 9.0 | 100 |
| | Non-Afrodescendent | 22.4 | 64.9 | 12.7 | 100 |
| Colombia, 2005 | Afrodescendent | 33.3 | 59.1 | 7.6 | 100 |
| | Non-Afrodescendent | 30.0 | 60.9 | 9.1 | 100 |
| Costa Rica, 2011 | Afrodescendent | 25.0 | 67.3 | 7.7 | 100 |
| | Non-Afrodescendent | 24.5 | 64.8 | 10.7 | 100 |
| Cuba, 2012 | Afrodescendent | 17.4 | 67.4 | 15.2 | 100 |
| | Non-Afrodescendent | 17.1 | 62.9 | 20.0 | 100 |
| Ecuador, 2010 | Afrodescendent | 32.6 | 60.6 | 6.7 | 100 |
| | Non-Afrodescendent | 30.7 | 59.8 | 9.5 | 100 |
| Uruguay, 2011 | Afrodescendent | 23.4 | 64.4 | 12.3 | 100 |
| | Non-Afrodescendent | 21.9 | 59.2 | 18.9 | 100 |
| Countries in which the Afrodescendent population has relatively fewer children and fewer older adults than the non-Afrodescendent population | | | | | |
| Argentina, 2010 | Afrodescendent | 24.7 | 64.4 | 10.9 | 100 |
| | Non-Afrodescendent | 25.6 | 60.2 | 14.2 | 100 |
| Bolivia (Plurinational State of), 2012 | Afrodescendent | 27.8 | 65.6 | 6.6 | 100 |
| | Non-Afrodescendent | 34.5 | 58.4 | 7.1 | 100 |
| Countries in which the Afrodescendent population has relatively fewer children and more older adults than the non-Afrodescendent population | | | | | |
| Honduras, 2013 | Afrodescendent | 31.8 | 59.5 | 8.7 | 100 |
| | Non-Afrodescendent | 35.2 | 57.5 | 7.3 | 100 |
| Nicaragua, 2005 | Afrodescendent | 35.6 | 56.5 | 7.9 | 100 |
| | Non-Afrodescendent | 37.2 | 56.8 | 6.1 | 100 |
| Panama, 2010 | Afrodescendent | 21.0 | 67.0 | 12.1 | 100 |
| | Non-Afrodescendent | 27.6 | 61.1 | 11.2 | 100 |
| Venezuela (Bolivarian Republic of), 2011 | Afrodescendent | 18.3 | 69.0 | 12.7 | 100 |
| | Non-Afrodescendent | 27.1 | 63.9 | 9.0 | 100 |

Source: Economic Commission for Latin America and the Caribbean (ECLAC), on the basis of census data.
Note: The non-Afrodescendent population does not include people who self-identify as indigenous or whose ethno-racial status is unknown. In the case of Panama, the figures do not include persons of undeclared age.

From the first standpoint, the countries with the largest proportions of Afrodescendent children aged under 15 years are Colombia, Ecuador, Honduras and Nicaragua, where they represent roughly one third of the Afrodescendent population.[10] In contrast, the Bolivarian Republic of Venezuela, Cuba and Panama have the smallest proportions of children and adolescents, ranging from 17.4% to 21% of their total Afrodescendent populations. At the other extreme of the population pyramid, the proportions of older Afrodescendent people (60 years of age and over) are highest in Argentina, the Bolivarian Republic of Venezuela, Cuba, Panama and Uruguay, where they represent more than 10% of the total Afrodescendent population and as much as 15.2% in Cuba. In Ecuador and the Plurinational State of Bolivia, older Afrodescendants account for less than 7%. In short, although there is some convergence with respect to the factors that shape the age composition of the Afrodescendent population, this also reveals different situations between the countries of the region, displaying older structures to a greater or lesser degree. Moreover, the discontinuities revealed by a closer examination of the age composition also suggest a differential declaration of ethnic identification according to age and gender (box V.3 illustrates this). Accordingly, this is a field that requires a detailed analysis to elucidate how processes of acculturation or cross-breeding or ethno-racial revitalization interact and combine with the demographic dynamics and their inherent components (fertility, mortality and migration).

A second reading of table V.2, which complements the foregoing, shows that although the Afrodescendent population is in the middle, or at an advanced stage, of its demographic transition, in most countries Afrodescendent populations are relatively younger than the rest of the population. This can be clearly seen in Cuba and Uruguay, which are already at a post-transitional stage, but whose Afrodescendent populations are younger than the rest of the population. The opposite is true in the Bolivarian Republic of Venezuela, Honduras, Nicaragua and Panama; in other words, their Afrodescendent populations are older than the rest of the population. In the last three of these countries (Honduras, Nicaragua and Panama), this would at least be consistent with Afrodescendent fertility levels, which, according to indirect estimations based on censuses, are lower than those of the rest of the population. In contrast, in the Bolivarian Republic of Venezuela, the fertility of the Afrodescendent population is above that of non-Afrodescendants, but the population pyramid of the former shows greater ageing; this suggests that there might be a differential ethno-racial declaration according to sex and age, which results in a significant understatement of the number of Afrodescendent children, and also of women (see box V.3).[11]

The information as a whole also shows favourable demographic dependency ratios: the proportion of working-age people outweighs those who are potentially inactive. This demographic dividend is even more favourable among Afrodescendants (which means they have lower dependency indices). Nonetheless, taking advantage of the demographic dividend means, firstly, strengthening education policies; ensuring that Afrodescendent children, adolescents and young people not only complete primary and secondary schooling, but also have equal access to higher education levels, where deep inequalities persist with respect to the national averages, as will be discussed in section C. It is also crucial to address health inequalities throughout the life cycle, as discussed in that section, because otherwise the demographic pressures caused by ageing will mean that cumulative risks will cause these inequalities to widen in old age.

---

[10]  This comparison must be made with caution, because the timeframes of the figures for Colombia and Nicaragua are earlier than those of the other two countries.

[11]  For the Bolivarian Republic of Venezuela, through the 2011 census, a global fertility rate of 2.5 children was estimated for the Afrodescendent population and 2.2 among the non-Afrodescendent population, so in principle relatively more children would be expected among the former group than the latter, which is not in fact the case. The base of the Afrodescendent population pyramid —where the children are— is suspiciously narrow or small. In addition, there is a clear imbalance in the sex composition: whereas the non-Afrodescendent population has 103 women for every 100 men, the Afrodescendent population recorded just 68 women per 100 men.

Box V.3
Composition of the Afrodescendent population by ages and sex, as a fundamental input for gender equality, racial equality and life-cycle policies

The census data of the 2010 decade enhances understanding of the demographic dynamic of Afrodescendent populations in various countries of the region, as never before. This dynamic, which is driven by reproductive, mortality and migration patterns, is affected in some cases by identity processes of Afrodescendent people that are not necessarily experienced equally across the generations or between men and women. Hence, it is necessary to investigate these issues in depth in each country, to understand the dynamic in an unbiased way; and, secondly, to improve the quality of information on ethno-racial identification.

The charts below show the gender composition of the Afrodescendent and non-Afrodescendent populations of the Bolivarian Republic of Venezuela, Brazil, Costa Rica and Cuba, through femininity indices (the number of women for every 100 men) by five-year age groups. The "expected" behaviour of the femininity index of the population by age groups assumes that in the early years of life the index would be below 100, since in all populations there is a larger number of male than female births, with the difference gradually declining in the early years of life owing to higher male mortality. Then the index fluctuates around 100 —which means demographic equality between men and women— with an increase in the older age groups owing to women's longer life expectancy.

Latin America (four countries): femininity indices by five-year age groups
(Number of women per 100 men)

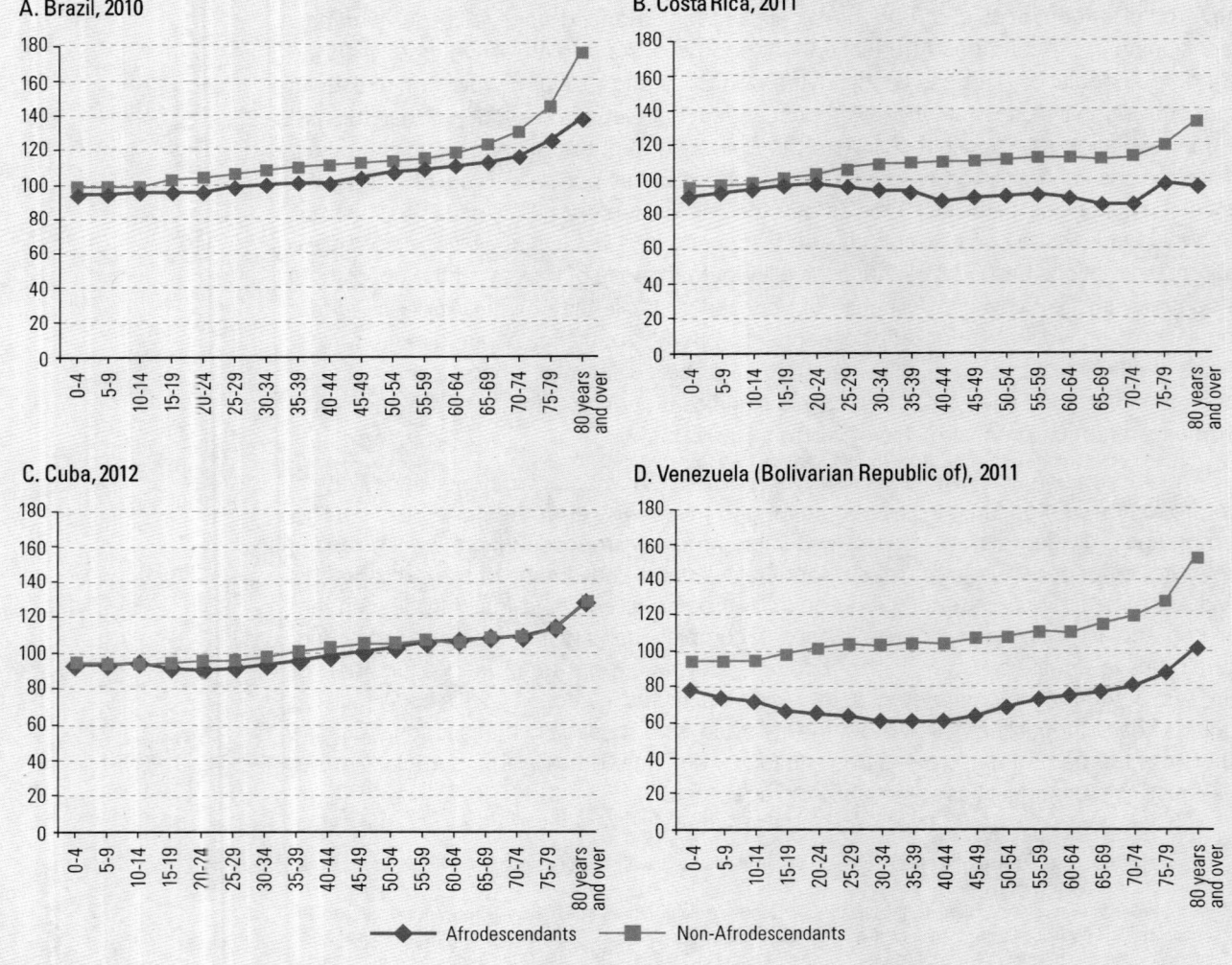

A. Brazil, 2010

B. Costa Rica, 2011

C. Cuba, 2012

D. Venezuela (Bolivarian Republic of), 2011

◆ Afrodescendants    ■ Non-Afrodescendants

Box V.3 (concluded)

The figures for the Afrodescendent population in Brazil seem to display the expected pattern; nonetheless, compared to Afrodescendants, the preeminence of women in the older age groups is significantly higher in the latter group; in other words, taking the population of 65 years of age and older, among Afrodescendants there are 120 women for every 100 men, whereas in the non-Afrodescendent population there are 139, which could indicate a shorter life expectancy for Afrodescendent women than for non-Afrodescendent women.

The case of Costa Rica illustrates an unexpected pattern in the Afrodescendent population: as from 30 years of age, the number of women is smaller than the number of men. These changes would suggest the impact of differential sociodemographic phenomena according to sex and age. In this case, and as a hypothesis, an index below 100 in productive age groups could be indicative of high rates of maternal mortality among Afrodescendent women, significant international emigration by those women or substantial international immigration by Afrodescendent men; but it is also impossible to rule out differential self-identification between Afrodescendent men and Afrodescendent women.

The situation described for Costa Rica is even clearer in the case of the Bolivarian Republic of Venezuela, where male numerical superiority appears as from five years of age, and balance between men and women is only attained in the 80 and over age bracket, a pattern that is certainly atypical.

Lastly, the behaviour of this index in Cuba not only follows the expected pattern for both the Afrodescendent and the non-Afrodescendent populations, but it also seems to show very low levels of inequality, particularly in mortality rates by gender in the older age groups, reflecting the sustained universal policies that are characteristic of that country, particularly in health care and education.

**Source**: Economic Commission for Latin America and the Caribbean (ECLAC), on the basis of special processing of census microdatabases.

## C. Intertwined inequalities: disparities in the exercise of economic and social rights

Ethno-racial inequalities constitute one of the structural axes of the matrix of social inequality in Latin America. This can be seen in the deep ethno-racial gulfs in areas such as health, education and work. In most countries, people of African descent have higher levels of maternal and infant mortality, lower access to secondary and higher education, higher levels of unemployment and lower labour incomes than non-Afrodescendants. These inequalities are intertwined with those of gender; and they put Afrodescendent women in the most disadvantaged situations.

As noted by ECLAC (2016b), ethno-racial inequalities, together with those of gender, territory and life cycle, are the structuring pillars of the social inequality matrix in Latin America. Although it is argued that these inequalities are intertwined and empower each other, the outcome is not necessarily linear and therefore requires more in-depth analysis. This section does that by drawing on census data to expand, for certain indicators, the range of countries analysed in the document *The matrix of social inequality in Latin America* (ECLAC, 2016b); in some cases, the data are broken down by gender so as to also examine interrelationships between ethno-racial and gender inequalities.

Except for a few Latin American countries, lack of systematic information has been one of the main obstacles to visualizing ethno-racial disparities. Nonetheless, a good number of countries have addressed the issue of African descent in its historical, political and sociocultural dimensions, through the work of academia and Afrodescendent organizations themselves. In fact, there is a large bibliography that reflects on the importance of the phenomenon of Afrodescendancy in the Americas, particularly studies that stress ethnicity and racial policies targeting persons of African descent.[12]

With some national and local exceptions, the region has made progress in the production of data with ethno-racial breakdowns, but these have been insufficiently exploited to generate information and knowledge. Accordingly, the following sections try to provide an overview, albeit partial, of this matrix of inequalities that affect the Afrodescendent population in the domains of income distribution, health, education and employment, by processing unpublished data from census microdata and household surveys available at ECLAC. It is acknowledged that the information still has shortcomings, and is insufficient to answer the various questions that arise on demographic and socioeconomic issues; nonetheless, identifying shortcomings and gaps in the production of information is also part of the results of this overview.

## 1. The Afrodescendent population is overrepresented in the lower income strata

As analysed in chapter I, income inequality as measured by the Gini coefficient fell significantly in Latin America between 2002 and 2015, amid notable progress in reducing poverty and extreme poverty (ECLAC, 2016a). This gain was the result of active policies implemented by the countries of the region in the production, social and labour market domains, in a favourable economic setting of advanced demographic transition (which facilitated an increase in labour market participation and reduced the dependency rate), and in which the goals of eradicating poverty, promoting social inclusion and reducing inequality gained unprecedented space on the public agenda and in development strategies.

The reduction in income inequality between individuals and households in that period was associated, in general, with a larger increase in income in the first quintile than in the fifth. This occurred across the main sources of household income (labour income from wage and independent work, retirement pensions and transfers). Owing to its weight in the composition of household income, labour income had the largest impact of all on the decline in inequality over the period, resulting from the improvements in the labour market, including higher employment and rises in minimum wages.

Nonetheless, high concentration in personal and household income remains a serious structural problem in Latin America. On average, according to 2015 figures, for every 100 monetary units received by each member of the lowest income quintile, each member of the highest income quintile receives 1,220. What is more, as noted in the previous chapters, women, children and adolescents are overrepresented in the lower income quintiles.

The same occurs in the Afrodescendent population. As shown in figure V.2, a higher proportion of the Afrodescendent population than the non-Afrodescendent population is in the first quintile (those with the lowest income) in all four countries with information available for 2014. By the same token, a much larger percentage of the non-Afrodescendent population than the Afrodescendent population figures in the fifth quintile (those with the highest income). This pattern is especially marked in Brazil and Uruguay, where the proportion of Afrodescendants in the first quintile is double the proportion of non-Afrodescendants (more than double, in the case of Brazil), while the fifth quintile has three times the proportion of non-Afrodescendants as Afrodescendants in Brazil, and almost four times in Uruguay.

---

[12]　Recent studies that compile work of various authors include: Lechini (2008); Anton, Avendaño and Tapia (2011); Mosquera and others (2010).

**Figure V.2**

Latin America (4 countries): distribution of the population by per capita household income quintile and ethno-racial status, 2014
(Percentages)

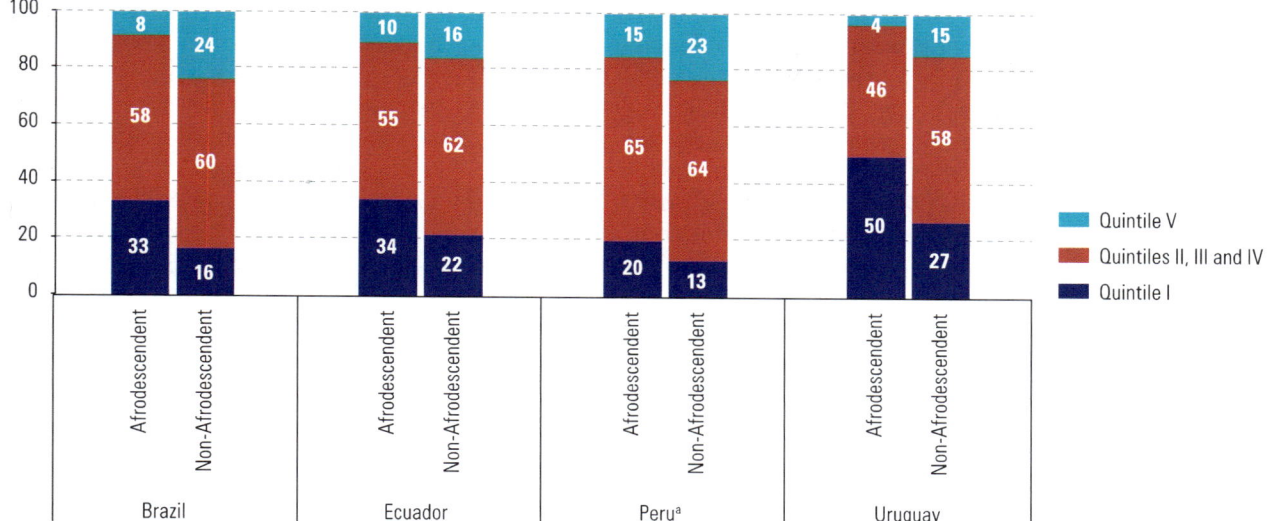

**Source**: Economic Commission for Latin America and the Caribbean (ECLAC), on the basis of data from the Household Survey Data Bank (BADEHOG.
**Note**:    The non-Afrodescendent population does not include those who self-identify as indigenous or those whose ethno-racial status is unknown.
ᵃ Does not include the population aged under 13 years in the case of Peru.

The magnitude of the differences between Afrodescendent and non-Afrodescendent population at the extremes of the income distribution testifies to the economic inequality between the two groups, even in countries whose overall poverty and income inequality levels are among the region's lowest, such as Uruguay. These data are evidence of the need for policies and strategies aimed at reducing income inequality to acknowledge the existence and magnitude of ethno-racial inequalities and adopt active measures to tackle them.

## 2.    Health inequalities

The right to health, including sexual and reproductive health, has been enshrined in various international human rights instruments and in international declarations and agreements that stress the need to approach health issues comprehensively, taking account of emotional, physical and social well-being, and recognizing the links that exist between health and other priorities such as education, peace, the environment and economic productivity.

In this connection, the Durban Declaration and Programme of Action propose the adoption of affirmative action measures, urging States to "establish programmes to promote the access, without discrimination, of individuals or groups of individuals who are victims of racism, racial discrimination, xenophobia and related intolerance to health care, and to promote strong efforts to eliminate disparities, inter alia in the infant and maternal mortality rates, childhood immunizations, HIV/AIDS, heart diseases, cancer and contagious diseases" (United Nations, 2001). In the 2030 Agenda for Sustainable Development, Goal 3, "Ensure healthy lives and promote well-being for all at all ages", includes 13 targets relating to health and its premise of "no one left behind", the central element of the Agenda, implies the need to make the situation of Afrodescendent men and women statistically visible and address the situations of special disadvantage in which they find themselves in several of the region's countries.

The magnitude of the differences between Afrodescendent and non-Afrodescendent population at the extremes of the income distribution testifies to the economic inequality between the two groups.

In the regional domain, there are explicit commitments on this topic: under priority measure 95 in the Montevideo Consensus on Population and Development, governments agree to "Ensure that Afro-descendent persons, in particular Afro-descendent girls, adolescents and women, can exercise the right to health, particularly the right to sexual health and reproductive health, taking into account the specific socio-territorial and cultural features and the structural factors, such as racism, that hinder the exercise of their rights" (ECLAC, 2013). It is important to stress the key role of civil society in each of the international and regional processes, including Afrodescendent organizations and activists, and also the contribution of academia. Moreover, Afrodescendent organizations in the region, particularly those of women and young people, have raised those issues in various forums and meetings. At the first World Summit of Afrodescendants (held in, 2011), they agreed to promote and implement the Plan of Action of the La Ceiba Declaration, which includes the following: "Demand that health systems must guarantee access to quality and sensitive health services, including Afrodescendent traditional medicine, so that we can abolish inequalities in indicators of maternal mortality, chronic diseases and HIV/AIDS, among others, that afflict Afrodescendent peoples" (paragraph XV); and in relation to Afrodescendent youth, procure adequate sexual health, and prevention of early pregnancy and HIV/AIDS.

> Afrodescendent people face situations that infringe their rights and directly affect their health status. The factors that generate exclusion and marginalization are expressed most permanently in damage to health.

Throughout their lives, Afrodescendent people face situations that infringe their rights and directly affect their health status. In terms of social determinants, the factors that generate exclusion and marginalization, such as discrimination and racism, are expressed most permanently in damage to health, producing significant differences in mortality levels and life expectancy, among many other indicators. Thus, inequity in health is associated with profound, unjust and avoidable social inequalities that can be overcome with relevant and timely interventions.

The findings discussed in section B on the demographic transition have a direct bearing on the epidemiological transition, since morbidity and mortality patterns change according to population age structures. This transition basically involves communicable diseases losing predominance to non-communicable ones, a shift in morbi-mortality from younger to older people, and the predominance of morbidity over mortality. Nonetheless, the structural inequalities that characterize the region lead to a peculiar epidemiological polarization, in which infectious diseases coexist with other chronic and degenerative ones, which is consistent with the axes of the social inequality matrix and, thus, with the ethno-racial differences.

A serious problem in visualizing the ethno-racial dimension of the epidemiological profiles of the region is the lack of systematic and up-to-date information; this is firstly due to a major deficit in data on Afrodescendent identification in health statistics systems. Nonetheless, fragmentary information indicates that the most worrying illnesses for Afrodescendants include diabetes, arterial hypertension and sickle-cell diseases (see box V.4). Even in Brazil, which has included the race/skin-colour variable in health statistics systems since the mid-1990s, and where the quality of the information has improved significantly over the years, it is still hard to find detailed, exhaustive, timely and up-to-date studies of epidemiological profiles for the Afrodescendent population. This represents an imperative in the region, because it is necessary to know the epidemiological patterns of Afrodescendent people, also taking account of differences relating to the various stages of the life cycle, sex and territorial location. Without this information, it will be difficult to design policies and programmes with health objectives that make sense for these population groups.

Box V.4
Some figures on the
epidemiological profile
of Brazil

According to figures from the Ministry of Health of Brazil, the Afrodescendent population[a] displays the highest prevalence of diabetes. Mortality from diabetes mellitus increased between 2000 and 2012 among that population group and declined among the white population. In 2012, the mortality rate recorded in the "black" (*preta*) population was 34.1 per 100,000 inhabitants; in the "brown" (*parda*) population it was 29.1, and among the "white" (*branca*) population it was 22.7 per 100,000 inhabitants. In other words, the highest rates are among Afrodescendants.

In the case of arterial hypertension, there has also been an increase among the Afrodescendent population between 2005 and 2012. The mortality rate from hypertension among the "black" population was 32.3 per 100,000 inhabitants, among the "brown" population it was 25 and among "whites" it was 17 per 100,000. Hypertension also leads to higher mortality risks among the Afrodescendent population, which concurs with the results of numerous studies performed for Afrodescendants in the United States.

As regards mortality from sickle-cell diseases, the rate in 2012 was 0.73 per 100,000 inhabitants among the "black" population, 0.28 among the "brown" population and 0.08 per 100,000 inhabitants among "whites". This is one of the most common hereditary diseases in Brazil, which occurs from the early years of life, for which reason it is considered in public policies.

**Source:** Economic Commission for Latin America and the Caribbean (ECLAC), on the basis of data from Ministry of Health of Brazil [online] http://portalsaude.saude.gov.br/index.php?option=com_content&view=article&id=15580&Itemid=803.
[a] In the censuses and household surveys of Brazil, as indicated above (see the footnote to box V.2), the self-identification of Afrodescendants is done through two categories related to skin colour (out of a total of five): black (*preta*) and brown (*parda*).

## (a) Achievements on mother-and-child health have not been fully inclusive: equity disparities persist to the detriment of Afrodescendent women and children

As analysed in chapter III, inequality manifests itself in different ways at different stages of the life cycle. One of the most eloquent indicators of this is the inequality observed between the Afrodescendent and non-Afrodescendent populations in child mortality rates (figure V.3). In a group of eight countries for which this information is available, childhood mortality among Afrodescendants as estimated in 2010 varies from 10 per 1,000 live births in Costa Rica to 26 per 1,000 in Colombia. Nonetheless, irrespective of its level, the chances that an Afrodescendent boy or girl will die before his or her first birthday are systematically higher than for non-Afrodescendants, except in the data reported by Argentina. The largest gaps occur in Colombia, Uruguay, Panama and Brazil, where the probability of an Afrodescendent child dying before his or her first birthday varies between 1.6 and 1.3 times that of a non-Afrodescendent child. Moreover, these inequalities persist even after controlling for area of residence. Apart from the urban areas of Argentina, infant mortality is always higher among Afrodescendants than among non-Afrodescendants, both in cities and in the countryside. Although urban areas generally display lower levels of infant mortality than rural areas, in some cases the relative ethno-racial disparities widen in the cities, as in Brazil, Costa Rica and Panama (see table V.3).

One of the most eloquent indicators of inequality between the Afrodescendent and non-Afrodescendent populations is the child mortality rate.

**Figure V.3**
Latin America (8 countries): estimates of infant mortality by ethno-racial status, 2010
*(Number of deaths per 1,000 live births)*

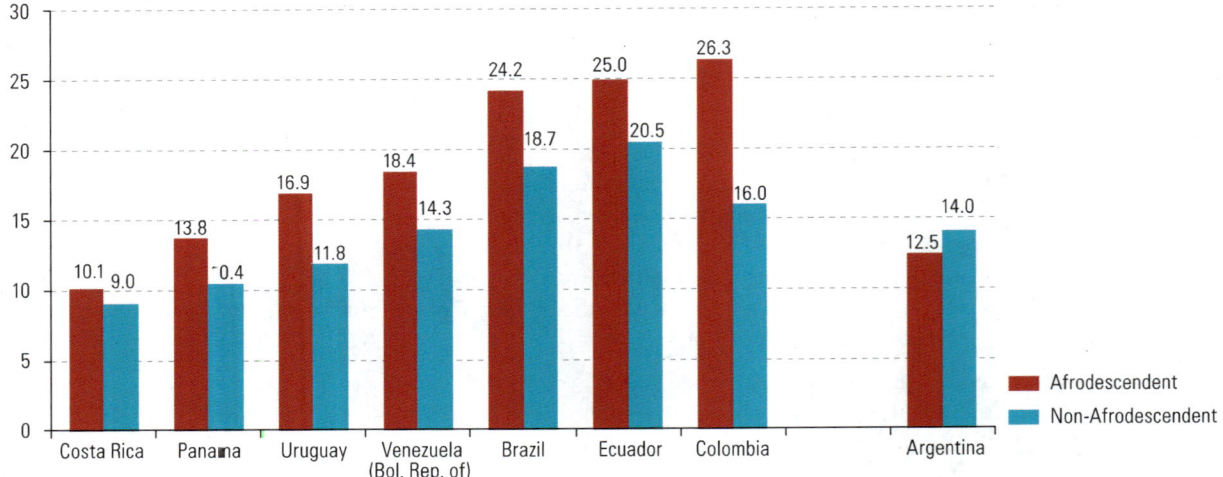

**Source**: Economic Commission for Latin America and the Caribbean (ECLAC), on the basis of indirect estimations from census microdata.

**Table V.3**
Latin America (8 countries): estimates of infant mortality by ethno-racial status, 2010[a]
*(Number of deaths per 1,000 live births)*

| Country | Ethnic-racial group | | | | | | Ethnic-racial gaps[c] | | |
| --- | --- | --- | --- | --- | --- | --- | --- | --- | --- |
| | Afrodescendent | | | Non-Afrodescendent[b] | | | | | |
| | Urban | Rural | Total | Urban | Rural | Total | Urban | Rural | Total |
| Argentina | 11.9 | 18.6 | 12.5 | 13.8 | 15.4 | 14.0 | 0.86 | 1.21 | 0.89 |
| Brazil | 22.2 | 31.6 | 24.2 | 17.6 | 25.3 | 18.7 | 1.26 | 1.25 | 1.30 |
| Colombia | 21.2 | 36.5 | 26.3 | 14.2 | 21.4 | 16.0 | 1.49 | 1.71 | 1.64 |
| Costa Rica | 10.6 | 8.8 | 10.1 | 9.9 | 8.9 | 9.0 | 1.07 | 0.99 | 1.12 |
| Ecuador | 23.2 | 29.8 | 25.0 | 18.9 | 23.3 | 20.5 | 1.23 | 1.28 | 1.22 |
| Panama | 13.8 | 13.6 | 13.8 | 9.4 | 12.4 | 10.4 | 1.48 | 1.09 | 1.32 |
| Uruguay | 16.9 | 15.0 | 16.9 | 12.0 | 8.9 | 11.8 | 1.41 | 1.69 | 1.42 |
| Venezuela (Bolivarian Republic of) | 18.0 | 20.6 | 18.4 | 14.1 | 15.6 | 14.3 | 1.28 | 1.32 | 1.29 |

**Source**: Economic Commission for Latin America and the Caribbean (ECLAC), on the basis of indirect estimations from census microdata.
[a] The estimations were obtained through indirect demographic methods and a final adjustment of the mortality rate based on current official figures for the national total, according to *Demographic Observatory, 2016. Population Projections* (ECLAC, 2017).
[b] Does not include the indigenous population.
[c] Ratio of Afrodescendent to non-Afrodescendent infant mortality.

In addition to the above, the quality of health care and its accessibility are elements that need more in-depth study in the region. Some studies describe discriminatory and racist practices in health care which clearly affect its quality.[13] Moreover, in certain national contexts, it is important to culturally adapt health services by including the knowledge and practices of African races that still persist in several Latin American countries. On this point, the first Afrodescendent Congress of the Americas and Caribbean on Health, Ancestral Medicine and Inter-culturality was held in 2011 in Ecuador, convened by that country's Ministry of Health. The Congress aimed to generate inputs to formulate public health policies, strengthen ancestral medicine and strategies for exercise of the inter-culturality of Afrodescendent men and women of the Americas and the Caribbean, from a rights perspective.[14]

---

[13]    Among other studies, see for example, Hurtado-Saa (2012); Defensoría del Pueblo del Ecuador (2012); and Mallú and others (2013).
[14]    For example, see the case of Peru in the next section of this chapter.

There is a wide-ranging literature on the social and economic factors that generate differentials in infant mortality rates, such as education or income, which operate through a set of proximal determinants that directly affect the risk of morbidity and mortality in the early years of life, such as access to health services or the characteristics of the mother (age, spacing of pregnancies, nutritional status, among others). Nonetheless, the interactions between the socioeconomic and proximal factors and their impact on infant mortality differentials have scarcely been studied for Afrodescendent populations, largely owing to lack of basic information as noted above.

Figure V.4 shows that Afrodescendent women receive less antenatal care than non-Afrodescendent women in three of the four countries with data available. Nonetheless, the differences are not large enough to explain the disparities in infant mortality for the same countries. The situation is broadly similar in relation to childbirth attended by qualified personnel (see figure V.5). Nonetheless, the details of the operational definitions of these indicators may conceal greater inequalities. In 2012, the Ministry of Health of Brazil reported that 55.7% of "black" women claimed having seven or more antenatal checkups, compared to 54.2% among "brown" women and 74.5% among "white" women.

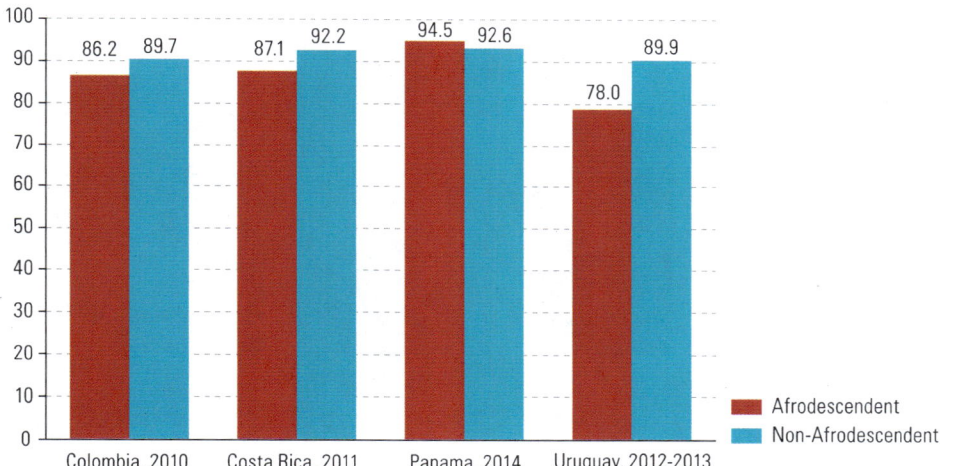

**Figure V.4**
Latin America (4 countries): proportion of women receiving at least four antenatal checkups, by ethno-racial status, around 2010
*(Percentages)*

**Source**: Multiple Indicator Cluster Surveys (MICS) for Costa Rica, Panama and Uruguay; and Demographic and Health Survey for Colombia.

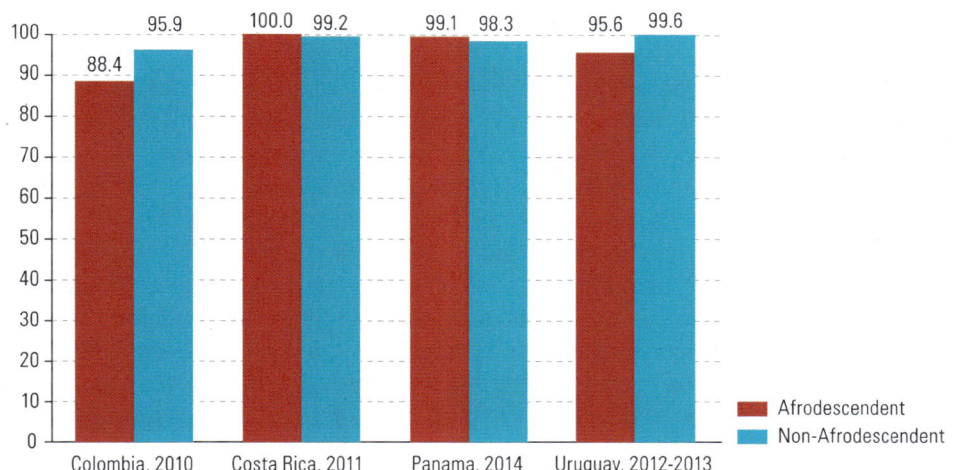

**Figure V.5**
Latin America (4 countries): proportion of deliveries attended by qualified personnel, by ethno-racial status, around 2010
*(Percentages)*

**Source**: Multiple Indicator Cluster Surveys (MICS) for Costa Rica, Panama and Uruguay; and Demographic and Health Survey for Colombia.

The poverty conditions that Afrodescendent women endure in the region impair their health status, which is further compounded by limited access to and cultural accessibility of the health services provided, including sexual and reproductive health care. Against this backdrop, although maternal mortality has dropped in the region, it remains high among Afrodescendent women, as shown by the figures for countries with data available. Based on the vital statistics of Brazil, Colombia and Ecuador, the fact that birth and death records have included ethno-racial identification reveals glaring inequalities to the detriment of Afrodescendent women (figure V.6). In Colombia, in 2010-2013, the maternal mortality rate for Afrodescendent women is just over twice the national average, and in Ecuador it is four times higher. In Brazil, the inequalities are much smaller; nonetheless in 2011 the Afrodescendent mortality ratio was 1.4 times the figure for "white" women. Those data show the importance and urgency of having timely and high-quality figures available on maternal mortality, both for women in general and for Afrodescendants in particular.

**Figure V.6**
Brazil, Colombia and Ecuador: maternal mortality rate by ethnic-racial status, around 2011
*(Number of deaths per 100,000 live births)*

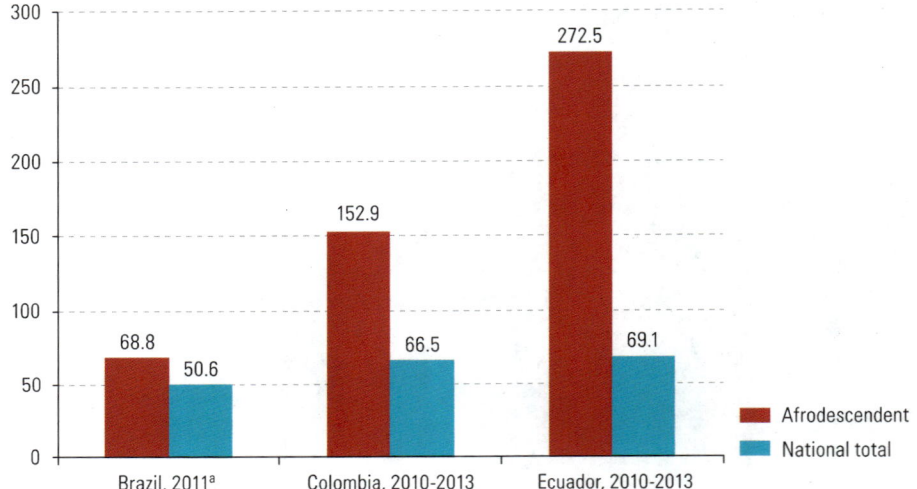

Source: Economic Commission for Latin America and the Caribbean (ECLAC), on the basis of data from Ministry of Health of Brazil [online] http://portalsaude.saude.gov.br/index.php?option=com_content&view=article&id=15580&Itemid=803; and in the cases of Colombia and Ecuador, databases of vital statistics supplied by the statistical institutes of each country.
[a] Total corresponds to the "white" population and not the national total.

## (b) Adolescent pregnancy: the need for policies that take account of sociocultural diversity

Pregnancy in adolescence is another manifestation of inequality to the disadvantage of Afrodescendent youth. Here, the interaction of generational and gender inequalities in terms of sexual and reproductive rights is made even more acute by the ethno-racial factor. It should be noted that early-age reproduction in the region is a public policy issue for several reasons; firstly because, despite the considerable drop in general fertility, adolescent fertility has not followed the same trend. In fact, in nearly all the region's countries, the levels have either remained constant or have even increased in some period. The second reason is that early-age reproduction is associated with socioeconomic inequalities, since it is much more frequent among the poor and less educated groups, in which Afrodescendants are overrepresented. In fact, it has been seen as a factor that reduces the chances of escaping poverty for several generations at a time (Rodríguez, 2014). It is also related to gender inequality, because responsibilities for upbringing and care fall mainly on young women, their mothers and grandmothers, irrespective of the young woman's conjugal status or whether or not she is living with the baby's father (Rodríguez, 2014).

Figure V.7 shows that the percentage of Afrodescendent adolescent girls between 15 and 19 years of age who are mothers remains high; and, in 7 of the 10 countries with data available, higher than among non-Afrodescendants of the same ages. In those 10 countries, between 14% and 25% of Afrodescendent adolescent girls have had at least one child, the highest proportion being in Ecuador. The largest inequalities are recorded in Brazil and Uruguay, which shows that even countries that have implemented integrated and universal health policies for youth, including policies to reduce unwanted adolescent pregnancy, have not been able to eliminate ethno-racial inequality. Weak government responses in combating violence, the near total absence of sex education programmes in health services that include the ethno-racial dimension, and the deterioration of public services in areas that have larger Afrodescendent concentrations, are some of the critical factors that wreak havoc on the lives of women, girls, adolescents and young people in this population group.

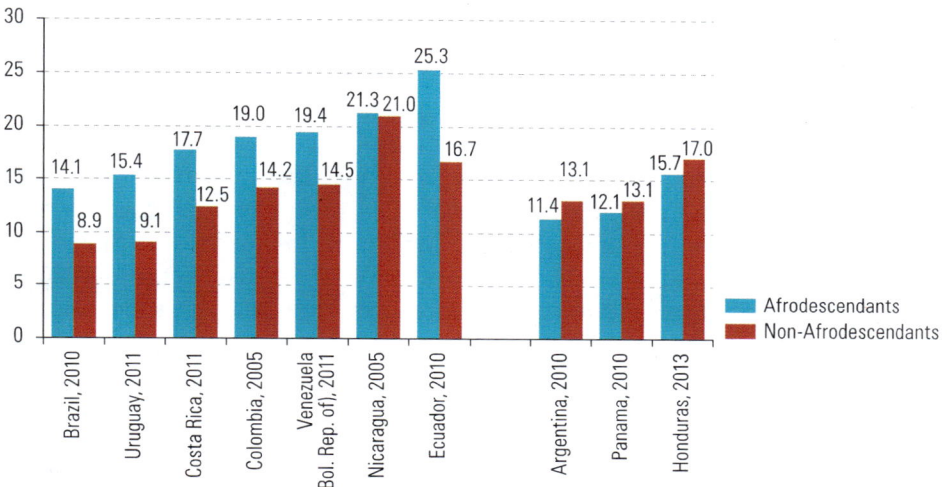

**Figure V.7**
Latin America (11 countries): proportion of adolescent girls aged 15-19 years who are mothers, by ethno-racial status, around 2010
(*Percentages*)

**Source**: Economic Commission for Latin America and the Caribbean (ECLAC), on the basis of special processing of census microdatabases using REDATAM 7.
**Note**: The non-Afrodescendent population does not include people who self-identify as indigenous or whose ethnic-racial status is unknown.

## 3.   Inequalities in education

The right to education is a fundamental tool of social change towards equality and the formation of a society build on solidarity and respect for cultural diversity; and the State is directly responsible for guaranteeing fulfilment of that right and implementing public policies to that end. Moreover, the right to education facilitates the achievement of other rights. In the region, the distribution of income and well-being is transmitted from one generation to another, and its determinant factors are education, wealth, demographic characteristics and opportunities for access to a productive and quality job and to decent work.

Major progress has been made on expanding education coverage and access in the last three decades in Latin America. On average, access to primary education is now practically universal throughout the region; and access to secondary school has also grown significantly, although major retention challenges persist, particularly at the upper secondary level. Illiteracy has declined, and the primary school gender gap is now virtually non-existent. Despite this progress, substantial heterogeneity in terms of education levels persists, both between countries and within them. The gaps reflect not only the country's development level, but also internal factors of inequality, including the level of household incomes (in 2013, while 80% of young people between 20 and 24 years of age belonging to the fifth income quintile had completed secondary school, the figure was only 34% among young people from the first quintile (ECLAC, 2016c)). In post-secondary education (particularly university) the gaps are even wider, because young people from households in the first income quintile have virtually no access to higher education. These inequalities are often rendered invisible when the analysis goes no deeper than national averages.

That means that each of the countries of the region have population groups with major education deficits, which in turn are projected on to other basic domains such as paid work, health, housing, infant mortality and life expectancy. Such is the case in most countries for Afrodescendent and indigenous youth.

In view of this reality, the Durban Programme of Action urges governments to: (i) commit themselves to ensuring access to education, including access to free primary education for all children, both girls and boys, and access for adults to lifelong learning and education, based on respect for human rights, diversity and tolerance, without discrimination of any kind; (ii) adopt and implement laws that prohibit discrimination on the basis of race, colour, descent or national or ethnic origin at all levels of education, both formal and non-formal; (iii) take all appropriate measures to eliminate obstacles limiting the access of children to education; and (iv) ensure that all children have access without discrimination to education of good quality. In the Plan of Action of the La Ceiba Declaration (issued at the First World Summit of Afrodescendants in 2011), Afrodescendent organizations asserted that: "Education systems must guarantee access to a quality education with an ethnic-racial perspective that educates students on the history and contributions to mankind of the African and Afrodescendent peoples written by themselves"(paragraph X); and "Work to ensure that national governments promote, in their education systems, ethno-education, the promotion of Afrodescendent mother tongues, the history and contributions to mankind of the peoples of Africa" (paragraph XI).

## (a) Access of children, adolescents and young people to the education system

Systematic efforts to expand the coverage of the education system have virtually eliminated ethnic-racial disparities in primary school access for 6-11 year-olds in the region today, at least in relation to national totals (although gaps may persist in certain geographic areas inside each country). Nonetheless, at higher ages the gaps are widening. Figure V.8 shows the proportion of children and adolescents aged 12-17 who were attending an educational establishment at the time of the census. Attendance rates among Afrodescendent children and youth vary from 71.7% in Honduras to 92.8% in Panama.

Moreover, in 7 of the 11 countries with data available, Afrodescendent school attendance is lower than that of other children and adolescents. The gaps are greatest in the Bolivarian Republic of Venezuela, Ecuador and Uruguay, although the differences are not large. Nor are there significant gender differences: even girls and adolescents aged 12 to 17 years, irrespective of their ethno-racial group, display school attendance rates that are slightly higher than those of their male peers. Accordingly, in the seven countries in which the indicators are less favourable for Afrodescendants, the overlap with the gender variable puts Afrodescendent boys in the worst situation and non-Afrodescendent girls in the best.

Moreover, in 7 of the 11 countries with data available, Afrodescendent school attendance is lower than that of other children and adolescents.

**Figure V.8**

Latin America (11 countries): proportion of boys, girls and adolescents aged 12-17 years attending an educational establishment, by ethno-racial and gender status, around 2010
*(Percentages)*

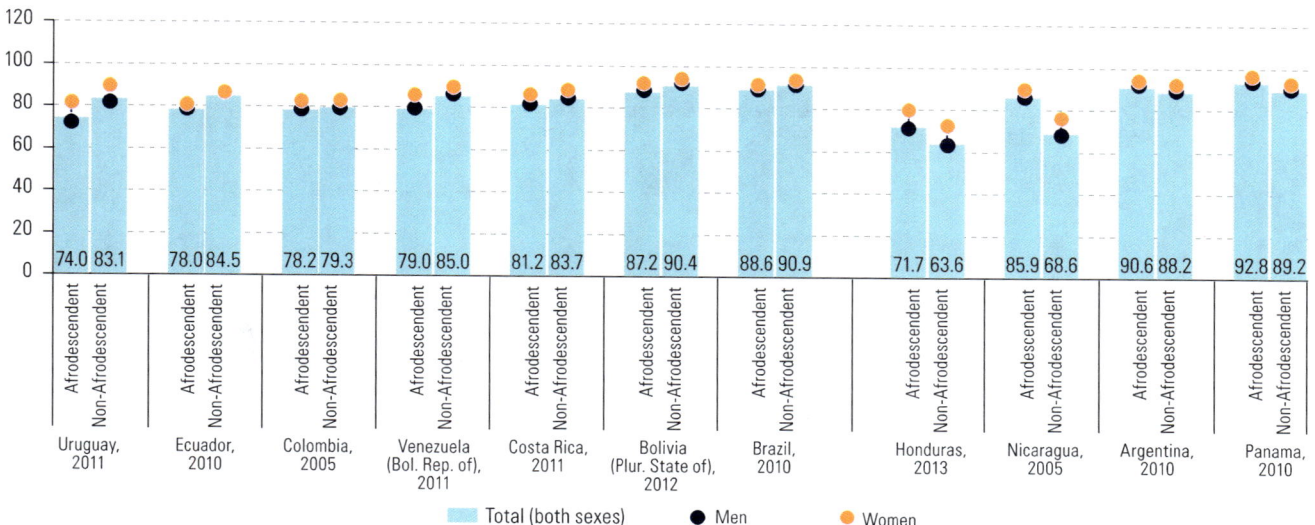

**Source**: Economic Commission for Latin America and the Caribbean (ECLAC), on the basis of special processing of census microdatabases using REDATAM 7.
**Note**:    The non-Afrodescendent population does not include people who self-identify as indigenous or whose ethno-racial status is unknown.

Figure V.9 reports the rate of school attendance among young people aged between 18 and 24 years in 11 of the region's countries. The data are "gross" attendance figures, in other words they do not distinguish whether the young people in question are at the primary level (behind the grade for their age), or whether they are proceeding through secondary school along with their age cohort. This is another aspect that needs to be developed further, because secondary education is compulsory in several of the region's countries. Nonetheless, looking beyond the legal framework and even current criticisms of the education system, the truth is that in the region's development context this should be the minimum floor for all young people, both men and women.[15] In this connection, although the figures only measure attendance, they also show that access is still not universal for Afrodescendent adolescents.

The generation gaps in access to education are eloquent when the data of figure V.8 are compared with those of figure V.9. The proportion of young people aged 18-24 who are attending an educational establishment is significantly lower than that of 12-17-year-olds. School enrolment among Afrodescendent youth aged 18-24 varies between 16.9% in Uruguay and 41.4% in Argentina. Moreover, the ethno-racial gaps widen in that age bracket to the detriment of Afrodescendent youth, and they are replicated in the same seven countries where that situation pertains among adolescents aged 12-17. In contrast, in Argentina, Honduras, Nicaragua and Panama, school attendance by Afrodescendent children, adolescents and young people is slightly higher than that of non-Afrodescendants (see figures V.8 and V.9). The greatest inequalities occur in Uruguay, where Afrodescendent school enrolment in the 18-24 year age group is just under half of the rate among non-Afrodescendent youth; followed by the Bolivarian Republic of Venezuela and Ecuador, with Afrodescendent school attendance rates that are 35%

---

[15]    Completing secondary education, at least, has important effects in terms of the possibility of avoiding being poverty in adulthood (ECLAC, 2016c); moreover, secondary education can also be crucial for participation in political mechanisms. In addition, high levels of education, particularly among women, are associated with better educational and health outcomes for their children.

and 25% lower, respectively, than those of non-Afrodescendent youth. In conjunction with this, the gender gaps are also larger in this age group than the previous one, both among Afrodescendent youth and among non-Afrodescendants; and here again they put Afrodescendent males at the greatest disadvantage.

**Figure V.9**
Latin America (11 countries): proportion of young people aged 18-24 years attending an educational establishment, by ethno-racial and gender status, around 2010
*(Percentages)*

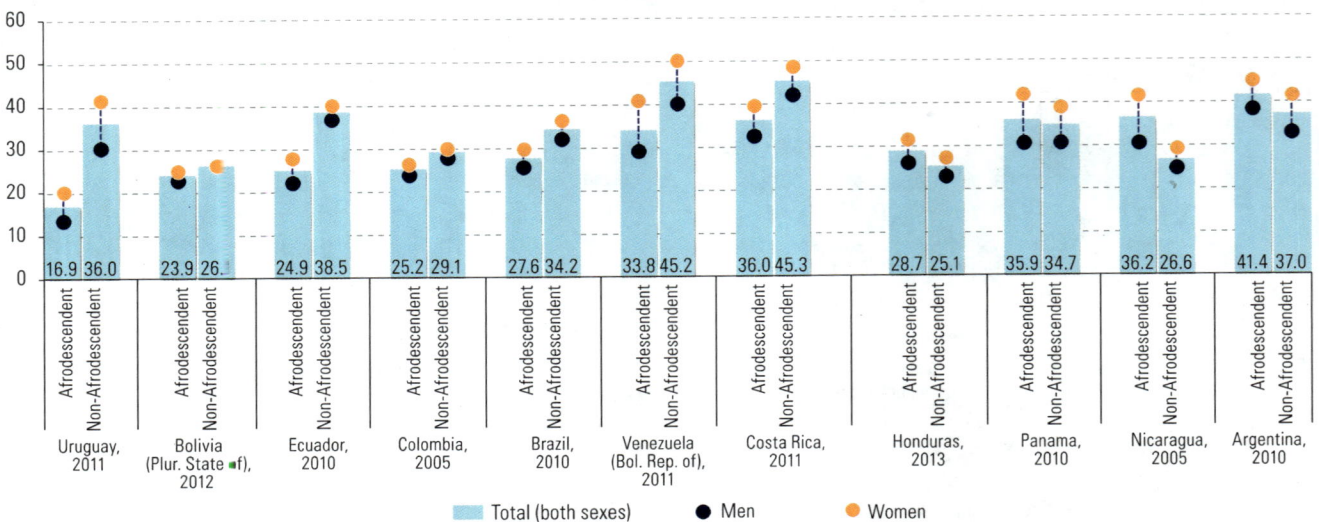

Source: Economic Commission for Latin America and the Caribbean (ECLAC), on the basis of special processing of census microdatabases using REDATAM 7.
Note:    The non-Afrodescendent population does not include people who self-identify as indigenous or whose ethnic-racial status is unknown.

To complement this overview, table V.4 reports access to tertiary or post-secondary education by young people aged 20-29 years, either at university level or otherwise. The range in this case for Afrodescendent youth is from 8.5% in Uruguay to 38.3% in Cuba. The pattern of ethno-racial inequality to the detriment of these young people is systematic in the seven countries mentioned, with gaps that are even wider at this level of education.[16] Brazil, Ecuador and Uruguay display the largest differences, in which the percentage of non-Afrodescendent youth who succeed in entering tertiary education more than triples or doubles the percentage corresponding to their Afrodescendent counterparts. In other words, whereas in Uruguay, for example, 28 of every 100 non-Afrodescendent young people enter higher education, only eight of every 100 Afrodescendent young people do so. In the construction of this indicator, data were available from Cuba, where the ethno-racial differences are smaller. In Argentina, Honduras, Nicaragua and Panama the situation appears to be more favourable for Afrodescendent youth, both male and female.

In all countries, women have greater access to higher education than men, irrespective of their ethnic status; so once again in most countries the overlap of inequalities in access to education puts Afrodescendent men in the least favourable situation, in direct contrast to the quality of their engagement in the labour market and the wages they receive (compared to the situation of Afrodescendent women).

---

[16]    The data shown in figure 10 reflects the access of young people to an educational establishment, without specifying the level attained (in other words, they could be attending primary, secondary or higher education).

Table V.4
Latin America (12 countries): proportion of young people aged between 20 and 29 years who gained access to higher education, by ethno-racial status and gender, around 2010
(Percentages)

| Country and year | Ethno-racial status | Non-university | | | University | | | Total (university and non-university) | | |
|---|---|---|---|---|---|---|---|---|---|---|
| | | Men | Women | Total | Men | Women | Total | Men | Women | Total |
| Argentina, 2010 | Afrodescendent | 8.1 | 15.3 | 11.5 | 21.4 | 26.1 | 23.7 | 29.5 | 41.4 | 35.2 |
| | Non-Afrodescendent | 7.5 | 13.7 | 10.7 | 17.9 | 22.7 | 20.3 | 25.4 | 36.4 | 30.9 |
| Bolivia (Plurinational State of), 2012 | Afrodescendent | 3.5 | 4.7 | 4.1 | 16.7 | 17.8 | 17.2 | 20.2 | 22.5 | 21.2 |
| | Non-Afrodescendent | 4.9 | 7.0 | 6.0 | 30.0 | 32.6 | 31.3 | 34.9 | 39.6 | 37.3 |
| Brazil, 2010[a] | Afrodescendent | ... | ... | ... | ... | ... | ... | 10.3 | 14.8 | 12.5 |
| | Non-Afrodescendent | ... | ... | ... | ... | ... | ... | 27.6 | 34.3 | 31.0 |
| Colombia, 2005 | Afrodescendent | 5.9 | 8.1 | 7.0 | 8.5 | 10.1 | 9.3 | 14.4 | 18.1 | 16.3 |
| | Non-Afrodescendent | 6.9 | 10.2 | 8.6 | 15.9 | 18.4 | 17.2 | 22.8 | 28.6 | 25.8 |
| Costa Rica, 2011 | Afrodescendent | 1.7 | 2.2 | 2.0 | 13.3 | 18.2 | 15.7 | 15.0 | 20.4 | 17.7 |
| | Non-Afrodescendent | 2.5 | 2.6 | 2.6 | 23.6 | 29.8 | 26.8 | 26.1 | 32.4 | 29.3 |
| Cuba, 2012 | Afrodescendent | 25.9 | 22.3 | 24.3 | 11.0 | 17.8 | 14.0 | 36.9 | 40.2 | 38.3 |
| | Non-Afrodescendent | 27.4 | 23.5 | 25.5 | 11.3 | 19.0 | 15.0 | 38.7 | 42.5 | 40.6 |
| Ecuador, 2010 | Afrodescendent | 1.8 | 2.4 | 2.1 | 10.7 | 15.1 | 12.9 | 12.5 | 17.5 | 14.9 |
| | Non-Afrodescendent | 2.3 | 2.4 | 2.3 | 27.8 | 32.7 | 30.3 | 30.0 | 35.0 | 32.6 |
| Honduras, 2013 | Afrodescendent | 3.1 | 4.2 | 3.7 | 7.3 | 9.5 | 8.4 | 10.4 | 13.7 | 12.1 |
| | Non-Afrodescendent | 3.1 | 3.3 | 3.2 | 6.5 | 7.9 | 7.3 | 9.7 | 11.2 | 10.5 |
| Nicaragua, 2005[a] | Afrodescendent | ... | ... | ... | ... | ... | ... | 10.8 | 22.9 | 17.2 |
| | Non-Afrodescendent | ... | ... | ... | ... | ... | ... | 12.2 | 15.2 | 13.7 |
| Panama, 2010 | Afrodescendent | 2.6 | 3.0 | 2.8 | 20.4 | 34.9 | 27.4 | 23.0 | 37.9 | 30.2 |
| | Non-Afrodescendent | 2.1 | 2.6 | 2.4 | 19.5 | 30.4 | 25.0 | 21.6 | 33.0 | 27.3 |
| Uruguay, 2011 | Afrodescendent | 2.0 | 4.7 | 3.4 | 3.7 | 6.6 | 5.2 | 5.7 | 11.3 | 8.5 |
| | Non-Afrodescendent | 5.2 | 9.5 | 7.4 | 16.7 | 24.0 | 20.4 | 21.9 | 33.5 | 27.8 |
| Venezuela (Bolivarian Republic of), 2011 | Afrodescendent | 5.2 | 7.7 | 6.2 | 13.9 | 23.9 | 17.8 | 19.1 | 31.6 | 24.0 |
| | Non-Afrodescendent | 7.6 | 10.2 | 8.9 | 23.0 | 34.9 | 29.0 | 30.6 | 45.1 | 38.0 |

Source: Economic Commission for Latin America and the Caribbean (ECLAC), on the basis of special processing of census microdatabases using REDATAM 7.
Note:   The non-Afrodescendent population does not include people who self-identify as indigenous or whose ethnic-racial status is unknown.
[a] It was impossible to establish the distinction between non-university and university at the higher education levels.

Access to university, and completion of that level of education, is one of the aspects that Afrodescendent organizations consider crucial for their advancement in terms of social inclusion and equality. Accordingly, major efforts are being made by both civil society and governments in the region to enable Afrodescendent youth to access and complete higher-level studies. For example, Nicaragua, one of the few countries in the region where education indicators report a better situation for Afrodescendants, has two community universities on the Caribbean coast —Bluefields Indian and Caribbean University (BICU) and the University of the autonomous regions of the Nicaraguan Caribbean coast (URACCAN)— which have made significant contributions to education and the development of ethnic and Afrodescendent communities (Sánchez, 2005). Brazil, as described in the next section, has implemented a systematic affirmative action policy to help Afrodescendent youth gain admission to universities (public and private). The policy has achieved significant results: according to the Brazilian Geographical and Statistical Institute (IBGE) (2015), 16.7% of Afrodescendent ("black" and "brown") youth aged 18-24 were attending higher education in 2004; and the proportion had risen to 45.5% by 2014. In the case of "white" young men and women, access to higher education was 47.2% in 2004 and had risen to 71.4% 10 years later. Although ethno-racial inequalities to the detriment of Afrodescendent youth clearly still persist, the data also show that they have been reduced significantly, because the higher education access rate for Afrodescendent youth has risen faster than that for "whites". Thus, in 2004, the higher education attendance rate for Afrodescendent youth was just over one third of the figure for "whites", but nearly two thirds by 2014.[17]

An analysis of census data yields important insights into the extent to which the right to education is being fulfilled; but this is insufficient in itself, particularly if the aim is to evaluate the quality of education received by Afrodescendent children, adolescents and young people. The discrimination and structural racism that they suffer in the education domain continues to manifest itself in various ways and on several levels in Latin American countries. The scarcity of culturally appropriate education policies, which recognize the history, identity and contribution of Afrodescendent peoples to the development of their countries, and the lack of effective participation mechanisms or affirmative action policies that are capable of reducing the existing gaps, combine with discrimination inside the classroom to generate deeper inequalities in an even more dramatic situation than just less access to educational establishments. This is another of the domains that require urgent and detailed analysis in the region's countries.

### (b) Young people who are neither studying and nor employed in the labour market

The situation of young people, both men and women, who are neither in the education system nor participating in the labour market, is a focus of attention in the region for several reasons. Although this is a heterogeneous group that combines structural situations with other more circumstantial ones, there is evidence that these young people are at a disadvantage and a greater risk of falling into poverty, or else have less chance of moving out of it. They also suffer from stigmatization (ECLAC 2014a). In reality, this is a group strongly differentiated by income quintile (roughly half of members of this group belong to the two first quintiles), and it consists chiefly of women living in urban areas, of whom a large proportion are already mothers with a heavy burden of unpaid work in their homes. This is precisely why it is difficult for them to continue or complete their studies and enter the labour market, given the lack of care systems and policies to reconcile study, work and personal and family life (ECLAC, 2014c and 2016e).

That situation is more acute in the case of Afrodescendent youth. Figure V.10 shows that the proportion of Afrodescendent young people not in education or employment is larger than that of non-Afrodescendent youth, a situation that also prevails in 7 of the 11 countries for which data are available.[18] In the other four countries (Argentina, Honduras, Panama and the Plurinational State of Bolivia) the situation is reversed, although in this case the ethno-racial gaps are considerably smaller. When the gender dimension is introduced into the analysis, a greater proportion of Afrodescendent than non-Afrodescendent young women are seen to be not in education or employment in 6 of the 11 countries. The gap is as large as 14 percentage points, as occurs in Uruguay, where 38% of Afrodescendent young women are in this situation, compared to 24% of non-Afrodescendent young women.

The proportion of Afrodescendent young people not in education or employment is larger than that of non-Afrodescencent youth, in 7 of the 11 countries.

---

[17]    Access by Afrodescendent young men and women to higher education needs to be complemented with the completion of the cycle. Preliminary data processed by CELADE from census microdata for the adult population (25-59 years of age) show that the completion of higher education is generally less frequent among Afrodescendent in 8 out of 12 countries. These figures are currently under review and will be published shortly in a document on the situation of the Afrodescendent population in the region, being prepared by ECLAC in conjunction with the United Nations Population Fund (UNFPA) and the Pan American Health Organization (PAHO).

[18]    Earlier parts of this section C provided evidence on the lower rate of school attendance and higher rates of adolescent maternity among young Afrodescendent women.

**Figure V.10**
Latin America (11 countries): young people aged between 15 and 29 years who are not in education or employed
in the labour market, by ethno-racial status and gender
*(Percentages)*

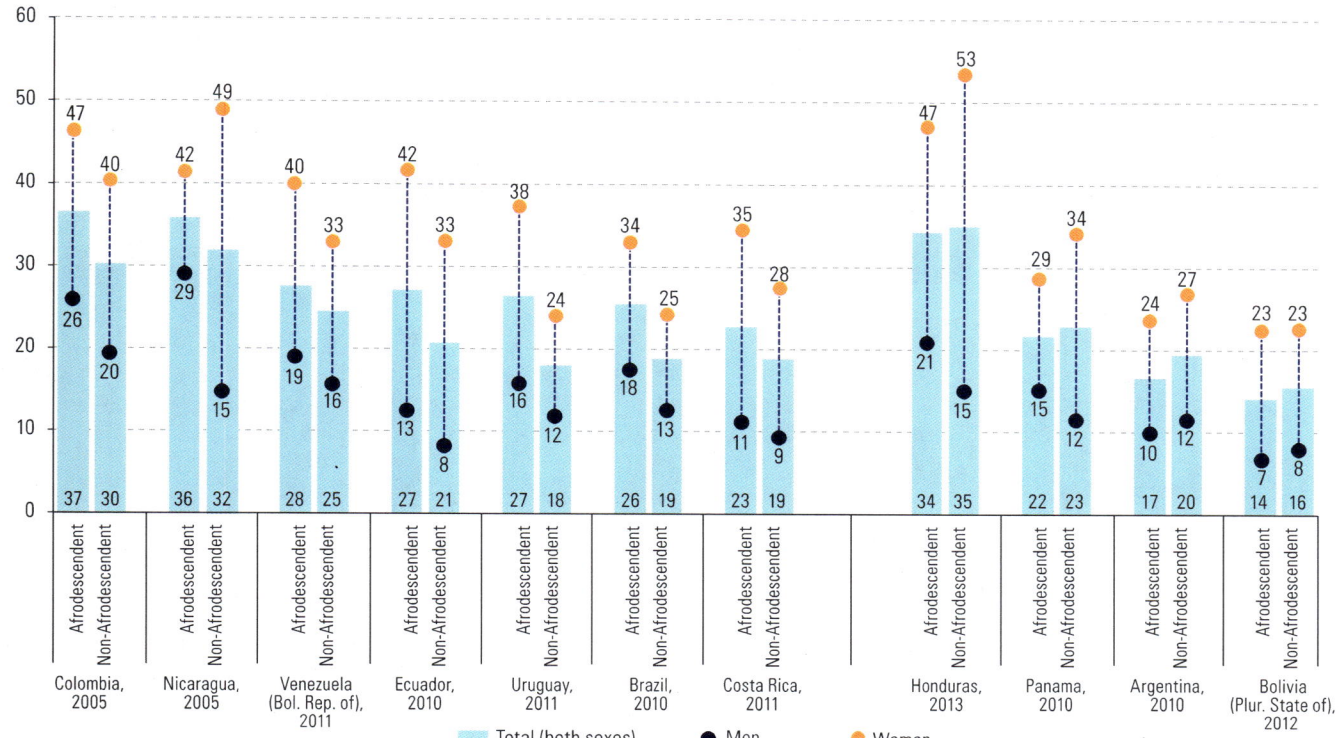

**Source**: Economic Commission for Latin America and the Caribbean (ECLAC), on the basis of special processing of census microdatabases using REDATAM 7.
**Note**:    The non-Afrodescendent population does not include people who self-identify as indigenous or whose ethnic-racial status is unknown.

Comparison of young Afrodescendent women to young non-Afrodescendent men shows wide gaps in all the countries with information available: the percentage of young Afrodescendent women not in education or employment exceeds the percentage of young non-Afrodescendent men in the same situation by at least a factor of 2 in Argentina, by a factor of 2.5 in four countries (Bolivarian Republic of Venezuela, Brazil, Colombia and Panama), by a factor of around 3 in another four countries (Honduras, Nicaragua, Plurinational State of Bolivia and Uruguay), by almost 4 in Costa Rica and over 5 in Ecuador.

The information contained in figure V.11 confirms that the main reason why young women are neither studying nor employed in the labour market is that they are performing unpaid domestic or care work in their own homes.

**Figure V.11**
Latin America (9 countries): proportion of women aged between 15 and 29 years who are not in education
or employed in the labour market, by ethno-racial status, around 2010
*(Percentages)*

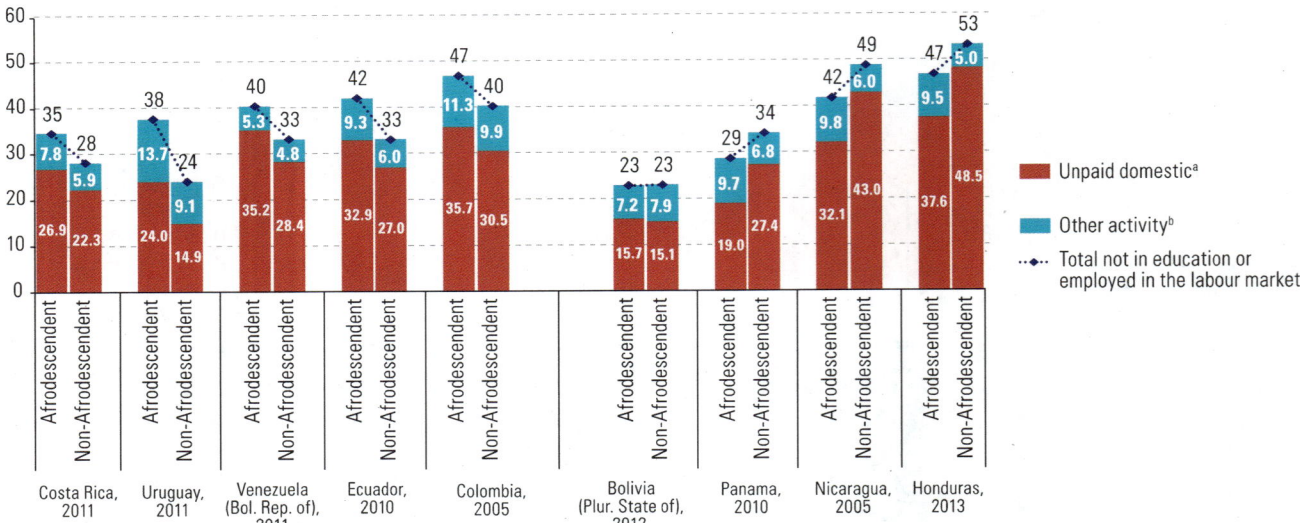

**Source**: Economic Commission for Latin America and the Caribbean (ECLAC), on the basis of special processing of census microdatabases using REDATAM 7.
**Notes**:   The non-Afrodescendent population does not include people who self-identify as indigenous or whose ethnic-racial status is unknown.
[a] Does not include Argentina or Brazil, because it is impossible to distinguish the "domestic work" category in these countries.
[b] Includes young people who are unemployed or economically inactive.

## 4.    Inequalities in the labour market

Concerns about discriminatory practices against individuals and the need to avoid them are long-standing, and have been embedded in various international regulations and United Nations instruments, as noted at the start of this chapter in relation to racial discrimination. In fact, even before the issuance of international regulations of a general nature, condemning racial discrimination in all spheres, in 1958 the International Labour Organization (ILO) adopted the first international regulation against discrimination, specifically targeting the employment sphere. This was ILO Convention No. 111 on Discrimination (Employment and Occupation) of 1958 (Convention No. 111), which identifies several domains of discrimination to be eliminated, including race/colour and sex, as well as defining the need for a national policy to promote equality of opportunities and treatment.[19]

ECLAC believes that work is the key to equality; together with education, work is the highway to social inclusion. In Latin America, incomes from work represent roughly 80% of total household income (ECLAC, 2016a). Accordingly, what happens in the sphere of work (opportunities and the quality of work to which individuals can accede)

---

[19]    The first paragraph of Article 1.1 asserts: "For the purpose of this Convention the term discrimination includes: (a) any distinction, exclusion or preference made on the basis of race, colour, sex, religion, political opinion, national extraction or social origin, which has the effect of nullifying or impairing equality of opportunity or treatment in employment or occupation; (b) such other distinction, exclusion or preference which has the effect of nullifying or impairing equality of opportunity or treatment in employment or occupation as may be determined by the Member concerned after consultation with representative employers' and workers' organisations, where such exist, and with other appropriate bodies." Article 2 adds that "Each Member for which this Convention is in force undertakes to declare and pursue a national policy designed to promote, by methods appropriate to national conditions and practice, equality of opportunity and treatment in respect of employment and occupation, with a view to eliminating any discrimination in respect thereof." See [online] http://www.ilo.org/dyn/normlex/es/f?p =NORMLEXPUB:12100:0::NO::P12100_ILO_CODE:C111.

strongly influences the chances of avoiding or escaping poverty and enjoying adequate levels of well-being. In other words, work is the main driver of poverty reduction, social and economic integration, equality, access to well-being and social protection; and it is also a fundamental mechanism for constructing autonomy, identity, personal dignity and broader citizenship (ECLAC, 2010, 2012a, 2012b, 2012c, 2014, 2016a and 2016b).[20]

For that reason, and considering the heavy presence of racial discrimination in the region and the structural gaps that exist, for example in the areas of health and education, it is crucial to analyse the existence and reproduction of ethno-racial inequalities in the world of work, and how they intertwine with other structural axes of the social inequality matrix, such as gender, age and territory. As reported in other ECLAC publications (ECLAC, 2016b and 2016g) and in previous sections of this chapter, the situation of multiple inequalities and discrimination endured by Afrodescendent women is one of the clearest manifestations of these intersecting inequalities.

This section draws on data from two different information sources: population censuses (for the education level of the employed population, the unemployment rate and occupational status) and household surveys (for labour incomes).

> It is crucial to analyse the existence and reproduction of ethno-racial inequalities in the world of work, and how they intertwine with other structural axes of the social inequality matrix, such as gender, age and territory.

## (a) The education level of employed people

As noted above, ECLAC views work and education as the two most powerful routes to social inclusion and the reduction of inequalities. Adequate levels of education, and its quality and relevance, are a key factor for good integration into the labour market (in productive, quality jobs with better incomes, access to rights and social protection). Nonetheless, educational attainments do not translate automatically to the labour market, particularly in the case of women, who, despite having higher levels of schooling, continue to earn less than men, even after controlling for hours worked (ECLAC, 2012a; 2011 and 2016f). In this context, secondary education is increasingly becoming a minimum floor from which to join the dynamic of productivity increases needed for sustainable development, and to mitigate the intergenerational reproduction of poverty, inequality and exclusion through access to decent work (ECLAC, 2016c).

When the educational attainment of the Afrodescendent and non-Afrodescendent employed population is compared (figure V.12), different trends can be discerned among the 10 countries for which there is information. In five cases, employed Afrodescendants (first group) are at a greater disadvantage, whereas in the other five either employed Afrodescendants have a slight advantage, or else no significant disparities are observed (second group). Considering employed persons with 13 or more years of schooling, Brazil and Uruguay stand out as countries in which the proportion of Afrodescendants is roughly one third that of non-Afrodescendants in that schooling bracket. In countries where employed Afrodescendants have the advantage (particularly Nicaragua, Honduras and the Plurinational State of Bolivia) the differences are much smaller. The size of the gaps that exist among countries in the first group shows the importance of affirmative action policies based on social and ethno-racial status that are being implemented by some of them, both in university education and in technical and vocational education (at secondary and tertiary level), and also in vocational training programmes, a topic that will be analysed in the last section of this chapter.

---

[20]   In Latin America and the Caribbean, the labour market has historically served as the link between a highly heterogeneous productive structure weighted towards low productivity sectors and a high level of household income inequality. Nonetheless, in the recent period (particularly between 2002 and 2014), as described in chapter I, the labour market has been a key factor for reducing poverty and inequality, owing basically to the reduction in unemployment, the growth of labour incomes, particularly minimum wages, a significant process of formalization of employment, and the extension of contributory social protection (health and pensions) and an increase in women's participation rate, which increases the number of income-earners per household and reduces the percentage of women without their own income (ECLAC, 2016a and 2016c).

**Figure V.12**

Latin America (10 countries): distribution of the total employed population aged 15 years and older, by years of schooling and ethno-racial status, around 2010

*(Percentages)*

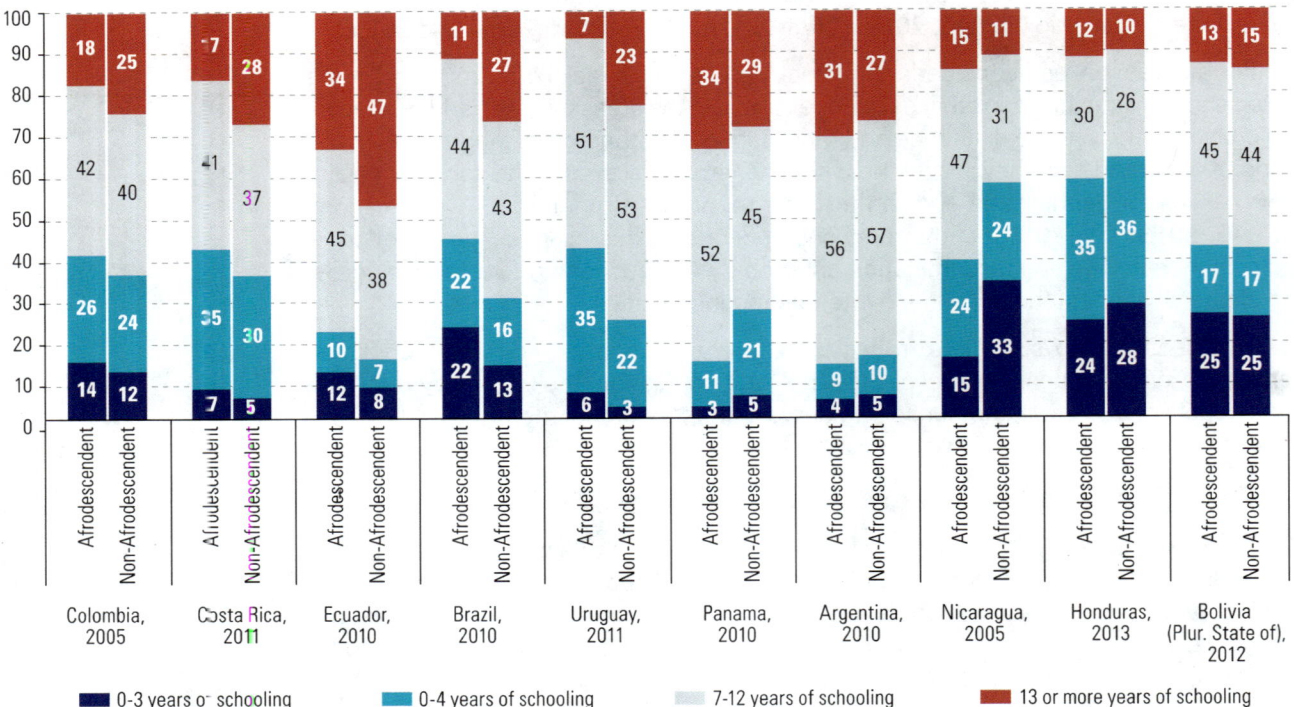

An analysis of gender inequalities in conjunction with ethno-racial inequalities among employed persons with 13 or more years of schooling (see figure V.13) shows that non-Afrodescendent women, and secondly Afrodescendent women, are better placed than men. Moreover, it is possible to distinguish two groups, the first consisting of six countries in which the percentage of the employed non-Afrodescendent population with that level of education exceeds the proportion of employed Afrodescendants (both men and women). In this case, the largest gaps are found in Uruguay and Brazil, where employed non-Afrodescendent women with 13 or more years of schooling are three times and twice, respectively, the number of employed Afrodescendent women with that level of schooling. The second group, consisting of four countries, also displays a more favourable situation for women (whether or not Afrodescendent) compared to men (Afrodescendent and otherwise); it is Afrodescendent women who are in the best position, although the differences are smaller. Panama is a special case, where the gender gap in favour of women is around 20 percentage points, among both Afrodescendants and non-Afrodescendants, representing a significant female advance and male retreat in this indicator.

**Source**: Economic Commission for Latin America and the Caribbean (ECLAC), on the basis of special processing of census microdatabases using REDATAM 7.
**Note**:    The non-Afrodescendent population does not include people who self-identify as indigenous or whose ethnic-racial status is unknown.

**Figure V.13**

Latin America (10 countries) proportion of the employed population with 13 or more years of schooling, by gender and ethnic-racial status, around 2010

*(Percentages)*

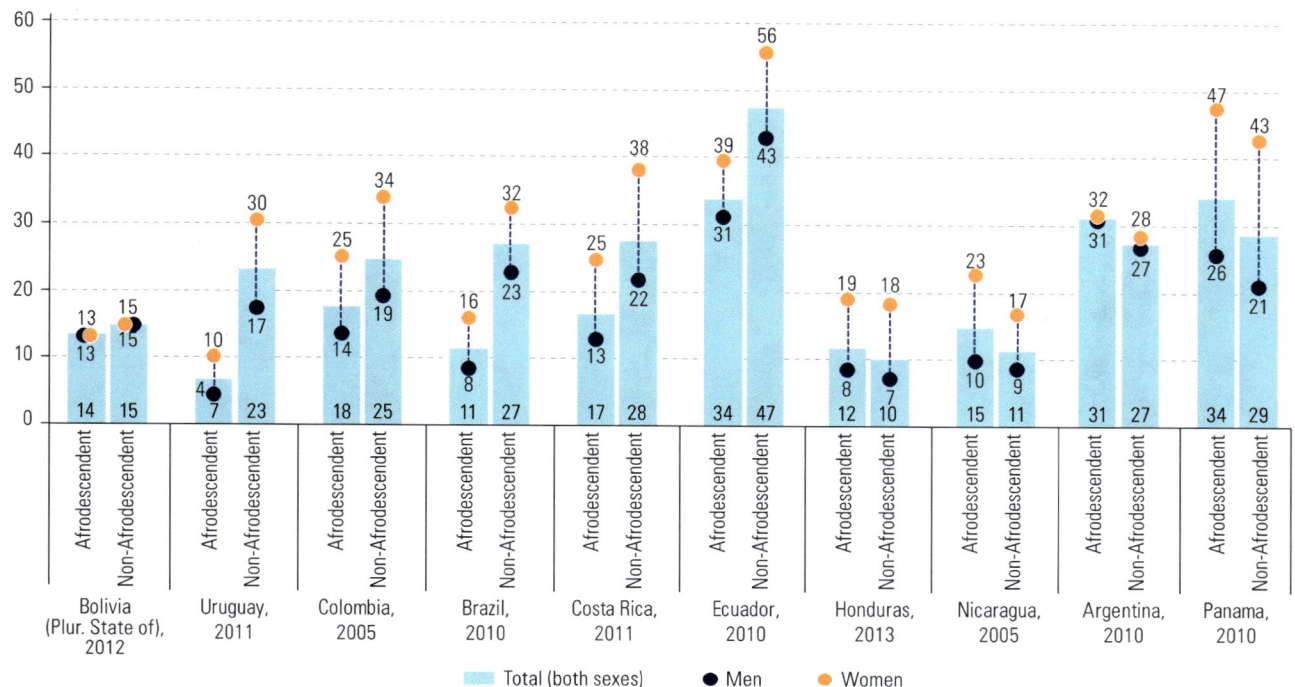

**Source:** Economic Commission for Latin America and the Caribbean (ECLAC), on the basis of special tabulations of data from household surveys conducted in the relevant countries.

**Note:** The non-Afrodescendent population does not include people who self-identify as indigenous or whose ethnic-racial status is unknown.

## (b) Unemployment rate

Unemployment is one of the main indicators of labour market exclusion; and it generally affects women and young people to a greater extent in all regions of the world, including Latin America. Several analyses of the labour market in Latin American countries, which incorporate the ethno-racial dimension, have also shown that unemployment disproportionately affects individuals belonging to indigenous peoples and Afrodescendants, and, particularly, the women and youth of those groups (IPEA, 2011; ECLAC/UNFPA 2011; 2014b; 2013 and 2016c; Guimarães, 2012; Borges, 2004).

According to census data (see figure V.14) the unemployment rate is higher among Afrodescendants than in the rest of the population (male or female) in 10 of the 11 countries considered (the Plurinational State of Bolivia being the exception). In both Argentina and the Bolivarian Republic of Venezuela, Afrodescendent and non-Afrodescendent unemployment rates differ little; nonetheless, Afrodescendants remain at a disadvantage.

In addition, in five countries (Argentina, Brazil, Ecuador, Panama and Uruguay) unemployment rates among Afrodescendent women are significantly higher than those of their male counterparts. They are also higher in comparison both with the unemployment rates of non-Afrodescendent women and those of non-Afrodescendent men in all cases except for the Bolivarian Republic of Venezuela and the Plurinational State of Bolivia.

**Figure V.14**

Latin America (11 countries): unemployment rate among the population aged 15 years and older, by gender and ethno-racial status, around 2010

*(Percentages)*

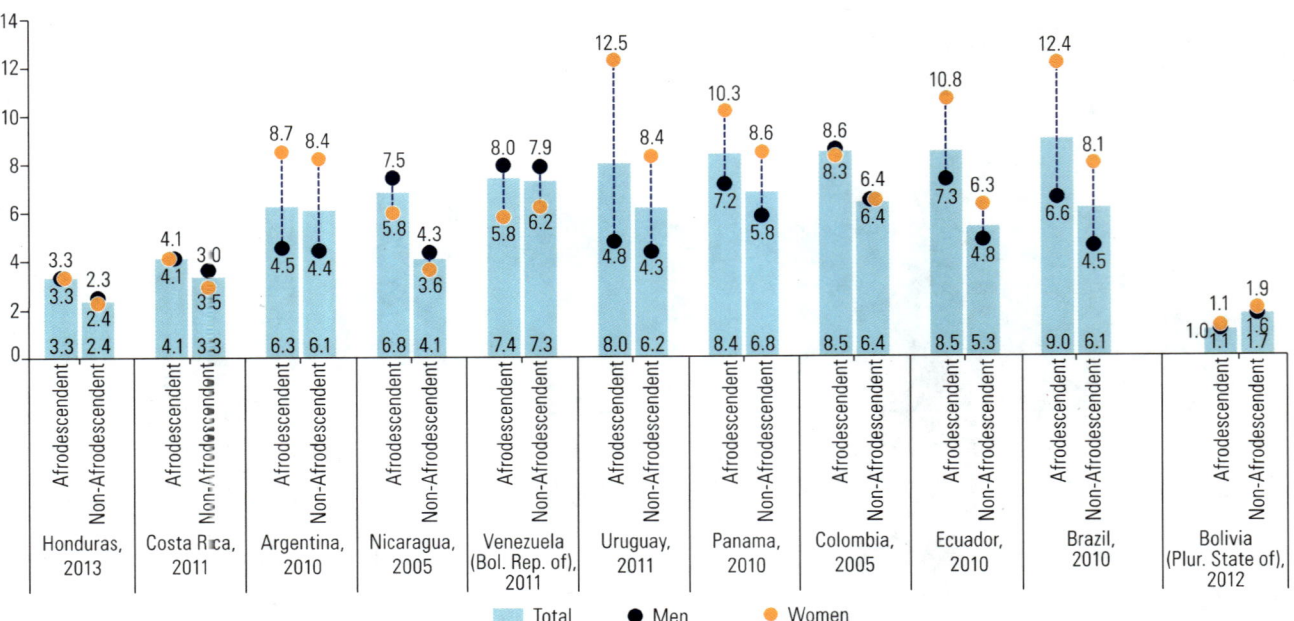

**Source:** Economic Commission for Latin America and the Caribbean (ECLAC), on the basis of special processing of census microdatabases using REDATAM 7.

**Note:**    The non-Afrodescendent population does not include people who self-identify as indigenous or whose ethnic-racial status is unknown.

As analysed in ECLAC (2016b), those data show the existence of a "dissonance" between the unemployment rate and the level of schooling attained; in other words, higher levels of schooling do not have the same employment effects for the different groups. This is a manifestation of the exclusion and discrimination against women that persists in the labour market (ECLAC, 2016f); and it is most pronounced in the case of Afrodescendent women.

## (c) Labour incomes

Just as levels of schooling do not translate automatically into possibilities of access to employment for Afrodescendants and others, both men and women, as analysed in ECLAC (2016b) and noted in the foregoing section in relation to unemployment rates, the same is true of one of the most important indicators of job quality, namely labour incomes.

Analysis of labour incomes per hour worked (see figure V.15) shows that Afrodescendent women are systematically lower on the income scale, even when education level is controlled for; and non-Afrodescendent men are in the best situations, as noted in ECLAC (2016b and 2016c). The data show the intertwining of ethno-racial and gender inequalities in the labour market, and also bear out what has been noted in many studies on gender-based income gaps: the gaps are larger the higher the levels of schooling.

Accordingly, among employed persons with the highest level of schooling (tertiary), Afrodescendent women receive an income equivalent to 58% of what non-Afrodescendent men receive. Afrodescendent men earn the equivalent of 73% of the income of non-Afrodescendent men; and non-Afrodescendent women earn 75% of the incomes of their male counterparts.

**Figure V.15**
Latin America (simple average of four countries): hourly income of the employed population aged 15 years or older, by level of schooling, gender and ethnic-racial status, 2014.
*(Dollars, in purchasing power parity, at 2010 prices)*

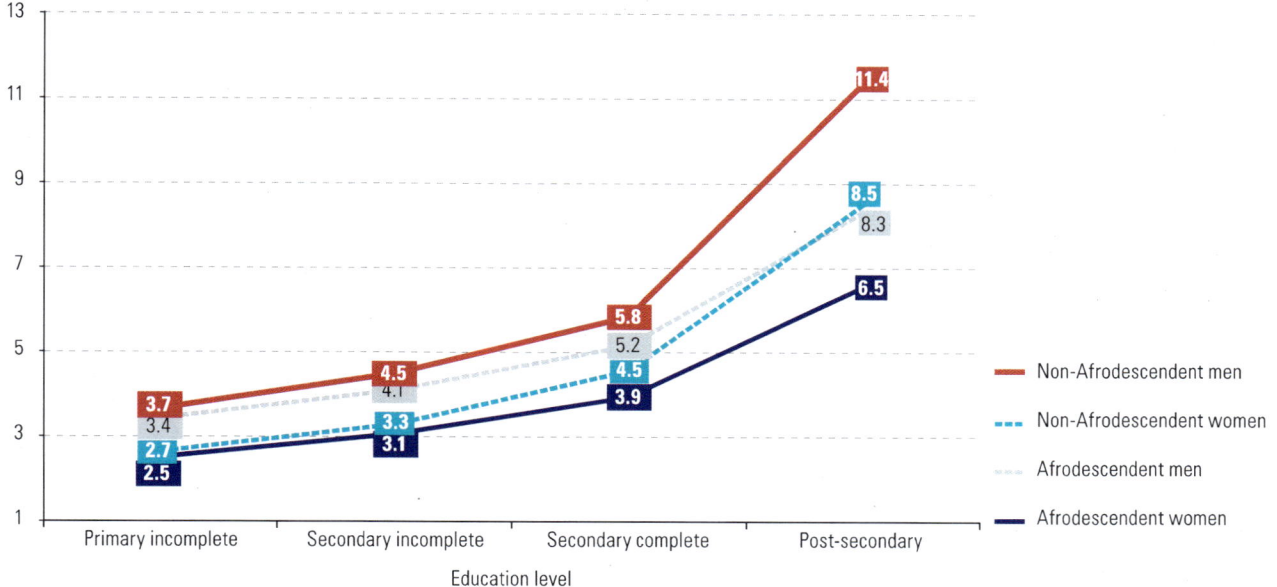

**Source**: Economic Commission for Latin America and the Caribbean (ECLAC), on the basis of special tabulations of data from household surveys conducted in the relevant countries.
**Note**:   The non-Afrodescendent population does not include people who self identify as indigenous or whose ethnic-racial status is unknown.

## (d) Paid female domestic workers: socioeconomic, gender and racial inequalities

One of the most telling pieces of evidence of the intertwining of socioeconomic, gender and racial/ethnic inequalities in society and in the labour market is the situation of paid female domestic workers. That is one of the occupations that generates most job sources for women in Latin America and the Caribbean, accounting for 13.7% of total female employment in urban areas (ILO, 2015).[21] Nonetheless, it is one of the activities least valued socially and economically, as expressed in low wages (female domestic workers gain on average equivalent of just over 50% of the income of all employed women),[22] poor working conditions and very low social protection coverage.[23] Moreover, those who work in this employment category in many countries are at a clear disadvantage in terms of labour regulations, compared to other wage-earners, on issues that are crucial for decent work, such as the minimum wage, maternity leave, access to social security, paid weekly rest period and vacations (ECLAC, 2007 and 2012a; Loyo and Velásquez, 2009; Valenzuela and Mora, 2009). This situation reflects explicit discriminatory patterns, based on the "argument that this work has particular features linked to the demands of care and social reproduction of households and families" (ECLAC, 2007), a characteristic which clearly does not prevent this occupation from being able to attain higher degrees of regulation to align it with other professional categories.

---

[21]   Weighted average, data for 2014.
[22]   Simple average for 18 countries, see annex table 22.1 (ECLAC, 2016a) [online] http://www.cepal.org/es/publicaciones/39965-panorama-social-america-latina-2015.
[23]   See (online) http://ilo.org/americas/publicaciones/notas-trabajo-dom%C3%A9stico-remunerado/lang--es/index.htm.

It is well known that the gender composition of domestic service (high proportion of women and very low participation by men) is one of the clearest manifestations of gender-based occupational segmentation. Many women who want to obtain a paid job, whether for the first time or otherwise, achieve this through that occupation, because the only experience similar to the labour market environment is the work they have done in their own homes (ECLAC, 2015).

Using 2010 census data from eight countries[24] that permits this occupational category to be distinguished, it was found that the number of people in domestic employment was upwards of 7 million, of whom 95% were women, and 71% lived in urban areas. Of those, just over 4.5 million (63%) were Afrodescendants.

Consideration of the ethno-racial dimension reveals a heterogeneous situation (see figure V.16): the proportion of domestic workers in total female employment varies from 3% (in the case of non-Afrodescendent women in Colombia) to about 20% (in the cases of Ecuador nationwide, in rural areas of Nicaragua and Panama, and in the urban parts of Brazil). In the case of employed Afrodescendent women, roughly one in every five is a paid domestic worker in Ecuador, in the urban areas of Brazil and in the rural areas of Costa Rica, Ecuador and Nicaragua. In three countries (Costa Rica, Honduras, Nicaragua and Panama, considering national totals), that proportion is 10% or above. The same is true of the urban areas of Costa Rica, Honduras and Nicaragua and the rural areas of Brazil.

**Figure V.16**
Latin America (8 countries): paid female domestic workers aged 15 years and older, by ethno-racial status and area of residence, around 2010
*(Percentages of total women employed in each zone of residency)*

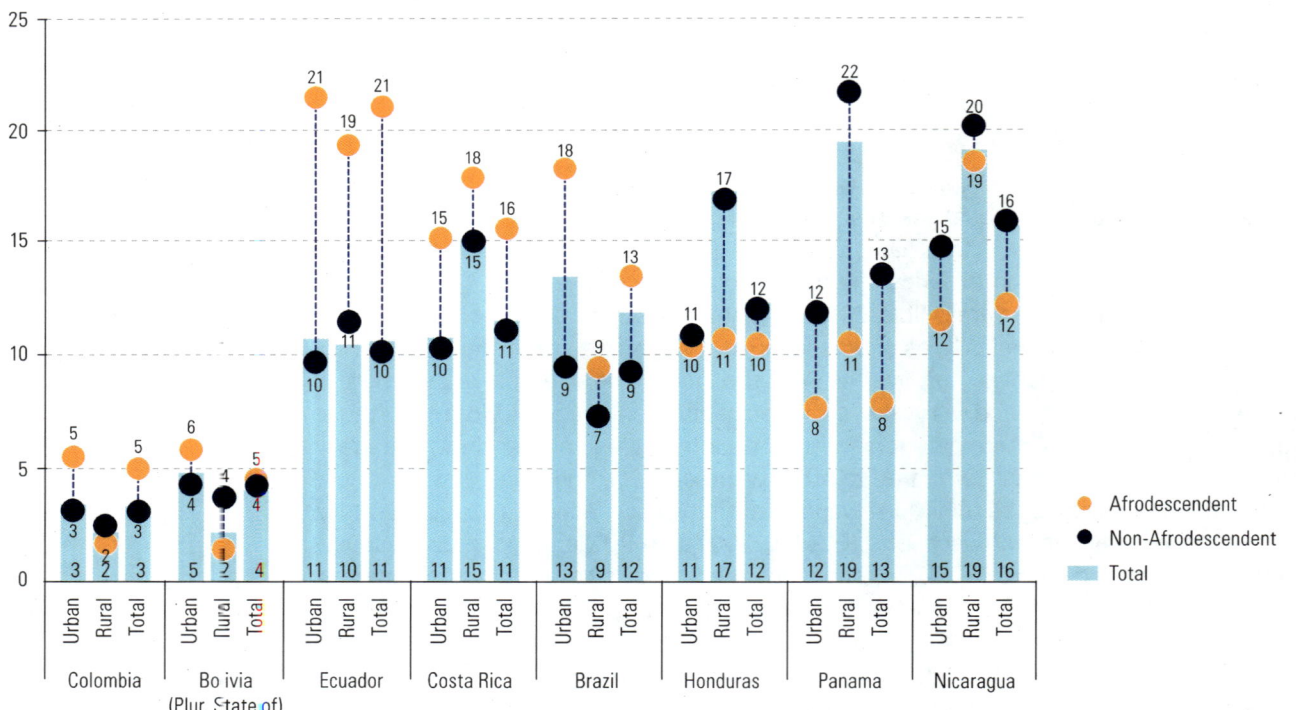

**Source**: Economic Commission for Latin America and the Caribbean (ECLAC), on the basis of special processing of census microdatabases using REDATAM 7.
**Note**:    The non-Afrodescendent population does not include people who self-identify as indigenous or whose ethnic-racial status is unknown. The countries are listed according to their ranking in the total.

---

24    Brazil, Colombia, Ecuador, Costa Rica. Honduras, Nicaragua, Panama and the Plurinational State of Bolivia.

That heterogeneity is also manifested when the proportion of paid domestic work in total female employment is compared between Afrodescendants and non-Afrodescendants: in four countries, a higher proportion of Afrodescendent women than non-Afrodescendent women are employed as domestic workers (Brazil, and Ecuador, where the ratio is almost double, and Colombia and Costa Rica); in another three countries (Honduras, Nicaragua and Panama), the proportion is smaller; and in the Plurinational State of Bolivia no differences are observed in the national totals. In urban areas (in comparison with national totals) the same trends basically are maintained, with the following differences: the gaps grow in Brazil and Ecuador; decrease slightly in Honduras, Nicaragua and Panama; and in the Plurinational State of Bolivia the proportion of Afrodescendent women in domestic work is slightly higher than the proportion of non-Afrodescendants.

## D. Institutional framework and policies for the Afrodescendent population

Most countries in the region have an institutional framework for matters pertaining to Afro-descendants or the promotion of racial equality. In addition, progress is being made on policies to prevent and combat racism and on policies to promote racial equality in various areas. Some countries have taken affirmative action, mainly in education and the labour market, but few have made progress in strengthening traditional communities —including cultural integrity rights and territorial rights in historically occupied land— and much remains to be done in terms of political participation. It is, therefore, necessary to redouble efforts to consolidate and these actions and ensure the continuity.

Over the last decade and a half, the region has seen sustained growth in the number of institutions responsible for social issues, reflecting a progressive institutionalization of social policies, particularly those on poverty reduction and social protection (ECLAC, 2016a). At the same time, government mechanisms responsible for Afrodescendent-related issues also saw growth and institutional strengthening, despite a number of setbacks. Currently, 14 Latin American countries have a government mechanism devoted to Afrodescendent affairs, which is the outcome of long-term advocacy by Afrodescendent social movements, other civil society organizations, governments and international organizations (Rangel, 2016).

The following paragraphs analyse those mechanisms on the basis of the main characteristics of their legal and regulatory frameworks and their organizational forms, and they review some of the most relevant policies implemented in the region to promote racial equality

## 1. Government mechanisms for promoting racial equality

The vast majority of government mechanisms for promoting racial equality were created after the year 2000, as part of the intensification of preparatory process for the World Conference against Racism, Racial Discrimination, Xenophobia and Related Intolerance, which was held in Durban (South Africa) in 2001; and, subsequently, to follow up and fulfil the commitments assumed by States in relation to Afrodescendent rights.

## (a) Legal and regulatory framework

The international legal framework for developing mechanisms to promote racial equality is based on international and regional human rights instruments that are fundamental for protecting the rights of Afrodescendants, particularly when this group is explicitly mentioned.[25]

In the case of national frameworks, anti-racism laws and those targeting Afrodescendent peoples have gained significant ground in Latin America, despite great heterogeneity between the different countries. Thirteen of the countries[26] have constitutional provisions against discrimination on the grounds of race or colour. In another seven,[27] the constitution does not refer to Afrodescendent populations, black populations, race or skin colour, although many of them do mention equality and non-discrimination. The constitution that refers most to Afrodescendent peoples is that of Ecuador (2008), which devotes a whole chapter exclusively to "black or Afro-Ecuadorian peoples"; the 2009 Constitution of the Plurinational State of Bolivia recognizes the Afrodescendent population for the first time. The 1998 Constitution of Brazil recognizes collective legal entities, establishes racism as a crime with no statute of limitations or right to bail (subject to a prison sentence), and recognizes Afrodescendants who occupy ancestral lands as having definitive ownership of those lands, so the State must issue them with land titles and safeguard historical documents and sites. The Constitution of Colombia also provides for collective ownership of the land. Lastly, several countries have framework laws specifically targeting the rights of Afrodescendent peoples.[28]

## (b) Organizational characteristics

Most of the region's racial equality promotion mechanisms (see table V.5) have legal backing and were created through laws or presidential decrees.[29]

Mechanisms for promoting racial equality have a variety of arrangements or institutional mechanisms that occupy different places in the State hierarchy: directorates, councils, institutes, secretariats, commissions, among others. The specific mechanism used is closely related to how governments address the crosscutting nature of ethnic-racial policies and the priority they give to the issue —given that those policies require articulation between the different government mechanisms, both sectorally and between the national, provincial and local levels.

As well as the type of authority, other key components of the organizational design for policy implementation are communication, coordination and linkaging between actors. For the development and implementation of government plans related to Afrodescendants, mechanisms for promoting racial equality are linked with different types of organization at various levels. This is fundamental, given the characteristics of this type of mechanism, which targets specific population groups with varied scopes of action.

---

[25]    The international instruments are: the ILO Convention on Discrimination (Employment and Occupation) Convention, 1958 (No. 111); the International Convention on the Elimination of All Forms of Racial Discrimination (1965); the International Covenant on Civil and Political Rights (1966); the International Covenant on Economic, Social and Cultural Rights (1966); the International Convention on the Suppression and Punishment of the Crime of Apartheid (1973); and the Indigenous and Tribal Peoples Convention, 1989 (No. 169). The regional conventions are: the American Convention on Human Rights (1969) and the Andean Charter for the Promotion and Protection of Human Rights (2002). See also ECLAC, 2016 and Rangel, 2016.

[26]    The Bolivarian Republic of Venezuela, Brazil, Colombia, Cuba, Dominican Republic, Ecuador, El Salvador, Honduras, Mexico, Nicaragua, Panama, Peru, the Plurinational State of Bolivia.

[27]    Argentina, Chile, Costa Rica, Dominican Republic, Guatemala, Haiti, Paraguay and Uruguay.

[28]    For example, in Brazil, the Racial Equality Statute 12.288 of 2010); in Colombia, the Negro Communities Law (Law No. 1993); in Ecuador, the Law on the Collective Rights of Negro or Afro Ecuadorian Peoples (Law No. 275 del 2006); in Bolivia, Law 234 of 2008; in Honduras, Law No. 82 of 2004; in Nicaragua, Law 445 of 2002; and, in Peru, el Supreme Decree No. 004 of 2015.

[29]    In Chile, although no specific institutional framework has been created, an Originating People's Department of the National Council of Culture and Arts also has responsibility for handling Afrodescendent affairs.

Table V.5
Latin America (15 countries): institutions responsible for issues related to the Afrodescendent population[a]

| Country | Name of institution | Legal instrument creating the institution | Institutional affiliation | Years |
|---|---|---|---|---|
| Argentina | National Institute against Discrimination, Xenophobia and Racism (INADI) | Law No. 24.515 | Ministry of Justice, Security and Human Rights | 1995 |
| Bolivia (Plurinational State of) | Committee against Racism and Discrimination | Law No. 045 | Directorate General of the Fight against Racism/Ministry of Cultures | 2010 |
| Brazil | Special Secretariat for Policies to Promote Racial Equality (SEPPIR) | Law No. 10.678 | Office of the President of the Republic[b] | 2003 |
| | National Secretariat for Policies to Promote Racial Equality (SEPPIR) | Provisional Measure 768 | Ministry of Human Rights | 2017 |
| Colombia | Office of Black, Afro-Colombian, Raizal and Palenquera Community Affairs | Law No. 70 | Ministry of the Interior and Justice | 1993 |
| | Populations Office (for all populations, including black communities) | Decree No. 4827 | Ministry of Culture | 2008 |
| Costa Rica | National Afro-Costa Rican Commission to Celebrate the Year of African Descent in Costa Rica and Related Activities Developed in Subsequent Years | Executive Decree No. 36.645 | Ministry of Foreign Relations and Worship | 2011 |
| | Commissioner of the Office of the President of the Republic for Afro-Costa Rican Community Affairs | Executive Decree No. 38.835 | Office of the President of the Republic | 2015 |
| Ecuador | Afro-Ecuadorian Development Corporation (CODAE) | Executive Decree No. 1747 | Office of the President of the Republic | 1998 |
| | National Council for Equality, Peoples and Nationalities | Executive Decree No. 686 | Office of the President of the Republic | 2015 |
| Guatemala | Presidential Commission against Discrimination and Racism against Indigenous Peoples in Guatemala-CODISRA | Government Decision No. 390 | Office of the President of the Republic | 2002 |
| Honduras | National Commission against Racial Discrimination, Racism, Xenophobia and Related Forms of Intolerance | Executive Decree | Secretariat of Governance and Justice | 2004 |
| | Directorate of Indigenous and Afro-Honduran peoples (DINAFROH) | Decree Law No. 203 | Secretariat of Development and Social Inclusion | 2010 |
| Mexico | National Council to Prevent Discrimination (CONAPRED) | Federal Law | Secretariat of Governance | 2003 |
| Nicaragua | National Commission for the Elimination of Racial Discrimination[c] | | | 2001 |
| | Secretariat for Indigenous and Afrodescendent Affairs (SAIA) | Presidential Decree No. 21 | Ministry of Foreign Relations | 2008 |
| Panama | National Commission against Discrimination | Law No. 16 | Ministry of the Office of the President of the Republic | 2002 |
| | National Council of Negro Ethnicity (CONEN). | Executive Decree No. 116 | Ministry of the Office of the President of the Republic | 2007 |
| | Secretariat of Negro Ethnicity | Draft Law No. 214 | Ministry of the Office of the President of the Republic | Presented in 2015 |
| Peru | National Institute for the Development of Andean, Amazonian and Afro-Peruvian Peoples (INDEPA) | Law No. 28.495 | Office of the President of the Council of Ministers | 2005 |
| | Directorate of Policies for the Afro-Peruvian Population | Law No. 29.565 | Vice Ministry of Interculturality of the Ministry of Culture | 2010 |
| Uruguay | Commission against Racism, Xenophobia and All Other Forms of Discrimination | Law No. 17.817 | Human Rights Directorate of the Ministry of Education and Culture | 2004 |
| Venezuela (Bolivarian Republic of) | Presidential Commission for the Prevention of All forms of Racial Discrimination | Decree No. 3.645 | Ministry of Popular Power for Culture | 2005 |
| | National Institute against Racial Discrimination (NCODIR) | Organic Law against Racial Discrimination | Office of the Vice President of the Republic | 2011 |

**Source**: Economic Commission for Latin America and the Caribbean (ECLAC).
[a] For each country, the first institution established and the one currently existing are given, in cases where they are not the same.
[b] Between 2008 and 2015 SEPPIR had ministerial rank.
[c] Never officially implemented or made operational.

The instability or weakness of the hierarchical position of those mechanisms not only endangers the stability of the effort to defend the rights of Afrodescendent people and combat racism and promote racial equality, but it also influences the resources that are allocated to them, and restricts their scope of action. Institutionally, these mechanisms usually report to the Office of the President of the Republic, or else to different ministries. Direct reporting to the Office of the President, together with greater authority, can improve the coordinating role, making racial equality policies more effective, as happened in Brazil with SEPPIR which, in addition, has been the only one of these entities to have had ministerial status (between 2008 and 2015).

The main objectives
of racial equality
mechanisms, as
defined in their
founding instruments,
are to coordinate
ethno-racial issues,
develop policies to
combat racism and
discrimination, and
promote racial equality
and an intercultural
citizenry.

The main objectives of racial equality mechanisms, as defined in their founding instruments, are to coordinate ethno-racial issues, develop policies to combat racism and discrimination, and promote racial equality and an intercultural citizenry. They do this by implementing policies aimed at guaranteeing the full exercise of the rights of individuals subject to ethno-racial discrimination, and at reducing the economic, social, political and cultural inequalities that these peoples experience.

The functions performed depend on the size and scope of action of the institution in question, which are also highly heterogeneous. Some of these mechanisms have fewer staff and a smaller budget than others; so they have more narrowly defined functions. The primary function is to formulate and implement policies to mainstream racial equality in public policies. Other functions include conducting research, providing free legal advice to victims of racism, assisting judicial entities, stimulating inclusion of the topic in school education materials, promoting culture, fostering participation in the formulation and execution of policies, disseminating State commitments to international regulations, promoting their fulfilment and monitoring their implementation.[30]

As can be seen, the mechanisms responsible for promoting racial equality are highly heterogeneous. They also form a world that is in constant advance and retreat, owing to their sensitivity to business cycles and the political cycles triggered by changes in governments, which have resulted in major changes in the legal instruments in the past few years. Most of these changes have strengthened race equality mechanisms and given them more power to affect policies, and greater stability and resources. Nonetheless, institutional setbacks can also occur as a result of the political context; recent developments with SEPPIR in Brazil being an example.[31]

In some cases, racial equality mechanisms are almost symbolic and never actually function effectively; or, if they do, they are not in a position to play a coordinating and influential role.[32] The legal form of government agencies on racial equality is crucial,

---

[30]    They may also fulfil specific functions such as, for example, in Argentina, verifying and reporting the presence of persons in the country who, during the Second World War, participated in deaths and persecutions motivated by race, religion, nationality or opinion, and propose extradition treaties see [online] http://www.inadi.gob.ar/.

[31]    In 2003, the Special Secretariat of Policies to Promote Racial Equality (SEPPIR) was created, with a direct link to the Office of the President of the Republic. The head of the Secretariat had the rank of Minister of State and participated in ministerial and interministerial meetings on an equal footing with other ministers. In 2008, SEPPIR gained ministerial status and held this until October 2015, when it was incorporated, as a secretariat, into the recently created Ministry for Women, Racial Equality and Human Rights. Between 2015 and 2017, SEPPIR was twice brought under a newly created ministry that was subsequently dissolved. Its current ministerial affiliation is to the Ministry of Human Rights. So many institutional changes in such a short period of time, and the budget cuts suffered, send worrying signals that consolidation and progress of the important work done by SEPPIR between 2003 and 2015 could be compromised. The work of SEPPIR had been outstanding in the region, in terms of formulating and implementing public policies to combat racism and promote racial equality in various areas, such as health, education, employment and work, poverty reduction, promotion of family farming and agrarian reform, recognition and titling of *quilombola* lands, research and establishment of indicator systems.

[32]    For example, in Nicaragua, the National Commission for the Elimination of Racial Discrimination was never made official and never functioned. See [online] http://www.acnur.org/t3/fileadmin/Documentos/BDL/2012/8795.pdf?view=1. In Panama, the Executive Secretariat of CONEN never had its own offices and operated with a minimal budget. See [online] http://tbinternet.ohchr.org/Treaties/CERD/Shared%20Documents/PAN/INT_CERD_NGO_PAN_76_9859_E.pdf. Moreover, the 2016 budget makes no reference to CONEN or to Afrodescendent peoples. (http://www.mef.gob.pa/es/direcciones/presupuestoNacion/Documents/pre_2016_Law.pdf).

because it affects their power to propose and influence policy design and implementation. Their legal standing also affects their scope of action and volume of resources and, hence, capacity to help reduce the racial discrimination in each country.

It is also necessary to analyse articulation between racial equality mechanisms and other institutions. Articulations with other government organizations occur both horizontally (with other ministries and institutions responsible for sectoral policies) and vertically (provinces and cities). The National System for the Promotion of Racial Equality (SINAPIR) of Brazil, for example, seeks to link the federal domain with state and municipal governments to implement policies targeting Afrodescendants.

Racial equality mechanisms also exist in other State entities, such as parliament and the judiciary. In the first case, this can occur through the creation of commissions and round tables (for example the Andean, Amazon and Afro-Peruvian Peoples and Environment and Ecology Commission, and the Afro-Peruvian Roundtable of the Congress of the Republic). In terms of links with the justice system, in Brazil the National Coordination for the Promotion of Equal Opportunities and Elimination of Discrimination at Work (COORDIGUALDADE) has been operating since 2002 in the Office of the Attorney General on Employment; in the subnational domain, the Office of the Attorney General of Pernambuco has been coordinating work to combat institutional racism since 2013. Lastly, there are several instances of coordination with social organizations and movements. For example, in 2014, Peru created the Round Table against Racism as part of the work of the National Human Rights Coordination Unit, which led a national campaign against racism, encompassing human rights organizations (Ardito, 2010); Brazil held three national conferences to promote racial equality (CONAPIR) between 2005 and 2013, with a wide-ranging process of citizen participation and consultation on public policies for racial equality, organized from the municipalities up to the national level.[33] Also in Brazil, the National Council to Promote Racial Equality (CNPIR) works with 19 civil society entities.[34]

Lastly, with respect to the fiscal dimension, the resources allocated to each government function can be considered an indicator of the priority assigned to it and, to some extent, they also reflect the impact of economic or political crises. In other words, business cycles can strongly favour or obstruct the allocation of resources and sustainability and institutional strengthening of the organizations and social policies (ECLAC, 2016a). This is also the case of racial equality policies, which can be affected by different circumstances. Nonetheless, despite the importance of the funding dimension for the sustainability of racial equality policies, a regional comparative study remains a pending task.

## 2.    Key policies targeting persons of African descent

In the last few years, several Latin American countries have been developing a set of policies to combat racism and promote racial equality. This has been in response to the Afrodescendent movement, a result of commitments undertaken internationally (either through the Durban Programme of Action or through international legal instruments signed previously), or a reflection of more decisive mainstreaming of the rights agenda and equality perspective by the governments of several countries. In addition, the powers and actions of racial equality mechanisms themselves have had an impact on the policy process.

Without claiming to be exhaustive, this section identifies key racial equality and anti-discrimination policies that have been developed in the last few years. The policies

---

[33]    On national conferences on public policies in Brazil, see Abramo, Araujo and Bolzon (2013 and 2014).

[34]    See [online] http://www.seppir.gov.br/articulacao/cnpir.

were classified in three groups, following the proposal by Jaccoud (2009): (i) policies to prevent and tackle racism; (ii) affirmative and enhancing actions —policies of positive discrimination and valuation of Afrodescendent culture and traditions; (iii) strengthening of traditional communities —those in the lands where the descendants of African slaves and former slaves live. A further group (iv) has been added on participation in decision-making and inclusion in national development plans.

## (a) Preventing and tackling racism

Over the last few years, Latin American countries have implemented several types of policy for preventing and tackling racism, ranging from laws to prohibit racist expression, and define the offence of racism, to the receiving of complaints, creation of observatories and conduct of tolerance training. Fourteen countries[35] have adopted legislation that prohibits racial discrimination and defines it as a crime punishable by imprisonment, which is consistent with the fact that 13 countries[36] have constitutional provisions against ethno-racial discrimination. Nonetheless, only eight countries have both provisions.[37] In addition, some countries have developed more comprehensive policies to eliminate racial discrimination, such as Ecuador, with the Plurinational Plan to Eliminate Racial Discrimination and Ethnic and Cultural Exclusion 2009-2012 (Ministry of Capital Coordination of Ecuador, 2009); Guatemala, with the Policy for Coexistence and Elimination of Racism and Racial Discrimination (Guatemala, Government of, 2006); and Brazil, with the National Plan to Promote Racial Equality (Brazil, Government of, 2009).

Another way of combating racism is by targeting territories with a larger Afrodescendent presence, high levels of violence and a large presence of certain groups at social risk (such as young people). Such is the case of Brazil, with the Living Youth (*Juventude Viva*) plan, launched in 2012. In education, Colombia has developed online training courses and workshops on recognition, justice and development for Afro-Colombians, targeting civil servants and the citizenry. Other initiatives include offices to receive complaints of racism, and provide victims with legal support (Argentina and the Plurinational State of Bolivia), observatories and platforms against discrimination (Argentina, Colombia and Peru), and local regulations.[38]

## (b) Affirmative and status enhancing actions

The affirmative actions undertaken in the region mainly involve quotas reserved for Afrodescendants in universities and jobs, in addition to the awarding of scholarships. On this issue, Brazil has been one of the countries to achieve the most progress, with quotas reserved for Afrodescendent and indigenous students at universities and public technical education institutes,[39] in addition to a scholarship programme in private universities[40] (some postgraduate programmes have also adopted a quota system). Scholarships have also been awarded for Afrodescendants to train for admission to a diplomatic career, and a 10% quota has been set for Afrodescendants in the first

---

[35]    Argentina, Brazil, Chile, Costa Rica, Cuba, Dominican Republic, Ecuador, El Salvador, Guatemala, Mexico, Nicaragua, Panama, Peru and Uruguay.

[36]    The Bolivarian Republic of Venezuela, Brazil, Colombia, Cuba, Dominican Republic, Ecuador, El Salvador, Honduras, Mexico, Nicaragua, Panama, Peru and the Plurinational State of Bolivia.

[37]    Brazil, Cuba, Ecuador, El Salvador, Mexico, Nicaragua, Panama and Peru,

[38]    The Metropolitan Social Council for the Elimination of Racial Discrimination (Quito, Ecuador) and, in Peru, municipal ordinances that prohibit any type of discrimination and mayoralties (Callao) that have powers to investigate discriminatory acts in job offers and labour relations.

[39]    Since 2001, several public universities have voluntarily adopted various modalities of quotas based on ethno-racial criteria; but under law 12.711 (2012) those criteria were standardized.

[40]    Law 11.096/2005, University for all Programme (PROUNI).

phase of the selection process for the diplomatic service (OAS, 2011). Quotas have been established in competitive selection tenders for public administration and state suppliers. Other countries, such as the Bolivarian Republic of Venezuela, Colombia, Peru, the Plurinational State of Bolivia and Uruguay, have also engaged in affirmative action.[41]

Appreciatory policies include the establishment of days celebrating African descent in 14 of the region's countries;[42] the teaching of African history and culture in schools;[43] and the implementation of policies that incorporate ancestral visions and health practices and which target diseases that particularly affect Afrodescendants, among other things.[44] The acknowledgement of Afrodescendent heroes and recognition of Afrodescendent cultural practices as historical heritage —as in the Plurinational State of Bolivia— is another important step. Similar steps have been taken by Nicaragua, with the declaration of Garífuna culture as national heritage; Panama, which has drawn attention to the contribution of Afrodescendent culture to society; and Peru, which has officially acknowledged the Afrodescendent contribution to the national identity and defence of the nation.

## (c) Strengthening of traditional Afrodescendent communities

Traditional Afrodescendent communities are concentrated in areas that were historically occupied by individuals fleeing from slavery (known as *cimarrones*).[45] Policies for strengthening these communities are not widespread, although there are examples in Brazil and Colombia. The Brazilian Constitution recognizes definitive titles of ownership of the occupied land for individuals resident in *quilombos*; and the State is required to issue their property titles. Nonetheless, it was not until 2003 that the rights of *quilombola* communities were regulated.[46] Then, in 2004, the *Brasil Quilombola* programme, designed to consolidate a comprehensive policy approach, began to be implemented. In Colombia, Decree No. 1.745 of 1995 regulates recognition of the right to collective ownership of Afro-Colombian land and land title; and the Directorate of Black Community Affairs (DACN) provides assistance to communities, support in dispute settlement and training on rights.

Other examples are Ecuador and the Plurinational State of Bolivia. In the latter, the National Agrarian Reform Institute (INRA) has awarded agrarian titles to hundreds of farmers and hundreds of Afro-Bolivian and Aymaran families; and the 2006 Community Agrarian Land Reform Act benefits them in the ongoing agrarian revolution. In Ecuador, the Law on Collective Rights of Afro-Ecuadorian peoples (2006) grants rights over ancestral land.

[41]   In the Plurinational State of Bolivia, an annual quota of 20% was set for indigenous and Afro-Bolivian students in higher education teacher training institutions, to which they can be admitted without a prior examination provided they have a certain school average. In Colombia there are non-reimbursable loans for Afrodescendent students in higher education (Decree No. 1.627 of 1996); and the mayoralty of Bogota gives preferential treatment to Afrodescendants. In Peru, some universities and higher technical institutes have differential admission mechanisms. Uruguay allocates 8% of jobs in state organizations and at least 8% of student scholarships to Afrodescendants (Law No. 19122 of 2013). The Bolivarian Republic of Venezuela has quotas and scholarships for Afrodescendants in training institutes (Decree No. 3645 of 2009).

[42]   Argentina, the Bolivarian Republic of Venezuela, Brazil, Colombia, Costa Rica, Ecuador, Guatemala, Honduras, Nicaragua, Panama, Paraguay, Peru, the Plurinational State of Bolivia and Uruguay.

[43]   For example, in the Bolivarian Republic of Venezuela, Brazil, Colombia and Uruguay. With regard to languages, in Guatemala, Garífuna is an official language and a compulsory subject in public and private schools; in Nicaragua, this language must be taught in schools in parts of the country where it is in official uses.

[44]   Examples include the following: in Brazil, the National Integrated Health Policy of the Black Population; in Ecuador, the Afro-Ecuadorian People's Collective Rights Act, which recognizes the right to traditional health practices; in Nicaragua, legislation that protects and promotes traditional Afrodescendent medicine; in Peru, an intercultural dimension has been incorporated into health services, valuing Afrodescendent practices and recognizing specific diseases; in addition, a start was made on including ethnic affiliation in administrative records, and an intercultural health policy was established.

[45]   These communities are known as *quilombos* in Brazil.

[46]   Article 2 of Decree 4887 defines *quilombola* communities as ethno-racial groups, under self-identification criteria, with their own historical tradition, endowed with specific territorial relations, and a presumed negro ancestry related to the resistance to historical oppression. This definition is in keeping with that of ILO Convention 169, which permits identification of collective rights for Afrodescendants.

### (d) Participation in decision-making and inclusion in development plans

Participation in decision-making and inclusion in development plans are crucial for overcoming racial inequalities. When decisions on development planning are taken on a participatory basis, the policies ultimately implemented tend to be more effective.

There are several Afrodescendent participation mechanisms at the regional level. The Inter-American Commission on Human Rights (IACHR) has the Rapporteurship on the Rights of Persons of African Descent and against Racial Discrimination; in the Organization of American States (OAS), the Secretariat for Access to Rights and Equity monitors and tracks the implementation of the Plan of Action of the Decade of African Descent in the Americas (2016-2025). The Black Parliament of the Americas was set up in 2005[47] and, since that year, the Ibero-American Secretariat (SEGIB) has recognized the rights of Afrodescendent people. In various Ibero-American declarations,[48] issued at the annual meetings with government representatives, it has been agreed to guarantee those rights in several domains.

At the subregional level, in the framework of the Andean Integration System, in 2011 the Afrodescendent Peoples Roundtable of the Andean Community of Nations was created; the Central American Integration System (SICA) has the Permanent Commission of Indigenous and Afrodescendent Peoples of the Central American Parliament (PARLACEN); and, in 2015, the Southern Common Market (MERCOSUR) approved the creation of the Meeting of Authorities on Afrodescendent Rights (RAFRO).[49] These mechanisms involve participation by representatives of Afrodescendent civil society organizations in various countries.[50]

In the case of national participation mechanisms, the Plurinational State of Bolivia has participatory planning processes with Afrodescendent organizations; Brazil holds National Conferences for the Promotion of Racial Equality (CONAPIR),[51] which are a consultation mechanism between the government and civil society; Colombia created a Vice-Ministry for Participation and Equal Rights, with jurisdiction on ethnic issues, and has the Special National Constituency for Black Communities and a Special Constituency in the Chamber of Representatives at the parliamentary level, in addition to consultative commissions at the departmental, district and sectoral levels; Ecuador has the Secretariat of Peoples, Social Movements and Citizen Participation, as well as National Councils for Equality, with membership equally split between civil society and State representatives, one of which is devoted to peoples and nationalities. Peru adopted a National Policy for Mainstreaming the Inter-Cultural Approach in 2015 (Ministry of Culture of Peru, 2015), with participation by Afro-Peruvian organizations; and the Bolivarian Republic of Venezuela created the Afrodescendent Communities Liaison Office. In Colombia, Ecuador and the Plurinational State of Bolivia, Afrodescendants are entitled to prior consultation for exploitation of the natural resources located in their territories.

In terms of inclusion in development plans, in Brazil Afrodescendants have been included in multi-year investment plans since 2004. In Colombia, development plans

> Participation in decision-making and inclusion in development plans are crucial for overcoming racial inequalities. When decisions on development planning are taken on a participatory basis, the policies ultimately implemented tend to be more effective.

---

[47]   In the context of the International Decade for People of African Descent, in 2016 the fifth meeting of Afrodescendent Parliamentarians and Political Leaders of the Americas and the Caribbean was held, with the aim of defining the Afrodescendent political agenda to 2025 ("Recognition, justice and development"), and also mechanisms for monitoring the actions that governments should promote to reduce the ethnic-racial development gaps. This inter-parliamentary meeting, which was held in Costa Rica (https://www.facebook.com/V-Encuentro-de-Parlamentarios-Parlamentarias-y-L%C3%ADderes-Afrodescendientes-155129984911989/?ref=page_internal), launched a Declaration of Women Parliamentarians and Leaders. See [online] https://amuAfroc.files.wordpress.com/2016/09/declaratoria-final_dialogo-de-parlamentarias-y-lideresas_agosto2016-final.pdf.

[48]   See the declarations made by the Ibero-American Culture Conferences held in Córdoba (Spain) (2005), Montevideo (2006), Valparaíso (Chile) (2007), San Salvador (2008), Lisbon (2009), Buenos Aires (2010), Asunción (2011), Salamanca (Spain) (2012), Panama (2013), Mexico City (2014) and Cartagena de Indias (Colombia) (2016) [online] http://www.oei.es/acercade/declaraciones.

[49]   See [online] http://www.mercosur.int/innovaportal/file/6956/1/dec_009-2015_es_rAfro.pdf.

[50]   For further information on Afrodescendent organizations in Latin America, see Rangel, 2009; Pascale, (undated) and García, 2016.

[51]   The most recent conference, held in 2013, mobilized around 48,000 people in 500 municipal conferences, 26 state-level conferences and three meetings for traditional communities (SEPPIR, 2014 in Rangel, 2016).

have been prepared with representation from black communities since 1994. In Costa Rica, the National Plan for Afrodescendants 2015-2018, Recognition, Justice and Development, aims to reduce disparities in living conditions with respect to the rest of the population (Costa Rica, Government of, 2015). In Guatemala, the National Policy for the Advancement and Comprehensive Development of Women (PNEDIM) and the Equal Opportunities Plan 2008-2023 (Guatemala, Government of, 2009) includes the comprehensive development of Garífuna women among its objectives; in Peru, the National Human Rights Plan 2014-2016 includes a specific chapter on Afrodescendants; and the National Development Plan for the Afro-Peruvian Population (PLANDEPA-2015-2024) forms part of the country's commitment in the framework of the International Decade of African Descent. Lastly, in Uruguay, the Action Plan for the Rights of Afrodescendants (2010-2015) aimed to bridge the racial gap in Montevideo.

Box V.5
Afrodescendent women's social movement and effect on institutionalization

Afrodescendent women are still too underrepresented in institutional decision-making processes and their participation does not reflect their demographic weight in societies. Nonetheless, they have a long track record of social and political participation, with societal leadership historically linked to the fight for better living conditions, such as access to drinking water, efficient electric energy, construction of community centres, health centres, public safety, among many other demands that contribute to the welfare of their communities.

Meetings of Afrodescendent women, both nationally and regionally, have helped to strengthen their cultural identity from an intersectional perspective and to develop organizational identities in the region. This has done much to generate and increase the political visibility of collective women's leaderships vis-à-vis the region's States.

The fruitful debates held on institutions and public policies for the equality and autonomy of Afrodescendent women in civil society produce, albeit more slowly than desired, institutional responses that lead to innovations in public policy, as new subjects of law are recognized and, in turn, new social and political actors are integrated into certain areas of development, thus affecting the generation of specific public policies in different sectors. Nonetheless, as analysed in this chapter, this institutional framework is still insufficient and displays uneven progress in countries in the region that have a larger Afrodescendent presence.

A review of progress made in constructing a gender institutional framework for Afrodescendent women shows that it has been slow and sparse in the region. Analysis of the experience of lobbying for public policy impact in Brazil shows links with the history of women's rights since the 1980s. It was as part of the process relating to the Third World Conference on Women, held in 1985 in Nairobi, that the Council of State for Women began to consider the situation of black women (Carneiro and Santos, 1985). It was also during this period that black women were integrated into the Council of State for Women, through the Black Women's Commission, and in 1988, the National Council for Women's Rights (CNDM) created a department coordinating the black women's programme. This process was linked with various state-level meetings of black women, leading to the First National Meeting of Black Women in 1988, with representatives from 19 Brazilian states (Carneiro, 1993). Nearly 15 years later, in 2003, the National Secretariat for Policies to Promote Racial Equality was created; and an articulated process was launched to address the priorities set in the National Plan on Policies for Women, the National Plan to Promote Racial Equality, and the Racial Equality Statute, working in coordination with a special Secretariat for Policies for Women.

In Uruguay, the Afrodescendent women's movement has two decades of experience of public policy efforts. In 1992, the first meeting of Afrodescendent women was held, with the aim of drawing attention to the multiple discrimination endured by women in Uruguay. It was not until 13 years later, in 2005, that the Afrodescendent Women's Department was created in the National Institute of Women (INMUJERES). Public policy influence is achieved mainly at the sectoral level, and women leaders of the Afrodescendent community have succeeded, based on an initiative of the UFAMA cooperative in the south of Montevideo, in obtaining a joint resolution issued by the Ministry of Housing, the Office of the Governor of Montevideo and Afro-Uruguayan women's cooperatives, for the construction of housing and cultural centres for women breadwinners in restored areas of the city's residential neighbourhoods.

**Source**: Economic Commission for Latin America and the Caribbean (ECLAC), "Mujeres Afrodescendientes en América Latina y el Caribe. Deudas de igualdad", Santiago, unpublished, 2017; N. Iraci Silva (ed.), "Mulher negra", *Cadernos Geledés*, No 4, São Paulo, Geledés/Black Women's Institute, November 1993 [online] http://www.geledes.org.br/wp-content/uploads/2015/05/Mulher-Negra.pdf; S. Carneiro, "A Organização Nacional das Mulheres Negras e as perspectivas políticas", "Mulher negra", N. Iraci Silva (ed.), Op. cit.; Presidencia de la República Oriental del Uruguay, "Sinergia y tenacidad impulsaron la concreción del proyecto Cooperativa UFAMA al Sur", 23 June 2010 [online] http://archivo.presidencia.gub.uy/sci/noticias/2010/06/2010062308.htm; Building and Social Housing Foundation (BSHF), "Cooperative UFAMA al Sur, Montevideo" [online] https://www.bshf.org/es/premios-mundiales-del-habitat/ganadores-y-finalistas/cooperative-ufama-al-sur-montevideo/; Fundación Habitat Colombia [online]http://americalatinagenera.org/newsite//images/649_cooperativaufamaalsur.pdf.

# E.   Conclusions

This chapter has aimed to contribute to the recognition of Afrodescendent persons in Latin America, one of the fundamental pillars for progress in guaranteeing their rights. The statistical visibility of Afrodescendants in official information systems is both a practical expression and a condition of such recognition, and has been a systematic and growing demand from Afrodescendent organizations. In Latin America, these demands have received significant responses in the current century, mainly in the last decade. Nonetheless, much remains to be done in terms of producing information with an ethno-racial status breakdown.

The figures obtained from recent censuses show that the Afrodescendent population extends throughout Latin America. The tremendous demographic and territorial diversity between and within the countries of the region is a result of the processes arising from nearly 400 years of slavery of African people and resistance by them and their descendants. Although history and national context have also shaped socioeconomic heterogeneity between Afrodescendent groups, the information presented here shows that ethno-racial inequality continues to be a deep-rooted structural feature of Latin American societies and an expression of the discrimination and racism from which the region suffers. Although the region has made significant progress in reducing income inequality, Afrodescendent populations are still overrepresented among the poor, at least in the four countries with data available.

The information also reveals the systematic presence of ethno-racial inequalities in the different spheres of development and individual well-being, such as health, education and work. In most countries, Afrodescendent populations display higher rates of infant and maternal mortality than non-Afrodescendants, as well as poorer access to education, particularly at the secondary and higher levels. The intertwining of ethno-racial and gender inequalities shows that, although their education levels have risen, Afrodescendent women earn lower labour incomes, have higher rates of unemployment and are engaged proportionately more in domestic work, whether paid or unpaid.

The general trends described have their exceptions, however. In some of the indicators presented in this chapter, Afrodescendent populations display a better situation than non-Afrodescendants, particularly in a few Central American countries such as Honduras, Nicaragua and Panama. Argentina also fits this pattern. Several hypotheses can be put forward for this. One relates to potential biases in ethno-racial self-identification in the data sources, particularly in countries that included self-identification for the first time in the 2010 census round. Biases occur not only because of the conceptual and methodological approaches used in formulating the questions, but also because of other aspects of the census process, such as training, awareness-raising, and participation by Afrodescendent people, to mention a few of the most relevant. another, different reading refers to historical processes that determine who Afrodescendent men and women are in each country today. In the Central American countries, there is at least one distinction between the so-called "colonial blacks" and "Antillean blacks" or "English blacks" (as they are called in Panama and Honduras, respectively). Although both groups descend from enslaved Africans, they have suffered the impacts of slavery differently, and they also have different positions in the social structures that were formed during the creation and consolidation of the nation States. Nonetheless, a more in-depth analysis is needed of the Afrodescendent situation in each socio-historical context, as well as better evaluation of measurements to improve their quality.

Beyond the possible explanations for these trends, the incorporation of ethno-racial identification in censuses and, to a lesser extent, in certain household surveys, has provided new and important evidence, albeit with certain limitations. For example, the figures show consistently that inequality disadvantaging Afrodescendent populations is much deeper than inequality in the other direction. The analysis of inequalities also shows that, even in countries that have the highest levels of well-being at the national level —according to their social indicators— ethno-racial disparities have persisted and even worsened, such as in Uruguay. In addition, in countries that have managed to sustain universal or affirmative-action policies over time, these inequalities tend to decline significantly —as shown in Cuba or Brazil, in terms of young Afrodescendants' access to universities.

The chapter also shows that in the last few decades, the countries have made progress, albeit in different degrees, in creating regulatory and institutional frameworks for combating racial discrimination, and also for applying affirmative action and inclusion policies with an ethnic-racial approach. Afrodescendent organizations continue to fight and lobby to close implementation gaps between regulatory frameworks and the daily realities of Afrodescendent people, who face numerous difficulties in effectively exercising their rights.

The foregoing shows the urgent need to strengthen the generation of knowledge from multiple dimensions of each problem. A necessary condition for this is the inclusion of ethno-racial self-identification in the various data sources, following the international and regional recommendations on the subject. Moreover, broader and more comprehensive approaches are needed, combining conventional with alternative sources, including qualitative methodologies. This knowledge should be an input for policy design, and is a condition for fulfilling the priority measures of the Montevideo Consensus on Population and Development, and one of the central aims of the 2030 Agenda for Sustainable Development, to "leave no one behind". In order to expand the coverage and raise the quality of social services, strategies are needed to guarantee full participation by Afrodescendent populations. Such strategies must consider the variety of situations that exist between and within countries, as well as overlaps with other dimensions of social inequality in Latin America, such as inequalities related to gender, life cycle, territory and migratory status. For example, some Afrodescendent communities have worldviews, understandings of reality and particular languages that should form the basis of programmes and policies framed in the recognition and guarantee of their rights.

The 2030 Agenda for Sustainable Development and the International Decade for People of African Descent represent both a major challenge and a great opportunity. International standards exist on the rights of Afrodescendent peoples, and achievements have been made in terms of recognition in all countries of the region, to a greater or lesser extent. It is now crucial to build on this by consolidating those recognition processes and designing and implementing policies for practical progress in reducing gaps and guaranteeing the rights of Afrodescendent persons, as has been agreed at the global level. This imperative arises from the principle of universalism that is difference-sensitive and from the urgency of shedding the culture of privilege in favour of a culture of equality.

# Bibliography

Abramo, L., A. Araujo and A. Bolzon (2014), "La importancia de los procesos participativos: la experiencia de las conferencias nacionales de políticas públicas de Brasil", *Pactos sociales para una protección más inclusiva*, Seminarios y Conferencias series, No. 76 (LC/L.3820), Santiago, Economic Commission for Latin America and the Caribbean (ECLAC).

Agudelo, C. (2012), "Los garifuna. Múltiples identidades de un pueblo Afrodescendiente de América Central", *Las poblaciones Afrodescendientes de América Latina y el Caribe. Pasado, presente y perspectivas desde el siglo XXI*, Universidad Nacional de Tres de Febrero/Universidad Nacional de Córdoba.

Amarante, A. and R. Arim (eds.) (2015), *Desigualdad e informalidad: un análisis de cinco experiencias latinoamericanas*, Libros de la CEPAL, No. 133 (LC/G.2637-P), Santiago, Economic Commission for Latin America and the Caribbean (ECLAC).

Antón, J. (2011), "Panorama general de los Afrodescendientes", *Pueblos Afrodescendientes y derechos humanos*, Ministry of Justice, Human Rights and Worship of Ecuador/Office of the United Nations High Commissioner for Human Rights.

____(2010), "Territorios ancestrales Afroecuatorianos: una propuesta para el ejercicio de la autonomía territorial y los derechos colectivos", *La autonomía a debate: autogobierno indígena y Estado plurinacional en América Latina*, Latin American Faculty of Social Sciences (FLACSO).

____(2007), "Afroecuatorianos: reparaciones y acciones afirmativas", *Afro-reparaciones: memorias de la esclavitud y justicia reparativa para negros, Afrocolombianos y raizales*, C. Mosquera Rosero-Labbé and L. Claudio Barcelos (eds.), Bogotá, National University of Colombia, Faculty of Human Sciences.

Antón, J., V. Avendaño and D. Tapia (eds.) (2011), *Pueblos Afrodescendientes y derechos humanos*, Ministry of Justice, Human Rights and Worship of Ecuador/Office of the United Nations High Commissioner for Human Rights.

Antón, J. and others (2009), "Afrodescendientes en América Latina y el Caribe: del reconocimiento estadístico a la realización de derechos", *Población y Desarrollo series*, No. 87 (LC/L.3045-P), Santiago, Economic Commission for Latin America and the Caribbean (ECLAC).

Ardito, W. (2010), "La experiencia de la mesa contra el Racismo" [online] http://studylib.es/doc/197079/el-movimiento-contra-el-racismo-en-el-per%C3%BA.

Bárcena, A. and W. Byanyima (2016), "Latin America is the world's most unequal region. Here's how to fix it", Santiago, Economic Commission for Latin America and the Caribbean (ECLAC) [online] http://www.cepal.org/en/articles/2016-latin-america-worlds-most-unequal-region-heres-how-fix-it.

Borges, R. (2004), "Desigualdades raciais e políticas de inclusão racial: um sumário da experiência brasileira recente", *Políticas Sociales series*, No. 82 (LC/L.2082-P), Santiago, Economic Commission for Latin America and the Caribbean (ECLAC).

Brah, A. (2013), "Pensando en y a través de la interseccionalidad", *La interseccionalidad en debate*, M. Zapata Galindo, S. García Peter, J. Chan de Avila (orgs.), Berlin, Institute for Latin American Studies (LAI), Freie Universität Berlin.

Brazil, Government of (2009), *Plano Nacional de Promoção da Igualdade Racial-PLANAPIR*, Brasilia.

Carneiro, S. and T. Santos (1985), *Mulher negra*, São Paulo, Nobel/Consejo Estadual de la Condición Femenina.

Contreras, D. and S. Gallegos (2007), "Descomponiendo la desigualdad salarial en América Latina: ¿una década de cambios?", *Estudios Estadísticos y Prospectivos series*, No. 59 (LC/L.2789-P), Santiago, Economic Commission for Latin America and the Caribbean (ECLAC).

Coordinating Ministry of Heritage of Ecuador (2009), *Plan Plurinacional para Eliminar la Discriminación Racial y la Exclusión Étnica y Cultural 2009-2012*, Quito.

Costa Rica, Government of (2015), *Plan Nacional Para Afrodescendientes 2015-2018. Reconocimiento, Justicia y Desarrollo*, San José.

Del Popolo, F., M. López and M. Acuña (2009), *Juventud indígena y Afrodescendiente en América Latina: inequidades sociodemográficas y desafíos de políticas*, Madrid, Ibero-American Youth Organization (OIJ)/Economic Commission for Latin America and the Caribbean (ECLAC).

Del Popolo, F. and S. Schkolnik (2013), "Pueblos indígenas y Afrodescendientes en los censos de población y vivienda de América Latina: avances y desafíos en el derecho a la información", *Notas de Población*, No. 97 (LC/G.2598-P), Santiago, Economic Commission for Latin America and the Caribbean (ECLAC).

ECLAC (Economic Commission for Latin America and the Caribbean) (2017), *Demographic Observatory of Latin America. Population Projections* (LC/PUB.2017/3-P), Santiago.

_____(2016a), *Social Panorama of Latin America 2015* (LC/G.2691-P), Santiago.

_____(2016b), *The social inequality matrix in Latin America* (LC/G.2690), Santiago.

_____(2016c), *Inclusive Social Development: The next generation of policies for overcoming poverty and reducing inequality in Latin America and the Caribbean* (LC.L/4056/Rev.1), Santiago.

_____(2016d), *Economic Survey of Latin America and the Caribbean, 2016* (LC/G.2684-P), Santiago.

_____(2016e), "Interrelationship of the autonomies" [online] http://oig.cepal.org/en/autonomies/interrelationship-autonomies.

_____(2016f), "The wage gap persists between men and women", *Notes for Equality*, No. 18, Gender Equality Observatory for Latin America and the Caribbean [online] http://oig.cepal.org/sites/default/files/note_18_wage_gap_.pdf.

_____(2016g), *Equality and women's autonomy in the sustainable development agenda* (LC/G.2686(CRM.13/3)), Santiago.

_____(2016h), *40 years of the regional gender agenda* (LC/G.2682), Santiago.

_____(2015a), *Social Panorama of Latin America, 2014* (LC/G.2635-P), Santiago.

_____(2015b), *Latin America and the Caribbean: looking ahead after the Millennium Development Goals. Regional monitoring report on the Millennium Development Goals in Latin America and the Caribbean* (LC/G.2646), Santiago.

_____(2014a), *Guaranteeing indigenous people's rights in Latin America Progress in the past decade and remaining challenges. Summary* (LC/L.3893/Rev.1), Santiago.

_____(2014b), *Compacts for Equality: Towards a Sustainable Future* (LC/G.2586(SS.35/3), Santiago.

_____(2014c), *Social Panorama of Latin America, 2014* (LC/G.2635-P), Santiago.

_____(2013a), "Mujeres indígenas en América Latina: dinámicas demográficas y sociales en el marco de los derechos humanos", *Project Documents* (LC/W.558), Santiago.

_____(2013b), "Santo Domingo Consensus", *Report of the twelfth session of the Regional Conference on Women in Latin America and the Caribbean* (LC/L.3789), Santiago.

_____(2013c), *Demographic Observatory 2012* (LC/G.2569-P), Santiago.

_____(2013d), *Montevideo Consensus on Population and Development* (LC/L.3697), Santiago [online] http://repositorio.cepal.org/bitstream/handle/11362/21835/S20131037_es.pdf?sequence=4.

_____(2012a), *Social Panorama of Latin America, 2012* (LC/G.2557-P), Santiago.

_____(2012b), *Eslabones de la desigualdad: heterogeneidad estructural, empleo y protección social* (LC/G.2539), Santiago.

_____(2012c), *Structural Change for Equality: An Integrated Approach to Development* (LC/G.2524(SES.34/3)), Santiago.

_____(2011), *Social Panorama of Latin America, 2010* (LC/G.2481), Santiago.

_____(2010), *Time for Equality: Closing Gaps, Opening Trails* (LC/G.2432(SES.33/3)), Santiago.

_____(2009), "Censos 2010 y la inclusión del enfoque étnico: hacia una construcción participativa con pueblos indígenas y Afrodescendientes de América Latina", *Seminarios y Conferencias series*, N° 57 (LC/L.3095-P), Santiago.

_____(2007), *Women's contribution to equality in Latin America and the Caribbean* (LC/L.2738-P), Santiago.

_____(2004), "Poverty and inequality from a gender perspective", *Social Panorama of Latin America, 2002-2003* (LC/G.2209-P), Santiago.

_____(2000), *The Equity Gap: A Second Assessment*, Santiago.

ECLAC/ILO (Economic Commission for Latin America and the Caribbean/International Labour Organization) (2014), "Employment formalization and labour income distribution", *The Employment Situation in Latin America and the Caribbean*, No. 11 (LC/L.3904), Santiago, October.

ECLAC/UNFPA (Economic Commission for Latin America and the Caribbean/United Nations Population Fund) (2011), Juventud Afrodescendiente en América Latina: realidades diversas y derechos (in)cumplidos, Santiago, October [online] http://www.unfpa.org.br/Arquivos/informe_Afro.pdf.

ECLAC/UNICEF (Economic Commission for Latin America and the Caribbean/United Nations Children's Fund) (2012), "Pobreza infantil en pueblos indígenas y Afrodescendientes de América Latina", *Project Documents* (LC/W.477), Santiago.

Ecuadorian Ombudsman's Service (2012), *El pueblo Afrodescendiente en el Ecuador. Informe temático*, Quito.

García, S. (2016), *Organizaciones de la población Afrodescendiente de América Latina 2016*, Madrid, Ibero-American Secretariat (SEGIB) [online] http://segib.org/wp-content/uploads/Organizaciones-Poblacion-Afrodescendiente-ESP-Baja.pdf.

Guatemala, Government of (2009), *Política Nacional de Promoción y Desarrollo Integral de las Mujeres —PNPDIM— y Plan de Equidad de Oportunidades —PEO-2008-2023*, Presidential Secretariat for Women (SEPREM).

___(2006), *Política para la Convivencia y la Eliminación del Racismo y la Discriminación Racial*, Guatemala.

Guimarães, J.R.S. (2012), *Perfil do trabalho decente no Brasil: um olhar sobre as Unidades da Federação durante a segunda metade da década de 2000*, Brasilia, International Labour Organization (ILO).

Hooker, A. (2012), "Las poblaciones Afrodescendientes en Nicaragua", *Las poblaciones Afrodescendientes de América Latina y el Caribe. Pasado, presente y perspectivas desde el siglo XXI*, Universidad Nacional de Tres de Febrero/Universidad Nacional de Córdoba.

Hurtado-Saa, T., R. Rosas-Vargas and A. Valdés-Cobos (2012), "Servicios de salud, discriminación y condición étnica/racial: un estudio de caso de la problemática en México y Colombia", *Revista Ra Ximhai*, vol. 9, No. 1, Autonomous Indigenous University of Mexico (UAIM).

IBGE (Brazilian Geographical and Statistical Institute) (2015), *Síntese de Indicadores Sociais 2015 - uma análise das condições de vida da população brasileira*, Brasilia.

ILO (International Labour Organization) (2015), *Panorama Laboral de América Latina y el Caribe, 2015*, Lima.

IPEA (Institute of Applied Economic Research) (2014), *Situação social da população negra por estado*, Brasilia.

___(2011), *Retrato das desigualdades de gênero e raça*, Rio de Janeiro [online] http://www.ipea.gov.br/retrato/pdf/ revista.pdf.

Jaccoud, L. (2009) (org.), *A construção de uma política de promoção da igualdade racial: uma análise dos últimos 20 anos*, Brasilia, Institute of Applied Economic Research (IPEA).

Lechini, G. (comp.) (2008), *Los estudios Afroamericanos y africanos en América Latina*, CLACSO ediciones.

Loyo, M.G. and M. Velásquez (2009), "Aspectos jurídicos y económicos del trabajo doméstico remunerado en América Latina", *Trabajo doméstico: un largo camino hacia el trabajo decente*, M.E. Valenzuela and C. Mora (eds.), Santiago, International Labour Organization (OIT).

Mallú, P. and others (2013), "Discriminação racial no cuidado em saúde reprodutiva na percepção de mulheres", *Texto & Contexto-Enfermagem*, vol. 22, No. 2, Florianopolis.

Milosavljevic, V. (2007), "Estadísticas para la equidad de género. Magnitudes y tendencias en América Latina", *Cuadernos de la CEPAL*, No. 92 (LC/G.2321-P), Santiago, Economic Commission for Latin America and the Caribbean (ECLAC).

Ministry of Culture of Peru (2015), *Política Nacional para la Transversalización del Enfoque Intercultural 2015*, Lima.

Mosquera, C. and others (eds.) (2010), "Debate sobre ciudadanía y políticas raciales en las Américas Negras", *Lecturas CES*, National University of Colombia/Universidad del Valle.

Mosquera, C. and others (2002), *Afrodescendiente en las Américas. Trayectorias sociales e identitarias*, National University of Colombia.

OAS (Organization of American States) (2011), *II Taller de Expertos/as de la Temática Afrodescendiente en las Américas Medidas de Acción Afirmativa, Legislación, Políticas Públicas y Buenas Prácticas Ecuador, Panamá, Estados Unidos, Brasil*, Washington, D.C.

Pascale, P. (n/d), "Actualidad Afrodescendiente en Iberoamérica. Estudio sobre organizaciones civiles y políticas de acción afiramativa", *Cuadernos SEGIB-PNUD*, No.1, Madrid, Ibero-American Secretariat (SEGIB)/United Nations Development Programme (UNDP) [online] http://segib.org/wp-content/uploads/Actualidad-Afrodescendiente-Iberoamerica.pdf.

Peña, X. and others (2016), *La propiedad colectiva mejora las inversiones de los hogares: lecciones de la titulación de tierras a las comunidades Afrocolombianas*, Bogotá, Centre for Economic Development Studies (CEDE), Los Andes University.

Public Prosecutor's Office of Pernambuco (2013), *No país do racismo institucional: dez anos de ações do GT Racismo no MPPE*, Recife, Office of the Attorney General.

Putnam, L. (2002), "La población Afrocostarricense según los datos del Censo 2000", paper presented at the Symposium "Costa Rica a la Luz del Censo 2000", San José, 5-6 August.

Rangel, M. (2016), "Políticas públicas para Afrodescendientes: marco institucional en el Brasil, Colombia, el Ecuador y el Perú", *Políticas Sociales series*, No. 220 (LC/L.4275), Santiago, Economic Commission for Latin America and the Caribbean (ECLAC).

___(2009), "Una panorámica de las articulaciones y organizaciones de los Afrodescendientes en América Latina y el Caribe", *Afrodescendientes en América Latina y el Caribe: del reconocimiento estadístico a la realización de derechos*, Población y Desarrollo series, No. 87 (LC/L.3045-P), Santiago, Economic Commission for Latin America and the Caribbean (ECLAC).

Rodríguez, J. (2014), "Fecundidad adolescente en América Latina: una actualización", *Comportamiento reproductivo y fecundidad en América Latina: una agenda inconclusa*, S. Cavenaghi and W. Cabella (coords.), Rio de Janeiro, Latin American Population Association (ALAP).

Rodríguez, R. (2004), "Entramos negros y salimos Afrodescendientes", *Revista Futuros*, vol. 2, No. 5.

Sánchez, T. (2005), "Condiciones sociales, culturales y económicas que afectan el acceso y permanencia de las mujeres Afrodescendientes de URACCAN, Recinto Bluefields, 2001-2005", unpublished.

SEPPIR (Special Secretariat for the Promotion of Policies of Racial Equality) (2015), *Guía de políticas públicas para comunidades quilombolas*, Brasilia.

UNDP (United Nations Development Programme) (2010), *Derechos de la población Afrodescendiente de América Latina: desafíos para su implementación*, Panama.

UNESCO (United Nations Educational, Scientific and Cultural Organization) (2010), "Slaves Route: A Global Visión. Documentary" [excerpt online] http://www.unesco.org/new/es/social-and-human-sciences/themes/slave-route/right-box/related-information/slave-routes-a-global-vision/.

United Nations (2001), Report of the World Conference against Racism, Racial Discrimination, Xenophobia and Related Intolerance (A/CONF.189/PC.2/23), New York, 18 April.

Urrea-Giraldo, F. (2006), "La población afrodescendiente en Colombia", *Pueblos indígenas y afrodescendientes de América Latina y el Caribe: información sociodemográfica para políticas y programas*, Project Documents (LC/W.72), Santiago, Economic Commission for Latin America and the Caribbean (ECLAC).

Valdés, A. (2016), "La intereseccionalidad como herramienta en la construcción de sujetas de derechos", paper presented at the meeting "Afrouruguayas en diálogo con el Estado: la mirada étnico racial en las políticas de género", Montevideo, Ministry of Social Development (MIDES)/National Women's Institute of Uruguay (INMUJERES), 22 June. Valenzuela, M.E. and C. Mora (eds.) (2009), *Trabajo doméstico: un largo camino hacia el trabajo decente*, Santiago, International Labour Organization (ILO).

Valdivia, N. (2013), *Las organizaciones de la población afrodescendiente en el Perú: discursos de identidad y demandas de reconocimiento*, Lima, Development Analysis Group (GRADE).

Valenzuela, R. (2003), "Inequidad, ciudadanía y pueblos indígenas en Chile", *Políticas Sociales series*, No. 76 (LC/L.2006-P), Santiago, Economic Commission for Latin America and the Caribbean (ECLAC).

World Bank (2015), *Indigenous Latin America in the Twenty-First Century: The First Decade*, Washington, D.C.

# Publicaciones recientes de la CEPAL
## *ECLAC recent publications*

## www.cepal.org/publicaciones

### Informes periódicos / *Annual reports*
**También disponibles para años anteriores /** *Issues for previous years also available*

- Estudio Económico de América Latina y el Caribe 2016, 236 p.
  *Economic Survey of Latin America and the Caribbean 2016, 232 p.*

- La Inversión Extranjera Directa en América Latina y el Caribe 2016, 170 p.
  *Foreign Direct Investment in Latin America and the Caribbean 2016, 164 p.*

- Anuario Estadístico de América Latina y el Caribe 2016 / *Statistical Yearbook for Latin America and the Caribbean 2016, 132 p.*

- Balance Preliminar de las Economías de América Latina y el Caribe 2016, 132 p.
  *Preliminary Overview of the Economies of Latin America and the Caribbean 2016, 124 p.*

- Panorama Social de América Latina 2015, 226 p.
  *Social Panorama of Latin America 2015, 222 p.*

- Panorama de la Inserción Internacional de América Latina y el Caribe 2016, 174 p.
  *Latin America and the Caribbean in the World Economy 2015, 170 p.*

### Libros y documentos institucionales / *Institutional books and documents*

- Panorama fiscal de América Latina y el Caribe 2017: la movilización de recursos para el financiamiento del desarrollo sostenible, 2017, 115 p.
  *Fiscal Panorama of Latin America and the Caribbean 2017: Mobilizing resources to finance sustainable development, 2017, 108 p.*

- *ECLAC Thinking. Selected Texts (1948-1998), 2016, 520 p.*

- La matriz de la desigualdad en América Latina, 2016, 96 p.
  *The social inequality matrix in Latin America, 2016, 94 p.*

- Autonomía de las mujeres e igualdad en la agenda de desarrollo sostenible, 2016, 184 p.
  *Equality and women's autonomy in the sustainable development agenda, 2016, 168 p.*
  *Autonomia das mulheres e igualdade na agenda de desenvolvimento sustentável.*
  *Síntese, 2016, 106 p.*

- La Unión Europea y América Latina y el Caribe ante la Agenda 2030 para el Desarrollo Sostenible: el gran impulso ambiental, 2016, 112 p.
  *The European Union and Latin America and the Caribbean vis-à-vis the 2030 Agenda for Sustainable Development: The environmental big push, 2016, 112 p.*

- Horizontes 2030: la igualdad en el centro del desarrollo sostenible, 2016, 176 p.
  *Horizons 2030: Equality at the centre of sustainable development, 2016, 174 p.*
  *Horizontes 2030: a igualdade no centro do desenvolvimento sustentável, 2016, 176 p.*

- 40 años de agenda regional de género, 2016, 130 p.
  *40 years of the regional gender agenda, 2016, 128 p.*

- La nueva revolución digital: de la Internet del consumo a la Internet de la producción, 2016, 100 p.
  *The new digital revolution: From the consumer Internet to the industrial Internet, 2016, 100 p.*

## Libros de la CEPAL / *ECLAC books*

145 Política industrial rural y fortalecimiento de cadenas de valor, Ramón Padilla, (ed.), 2017, 242 p.

144 Desde el gobierno abierto al Estado abierto en América Latina y el Caribe, Alejandra Naser, Álvaro Ramírez-Alujas, Daniela Rosales (eds.), 2017, 466 p.

143 Proteccion social en América Latina: la desigualdad en el banquillo, Ana Sojo, 2017, 246 p.

142 Consensos y conflictos en la política tributaria de América Latina, Juan Carlos Gómez Sabaini, Juan Pablo Jiménez y Ricardo Martner (eds.), 2017, 446 p.

141 Brechas y transformaciones: la evolución del empleo agropecuario en América Latina, Jürgen Weller (ed.), 2016, 274 p.

140 Protección y formación: instituciones para mejorar la inserción laboral en América Latina y Asia, Alberto Isgut, Jürgen Weller (eds.), 2016, 428 p.
*Protection and training: Institutions for improving workforce integration in Latin America and Asia, Alberto Isgut, Jürgen Weller (eds.), 2016, 428 p.*

139 Hacia una nueva gobernanza de los recursos naturales en América Latina y el Caribe, Hugo Altomonte, Ricardo J. Sánchez, 2016, 256 p.

## Páginas Selectas de la CEPAL / *ECLAC Select Pages*

- Planificación y prospectiva para la construcción de futuro en América Latina y el Caribe. Textos seleccionados 2013-2016, Jorge Máttar y Mauricio Cuervo (comps.), 2016, 222 p.

- Desarrollo inclusivo en América Latina. Textos seleccionados 2009-2016, Ricardo Infante (comp.), 2016, 294 p.

- Globalización, integración y comercio inclusivo en América Latina. Textos seleccionados 2010-2014, Osvaldo Rosales (comp.), 2015, 326 p.

- El desafío de la sostenibilidad ambiental en América Latina y el Caribe. Textos seleccionados 2012-2014, Carlos de Miguel, Marcia Tavares (comps.), 2015, 148 p

## Copublicaciones / *Co-publications*

- El imperativo de la igualdad, Alicia Bárcena, Antonio Prado, CEPAL/Siglo Veintiuno, Argentina, 2016, 244 p.

- Gobernanza global y desarrollo: nuevos desafíos y prioridades de la cooperación internacional, José Antonio Ocampo (ed.), CEPAL/Siglo Veintiuno, Argentina, 2015, 286 p.

- Decentralization and Reform in Latin America: Improving Intergovernmental Relations, Giorgio Brosio and Juan Pablo Jiménez (eds.), ECLAC/Edward Elgar Publishing, United Kingdom, 2012, 450 p.

- Sentido de pertenencia en sociedades fragmentadas: América Latina desde una perspectiva global, Martín Hopenhayn y Ana Sojo (comps.), CEPAL/Siglo Veintiuno, Argentina, 2011, 350 p.

## Coediciones / *Co-editions*

- Perspectivas económicas de América Latina 2017: Juventud, Competencias y Emprendimiento, 2016, 338 p.
*Latin American Economic Outlook 2017: Youth, Skills and Entrepreneurship, 2016, 314 p.*

- Desarrollo e integración en América Latina, 2016, 314 p.

- Hacia un desarrollo inclusivo: el caso del Uruguay, 2016, 174 p.

- Perspectivas de la agricultura y del desarrollo rural en las Américas: una mirada hacia América Latina y el Caribe 2015-2016, CEPAL/FAO/IICA, 2015, 212 p.

## Documentos de proyecto / *Project documents*

- La transversalización del enfoque de género en las políticas públicas frente al cambio climático en América Latina, Marina Casas Varez, 2017, 101 p.

- Financiamiento para el cambio climático en América Latina y el Caribe en 2015, Joseluis Samaniego y Heloísa Schneider, 2017, 76 p.

- El cambio tecnológico y el nuevo contexto del empleo: tendencias generales y en América Latina, Sebastian Krull, 2016, 48 p.

- Cambio climático, políticas públicas y demanda de energía y gasolinas en América Latina: un meta-análisis, Luis Miguel Galindo, Joseluis Samaniego, Jimy Ferrer, José Eduardo Alatorre, Orlando Reyes, 2016, 68 p.

- Estado de la banda ancha en América Latina y el Caribe 2016, 2016, 46 p.

## Cuadernos estadísticos de la CEPAL

44 Las cuentas de los hogares y el bienestar en América Latina. Más allá del PIB, 2016.

43 Estadísticas económicas de América Latina y el Caribe: Aspectos metodológicos y resultados del cambio de año base de 2005 a 2010

## Series de la CEPAL / *ECLAC Series*

Asuntos de Género / Comercio Internacional / Desarrollo Productivo / Desarrollo Territorial / Estudios Estadísticos / Estudios y Perspectivas (Bogotá, Brasilia, Buenos Aires, México, Montevideo) / *Studies and Perspectives* (The Caribbean, Washington) / Financiamiento del Desarrollo / Gestión Pública / Informes y Estudios Especiales / Macroeconomía del Desarrollo / Medio Ambiente y Desarrollo / Población y Desarrollo / Política Fiscal / Políticas Sociales / Recursos Naturales e Infraestructura / Seminarios y Conferencias.

## Manuales de la CEPAL

5   Estimación de las erogaciones sociales a partir del sistema de cuentas nacionales: una propuesta para las funciones de educación, salud y protección social, María Paz Colinao, Federico Dorin, Rodrigo Martínez y Varinia Tromben, 2016, 63 p.

4   Territorio e igualdad: planificación del desarrollo con perspectiva de género, 2016, 84 p.

3   Manual de formación regional para la implementación de la resolución 1325 (2000) del Consejo de Seguridad de las Naciones Unidas relativa a las mujeres, la paz y la seguridad, María Cristina Benavente R., Marcela Donadio, Pamela Villalobos, 2016, 126 p.

2   Guía general para la gestión de residuos sólidos domiciliarios, Estefani Rondón Toro, Marcel Szantó Narea, Juan Francisco Pacheco, Eduardo Contreras, Alejandro Gálvez, 2016, 212 p.

## Revista CEPAL / *CEPAL Review*

La Revista se inició en 1976, con el propósito de contribuir al examen de los problemas del desarrollo socioeconómico de la región. La *Revista CEPAL* se publica en español e inglés tres veces por año.

*CEPAL Review first appeared in 1976, its aim being to make a contribution to the study of the economic and social development problems of the region. CEPAL Review is published in Spanish and English versions three times a year.*

## Observatorio demográfico / *Demographic Observatory*

Edición bilingüe (español e inglés) que proporciona información estadística actualizada, referente a estimaciones y proyecciones de población de los países de América Latina y el Caribe. Desde 2013 el *Observatorio* aparece una vez al año.

*Bilingual publication (Spanish and English) proving up-to-date estimates and projections of the populations of the Latin American and Caribbean countries. Since 2013, the Observatory appears once a year.*

## Notas de población

Revista especializada que publica artículos e informes acerca de las investigaciones más recientes sobre la dinámica demográfica en la región. También incluye información sobre actividades científicas y profesionales en el campo de población. La revista se publica desde 1973 y aparece dos veces al año, en junio y diciembre.

*Specialized journal which publishes articles and reports on recent studies of demographic dynamics in the region. Also includes information on scientific and professional activities in the field of population. Published since 1973, the journal appears twice a year in June and December.*

**Las publicaciones de la CEPAL están disponibles en:**
***ECLAC publications are available at:***

# www.cepal.org/publicaciones

**También se pueden adquirir a través de:**
***They can also be ordered through:***

# www.un.org/publications

United Nations Publications
PO Box 960
Herndon, VA 20172
USA

Tel. (1-888)254-4286
Fax (1-800)338-4550
Contacto / *Contact*: publications@un.org
Pedidos / *Orders*: order@un.org